Studies in Church History

28

THE CHURCH AND THE ARTS

Frontispiece Christ in Majesty, Godescalc Evangelistary (781–783), Paris, BN, MS nouvelle acquisition latine, 1203, fol. 3r.

THE CHURCH AND THE ARTS

PAPERS READ AT
THE 1990 SUMMER MEETING AND
THE 1991 WINTER MEETING OF
THE ECCLESIASTICAL HISTORY SOCIETY

EDITED BY

DIANA WOOD

PUBLISHED FOR
THE ECCLESIASTICAL HISTORY SOCIETY
BY
BLACKWELL PUBLISHERS
1992

First published 1992

Blackwell Publishers
108 Cowley Road, Oxford OX4 1JF, UK

Three Cambridge Center,
Cambridge, Massachusetts 02142, USA

British Library Cataloguing in Publication Data

A CIP record for this book is available from the British Library.

Library of Congress Cataloging in Publication Data

Ecclesiastical History Society. Summer Meeting (1990: Bishop Otter College)
The church and the arts: papers read at the 1990 Summer Meeting and the 1991 Winter Meeting of the Ecclesiastical History Society / edited by Diana Wood.
p. cm.—(Studies in church history; 28)
Includes bibliographical references.
ISBN 0-631-18043-5
1. Christianity and the arts—Congresses. I. Wood, Diana, 1940— . II. Ecclesiastical History Society. Winter Meeting (1991: King's College London) III. Title. IV. Series.
BR115.A8E25 1990
270 s—dc20 91-35624
[246'.09] CIP

Typeset in 11 on 12 pt Bembo
by Joshua Associates Limited, Oxford
Printed in Great Britain by Billing and Sons Ltd, Worcester

CONTENTS

CONTENTS

CONTENTS

PREFACE

The theme of The Church and the Arts, chosen for the year 1990–1 by the Society's President Dr J. C. G. Binfield, was a particularly challenging one, and members responded in a variety of ways, discussing art and architecture, liturgy and iconography, church furnishings and decor, literature and music, drama and film, as well as the piety, the patronage, and the politics which gave rise to their creation. The volume contains a selection of the papers presented at the summer and winter conferences. Both these meetings will be remembered especially for the spectacular slides shown and for a welcome emphasis on church music. It was especially fitting that the summer conference closed with a harpsichord recital based on church tunes from Tallis to Bach, given by Dr Alan Brown of the University of Sheffield, for which the Society would like to thank him warmly.

Our gratitude must also be expressed to Bishop Otter College, Chichester, for its generous hospitality at the summer conference, and to King's College London, once again, where the winter meeting was held.

Diana Wood

ACKNOWLEDGEMENTS

The Editor would like to record her warmest thanks to Jan Chamier and Ann McCall of Blackwell Publishers for their unfailing and good-humoured help in dealing with a difficult typescript.

Grateful acknowledgement is also due to the many museums, libraries, archives, institutions, and people who have allowed reproduction of their illustrations or have allowed authors to take photographs. In most cases, individual acknowledgements appear beneath each illustration, and every effort has been made to ensure that permission has been obtained. However, if any have been overlooked the Editor and Publishers will be pleased to make the necessary arrangement at the first opportunity.

LIST OF CONTRIBUTORS

CLYDE BINFIELD (*President*)
Reader in History, University of Sheffield

BERNARD ASPINWALL
Senior Lecturer in Modern History, University of Glasgow

MARGARET ASTON

BRENDA M. BOLTON
Senior Lecturer in History, Queen Mary and Westfield College, University of London

LOUISE BOURDUA
Lecturer in History and History of Art, University of Aberdeen

ROGER BOWERS
University Lecturer in Music, University of Cambridge

LINDSAY BOYNTON
Reader in History, Queen Mary and Westfield College, University of London

AVERIL CAMERON
Professor of Late Antique and Byzantine Studies, King's College, University of London

KENNETH W. T. CARLETON
Research Student, King's College, University of London

DONALD DAVIE
Emeritus Professor of the Humanities, Vanderbilt University, Nashville, Tennessee

MARTIN DUDLEY
Vicar of St George in Owlsmoor, Berkshire

JACQUELINE EALES
Lecturer, Hollins College, London

JUDY ANN FORD
Research Student, Fordham University, New York

SHERIDAN GILLEY
Senior Lecturer in Theology, University of Durham

ALICE L. HARTING-CORRÊA
Research Student, University of St Andrews

WALTER HILLSMAN
Member of the Faculty of Music, University of Oxford

W. M. JACOB
Warden of Lincoln Theological College

FLORA LEWIS

G. I. T. MACHIN
Professor of British History, University of Dundee

ANDREW MARTINDALE
Professor of Visual Arts, University of East Anglia

HENRY MAYR-HARTING
Fellow and Tutor, St Peter's College, Oxford

STUART MEWS
Lecturer in Religious Studies, University of Lancaster

MARY CHARLES MURRAY
Lecturer in Theology, University of Nottingham

KEITH A. NEWMAN

SUSAN O'BRIEN
Principal Lecturer in History, Anglia Polytechnic, Cambridge

HENRY R. SEFTON
Master of Christ's College and Lecturer in Church History, University of Aberdeen

R. N. SWANSON
Senior Lecturer in Medieval History, University of Birmingham

JOHN NELSON TARN
Roscoe Professor of Architecture, Liverpool School of Architecture and Building Engineering, University of Liverpool

BRIAN TAYLOR
Rector of Guildford St Nicholas'

GARTH TURNER
Rector of Tattenhall and Handley, Cheshire

BRETT USHER

A. F. WALLS
Professor and Director, Centre for the Study of Christianity in the Non-Western World, University of Edinburgh

W. R. WARD
Emeritus Professor of Modern History, University of Durham

GROVER A. ZINN, JR
Danforth Professor of Religion, Oberlin College, Ohio

ABBREVIATIONS

Abbreviated titles are adopted within each paper after the first full citation. In addition, the following abbreviations are used throughout the volume.

AFH	*Archivum Franciscanum historicum* (Quaracchi, 1908ff.)
AHDL	*Archives d'histoire doctrinale et littéraire du moyen-âge* (Paris, 1926ff.)
AHR	*American Historical Review* (New York, 1895 ff.)
AnBoll	*Analecta Bollandiana* (Brussels, 1882ff.)
AV	Authorized Version
BL	British Library, London
BM	British Museum, London
BN	Bibliothèque nationale, Paris
CalSPD	*Calendar of State Papers: Domestic* (London, 1856ff.)
CChr.SG	*Corpus Christianorum, series Graeca* (Turnhout, 1974ff.)
CHB	*Cambridge History of the Bible*, 1, ed. P. R. Ackroyd and C. F. Evans (Cambridge, 1970); 2, ed. G. W. H. Lampe (1969); 3, ed. S. L. Greenslade (1963)
Clm	Codex latinus Monacensis = MS collection, Munich, Bayerische Staatsbibliothek
CPG	*Clavis patrum Graecorum*, ed. M. Geerard (Turnhout, 1974) = *CChr.SG*, 1–4
CPR	*Calendar of Patent Rolls preserved in the Public Record Office* (London, 1892ff.)
CYS	*Canterbury and York Society* (London, 1907ff.)
DNB	*Dictionary of National Biography* (London, 1885ff.)
DOP	*Dumbarton Oaks Papers* (Cambridge, Mass., 1941ff.)
EETS	*Early English Text Society* (London/Oxford, 1864ff.)
EHR	*English Historical Review* (London, 1953ff.)
HMC	*Historical Manuscripts Commission*
HThR	*Harvard Theological Review* (New York/Cambridge, Mass., 1908ff.)
InR	*Innes Review* (Glasgow, 1950ff.)
JEH	*Journal of Ecclesiastical History* (Cambridge, 1950ff.)
JThS	*Journal of Theological Studies* (London, 1899ff.)
JWCI	*Journal of the Warburg and Courtauld Institutes* (London, 1937ff.)
Mansi	J. D. Mansi, *Sacrorum conciliorum nova et amplissima collectio*, 31 vols (Florence/Venice, 1757–98); new impression and continuation, ed. L. Petit and J. B. Martin, 60 vols (Paris, 1899–1927)
MGH	*Monumenta Germaniae Historica inde ab a. c.500 usque ad a. 1500*, ed. G. H. Pertz *et al.* (Hanover, Berlin, etc., 1826ff.)
MGH.Cap	*Capitularia regnum Francorum* (1883–97, repr. 1960) = *MGH.L*, sectio 2
MGH.Const.	*Constitutiones et acta publica imperatorum et regnum* (1893ff.) = *MGH.L*, sectio 4
MGH.Ep	*Epistolae* (1887ff.)
MGH.L	*Leges* (in folio) (1835–89) —2. Sectio: *MGH.Cap*
MGH.PL	*Poetae Latinae medii aevi* (1880ff.)
nd	no date

np	no place
ns	new series
PaP	*Past and Present. A Journal of Scientific History* (London, 1952ff.)
PD	*Hansard's Parliamentary Debates*
PG	*Patrologia Graeca*, ed. J. P. Migne, 161 vols (Paris, 1857–66)
PL	*Patrologia Latina*, ed. J. P. Migne, 217 + 4 index vols (Paris, 1841–61)
PO	*Patrologia Orientalis*, ed. J. Graffin, F. Nau, *et al.* (Paris, 1903ff.)
Potthast	*Regesta pontificum Romanorum inde ab a. post Christum natum 1198 ad a. 1304*, ed. A. Potthast, 2 vols (Berlin, 1974–7, repr. Graz, 1957)
PRO	Public Record Office, London
PS	*Parker Society* (Cambridge, 1841–55)
RBen	*Revue bénédictine de critique, d'histoire et de littéraire religieuses* (Maredsous, 1884ff.)
RGG	*Die Religion in Geschichte und Gegenwart*, 3rd edn (Tübingen, 1956–65)
RHE	*Revue d'histoire ecclésiastique* (Louvain, 1900ff.)
s.a.	*sub anno*
SC	*Sources chrétiennes*, ed. H. de Lubac and J. Danielou (Paris, 1941ff.)
SCH	*Studies in Church History* (London/Oxford, 1964ff.)
ScHR	*Scottish Historical Review* (Edinburgh/Glasgow, 1904ff.)
SS	*Surtees Society* (Durham, 1835ff.)
STC	*A Short-title Catalogue of Books Printed in England, Scotland, and Ireland, and of English Books Printed Abroad, 1475–1640*, ed. A. W. Pollard and G. R. Redgrave (London, 1926, repr. 1945, 1950)
s.v.	*sub verbo*
VCH	*Victoria County History* (London, 1900ff.)

INTRODUCTION

'The Church and the Arts' is an obvious theme for an Ecclesiastical History Society to explore. It is also an impossible theme, which is perhaps why it was not explored before the Society's 1990–1 session. It is impossible because it lacks focus or definition. Is it, for example, 'The Church and the Arts' or is it 'Church and Art'? The former is down-to-earth, as much a matter of hassocks and umbrella-stands as *pietàs* and chorales, the latter is cerebral and full of doctrine. Both were in the Society's collective mind and both emerge in the papers collected here, although the majority, being perhaps easier to write, reflect the title of this volume: 'The Church and the Arts'.

What is done here beyond peradventure suggests an agenda for future themes, each demanding a volume of its own: Church and Music, Church and Architecture, Church and Literature, and Pictorial Art, and Aesthetics. Here hares are started and wild geese chased in the hope that they might be swans. At least this volume is comprehensively suggestive. Its horizons contain art and craft; aesthetics and the ascetic; Word, words, and liturgy; music. Cathedrals are juxtaposed with chapels. The theme embraces women, war, and the cinema as well as drama, Puritanism, and, of course, theology, often promiscuously. Geographically the volume is Eurocentric. It is, for example, the *Western* discovery of Non-Western Christian art that is considered, and then only in the last paper. Again, while the range within Europe is from Byzantium to the Netherlands, via Rome, Padua, and Burgundy, the concentration is English: London, Liverpool, Northampton, Chichester, a font at Hook Norton, parishes in Kent. There is inevitably an insistent clash of theme: the incursion of the secular into the sacred; the implications of patronage, whether of emperor, squire, dean, or mere incumbent; the fear of images as well as their allure; the place of hymn-book, prayer-book, and Bible.

The value of so apparently random a collection of gems, wild-geese, hares, and graces is that it allows scholars whose interests are separated less by theme than place or century to discover that they have common cause. The stimulus of such interaction is productive and not just antiquarian. That, helped immensely by unexpected discussion and the unique light shed at each moment by fresh images, was experienced at Chichester. Although here reduced to a book, and with the passing image given the permanence of illustration, and away from what was literally the heat of the moment in the summer of 1990, the Chichester experience has not been entirely lost.

And there is in fact a structure, of time, place, and theme set by the main lectures. In them Byzantium, the Empire of Charlemagne, the Netherlands of the latest Middle Ages, combine with aspects of English baroque, Dissenting Gothic, and that nagging contradiction in terms, the twentieth-century cathedral, to focus on image-consciousness, patronage, music, literature, and architecture. Around these main papers the others cluster, exploring issues touched by them, interweaving doctrine, culture, personality, capability, and pure necessity. If, at the end, the task's impossibility is clearer than ever, that too keeps faith with the subject, for 'The Church and the Arts' is about the setting of the infinite within constraints. That is art; it is artifice. Yet, just as architecture is the enclosure of space to create space, and great architecture is a liberation of space, so, for all the arts, where the spirit is allowed to roam more freely than might otherwise have happened, there is Art justified, even in relation to the Church.

Clyde Binfield

THE LANGUAGE OF IMAGES: THE RISE OF ICONS AND CHRISTIAN REPRESENTATION*

by AVERIL CAMERON

INTRODUCTION

ONE has to be brave to return to the subject of Byzantine Iconoclasm, a subject which, we may feel, has been done to death.[1] But the division in Byzantine society which lasted off and on for over a century, from 726 to the 'restoration of orthodoxy' in 843, was so profound that any Byzantine historian must at some time try to grapple with it. This is especially so if one is trying to understand the immediately preceding period, from the Persian invasions of the early seventh century to the great sieges of Constantinople by the Arabs in 674–8 and 717. It is well recognized by historians that this was a time of fundamental social, economic, and administrative change, which coincided with, but was by no means wholly caused by, the loss of so much Byzantine territory to the Arabs.[2] However, the connection, if any, of this process of change with the social and religious upheaval known as Iconoclasm still leaves much to be said; indeed, no simple connection is likely in itself to provide an adequate explanation. In this paper I want to explore further some of the background to the crisis, without attempting here to provide a general

* Earlier versions of the present paper were given at the Institute of Classical Studies, London, the Collège de France, and at the Symposium on 'The Holy Image', organized by Professors H. Belting and H. Kessler at Dumbarton Oaks, 27–9 April 1990.

1 See, for instance, Anthony Bryer and Judith Herrin, eds, *Iconoclasm* (Birmingham, 1977); D. Stein, *Der Beginn des byzantinischen Bilderstreites und seine Entwicklung in die 40er Jahre des 8 Jahrhunderts* (Munich, 1980); S. Gero, *Byzantine Iconoclasm during the Reign of Leo III* (Louvain, 1973) and *Byzantine Iconoclasm during the Reign of Constantine V* (Louvain, 1978); A. Grabar, *L'Iconoclasme byzantin* (Paris, 1957); Robin Cormack, *Writing in Gold* (London, 1985).

2 See now John Haldon, *Byzantium in the Seventh Century. The Transformation of a Culture* (Cambridge, 1990), with his earlier articles 'Some remarks on the background to the Iconoclast Controversy', *Byzantine Studies*, 38 (1977), pp. 161–84, and especially 'Ideology and social change in the seventh century: military discontent as a barometer', *Klio*, 68 (1986), pp. 139–90; Alan Harvey, *Economic Expansion in the Byzantine Empire 900–1200* (Cambridge, 1989), pp. 15–34. The contrasting view (emphasizing continuity) put forward by W. E. Kaegi, Jr., 'Visible Rates of Seventh-century Change', in F. M. Clover and R. S. Humphreys, eds, *Tradition and Innovation in Late Antiquity* (Madison, Wisc., 1989), pp. 191–208, depends mainly on institutional and military evidence from the reign of Heraclius itself and does not conflict with the perception of profound change over a longer period (see further below).

explanation for Iconoclasm itself. I shall not venture beyond the first phase of Iconoclasm, which ended with the Second Council of Nicaea in 787, and after which the argument is somewhat different. Indeed, I shall be focusing here not even on the period known as 'first Iconoclasm', but mainly on the preceding period, when the issues inherent in the controversy were already, and increasingly, making themselves felt. Though we shall inevitably be concerned with some of the arguments brought against icons by their opponents, it is the place of images themselves in the context of the pre-Iconoclastic period which will be the main issue. Finally, while I want to offer a different way of reading the rise of icons, I do not pretend that it is the only one, or even possibly the most important. I do suggest, though, that it can help us to make sense of some of the issues that were involved.

It is clear that the suspicion of religious images which took such an extreme form in Byzantine Iconoclasm followed a period of intense questioning about the legitimacy of Christian representation.[3] In 691, for example, the well-known canon 82 of the Council in Trullo forbade the representation of Christ as a lamb or otherwise in symbolic form; he was to be depicted only in human form, so that 'we may recall to memory his conversation in the flesh, his passion and salutary death and his redemption which was wrought for the whole world.' Here I should like to broaden the enquiry beyond the immediate iconographical issue. The first part of the paper will argue that in the period of the 'rise of icons', from the later sixth to the eighth centuries, religious images, which were held by iconophiles to represent objective truth, came to be seen as one of the guarantors of knowledge, and were thus an important component in the evolving belief system of Byzantine society at the time.

One of the functions of religion as a cultural system is to provide a way of making sense of the disasters, injustices, and problems with which people are faced in the world. At this time there were indeed many reasons for uncertainty. First, the period from, say, the late sixth century to the beginnings of Iconoclasm (conventionally set in 726) was precisely the time during which Classical Antiquity finally did become Byzantium. The Greek cities, which until the sixth century had still been the centres of culture and education, were either devastated by invasion or else turned into medieval towns. With them went much of the old educational system, and, with it, access to classical books. By the eighth century it was

[3] See on this Charles Barber, 'The Koimesis Church, Nicaea. The limits of representation on the eve of Iconoclasm', *Jahrbuch der österreichischen Byzantinistik* 41 (1991), pp. 43–60.

a difficult thing to get hold of a classical text even in Constantinople itself, let alone the provinces, and in any case, attention was directed to more immediate concerns elsewhere. Of course, one can exaggerate. But it seems that even educated people now had little idea of their past history beyond legend and fantasy. As for the classical statues which still survived in large numbers even in the shrunken city of eighth-century Constantinople, they were often misidentified, misunderstood, and more often feared as potentially dangerous.[4] During this Byzantine Dark Age, Classical Antiquity was no longer part of the average consciousness.

The reign of the Emperor Heraclius (610–41) probably saw the last manifestation of traditional learning for many years to come. During that period scholarly history was still possible, as were classicizing art, epic poetry, and philosophy; by contrast, the next period is so ill-documented that it was hardly known to the chronicler Theophanes or the Patriarch Nicephorus, to whom we owe the basic Byzantine historical accounts.[5] Classicizing literary forms are not to be found again for nearly three centuries, not until after the end of Iconoclasm and the establishment of a new dynasty in Constantinople. Heraclius's reign also saw tremendous reversals: difficult but successful wars against Persia, followed closely by the loss of most of the eastern provinces of the Empire to the Arabs. In the course of these events the holy city of Jerusalem, the location of the True Cross, was lost, regained, and lost again within the space of twenty-five years. The reign ended in a confusion of religious division. The mental dislocation caused by all this can hardly be exaggerated.[6]

Heraclius's campaigns against the Persians were accompanied by a marked amount of eschatological propaganda; affecting as they did the eastern provinces which were to be the focus and crucible for religious change on a scale as yet undreamt of by the unfortunate Byzantines, they stimulated deep soul-searching, expectation, and then disappointment among the local populations.[7] I shall argue here that as well as representing

[4] For a fascinating range of examples, see Cyril Mango, 'Antique statuary and the Byzantine beholder', *DOP*, 17 (1963), pp. 53–75.

[5] See the discussion in Cyril Mango, ed., *Patriarch Nikephoros of Constantinople. Short History* (Washington, DC, 1990), pp. 12–18.

[6] See also Averil Cameron, *Christianity and the Rhetoric of Empire* (Berkeley and Los Angeles, 1991), ch. 6, and 'New Themes and Styles in Greek Literature, 7th–8th Centuries', in Averil Cameron and Lawrence I. Conrad, eds, *The Byzantine and Early Islamic Near East I: Problems in the Literary Source Material = Studies in Late Antiquity and Early Islam*, 1 (Princeton, 1991), pp. 81–105.

[7] See Michael Whitby, 'Greek Historical Writing after Procopius: Variety and Vitality', in Cameron and Conrad, *Problems in the Literary Source Material*, pp. 25–80, with the papers by G. J. Reinink and Han Drijvers in the same volume.

a revival of the Church's own longstanding hesitation about religious images, Iconoclasm was a manifestation of an uncertainty which people felt about their own thought-world. As for the extreme proliferation of religious images itself, together with the massive amount of attention which is given to them in the literature of the seventh century onwards, this can be read in its Byzantine context as part of the replacement for the lost horizons of Classical Antiquity, and indeed as part of an urge to assert a new authority.[8] Images form part of the intellectual framework round which we can see Byzantium reorientating itself. They are an important element in a sign-system through which knowledge, no longer accessible in the old way, could still be reliably assessed. Yet the implications of such a realignment were not to be fully realized or accepted without a profound struggle, of which the seventh century reveals many indications; to be aware of its extent, we have only to look at the anxious canons of the Quinisext Council of 691–2, or at some of the question-and-answer literature from the seventh century, which may be taken to reflect contemporary concerns. When official Iconoclasm began, even though it seems to have been mainly imposed from the top and to have lacked real popular support, the religious divisions which it opened up were often bitter and hard to resolve. Moreover, they happened against a background of equally profound administrative, social, and economic change, in the course of which Byzantium shed the structures still remaining from Classical Antiquity and adopted the medieval appearance of the Middle Byzantine State.[9] But having passed through this painful phase, of which Iconoclasm was the culmination, Byzantium can clearly be seen from the ninth century onwards to be entering a phase of renewed confidence and to have found a level of integration which was to permit advances in new directions.

It is mainly during the late sixth and seventh centuries that the veneration of icons seems to have taken off in Byzantium. Few pre-Iconoclastic icons have survived the efforts of the Iconoclasts (the most famous and striking examples come from the monastery on Mount Sinai); nevertheless, the visual evidence that we do have is sufficiently scattered geo-

[8] For this emphasis (against 'decline'), see Robin Cormack, 'Byzantine Aphrodisias. Changing the symbolic map of a city', *Proceedings of the Cambridge Philological Association*, 216, ns 36 (1990), pp. 26–41.

[9] This is particularly stressed by Haldon: see n. 2 above, and for signs of ideological dislocation, see also G. Dagron, 'Le Saint, le savant, l'astrologue. Étude de thèmes hagiographiques à travers quelques recueils de "Questions et réponses des Ve-VIIe siècles"', in *Hagiographie, cultures et sociétés (IVe–VIIe s.)* (Paris, 1981), pp. 143–55; for administrative change see F. Winkelmann, *Byzantinische Rang- und Ämterstruktur im 8. und 9. Jahrhundert = Berliner byzantinische Arbeiten*, 54 (Berlin, 1985); the origins of the highly contentious 'theme-system' also belong to this period.

graphically, and we have enough references in other sources to the use of icons in public and private contexts to make it clear that this was a widespread contemporary development.[10] While we tend to think of icons typically as portable images painted on wood, it is important to realize that it was neither the material nor its portability that made a picture into an icon; the Greek word *eikon* in itself simply means 'image'. Nor, for this early period, should we think in terms of the arrangement and use of icons familiar from later Byzantine churches or indeed from Orthodox churches today; whereas in later Byzantine times, a set of protocols developed for their subject-matter and types, together with their position in the church and their liturgical use, this had not yet happened in our period, and some churches, including Hagia Sophia in Constantinople, seem to have had no figural decoration among their furnishings.[11] It would, however, appear that in some cases at least portable icons were indeed displayed in churches. We learn, for example, in the seventh-century *Miracles of Artemius*, a collection of miracle stories associated with the Constantinopolitan church of St John the Baptist at Oxeia, of an icon hanging in the left nave of the church, and of the clergy lending an icon to a great lady, who was so devoted to it that she was reluctant to leave the church.[12] But while there seem to have been several icons in this church, they would not yet have been hung on the familiar closed iconostasis, which is also a later development.[13] Several of the images which attracted the hostility of the Iconoclasts in fact took the form of fixed decoration in churches, in mosaic or fresco; it is rather the subject and treatment of the picture that qualifies it for the term 'icon'—surviving early examples include ivories and textiles as well as wall and ceiling decorations and the portable images painted on wood with which we usually associate the term.[14] This fluidity of Greek terms used for visual art means that where the evidence is literary and the object itself has been lost, as is often the

[10] See, in particular, E. Kitzinger, 'The cult of images in the period before Iconoclasm', *DOP*, 8 (1950), pp. 85–150; K. Weitzmann, *The Icon. Holy Images—Sixth to Fourteenth Century* (New York, 1978), pp. 7–23. Marlia Mundell, 'Monophysite Church Decoration', in Bryer and Herrin, *Iconoclasm*, pp. 59–74, collects examples of iconic and aniconic decoration in contemporary churches.

[11] On this question see Mundell, 'Monophysite Church Decoration', at p. 70.

[12] *Miracula Artemii* [hereafter *Mir. Art.*] ed. A. Papadopoulos-Kerameus, *Varia graeca sacra* (St Petersburg, 1909), chs 6, 31. For discussion see V. Déroche, 'L'Authenticité de l'"Apologie contre les Juifs" de Léontios de Néapolis', *Bulletin de Correspondance Hellénique*, 110 (1986), pp. 655–69, at pp. 658–9.

[13] See T. F. Mathews, *The Early Churches of Constantinople: Architecture and Liturgy* (University Park, Pennsylvania, 1971), pp. 168ff.

[14] See also Weitzmann, *The Icon*.

Plate 1 Ivory showing the Nativity and the Adoration of the Magi, Syria or Egypt, sixth century (Medieval and Later Antiquities 1904, 7–2, 1, by courtesy of the Trustees of the British Museum).

Plate 2 Ivory Diptych of Christ between Saints Peter and Paul and the Virgin Enthroned with Angels, sixth century (Berlin, Staatliche Museen).

case, it can often be difficult to know exactly what medium is being referred to.[15]

What, then, made a Christian work of art into an icon? By the seventh and eighth centuries the argument over *eikones* was understood to refer to holy images which received special veneration, and particularly to images depicting Christ, the Virgin, or the saints, usually in non-narrative

[15] For the ambiguity see Averil Cameron, Judith Herrin, *et al.*, eds, *Constantinople in the Eighth Century: the* Parastaseis Syntomoi Chronikai (Leiden, 1984), pp. 31 (as applied to statues), 48–52 (often mentioning different materials used, but still in the same general vocabulary).

Plate 3 Tapestry Panel of the Virgin Enthroned, wool, sixth century (The Cleveland Museum of Art, Leonard C. Hanna, Jr, Fund 67.144).

representations, that is, in the familiar frontal poses adopted in the great Sinai icons of this period representing the Virgin and Child with archangels and saints, Christ, and St Peter (colour plate 1 and plates 4 and 5). Similar images, as we have seen, might also appear in fixed form on the walls of churches, whether in mosaic or fresco; famous surviving examples include the mosaic of the Virgin and Child from Kiti in Cyprus, usually dated to the sixth century (plate 6), the seventh-century mosaics from the church of St Demetrius in Thessaloniki (plate 7), and the frescos in the seventh-century Roman church of S. Maria Antiqua. An encaustic icon of the Virgin also survives from the church of S. Maria in Trastavere, in Rome (plate 8). In addition, there is plentiful evidence for small images owned by private individuals, either fixed in their houses or capable of being carried around.[16] The kind of veneration offered to such images is shown in later illustrations; it consisted of *proskynesis* (bowing, kneeling) and *aspasmos* (kissing the image, as today). These practices, too, become more formalized (though still leaving a good deal to individual habit)[17] only after the final defeat of Iconoclasm. That they were already in use in our period is, however, clear from the fact that they are explicitly discussed by Leontius of Neapolis and others in the seventh century, who defended the practice in terms which were later taken up by John of Damascus and by the Second Council of Nicaea.[18] It is interesting to see that the practice of kissing and bowing down before images is associated in these texts with venerating the Cross, a practice which was also becoming more important in this period, with the acquisition by Justin II of the fragment of the True Cross from Apamea, and still more with the recovery by Heraclius of the True Cross from Jerusalem after its capture by the Persians, and its subsequent transfer to Constantinople.[19] Again, it

[16] Cyril Mango, *The Art of the Byzantine Empire, AD 312 to 1453* (Englewood Cliffs, 1972), pp. 113ff., 133–41, gives an excellent introduction to the literary evidence.

[17] See Bishop Kallistos of Diokleia, 'The Meaning of the Divine Liturgy for the Byzantine Worshipper', in R. Morris, ed., *Church and People in Byzantium* (Birmingham, 1990), p. 13.

[18] Mansi, 13, 284A–B; cf. 377E; see N. Baynes, 'The Icons before Iconoclasm', *HThR*, 45 (1951), pp. 93–106, repr. in his *Byzantine Studies and Other Essays* (London, 1955), pp. 226–39, at pp. 232–4. For John of Damascus, veneration of icons, veneration of the Cross, and praying towards the East are main issues. With the increasing awareness of Islam among Christian writers the justification of *proskynesis* becomes even more of an urgent theme.

[19] Justin II: Michael the Syrian, *Chronicle*, ed. J. B. Chabot, 4 vols (Paris, 1899–1910), 2, p. 285 for Jerusalem, see further below. *Mir. Art.*, ch. 33, refers to the adoration of the Cross as a regular rite, and the Feast of the Exaltation of the Cross seems to have received a special impetus with its restoration by Heraclius. See, in general, A. Frolow, *La Relique de la vraie croix. Recherches sur le développement d'un culte* (Paris, 1961), and see Averil Cameron, 'Byzantium in the Seventh Century. The Search for Redefinition', in J. Fontaine and J. Hillgarth, eds, *The Seventh Century: Change and Continuity* (London, forthcoming).

Plate 4 Encaustic Icon of the Virgin Enthroned between St Theodore and St George, Monastery of St Catherine, Mount Sinai (by permission of Princeton University Press).

Plate 5 St Peter, Monastery of St Catherine, Mount Sinai (by permission of Princeton University Press).

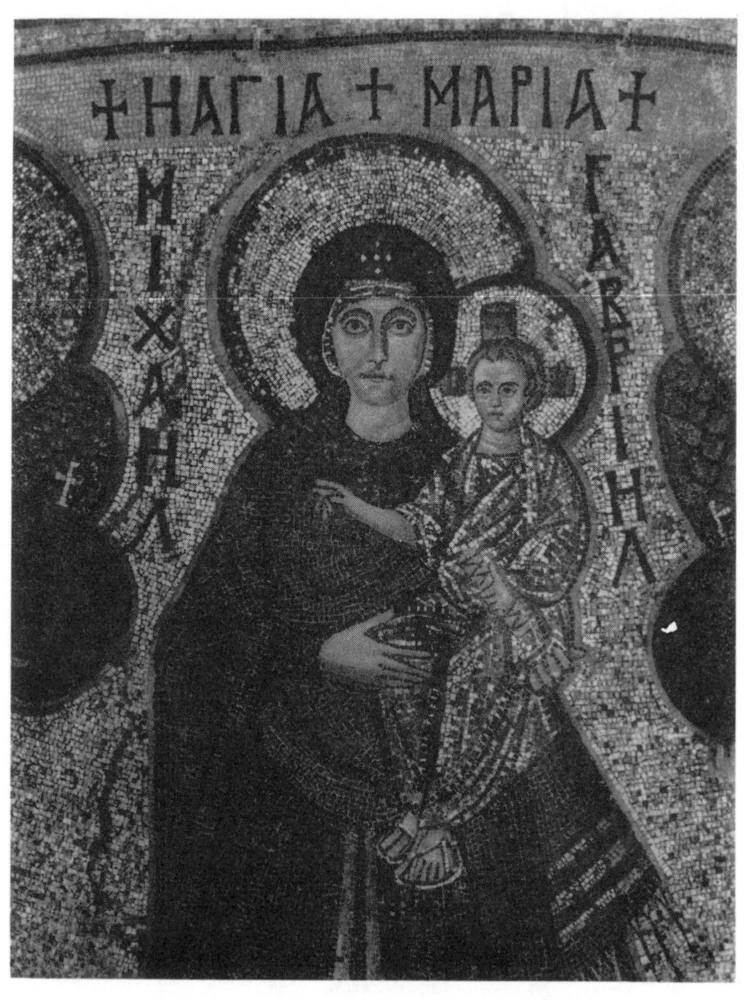

Plate 6 Apse Mosaic, Virgin and Child, Kiti, Cyprus.

Plate 7 Mosaic of St Demetrius between a Bishop and a Dignitary, Church of St Demetrius, Thessaloniki.

Plate 8 Encaustic Icon of Madonna and Child with Archangels (Rome, Santa Maria in Trastevere).

is clear that it was not only the liturgy as such that was in the process of evolution during these years, but also the actual practices of individual Christians in churches. Not all the argument over images was on the level of high theory; it was also directed at these and other practical manifestations in Christian piety, especially, as we shall see, the customs to be followed when taking the Eucharist.[20] At one level the questioning of images was part of the response to a period of unusual innovation and development in church practice.

If we wish to discover what it was that made these particular images 'holy' in a sense which set them apart, even, perhaps, at this period, from other sorts of religious art, we must, I think, consider both their subject and the sense of divine presence; the images in question were taken to be not 'works of art' in the modern sense, but depictions of objective reality, and, as such, were held to bring the very presence of the divine to the worshipper.[21] Images 'recalled' the Gospel narrative or the saint who was depicted,[22] but they were also regarded as having all the power of the personage represented. Looking at the great Sinai icons, with their intense gaze, it is easy to see how this could be so.

SCHOLASTICISM AND THE SEARCH FOR AUTHORITY

But if icons claimed to represent the truth, it was indeed precisely the issue of knowledge, that is, of access to the truth, that was now in question. The period before Iconoclasm, that of the 'rise of icons', saw a drastic revision of what now counted as 'knowledge', and coincided with some fundamental developments: the evolution of fanciful *patria* in the place of history, the relegation of Constantine the Great to legend and sainthood, the end of the flourishing Neoplatonism of Late Antiquity,[23] the mushrooming of collections of miracle stories testifying to divine

[20] See n. 119 below.

[21] For the former distinction, see H. Belting, *Bild und Kunst. Eine Geschichte des Bildes vor dem Zeitalter der Kunst* (Munich, 1990); for the idea of presence, cf. Bishop Kallistos, 'The Meaning of the Divine Liturgy', pp. 8–11, citing the *Life of S. Stephen the Younger*: 'the icon may be termed a door' to the heavenly realm (*PG* 100, col. 1113A).

[22] Mansi 13, 288C.

[23] Whatever actually happened to the Athenian philosophers who left the Academy of Athens in 529, Byzantium in the seventh century no longer had the great philosophical schools of Late Antiquity where Christians and pagans could learn side by side; for a brief and lively description of the latter see P. Chuvin, *A Chronicle of the Last Pagans* (Cambridge, Mass., 1990), pp. 91–118, 131–50, and on the Athenian philosophers, especially Simplicius, see I. Hadot, 'The Life and Work of Simplicius in Greek and Arabic Sources', in R. Sorabji, ed., *Aristotle Transformed. The Ancient Commentators and their Influence* (London, 1990), pp. 275–303.

intervention, a sharp decrease in the availability of traditional secular learning, with the establishment of the Byzantine chronicle tradition, the avid collection of proof-texts for dogmatic use—handlists of useful arguments and quotations from the Scriptures and the Fathers, and the growth of a literature of question and answer providing a vade-mecum for seventh- and eighth-century Byzantines.[24] Attention has been drawn by others to this period as marking an incipient Byzantine scholasticism and the formulation of a conception of authority as resting in a fixed canon of the Fathers.[25] The concern for codification intensified in inverse proportion as access to the old knowledge receded, and is vividly illustrated in the lengthy strings of authorities cited by both sides in the proceedings of the Sixth and Seventh Ecumenical Councils. Such a technologizing of religious authority inevitably gave rise to fakes and bogus citations, and laborious measures were taken at the Sixth Council in 680–1 to check authenticity—an interesting reflection on the morality of seventh-century churchmen.[26] The concern for textual evidence and the manufacture of authoritative documents is shown in a story told by Anastasius of Sinai of how a Monophysite *praefectus augustalis* of Egypt employed fourteen scribes to make multiple copies of patristic texts, especially the works of Cyril of Alexandria, rewritten in order to make them into Monophysite propaganda.[27] The same Anastasius argues elsewhere that material signs are superior to written texts, just because texts are so likely to be falsified.[28] It was not easy to get hold even of important texts, and even those who, one might have thought, were well placed to have access to them did not always know the works which are central to our own discussion. Thus Patriarch Germanos in Constantinople did not have access to the *Apology* of Leontius of Neapolis, although it was known to John of

[24] See for the *patria* and the question and answer literature respectively, G. Dagron, *Constantinople imaginaire* (Paris, 1984) and 'Le Saint, le savant, l'astrologue'. Constantine the Great: see n. 115 below.

[25] See Patrick Gray, 'The "Select Fathers": canonizing the patristic past', *Studia Patristica*, 23 (1989), pp. 21–36, and 'Neochalcedonianism and the tradition: from patristic to Byzantine theology', *Byzantinische Forschungen*, 8 (1982), pp. 61–70; Averil Cameron, 'Models of the Past in the Late Sixth Century: the Life of the Patriarch Eutychius', in G. Clarke, ed., *Reading the Past in Late Antiquity* (Canberra: 1990), pp. 205–23.

[26] See Judith Herrin, *The Formation of Christendom* (Oxford, 1987), p. 278; examples: Mansi, 11, 225B–9A; 332D; 336D; 381–449; see also G. Bardy, 'Faux et fraudes littéraires dans l'antiquité chrétienne', *RHE*, 32 (1936), pp. 290–2, and esp. P. Van den Ven, 'La patristique et l'hagiographie au concile de Nicée en 787', *Byzantion*, 25–7 (1955–7), pp. 325–62.

[27] *Hodegos*, X.2.7, ed. K.-H. Uthemann, *Anastasii Opera. Viae Dux*, *CChr.SG*, 8 (1981); *PG* 89, cols 184–5.

[28] *Hod.*, XII.3, *PG* 89, col. 198; see the very interesting discussion by A. Kartsonis, *Anastasis* (Princeton, 1986), pp. 40–63.

Damascus in Jerusalem; it is some measure of the general difficulty of access to books that it was brought to the notice of the Second Council of Nicaea by legates from Rome.[29] The Second Council of Nicaea cited the *Miracles of Cosmas and Damian*, but not those of Artemius, and despite the prominence it gave to John of Damascus as a defender of images, did not cite directly from his works. Ironically, we may feel, a new sort of textual criticism evolved in response to this situation, and, in particular, to the attempts to bend the record, which were evidently a serious problem: in order to check authenticity, extraordinary measures were taken to seek out complete texts of works commonly cited only in second-hand extracts, a particularly elaborate procedure of citation, proof-texts, and checking being employed at the Second Council of Nicaea in 787,which ended the first phase of Byzantine Iconoclasm. The florilegia of scriptural and patristic citations, which are so prominent a feature of this period, are yet another indicator of this desire to claim authority for approved texts, and thus to guarantee access to genuine knowledge.[30] Very naturally in such circumstances, iconophiles, attacked by Iconoclasts as innovators, made particular use of the appeal to tradition and authority, though it is also true that in so doing they were selective about the precise elements in the past history of the Church which were to be accepted.[31] Indeed, the appeal to unwritten as well as written tradition is a basic argument used in John of Damascus's apologies in defence of images.

Amongst their other properties, then, icons—religious images—functioned as a component in the system of knowledge which evolved as Byzantine society shed its classical past.[32] Of course, that is far from being the whole story. But let us see what it might add to the existing explanations for Byzantine Iconoclasm.

[29] See Déroche, 'L'Authenticité de l'"Apologie contre les Juifs"', pp. 667–8.

[30] See Cyril Mango, 'The Availability of Books in the Byzantine Empire, A.D. 750–850', in *Byzantine Books and Bookmen* (Washington, DC, 1975), pp. 29–46, esp. 30–1.

[31] N. Baynes, 'Idolatry and the Early Church', in his *Byzantine Studies and Other Essays* (London, 1955), pp. 116–43, esp. p. 141; J. McGuckin, 'The Theology of Images and the Legitimation of Power in Eighth-Century Byzantium', forthcoming. The iconophile argument in Germanos's *De haeresibus et synodis* (*PG* 98, cols 40–88) and elsewhere rests on the idea that images belong to the tradition of the Ecumenical Councils, whereas Iconoclasm is a flagrant example of heresy. See also Leslie Brubaker, 'Byzantine art in the ninth century: theory, practice and culture', *Byzantine and Modern Greek Studies*, 13 (1989), pp. 23–93, at pp. 42–56, emphasizing the role of the florilegia, of which the *Sacra Parallela* attributed to John of Damascus is the most conspicuous example, and which was duly illustrated with approved miniatures: see K. Weitzmann, *The Miniatures in the Sacra Parallela* (Princeton, 1979).

[32] See also the stimulating article by G. Dagron, 'Le Culte des images dans le monde byzantin', in his collection *La Romanité chrétienne en Orient* (London, 1984), no. XI.

These arguments take various forms, with varying degrees of nuance and plausibility. Aside from the view of Iconoclasm as a purely theological quarrel, some theories focus narrowly on the contemporary context; thus it is often argued that Byzantine Iconoclasm took its impetus from contemporary Islam, sometimes with reference to the Syrian origin of the first iconoclastic emperor, Leo III. It is thus connected straightforwardly with imperial personalities. But it has also received broader explanations, being seen, for instance, as essentially puritanical; a reform movement within the religious life of Byzantium inspired by the sense that the recent problems of the Empire were a punishment from God as well as, perhaps, by a sense of justified criticism from Jews, Muslims, or traditionalist Christians. Alternatively, it has been interpreted as a social movement, or as a matter of the assertion of imperial authority, whether over and against an overly-independent Church, represented particularly by the monks, or, in political terms, after decades of danger and insecurity.[33] Lastly, this was a historical crisis of major proportions, which centred on questions of visual art; naturally, therefore, it has also been seen primarily as a problem in art history.[34]

In the case of the 'rise of icons', one version of what we might term the social explanation is represented by the persistent claim that devotion to icons represents a type of popular religion.[35] Peter Brown has argued to some extent against this view, by emphasizing the appeal of icons to 'human', not 'popular', needs: 'Rather than assume that the worship of icons rose like a damp stain from the masses, we should look into the

[33] See Cormack, *Writing in Gold*, pp. 106–18, for an excellent analysis of the range of explanations listed above. Muslim iconoclasm: see G. R. D. King, 'Islam, Iconoclasm and the declaration of doctrine', *Bulletin of the School of Oriental and African Studies*, 48 (1985), pp. 267–77.

[34] Discussion of the coins of Justinian II and their possible relation to contemporary Islamic coinage (Cormack, *Writing in Gold*, pp. 96–106) is part of the story. See also J. Moorhead, 'Byzantine Iconoclasm as a problem in art history', *Parergon*, ns 4 (1986), pp. 1–18. The style and development of icons themselves in the sixth and seventh centuries is still a controversial matter, being hampered by the paucity of surviving material and the lack of external dating criteria; see especially the works of E. Kitzinger, 'On Some Icons of the Seventh Century', in K. Weitzmann *et al.*, eds., *Late Classical and Medieval Studies in Honor of A. M. Friend* (Princeton, 1955), pp. 132–50; 'Byzantine art in the period between Justinian and Iconoclasm', *Berichte zum XI. internationalen Byzantinisten Kongress* (Munich, 1958), pp. 1–50; *Byzantine Art in the Making* (Cambridge, Mass., 1977), and for some discussion of the issues, J. Trilling, 'Sinai Icons: another look', *Byzantion*, 53 (1983), pp. 300–11. After writing this paper I found many parallelisms of approach with the valuable discussion of the later phase of Byzantine Iconoclasm by Brubaker, 'Byzantine art in the ninth century' (see esp. pp. 23–4).

[35] See Cyril Mango, *Byzantium. The Empire of New Rome* (London, 1980), p. 98 ('popular piety') and especially Kitzinger, 'The Cult of Images'; Herrin, *The Formation of Christendom*, p. 307.

needs which the piety of Late Antique men sought to satisfy in looking at them.'[36] Icons are also held to have a characteristically 'private' role—hence their tendency to be cited in stories about women, who are always seen as the denizens of the private sphere.[37] But their appeal was universal: a good deal of contemporary anecdotal evidence suggests that they were seen by high and low alike as offering the power of emotional solace and access to the divine. This might affect emperors and empresses as much as humble people; they too had their favourite icons, and displayed them in public as well as private life. The first major public icons, including the image of Christ 'not made by human hands' from Camuliana, appeared in the context of the wars against Persia in the late sixth century, when they were publicly paraded,[38] and in Constantinople, too, public images, like relics, were brought out at times of crisis, especially when the city was attacked; it is in this period that the Virgin, through her icon and relics, acquired her status as the protectress of the city.[39] Rich donors were also quick to associate themselves with images of Christ, the Virgin, and the saints in the decorative schemes which they financed.[40] Here, too, public and private merge. Robin Cormack emphasizes the role played by icons in the story of the life of Theodore of Sykeon; in only one of several such interventions, the saints Cosmas and Damian come out of their icon to cure him and to go off to Heaven for help on his behalf.[41] But the icons demonstrate the power of the saint to individuals: in their role as 'supernatural defenders' they also protected the state and society at large.[42]

It has generally been held that the disturbed social conditions which prevailed in the Byzantine 'Dark Age' fostered the popularity of religious images. In most of its forms such a view is not only functionalist (icons serve a useful purpose in assuaging anxiety), but also essentially reductionist

[36] 'A Dark-Age crisis: aspects of the Iconoclastic Controversy', *EHR*, 88 (1973), pp. 1–34, repr. in his *Society and the Holy in Late Antiquity* (Berkeley and Los Angeles, 1982), pp. 251–301, esp. p. 274; earlier, he had written of the 'democratization' of culture in Late Antiquity: see *The World of Late Antiquity* (London, 1971), pp. 74–180ff., on which see Averil Cameron, 'Images of authority: elites and icons in late sixth-century Byzantium', *PaP*, 84 (1979), pp. 3–35, esp. 24–5.

[37] See Herrin, *The Formation of Christendom*, pp. 309f. and other works cited there; *Christianity and the Rhetoric of Empire*, pp. 201–3.

[38] Ps. Zacharias Rhetor, *Historia ecclesiastica*, XII.4, tr. in Mango, *Art of the Byzantine Empire*, pp. 114–15.

[39] See further Cameron, 'Images of authority'.

[40] Cf. also the analysis of the *Miracles of S. Demetrios* and the mosaics of the church of St Demetrios at Thessaloniki: Cormack, *Writing in Gold*, pp. 50–94.

[41] *Writing in Gold*, p. 46; analysis of the *Life of Theodore of Sykeon*, pp. 39–47.

[42] See N. Baynes, 'The supernatural defenders of Constantinople', *AnBoll*, 67 (1949), pp. 165–77 and 'The icons before Iconoclasm', *HThR*, 44 (1951), pp. 116–43 (both in his *Byzantine Studies and Other Essays*, pp. 248–60 and 226–39 respectively).

Plate 9 Fresco with Virgin Enthroned between St Felix and St Adauctus, with Turtura, in whose honour the fresco was dedicated by her son, sixth century (Rome, Catacomb of Commodilla).

(icons are to be explained in terms other than religious ones). Whatever its merits, it does not do full justice either to the seventh-century developments or to the extraordinary persistence and eventual victory of the iconophiles in the ninth century, which ensured the centrality of icons in the Orthodox Church to this day. Nevertheless, it is possible to avoid these pitfalls while still focusing on the seventh to eighth centuries as a period of major change.

This change affected the very structure of Byzantine society, and thus the relationships within it, usually in drastic ways—between town and country, capital and provinces, civil and military. Especially after the death of Heraclius in 641, and the dismal times which followed for the Empire, imperial authority diminished, leaving more and more of a leadership role to the Church and the higher clergy. The latter should not be seen as an isolated sector of society; a substantial number of bishops in this period had also held civil office, and in the siege of Constantinople in 626 nobody found it odd for authority to be vested in the patriarch, nor for the military despatches later sent back from the Emperor Heraclius's campaigns against the Persians to be read out from the ambo in Hagia Sophia, also the scene of political demonstrations.[43] The interdependence in these events of civil and ecclesiastical authorities, and indeed personnel, is very striking; indeed, the responses to the military danger included actual liturgical innovation.[44] The early seventh century saw some important developments in the patriarchal liturgy of Hagia Sophia in Constantinople, which collectively can only have enhanced the position and authority of the patriarch himself.[45] The triumphal return of the Emperor from his Persian wars, when he was formally met at Hieria by his son and the patriarch Sergius, also combined liturgical features with traditional imperial ceremony.[46] The Church's position changed in other ways, too. Its wealth, if anything, had been increasing; even small and obscure Syrian churches in the seventh century owned vast amounts of liturgical silver, which continue to present us with surprises in relation to the overall economic picture (plate 10).[47] The Quinisext Council of 691–2 was

[43] *Chronicon Paschale, 284–628 AD*, ed. and tr. Michael and Mary Whitby (Liverpool, 1989), *s.a.* 626, 628.

[44] Ibid., *s.a.* 624, and cf. also *s.a.* 615; for all this account see the valuable translation and notes by Michael and Mary Whitby, esp. pp. 166ff., referring to further bibliography; the 626 siege marked an important moment in the formation of the idea of Constantinople as specially protected by God and especially the Virgin, although the famous icon of the Virgin at Blachernae (no longer surviving) is not securely attested at this date (see Averil Cameron, 'The Virgin's robe; an episode in the history of early seventh-century Constantinople', *Byzantion*, 49 (1979), pp. 47–8). The editors comment that the liturgical changes of 615 and 624 were 'intended to emphasise that God was present with the congregation, a reliable source of protection in troubled times' (p. 168, n. 454).

[45] See, e.g., H.-J. Schulz, *The Byzantine Liturgy*, Eng. tr. (New York, 1986), pp. 38–40, 164–72.

[46] Theophanes, *Chronographia*, ed. C. de Boor (Leipzig, 1883), 1, anno mundi 6119, pp. 327–8; cf. Nicephorus, *Breviarum*, 19, and see Michael McCormick, *Eternal Victory* (Cambridge, 1986), pp. 70–2. On the chronological problems and the question of whether or not these two accounts refer to the same occasion, see Mango, *Patriarch Nikephoros*, pp. 185–6.

[47] See now Marlia Mundell Mango, 'The Uses of Liturgical Silver, 4th–7th Centuries', in Morris, ed., *Church and People in Byzantium*, pp. 245–62; cf. also M. Kaplan, 'L'Eglise byzantin des VIe–XIe siècles: terres et paysans', in ibid., pp. 109–23; according to Procopius, *De*

Plate 10 Silver Paten from Stuma Treasure, showing the Communion of the Apostles, Syria, late sixth century (Istanbul Archaeological Musem).

justifiably worried about the situation of bishops and clergy whose sees had been taken over by 'barbarians'; but even as these lands were lost, the growth of monastic holdings changed the balance of ecclesiastical to secular property in the territories which remained. While these major

aedificiis, ed. J. Haury, rev. G. Wirth (Leipzig, 1913), I. 1. 65, the original sanctuary furnishings of St Sophia in Constantinople amounted to 40,000 lbs of silver; the altar was of gold, with gold columns and a ciborium of silver (Paul the Silentiary, *Ekphrasis on Hagia Sophia*, ed. P. Friedländer, *Johannes von Gaza und Paulus Silentiarius* (Leipzig and Berlin, 1912), lines 720–54). The same period saw changes in the monetary and fiscal structure as basic as any of the military and administrative developments: see the contributions by C. Morrisson, J. Durliat, and R. Delmaire in *Hommes et richesses dans l'empire byzantin, IVe–VIIe siècle* (Paris, 1989).

changes were affecting the place of churches, monasteries, and ecclesiastics in Byzantine society, we see a parallel move towards the interpretation of the liturgy and the churches themselves. In several contemporary works the Church is interpreted as the image or microcosm of heaven, and the liturgy itself as a symbolic enactment which also implied the real presence of God. Church furniture, vestments, icons were all parts that made up the whole, as a series of writers pointed out.[48]

Why did images become so much more of an issue in the East than in the West? While not neglecting the inheritance of debate about Christian art, we must also place the rise of icons in its contemporary context. We have already noted the extent of general social change in the East in the seventh century, and the fact that icons also came to prominence simultaneously with an increasing splendour in the celebration of the liturgy, accompanied by a theoretical exposition in symbolic terms, and a focusing of attention on the meaning of the Eucharist and on all aspects of church decoration, furniture, and ceremony. We shall see that the opponents of icons were concerned not only with the Platonizing concepts of image and prototype, but also with questions of materiality and symbolism which arose in several other seventh-century contexts. Already in the sixth century the patriarch Eutychius had argued against a symbolic interpretation of the Eucharist,[49] and we shall see during the seventh century a shift away from the more symbolic interpretation of Maximus Confessor in the direction of literal realism, associated with Patriarch Germanos I (715–30). Thus the debate in which religious images were a part was both more immediate and more continuous in the Eastern context, where the history of Christian opposition to images combined with the particular circumstances of the seventh century to make them the focus of existing tensions between symbolism and realism.

[48] See Bishop Kallistos, 'The Meaning of the Divine Liturgy', and further below. Symbolic interpretations of church buildings: Corippus, *In laudem Iustini*, IV. 288–311, ed. with tr. and comm. Averil Cameron (London, 1976), with pp. 206–7; Paul the Silentiary, *Ekphrasis on H. Sophia*, on which see R. Macrides and P. Magdalino, 'The architecture of Ekphrasis: construction and context of Paul the Silentiary's Ekphrasis of Hagia Sophia', *Byzantine and Modern Greek Studies*, 12 (1988), pp. 47–82; Andrew Palmer, with Lyn Rodley, 'The inauguration anthem of Hagia Sophia in Edessa: a new edition and translation with historical and architectural notes and a comparison with a contemporary Constantinopolitan kontakion', ibid., pp. 117–67; Mathews, *The Early Churches of Constantinople*, and on the symbolism of church architecture in the ninth century and later, cf. also 'The Transformation Symbolism in Byzantine Architecture and the Meaning of the Pantokrator in the Dome', in Morris, ed., *Church and People in Byzantium*, pp. 191–214.

[49] Eutychius, *Sermo de paschate et eucharistia*, *PG* 86, 2.2400–1.

THE PROBLEM OF CHRISTIAN REPRESENTATION

But the immediate circumstances of the late seventh and early eighth centuries do not provide the whole explanation for the concerns voiced about religious images, for besides the traditional prohibition of figural art, the question of religious images also relates to longstanding problems which Christians had had with the verbal representation of religious truth.[50] The Iconoclasts claimed that only the human, not the divine, nature of God could be represented in visual terms.[51] A very similar difficulty had been felt in relation to language by Christian writers for centuries, especially by the Cappadocians; indeed, the representation of God in linguistic terms is still an issue today. One author who followed in the tradition of negative theology set by the Cappadocians was Pseudo-Dionysius the Areopagite, and, sure enough, during the period of the 'rise of icons' the Pseudo-Dionysius's works gained increasing importance. Several sets of scholia on his works were put together in the sixth and seventh centuries, culminating with the work of John Damascene in the eighth. In contrast to theologians, many historians have tended to neglect such works as peripheral to their concerns, yet the fact that the Pseudo-Dionysius, who posed in the sharpest possible way the central problem of Christian representation, and did so exactly as the rival secular culture was on the verge of yielding, rapidly became canonical for all parties is in itself surely significant.

In a famous passage Pseudo-Dionysius the Areopagite writes of the ultimate darkness of religious experience. Taking up themes from Gregory of Nyssa's *Life of Moses* and from Gregory of Nazianzus, he describes how, when Moses knows God, he plunges into the 'truly mysterious darkness of unknowing'.[52] His briefest work, the *Mystical Theology*, begins with a prayer to the Trinity:

> Lead us up beyond unknowing and light,
> up to the farthest, highest peak
> of mystic scripture,

[50] For discussion of earlier patristic views see Charles Murray, 'Art in the Early Church', *JThS*, ns 28 (1977), pp. 303–45; 'Le Problème d'iconophobie et les premiers siècles chrétiens', in F. Boespflug and N. Lossky, eds, *Nicée II 787–1987* (Paris, 1987), pp. 39–49.

[51] See P. Henry, 'What was the Iconoclastic Controversy all about?' *Church History*, 45 (1976), pp. 21–5.

[52] *Mystical Theology*, 1001A, tr. C. Luibheid and P. Rorem, *Pseudo Dionysius: the Complete Works* (London, 1987), p. 137; cf. V. Lossky, *The Mystical Theology of the Eastern Church*, tr. Members of the Fellowship of St Alban and St Sergius (Cambridge, 1957), p. 35.

> where the mysteries of God's Word
> lie simple, absolute and unchangeable
> in the brilliant darkness of a hidden silence.

This is the culmination of negative theology—one cannot describe but only experience in direct contemplation. The logical outcome should have been silence, an end to theology and to all attempts to describe the truth.

In practice, of course, churchmen continued to try to describe the divine. The Pseudo-Dionysius himself discusses the implications of the view that God can only be assessed through images. While he presents this as a linguistic dilemma, he also discusses the imagery commonly used of God in more visual terms. In letter 9, for instance, he describes how in the lost *Symbolic Theology* he had discussed the physical imagery used of God in the Old Testament, including the cruder forms of anthropomorphism; these are to be found, he argues, 'so that what is hidden may be brought out into the open and multiplied, what is unique and undivided may be divided up and multiple shapes and forms be given to what has no shape or form.'[53] Similarly, the ranks of angels are represented as creatures on thrones, not 'for the sake of art', but 'as a concession to the nature of our own mind',[54] for the real simplicity of the heavenly creatures cannot be depicted at all. The author is not concerned with religious images in the sense of icons, but rather with the much more basic question of how God can be apprehended in the first place. These images do not operate through likeness but because they are dissimilar, and this is, in the mind of the Pseudo-Dionysius, the superior form of representation since it does not pretend to portray what is actually transcendent and indescribable.[55]

But the author is indeed in a dilemma. He takes up the Pauline saying at Romans 1.20, according to which the invisible truth is to be understood through the visible world;[56] 'the visible is truly the plain image of the invisible',[57] even while, again like Paul, he emphasizes the mysteriousness of God, which cannot be expressed directly but only through signs, as in the case of the parables of Jesus.[58] The Pseudo-Dionysius was not writing about the religious images that we call icons, that is, direct representations

[53] Letter 9, 1105C, pp. 282–3.
[54] *Celestial Hierarchies*, 2, 137B, p. 148.
[55] Ibid., 140D, p. 149.
[56] Letter 9, 2, 1108B, p. 284.
[57] Letter 10, 1117B, p. 289.
[58] Letter 9, 1105D, p. 283.

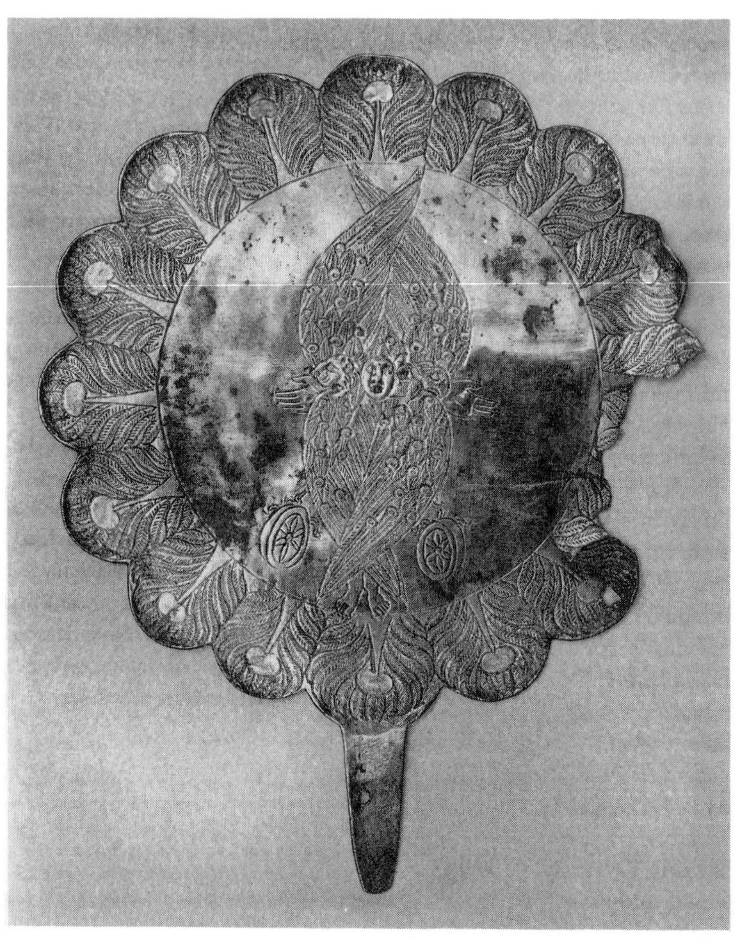

Plate 11 Silver-gilt Rhipidion (liturgical fan) from Riha, Syria, late sixth century, with cherub flanked by fiery wheels, as in the Vision of Ezekiel (cf. Ezekiel 1. 5–14) (Byzantine Visual Resources, © 1991, Dumbarton Oaks, Washington, DC).

of Christ, the Virgin, and the saints, but about the figural depictions of God and the cherubim to be found in the Old Testament. But the cherubim of Solomon and Ezekiel, like the brazen serpent of Moses, were to feature in the catalogues of Old Testament representations to which iconophiles turned for supporting evidence.[59] Indeed, his preoccupation with the general issue of representation of the divine made him a natural source for the iconophile writers, who selected the parts of his argument most congenial to their needs. As has been noted, Hypatius of Ephesus in the sixth century had already justified Christian art along the lines of interpretation laid down by the Pseudo-Dionysius.[60] But the Pseudo-Dionysius is not to be seen as wholly symbolist;[61] a more realist reading is also possible, which lays emphasis on the liturgy and the sacraments, and this approach was indeed taken up in the course of the greater emphasis on literalism in the late seventh century. Accordingly, the Iconoclasts were also able to claim his support at the Iconoclast Council of Hieria in 754, as the acts of the Seventh Council make clear: 'Since they put as a preface the patristic words of Dionysius the revealer of God, would that they had preserved his teachings, as well as those of all our holy Fathers, unbroken.'[62] But he was particularly cited by iconophiles: the account of the decoration of Hosios David at Thessaloniki, for instance, refers directly to the Pseudo-Dionysius's discussion of cherubim.[63] Iconophiles were able to find in the corpus a justification both for the double concept of the Eucharist as image and as the Real Presence, and were thus able to deny that the Eucharist was '*only* an image'.[64] In one sense, the thrust of the writings of the Pseudo-Dionysius led to the path of contemplation, mystical silence, and this was

59 E.g. Joh. Dam., *Oratio* III.22, *De imaginibus*; Theodore Abu Qurrah, *De cultu imaginum*, ed. I. Dick, *Théodore Abuqurra, Traité du culte des icones* (Jounieh and Rome, 1986, ch. 15); see Sidney H. Griffith, 'Theodore Abu Qurrah's Arabic Tract on the Christian practice of venerating images', *Journal of the American Oriental Society*, 105 (1985), pp. 53–73. I am grateful to Sidney Griffith for his generosity in sharing his translation with me in advance of publication, and for continued help in other ways.

60 Kitzinger, 'Cult of images', pp. 137f., with Charles Murray, 'Artistic Idiom and Doctrinal Development', in Rowan Williams, ed., *The Making of Orthodoxy. Essays in Honour of Henry Chadwick* (Cambridge, 1989), pp. 288–308, at p. 298, and Baynes, 'The icons before Iconoclasm', pp. 226–8.

61 As, for instance, J. Meyendorff, *Christ in Eastern Christian Thought* (Washington, 1969), p. 79; see, however, P. Rorem, *Biblical and Liturgical Symbols within the Pseudo-Dionysian Synthesis = Studies and Texts*, 71 (Toronto, 1984); A. Louth, 'Pagan theurgy and Christian sacramentalism in Denys the Areopagite', *JThS*, ns 37 (1986), pp. 432–8, and see his *Denys the Areopagite* (London, 1989).

62 Mansi, 13, 212A, tr. D. Sahas, *Icon and Logos: Sources in Eighth-Century Iconoclasm* (Toronto, 1986), p. 54.

63 Ignatius Monachus, *Narratio de imagine Christi in monasterio Latoni*, 6, tr. in Mango, *Art of the Byzantine Empire*, p. 155.

64 See Bishop Kallistos, 'The Meaning of the Divine Liturgy', p. 17.

certainly a strong element in the theology of Maximus;[65] signs and symbols pointed the seeker of truth on his way, not logical argument.

Thus knowledge of God, if it cannot be adequately expressed in language, must come through signs. Pseudo-Dionysius was voicing an emphasis on the hiddenness of divine truth and the need for revelation through signs which had been present in Christian discourse from the earliest times. In the *Ecclesiastical Hierarchy* he understands the liturgy in this way. The language is difficult; the synaxis itself is said to be surrounded by 'symbolic garments of enigmas', yet the Sacrament can nevertheless show itself clearly and 'fill the eyes of our mind with a unifying and ineffable light'.[66] As the Pseudo-Dionysius insists, it is St Paul's emphasis on mystery and paradox that lies behind this thinking. Paul too lays heavy stress on the hiddenness of divine truth, how God's 'foolishness has confounded the wisdom of the world' by the paradox of the Cross and how now 'we see through a glass, darkly'.[67] Augustine, in his turn, had struggled to define the source and nature of divine knowledge, citing the same Pauline arguments in doing so;[68] he too arrived at the view that knowledge of God came through revelation, and spoke of the Scriptures as the 'fleshly wrappings' of the truth.[69] Following Paul, Christian discourse itself was essentially figural, and our consciousness of the long-standing conflict over biblical interpretation between Alexandrian allegorizers and Antiochene literalists should not be allowed to obscure the fact that all Christian writers alike, from Paul onwards, used a vocabulary of mystery and hidden meaning.

After all, Christian discourse appealed to faith: 'He that hath ears, let him hear', and 'It is given unto you to know the mysteries of the kingdom of heaven.'[70] Fundamental to it was the idea of a complex of signs and symbols requiring interpretation but capable of revealing the truth; despite the Old Testament prohibition on graven images, it was only a very short step from this figural discourse to the resort to actual visual images.[71] When Anastasius of Sinai preferred pictorial representations to

65 Cf. R. Mortley, *From Word to Silence*, 2 vols, Theophaneia, 34–35 (Bonn, 1986), esp. 2, pp. 221–41; Maximus: see H. U. von Balthasar, *Kosmische Liturgie. Das Weltbild Maximus des Bekenners*, 2nd edn (Einsiedeln, 1961).

66 *Eccl. Hier.* 2, 428C, p. 212.

67 I Cor. 1. 18f.; 13. 12.

68 *De doctrina christiana*, I.11.11, 12.11; see Cameron, *Christianity and the Rhetoric of Empire*, pp. 66–7.

69 Cf. *De rudibus catechizandis*, 9.13.

70 Mark 4. 9; Matt. 13. 43; Luke 14. 15; Matt. 13. 11.

71 See on this Cameron, *Christianity and the Rhetoric of Empire*, ch. 2, esp. pp. 47–8, 56–7. For revelation by 'signs' and the view of creation as containing 'signs' of God's purpose in the Early Christian period see R. M. Grant, *The Letter and the Spirit* (London, 1957).

written ones, he was only voicing a version of the arguments by which earlier Christian writers had justified and praised religious pictures as a means of instruction.[72] His argument is the converse of the Iconoclast privileging of writing over pictures; by contrast, images and writing were often at this stage simply equated by iconophiles, for whom it was necessary to show that images had the same status as the Scriptures.[73] In the words of John of Damascus, the way was clear: depiction of God in human form was not merely allowable but even incumbent. 'How depict the invisible? How picture the inconceivable?' In his view pictures could help: 'When he who is without form or limitation . . . takes upon himself the form of a servant in substance and a body of flesh, then you may draw his likeness and show it to anyone willing to contemplate it.'[74]

REVELATION THROUGH SIGNS

At this point, however, a shift takes place. Images were not the only indicators of divine truth. Moreover, while symbolism was indeed an issue in this period, it is misleading to talk of symbols in relation to the signs which are the ways of revelation; rather, the signs which are often listed in seventh- and eighth-century authors as ways to an understanding of God are not symbols in the usual sense in which we use the term—when one thing stands for another—but, to quote Lossky, real 'material signs of the presence of the spiritual world'.[75]

These 'signs' by which God reveals himself are variously listed, but typically include the Cross, the Scriptures, the trappings of the liturgy—incense, candles, water, as well as, for instance, the Ark and the Burning Bush. The listing of signs had also begun early;[76] from now on, however, they begin to acquire the status of canonical lists, and holy images to figure as one of the items included.[77] Iconophile writers claim for images the same status as the Cross and the Gospels, deserving of veneration,

[72] See Cameron, *Christianity and the Rhetoric of Empire*, p. 150.

[73] See Brubaker, 'Byzantine art in the ninth century', pp. 70–5 for examples. In later versions of the iconophile argument the point is made that pictures are universal, whereas writing is circumscribed by having to use a specific language.

[74] *Oratio I de imaginibus*, 16, ed. B. Kotter, 3 (Berlin, 1975), pp. 89–90; *PG* 94, col. 1245.

[75] Lossky, *Mystical Theology*, p. 189; this judgement draws on contemporary statements, but cf. also D. Sperber, *Rethinking Symbolism*, Eng. tr. (Cambridge, 1975), p. 85: 'symbols are not signs'.

[76] See, e.g., Cyril of Jerusalem, *Catechetical Homilies*, 10.19.

[77] E.g. John Dam., *Oratio III de imaginibus* 22, Kotter, 3, p. 129, cf. *Or.* I.12 (the Burning Bush, the dew upon the fleece (Judges 6. 40), Aaron's Rod, manna, the brazen serpent (Num. 21.9), the sea, water, and clouds).

though not of worship; as icons are a 'sign', so the other 'signs' could be read as icons.[78] Again, the case of the Cross is instructive: the terms applied to it in the Christian apologiae against the Jews in order to rebut charges of idolatry, include both *typos* and *semeion* (sign);[79] during 'second Iconoclasm' debates about terminology reached a highly sophisticated level in the works of Nicephorus and Theodore the Studite, but in the early stages of the controversy the very ambiguity of the Greek terminology may have helped the equation.

The listings of signs indicates an authoritarian view of divine knowledge, based on revelation; it works on the premise that knowledge is not to be found through secular learning but by direct revelation. But this revelation is not arbitrary; on the contrary, it comes only through the channels which have been officially approved as orthodox by the Church. Thus the arguments about the nature of images, as about material and created signs in general, were indeed arguments about authority, about the licensing of signs. In our period, the learning of the world really does fall away, and as it does, holy images begin to claim the authoritative status of divine 'signs'. The argument on their behalf made large claims: Theodore Abu Qurrah's ninth-century defence of images argues that as Christianity is based on a mystery, to reject icon-veneration is to reject all the other mysteries of Christianity as well. He, too, invokes St Paul, this time for an answer to the accusation that icon-veneration is foolish: had not the Apostle said that Christianity itself was based on foolishness in the eyes of the world—'We speak of God's wisdom in a mystery' and 'The world's wisdom is foolishness with God'?[80] Religious images were a way out of this dilemma; they fell naturally into place as one of the signs by which the impossibility of understanding God through language could be circumvented.[81] But the repertoire of these images was potentially vast, and their doctrinal and other implications could be alarming if uncontrolled. What we see therefore are progressive attempts by iconophiles and Iconoclasts alike to do just that, that is, to regulate the signs and define their meaning.

Miracle afforded another means by which to read the providence of God. As icons are not simply indicators of popular religion, so miracle can be read not just as a manifestation of popular credulity, but as providing

[78] The same idea transferred into Arabic: Abu Qurrah, *De cultu imaginum*, 15: 'the greatest, the most famous icon, the tablets of the Law'.

[79] See Déroche, 'L'Authenticité de l'"Apologie contre les Juifs"', p. 661; see further below.

[80] I Cor. 2. 7; 3. 19, cited by Abu Qurrah, *De cultu imaginum*, 3.

[81] Cf. Brubaker, 'Byzantine art in the ninth century', pp. 75–81.

direct access to knowledge of God, and as a further alternative to secular learning. The period of the so-called 'rise of icons' also saw a proliferation of miracle collections attached to shrines and a great increase in stories of miraculous intervention, often featuring the Virgin or with reference to icons.[82] Like our reading of the significance of icons, how we view the collections of such stories in the *Miracles of Artemius* or the *Miracles of S. Demetrius* (to name only two) is partly a matter of emphasis. While they do certainly testify in our terms to popular credulity, we are equally entitled to see them as yet another example of the impulse towards an authoritative codification of the signs which could lead to religious knowledge.

The Virgin, the Mother of God, is the agent in many of the miracle stories, typically as a beautiful lady dressed in purple or blue, and is frequently mentioned in iconophile argument. Of the surviving pre-Iconoclastic images, a high proportion depict the Virgin and Child, a fact which is indicative of her Christological importance, and which, in itself, illustrates the way in which visual art was being used to make doctrinal points. The period of the rise of icons also saw the establishment of the cult of the Virgin as the special protectress of Constantinople; the 'restoration of orthodoxy' took place in 843, but it was with the dedication by Photius in 867 of an image of the Virgin and Child in the apse of St Sophia that the ending of Iconoclasm was finally confirmed. In the West, from the sixth century onwards, we can see the beginning of the collections of 'Mary miracles' which continue into the medieval period.[83] But while there was nothing quite like this in the East, it was, indeed, precisely now that the icons of the Virgin leapt to prominence in the sieges of 626 and 717; indeed, the great Akathistos hymn was elaborated as a hymn of triumph to the Virgin after the city's deliverance in 626. Now, too, I believe, the Marian relics in Constantinople, the Virgin's robe and girdle, were equipped with their highly elaborated stories.[84]

The Cross, the Mother of God, miracles, the holy images—these must be taken together. I find it hard to separate consideration of icons either from consideration of the other 'signs' or from verbal representation. All were seen as ways of perceiving truth, and truth was seen as absolute and

[82] See Cameron, *Christianity and the Rhetoric of Empire*, pp. 208–13. For some examples, see Mango, *Art of the Byzantine Empire*, pp. 133–9.

[83] See Benedicta Ward, *Miracles and the Medieval Mind. Theory, Record and Event 1000–1215* (London, 1987), pp. 132ff.; Cameron, *Christianity and the Rhetoric of Empire*, pp. 212ff. (also associated with miracle stories focused on the Eucharist).

[84] Cameron, 'Images of authority', pp. 18–24.

objectively real. But such a conception of knowledge was, of course, also political. Again we turn to the Pseudo-Dionysius. Besides his emphasis on mystery and the need for revelation, his most striking characteristic is his insistence on hierarchy, as shown by the titles of his works known as the *Celestial* and *Ecclesiastical Hierarchies*. Being is constituted for him in an ascending hierarchy, from the natural world at the bottom to the divine truth at the summit; heaven and the Church are each similarly constructed. From this it follows that knowledge will be a matter of gradual ascent towards the ultimate. There is no need to labour the Platonic framework within which he writes, except to stress that like Plato he, too, was an advocate of the closed society. For the Pseudo-Dionysius, too, there is no logical way of dissent; it is knowledge, not opinion, about which he writes, *episteme* rather than *doxa*, and knowledge, like Plato's *episteme*, is only of truth. The codification of hierarchies, the marshalling of instances of divine intervention, the listing of patristic and scriptural citations were all striving for this certainty, for which the Pseudo-Dionysius taught that the soul longed with a natural desire (*eros*). It is no coincidence that both the great followers of the Pseudo-Dionysius, Maximus Confessor and John Damascene, each sought effectively to produce great syntheses of Christian knowledge, as though a complete listing of the routes to religious understanding would guarantee the eventual perception of truth.[85]

In such an intellectual climate the various components of the system locked together to form an overall coherence. I am suggesting that we should see icons as part of this complex. The importance of icons is not just a problem in Byzantine art, though, of course, it may be that too. Nor are they to be seen just in social terms, whether in relation to patronage or to private piety. Rather, they provided one of the answers to the problem of how God could be apprehended, a problem which had been inherent in Christianity from the very beginning and which only became more acute as time went on. They were the guarantors of truth;[86] while at the same time a way of controlling true belief. And as the classical alternative fell away, Christian knowledge *was* social knowledge.

[85] Cameron, *Christianity and the Rhetoric of Empire*, pp. 218–19. In John Damascene the defence of images went together with the exposition of the faith (cf. his *De fide orthodoxa*, ed. B. Kotter, *Die Schriften des Johannes von Damaskos*, 2 (Berlin, 1973). For John of Damascus and the idea of a hierarchy of images and approved ways to God, see also John Elsner, 'Image and Iconoclasm in Byzantium', *Art History*, 11 (1988), pp. 471–91, esp. pp. 477–91.

[86] Thus the iconophiles condemned iconophile 'innovation' and claimed their own obedience to apostolic, patristic, and ecclesiastical tradition: Mansi, 13, 208C, tr. Sahas, *Icon and Logos*, p. 52; see Brubaker, 'Byzantine art in the ninth century', pp. 48–9.

This is not the old question of the theology of the icon, but an attempt to place the rise of icons in the context of a general intellectual realignment, in effect, the replacement of the remaining vestiges of classical culture by a codification of knowledge based on religious truth. It has the advantage for the historian that explanations for the rise of icons are neither detached from the general cultural context, as they often are, or too closely linked to particular external circumstances. For while if one could get away from functional explanations altogether, history would probably not be history, historical explanations are much more satisfying if they can embed the phenomena they are trying to explain in a really thick context.

REALISM AND TRUTH

Seeing icons in this way raises some other questions. One is that of realism; for if icons are to be seen not just as a specialized form of Byzantine art, but as having a connection with the sociology of knowledge, the old art-historical problem of realism as opposed to abstractionism has to be reopened. However, the reason why this should be a problem lies more with ourselves and with the way in which we frame the question than with the icons. Contemporaries did not doubt that they were true representations of actual reality, a conviction which explains the accusations of idolatry from Iconoclasts and Muslims alike. To us, Byzantine religious art usually appears anything but realistic.[87] Nor, on the whole, do modern historians share the contemporary beliefs either in the religious entities themselves (or at any rate, not in these objectified forms) or in the notion that language, verbal or artistic, represents objective reality. But the question of realism remains. Photius on the restored image of the Virgin in Hagia Sophia and the French realist painters of the nineteenth century alike claimed that art was a reflection of reality. Both had supreme confidence; neither would have tolerated for a moment the modern difficulty that 'realism' is itself relative.

But during the centuries before Iconoclasm—the period of the rise of icons—the conception of reality itself had changed. Confusingly for us, Erich Auerbach's famous book, *Mimesis*, made 'realism' the touchstone of Christian and medieval, as opposed to classical, representation. His classic

[87] On these issues see L. Brubaker, 'Perception and conception: art, theory and culture in ninth-century Byzantium', *Word and Image*, 5 (1989), forthcoming, with 'Byzantine art in the ninth century', pp. 24–6.

analyses of the Gospel account of Peter's denial of Christ and of the arrest of Peter Valvomeres in the history of Ammianus Marcellinus put forward an antithesis between the formalities of classical representation, with its emphasis on levels of style, and the contrasting realism of Christian and medieval description.[88] Christianity provided the touchstone: to quote from his epilogue, 'It was the story of Christ, with its ruthless mixture of everyday reality and the highest and most sublime tragedy, which had conquered the classical rule of styles.'[89] Christianity and Christianization are therefore made the keys to understanding changing types of representation in Late Antiquity generally. But this is the realism of Huizinga's late Western Middle Ages, with its earthy juxtaposition of opposites, and disregard for the unity of styles. It is not at all the same as the realism of Byzantine icons; indeed, the East, with its continuous theological tradition, went in quite another way. Auerbach's antithesis is embedded in the context of interpretation in which Late Antiquity is seen as demonstrating encroaching gloom, the descent into irrationality, 'something sultry and oppressive', a 'darkening of the atmosphere of life'—all the familiar spectres of old-fashioned history, and categories which, if they belong anywhere, belong to the fragmentation of the early medieval West rather than to Byzantium.

In contrast, the realism claimed for religious images by contemporaries in early Byzantium has to do with authority. The ultimate reality, God himself, cannot be represented directly, either in visual art or in language, and can only be known by entering the 'cloud of unknowing' described by the Pseudo-Dionysius. But the images of Christ in human form, and of the Virgin and the saints, function as guarantees, ways to perceiving truth.

Obviously the Christianization of society was indeed vital to the rise in importance of religious images, though not in Auerbach's sense, and although this process was slow, the sixth century can plausibly be seen as the critical stage in the East. From now on, social and economic circumstances also increasingly undermined the classical culture which had survived tenaciously for so long. What effect it continued to exert on Byzantium in later centuries is another story. Meanwhile, religious images represented one element in the necessary construction of an alternative world-view.

[88] E. Auerbach, *Mimesis. The Representation of Reality in Western Literature*, Eng. tr. (Princeton, 1953), pp. 40ff., 53f., 63, 74ff.; cf. *The Literary Language and its Public in Late Latin Antiquity and in the Middle Ages*, Eng. tr. (London, 1965), pp. 22, 60f.

[89] *Mimesis*, p. 555.

MATERIALITY, CREATED OBJECTS AND LITERALISM

Yet some powerful counter-arguments existed, which we can clearly see in prototype during the seventh century. One of the charges made most often by the eighth-century Iconoclasts was that of idolatry: veneration of an image was simply veneration of a material object, and therefore constituted idolatry.[90] If indeed icons were considered as a 'real material sign' the charge was fully understandable. It was not, however, an argument brought against icons alone, but against the veneration of all created objects, and indeed the status of matter. It was, most notably, at the heart of Christian-Jewish argument, and it is very striking to note the degree to which an intensified Christian polemic against Jews is already apparent, in which the same argument was directed at Christian veneration of the Cross, well before images as such came under attack. Anti-Jewish arguments creep into a strikingly high proportion of the surviving theological writings of the period, not to mention the anti-Jewish polemic we hear of but which does not survive.[91] In the seventh-century context, the argument appears particularly in connection with Palestine, and especially with Jerusalem, after its capture by the Persians in 614 and surrender to the Arabs in 638.[92] The Jews were accused of assisting the Persians in their invasion, and after his triumphal return to Constantinople and the restoration of the True Cross (seized by the Persians in 614), the Emperor Heraclius (610–41) decreed forced baptism for Jews, a measure repeated according to Theophanes by Leo III in 721–2 on the eve of Iconoclasm.[93] In the several anti-Jewish polemical works which survive from the immediately following period, from the *Doctrina Jacobi nuper baptizati*, a

[90] See the letter of Germanos I to Thomas of Klaudiopolis, *PG* 98, cols 156C–D, 176D, on which see Herrin, *The Formation of Christendom*, pp. 331–2; Brubaker, 'Byzantine art in the ninth century', p. 34; see also Dagron, 'Le Culte des images', pp. 141–2.

[91] Rebuttal of supposed Jewish arguments is still a strong theme in Abu Qurrah's tract, which goes through the whole repertoire of created objects which receive veneration in the Old Testament; see Griffith, 'Theodore Abu Qurrah's Arabic Tract', pp. 59–62; also Sidney H. Griffith, 'Anastasios of Sinai, the *Hodegos* and the Muslims', *Greek Orthodox Theological Review*, 32 (1987), pp. 341–58, at pp. 345ff. For the importance of the theme in the seventh century see also Dagron,'Le culte des images', p. 143 ('cette nouvelle appréciation de l'héritage judaïque'). The hardening of Christian attitudes to Judaism is not so much a cause of Iconoclasm as a parallel development.

[92] See recently G. G. Stroumsa, 'Religious contacts in Byzantine Palestine', *Numen*, 36 (1989), pp. 16–42.

[93] See, e.g., A. Sharf, *Byzantine Jewry from Justinian to the Fourth Crusade* (London, 1971), pp. 48–57. Leo III: Theoph., *Chron.*, anno mundi 6214, p. 401, de Boor; according to Theophanes the iconoclastic edict of Caliph Yazid II which belongs to 722 was also inspired by 'a Jewish wizard'.

kind of Christian catechism for Jewish converts in the form of a dialogue, to the *Apology* of Leontius of Neapolis and the so-called *Trophies of Damascus*, the Christian worship of material objects, in particular the Cross, is represented as a major Jewish accusation to be rebutted.[94] It is answered by two strategies—resort to lists of citations from the Old Testament, indicating the material objects honoured by Jews themselves (the tablets of the law, the Ark, the Burning Bush, and so on), and the argument, also on the basis of Scripture, that the Cross is venerated for what it represents, not as a piece of wood.[95] The dramatic reversals in the fate of Jerusalem, and especially the vicissitudes of the True Cross in this period, made such a focus particularly apt, and also helped to stimulate an increased interest in Constantine the Great as the traditional discoverer of the True Cross and builder of Christian Jerusalem.[96] Both Christians and Jews had had brief periods of renewed hope in relation to Jerusalem, and both were disappointed. Doing their best to save the situation, the Christian anti-Jewish dialogues make much of the fact that the Temple had never been rebuilt, while the Christian Empire could still just about be said to have survived.[97]

The Christian apologiae for veneration of the Cross thus had a strongly political flavour. But they also fit into the wider context of Christian concern about materiality; when the examples chosen in the anti-Jewish literature broaden to include icons they do so in relation to their physical nature as images on wood or other materials. Were not Christians idolaters and worshippers of the material? The counter-argument followed the teaching of the Pseudo-Dionysius that the visible world signifies God; thus we read in Leontius of Neapolis how God is worshipped through creation and created objects, which embrace not only 'heaven and earth and sea', but also 'wood and stone . . . relics and church-buildings and the cross'.[98] Creation itself, it is argued, is a sign and mirror of God; the material objects which he has created are the signs through which he is recognized and represented. A similar defence of

[94] On this genre and its main themes see Déroche, 'L'Authenticité de l'"Apologie contre les Juifs"', discussing its purpose at pp. 668–9.

[95] See N. Gendle, 'Leontius of Neapolis: a seventh century defender of holy images', *Studia Patristica*, 18 (1985), pp. 135–9.

[96] See Averil Cameron, 'Byzantium in the Seventh Century. The Search for Redefinition', in J. Fontaine and J. Hillgarth, eds, *The Seventh Century: Change and Continuity* (London, forthcoming).

[97] See, e.g., *Trophies of Damascus*, ed. G. Bardy, *Patrologia Orientalis*, 15 (1927), pp. 169–292, at p. 221.

[98] Leontius of Neapolis, *PG* 93, col. 1604B.

veneration of material objects such as the Cross is an important part of John of Damascus's apologia for images; he links veneration of the Cross explicitly with such material signs of the death and resurrection of Christ as the rock of Calvary, the tomb, and the stone.[99] The Jews may have accused Christians of idolatry, but the Christian argument itself was about signification, what signified, and how.

Whatever else it may have been, Byzantine Iconoclasm was certainly an argument about the correct representation of God. According to the Iconoclasts, only certain signs were to be allowed, principally the Eucharist, the 'one true image' of God.[100] They thus claimed it for themselves, while denying the legitimacy of other signs favoured by their opponents. This is why actual icons and figural decoration in churches were destroyed, whitewashed, or replaced. Needless to say, the Iconoclast argument, including Constantine V's understanding of the Eucharist, was hotly rebutted.[101] Both sides in the controversy, however, drew on the arguments of the preceding century. One such was a renewed stress on the suffering of Christ in the flesh, that is, in his human and physical form, which constituted a major concern of late seventh-century Eastern theology, and which now also began to manifest itself in the late appearance in Byzantine art of representations of the dead Christ on the Cross.[102] Again, the emphasis is on materiality; Christ suffered in the body, not symbolically. But this posed major Christological problems: in which nature did Christ suffer? Theopaschites and others who wished to restrict his suffering to one nature only were now again formally condemned.[103] The two natures had to be realized somehow in every part of the divine economy, and in every portrayal of it. It is obvious that any picture of Christ would raise the issue of exactly what it was that was represented,

[99] Scorn for matter is represented as a Manichaean error: *Oratio* II.13, Kotter, 3, p. 104; *PG* 94, col. 1300B, cf. 1245B (other material signs; see n. 77 above).

[100] As argued in the *Peuseis* of the Emperor Constantine V: see S. Gero, 'Notes on Byzantine Iconoclasm in the eighth century', *Byzantion*, 44 (1974), pp. 23–42; 'The eucharistic doctrine of the Byzantine Iconoclasts and its sources', *Byzantinische Zeitschrift*, 68 (1975), pp. 4–22.

[101] See, e.g., Nicephorus, *Antirrhetici*, II.2: *PG* 100, col. 333B–D, usefully tr. with notes M.-J. Mondzain-Baudinet, *Nicéphore, Discours contre les iconoclastes* (Paris, 1990).

[102] See the discussion by Anna Kartsonis, *Anastasis. The Making of an Image* (Princeton, 1986), pp. 33–60; Brubaker, 'Byzantine art in the ninth century', p. 39. Interestingly, a miniature in the Chludov Psalter (ninth century) shows the figure of Pseudo-Dionysius as a witness to the Crucifixion, illustrating the text of Ps. 45.7, 'Nations may be in turmoil and thrones totter'; see Cormack, *Writing in Gold*, p. 134.

[103] Theopaschism, condemned by the Fifth Ecumenical Council of 553, was also condemned in 691–2 (canon 81, see below), and at the Second Council of Nicaea, 787.

over and above the existing doubts about materiality in relation to the objects themselves.

These worries also showed themselves in other ways. The greatest theologian of the seventh century, Maximus Confessor, composed scholia on the writings of the Pseudo-Dionysius, and emphasized symbolism and mystery in his own work on the liturgy, the *Mystagogia*. The practice of commenting on and interpreting the liturgy was taken up again on the eve of Iconoclasm by Germanos I in his *Historia ecclesiastica*.[104] By this time, however, a new strain of realism is evident, with an emphasis on the human and physical aspects of the life of Christ signified in the Eucharist; undue emphasis on symbolism was reined in by stressing the realistic details of the Incarnation, as in canon 82 of the Council in Trullo, where symbolic representations of Christ are forbidden.[105] Behind this, there seems to have been something of a move in the direction of Antiochene literalism in reaction against an over-symbolic theory of interpretation. It was a long-standing difference; the theology of Theodore of Mopsuestia, condemned by the Fifth Council, nevertheless provided the basis for this more literal reading.[106] The Sixth Ecumenical Council of 680–1, which condemned Monothelitism, laid a heavy emphasis on the human nature of Christ and his existence on earth in the flesh, while the passage in Anastasius of Sinai already cited, insisting on material representations rather than mere words, may belong to the period shortly before.[107] In his *De haeresibus*, Germanos argued that the human representation of Christ was necessary in order to remember his life in the flesh, his suffering, and

[104] Germanos's exposition of the meaning of the Eucharist also follows in the tradition of the Pseudo-Dionysius, and draws on Maximus. The Migne text of his *Historia ecclesiastica* or *Historia mystagogica* (*PG* 98, cols 384–453) is late and interpolated, but the original can be reconstructed from other versions, including the Latin translation of Anastasius Bibliothecarius: see R. Taft, 'The Liturgy of the Great Church: an initial synthesis of structure and interpretation on the eve of Iconoclasm', *DOP*, 34–5 (1980–1), pp. 45–76, and on the Urtext, R. Bornert, *Les Commentaires byzantins de la divine liturgie du VIIe au XVe siècle* (Paris, 1966), pp. 125–42; for the extant versions see *CPG*, 3, 8023, and see J. Meyendorff, *On the Divine Liturgy* (*Historia ecclesiastica*), ed. and tr. (Crestwood, NY, 1984); for Maximus's *Mystagogia*, see J. Stead, ed. and tr., *The Church, the Liturgy and the Soul of Man: the Mystagogia of St. Maximus the Confessor* (Still River, Mass., 1982).

[105] On the development from Pseudo-Dionysius to Germanos see Taft, 'The Liturgy', p. 58, and cf. pp. 67ff., with p. 71 on Maximus; see also Barber, 'The Koimesis Church, Nicaea'. Cf. also the similar emphasis in the Acts of II Nicaea, Mansi, 13, 288C–E: the coming of Christ in the flesh justified the place of the material in the divine economy against the Iconoclast view that matter was evil (280D).

[106] For a brilliant short exposition of the implications of Antiochene literalism versus Alexandrian allegory see H. Chadwick, 'Philoponus the Christian Theologian', in R. Sorabji, ed., *Philoponus* (London, 1987), pp. 42–6.

[107] Sixth Council: see Barber, 'The Koimesis Church'; Anastasius: above, n. 28.

his death, and maintained that rejection of the Sixth Council implied rejection of all the rest,[108] while the argument of his *Historia ecclesiastica* contains an emphatic reading of the Eucharist as a memorial of Christ's passion and death, and the gifts at the Great Entrance as signifying the body of the dead Christ, and employs a realism which Father Taft compares to the realism of visual art.[109] This was certainly a political as well as a religious dispute: the Sixth Council, with its emphasis on the humanity of Christ, had been emphatically rejected by the Emperor Philippicus (711–13), who had even removed a depiction of it from the imperial palace, provoking the Pope to set up an image of the Six Councils in St Peter's.[110] It is a sign of the twists and turns of ecclesiastical and political life in the period that the same Germanus who now supported the Sixth Council so warmly is listed by Theophanes as being among Philippicus's supporters.

But the issue of symbolism versus literalism was a real one. It was not a matter of mutually exclusive alternatives, but rather of achieving the right balance; the symbolic interpretation of church buildings and of the liturgy itself, which is characteristic of this period, did not preclude an emphasis on the materiality of the buildings or the divine elements. The iconophiles indeed rested part of their case for images on the argument of the Pseudo-Dionysius about the efficacy of material aids towards religious understanding.[111] The attention paid by writers of this period to the interpretation of the elements of the Eucharist, also material signs until transformed into the Body and Blood of Christ, is part and parcel of the debate. Thus when the Iconoclasts claimed the Eucharist as the only true image of Christ, they were paradoxically appropriating a eucharistic emphasis which was already a major feature of the thought of the supporters of images and the sources on which they depended; both Iconoclasts and iconophiles alike had to find ways of explaining the eucharistic elements in relation both to materiality and to representation.

It is not surprising that Byzantines of the same period were also worried about what was actually represented by the classical statues which still survived, especially in Constantinople itself.[112] When the exact nature of

[108] *PG* 98, cols 80A, 81B.

[109] Taft, 'The Liturgy', p. 58.

[110] Theoph., *Chron.*, anno mundi, 6203, pp. 381–2, de Boor; *Liber Pontificalis*, ed. L. Duchesne, 2 vols (Paris, 1886–92), *s.v.* Constantine I (708–15); Herrin, *Formation of Christendom*, p. 312.

[111] See Bishop Kallistos, 'The Meaning of the Divine Liturgy', pp. 12–15; Brubaker, 'Byzantine art in the ninth century', pp. 65–7.

[112] See Mango, 'Antique Statuary'; Cameron and Herrin, *Constantinople in the Eighth Century*, intro., pp. 31–4.

what was depicted in religious pictures had become such a matter of attention and controversy, it was only natural that representations of pagan gods and mythological characters should become a major anxiety, especially when their very identification had often been forgotten. It was tempting to ascribe magic powers to them, or to believe that they had been bewitched.[113] Lurking behind this fear of ancient statues is the same suspicion of idolatry which was directed at religious images; thus in the eighth-century *Parastaseis* Christian emperors are credited with destroying pagan statues, and the pagan Emperor Julian with tricking people into venerating idols in the guise of imperial images.[114] Whatever powers that ancient statues might possess, nobody imagined that they could be beneficent. The historical past, even the reign of Constantine, had receded into half-remembered fantasy.[115] As for classical statues, if a picture of the Virgin and Child, or someone's favourite saint, was now suspect, how much more suspect were Apollo and Aphrodite? The story of a mosaicist whose hand was struck by a demon as he tried to remove a depiction of Aphrodite exactly expresses how people felt.[116] If nothing else, Iconoclasm demonstrated that the representation of Classical Antiquity no longer had a place in medieval Byzantium.

IMAGES AS GUIDES TO TRUTH

The 'rise of icons' and the attack made on them by the Iconoclasts have received a vast amount of attention in histories of Byzantium. I have tried to show that one way of reading both is in relation not just to 'society', or to theology, or to the disasters of the seventh century, but in relation to the intellectual and imaginative framework of contemporary society. A massive intellectual adjustment was necessitated by the final demise of the classical world and the new circumstances of the early medieval one.[117] As

[113] Cameron and Herrin, *Constantinople in the Eighth Century*, intro., p. 33.

[114] *Parastaseis Syntomoi Chronikai*, chs 53, 57, 47, ed. Th. Preger, *Scriptores Originum Constantinopolitanarum*, I (Leipzig, 1901, repr. New York, 1975); cf. Cameron and Herrin, eds, *Constantinople in the Eighth Century*, p. 33.

[115] See ibid., pp. 34ff. But not only as the discoverer of the True Cross but also as the founder of Constantinople as a Christian city, contrasted with another imperial builder, the pagan Emperor Septimius Severus, Constantine also acquired a new prominence; see also Cameron, 'Byzantium in the Seventh Century'.

[116] Eustratius, *Vita Eutychii*, 53, *PG* 86.2.2333, tr. Mango, *Art of the Byzantine Empire*, pp. 133–4.

[117] Cf. Dagron, 'Le culte des images', p. 143: 'un long processus d'acculturation, au cours duquel la Byzance chrétienne apprend ce qu'elle eut revendiquer de son passé romano-hellénique et ce à quoi il lui faut renoncer.'

the traditional systems crumbled, the nature of truth and the foundations of knowledge were themselves called into question. We can see this sharply confirmed by the extreme concern for the citation of genuine texts and authorities shown at the councils of 680–1 and 787. Which authorities one should accept was precisely the issue.[118]

Truth being redefined as religious knowledge, images were seen by many as one, though only one, of the ways by which access to this truth was possible (see colour plate 2). They occupied this privileged position not least because of the long struggle in Christian thought to find a language by which God could be represented and in relation to the emphasis placed by writers such as the Pseudo-Dionysius, Maximus, and Germanos on symbolic interpretation and revelation through signs. But they also raised fundamental issues about matter and about what they could actually be held to represent, in a period concerned about charges of idolatry and still dominated by basic Christological issues. The same Quinisext Council which sought to regulate the visual representation of religious subjects also laid down stricter principles for the celebration of the Eucharist, condemned surviving pagan practices, and anathematized those who upheld the addition of the words 'who was crucified for us' to the Trisagion as implying that God could suffer on the Cross.[119] The regulation of images ran parallel to the regulation of behaviour and doctrine as part of the closer definition of the truth. As the Christological arguments of the seventh century centred on the exact definition of the physical life and suffering of Christ, so religious images began to be seen as a means of demonstrating doctrine even more exactly than could be done in words; their potential in this regard is explicitly defended in the powerful argument put by Anastasius of Sinai to which I have already referred, according to which pictures are a more effective way of convincing people of true doctrine than quotations from the Scripture and the Fathers.[120]

The Iconoclastic movement in Byzantium is a perfect illustration of how history proceeds by the convergence of multiple factors, all of which

[118] For a similar process at work in the late sixth century see Cameron, 'Models of the Past'.

[119] Canons 73 (Cross not to be used to decorate floors), 82 (Christ not to be represented as a lamb, but in human form, so as to remember the physical suffering of Christ in the flesh); 23, 28, 29, 31, 32, 58, 70 (women must be silent during the liturgy), 83, 101 (Eucharist); 57, 61, 62, 65 (pagan practices; many other canons regulate custom, dress, and entertainment); 81 (Trisagion). On canon 81, condemning Theopaschism, see Kartsonis, *Anastasis*, p. 37.

[120] Above, n. 28; Anastasius's argument also appears in the context of an attack on Theopaschism.

must be given their due. One can read post-Iconoclastic Byzantine art as the vindication of the sign-system which images implied.[121] But I hope to have shown that we must overlook either the place of images in the intellectual framework which had evolved as a replacement for the secular tradition, or the fact that they were seen as representing truth. 'Icons are equivalent to writing';[122] they claimed to be part of the grammar of Byzantine representation. It was hardly surprising that this flight to icons created as many problems as it seemed to solve, but one is sometimes inclined to forget that in the long run the defenders of icons won out, and the system of which icons formed a part was confirmed.

King's College London

[121] Brubaker, 'Byzantine art in the ninth century', deals mainly with the art of the ninth century in this light.

[122] Abu Qurrah, *De cultu imaginum*, 13.

CHARLEMAGNE AS A PATRON OF ART

by HENRY MAYR-HARTING

THE lesson that people hold radically differing views about church art is the harder to learn when one comes to it from the iconodulistic side. Looking back on my own Roman Catholic schooling, and the place of statues and holy pictures in the religious devotions of that milieu, I realize that once sacramental awareness develops, it is not always easily confined to the matter of the theological sacraments themselves. The beheading of the statues in the Lady Chapel at Ely, which I visited at the age of eleven, seemed a shocking circumstance whose motivation was totally incomprehensible, even allowing for the fact that it was the work of Protestants, and the Old Testament, which might have brought the dawn of understanding, was, of course, no part of an ordinary Catholic education at that time. In short, the author of Charlemagne's *Libri Carolini* would have found much upon which to make adverse comment in me, my fellows, and the monks who taught us. With the first artistic love of my student days, which was Romanesque sculpture, came an awareness of the voices and practice of those great medieval Protestants, the Cistercians. But only in the later encounter with Charlemagne was I forced to listen seriously to the moral and theological arguments against the unbridled use of figural art in the service of the Church.

It is on the relation of these discussions in Charlemagne's circle to actual artistic production that I focus; not that I am the first person to do so, but so many perceptive general surveys of Charlemagne's art have been made by scholars of German, French, and English nationality that it would be pointless to make another of those.[1] I raise two questions. One is why the Gospel books of Charlemagne's court school are so sparing in their representations of Christ and scenes from his life, while the ivories of that school are so profuse in them. The second is the effect of the arguments under Charlemagne on the practice of artists, in and outside the court circle.

[1] For instance, Florentine Mütherich, 'Die Buchmalerei am Hofe Karls des Grossen', in W. Braunfels, ed., *Karl der Grosse*, 3 (Düsseldorf, 1965), pp. 9–53; Wilhelm Köhler, *Die Karolingischen Miniaturen*, 2 (Berlin, 1958), 3 (Berlin, 1960); C. R. Dodwell, *Painting in Europe, 800–1200* (Harmondsworth, 1972); J. Hubert, J. Porcher, and W. F. Volbach, *Carolingian Art* (London, 1970); John Beckwith, *Early Medieval Art* (London, 1964); *Libri Carolini* [hereafter *L.C.*], *Caroli Magni Capitulare de Imaginibus*, ed. H. Bastgen, *MGH.Conc.* II, *Supplementum* (Hanover, 1924).

GOSPEL BOOKS

First the Gospel books and ivories. Every important surviving manuscript of the court school is a Gospel book, with the exception of the Dagulph Psalter of *c.*795. In the universally accepted chronology of Wilhelm Köhler, the series begins with the Godescalc Evangelistary of 781–3, so called from the name of its scribe mentioned in the colophon, and ends with the Lorsch Gospels at least thirty years later.[2] These are the first and last manuscripts of the Ada group, so called from the reference to *Ada Christi ancilla* in the Trier manuscript, a group consisting of seven books plus Dagulph. Alongside this group is another of four Gospel books, of which the Vienna Coronation Gospels dates from the 790s and the others, in Aachen, Brescia, and Brussels, from late in Charlemagne's reign, as can be established from the relations between their texts and the developing texts and textual emendations of the Ada group.[3] That is eleven surviving Gospel books in all.

This steady production of Gospel books, finely ornamented, may in itself appear singular for a culture whose devotion to the Old Testament is proverbial, and in consideration of the great full Bibles emanating from the scriptorium of Carolingian Tours in the next generation.[4] The answer must be mainly, when we take into account the surviving sixth-century Mediterranean Gospel books, that this was the principal form in which their Late Antique artistic models came to Charlemagne's artists.[5] Partly, also, these were liturgical books, in that each has a *capitulare*, or list of Gospel readings for the liturgical year. In addition, for the very reason that the people of this period were so much *en rapport* with the Old Testament and its ethos, Carolingian churchmen conceivably wanted to nudge them more on to the New Testament. The *Libri Carolini*, which revel in the Old Testament, explicitly state that it is but an adumbration of the New,[6]

[2] Köhler, *Karolingischen Miniaturen*, 2, pp. 9–14.

[3] Ibid., 3, esp. pp. 40–2.

[4] See the fine study by Herbert Kessler, *The Illustrated Bibles from Tours* (Princeton, 1977).

[5] Especially the Sinope Codex: A. Grabar, *Les Peintures de l'Evangéliaire de Sinope* (Paris, 1948); the St Augustine's Gospels; Francis Wormald, repr. in *Collected Writings*, 1 (London, 1984), pp. 13–35; *Rabbula Gospels*, ed. C. Cecchelli *et al.* (Olten and Lausanne, 1959); Rossano Gospels: *Il Codice Purpureo di Rossano*, ed. Ciro Santoro (Rome, 1975). See also Mütherich, 'Die Buchmalerei', esp. pp. 14–16, 28; D. A. Bullough, 'Roman books and Carolingian *renovatio*', *SCH*, 14 (1977), pp. 23–50. As an example one may note the roundels used for the title-page of the Harleian Gospels, fol. 12v, Braunfels, ed., *Karl der Grosse*, 3, plate VI, and in the Rossano Gospels (sixth century), Tavola 9, p. 94.

[6] See W. Hoffmann *et al.*, eds, *Der Stuttgarter Bilderpsalter*, 2 vols (Stuttgart, 1965), esp. Florentine Mütherich in the volume of Untersuchungen, 22, pp. 175–90, where the dependence of the Christological scenes on exegetical works is also stressed.

while both the Utrecht Psalter (*c.*830) in art and the *Heliand* in Old High German poetry sought to absorb Christ into the Germanic warrior ethic,[7] whose natural biblical expression was in books of the Old Testament.[8]

The Godescalc Evangelistary (781–3) has as its frontispiece a representation of Christ seated in majesty, undoubtedly derived from a Mediterranean (even Roman) prototype, with panels of Mediterranean and insular motifs round its borders (see frontispiece).[9] There is no further example of a *maiestas* in the court school until we come to the St Médard of Soissons Gospels, late in the series (*c.*810–14), and the Lorsch Gospels, positively the last.[10] Schrade believed this hiatus of some thirty years to be explained not by any dispute about images, but by gaps in our evidence.[11] I am not persuaded. Between Godescalc and St Médard, we have Arsenal, Harley, Abbeville, and possibly Ada, all without the *maiestas*. In addition, there is evidence of at least two lost Gospel books of the Ada group, which supplied models for later manuscripts, one of which was at Fulda and the other at Salzburg; the Salzburg manuscript shows no sign of having had a *maiestas*, while that at Fulda almost certainly lacked it.[12] One should not exaggerate the gap in our evidence. Perhaps this would be a place to add that while recognizing that Schnitzler could not *prove* that the Worship of the Lamb rather than of the *maiestas* by the Twenty-four Elders was the original subject of the dome mosaic of Charlemagne's church at Aachen, which must certainly have dated from some time between Godescalc and St Médard, I differ from some historians in that I find Schrade's counter-arguments still less convincing.[13]

[7] Utrecht Psalter: Christ and the Apostles as an army and its leader, illustration to Psalm 23 (24), fol. 13v, in *Utrecht Psalter*, ed. K. van der Hoerst and J. H. A. Engelbregt (Graz, 1984). For the *Heliand*, J. M. Wallace-Hadrill, *The Frankish Church* (Oxford, 1983), pp. 384–5.

[8] Though not its only expression, e.g., *The Dream of the Rood*, in Richard Hamer, ed., *A Choice of Anglo-Saxon Verse* (London, 1970),pp. 159–71.

[9] See in Beckwith, *Early Medieval Art*, p. 31, stylistic comparison with an icon of Mary made for the oratory of Pope John VII (705–7).

[10] Lorsch Gospels, fol. 18v; St Médard Gospels, fol. 124r, Mütherich, 'Die Buchmalerei', colour plate XV, even here not full-page, but tucked into the 'Q' of the opening of St Luke.

[11] Hubert Schrade, 'Zum Kuppelmosaik der Pfalzkapelle und zum Theoderich-Denkmal in Aachen', *Aachener Kunstblätter*, 30 (1965), pp. 25–37, esp. p. 28.

[12] The lack of a *maiestas* in the Codex Wittekindeus of Fulda, *c.*970, which gives apparently a quite precise picture of its lost Ada prototype, is highly suggestive, especially as the Gero Codex of about the same date, which follows the Lorsch Gospels, repeats the latter's *maiestas*: *Der Codex Wittekindeus*, ed. A. Boeckler (Leipzig, 1938), pp. 15–17. For the lost Salzburg manuscript, see Mütherich, 'Die Buchmalerei', pp. 42–3.

[13] Schrade, 'Zum Kuppelmosaik', p. 29, rather gives his own point away with his citation from the Synod of Frankfurt (794) concerning the Lamb of God; he does not give due weight to the appearance of the Worship of the Lamb in the St Médard of Soissons Gospels (nor to the

It might be true that Theodulph of Orleans, who as a result of Ann Freeman's researches is almost universally accepted as the author of the *Libri Carolini*,[14] would not have approved of either subject (just as we know that Alcuin approved of both), but for those who had imbibed the spirit of the *Libri Carolini*, the *maiestas* would be the more dangerous. For in the Byzantine Empire which the *Libri* so abhorred, images of Christ and the Emperor approximated to each other, and images of the Emperor were venerated as divine; it was part of their rulers' 'Babylonic' pride which had caused them to lose the Roman Empire.[15] This presumably is also why there is not one surviving image of Charlemagne in all his court manuscripts, a striking contrast with later Carolingians, although he was forced for practical purposes to imitate Byzantium by placing his image on his coins and seals. As Donald Bullough has said of the *Libr' Carolini*, 'A condemnation of images of the ruler as such is avoided, although at times the author's arguments seem to be tending in that direction.'[16]

Even more striking in this series of Gospel books, adorned by the consummate artists of their age with magnificent canon tables, evangelist pictures, and *initium* pages, is the near absence of all scenes illustrating the life of Christ, when it is virtually certain that the court had large Christ cycles available to it as models.[17] We encounter them for the first time only in St Médard, tiny scenes in the spandrels of the arches on evangelist and *initium* pages, like those illustrating the baptism of Christ and his being comforted by angels after the temptations at the beginning of St Mark (plate 1); they are more like a variation on Tironian marginal notes, reminding the reader of the early content of the Gospel, than illustrations to the text (I am sceptical of the claim that the lost pericopes book of the Ada group, attested by a surviving fragment, contained a cycle of Christ

---

Lamb with crossed nimbus in the initial 'I' of St John's Gospel in the Harleian Gospels: Köhler, *Karolingischen Miniaturen*, 2, Tafeln 2, p. 61); and, considering that this was the subject of the facade mosaic of St Peter's, Rome, he exaggerates both the unlikelihood of Charlemagne's imitating it and the difficulties of adapting it to the Aachen dome, p. 30.

14 Ann Freeman, 'Theodulf of Orleans and the *Libri Carolini*', *Speculum*, 32 (1957), pp. 663–705, and 'Further studies in the *Libri Carolini*', ibid., 40 (1965), pp. 203–89.

15 For images of Christ and the Emperor, A. Grabar, *L'Empereur dans l'art Byzantin* (Paris, 1936). For the effects of 'Babylonic' pride of the East, *L.C.*, III, 15, p. 135, and Robert Folz, *The Coronation of Charlemagne*, tr. J. E. Anderson (London, 1974), pp. 92–3.

16 Donald Bullough, '*Imagines regum* and their significance in the early medieval West', in Giles Robertson Henderson, eds, *Studies in Memory of David Talbot Rice* (Edinburgh, 1975), p. 224.

17 See Florentine Mütherich, 'Ottonian Art: changing aspects', *Romanesque and Gothic Art: Acts of the 20th International Congress of the History of Art*, 1 (Princeton, 1963), p. 29; Donald Bullough, *The Age of Charlemagne* (London, 1965),p. 137; Wormald, *Collected Writings*, 1, p. 172, n. 40.

Plate 1 *Initium* Page of St Mark's Gospel, St Médard of Soissons Gospels (*c*.800–814), Paris, BN, MS lat. 8850, fol. 82r.

illustration).[18] They recall past events and give little jogs to the memory. Christological scenes again figure in the cameos set into the canon-table arches of the Lorsch Gospels (plates 2 and 14), a fascinating reflection, in their combination of Christian content and classical forms, of the very way in which Einhard cast his perception of Charlemagne.[19] These cameos are at the heart of the Carolingian Renaissance, but they are not the height of uninhibitedness in Christ imagery.

Whatever the explanation for the inhibitions, there are scholars who would question whether they had much to do with the views of the *Libri Carolini*. This work makes it clear that it is not against images, but only against their veneration as if purely material paint or stone could contain any of the spiritual reality, the mystical properties, of what was depicted. Theodulph of Orleans himself was a great lover of art and colour, of precious metal with engraving, and of stucco ornament. The *Libri Carolini* acknowledge the function of images to instruct the unlettered, according to a famous letter of Pope Gregory the Great, which they cite with approval; though obviously pictures in books could have nothing to do

[18] Florentine Mütherich and Joachim Gaehde, *Carolingian Painting* (London, 1977), p. 45 and n. 7. This form of Christ illustration in the St Médard Gospels may have been suggested by something like the sixth-century Rabbula Gospels, with Christ illustrations to the side of the canon tables: Kurt Weitzmann, *Late Antique and Early Christian Book Illumination* (London, 1977), plate 34. On the fragment from an otherwise lost pericopes book of the Ada group, representing Zachary and the Angel, in BL, MS Cotton Claudius B.V., see W. Koehler, 'An illustrated Evangelistary of the Ada School', *Journal of the Warburg and Courtauld Institutes*, 15 (1952), pp. 48–66. I do not now doubt the argument that there was a Late Antique pericopes book available to the Charlemagne Court School, as to the artists of the early Ottonian Christ cycles: see the *Retractatio* at the end of part ii of my *Ottonian Book Illumination; an Historical Study* (London, 1991), with illustrations incorporated into the relevant places in the texts. But I am sceptical of Köhler's argument that the supposed comparative rarity of the Zachary subject indicates that the miniatures in the lost Carolingian book were fairly numerous (pp. 59–60). The subject is repeated in the Soissons book, where scenes of the life of Christ, besides being tiny, are hardly numerous, and it is the *only* New Testament subject to appear in the whole of the Harleian Gospels, conceivably for the very reason that it was not a Christ scene. If it had been the only illustration to the texts in the lost book, that might explain why Sir Robert Cotton had cut it out of one book and stuck it into another. One could be tempted to think that the reason why it survived, however, was not because it was the only illustration in the book, but because it was the first, in a book whose liturgical readings one might imagine to have begun with Advent. But both types of *capitulare*, i.e., list of Gospel readings for the liturgical year, used at Charlemagne's court started not with Advent but with Christmas, and in both, the Zachary story is the reading for the Vigil of St John the Baptist, which would come late in a pericopes book, and not for an Advent reading. See T. Klauser, *Das römische Capitulare Evangeliorum* (Münster, 1972), p. 76, no. 157; p. 116, no. 156.

[19] Such cameos are already found in the canon tables of the St Médard Gospels, e.g., the Annunciation at fol. 7r, the Transfiguration at fol. 9r, and the victorious Christ as in the Douce 176 ivory at fol. 10v. Einhard's Suetonian form and model is a commonplace; the idea of his Christian content may raise eyebrows, but see Wallace-Hadrill, *Frankish Church*, p. 203.

Plate 2 Page of Canon Tables, Lorsch Gospels (*c.*810–814), Julia Alba, Rumania, fol. 11v.

with the world of the illiterate, and Gregory's letter refers to wall-painting in churches. The *Libri Carolini* also allow that images can enable the onlooker to recall past events and can add to the beautification particularly of fine materials.[20] I would not dismiss too lightly, however, the influence on Charlemagne's art of the *Libri Carolini*, or their ideas—ideas put forward with such intelligence, force, and comprehensiveness that it would be astounding had they represented a mere lone voice in Carolingian culture. For behind the objection to veneration of images there is another argument: that illustration can never be the *best* way to understand the Scriptures, even for the illiterate. Writing and words are in principle better. Not pictures, but Scriptures have been granted to us for the knowledge of our faith. Painters can remind one of events which have occurred, but these too can be just as well expressed in words. When Psalm 26 says 'I will seek the face of the Lord', this is not to be taken to mean 'seek through images'.[21] Furthermore, this argument is couched in the tone of one who has taken the high moral ground. As Hans Liebeschütz has said, the *Libri Carolini*'s antagonistic philosophy of art tried to demonstrate the essentially pagan character of, and lack of *religious meaning* in, Byzantine art.[22] Images cannot teach one the moral or spiritual sense of things; one cannot derive the *virtus sensuum* from them. 'God is to be sought not in visible or manufactured things, but in the heart; he is to be beheld not with the eyes of the flesh but only with the eye of the mind.'[23] At best, the *Libri Carolini* tolerated only religious images.

There is another point about the curb on Christological scenes in court Gospel books: the debate on images must be taken in conjunction with the attack on the heresy of Adoptionism, which held that Christ was not the

[20] Freeman, 'Theodulf of Orleans', pp. 695–9; *L.C.*, I, 29, p. 57, 'Lord I have loved the beauty of thy house', etc., not a material but a spiritual dwelling; *L.C.*, I, 16, pp. 38, 44, lack of mystical properties in art; *L.C.*, p. 137, line 36, value of materials; *L.C.*, III, 16, p. 138, lines 1–2, and IV, 29, quote Gregory; *L.C.*, III, 16, p. 138, lines 3–4, 'non ad adorandum sed ad memoriam rerum gestarum et venustatem parietum habere permittimus'—even so, there is a warning to those who cannot remember Christ without pictures, *L.C.*, IV, 2, p. 176, lines 23–7.

[21] *L.C.*, II, 30, pp. 92–3, see David Ganz, 'The preconditions for Caroline minuscule', *Viator*, 18 (1987), esp. pp. 29–34, 'in libris non in imaginibus doctrinae spiritalis eruditionem diximus', *L.C.*, ibid.; Psalm 26 is cited at *L.C.*, I, 23, p. 51; furthermore, 'lumen ergo vultus Dei . . . non in materialibus imaginibus est accipiendum . . . sed in vexillo crucis', I, 23, p. 51, lines 37–9.

[22] Hans Liebeschütz, 'Western Christian thought from Boethius to Anselm', in A. H. Armstrong, ed., *Cambridge History of Later Greek and Early Medieval Philosophy* (Cambridge, 1967), p. 566.

[23] *L.C.*, IV, 2, p. 176, quoted by Celia Chazelle, 'Matter, spirit and image in the *Libri Carolini*', *Recherches Augustiniennes*, 21 (1986), p. 176 and n. 75. The phrase *in virtute sensuum* is used at II, 30, p. 97, line 34.

true but only the adoptive son of God, and thus denied his divinity. Charlemagne issued the *Libri Carolini* at the Synod of Frankfurt in 794, the meeting which also saw a condemnation of the Spanish heresy after a first round of discussion and correspondence among churchmen in which Alcuin was deeply involved.[24] Adoptionism, which had entered Charlemagne's empire through the writings of Felix of Urgel, a bishop in his Spanish march, would obviously undermine the whole idea of Christian salvation on which Carolingian society was based, and as the human body despatches resources from everywhere in order to heal a wound inflicted upon it, so did the Carolingians concentrate their cultural resources to sustain the divinity of Christ.[25] Pictures of his human life would perhaps not have been the most immediately effective way of achieving this end. An argument of this kind is not put directly in the *Libri Carolini* because of their anxiety to avoid outright condemnation of images as such, but it is implied. As Celia Chazelle has rightly commented, the emphasis there on Christ's divine attributes is such that his humanity largely disappears from view, diminishing still further the value of artists' representations of him.[26] That Christ illustrations deny his divinity is an explicit argument, however, in the Byzantine iconoclastic council of 754:

[24] Wilhelm Heil, 'Der Adoptianismus, Alcuin und Spanien', in Bernhard Bischoff, ed., *Karl der Grosse*, 2 (Düsseldorf, 1965), discusses finely the principal opponents of the Adoptionists: in Spain Beatus of Liebana, and in Charlemagne's circle Paulinus of Aquileia and Alcuin. For Beatus on Christ's divinity, esp. pp. 128–9; for Paulinus' distinction between adoption and assumption (*redemptor noster perfectum hominem adsumpsit in Deum*), pp. 131–2; for Alcuin's use of conciliar and Roman teaching (which Heil perhaps overstates at the expense of his theological grasp), pp. 136–53. See also Donald Bullough, 'Alcuin and the Kingdom of Heaven', in Uta-Renate Blumenthal, ed., *Carolingian Essays* (Washington, DC, 1983), pp. 49–56.

[25] Angilbert's inscription for the west apse of St Ricquier, beginning, 'Almighty God who rulest the heights and the depths', J. von Schlosser, *Schriftquellen zur Geschichte der karolingischen Kunst* (Vienna, 1892) [hereafter Schlosser], no. 783, pp. 257–9, is an example, as is Alcuin's grace, in which to Christ are attributed deeds of the Father in the Old Testament as well as of himself in the New, ibid., p. 318, and also several of Alcuin's inscriptions for churches, e.g., for Trier, St Amand, and Gorze, ibid., pp. 12, 180. There are, it is true, a number of hymns and inscriptions in which Christ is addressed directly, e.g., Alcuin's Cologne inscription, beginning, *Mitissime Christe* (ibid., no. 155, p. 45), and Hrabanus Maurus continued this feature at Fulda, ibid., nos. 147, 148, 211, but even Christ-centred poems tend to remember or even emphasize the Divinity, e.g., the poems referring to Christ seated as the *species hominis*, the *image* of man, ibid., nos. 801–5. The emphasis on the Trinity in Carolingian religious culture is noteworthy, as in the arrangement of the three churches at St Ricquier (*Quia igitur omnis plebs fidelium sanctissimam atque inseparabilem Trinitatem confiteri, venerari et mente colere firmiter credere debet*, etc., ibid., no. 782, p. 254). Alcuin's treatise on the Trinity may be considered as the culmination of his writing on Adoptionism, Heil, 'Der Adoptianismus', pp. 147–8. For Alcuin's use of Augustine's Commentary on St John rather than his *De Trinitate* in order to give proper stress to the divinity of Christ, see Bullough, 'Alcuin', pp. 52, 59.

[26] Chazelle, 'Matter, spirit and image', pp. 176–7.

> The painter . . . makes an image and calls it Christ. Now the name Christ means both God and man. Hence he has either included according to his vain fancy the uncircumscribable Godhead in the circumscription of created flesh, or he has confused that unconfusable union . . . and in so doing has applied two blasphemies to the Godhead, namely through the circumspection and the confusion. . . . [The painter of such images] severs the flesh from the divinity.

I have used here the translation of Cyril Mango, who notes that 'circumscribable' and 'uncircumscribable' were technical terms in the Iconoclastic Controversy, the one meaning anything finite, bounded, and visible, and hence admitting of representation, the other what is infinite and invisible.[27] It is clear that Theodulph knew this argument, and used it in all but name, which would have meant recognizing good in something Byzantine. For he says that there is nothing which can be painted in God's command, given through Moses, 'Hear, O Israel, the Lord thy God is One', and adds, 'Why is it necessary to adore God in image, who is uncircumscribed (*incircumscriptus*), who is One everywhere, and who is not circumscribed by place?'[28] The Byzantine council of 754 concludes that the only true image of Christ is the bread and wine of the Eucharist, as he himself indicated; likewise Theodulph says that Christ constituted the commemoration of his Passion not through mundane works of art (*non in mundarum artium opificiis*), but in the consecration of his Body and Blood.[29]

The glory of the Ada group, as we have implied, lies in canon tables, evangelist pictures, and *initium* pages. In the canon tables, with their sun-drenched colours, their bright birds, their exotic-looking plants and antique ornamental motifs, we experience almost physically how the Carolingians have entered the Mediterranean world. With Wilhelm Köhler and Florentine Mütherich we can study the influx into the court-school of Mediterranean models, eastern and western, almost from one manuscript to the next; and with them we can watch the conquest of the three-dimensional, the growing capacity to depict the human figure in space, and the development of an architectonic quality in the arches of the canon tables, where marbled pillars succeed to two-dimensional strips adorned with flat panels of insular-type interlace.[30] The Harleian Gospels

27 Cyril Mango, *The Art of the Byzantine Empire 312–1453* (New Jersey, 1972), p. 166, and n. 69.
28 *L.C.*, III, 15, p. 135, lines 2–4.
29 *L.C.*, II, 27, p. 88, lines 19–23; and Mango, *Art of the Byzantine Empire*, p. 166.
30 Mütherich, 'Die Buchmalerei', pp. 14–18. Such panels of interlace, still in the Harleian Gospels, have disappeared in the Lorsch Gospels.

have the evangelical symbols above each arch in Late Antique western style (those with an angel carrying a title-table being more eastern),[31] and a tree of life in one of the tympana (plate 3), which according to a shrewd suggestion of Elizabeth Rosenbaum probably derives its shape from a sixth-century Ravenna manuscript.[32] It is doubtful whether the canon tables were actually used for the workaday study and harmonization of the Gospel texts in such de luxe manuscripts, although the Eusebian divisions of text listed in the tables are noted in the margins.[33] Whatever the case, however, the magnificent embellishment of these tables, alongside the near absence of Christ scenes, serves to convey a lesson, almost to promulgate a manifesto, that biblical texts should be objects not of magic, but of study. Thus their very splendour highlights the teaching function of Charlemagne's priestly kingship.

Exactly the same may be said of the evangelist pictures. There are those, such as Schrade, who would maintain that had the court school a consistent abhorrence of images, it would have excluded images of the Evangelists along with those of Christ, and Köhler cleverly insinuated into his writing the aspersion that the Ada group Evangelists were iconodulistic. The foreign artists (probably from Italy), who came to Charlemagne's court and were commissioned to paint the Vienna Gospels and its successors in that group, are praised by him for their Antique figures and pure Hellenic illusionism; the Ada group Evangelists of the court artists (plate 4) are by contrast branded as 'idols far from reality' (*wirklichkeitsferne Idole*).[34] But at least the evangelist pictures signify, albeit paradoxically, what was one of the principal dictates of the *Libri Carolini*, that it was writing not pictures which had been given to us for our salvation, and all the evangelist pictures of Charlemagne's court school show the Evangelists writing, or drawing inspiration while in the process of writing, never, like some of the Ottonian depictions, staring into space with hieratic ecstasy.[35] The Aachen Gospels, a manuscript of the Vienna Gospels group and late in Charlemagne's reign, brings in a new and up to that time rare iconography of the Evangelists working away together in the same rocky

[31] Ibid., p. 28. For the early development of canon tables and the various branches of their development, see the monograph of Carl Nordenfalk, *Die spätantiken Kanontafeln*, Textband und Tafelband (Göteborg, 1938).

[32] Elizabeth Rosenbaum, 'The Evangelist Portraits of the Ada School and their models', *Art Bulletin*, 38 (1956), pp. 81–90.

[33] For example, Braunfels, ed., *Karl der Grosse*, 3, colour plate X (Harleian Gospels).

[34] Köhler, *Karolingischen Miniaturen*, 3, p. 50.

[35] For example, St Matthew in the Gospel Book of Otto III, MS Clm 4453, illustrated in Hanns Swarzenski, *Early Medieval Illumination* (London, 1951), plate X.

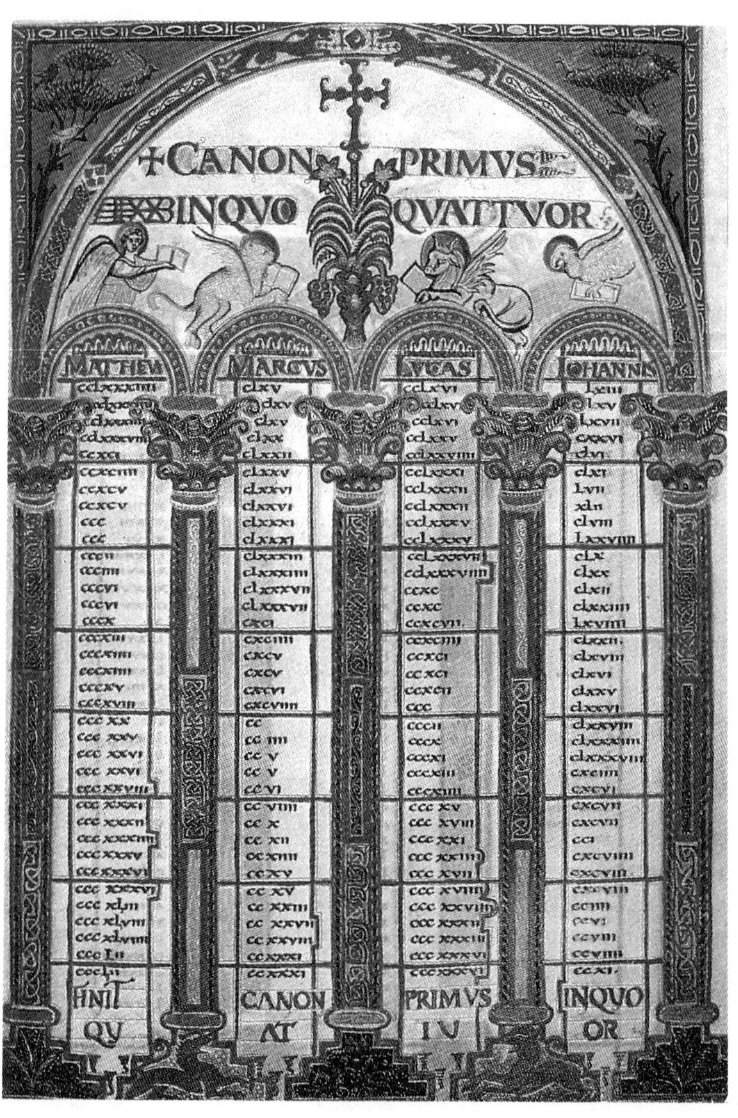

Plate 3 Page of Canon Tables, Harleian Gospels (*c.*795–800), London, British Library, MS Harley 2788, fol. 6v.

Plate 4 St Mark, Ada Gospels (*c.*810–814), Trier Stadtbibliothek, MS 22, fol. 59v.

landscape (colour plate 3), the very picture of industry and concentration which Charlemagne would have wished to conceive in the scriptoria of his empire. The landscape is a wonderful symphony of blues and reveals a fine grasp of Antique spatialism; the wispy trees on the horizon would appear again in the Rheims school under Archbishop Ebbo, who had been court librarian.[36] The artist, for all his Byzantine stylistic elements, was most likely an Italian at Charlemagne's court; the same motif of white-clad Evangelists in a blue and rocky landscape, with their symbols perched on nearby precipices, is found in the sixth-century mosaics of San Vitale, Ravenna, a place whose art was almost as vital a source of artistic inspiration to Charlemagne as was Rome itself.[37] What the Aachen scene signifies above all else is that, if one studies them, the Evangelists work in harmony to produce four Gospels which hang together as an account of Christ. It is the same lesson as that of the canon tables, and the patristic text which above all conveyed it, a text of interest to Carolingian scholars, was Augustine of Hippo's *De consensu Evangelistarum*.[38]

None the less, that the existence of evangelist pictures in the court manuscripts may be considered a breach at least in the spirit of the *Libri Carolini* is suggested by the fact that Theodulph of Orleans's own Bibles, which contain ornamented canon tables, lack Evangelists.[39] We may say in parentheses that it is obvious from the textual history of the Gospels in Charlemagne's time that neither Theodulph nor Alcuin, the two greatest of his court scholars, could have had a commanding influence on the production of court Gospel books. Theodulph used Italian textual models eclectically, and the format of his Bibles, incorporating constant revisions as he worked, is quite different from anyone else's. Alcuin based himself on the Vulgate, at least for the Gospels, but it was primarily the Wearmouth-Jarrow text as reflected in the Codex Amiatinus, whereas the Vulgate of the Ada group (to which the Vienna Gospel group is closely related) had an Irish strand in it and was most probably derived from the circle of St Boniface's monasteries.[40] Amongst the variations in the far

[36] Mütherich and Gaehde, *Carolingian Painting*, plate 14, p. 60.

[37] See with regard to the parallel case of Charlemagne as a collector of books, Bernhard Bischoff, 'Die Hofbibliothek Karls des Grossen', in Bischoff, ed., *Karl der Grosse*, 2, p. 46.

[38] For example, Karlsruhe, MS Aug. XCVIII (Reichenau); Wolfenbüttel, MS Weissenburg 30; E. Lesne, *Histoire de la propriété ecclésiastique en France*, 4 (Lille, 1938), pp. 433–4 (Lyon).

[39] Schrade, 'Zum Kuppelmosaik', p. 27; Raphael Loewe, 'The Medieval History of the Latin Vulgate', in *Cambridge History of the Bible*, 2, ed. G. W. H. Lampe (Cambridge, 1969), p. 127; Bonifatius Fischer, 'Bibelausgaben des frühen Mittelalters', *Settimane di Studio*, 10 (1963), pp. 593–6.

[40] Fischer, 'Bibelausgaben', pp. 586–97; Loewe, 'Latin Vulgate', pp. 126–40.

from standardized texts of the late eighth century the court was under nobody's thumb. If the ideas embodied in the *Libri Carolini* had influence, therefore, this can have had nothing to do with the direct influence of their author on court manuscripts.

We said first that these were liturgical books, each with its *capitulare* of Gospel readings for the liturgical year, and now we have treated them like a call to biblical study. These two aims are, of course, eminently compatible, but it is always important to strike the right balance between liturgy and what one might call ethic in considering Charlemagne. We know that Charlemagne was deeply interested in the liturgy (which can itself have either a magical or an educational aspect), acquiring a Roman sacramentary, following the chants, and helping to build churches which formed the noblest of its settings.[41] But in contrast to his grandson, Charles the Bald, for instance, he did not regard his own person as an integral part of the court liturgy, a Christ figure round whom the Easter liturgy might revolve or whose image might replace that of Christ in a Gospel book.[42] That would have been too Byzantine for him. And there is one striking change of emphasis, away from liturgy and towards study, within the court school manuscripts.

Godescalc, the first of the Ada group, is a pericopes book, a book of Gospel readings arranged by the cycle of the liturgical year. Such books, which become so common under the Ottonians, were relatively uncommon in the eighth century, and the prototype of Godescalc is likely to have been, once again, a sixth-century Ravenna pericopes book.[43] Thereafter, almost every surviving court Gospel book was a whole and continuous text of the four Gospels.[44] I would suggest that the obvious rationale of this change is contained in Charlemagne's charge, known as

[41] For example, Bischoff, 'Hofbibliothek', p. 44; Einhard, *Vita Karoli*, ed. L. Halphen (Paris, 1947), c.26, pp. 76–8; Schlosser, no. 782, p. 256, for Charlemagne's generosity to St Ricquier.

[42] For Charles the Bald's manuscripts, Kessler, *Illustrated Bibles*, ch. 9; *Der Codex Aureus der bayerischen Staatsbibliothek in München*, 3 vols (Munich, 1921), Textband, pp. 20–2. A liturgical example is provided by Nithard' from as early as 841, see Janet Nelson, 'Public History and Private Histories in the work of Nithard', in her *Politics and Ritual in Early Medieval Europe* (London, 1986), pp. 205–6.

[43] See Adolf Weis, 'Die spätantike Lektionar-Illustration im Skriptorium der Reichenau', in Helmut Maurer, ed., *Die Abtei Reichenau* (Sigmaringen, 1974), pp. 326–7.

[44] The exception is the lost pericopes book of the Ada group reconstructed by Köhler, 'An illustrated Evangelistary', but he shows at pp. 49–50 that this must again have been early in the series, at latest contemporary with the Harleian Gospels. The four pericopes books of the Charlemagne period known to Köhler are listed at p. 59, n. 1. It is interesting to note that he sees Rome and Ravenna as two sides of the same coin where stylistic influences on the Court School are concerned, pp. 61–6.

the *De literis colendis*, and its premium on the study of Scripture: 'Wherefore we exhort you not only not to neglect the study of letters, but also, with most humble and God-pleasing application, to learn zealously for a *purpose*, namely, that you may be able the more easily and the more correctly to penetrate the mysteries of divine scripture.'[45] I do not argue that the issuing of this precept itself caused the change, for one cannot date the *De literis colendis* precisely enough to know this; only that it was the idea expressed in the precept, that Scripture needed study, which was influential.

IVORIES

The ivories of the court school, which have been comprehensively catalogued and surveyed by Goldschmidt, present a very different iconographic picture from the manuscripts, bursting as they are with Christ scenes. The Douce ivory in Oxford alone has eleven of them, besides the victorious Christ, with Cross slung over his shoulders, trampling on the beasts (colour plate 4).[46] A pyx in the British Museum is carved with the Healing of the Leper (plate 6).[47] The covers of the Lorsch Gospels depict the Magi, beneath the victorious Christ, a natural (indeed, an Orosian) association of ideas.[48] A book-cover formerly at Schloss Hradek, in Bohemia, has the Annunciation, Nativity, Crucifixion, and Three Women at the Tomb. A fragment of an Ascension at Darmstadt has a vivid rendering of Mary and the Apostles. And a pair of book-covers at Aachen has six scenes of Christ's appearances after his death.[49] There is no doubt that these ivories, and others which I have not mentioned, emanate from Charlemagne's court. The association of several with court manuscripts, their value as objects and closeness in size and format to late Roman consular or imperial diptychs, and the correspondence of their figural style, with Late Antique calm and gestures, round soft heads, curly hair, wide-open eyes, and broad noses, to the style of the Ada group Evangelists, all make this clear.[50]

To ask how one can account for this iconographic difference is to attempt more than the mere solution of an intriguing conundrum; it is to

[45] Translation of P. D. King, in *Charlemagne: Translated Sources* (Kendal, 1987), p. 233.

[46] Adolph Goldschmidt, *Die Elfenbeinskulpturen aus der Zeit der Karolingischen und Sächsischen Kaiser*, repr. 2 vols (Oxford, 1960), 1, p. 10 [hereafter Goldschmidt].

[47] Ibid., p. 11.

[48] Ibid., p. 13. For the Orosian theme, see my *Ottonian Book Illumination*, part i, p. 159, using the work of Konrad Hoffmann.

[49] Goldschmidt, pp. 14–17.

[50] Ibid., p. 10; Peter Lasko, *Ars Sacra 800–1200* (Harmondsworth, 1972), p. 27.

seek an enlarged understanding of the court culture which can accommodate the difference. I would like to suggest four possible lines of answer.

The first line of answer, almost too obvious to state, is that there was perhaps a disagreement about whether such depictions facilitated devotion or were a self-indulgence bordering on the superstitious for educated men. Ann Freeman has brought out how the *Libri Carolini* themselves represent a moderation of the author's extreme views after taking account of critics with whom he must have entered into vigorous argument, and she suggests that the numerous corrections in the *Libri Carolini* manuscript resulted from 'a reading before a round-table of Carolingian theologians'.[51] Controversy and disagreement on every kind of topic would appear almost endemic in Charlemagne's court circle. Peter Godman has taught us, with relish, to think of a high degree of public debate and point-scoring against one another among Charlemagne's scholars, expressed in their poetry.[52] Schrade thinks that the small triumphal arch which Einhard had carved for the church of St Servatius, Maastricht, expressed disapproval in its iconography of Charlemagne's acquisition from Italy of the statue of Theoderic, a great Germanic hero of the past, but also an Arian heretic. It is possible; others certainly disapproved.[53] Alcuin's ideas on how the Saxons should be converted to Christianity—by persuasion rather than force—were not those of Charlemagne, yet Charlemagne apparently allowed himself to be freely criticized on the point.[54] These clashes cannot be explained by prosopography or faction; they are disagreements about intellectual or ethical matters, natural to a group of men who are making huge advances in their understanding of classical culture, biblical learning, and theological doctrine.

There were deep divisions in the eighth century about the nature of religious art itself. The protestations of *Libri Carolini* show that their author faced opposition and suggest that not all of it was in the East. Equally, Bede, who had a much more positive view of figural art, propounded in his Commentary on Solomon's Temple, knew that he faced opposition, for he says defensively: 'There are some who believe that God's law forbids us to sculpture or to paint, whether in a church or

[51] Freeman, 'Theodulf of Orleans', p. 667; '*Libri Carolini*', p. 221.
[52] Peter Godman, *Poetry of the Carolingian Renaissance* (London, 1985), pp. 4–15.
[53] Schrade, 'Zum Kuppelmosaik', pp. 31–5.
[54] For example, Alcuin's letter to Charlemagne (796) urging him not to commit the same wrong of forcible conversion to Christianity in the case of the Avars as he had committed with the Saxons, *MGH.Ep.* 4, ii, ed. E. Dümmler, no. 110.

any other place, the figures of men or animals, on the grounds that it is said in the Decalogue, "Thou shalt not make unto thyself a graven image", etc.'[55] That the opposition to Bede's point of view was actually all round him is suggested by the fact that many insular artists, superb draughtsman as they were, so often reduced the human figure when they ventured on it at all to an almost barbaric geometricality, in contrast to the art of his own monasteries as represented in the Codex Amiatinus.[56] No doubt logicians could prove that basically the views of Bede and Theodulph are not at odds with each other, but there is a sizeable practical difference between Bede's desire to justify historiated sculptures and paintings of stories about Christ and his saints, and Theodulph's 'is-your-picture-really-necessary?' approach. And Bede's *De templo* was certainly well known in the Carolingian schools.[57]

A second possible line of answer is that in Charlemagne's time, despite the stylistic connections between ivories and manuscripts, ivories operated in a world of their own as to iconography, almost hermetically sealed off from the iconographic world of manuscripts; and that Carolingian artists and scholars had not yet so harmonized their culture that they could see every aspect of it in the light of every other aspect, or at least could reconcile every aspect. It is remarkable how often Charlemagne ivories can be shown or reasonably surmised to have had their prototypes in earlier ivories. In the case of the Douce book-cover, used for a pericopes book belonging to the royal nunnery of Chelles, the form is that of a five-part diptych, and of the eleven Christ scenes on the four parts around the victorious Christ, six had a fifth-century ivory model, whose panels survive at Paris and Berlin (plate 5), and three more are so similar to a Carolingian fragment of a five-part ivory diptych in the British Museum that they are presumed to have a common Late Antique ivory prototype.[58] In this way, nine of the eleven scenes are directly

[55] Cited (in his own translation) by Paul Meyvaert, 'Bede and the church paintings of Wearmouth-Jarrow', *Anglo-Saxon England*, 8 (1979), pp. 68–9.

[56] For example, Carl Nordenfalk, *Celtic and Anglo-Saxon Painting* (London, 1980), plates 4, 9, 14, 24, 25; R. L. S. Bruce-Mitford, 'The art of the Codex Amiatinus', *Journal of the British Archaeological Association*, ser. 3, 32 (1969), pp. 1–25.

[57] M. L. W. Laistner, *A Hand-List of Bede Manuscripts* (Ithaca, NY, 1943), pp. 75–7. The fact that most manuscripts listed there are later, i.e., twelfth to thirteenth century, should not make one conclude that the work was little known in the Carolingian period, for as Lesne, *Histoire de la propriété ecclésiastique*, 4, p. 57, observed, Carolingian manuscripts of Bede were so well used that they were heavily replaced. Hrabanus Maurus used this work heavily for his Commentary on Chronicles: see Mayr-Harting, *Ottonian Book Illumination*, part ii, ch. 4.

[58] Goldschmidt, p. 10.

Plate 5 Panels of a Fifth-century Roman Book-cover, Ivory, with Scenes from the Life of Christ, Berlin, Preussischer Kulturbeseitz, and Paris, Louvre.

accounted for by earlier ivories. The pyx in the British Museum (plate 6) is likely to come from an early medieval ivory, since this was a common sort of ivory artefact, and the scene is rather different from the normal iconographic canon of early medieval manuscripts, eastern and western, one of whose representatives is a Carolingian drawing now at Düsseldorf

Plate 6 Healing of the Leper, Ivory Pyx (*c.*800), Charlemagne Court School, London, British Museum.

(plate 7).[59] One could easily put together more evidence or arguments along these lines.

The third possible approach is the important difference which it made to the acceptability of figural art, not least of Christ, that ivory was a precious material. The *Libri Carolini* have the argument that art was the materials used (in book illumination the paint on the parchment), together with the skill of the craftsman; nothing more. Works of art were mere mundane artefacts, or *opificia*. To attribute to the material substance any of the mystical properties in the object or person represented was tantamount to blasphemy. Hence it was the value of the material, not any mystical property, which gave the work of art its worth. It was as if the author would say that it was foolish to attach some absolute value to musical notes simply because they were composed by the genius Mozart, regardless of whether they were played on the mouth-organ or the

[59] For the drawing see Eberhard Galley, 'Das karolingische Evangeliarfragment aus der Landes- und Stadtbibliothek Düsseldorf', *Düsseldorfer Jahrbuch*, 52 (1966), pp. 120–7.

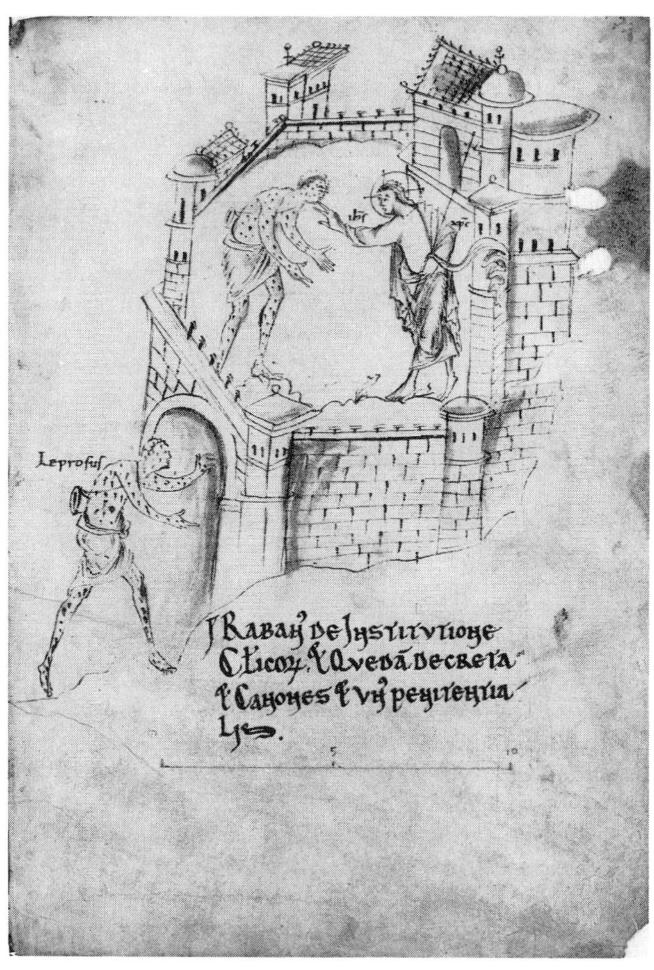

Plate 7 Healing of the Leper, from fragment of a ninth-century pericopes book (?Rhineland), Düsseldorf, MS B. 113, fol. 5r.

instruments for which Mozart had composed them. Theodulph himself approved of finely engraved silver cups for liturgical use, and he adorned his church of Germigny with stucco reliefs, although there is apparently no evidence of his interest in ivory carvings.[60] But ivory was an exceptionally valued substance in Charlemagne's time, every piece of which was elephant tusk or bone and so had to come from the East, since the substitutes of walrus and whale were at that time unknown, unless perchance for the rare good fortune of a stranded whale, such as the maker of the Franks Casket enjoyed.[61] The most cursory perusal of early medieval treasure lists will convince one of the contempt in which the illumination of books was held compared with the art of their precious covers, including ivories.[62] If one were going to have ivory book-covers, it was drab to leave them uncarved; consider (say) the wonderful life and movement of Mary and the Apostles, the subject of the Ascension fragment at Darmstadt, as an example of the beautification of the material by carving. In 801 or 802, Bishop Hildoard of Cambrai had two ivory panels sculpted beautifully, 'as anyone can see who looks at them', adds the historian of the bishopric. Ansegis, Abbot of St Wandrille (822–33), placed a silver cross before the altar, 'decorated with silver images'; silver, too, made figural art more acceptable.[63]

The fourth possible line of answer is that these ivories performed a function in relation to private prayer and meditation, and in so far as the books they adorned were liturgical books (Douce 176, for instance, is a book of Gospel readings for the liturgical year), this function could actually be better performed when the book was closed than when it was open, particularly when one remembers it might well have remained closed until the moment of the Gospel reading.[64] A deacon could hardly ponder illustrations of the life of Christ while he was chanting the Gospel. Let me suggest that the covers of the Gospel book could be used for the lightning meditation of a priest or deacon or abbess immediately before Mass. When the author of the *Libri Carolini* allows images, not for adoration but *ad memoriam rerum gestarum*,[65] he is not making a small concession, referring to mere *aides-mémoire* (though that is part of it), but a very large

[60] See Freeman, 'Theodulf of Orleans', pp. 696–9, and *L.C.*, III, 16, p. 137, lines 40–2.

[61] See Henry Mayr-Harting, *The Coming of Christianity to Anglo-Saxon England* (London, 1972), p. 221.

[62] See Mary-Harting, *Ottonian Book Illumination*, part i, pp. 48–9.

[63] Schlosser, no. 26, p. 262; no. 981, p. 355. For approval of silver and comments on its allegorical significance, *L.C.*, I, p. 39.

[64] Mayr-Harting, *Ottonian Book Illumination*, part i, p. 49.

[65] *L.C.*, III, p. 138, lines 3–4. Excellent discussion of this point and comparison with Byzantium in Rosamond McKitterick, 'Text and image in the Carolingian world', in Rosamond McKitterick, ed., *The Uses of Literacy in Early Medieval Europe* (Cambridge, 1990), pp. 298–300.

one. For *memoria* here is a word with profound meaning, derived from Augustine of Hippo, as the learned author was certainly aware. Augustine was especially interested in the memory at prayer. When a man summons something back to his memory and recalls it in meditation, he is like a ruminating animal. Memory recalls the past, indeed, but it is not absurd to speak of it also in the present; it is the condition in which the mind is present to itself and directs the will to the right kind of love.[66] Modern spiritual writers might call Augustine's *memoria* a state of recollection; and thus, to return to the language of the *Libri Carolini*, images could help to bring about prayerful recollection. This was not the least function of Angilbert's four stucco reliefs which, framed by gold, silver, and precious gems, he set up in the various parts of his church of St Ricquier, and whose style and iconography were likely to have been related to those of the court ivories. These stuccos could well give us a clue to the use of the Douce ivory carvings. They illustrated the Nativity, Passion, Resurrection, and Ascension.[67] At every Vespers, according to Angilbert's ritual order, the monks would pray before the Passion, and then, splitting into two choirs, one would pray before the Resurrection, the other before the Ascension. There would be prayer before the Passion and Resurrection on the Solemnity of St Maurice. The Palm Sunday procession would pause on entering the church to pray at the Nativity, which was in the vestibule or *porticus* of the west work; so also on the feast of St Richarius and other occasions.[68] Whether prayers were said aloud or in silence on such occasions is not clear, but one must remember that these men were following pre-eminently the Rule of St Benedict, which amidst all its liturgical stipulations did not neglect private prayer, though saying that it should be short and pure unless prolonged by the inspiration of God (chapter 20).

These four arguments, it will be clear, are not easily compatible with one another. The first presupposes unresolved tensions in the court culture, as does the second about the divided worlds of book painting and ivory carving (in the way I have stated it); whereas the third and fourth,

[66] Augustine of Hippo, *De Trinitate*, XIV, 11, 14, *PL* 42, col. 1048: 'Quapropter sicut in rebus praeteritis ea memoria dicitur qua fit ut valeant recoli et recordari, sic in re praesenti quod sibi est mens memoria sine absurditate dicenda est, etc.': quoted by G. B. Ladner, *The Idea of Reform* (Cambridge, Mass., 1969), p. 201, n. 51. See also Henry Chadwick, *Augustine* (Oxford, 1986), p. 70, commenting on the *Confessions*, and André Crépin, 'Bede and the Vernacular', in Gerald Bonner, ed., *Famulus Christi* (London, 1976), esp. p. 172.

[67] Schlosser, no. 979, p. 354. See also K. J. Conant, *Carolingian and Romanesque Architecture, 800–1200* (Harmondsworth, 1959), p. 12; J. Hubert, in Hubert, Porcher, and Volbach, *Carolingian Art*, p. 3.

[68] Edmund Bishop, 'Angilbert's Ritual Order for Saint-Ricquier', *Liturgica Historica* (Oxford, 1918), pp. 322, 327–8.

referring to the difference made by the materials and to the religious functions, imply coherence. For myself, while acknowledging that all is not amicable and tidy in history, I incline somewhat to the arguments of coherence in this case, not least because they are justified in one of the most sympathetic figures of Charlemagne's Renaissance, namely Angilbert, Abbot of St Ricquier. The patron of the carved stuccos was also the donor of one of the court Gospel books, the Abbeville Gospels, to his abbey.[69]

INFLUENCE OF THE *LIBRI CAROLINI* ON ART

We come now to the influence of the *Libri Carolini* on actual art. Here it is essential not to treat the books as if they were a carefully formulated, late medieval treatise on scholastic theology or canon law which could be applied *ad litteram* to given cases. We have said that they were the products of discussions, and it is the climate of artistic production, doubtless influenced by the discussions, on which I focus. The *Libri Carolini* allowed images but preferred words; they begged the reader to seek sacred truth within his own soul rather than in the mundane externals of images; they urged a high morality in which anything approaching superstitious veneration was abhorrent. C. S. Lewis says that after a Cambridge undergraduate had heard his lectures, which were published as *Studies in Words* (1960), he remarked, 'You have made me afraid to say anything at all.'[70] Perhaps likewise the effect of the discussions about images under Charlemagne was to make painters feel that they had been cautioned.

Whatever one sees as the reason for the Christ scenes in the court ivories, one already encounters a sense of caution here. Art historians have found models for almost all the Christ scenes on the Douce ivory, for instance, but I am not aware that anyone has ever claimed to have found a model in a similar context for such a figure as that in the top left-hand corner who initiates (as it were) the whole series of subsequent scenes, beginning with those of the Nativity. This is Isaiah, holding a scroll on which is written his own prophecy, 'Behold a Virgin shall conceive (*Ecce virgo concipiet*).' The *Libri Carolini* were very keen to stress the continuities between the Old and the New Testaments. 'As the body is pre-eminent over its shadow, truth over image, deed over figure, so is the New Testa-

[69] Köhler, *Karolingischen Miniaturen*, 2, pp. 9–11; and for the closeness of the Abbeville revision of the court text to that of the Vienna Gospels, ibid., pp. 50–1. Angilbert was a son-in-law of Charlemagne, and for his closeness to Alcuin, see Godman, *Poetry of the Carolingian Renaissance*, p. 10; Wallace-Hadrill, *Frankish Church*, p. 347.

[70] C. S. Lewis, *Studies in Words* (Cambridge, 1960), p. 6.

ment pre-eminent over the Old', says their author. 'The role of the Old Testament and its mysteries', as Paul Meyvaert concludes, 'was to foreshadow and offer intimations of the mysteries of the New Testament.'[71] The corollary is surely that it was a lesson of didactic value (which art *could* have) to show how the mysteries of the New Testament had followed from the words of the Old. Where the idea of the scroll-holding Isaiah came from is obvious; it must have been those Late Antique Gospel books like the sixth-century Rossano Gospels, which show New Testament scenes, and prophets pointing to them (like Isaiah in the ivory) while holding scrolls with relevant Old Testament texts in parallelism (plate 8).[72] To place this figure on the Douce ivory, which has the look of a Carolingian novelty in its context, is likely to be the idea of somebody at least taking account of *Libri Carolini* didacticism. It is worth noting that our largest Christ cycle in Carolingian book art comes amongst the illustrations of the Stuttgart Psalter (*c.*830), as if to show the wealth of Christ prophecies contained in the Psalms.[73]

Nor is the Douce the only court ivory in which the desire to relate the Christ scenes to the Old Testament is manifest. A pair of book-covers at Aachen itself depict appearances of Christ after his rising from the dead (plate 9); and there is an obvious meditational point in the concentration of subject matter itself. Three scenes illustrate the Journey to Emmaus, the Breaking of Bread there, and the Two Apostles reporting afterwards; also there is Doubting Thomas and Jesus blessing the Apostles before Bethany (Luke 24. 50). Finally, in the bottom left-hand panel, Jesus, holding a book in his left hand, explains the writings of Moses and the prophets concerning himself: 'And beginning at Moses and all the prophets, he expounded unto them in all the scriptures the things concerning himself', says Luke 24. 27 (compare 24. 44–5) about the journey to Emmaus. It would not adversely affect my argument if this were a common piece of iconography, but I think it must be rare.[74]

71 *L.C.*, I, 19, p. 44, lines 37–8; Paul Meyvaert, 'The authorship of the *Libri Carolini*', *RBen*, 89 (1979), pp. 53–4.

72 Weitzmann, *Book Illumination*, plates 29, 32.

73 Hoffmann *et al.*, eds, *Stuttgarter Bilderpsalter*: see n. 6 above.

74 Goldschmidt, no. 22, Tafel XII, and p. 17. Gertrud Schiller, *Ikonographie der christlichen Kunst*, 3 (Gutersloh, 1971), p. 89, and fig. 331a,b, calls it unique, at the same time presuming that an early (fifth to sixth century) North Italian cycle lies behind it. She points to a single leaf (London, V. and A., MS 661) similar to the Aachen scene of Jesus teaching the Apostles, English twelfth century, St Alban's school, ibid., pp. 106–8. E. Kirschbaum, ed., *Lexikon der christlichen Ikonographie* (Freiburg, 1968), 1, p. 671, on post-Resurrection appearances of Christ to the Apostles, mentions the Aachen ivories, but gives no other examples of the scene from Luke 24. 27 and 44–5.

Plate 8 The Raising of Lazarus, and Old Testament Prophets, Rossano Gospels (sixth century), Rossano Cathedral, fol. 1r.

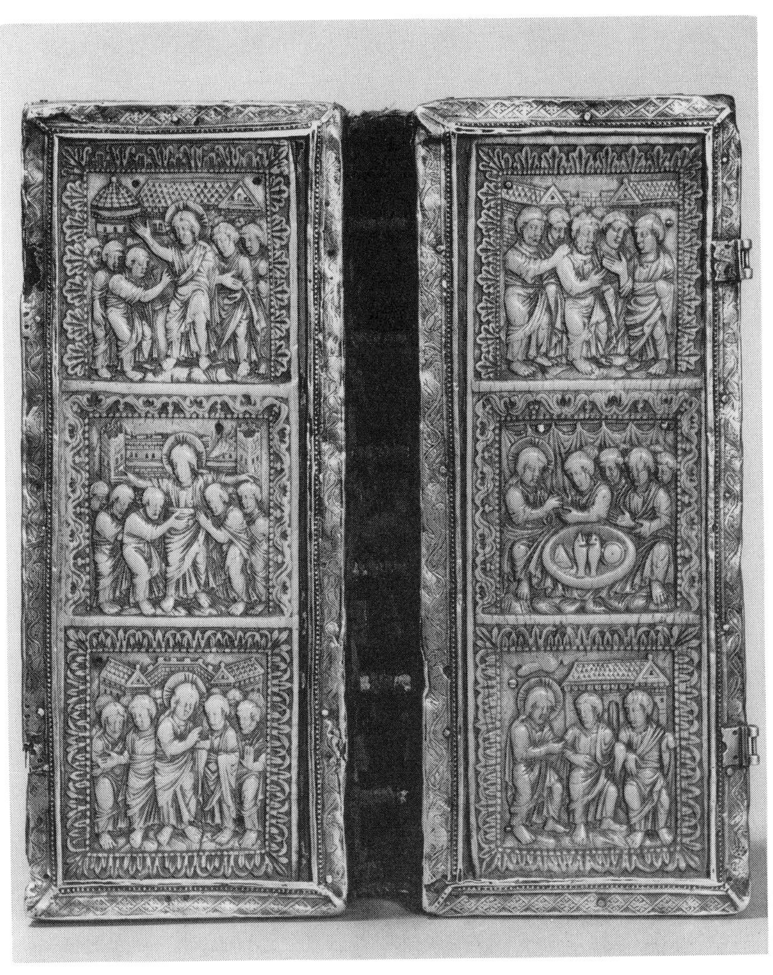

Plate 9 Post-Resurrection Appearances of Christ, Ivory Book-covers (*c*.800), Charlemagne Court School, Aachen Minster Treasury.

My next example takes us outside the court circle to Corbie, and may seem a trivial one, but it is indicative of the climate which reared it. It is a small initial 'S' of the early ninth century, in the shape of a fish, and standing at the head of an anti-Adoptionist tract in a canon law manuscript (plate 10).[75] An extraordinary amount of eighth- and ninth-century skill and imagination was channelled into fish initials, such as the 'D' for *Deus* in the eighth-century Gellone Sacramentary (plate 11), where a disembodied leg is slung casually over a ferocious fish. Teyssèdre, writing on the Gellone Sacramentary in 1930, in a chapter entitled *Abstracta vel disjecta membra*, managed to find this initial and others like it a return to (French) rationality from the wilder unrealisms of Celtic art, for they were based on juxtapositions of *disjecta membra* rather than interpenetrations, and they preferred familiar monstrous beasts to fabulous ones.[76] Be that as it may, the Gellone fish has little to do with either God or salvation, whereas our anti-Adoptionist fish is a triune fish, a fish whose head and body gives a special importance to the Second Person of the trinal composition, so to speak. This is certainly not the direct influence of the *Libri Carolini*, to which symbols such as lambs and fish did not recommend themselves any more than the actual images which they represented.[77] But the eschewing of frivolity and the drive towards moral and theological pointedness, which is not universal but characteristic in the Charlemagne and post-Charlemagne era, can be supposed to be a result of the discussions surrounding the *Libri Carolini*, while symbolic initials (as distinct from historiated initials, which seem to take their rise in eighth-century England) had a long history before them in Carolingian and Ottonian art, as can be seen from the emblematic baptism in a tenth-century Freising sacramentary (but the calligraphy Reichenau), in the initial for the Collect of St Paul, suitably enough (plate 12).[78]

One can see climate also affecting the practices of the scribes and artists of the Trier Apocalypse, this time more directly in line with the principles of the *Libri Carolini*. The Trier Apocalypse, a manuscript of about 800 or

[75] West Berlin, MS Hamilton 132; see *Zimelien: Abendländische Handschriften des Mittelalters aus den Sammlungen der Stiftung Preussischer Kulturbesitz, Berlin* (Wiesbaden, 1976), p. 18, illustration at p. 27.

[76] Bernard Teyssèdre, *Le Sacramentaire de Gellone et la figure humaine dans les manuscrits francs du VIIIe siècle* (Paris, 1930), esp. p. 47.

[77] Schrade, 'Zum Kuppelmosaik', pp. 28–9, *L.C.*, I, 23. A Carolingian manuscript of Paterius at Cologne, MS 97, fol. 198v, has a Trinitarian initial, an 'O', with a trefoil of Celtic design inside.

[78] Hartmut Hoffmann, *Buchkunst und Königtum in ottonischen und frühsalischen Reich* (Stuttgart, 1986), Textband, p. 334.

Plate 10 Fish Initial for an anti-Adoptionist Tract (early ninth century), West Berlin, MS Hamilton 32, fol. 248v.

very early ninth century, came from a north French scriptorium probably in touch with Tours. It would seem to be a direct derivative, with its seventy-three illustrations, of a sixth-century Italian prototype.[79] Folio 21 recto (plate 13) depicts 'four angels standing on the four corners of the earth, holding the four winds of the earth, that the wind should not blow on the earth, nor on the sea, nor on any tree (Apocalypse 7. 1).' For the personifications of the winds with wings on their heads, and even for their being on vases, there are Antique precedents.[80] One notes also the prominent Roman numerals in red, marking off the sixty-two divisions of the text (for our division into chapters is no earlier than the thirteenth century), another indicator of the importance of such manuscripts within

[79] *Trierer Apokalypse*, ed. R. Laufner and P. F. Klein (Graz, 1975), Textband, pp. 81–6.
[80] Ibid., p. 98, fig. 44, 45, 47.

Plate 11 Fish Initial from the Gellone Sacramentary (eighth-century West Frankish), Paris, BN, MS lat. 12048, fol. 164v.

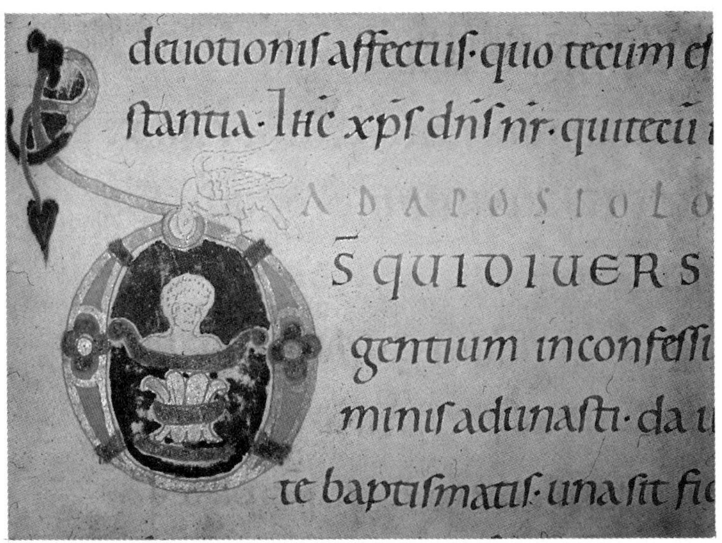

Plate 12 Baptism Initial, Feast of St Paul, Sacramentary of Bishop Abraham of Freising (957–993), Munich, Bayerische Staatsbibliothek, MS Clm 6421, fol. 116r.

Plate 13 The Four Winds restrained by Angels, Trier Apocalypse (early ninth century), Trier, Stadtbibliothek, MS 31, fol. 21r.

the context of schoolroom study, as the divisions of a symphonic score are for orchestral rehearsal. But the most interesting feature of this page is that it is the only page of the whole manuscript which contains any text on the same page as the illustrations. And whereas up to this point the picture had been on the recto, with the text corresponding to it on the other side of the page, on the verso, so that one could never read the text and see the relevant picture open together, from this point onwards there is an adjustment whereby picture is on the recto and relevant text is on the preceding verso. After folio 21 recto, for the first time in the manuscript, text and illustration lie together on the same opening, text on the left, illustration on the right. If words are always preferable to pictures, even when pictures are permissible, it is surely right that they should both be seen as closely in conjunction with each other as possible. If pictures are given for memory and recollection, then surely the same applies so that one can ponder the picture as one reads. Moreover, it is practically certain that this is a reorganization of text in relation to illustration made first in Trier itself and not in its model. For one leaf further on, a leaf between folios 22 and 23 was cut out of the original quire (making it the only incomplete quire in the book), which argues that it must have destroyed the new rhythm. Presumably the leaf had been written beforehand or in ignorance of the change in plan, or else there was some inadvertence of scribe or illuminator when not yet used to the new and more meaningful arrangement.[81]

The capitularies and edicts of Charlemagne are heavily impregnated with the idea that if only people are sufficiently taught, preached at, and pressurized, they will come to a responsible share in his own high sense of morality. 'Everybody is personally to strive to maintain himself in God's holy service', says the great capitulary of 802, 'for the lord emperor cannot himself provide the necessary care and discipline for each man individually.'[82] Scribes were particularly pressurized, being reminded that bad work would lead to improper prayer and misunderstanding of Scripture; and to judge by the fascinating recent work of scholars such as David Ganz and Rosamond McKitterick, it all had some effect.[83] Although

[81] Ibid., pp. 85–6.

[82] King, tr., *Charlemagne*, p. 234.

[83] Ganz, 'The preconditions', esp. pp. 29–34; Rosamond McKitterick, *The Frankish Church and the Carolingian Reforms, 789–895* (London, 1977), and *The Carolingians and the Written Word* (Cambridge, 1989). I am grateful to Richard Gameson for some helpful comments in the preparation of this paper, which has been the occasion of my studying more deeply some matters which arose in my work on Ottonian Book Illumination.

painters were no doubt a lesser breed in that society, if they were not scribes and calligraphers themselves, they too appear to have been pulled into the ambit of moral responsibility.

St Peter's College,
Oxford

Plate 14 'Cameo' in the Arch of a Lorsch Gospels Canon Table, with the Three Women and the Angel at the Tomb after the Resurrection, Lorsch Gospels (*c*.800–814), Julia Alba, Rumania, detail of fol. 11v.

Principal Surviving Court School Manuscripts Charlemagne 768–814

ADA GROUP

Godescalc Evangelistary 781–3, Paris, BN, MS nouv. acq. lat. 1203
Paris, Bibl. de l'Arsenal, MS 599
Ada Gospels I, Trier, Stadtbibliothek, MS 22
Dagulph Psalter *c.*795, Vienna, Nationalbibliothek, MS 1861
Zachary Fragment, *c.*790–800, London, BL, MS Cotton Claudius B.V.
Harleian Gospels *c.*795–800, London, BL, MS Harley 2788
Gospels from St Ricquier, Abbeville, Bibl. mun., MS 4
St Médard of Soissons Gospels, Paris, BN, MS lat. 8850
Ada Gospels II, Trier Stadtbibliothek, MS 22
Lorsch Gospels, Alba Julia, and Vatican, MS Pal. lat. 50

The above are listed in the generally accepted likely chronological order established by Wilhelm Köhler; in the Ada Gospels the canon tables are early, the Evangelists late.

VIENNA CORONATION GROUP

Vienna Coronation Gospels, *c.*790–800, Vienna, Schatzkammer
Aachen Gospels, Aachen Minster Treasury
Brescia Gospels
Brussels Gospels

The last three are all late Charlemagne.

Principal Ivories of the Charlemagne Court School Mentioned

Book-cover (for pericopes book from Chelles), Oxford, Bodleian Library, MS Douce 176
Pyx, with Healing of the Leper, London, British Museum
Covers of the Lorsch Gospels, Vatican and London, Victoria and Albert Museum

Covers of the Dagulph Psalter, with scenes of David and St Jerome, *c.*795, Paris, Louvre
Ascension Fragment, Darmstadt
Ivory Panel with Nativity scenes, London, British Museum
Book-covers at Aachen, with scenes of Christ's appearances after the Resurrection, Aachen Minster Treasury

MAKE A MERRY NOISE! A NINTH-CENTURY TEACHER LOOKS AT HYMNS

by ALICE L. HARTING-CORRÊA

FORTY years after Charlemagne's imperial coronation, Walahfrid Strabo, thirty-three-year-old abbot of the monastery of Reichenau, wrote a history of mid-ninth-century Frankish liturgy: *Libellus de exordiis et incrementis quarundam in observationibus ecclesiasticis rerum—A Little Book about the Origins and Development of Certain Aspects of the Liturgy*.[1] It was the first account of liturgical development, and the topics ranged widely over thirty-two chapters, from bells to baptism, language to litany. Most of the subjects were in a state of change or expansion. Where there was controversy—for example, should a priest celebrate the Eucharist more than once a day—the history of a practice would help to underline the essential elements and to demonstrate the Christian constants as opposed to cultural diversity. Where there was development, such as the increasing number of hymns available for the Liturgy of the Hours, the history of that practice was appropriate and timely.

This paper will introduce the author of the treatise, the relationship of liturgy to the text as a whole, and then look at chapter 26, 'About the canonical hours, kneeling, hymns, chants and their development'. This important chapter supports a recent argument that the Aachen court and chapel of Charlemagne's son, Louis the Pious, played a part in the growing development of a new hymnary and its transmission to both monasteries and some non-monastic churches.

A great deal is known about the author, Walahfrid Strabo, from several sources, such as the annals of Reichenau, where he was abbot from 838 to 849, his own poetry, and his vade-mecum, an extraordinary manuscript written for and largely by Walahfrid.[2] Briefly, Walahfrid was born in 808–9 and entered Reichenau as a *puer*, or young lad, from a poor

[1] *MGH Cap.*, II, ed. V. Krause (Hanover, 1897), pp. 473–516. I have recently completed a translation of and liturgical commentary on this text as my doctoral thesis in the University of St Andrews, publication forthcoming in *Mittellateinische Studien und Texte* (E. J. Brill).

[2] In his fundamental article, 'Eine Sammelhandschrift Walafrid Strabo', *Aus der Welt des Buches. Festschrift Georg Leyh* (Leipzig, 1950), pp. 30–48; (repr. *Mittelalterliche Studien*, 3 vols (Stuttgart, 1967), 2, pp. 34–51), Professor Bernhard Bischoff has convincingly demonstrated that St Gallen MS 878 was written for and largely by Walahfrid over a period of about twenty-four years. It is Walahfrid's commonplace book, or vade-mecum, a collection of texts and excerpts from texts that he found worthy of copying for additional study and use.

Swabian family. Strabo is not a family name. It is a nickname Walahfrid himself used: it means 'squinter', referring to what must have been an obvious visual defect. His contemporaries never used the term: they always wrote of 'Walahfrid'. He was a brilliant and precocious student: at the age of eighteen he rewrote a prose account of a death-bed vision of his teacher in Latin verse, in 945 hexameter lines.[3]

Walahfrid's student days ended in 829, when Louis the Pious summoned him to the Aachen court as tutor to the six-year-old Charles, the Emperor's youngest son and the future Charles the Bald. This was only fifteen years after the death of Charlemagne: the building of the Aachen complex, the palace and chapel, was one of Charlemagne's major projects. Louis the Pious was the next to rule from Aachen. Walahfrid resided with the royal family there for the next nine years—teaching, developing his poetic skills, worshipping at the chapel, and laying the foundation for his history of worship.

When the young Charles came of age at fifteen, the Emperor Louis appointed Walahfrid abbot of his own monastery at Reichenau, a position he held for eleven years, until his death in 849. In August of that year Walahfrid drowned, crossing the Loire while on a diplomatic mission between his former student, Charles the Bald, and Louis the German.[4]

During a two-year forced exile from his abbacy of Reichenau, Walahfrid completed in excellent Latin his history of the liturgy. Ahead of its time, the popularity of the text was limited and short lived: all the copies of the book were made in the next two hundred years; only five manuscripts contain the entire work, and four other manuscripts include just a few selected chapters. The Latin text was well edited in the late nineteenth century from all the known manuscripts.

In the ninth century scholars were of necessity educated in church or monastery, centres of most intellectual activity. Regardless of the degree of personal conviction, the liturgy was a common denominator, a part of daily life for most, a topic of correspondence, and the business of councils and synods. The year, the month, the week, and the day—the recurring divisions of life—were structured within prescribed liturgical actions which linked the activities of the Christian people to those of Christ, his

[3] The two most recent editions are *Visio Wettini*, ed. and tr. D. Traill (Bern, 1974) and *Visio Wettini*, ed. and tr. H. Knittel (Sigmaringen, 1986).

[4] Among several good accounts of Walahfrid's life see K. Langosch, *Die deutsche Literatur des Mittelalters: Verfasserlexicon*, 4 vols (Berlin, 1955), 4, pp. 734–70, with full references and extensive bibliographies; see esp. pp. 738–67, which provide an excellent analysis of Walahfrid's writings.

precursors, and his saints. Easter, with its Lenten preparation, determined special feasts and fasts, changes in the readings, the choice of hymns. Times for ordinations and baptisms were circumscribed by the calendar. The compilation of a hymnal for the Liturgy of the Hours exercised the royal palace as well as monasteries.

However, despite Charlemagne's educational and liturgical reforms and continuing attempts at standardization throughout the Frankish Empire, the period remained characterized by experimentation and diversity. Liturgical controversy and variety is a dominant theme in Walahfrid's *De exordiis*. The liturgy was in a state of flux, and for monk, priest, scribe, musician, bishop, and emperor participation in its development was a lively issue. A contemporary historical view of Carolingian liturgy written by a well-educated and intelligent ecclesiastic provides a means for seeing broad patterns of Christian constants and historical variables against which the details are more clearly defined.

Walahfrid's nine years at the Aachen court teaching the young Charles the Bald are crucial to the argument that Louis the Pious's court played a part in the development of the New Hymnary.[5] The young scholar and teacher, still in his twenties, would have been exposed to the lively liturgical issues involving ecclesiastical and lay members of family, court, chapel, and their visitors. The liturgical centre had shifted from Rome to Francia: one indication of this is the Frankish emphasis on Roman authority and tradition to give weight to Carolingian liturgical reform. Decisive liturgical assemblies at Aachen pressed for continuing standardization throughout the Empire: the 809 assembly, the 816 decrees for canons, and the 817 decrees for monks. As recounted in the 814 letter of the archchancellor, Helisachar, reformed liturgical texts were available at Aachen for copying.[6] This extraordinary letter also reveals his intense interest in the musical performance of chants and hymns in a period when texts still lacked notation.[7] It was during just these early years of the Carolingian era that manuscript evidence points to a crucial phase in the development of the New Hymnary.

The pre-Carolingian monastic hymnary has latterly been called the

[5] See D. A. Bullough and Alice L. Harting-Corrêa, 'Texts, Chant, and the Imperial Chapel', in Peter Godman and Roger Collins, eds, *Charlemagne's Heir* (Oxford, 1990), pp. 489–508.

[6] *MGH Ep.*, V, ed. E. Dümmler (Berlin, 1899), pp. 307–9.

[7] For an excellent summary of this interesting and complex aspect of early music see Giulio Cattin, *Music of the Middle Ages*, tr. Steven Botterill, 2 vols (Cambridge, 1984), 1, pp. 53–63, with full references.

Old Hymnary.[8] This term does not mean a stable collection of hymns, but simply those poetic texts which various kinds of evidence show to have been sung in the Liturgy of the Hours by communities as far apart as northern Italy and the north of England. It was a modest affair of no more than forty-five hymns; indeed, the composite Oxford Bodleian Library manuscript, Junius 25, contains twenty-six hymns, the greatest number recorded in a single source. That number is only reached because at Murbach in the (?)820s five hymns were added to a Reichenau collection of twenty-one written a few years earlier when Walahfrid was still a young boy there. Eight of the twenty-one hymns in the Reichenau collection were necessarily used in each of the eight Hours almost every day of the year; and, in fact, it was one of a group of hymnaries in which the Office of Lauds, the Office sung at daybreak, was also allocated a different (morning) hymn for each day of the week. That left only seven hymns with which to add seasonal variety.

An examination of three manuscripts, Cologne, Dombibliothek 106, folios 44r, 46r, and 46v,[9] Düsseldorf, Universitätsbibliothek cod. B. 3, folios 255v–71v, and Manchester, John Rylands University Library 116, folios 95r–104v, has shown that a new hymnary was in the process of formation in the early years of the ninth century, with hymns taken in part from the Old Hymnary and in part from other sources. On codicological, paleographical, and textual grounds it has been argued that the common source of the verse texts of the New Hymnary probably resided at the Aachen court. There would have been an *authenticum*, but not a single codex, probably a collection of small parchment books, perhaps even bifolia, mostly but not invariably rubricated, revised, extended, and recopied from time to time, disarranged and rearranged, and inevitably offering alternative texts for some Offices. Hence the slightly differing choices in substantially overlapping collections before the standardization of monastic and non-monastic hymnaries, and the variant order in which largely identical groups of hymns figure in these same collections.

Interest in every aspect of hymn-writing—suitability of text to the occasion, authorship, melody, and performance—would have been intense. And these are the very features Walahfrid addresses in chapter 26.

[8] The terminology has been widely accepted since H. Gneuss first proposed the terms, 'Alte Hymnar', 'revidierte Alte Hymnar' in *Hymnar und Hymnen im englischen Mittelalter* (Tübingen, 1968), pp. 10–40.

[9] The folio references supplement the material in Bullough and Harting-Corrêa, 'Texts, Chant and the Imperial Chapel', pp. 502–3.

I shall cite the major areas of his interest and then read excerpts from the chapter which will allow the text to speak for itself.

Meticulously noting his sources, Walahfrid introduces the fourth-century beginnings of hymn-writing, listing authors up to the eighth century; he distinguishes between unstructured, or what he terms general, hymns and hymns composed in [quantitative] metre and in rhythmical or accentual verse; the problem of the texts for hymns follows; he makes unexpected references to hymn-singing in the Mass; and finally he notes that there are Ambrosian and pseudo-Ambrosian hymns.

Walahfrid begins his history of hymn-writing in Western Europe in the fourth and fifth centuries:

> For, as blessed Augustine testifies in the books of his *Confessiones*, Ambrose of Milan, composing hymns of divine praise for the people, alleviated the persecution of Justina Augusta by the novelty of the hymns. Just as it is also written in the life of Ambrose himself: 'That is the time when antiphons, hymns and vigils began to be observed in the church of Milan.' Hilary of Poitiers also composed hymns, and it is written about Pope Gelasius that he composed . . . hymns after the custom of blessed Ambrose.

Walahfrid continues his account of fourth-century hymn-writing, but turns his attention to Eastern Europe, with a quotation from his source-text:

> Cassiodorus writes in the tenth book of his *Ecclesiastical History*, which is called the *Tripartita*, that John Chrysostom was the 'first to enrich prayers with evening hymns for this reason most particularly. The Arians (ostracized from the Orthodox Church for their heretical views of the Trinity) used to hold services outside the city. However, on Saturday and Sunday the Arians gathered inside the gates and along the arcades and sang hymns and antiphons composed according to the Arian doctrine; and having done this for the greatest part of the night, at dawn they went out, antiphons and all, through the middle of the city to the gate, and assembled at their church. They kept on doing this repeatedly, however, as if to spite the Orthodox, for they also sang this frequently: "Where are they who speak of the one with triple power?" Then, lest the simple people be attracted by hymns of this kind, John instructed his people so that they, too, should be occupied with night-time hymns both so that the Arians'

> activity would be obscured and the declaration of the faithful would be strengthened.'

Walahfrid resumes his own account:

> However, it should be remarked that not only were hymns sung which flow in [quantitative] metres or [accentual] rhythms, such as Ambrose and Hilary, Bede, priest of the English, and Prudentius, scholar of the Spaniards, and many other people composed, but also other chants of praise which were produced with suitable words and pleasant melodies; this is why among the Hebrews the book of Psalms is called the Book of Hymns. And although in some churches metrical hymns are not sung, nevertheless in all [churches] general hymns, that is praises, are sung.

By the fifth century newly composed texts for hymns had come under attack. This next section suggests that the subject has become controversial again. Walahfrid continues:

> The 633 council at Toledo indicated among other things that those hymns which were properly composed must be sung. [Walahfrid quotes the ruling of the council]: 'and because hymns are known to have been composed by some men with great devotion for the praise of God and for the triumphs of the apostles and martyrs, as indeed are those which the blessed doctors Hilary and Ambrose produced, nevertheless, certain people particularly condemn them because they did not arise from the writings of the holy Canons or the apostolic tradition: therefore, let them also reject that hymn composed by men which we sing daily in the public and private liturgy at the end of all the psalms: *Gloria et honor Patri et Filio et Spiritui sancto in saeculo saeculorum, amen*. And there is that hymn which the angels sang at Christ's birth in the flesh: *Gloria in excelsis Deo et in terra pax hominibus bonae voluntatis*; the ecclesiastical doctors composed the remaining [words] which follow on. Therefore, must those [hymns] not be sung in churches because they are not found in the books of holy scriptures? Masses and mass-set prayers and prayers and commemorations and laying-on of hands are composed from elements which, if none are sung in church, then all the ecclesiastical services are empty.'
>
> [Walahfrid comments on the ruling of the council:] From these words it is clear that many things are newly composed in the Church

> which must not be excluded if they are not inconsistent with the faith of truth.

In the ninth century, hymns were associated exclusively with the Liturgy of the Hours. Walahfrid's next remarks are all the more interesting:

> Metrical and rhythmical hymns are sung in the Ambrosian liturgy which some people were accustomed to adopt occasionally in the Mass because of the grace of remorse which is increased by the beautiful sweetness. For indeed tradition has it that Paulinus, the patriarch of Friuli, used hymns composed by himself and others quite frequently and particularly in private Masses at about the time of the offering of the sacraments. I would, in fact, have believed that so great a man and one of so great knowledge would not have done this either without authority or without the weight of reason.

Finally, Walahfrid puts to rest the widespread assumption that most hymns were composed by Ambrose:

> In the Offices, also, which blessed Abbot Benedict outstanding in all holiness established [that is, in the Rule which was the basis of ninth-century Reichenau observance], hymns are sung throughout the Liturgy of the Hours, [hymns] which he himself in calling [them] Ambrosian, wished to be understood either as those which Ambrose composed, or which others composed in imitation of Ambrosian hymns.
>
> Nevertheless, it must be understood that many hymns are thought composed by Ambrose which have by no means been produced by that man. For it seems incredible that he composed some [hymns] such as are found in substantial numbers, that is, [those] which, having no sequence of thought, show a rusticity in their vocabulary which is not customary in Ambrose.[10]

The part played by Louis's court and chapel in the formation of the New Hymnary and its transmission to monasteries and cathedrals over many decades has yet to be finally established. But Walahfrid's residence at court for nine of those years, his personal interest and involvement in liturgy and liturgical hymns (some of his own hymns established their place in the liturgy), and his responses in chapter 26 of *De exordiis* to the

[10] For the Latin text of all of the above quotations see *MGH Cap.*, II, pp. 505–6.

many issues arising from the compilation of the New Hymnary are strong supports for the argument.

During a period when there was still no musical notation, or only the most rudimentary indications of melody and rhythm, a discussion of the musical settings of hymns must necessarily be thwarted. That much of the liturgy was 'words plus music' is, however, clear from the texts. Helisachar's letter explained that skilled musicians (anonymous, of course, like most of the artists of the time) were summoned to the court to supply appropriate settings and pass them on orally, in conjunction with copies of the verses, to other cantors. The supposed specific examples of the transfer of settings of hymns in the Old Hymnary to others in the New are almost certainly false. But it seems clear that the interest and controversy generated by the compilation of the New Hymnary formed the basis of this fascinating chapter of Walahfrid's liturgical history.

University of St Andrews

THE CHRISTIAN ZODIAC ON A FONT AT HOOK NORTON: THEOLOGY, CHURCH, AND ART

by MARY CHARLES MURRAY

THIS paper is an attempt to offer a preliminary study of a Christian tradition of allegorizing the zodiac which is found in certain literary texts and artistic representations. What prompted the investigation from the artistic point of view was an examination of the twelfth-century baptismal font in the church of St Peter at Hook Norton, Oxfordshire, which is decorated with a mixture of selected signs of the zodiac and scriptural images (plate 1).[1] It raises the question of how early was the tradition in which the zodiac was linked with baptism in Christian thought, and what other connections there might be. So the question I should like briefly to illustrate here is the connection between Christian decorations which feature the zodiac, particularly in the medieval period, and an allegorical tradition which goes back to the early Church.

The zodiac, which is part of the solar universe with its order of planets, months, and seasons, always symbolizes in ancient Roman pagan iconography and its accompanying literature some aspect of the notion of time. The relationship of the zodiac to the year is the same as its relationship to the sun on its yearly course. Some of the best artistic examples illustrating the idea, from the purely chronological point of view, are the abstract or radial type of calendars, which express the annual course of the sun within

[1] The font is a small, white stone cylindrical drum, 2 feet 1½ inches high, with an upper diameter of 2 feet 7 inches and a lower of 2 feet 4 inches. It has two bands of decoration, one at the top and one at the bottom, encircling it. The upper band, 4 inches deep and running below the rim, is composed of a pattern of writhing branches and foliage; the bottom, half an inch smaller, is a running pattern of rimmed circles. The surface between the bands is carved with a single series of large figures, facing in such a way that they should be read from right to left, and all in excellent condition, despite the careless treatment the font has at some time received. The first two figures are a naked Adam and Eve, identified by a Latin inscription. Next to Eve is a formally designed Tree of Knowledge, identified by the apples, carefully arranged in a studded pattern on its curling branches. Next is Sagittarius, then Aquarius, then a lamb (Aries), standing above a Tree of Life. The circle is completed by a half-wild animal, a half-finned serpent, which appears to be a combination of the biblical serpent, Scorpio, and Capricorn. Beside the serpent is a three-leaved, flower-star rosette, corresponding to the large, formal four-leaved, star-like flower, which separates the figures of Adam and Eve. The Hook Norton allegory is complete, continuous, and carefully elaborated, and totally related to the baptismal purpose of the font.

Plate 1 The Romanesque Font, Church of St Peter, Hook Norton, Oxfordshire: Adam and Eve and the Tree of Life (photo: R. A. Markus).

the circle of the zodiac signs, or the months of the year, or both. A beautifully clear example of this use within the Jewish tradition in the Late Antique period is to be found in the famous zodiac mosaic of the Beth Alpha synagogue in Palestine, dating from the sixth century.[2] This kind of Sol-Zodiac composition was widespread, and it serves to indicate the familiarity of ordinary people with astronomical-astrological matters; for in the ancient world astronomy and astrology were not clearly separated, as in the modern distinction.

As an allegory, the zodiac was introduced into pagan iconography in the Hadrianic period in connection with the year, or the personification of time, on the coinage, and on imperial medallions; and it is exclusive to the new-year issues.[3] It was intended to propagate the idea of the acceptable year: the ideas of new birth, new life, and new prosperity which might be expected in the coming year. An early *aureus* of Hadrian, struck, as the legend SAE(CULUM) AVR(EUM) shows, to advertise the new reign as another golden age shows the *genius anni* or the *genius saeculi*, the Spirit of the Time, as a half-draped figure standing within an oval zodiac frame.[4] This figure appears on an analogous piece of the same date, a mosaic from Sentinum, now in Munich,[5] showing the same zodiac frame grasped by a similar personage and with it the seasons and Mother Earth in the lower part of the design. The security, peace, and prosperity ushered in by the new era are clearly indicated by the iconography. In the third century the *genius saeculi* is replaced by the figure of the emperor, who presides over the zodiacal year and becomes himself in propaganda terms *cosmocrator*. The coin legend, too, as is illustrated by a medallion of Tacitus, changes from the familiar new-year wish to AETERNITAS AUGUSTI, and the impression is unavoidable that there is a suggestion of a happy new year which will never end.[6] By the fourth century AD the zodiac iconography symbolizing time becomes, as a result of its use in imperial propaganda, shorthand for 'celestial' or 'divine' time, corresponding to the adjectives used in the imperial hymns and panegyrics.

This enrichment of the symbol in imperial art is probably what made

[2] See E. L. Sukenik, *Ancient Synagogues in Palestine and Greece* (London, 1934), pp. 33–5.

[3] See J. M. C. Toynbee, *Roman Medallions = Numismatic Studies*, no. 5 (New York, 1944), p. 90.

[4] H. Mattingly, *British Museum Catalogue of the Coins of the Roman Empire*, 3 (London, 1936), p. 278, no. 312.

[5] See J. M. C. Toynbee, *The Hadrianic School* (Cambridge, 1934), pl. 33, no. 3.

[6] For Tacitus, also Alexander Severus, Julia Mamaea, and Gordian III, see F. Gnecchi, *I Medaglioni Romani*, 3 vols (Milan, 1912), 2, plates 101, no. 10; 105, no. 7; 3, plate 156, no. 14 (pl. XLVII, 3). Toynbee, *Medallions*, p. 92.

the zodiac popular as a cosmic symbol in contemporary and later religious art of a non-imperial kind. It is not surprising to discover that some of the best non-imperial zodiac iconography is to be found within Mithraic contexts. On Mithraic monuments the zodiac appears most frequently in representations of the miraculous birth of Mithras. On a third-century altar found in conjunction with a Mithraic birth scene at Housesteads, on Hadrian's Wall, Mithras is described as *saecularis*, the eternal, the lord of time, and the lord of the golden age so praised in prose and poetry and on the imperial coinage, which will return for those devoted followers who receive immortality.[7] The zodiac has now become a religious symbol, carrying earthly time into the divine sphere, a symbol of new birth into divine life. This links it also with one of its commonest appearances within literary texts of the period: its use in horoscopes.

In the preceding paragraphs we have surveyed material on the use of the zodiac which has not yet been in any way adapted to the new Christian thought-world, but such a survey seemed necessary in order to provide the context for its adaptation for Christian use, for the same traditional thoughts which were associated with it could well be put to the service of Christianity.

The Christian literary allegorization of the zodiac in the early Church is confined to two contexts: that of Christian baptism and that of discussions of the functions of the Twelve Apostles, particularly with regard to their preaching. There is, so far as I know, only one early Christian text which allegorizes the zodiacal signs directly, that to be found in an Easter-night sermon of the fourth century bishop Zeno of Verona, on the occasion of the baptism of the neophytes.[8] Zeno expounds for them the horoscope of their new birth in Christ. Since, as he says, he knows their curiosity about such things in their former way of life, he gives each of the twelve signs, save Capricorn, a specifically Christian meaning. His text refers to the use of the zodiac in a non-iconographical form, that of horoscopes, but he is relevant for us in that he demonstrates that a link

[7] The iconographical evidence for Mithraism is still most easily accessible in M. J. Vermaseren, *Corpus inscriptionum et monumentorum religionis Mithriacae*, 2 vols (The Hague, 1956, 1958). For Housesteads see D. J. Smith, *Museum of Antiquities, Newcastle-upon-Tyne, an Illustrated Introduction* (Newcastle, 1974), no. 26, p. 23. Vermaseren, *Corpus*, 1, pp. 298–9, no. 860, fig. 226.

[8] Zeno of Verona, *Tractatus*, I, 38, ed. B. Lofstedt, *CChr.SL*, 22, pp. 105–6. This edition supplants for the text that of A. Bigelmair, *Bibliothek der Kirchenvater*, 2 (Munich, 1934), 10. But for the introduction Bigelmair is essential. For a largely inclusive discussion of both see G. Banterle, 'La Nuova Edizione dei Sermoni di S. Zeno', *Studi Zenoniani* (*in occasione del XVI centenario della morte di S. Zeno*). *Accademia di Agricoltura, Scienze e Lettere di Verona* (Verona, 1974).

was made at the level of popular preaching between the zodiac and the sacrament of baptism.

The second zodiac tradition represents a transfer of the pagan idea of zodiacal time. It is found in exegetical commentaries which deal with texts which speak of the baptism of Christ, the Lamb of God, and the Paschal Lamb, and the functions of the Apostles. In the characteristic manner of the exegesis of the period these elements are allegorized, and the commentaries compare Christ with the year and the Apostles with the signs of the zodiac and the months of the year. We may look at a few texts. The idea of referring to Christ as the 'year' was based on an old tradition within the Church which saw in the 'acceptable year' of Isaiah 61. 2 a prediction of the fact, as it was believed, that Christ's ministry had lasted only one year from his baptism.

This tradition was used and explained, for example, by Gregory of Elvira (d. after 392) commenting on the epithet 'one year old' as applied to the Paschal Lamb in Exodus 12. 5. He says Christ is called *anniculus* because after his baptism in the Jordan by John, the time of his preaching having been accomplished, he suffered in accordance with David's prophecy, 'You shall bless the crown of the year with your goodness.'[9] The theme is treated in longer form by Gaudentius of Brescia (fourth to fifth century): he is *anniculus* because one year elapsed from his baptism in the Jordan to the day of his Passion. That was the acceptable year of the Lord, which Jesus, reading in the synagogue, declared had been written concerning himself in the book of Isaiah. This is what the prophet had extolled in the psalm, 'You shall bless the crown of the year with your goodness.' It was the triumphant circle blessed by Christ's deeds of goodness.[10]

The theme is treated elsewhere, but the focus this time is on the Apostles, who are the months of the year, which is Christ, and sometimes by variation the twelve hours of the day, which is also Christ. This allegorization was popular, and we may just select some representative examples. In his commentary on Psalm 11. 2, Asterius the Sophist (d. after 341) makes the strange statement that Judas's betrayal has 'crippled the clock of the Apostles, and of the apostolic twelve hour day he has made one of eleven hours; he has also deprived the Lord's year of one month.'[11] Ambrose of Milan (*c.*339–97) also presents the same idea: if the duration of the world is a single day, then its hours are counted in centuries, since

[9] Greogry of Elvira, *Tractatus originis*, IX, 11–14, *CChr.SL*, 69, p. 73.
[10] Gaudentius of Brescia, *Sermo* III, *PL* 20, cols 865–6.
[11] Asterius the Sophist, *Homilies on the Psalms*, ed. M. Richard = *Symbolae Osloenses* (Oslo, 1956).

there are twelve hours in the day, this day must be mystically understood as Christ, who has his Twelve Apostles shining with heavenly light.[12]

Underlying these allegories in addition to the radial calendars is the ancient sundial, the horologion, which was decorated with the signs of the zodiac and was meant to express visually the cycle of the twelve-hour day and the twelve-month year. The iconographical representations for both the hours and the months was the zodiac.[13] In the texts just quoted the Apostles are substituted by suggestion for the signs. But that they had passed from association with the signs of the zodiac to complete identification with them, at least in certain Gnostic circles, is shown by the Gnostic Theodotus, as recorded by Clement of Alexandria (*c.*150–*c.*215). Clement says that he (Theodotus) says that the Apostles have been substituted for the twelve signs of the zodiac, for just as generation is governed by these, so regeneration is directed by the Apostles.[14] This text seems to be supported by some early Christian sarcophagi from France, which show the Twelve Apostles, each with a star above his head.[15] With this text we are again in the ambience of thought which we noted above with regard to Zeno of Verona, connecting the zodiac and horoscopes with the idea of the new birth of Christian baptism, and with the wealth of pagan imagery which associates the zodiac with figures who are *cosmocratores*.

The verse from the Gospel of Matthew (19. 28) which states that the Apostles would sit on twelve thrones, judging the twelve tribes of Israel, was also, and perhaps inevitably, connected with zodiac symbolism in early Christian commentary. As an example we note Origen, who gives an exegesis of the twelve tribes as signifying the celestial peoples, the fathers of the tribes are the twelve stars, and the celestial peoples will be judged by the Twelve Apostles. The Apostles are here again *cosmocratores*.[16] But in another commentary of Arian authorship the text is applied not to the

[12] Ambrose of Milan, *Expositio evangelii secundum Lucam*, VII, 222, *CChr.SL*, 14, p. 291.

[13] Boll shows that the *dodekaoros* represented the cycle of both the twelve hours and the twelve months; and that the sundial, the horologion, was decorated not only with the signs of the zodiac, but also with the twelve gods of Olympus. See F. Boll, *Sternglaube und Sterndeutung* (Leipzig, 1918), p. 75. There is an example, found at Gabies, in the Louvre. That the Apostles are here also being substituted for the Olympians is suggested by J. Danielou, *Primitive Christian Symbols* (London, 1964), p. 124, who gathers together useful material on the Apostles and the zodiac, to which I am indebted.

[14] Clement d'Alexandrie, *Extraits de Theodote*, ed. F. Sagnard, *Sources chrétiennes* (Paris, 1970), sect. A.1,2, p. 110.

[15] Instances from Arles and Manosque: see *s.v.* 'Astres', in *Dictionnaire d'archéologie chrétienne et de liturgie*, 1(2) (Paris, 1907), cols 3005–33.

[16] Origen, *In Matthaeum*, XV, 24, *PG* 13, cols 1323–6.

eschatological end-time, when the Apostles rule the world, but to the time after Christ's ascension when the Apostles baptize.[17]

Iconographically there is no trace of the representation of the zodiac in any specifically Christian context until the medieval period. It does not appear in the catacombs or on the related sarcophagi.[18] Why this is so is obvious; it was a vital and highly charged image in constant use in pagan art, where the astrological significance was clear, making its adoption for Christian decoration impossible. The Christianization of the signs was, as we have seen, taking place at the literary level, in learned exegetical commentary and in popular preaching.

We may now turn to the problem of how the zodiac tradition was carried and by whom, and in what ways it was modified in the intervening centuries between the early Church and its appearance in the medieval period on the doors of churches and on the Romanesque font at Hook Norton. During this transition period a third mode of Christian interpretation emerged, the emphasis being on the seasonal changes and the calendar, which expressed the daily-life concerns of a predominantly agricultural society and its connection with the Church's liturgical year. Here the signs are secularized and any trace of astral power disappears.

Through the influence of scholars such as Bede (*c.*673–735) the zodiac came to be adopted as a semi-scientific symbol, applicable to chronology, the weather, the labours of the months and seasons. Among the chief subjects of Bede's study was an interest in computing and calendars, expressed in his own works and in those attributed to him. His works were glossed and commented on in the medieval period, and provide a major literary context in which is found the allegory of the zodiac. In *De natura rerum*, chapter 17, he gives a purely classical zodiac allegory in a learned and scientific spirit meant to show the relationship of the twelve signs to the twelve months they govern. Chapter 16 of the *De temporum ratione*, often attributed to him, also contains a discussion in the same learned strain. But here the author has omitted the names of the signs drawn from Greek myth on the score that there is little fruit in repeating something in

[17] *Commentarium in Matthaeum Imperfectum*, *PL* 56, cols 813–14.

[18] There is a mosaic which appears from very imperfect photographs to have the heads of the twelve months, with a personification of the year, the four seasons, and the twelve zodiac figures, on the floor of the baths of Tallera, north of Maltezana harbour, on the island of Astypalaia, near Kos. Apart from its date in the Christian period, there seems nothing to identify it as either pagan or Christian. See S. Pelecanidis and P. Atzaca, *Corpus mosaicorum Christianorum vetustiorum pavimentorum Graecorum I, Graecia Insularis* (Thessaloniki, 1974), pp. 46–7, and pl. 5(a)(b). See also J. M. Cook, 'Archaeology in Greece', *Journal of Hellenic Studies*, 73 (1953), p. 126.

which the harm done to the ignorant would outweigh any profit to the wise, showing a distinct element of piety when dealing with his science. This same strain is shown by the very interesting gloss on the passage attributed to Byrhtferth (Bridefortus) of Ramsey. The author of the gloss introduces his own allegory by quoting *De natura rerum*, but displaces the learned discussion of the signs in terms of classical mythology with a deliberate religious substitution: the Ram is Abraham . . . the Bull Jacob . . . and so on.[19] 'Byrhtferth's' allegory, as is readily apparent, is not conceived in the same spirit as that of Zeno or with any comparable purpose. It is a matter of a bow in the direction of religion within a scientific context. Bede was the most widely-read scholar of his age, and in his works and those of his time the zodiac begins to lose its force as a Christian allegory, and becomes a secular symbol: a semi-scientific figure, applicable to chronology, the weather, the labours of the months and the seasons.

This generated the most widely-used context for the representation of the zodiac in Romanesque art: the twelve signs and the labours of the twelve months of the year.[20] This theme translates itself into pictorial embodiment in every artistic medium and occurs all over medieval Europe; but it is on Romanesque church doorways that the tradition is most interestingly to be studied. In England there is a clear example of zodiac imagery on the west door of St Mary the Virgin at Iffley, Oxford. In France the signs and months are finely sculptured on the northernmost of the three great portals of Amiens Cathedral, and the most perfect series is to be found on the principal doorway of the abbey church at Vézelay. The tradition is well represented in Italy also, the best-known example

[19] *De temporum ratione*, ch. 16, gloss = 361. There is some confusion about the works involved and the names and persons concerned. Genuinely of Bede, see C. W. Jones, *Bedae opera de temporibus* (Cambridge, Mass., 1943), is the *De natura rerum*, containing in ch. 17 a scientific analysis of the classical zodiac. The explanation is dependent on Isidore of Seville, *Etymologiarum libri XX*, book 3, 71. This allegory was commented on by an English monk of the eleventh century, Byrhtferth of Ramsey. Attributed to Bede is the *De temporum ratione*: see C. W. Jones, *Baedae pseudepigrapha—Scientific Writings Falsely Attributed to Bede* (Cornell and Oxford, 1939), pp. 21–38. This, in turn, was commented on in a gloss attributed to, but in fact in no way related to, Byrhtferth. The mistake seems to have been made in the first folio edition of Bede by Hervagius (Basle, 1563) and thence copied into subsequent editions.

[20] Many examples of this tradition are carefully arranged in a series of tables in the long article by J. Fowler, 'On mediaeval representations of the months and seasons', *Archaeologia*, 44 (1873), pp. 137–224. This tradition appears on fonts also, e.g. a type of lead font imported from France and found at Brookland, in Kent, illustrated in L. Stone, *Sculpture in Britain; the Middle Ages* (Harmondsworth, 1955), p. 89, fig. 66. Cf. also the font at Burnham Deepdale, Norfolk.

probably being the zodiac of the archivolt of the great west door of St Mark's, Venice.

It is the coupling of the signs of the zodiac with the labours of the months which defines the allegorical content of the iconography; and it is their context on the doors of churches which defines their place in the religious scheme. This time it is not a question of baptism or preaching, but the bringing of all the work of the year into the orbit of religion. Survey of the evidence shows at once that the signs of the zodiac in this form, though meaningful, are theologically much more attenuated. They belong more to the realm of piety than dogma, and are a matter rather of chronology than theology.

With regard to this widespread medieval tradition the Hook Norton zodiac, with its selected and striking series of signs, together with a naked and inscribed Adam and Eve, appears as an example of iconographic deviance. It is not possible to establish where the iconography of the font came from;[21] but it is a well-known fact that much continental culture was transmitted to England through the medium of Irish monastic learning. There is evidence which makes it possible to suggest a link with the theology of Zeno through this mediation. That there was a connection between Irish monasticism and Zeno seems clear. He was respected at this period chiefly as one of the founders of the church of Verona and was popular in Irish monastic circles. In a curious and fragmentary poem in elegiacs, apparently by an ex-monk of Bobbio teaching at Verona, he appears in conversation with Columban.[22] Secondly, there was a large body of learned Latin poetry about the zodiac, much of which survives. It usually restricts the allegorization to classical terms, but one of these poems, by a certain Hirenicus, is based directly on Zeno's sermon, since it contains a large number of verbal quotations from him.[23] Beyond this, it is not possible to go; but it does seem that in some curious way the Hook Norton baptismal font and Zeno of Verona are connected.

With the medieval symbolism of the months and the seasons and the unusual survival of the ancient baptismal link at Hook Norton the iconography of the Christian zodiac and its literary relationships comes to an end. It has been possible to trace to some degree its change and

21 That Bede and Northumbria are not the source is clear, though there are illustrated zodiac manuscripts from this area. See F. Saxl, *Verzeichnis astrologischer und mythologischer illustrierten Handschriften des lateinischen Mittelalters* (Heidelberg, 1927).

22 *MGH.PL*, III, 2, poem VI, pp. 688f. I owe this reference to Peter Levi, who generously made available to me his own unpublished work on the Hook Norton font.

23 *MGH.PL*, IV, poem CXVII, pp. 693f.

Plate 3 Hook Norton Font, Aquarius (photo: R. A. Markus).

Plate 2 Hook Norton Font, Sagittarius (photo: R. A. Markus).

development from the beginning of the Christian period to the High Middle Ages. The earlier Christian world was not based on one hard and fast perspective on dogma, but shifted its focus from period to period under the change of circumstances. The zodiac is a reflection of this, as an example of a religious image which was not reduced to a common denominator with a fixed content, until the time came for it to enter a period of great academic and theological systematization. It is an example of the taking over by the Christian Church of an interesting system of iconography, and the giving to it of a new content and meaning. It is an example also of a literary and visual tradition not deriving from Jewish sources, but sources already expressed in the classical terms of the cultural milieu before the foundation of Christianity.

University of Nottingham

HUGH OF ST VICTOR, ISAIAH'S VISION, AND *DE ARCA NOE*

by GROVER A. ZINN, JR

HUGH of St Victor's two treatises on Noah's Ark, *De arca Noe morali* and *De arca Noe mystica*, are major twelfth-century writings on the contemplative life with a significant relationship to the medieval iconographic tradition.[1] Both refer to a drawing that symbolically presents the spiritual teaching of the treatises. Unfortunately this drawing no longer exists, but *De arca Noe mystica* describes it in detail.[2] That description and passages in *De arca Noe morali* show that the drawing had three major iconographic elements:

(1) a figure of Christ 'seated in majesty' as seen in a vision by the prophet Isaiah (Isaiah 6);

(2) a symbolic cosmos, with the earth at the centre, surrounded by the regions of *aer* and *aether*; and

(3) a schematized drawing of Noah's Ark, depicting it as a three-storeyed, pyramidal vessel viewed from above.

These three 'units' were arranged so that the figure of Christ held the symbolic cosmos in front of his body (with only his head, hands, and feet visible), while the diagram of the Ark was placed in the centre of the symbolic cosmos so that the earth surrounded the Ark.

By drawing the pyramid-shaped Ark as if seen from above, Hugh could show length, width, and height in a two-dimensional drawing (see figure 1). The keel of the Ark, with the genealogy of Jesus and the succession of

[1] Texts in *PL* 176. *De arca Noe morali* [hereafter *A. mor.*], cols 617–80 (chapter divisions will follow the C.S.M.V. translation [see below], not Migne); *De arca Noe mystica* [hereafter *A. myst.*], cols 681–794. *A. mor.* tr. in Hugh of St Victor, *Selected Writings on Contemplation*, tr. by a Religious of C.S.M.V., intro. by Aelred Squire (London, 1962) [hereafter C.S.M.V.]. A critical edition of both works is being prepared for *Corpus christianorum, continuatio medievalis* by Patrice Sicard.

[2] For a description of the drawing, which was probably painted on a wall or on a large surface produced by sewing many parchment sheets together, see Grover A. Zinn, Jr., '*De gradibus ascensionum*: the stages of contemplative ascent in two treatises on Noah's Ark by Hugh of St. Victor', *Studies in Medieval Culture*, 5 (1975), pp. 61–79, and 'Mandala use and symbolism in the mysticism of Hugh of St. Victor', *History of Religions*, 12 (1972–3), pp. 317–41. Partial reconstruction of drawing in J. Ehlers, '*Arca significat ecclesiam*. Ein theologisches weltmodell aus der ersten Halfte des 12. Jahrhunderts', *Frühmittelalterlichen Studien*, 6 (1972), pp. 171–87. The relation of the drawing to a *mappa mundi* text now identified as being by Hugh is discussed by Patrick Gautier Dalché, *La 'Descriptio mappe mundi' de Hugues de Saint-Victor: Texte inédit avec introduction et commentaire* (Paris, 1988).

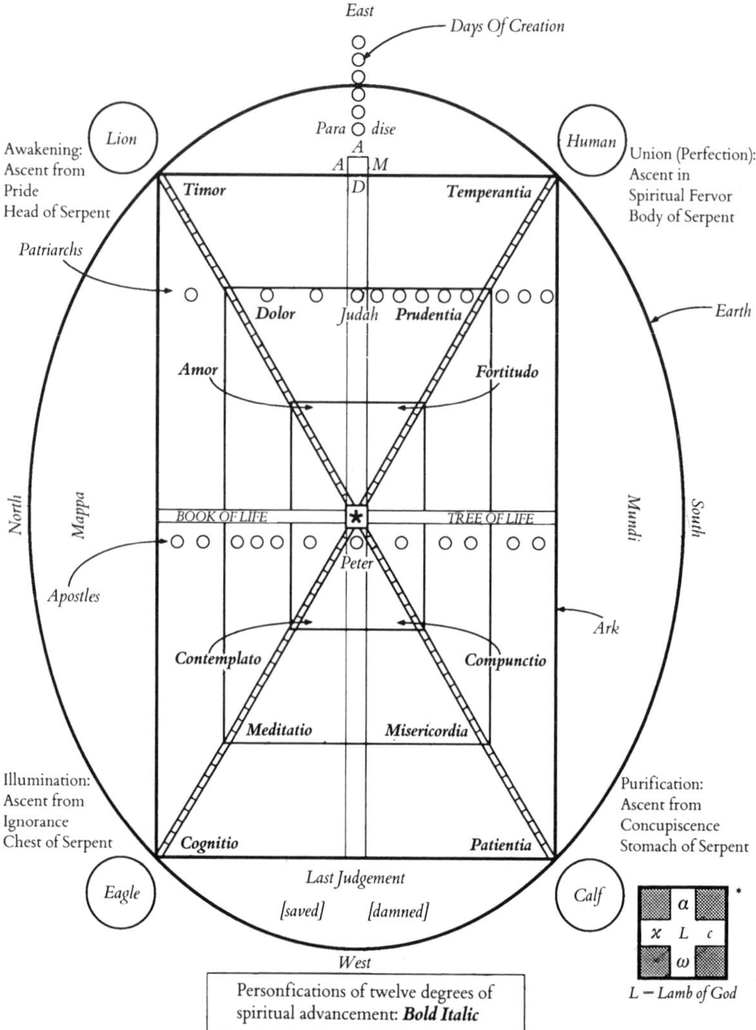

Figure 1 Partial Diagram of Drawing of Ark of Noah and Earth at the Centre of Hugh's Symbolic Cosmos held by Christ. Exact proportions of length/width not reproduced to assist in clarity. (Reconstruction by author; computer graphics by Geoff Duncan, Oberlin College, Ohio.)

bishops of Rome inscribed along the time-line from bow to stern, symbolized the temporal sequence of history from Creation to Last Judgement.[3] The Incarnation was located at the mid-point of the time-line and so corresponded with the cubit at the apex of the Ark. Paradise was depicted at the bow; the Last Judgement at the stern. The vertical dimension of the Ark was shown by drawing the floors of the three storeys.[4] The base, or first floor, was a large rectangle; the second floor, a smaller rectangle inside the first; the third floor, a still smaller one. The cubit at the peak of the Ark was shown as a square at the centre of the three nested rectangles. In each corner a series of three ladders linked the floors from bottom to top. In the symbolic interpretation of the Ark, each of the four basic stages of the contemplative quest (awakening, purification, illumination, and union [or perfection]) was divided into three parts and depicted as a movement up one of the series of three ladders placed at a corner. Inscriptions and complex iconographic devices associated with the ladders and storeys of the Ark gave visual expression to Hugh's teaching about the spiritual quest.[5]

This Ark, with its weighty iconographic cargo, was set in the centre of a symbolic cosmos similar in structure to one in a miniature from Hildegard of Bingen's *De operatione Dei*, written several decades after the Ark treatises.[6] Hildegard depicted the earth surrounded by *aer* (with the four seasons personified in four quadrants) and *aether* (with personifications of the twelve winds) (plate 1). Hugh's *aer* also had a diagram which showed the harmony of the seasons by correlating pairs of the four humours (dry, wet, hot, cold) with the seasons; his *aether* also had on the circumference representations of the twelve signs of the zodiac and a division for each of the twelve months.[7] In Hugh's drawing the earth surrounding the Ark functioned as a map of the world; it included places, mountains, rivers, fortresses, and towns (*loca, montes, flumina, castella, et oppida constituta*) with Egypt to the south, Babylon to the north, and Paradise to the east.[8] Unlike

[3] See *A. myst.*, iii–iv, cols 685A–8A.

[4] See Hugh's description of drawing the floors and central column of the Ark, ibid., ii, col. 684BC.

[5] For the four stages of the spiritual quest, the twelve ladders, and associated iconography, see *A. myst.*, vii–viii, cols 692B–7D, and my articles cited in n. 2, above.

[6] Lucca, Bibl. Governativa, MS 1942, fol. 38r. For a consideration of the manuscript, dating, and title (the title in Migne is *Liber divinorum operum*), see B. Newman, *Sister of Wisdom: St. Hildegard's Theology of the Feminine* (Berkeley, Los Angeles, and London, 1987), pp. 11, 19–22.

[7] See *A. myst.*, xiv, cols 700D–1A. Hildegard's *aer* and *aether* are subdivided into 'layers' in a way Hugh's are not.

[8] For the earth (*orbis terrae*) surrounding the Ark, see ibid., 700C; Hugh says that in the area of

[*See p. 103 for n. 8 cont.*]

Plate 1 Cosmos with Personifications of the Four Seasons and with the Twelve Winds, Hildegarde of Bingen, *De operatione Dei*, Lucca, Biblioteca Statale, MS 1942, fol. 38r. Reproduced by kind permission of the Biblioteca Statale, Lucca.

the circular earth in *De operatione Dei*, however, the earth in Hugh's drawing seems to have been oval-shaped, for he describes it as a 'circlus oblongus'.[9]

With the cosmos covering Christ's body, only his head and shoulders, his hands, and his feet were visible. In this formal aspect, the drawing resembles two later examples of a figure holding the cosmos or the world: a miniature from Hildegard of Bingen's *De operatione Dei* (plate 2) and the Ebsdorf world map.[10]

I

The figure of Christ holding the cosmos and accompanied by two seraphs forms the central focus of this paper. There has been little, if any, careful analysis of the figures of Christ and the seraphs in this drawing.[11] Isaiah's vision of the enthroned Lord and two seraphs is one of the major theophanies in the biblical tradition. Through the text of the *Sanctus*, based on the chant of the seraphs, it had an important place in the medieval liturgy. It also furnished important themes for programmes of monumental sculpture associated with major twelfth-century ecclesiastical structures.

The figure of Christ enthroned in majesty provides the actual point of departure in *De arca Noe morali* for introducing the idea of a drawing of Ark, cosmos, and Christ.[12] Indeed, the Ark treatises are most accurately understood as Hugh's spiritual 'unfolding' of the mysteries of Isaiah's

---

the earth in the drawing, a *mappa mundi* is to be depicted. In ibid., 702C the earth (and hence the *mappa*) is said to show 'loca, montes, flumina, castella et oppida constituta'. For the location of Egypt and Babylon, see ibid., 699D. The correlation of 'places' (on the *mappa*) and 'times' (on the time-line of the Ark) was important to Hugh; see comment ibid., 700CD: 'ut mirabili dispositione ab eodem principe decurrat situs locorum cum ordine temporum, et idem sit finis mundi, qui est finis saeculi.'

9 See *A. myst.*, xiv, col. 700D for 'circulus oblongus'. A few sentences later the 'circulus' bounding *aer* is described as 'paulo laxior' with no reference to being 'oblongus'.

10 For the Ebsdorf world map (now destroyed), see fig. 80a in Anna C. Esmeijer, *Divina Quaternitas: a Preliminary Study in the Method and Application of Visual Exegesis* (Amsterdam, 1978); brief discussion, p. 99. The miniature from Hildegard is Lucca, Bibl. Governativa, MS 1942, fol. 9r.

11 Ehlers, *Arca significat*, p. 176, mentions the seraphs but says no more. In *Hugo von St. Viktor: Studien zum Geschichtsdenken und zur Geschichtsschreibung des 12.Jahrhunderts = Frankfurter Historische Abhandlungen*, 7 (Wiesbaden, 1973), Ehlers mentions the seraphs briefly, pp. 121–2, when discussing Hugh's exegesis of Isaiah's vision, but he omits any reference to them when discussing the drawing of Christ and the cosmos, pp. 131–2. R. Baron, *Science et sagesse chez Hugues de Saint-Victor* (Paris, 1957), p. 185, does not discuss the seraphs. My earlier work (see n. 2 above) includes the seraphs, but this present paper develops the significance of Isaiah's vision in more detail.

12 *A. mor.*, I, vii, col. 622C; C.S.M.V., p. 52.

Plate 2 Figure Holding Cosmos, Hildegarde of Binge, *De operatione Dei*, Lucca, Biblioteca Statale, MS 1942, fol. 9r. Reproduced by kind permission of the Biblioteca Statale, Lucca.

theophanic experience for those who wish to be initiated. To the extent that scholars have overlooked the significance—and even the presence—of the elements of theophany here, a crucial aspect of the Ark treatises has been lost in current interpretation.

Viewed within the twelfth-century context, Hugh was not alone in his interest in elaborating a symbolic cosmos or symbolically depicting/describing a spiritual journey. One need only think of the platonizing cosmologies of the Chartrians, the mythologizing of William of Conches, the *Clavis physicae* of Honorius Augustodunensis, the cosmological poems of Alan of Lille, and the cosmological visions and speculations of Hildegard of Bingen.[13] Hugh stands apart, however, in connecting cosmological/spiritual interests directly with Isaiah's vision.

II

In *De arca Noe morali* Hugh introduces a drawing as a focus for meditation. He says that he will place before the brothers a drawing of Christ enthroned, 'as Isaiah saw Him', accompanied by two seraphs.[14] In it they will see delightful shapes and colours to guide them in shaping properly the interior self in a journey of spiritual development.

One initial problem in visualizing the drawing is that Hugh says that Christ is seated on a throne, yet he also says that the diagram of the cosmos covers Christ's body. How then can he be shown as seated? A possible suggestion requires that the ends of a benchlike throne protrude from 'behind' the cosmos, just below Christ's hands. The importance of the throne in Hugh's tropological interpretation of the seraphs and the Lord lends weight to the presumption that the throne was, in fact, visible in the drawing. One manuscript illumination that suggests how this might be accomplished is the Godescalc Evangelistary, which shows Christ seated on a benchlike throne extending beyond his body on either side (frontispiece).[15] Were Christ 'holding' a cosmos in such a drawing, the throne would be visible.

[13] On speculative cosmologies and the symbolic cosmos, see B. McGinn, *The Golden Chain: a Study in the Theological Anthropology of Isaac of Stella = Cistercian Studies Series*, 15 (Washington, DC, 1972); P. Dronke, *Fabula: Explorations into the Uses of Myth in Medieval Platonism* (Leiden, 1974); W. Wetherbee, *Platonism and Poetry in the Twelfth Century: the Literary Influence of the School of Chartres* (Princeton, 1972); B. Stock, *Myth and Science in the Twelfth Century: a Study of Bernard Silvester* (Princeton, 1972); and M.-T. d'Alverny, 'Le cosmos symbolique du xiie siècle', *AHDL*, 20 (1954), pp. 31–81.

[14] *A. mor.*, I, vii, col. 622C; C.S.M.V., p. 52; 'to make the illustration clearer for you I have depicted Christ's whole person, the Head with the members, in a form that you can see; . . . And I want to represent this Person to you in such wise as Isaiah testifies that he beheld Him.'

[15] Paris, BN, MS nouvelle acquisition lat. 1203, fol. 3.

In Hugh's drawing, one six-winged seraph is depicted on Christ's left side, the other on his right. Hugh interprets the phrase *stabant super illud* (Isaiah 6. 2) to mean that these two angelic beings stand *on* the throne.[16] This curious arrangement has no apparent precedent in earlier representations, but it is an important element in Hugh's spiritual interpretation of the seraphs and throne.[17]

Hugh follows neither biblical text nor exegetical tradition when describing the seraphs' wings. He says that each seraph covers its own body with two wings, flies with two wings, and with the remaining two covers the Lord's head with one and the Lord's feet with the other.[18] Two major departures from text and tradition occur here: (1) covering the bodies of the seraphs; (2) covering Christ's *head* but not his *face*.

The biblical text says that each seraph uses two wings to cover 'his face' (*faciem ejus*), two wings to cover 'his feet', and two wings to fly (Isaiah 6. 2). No mention is made of covering a seraph's body. Origen established the exegetical tradition by assuming the face and feet covered were those of the Person on the throne.[19] Jerome followed Origen on this point, making it standard in Western Latin exegesis.[20] Origen had gone on to suggest that the seated figure was God, and the seraphs were Christ and the Holy Spirit. Jerome emphatically rejected this interpretation and affirmed that the enthroned figure was Christ and the seraphs were members of the angelic choir who praise the Trinity with a threefold repetition of *sanctus*.[21]

Hugh offers no justification for departing from the usual disposition of the wings in the *commentary* tradition. Comparing his description with illustrations of seraphs in medieval manuscripts suggests, however, that the *visual*, not the *written*, tradition was his probable inspiration.[22]

[16] The text reads; 'Seraphim stabant super illud . . .': col. 623D. The interpretation presented here takes 'super illud' to mean 'upon that (= the throne)', in parallel with Isa. 6. 1: 'vidi Dominum sedentem super solium excelsum et elevatum . . .' ('I saw the Lord sitting upon a throne high and lifted up . . .'). Translating Isa. 6. 2, C.S.M.V. follows the AV, as elsewhere. 'Upon it' is more accurate in preserving the parallelism between the phrases for the seraphs and for God. When translating the phrase *in Hugh's text*, C.S.M.V. uses 'stand on the throne'; see *A. mor.*, I, ix, col. 624B; C.S.M.V., p. 55.

[17] See *A. mor.*, I, ix, col. 624AB; C.S.M.V., p. 55.

[18] Ibid., I, x, col. 624C; C.S.M.V., p. 56.

[19] Jerome, *Tr. hom. Origenis in visione Isaiae*, *PL* 24, col. 903A.

[20] Jerome, *Ep.* XVIII, iv, *PL* 22, col. 365.

[21] See ibid., col. 363, where Jerome adduces a passage from the Gospel of John as proof that the person on the throne is the Son, not the Father.

[22] For a general discussion of angels, including seraphs, in artistic representation, see E. Kirschbaum, ed., *Lexikon der christlichen Ikonographie*, 8 vols (Rome, Fribourg, Basle, and Vienna, 1968–76), 1, pp. 626–42.

Carolingian and later manuscript paintings show seraphs with one pair of wings covering the seraph's body (usually with feet uncovered), one pair free for flight, and the third pair raised vertically above the seraph's head. Good examples are found associated with the text of the *Sanctus* in the Metz Coronation Sacramentary and the Drogo Sacramentary.[23] The Metz manuscript shows the Lord enthroned with seraphs, with wings as described above, 'standing' on either side of Christ enthroned (plate 3). The Drogo Sacramentary superimposes on the text of the *Sanctus* a seraph with wings disposed in the same general way (plate 4). This 'formula' for representing seraphs probably came to the West from earlier Byzantine illustrations of Isaiah's vision and other representations of Christ enthroned in heaven or the Trinity in heaven.[24]

The second difference between the drawing and the biblical text is carefully justified. Hugh emphasizes that in his drawing the wings of the seraphs veil Christ's *head* while leaving his *face* uncovered.[25] Thus the wings must have been drawn 'covering' the top of Christ's head. This contradicts the biblical text, for there the Lord's *face* is said to be covered (Isaiah 6. 2). Hugh explains the difference by noting that although God said to Moses that in this life no one can see God as he is and still live, nevertheless full knowledge of the Godhead is promised to the saints in heaven. Paul's statement that in heaven God will be seen 'face to face' (I Corinthians 13. 12) is also cited. However, the crucial passage seems to be Jesus' statement (Matthew 18. 10) that the angels of little children always behold the face of God in heaven.[26] Leaving Christ's face *un*veiled is Hugh's way of underscoring this in a vivid visual manner. He even says at one point that certain matters should be taken in accord with the drawing, not Scripture.[27]

[23] Metz Coronation Sacramentary, BN, MS lat. 1141, fol. 6r; Drogo Sacramentary, BN, MS lat. 9428, fol. 15r. For these MSS see R. Calkins, *Illuminated Books of the Middle Ages* (Ithaca, NY, 1983), pp. 162–77.

[24] On the Greek tradition, see K. Weitzmann, *Illustrations in Roll and Codex: a Study of the Origin and Method of Text Illustration* = *Studies in Manuscript Illumination*, 2 (Princeton, 1947), pp. 88–91, 148–9, with illus 138, 139.

[25] *A. mor.*, I, x, col. 625AB; C.S.M.V., p. 57. See also ibid., col. 624BC; C.S.M.V. p. 57, and *A. myst.*, xv, col. 702C, where Hugh remarked that the wings cover the head, not the face of Christ ('velant caput majestatis et pedes, facie tamen intecta manente').

[26] See *A. mor.*, I, x, col. 625A; C.S.M.V., p. 57. For a discussion of the possibility of seeing God in this life see Hugh's *De sacramentis christianae fidei* [hereafter *De sac.*], I, xviii, 16–22, *PL* 176, cols 613A–18B, tr. Roy J. Deferrari, *On the Sacraments of the Christian Faith* (*De sacramentis*) [hereafter Deferrari] = *Mediaeval Academy of America Publications*, 58 (Cambridge, Mass., 1951), pp. 470–5.

[27] *A. mor.*, I, x, col. 625B; C.S.M.V., p. 57.

Plate 3 The Lord Enthroned with Seraphs, Metz Coronation Sacramentary, Paris, BN, MS lat. 1141, fol. 6r. Photograph by courtesy of the Bibliothèque nationale, Paris.

Plate 4 A Seraph, superimposed on the text of the *Sanctus*, Drogo Sacramentary, Paris, BN, MS lat. 9428, fol. 15r. Photograph by courtesy of the Bibliothèque nationale, Paris.

With the exegetical/theological move of unveiling Christ's face, Hugh propels the viewer/reader beyond Isaiah's earthly vision to the celestial vision experienced by angels and saints in eternity. Thus we should consider that the drawing refers to two levels:

(1) the manifestation of divinity *in time*, *in this world* (Isaiah's vision) and

(2) the manifestation of divinity *in heaven*, *in eternity* (the unveiled face).

In the drawing, seraphs *veil* and also *unveil* in order to represent theophany *in* time and *beyond* time.

The concluding sentences of *De arca Noe mystica* draw attention to another aspect of the drawing that relates angels to the figure of Christ enthroned. Hugh says that crowned representations of the nine orders of angels were drawn on either side of Christ in the space between his shoulders and the seraphs' wings.[28] These angels, gazing intently upon the unveiled face of Christ, underscore the celestial aspect of the drawing, for they behold the full and eternal manifestation of the divine in heaven.

The angels are arranged in nine horizontal rows, placed one above the other. The uppermost row on each side of Christ has two angels in it, the second has three, and so on, up to the ninth row with ten. The diagram thus has 108 angels. Hugh notes that when the angels fell, one fell from each of the nine orders, leaving a total of ninety-nine unfallen angels. This number he associates with the ninety-nine *un*lost sheep in Jesus' parable (Luke 15. 4–7). Jesus' recovery of the one lost sheep represents the salvation of fallen humanity and the restoration of the celestial city to the number 100. Hugh's presentation is terse, even elliptical. Some clue to the wider context can be gained from a sermon by Gregory the Great, in which he combines interpretations of the widow's lost coin and the lost sheep in considering the fall of the angels (the lost coin) and the completion of the heavenly society by saved humanity (the lost sheep).[29]

In the drawing, the angels provide a visual link between Isaiah's vision (indicated by the seraphs) and the vision of God enjoyed by angels in eternity and sought by those who begin the journey of discipline and deepening insight that culminates in the contemplative experience of divine presence in this life. Isaiah's vision provided a glimpse of the overwhelming experience of divine self-disclosure. Hugh's drawing offered a visual interpretation of that theophany and invited the reader/viewer to reshape life and thought so that the vision of Isaiah and its deeper meaning could become a transforming reality in this world in preparation for the next.

The veiling of Christ's head and feet in the drawing clearly links Christ's body to the cosmos and Ark that obscure the body.[30] In Hugh's

[28] *A. myst.*, xiv, col. 702CD: 'Sub alis autem seraphim desuper in eo spatio, quod est inter scapulas majestatis et alas ex utraque parte ordines angelorum consituuntur novem, ad contemplandam faciem majestatis conversi.'

[29] *Hom. in evang.*, *PL* 76, cols 1246A–59A, esp. sections 3–6, cols 1247B–9D. This homily also contains Gregory's only reference to Pseudo-Dionysius the Areopagite—and the reference is to his theory of angelic orders.

[30] *A. mor.*, I, x, cols 625C–6A; C.S.M.V., p. 58.

interpretation of this veiling (an interpretation that depends on Jerome[31]) the Lord's head represents that which was before the world's creation; his feet, that which will be after the end of the age. His body, which is 'in the middle', represents the time that exists between the beginning and the end. Since in this life humans can never discover the things represented by the head and feet, these are veiled by seraphs' wings. The body is fully visible, for 'we see the intermediate things that happen in the present age.' This body Hugh identifies with the Church.[32] The further step of identifying the Church with the Ark of Noah establishes the rationale behind the construction of a drawing in which the body of the enthroned Lord is covered by the drawing of a symbolic cosmos with the Ark at the centre.[33] The Lord's body becomes—literally and visually—the world and the drama of historical existence, centred on the unfolding panorama of salvation history, demonstrated visually in the disposition of time, places, and events on the time-line of the Ark and the world map of the cosmos in the drawing.

III

Elements from biblical theophanies other than Isaiah's vision also appear in the drawing: Ezekiel's vision of the Four Living Creatures, John's vision of the heavenly Jerusalem with Twenty-four Elders and Four Celestial Beings around the Lamb, and the coming of the Son of Man in judgement, from Matthew.[34]

Incorporating these produces a complex interweaving of themes of history and contemplation, time and eternity. On the time-line/keel of the Ark, Hugh inscribed the names of Christ's ancestors according to the flesh and the spiritual filiation extending from Christ through Peter and his successors as bishop of Rome.[35] (See plate 1.) Just after the name Jacob on the time-line Hugh drew twelve medallions set in a row across the Ark. They depicted the Twelve Patriarchs, Jacob's sons, whom Hugh described as the *senatus* of the City of God.[36] Further along, at Peter's name, Hugh

[31] See Jerome, *Comm. in Isaiah*, iii, *PL* 24, col. 94A.

[32] *A. mor.*, I, x, col. 625D; C.S.M.V., p. 58.

[33] Ibid., vii, col. 622C; C.S.M.V., p. 52: 'And because the ark denotes the Church, and the Church is the body of Christ, to make the illustration clearer for you I have depicted Christ's whole Person, the Head with the members, in a form that you can see . . .'

[34] See Ezek. 1. 10, Rev. 4. 7, and Matt. 25. 31–46, esp. vv. 33–4 and 41.

[35] *A myst.*, iii–iv, cols 685A–8A.

[36] Ibid., col. 686D.

drew another row of twelve medallions, this time depicting the Twelve Apostles. Thus twenty-four medallions (Hugh calls them icons) surrounded the square in the centre of the Ark diagram. That square contained the figure of a lamb representing Christ.[37] Hugh explicitly associates the twenty-four figures from the Hebrew and Christian traditions with the Twenty-four Elders of the Apocalypse, who offer eternal praise while gathered around the throne and the Lamb in the celestial Jerusalem.[38] (See Revelation 4. 1–14.) By identifying the Elders of the Apocalypse with Patriarchs and Apostles Hugh subtly links a vision of celestial praise with the history of salvation and the union of the two people (Jews and Gentiles) in the service of their one Lord throughout all history.[39]

A further presence of Apocalypse imagery occurs with four figures symbolizing Gospel writers, placed at the four corners of the Ark, and thus at the bases of the four series of ladders marking the stages of contemplative ascent.[40] The iconography is simple in presentation, complex in meaning. In *De arca Noe morali* Hugh presents Christ's Incarnation as an 'outward voice' calling people turned outward toward the material world to return to inward, spiritual realities.[41] This outward voice is now expressed in the Gospels, each of which Hugh associates with one of the four major stages of the contemplative quest. The lion (Mark) terrifies the proud and is associated with the stage of awakening in which pride, the root of all sin, is overcome. The calf (Luke) mortifies the flesh and is associated with asceticism and penance that overcomes concupiscence. The eagle (John) illumines the blind; it is associated with the stage of illumination leading to contemplative ecstasy. Finally, the human figure

[37] The lamb in the square is mentioned in the description of the complex diagram inscribed in the square, in ibid., i, col. 681C.

[38] Ibid., iv, col. 687A: '. . . ut ex una parte columnae duodecim patriarchae, et ex altera parte duodecim apostoli sint constituti ad similitudinem viginti quatuor seniorum in Apocalypsi in circuitu throne sedentium.'

[39] See *A. mor.*, I, x, col. 625D; C.S.M.V., p. 58, where Hugh speaks of the Church, 'which began with the beginning of the world and lasts until the end of the age.' The most moving instance of the unity of the 'two peoples' occurs in the prologue to *De sacramentis*, which describes the Incarnate Word as a king who has come into the world to do battle with the Devil (*cum diabolo*). The Word is accompanied by the holy ones (*sancti*)—those who lived before his advent are soldiers who go before their king; those who live after the advent, and up to the end of the world, follow their king into battle. See *De sac.*, prol., ii, col. 183B, Deferrari, pp. 3–4. In describing the square at the centre of the Ark drawing, Hugh repeatedly stresses the 'two people'; see *A. myst.*, i, cols 681A–2B.

[40] Ibid., viii, col. 696AB. The figures are from Rev. 4. 7; see the four faces of the four winged beings in Ezek. 1. 10.

[41] See esp. *A. mor.*, IV, ix, cols 669A–70C; C.S.M.V., pp. 132–4.

(Matthew) recalls people to their origin and is associated with the final stage of advancement in perfection as one progresses toward the state of knowledge and love of God from which the first humans fell.

At the corners of the Ark a serpent, personifying evil, coils about the base of each ladder.[42] The people who climb the ladders as they return along the spiritual way are shown trampling upon this serpent. Overcoming pride, one tramples the head of the serpent; overcoming concupiscence, the stomach; overcoming ignorance, the chest. In the fourth stage of increasing unity with God, both uprights of the ladder (representing body and soul) are thrust into the serpent's body as those ascending move beyond the serpent's reach.

The final theophanic motif to be mentioned is the Last Judgement. The drawing visually represents Christ's words in the Gospel of Matthew (Matthew 25. 31–7) concerning the separation of the saved and the damned at the general resurrection of the dead. This Judgement is depicted at Christ's feet, which are adjacent to the end of the time-line along the keel of the Ark, and thus are at the denouement of history. By Christ's right foot are the saved, with the words, 'Come, O blessed of my Father, inherit the kingdom prepared for you from the foundation of the world.' By his left foot are the damned, with, 'Depart from me, you cursed, into the eternal fire prepared for the devil and his angels.'[43]

Closer examination of the passage in Matthew provides two connections with other elements in the drawing. Matthew describes the Son of Man as seated on a 'glorious throne' and accompanied by 'all the angels' when he comes in judgement. As we have seen, the Lord on a throne and all the angels are major elements in Hugh's drawing. The relation of these elements to various 'units' of the drawing and to theophanic themes from the past, in heaven, and at the end of time, shows Hugh's skill and insight in crafting this richly symbolic drawing. The attentive reader/viewer would have grasped the subtle interweaving of history, contemplative journey, divine manifestation, and human experience.

IV

The material thus far presented has important connections with twelfth-century monumental sculpture. The tympanum at Moissac and the central tympanum of Abbot Suger's new west front for the Abbey of

[42] *A. myst.*, viii, cols 695D–6A.
[43] Ibid., xiv, xv, cols 700D, 702AB.

Saint-Denis at Paris both echo elements of Hugh's drawing.[44] Moissac shows, according to Louis Grodecki, the Lord enthroned with seraphs, as in Isaiah, joined with the Twenty-four Elders of the Apocalypse and the Four Living Beings representing the Gospels.[45] All are elements found in Hugh's drawing. The tympanum of Suger's church, surely one of the most striking iconographic constructs of the century in a public work of monumental scope, has the Lord enthroned with the Twelve Apostles, the Twenty-four Elders, the angelic hosts in heaven, and the resurrection of the dead, with the explicit (but marginal in the programme) separation of the saved and the damned, accompanied by the same biblical verses that Hugh employed.[46]

These parallels are striking indeed. At the very least, the appearance of major works employing theophanic themes exhibits a deep concern with the question of the manifestation of the divine in time, in personal experience, and at the end of time. This was not a new concern, but the artistic results in the early to mid-twelfth century are remarkable.[47] Moissac and Saint-Denis are eloquent in their visual impact and symbolic structure. In one crucial way they remain mute, though: they have no accompanying text. Only through observation, inference, and painstaking reconstruction can one tease out a reasonable conception of what the designer(s) and sculptor(s) had in mind. With Hugh's drawing we have two levels of eloquence:

(1) the description of a symbolic drawing that (when reconstructed) speaks like the church façades through a deep, rich, and interwoven visual representation;

[44] The material that follows expands on comments in my article, 'Suger, Theology, and the Pseudo-Dionysian Tradition', in Paula Lieber Gerson, ed., *Abbot Suger and Saint-Denis: A Symposium* (New York, 1986), p. 37. The development of sculptural programmes for Romanesque tympani has been studied by M. F. Hearn, *Romanesque Sculpture: the Revival of Monumental Stone Sculpture in the Eleventh and Twelfth Centuries* (Ithaca, NY, 1981). For Saint-Denis see Lieber Gerson, ed., *Abbot Suger and Saint-Denis*; Sumer McK. Crosby, ed. Pamela Z. Blum, *The Royal Abbey of Saint-Denis: from its Beginnings to the Death of Suger 471–1151* (New Haven, 1987), and Conrad Rudolf, *Artistic Change at Saint-Denis: Abbot Suger's Program and the Early Twelfth-Century Controversy over Art* (Princeton, 1990).

[45] Louis Grodecki, 'Le probleme des sources iconographiques du tympan Moissac', *Moissac et l'Occident au xie siècle: Actes du Colloque international de Moissac, 1963* (Toulouse, 1964), pp. 59ff.: cited by Hearn, *Romanesque Sculpture*, p. 174, n. 5.

[46] The west façade of Saint-Denis has been examined in detail by Paula Lieber Gerson, 'The West Façade of Saint-Denis: an Iconographic Study' (Columbia University Ph.D. thesis, 1970). This study stresses the importance of the Matthean judgement text for the iconography.

[47] See Hearn, *Romanesque Sculpture*, ch. 5, examining the rebirth of monumental stone sculpture in church portals with close attention to theophanic themes.

(2) the text that to some degree lays bare the *meaning* of the symbols situated so carefully in the cosmos, Ark, and vision of Isaiah.

For Hugh, the vision of Isaiah offers the inspiration to develop a drawing that represents the Divine Word as manifest in Creation, Incarnation, Providence, and Judgement, with these manifestations made known in the theophanic experiences of the prophets and the revelatory words of Jesus, the perfect theophany in this world. Joined to this evocation of theophanic/visionary experiences in the course of salvation history are powerful representations of the Lord's presence in the celestial world of the angels and at the Last Judgement with the Elders of the Apocalypse.

In indicating parallels and analogues, I have no intention of suggesting who might have influenced whom or to what degree we have the multiple appearances of ideas 'in the air', so to speak. In the first place, the dating of monumental sculpture in France is not an exact science, but rather like an art, with analyses of style, intuitions (some very profound) of precedence, and assumptions about the moment of completion for a particular programme (that is, at the time of consecration).[48] One can be certain, for example, that Hugh's drawing preceded Suger's tympanum.[49] Whether or not it preceded the tympanum at Moissac is less certain, although if one accepts M. F. Hearn's date of 1140 for Moissac, then the drawing does predate Moissac.[50]

Whatever one makes of questions of precedence and possible influence, the importance of Hugh's drawing should not be underestimated. As a correlation and symbolic unfolding of major theophanic instances and themes drawn from the biblical text, it is masterful. As an articulation of Hugh's spiritual teaching, it employs Isaiah's vision and Noah's Ark as vehicles for a profound expression of contemplative theology. The fact that these same theophanic themes and instances also provided powerful images for the new monumental sculpture of the first half of the twelfth century is yet to be reckoned with fully. The specific catalyst that brought the themes together may never be fully known. It is now clear, however,

[48] For an example of difficulties, see Hearn's discussion of the dating of the central portal of Vezelay and the Moissac portal, ibid., pp. 169–70, with references to literature, p. 170, n. 1.

[49] *A. myst.* dates before 1130, and most likely from 1128 or 1129; see Damien van den Eynde, *Essai sur la succession et la date des écrits de Hugues de Saint-Victor = Spicilegium Pontificii Athenaei Antoniani*, 13 (Rome, 1960), p. 80. The west façade of Saint-Denis was dedicated in 1140; M. F. Hearn dates the work as *c.*1137–40; see *Romanesque Sculpture*, pp. 191–2, n. 44.

[50] See n. 47 above. The author wishes to thank Jeffrey Hamburger and Joseph Romano (Oberlin College) and Patricia Stirnemann (Bibliothèque nationale, Paris) for generous assistance.

that in using Isaiah's vision, Hugh was in the forefront of iconographic developments in his day. This suggests that there is more to be explored in considering his symbolic construct and its place in the vital and revolutionary iconographic developments of the twelfth century.

Oberlin College, Ohio

ADVERTISE THE MESSAGE: IMAGES IN ROME AT THE TURN OF THE TWELFTH CENTURY[1]

by BRENDA M. BOLTON

ON at least three occasions during the pontificate of Innocent III, Gerald of Wales—failed bishop, celebrated story-teller, and inveterate and inventive pilgrim, made the journey to Rome.[2] There, having already carried out his preliminary research, he was always eager to examine two of the most outstanding images in Rome at close quarters. These two images—the Uronica at the Lateran and the Veronica at St Peter's—made such a deep impression upon him that his description and explanation of their importance was to form a central role in his *Speculum Ecclesiae*, which he wrote on his return home.[3] He clearly saw them as a pair, having similar names and being held in equal reverence, although perhaps their authenticity sprang from different roots.[4] His remarks would have greatly pleased Innocent, for this was precisely the approach which the pope aimed to achieve. He considered it essential that the long and damaging rivalry between the two great basilicas of the Lateran and the Vatican, which had existed for much of the twelfth century, should now be resolved.[5] It was a rivalry which had brought scandal to the papacy and grave detriment to the Church.[6] In this

[1] My deep gratitude to Dr Fabrizio Mancinelli of the Vatican Museums for granting me privileged access to the *confessio* of St Peter's and the *Sancta Sanctorum* in April 1989.

[2] Gerald of Wales (*c.*1145–1223), disputed the election to the bishopric of St David's and thereafter pursued his claim relentlessly at the Curia. *Giraldus Cambrensis opera*, ed. J. S. Brewer and J. F. Dimock, 8 vols, *RS* (London, 1861–91). See also *The Jewel of the Church: a Translation of the Gemma Ecclesiastica by Giraldus Cambrensis*, ed. J. J. Hagen (Leiden, 1979), pp. ix–xv [hereafter *Jewel of the Church*] for biographical and bibliographical information.

[3] Gerald of Wales, *Speculum Ecclesiae*, *RS*, 4 (1873), esp. *Distinctio* IV, pp. 268–85 [hereafter *Speculum Ecclesiae*], and *Jewel of the Church*, p. xiii, for the suggestion that this work was possibly his latest, still being added to in 1216.

[4] *Speculum Ecclesiae*, p. 278: 'De duabus igitur iconiis Salvatoris, Uronica scilicet et Veronica, quarum una apud Lateranum, altera vero apud Sanctum Petrum.'

[5] M. Maccarrone, 'La "Cathedra Sancti Petri" nel medioevo: da simbolo a reliquia', *Rivista di Storia della Chiesa in Italia*, 39 (1985), pp. 349–447, esp. pp. 395–432.

[6] Ibid., pp. 430–2; John the Deacon, *Descriptio Lateranensis Ecclesiae*, in R. Valentini and G. Zucchetti, *Codice topografico della città di Roma, Fonti per la storia d'Italia*, 4 vols (Rome, 1940–53), 3, pp. 319–73 [hereafter *Descriptio Lateranensis*]; *Petri Mallii Descriptio Basilicae Vaticanae aucta atque emendata a Romano Presbytero* [hereafter *Descriptio Vaticanae*], ibid., pp. 375–442, and esp. pp. 379–80 for two poems, *Contra Lateranensis*.

controversy the Lateran had some advantages, both historically—as the cathedral of Rome and hence of the world—and in the popular appeal of its fabulous relics.[7] A brief glance at a contemporary inventory shows the outstanding richness of this collection.[8] Innocent's aim was not to diminish the Lateran, but instead to raise the status of St Peter's, so that both became co-equal seats of the pope-bishop of Rome.[9] What Gerald of Wales had written confirmed Innocent's own reading of the *Liber Pontificalis*, which was to form the basis for his important reform of the liturgy at this time.[10] Nor was his approbation merely directed towards Gerald. It went to all observant pilgrims, particularly that small number of highly significant archbishops and metropolitans who came to Rome to collect their pallia on their appointments. That great show, the Fourth Lateran Council of 1215, saw almost all of them in attendance.[11] Here was a wonderful opportunity for Innocent to stress the underlying purpose of his artistic patronage, whereby Lateran and Vatican were to achieve co-equal status whilst, at the same time, the Church's real message was being strengthened.[12]

Innocent III's patronage of the arts, particularly in the field of small-scale works, although performing the task for which it was intended, has been neglected by art historians, with the notable exception of Mme Gautier, whose work well deserves close attention.[13] A full understanding

[7] L. Antonelli, *Memorie storiche delle sacre teste dei Santi Apostoli Piero e Paolo e della loro solenne ricognizione nella Basilica Lateranense*, 2nd edn (Rome, 1852); P. Lauer, *Trésor du Sancta Sanctorum. Extrait des monuments et mémoires publiés par l'Academie des Inscriptions et Belles-Lettres* (Paris, 1906); ibid., *Le Palais de Latran. Étude historique et archéologique* (Paris, 1911); P. Jounel, *Le Culte des Saints dans la basilique du Latran et du Vatican au douzième siècle* (Paris, 1911).

[8] *Descriptio Lateranensis*, pp. 356–8, *De Ecclesia Sancti Laurenti in Palatio*; *Speculum Ecclesiae*, pp. 272–4, for Gerald's own list.

[9] 13 March 1198, O. Hageneder and A. Haidacher, eds, *Die Register Innocenz' III*, I Band, *Pontifikatsjahr 1198/99* (Graz and Koln, 1964), [hereafter *Register* I], pp. 417–18; *Innocentii III: Opera omnia*, 4 vols (Paris, 1855), *PL* 214, cols 254–5; Potthast, 1, no. 46; 18 Jan. 1199, *Register* I, pp. 772–3; *PL* 214, cols 490–1; Potthast, no. 939; 21 Jan. 1204, *PL* 215, cols 513–17, esp. col. 513, 'quia ex tunc fecit Petrum stabilem sedem habere, sive in Laterano, sive in Vaticano'; Maccarrone, '"Cathedra"', pp. 430–1.

[10] S. J. P. van Dijk and J. Hazelden Walker, *The Origins of the Modern Roman Liturgy* (London, 1960), pp. 126–8 [hereafter *Origins of the Liturgy*].

[11] C. J. Héfèle and H. Leclercq, *Histoire des Conciles*, 5 (Paris, 1913), 'Liste des évêchés représentés au Concile de 1215', pp. 1723–33.

[12] B. M. Bolton, 'A show with a meaning: Innocent III's approach to the Fourth Lateran Council, 1215', *Medieval History*, 1 (1991), pp. 53–67.

[13] M. M. Gautier, 'La Clôture Émaillée de la Confession de Saint Pierre au Vatican hors du Concile de Latran, 1215', *Bibliothèque des Cahiers Archéologiques*, II, *Synthronon: art et archéologie de la fin de l'antiquité* (Paris, 1968), pp. 237–46; 'Observations préliminaires sur les restes d'un revêtement d'émail champlevé fait pour la Confession de Saint Pierre à Rome', *Bulletin de la*

of this patronage must surely start with an examination of his attitude to the Uronica and Veronica images and to relics associated with the basilicas. Although Innocent took pains to identify his patronage of several small works, it was by finely incised inscription only.[14] His chief personal identification occurred in his appearance as impresario in the reconstructed apse-mosaic of St Peter's, which was full of meaning for the Christian message.[15] Here, in his own lifetime, he ensured that both the message and his person received due prominence. Some fragments of this mosaic, including his head, have survived the demolition of the basilica which took place in the sixteenth century.[16]

Gerald's account of the Uronica and Veronica sets the scene. Legend attributed the Lateran Uronica to the painter St Luke, whose hand was guided by the Virgin Mary, and the work then completed by an angel.[17] Hence it was also called the *acheropita* or icon not made with human hand.[18] Gerald states that two or three such miraculous icons were made, the one in Rome being in the *Sancta Sanctorum* or papal chapel of S. Lorenzo at the Lateran.[19] This encaustic painting, with its burnt-black, fearsome image, both represented and contained the essential spirit of Christ. The truth of this was confirmed, to Gerald at least, by the blinding of an earlier and unnamed pope who had presumed to peer too closely at the icon.[20] Gerald's description refers to this image being covered with gold and silver, except for the right knee, from which oil constantly flowed.[21] What Gerald is clearly describing is the Uronica after its restoration by Innocent, who added a splendid new cover made of gilded silver,

---

Société Archéologique et Historique du Limousin, 91 (1964), pp. 43–70; 'L'art de l'émail champlevé en Italie à l'époque primitive du gothique', *Il Gotico a Pistoia nei suoi rapporti con l'arte gotica italiana = Atti del secondo convegno internazionale di studi, Pistoia, 24–30 aprile, 1966*, pp. 271–93. Cf. F. Vitale, 'Il frontale della confessione Vaticano', *Federico II et l'arte del ducento italiano*, 2 vols (Rome, 1980), 2, pp. 159–72.

14 Gautier, 'Clôture émaillée', p. 238.

15 A. Iacobini, 'Il mosaico absidale di San Pietro in Vaticano', *Fragmenta Picta: affreschi e mosaici staccati del medioevo romano* (Rome, 1989), pp. 119–29; A. Margiotta, 'L'antica decorazione absidale della basilica di S. Pietro in alcuni frammenti al Museo di Roma', *Bolletino dei Musei Communali di Roma*, ns 2 (1988), pp. 21–33; R. Krautheimer, *Rome: Profile of a City 312–1308* (Princeton, 1980), pp. 205–6.

16 Iacobini, 'Il mosaico absidale', pp. 66–8, plates 2, 3, and 4.

17 Hence Gerald of Wales, *Speculum Ecclesiae*, p. 278; *Descriptio Lateranensis*, p. 357.

18 H. Grisar, *Il Sancta Sanctorum ed il suo tesoro sacro* (Rome, 1907), p. 49.

19 Gerald of Wales, *Speculum Ecclesiae*, p. 278, 'Tales fecit duas vel tres, quarum una Romae habetur apud Lateranensem, scilicet in sancta sanctorum.'

20 Ibid., 'Cum papa quidam . . . inspicere praesumpsisset, statim lumen oculorum amisit.'

21 Ibid., 'Deinde cooperta fuit auro et argento tota praeter genu dextrum, a quo oleum indesinenter emanat.'

decorated with images portraying the message. Over the centuries this cover became subject to constant elaboration, but there is no record of it ever being removed until Pius X (1903–14) allowed the art historian J. Wilpert to do so.[22] Wilpert's comments bridge the gap between those of Gerald and, indeed, describe what Gerald himself might probably have seen. A full-length figure with traces of polychromy—the purple robe, a brown scroll, and a red cushion: the letters 'E' and 'EL', probably the inscription Emmanuel, in gold, on a *turchino* background: a gold nimbus and cross behind the bearded head.[23] Wilpert also described not only the sun, moon, and stars in the nimbus, but also, on the right side, a great round hole made for unction! Gerald's knee? Eight other holes covered with little silver discs engraved with birds and symbolic animals complete the image (plate 1).[24]

Innocent's cover stopped at neck level, leaving the face free. Flora Lewis is obviously correct when she says that even in full-length images, it is the face of Christ on which the observer focuses his gaze.[25] Today much of Innocent's work on the Uronica's silver cover is overlaid by later additions—a rectangular door for symbolic foot-washing, dating from the fourteenth century, a crown of flames, a baroque angel, and various medallions—but a closer inspection reveals much of the original design.[26] Innocent's cover is divided into four parts with a geometric decoration of stars and rosettes within circles—a complex design reminiscent of the patterns of cosmatesque pavements. Small figures of the highest quality further elaborate the design. At the top, nearest to Christ's face, are the evangelist symbols—Matthew and Mark to the left, Luke and John being identifiable on the right. Beneath them, to the left and right, are St Stephen and St Laurence, with his gridiron, both of whose relics were venerated in the oratory.[27] In the next row and on the left is a medallion with the *Agnus Dei*, matched on the right by a descending angel. The Virgin stands below on the left, and on the right a male figure in the act of

[22] J. Wilpert, 'L'*acheropita* ossia l'immagine del Salvatore della Capelle del *Sancta Sanctorum*', *L'Arte*, 10 (1907), pp. 159–77, 246–62, esp. pp. 162–5.

[23] Cf. W. F. Volbach, 'Il Cristo di Sutri e la venerazione del SS. Salvatore nel Lazio', *Pontificia Accademia Romana di Archeologia, Rendiconti*, 17 (1940–1), pp. 97–126.

[24] Wilpert, 'L'*acheropita*', p. 174 and esp. fig. 9.

[25] F. Lewis, 'The Veronica: image, legend and the viewer', in W. M. Ormrod, ed., *England in the Thirteenth Century, Proceedings of the Harlaxton Conference* (Woodbridge, 1985), pp. 100–6, especially p. 104.

[26] Wilpert, 'L'*archeropita*', pp. 246–62.

[27] *Descriptio Lateranensis*, p. 357.

Plate 1 Innocent III's Silver Cover for the Uronica or *Acheropita* (by courtesy of the British Library).

homage or *proskynesis*.[28] Next comes St Paul, with a pointed beard carrying a book, and opposite him, St Peter, with the pallium over his right hand and keys in the left. Then, nearest to the doorway, for the anointing of the Saviour's feet, are two small female figures, possibly S. Agnese and S. Prassede, whose actual heads were in reliquaries under the oratory's altar.[29] The cover is completed at the bottom with ten small, diamond-shaped champlevé enamel medallions, showing traces of green and yellow colouring.[30] Some of the figures previously encountered are repeated in this marginal frieze, which also includes a mitred bishop and a figure without a nimbus—possibly a donor figure—perhaps even Innocent himself? The inscription shows without any doubt that Innocent, its patron, had the whole cover made.[31]

The second of Gerald's images, this time found at St Peter's, was the cloth with which Christ's brow was wiped on his way to Calvary.[32] A clear and lasting impression of his suffering face had been left upon it.[33] This cloth was called the Veronica, after the Virgin Mary's maid-of-all-work, and meaning the *vera icona*, the true icon or image.[34] Such a play on words would have delighted the eloquent Welshman Gerald. In actual fact, the Veronica image, the so-called *sudarium* of Christ himself may, according to Wilpert, have had a painted image added to it at the end of the twelfth century.[35] Whether this is so or not, it would certainly have been in keeping with Innocent's aim to raise the standing and public veneration of so ancient but obscure an image already in the possession of St Peter's. A bull addressed to the canons of the basilica tells how the

28 Cf. G. B. Ladner, 'The gestures of prayer in papal iconography of the thirteenth and early fourteenth centuries', *Images and Ideas in the Middle Ages*, *Selected Studies in History and Art*, *Storia e Letteratura = Raccolta di Studi e Testi*, 155–6, 2 vols (Rome, 1983), 1, pp. 209–37, esp. pp. 209–11.

29 *Descriptio Lateranensis*, p. 357, 'et caput Sancta Praxedis et Sanctae Agnese reliquae cum aliis multis'. Wilpert, 'L'*acheropita*', p. 177, suggests that one might be the Magdalene, who herself anointed Christ's feet.

30 From left to right, Agnes with lamb and crown, St Paul with his sword, John the Baptist, a space, Madonna and Child, Peter with keys and a book, St Laurence, S. Prassede, a bishop, and a donor.

31 + INNOCENTIVS PP III HOC OPVS FECIT FIERI +.

32 E. V. Dobschütz, *Christusbilder, Untersuchungen zur christlichen Legende* (Leipzig, 1899), esp. pp. 197–262.

33 I. Wilson, *Holy Faces: Secret Places* (London, 1991); Lewis, 'The Veronica', pp. 100–3.

34 E. Delaruelle, 'Le problème de la pauvreté vu par les théologiens et les canonistes dans la deuxième moitié du xii siècle', *Cahiers de Fanjeaux*, 2 (Toulouse, 1967), pp. 48–63, esp. p. 62 for a discussion of Veronica as a poor saint.

35 J. Wilpert, *Die römischen Malereien und Mosaiken*, 2 vols (Freiburg, 1917), 2, p. 1123; Lewis, 'Veronica', p. 105, n. 15.

Veronica was to be presented to the people, contained within a *capsa* or casket of gold, silver, and precious stones, made specially for this purpose by a silversmith (*fabre facta*).[36]

In both images it was the face which was to convey the message to the people, hence Innocent's concentration on this feature. Yet the Uronica's dark, burnt-black, and fearsome face, with rigid nose, staring eyes, and enormous pupils, seems far less likely than the Veronica to show that Christ had suffered.[37] In the Veronica face the suffering was only too obvious. There were, of course, similarities, and not just in the features. In each, for example, a bruise appeared under the right eye. Perhaps wishing to demonstrate there was humanity in the Uronica image, Gerald speaks also of a scar on the forehead.[38] This he alleged to have been caused by a certain Jew who had thrown a stone at it. The stone thrower died, and many conversions subsequently took place. Gerald cites this story word for word from the *Ordines Romani XII* of Cencio Camerius, of about 1192, and explains that in his day it was still possible to see that the wound had actually bled.[39] We do not know now exactly how the Veronica looked. When Wilpert examined it in 1917 he saw only a square piece of discoloured and stained cloth.[40] Yet it had clearly once existed in a form by which the faithful could be moved to wonder at Christ's message, and its popularity in the later Middle Ages has never been in doubt.[41]

Although these images of the Uronica and the Veronica were the two most impressive in conveying the message, Rome, by the second half of the twelfth century, was one whole great storehouse of images and relics: a unique source of attraction and inspiration to citizen and pilgrim alike.[42] Something of that excitement experienced on being face to face with one or more of these images in the twelfth and thirteenth centuries must have been generated once more when the five surviving Roman icons of the Virgin were brought together at S. Maria Maggiore for two weeks in June

[36] 3 Jan. 1208, *PL* 215, col. 1270, 'recolitur infra capsam ex auro et argento et lapidibus pretiosis ad hoc specialiter fabrefactam venerabiliter deportetur.' Cf. Lewis, 'Veronica', p. 103, n. 15.

[37] Grisar, *Sancta Sanctorum*, p. 51.

[38] Gerald of Wales, *Jewel of the Church*, ch. 31, pp. 79–80.

[39] *Ordo Romanus XII*, *PL* 78, cols 1063–1106, esp. col. 1097.

[40] Lewis, 'Veronica', p. 105.

[41] For fourteenth-century representations of the pilgrim badge or 'vernicle', see M. Mitchiner, *Medieval Pilgrim and Secular Badges* (London, 1986), p. 273, and plates 1057–8.

[42] P. Jounel, *Le Culte des Saints*; *The Blessings of Pilgrimage*, ed. R. Ousterhout = *Illinois Byzantine Studies*, 1 (Urbana, 1990).

and July 1988.[43] The fifth-century icon of S. Maria Nova was the most venerable of them all and owed its miraculous origin to the unseen angelic hand.[44]

Such images were intended to arouse intense spirituality in the worshipping beholder.[45] The effect was heightened as the images were often surrounded by banks of lights—candelabra in the churches and torches in the streets. As Bernard of Clairvaux cynically commented, 'When golden reliquaries catch the eye, the purses open up', and again, 'The brighter the image of a saint appears, the holier the people imagine it to be.'[46] In her study of twelfth-century statues of the Virgin in France, Iylene Forsyth has indicated the importance of the use of precious metals, silver beaten to the thinness of tissue, carefully fastened to a wooden core, and decorated with dozens of precious stones, all producing an awe-inspiring effect.[47] The contours and folds of the metal collected the light and reflected it back, suggesting an intangible, mystical presence. The faithful observer might even have been tempted to endow the effigy with the ability to move, so easily was this shimmering illusion fostered.[48] One Master Gregory, an English tourist visiting Rome at the turn of the twelfth century, could have sworn that the colossal bronze head and hand of Constantine gave the appearance of being about to speak and move![49] A devout worshipper thus built up a close mutual relationship with an image. This was often heightened by the expressive, eloquent, or even terrifying fixed stare in the eyes of the image remarked upon by contemporaries.[50] Indeed, not only Gerald of Wales, but Gervase of Tilbury, who also saw both images, indicated that the *Sancta Sanctorum* image, the

[43] P. Amato, *De Vera Effigie Mariae: antiche icone Romane* (Rome, 1988); C. Bertelli, 'Icone di Roma', *Stil und Überlieferung in der Kunst des Abendlandes*, 2 vols (Berlin, 1967), 1, pp. 100–6.

[44] E. Kitzinger, 'A Virgin's face: antiquarianism in twelfth-century art', *Art Bulletin*, 62 (1980), pp. 6–19; M. Guarducci, *La più antica icone di Maria: un prodigioso vincolo fra oriente e occidente* (Rome, 1989).

[45] E. Dahl, 'Heavenly images. The statue of St Foy of Conques and the signification of the medieval "Cult-image" in the West', *Acta ad Archaeologicam et Artium Historiam Pertinentia = Institutum Romanum Norvegiae*, 8 (Rome, 1978) [hereafter *AAAHP*], pp. 175–92.

[46] *Sancti Bernardi Opera*, 3, ed. J. Leclercq and H. M. Rochais (Rome, 1963), *Apologia ad Guillelmum Abbatem*, p. 105.

[47] L. Forsyth, *The Throne of Wisdom: Wood Sculptures of the Madonna in Romanesque France* (Princeton, 1972), pp. 40–4.

[48] Dahl, 'Heavenly images', pp. 188–91.

[49] Master Gregory, *The Marvels of Rome*, tr. J. Osborne = *Medieval Sources in Translation*, 31 (Toronto, 1987), p. 23.

[50] Dahl, 'Heavenly images', pp. 190–1; S. Sinding-Larsen, 'Some observations on liturgical imagery of the twelfth century', *AAAHP*, pp. 192–212, esp. pp. 208–12.

Uronica, remained covered, possibly by closed doors, because of its fearsome effect on the viewer.[51] Gerald also comments upon the fact that curtains hung before the Veronica.[52] The wide-open eyes, combined with a hypnotic gaze frequently found in reliquary images, indicated to many of the faithful that the Holy Spirit was speaking directly to them.[53] Clearly the danger of idolatry was always present,[54] and steps were taken to protect the images from too frequent a public gaze. The Church legislated consistently against such a threat. Canon 62 of the Fourth Lateran Council decreed that relics were henceforth to be enclosed in reliquaries or behind impenetrable bars.[55] This instruction Innocent had already carried out when he secured the heads of Saints Peter and Paul at the Lateran behind a decorative grille.[56] This had the added advantage of preventing any tampering. Proliferation of relics was to be halted, and the need for solemn authenticity stressed. Sometimes this authentication had to be left to God himself, as Innocent remarked about Christ's foreskin and umbilical cord, both claimed as part of the collection in the *Sancta Sanctorum* of the Lateran.[57] His established practice, indeed, was to concentrate far more attention on images from which the message could be more readily expounded than on relics, the intrinsic characteristics of which were dubious, and which could easily divert attention from the Gospel.

Innocent was eager to bring the two main images out into the streets to meet the people, so following a practice common to all Italian towns in various matters, not merely religious. The Uronica had a venerable history of street theatre, but there is no similar evidence for the Veronica. In bringing the Veronica to the people, possibly for the first time, on 20 January 1208, the second Sunday after Epiphany, Innocent was not only giving them another image of great holiness to venerate, but was also emphasizing the importance of St Peter's, from whence it came.[58] The earliest mention of

[51] Gervase of Tilbury, *Otia Imperialia*, book 3, ed. G. G. Leibnitz, *Scriptores rerum Brunsvicensium* (Hanover, 1707), p. 967; Lewis, 'Veronica', p. 103.

[52] Gerald of Wales, *Speculum Ecclesiae*, p. 279, '. . . a nemine, nisi per velorum quae ante dependent interpositionem inspicitur.'

[53] Dahl, 'Heavenly images', pp. 186–91.

[54] Ibid., pp. 177–8.

[55] *Conciliorum oecumenicorum decreta*, ed. J. Alberigo *et al.*, 3rd edn (Bologna, 1973), pp. 263–4.

[56] Antonelli, *Memorie storiche*, p. 11; Grisar, *Sancta Sanctorum*, p. 24.

[57] *PL* 217, col. 877, 'Melius est Deo totum committere quam aliud temere definire.' Cf. Grisar, *Sancta Sanctorum*, p. 123, who notes that this relic was kept in a gemmed cross inscribed 'PREPUTIUM DNJC'.

[58] *PL* 215, col. 1270, for the privilege to the Hospital.

the ceremony of processing the Lateran Uronica occurs in the *Liber Pontificalis* under Sergius I (687–701).[59] He had laid down that

> from the time of the breaking of the Lord's body, the clergy and people should sing the *Agnus Dei* and on the occasion of the Annunciation, Dormition and Nativity of the Virgin, the procession should go out from the Church of San Adriano gathering people as it went, all meeting up at S. Maria Maggiore.

Stephen II (752–7), barefooted, carried on his shoulders the 'imago Dei et Salvatoris nostri Jesu Christi' across the city to counter the Lombard threat, all the Romans following.[60] By the time of Leo IV (847–55), such processing had become a matter of custom, and the Feast of the Assumption was developing into one of the most grandiose rites of medieval Rome.[61] On the vigil of this feast, 14 August, the procession of the *tabula* or image of Christ—what Gerald had called the Uronica—set out at midnight along lighted streets from the Lateran, past SS Quattro Coronati, the Colosseum, the Arch of Titus, and arrived at the steps of the Temple of Venus and Rome, in front of S. Maria Nova, nowadays S. Francesca Romana.[62] On its arrival, the feet of the image were washed with *basilicum*, whilst the people prostrated themselves and the *Kyrie* and *Christe eleison* were sung a hundred times.[63] At this climax, the image of the Virgin at S. Maria Nova met the image of her Son, which had been carried through the streets to her. By the twelfth century the Uronica was carried on a *portatorium*, borne high, surrounded by lighted candles and torches, to the accompaniment of psalms. It was led by twelve of the best-regarded dignitaries in Rome and twelve officials of the papal chapel.[64] The procession continued to S. Adriano, where the ritual foot-washing was repeated, and S. Maria Maggiore was finally reached as dawn was

[59] *The Book of Pontiffs* (*Liber Pontificalis*), tr. R. Davis (Liverpool, 1989), pp. 87–8; A. Mancini, 'La chiesa medioevale di S. Adriano nel Foro Romano', *Pontificia Accademia Romana di Archeologia, Rendiconti*, 40 (1967–8),pp. 191–245.

[60] *Liber Pontificalis*, ed. L. Duchesne, 3 vols (Paris, 1886–92), 1, p. 443; Grisar, *Sancta Sanctorum*, p. 50; Kitzinger, 'A Virgin's face', p. 12. Cf. D. de Bruyne, 'L'origine des processions de la Chandeleur et des rogations à propos d'un sermon inédit', *RBen*, 34 (1922), pp. 142–26.

[61] *Liber Pontificalis*, 2, pp. 110, 135; Volbach, 'Il Cristo di Sutri', p. 116.

[62] Grisar, *Sancta Sanctorum*, pp. 55–7; Kitzinger, 'A Virgin's face', pp. 12, 17; Mancini, 'S. Adriano nel Foro Romano', p. 223; Sinding-Larsen, 'Liturgical imagery', p. 211; Volbach, 'Il Cristo di Sutri', pp. 116–18.

[63] J. Mabillon, *Museum Italicum seu collectio veterum scriptorum ex bibliothecis Italicis*, 2 vols (Paris, 1724), 2, pp. 131, 134, 174; Kitzinger, 'A Virgin's face', p. 12.

[64] Benedictus Canonicus, *Liber Politicus*, in P. Fabre and L. Duchesne, *Le Liber Censuum de l'église romaine*, 3 vols (Paris, 1905–10), 2, p. 158.

breaking on 15 August. By tradition, the liturgical station for the Feast of the Assumption then followed, and Innocent used this occasion to preach his Sermon XXVIII on the Dawn.[65] The Virgin Mary was the dawn, marking the end of night and the beginning of day, the end of vice and the beginning of virtue in the world. Her Son was the Day-Star on high.[66]

This ceremony of the vigil of the Assumption was seen by Grisar,[67] and more recently by Kitzinger, as representing in a literal sense a visit by Christ to his mother on her great feast day.[68] This cult of the *acheropita* or Uronica seems to have been unique to Lazio, and the *ordo* and rite, as well as the image, were initiated throughout the little towns of the region around Rome.[69] Tivoli appears to have been particularly blessed, for as recently as August 1978, in the so-called *inchinata*, the Saviour and his mother bowed to each other as they met.[70]

Innocent wished to arrange something similar for the Veronica, which was first processed in January 1208. In the procession the special portable reliquary for the image was carried by the canons of St Peter's to Innocent's new hospital foundation of S. Spirito, by the Tiber, and its adjacent church of S. Maria in Sassia.[71] The Veronica was there venerated by 'a flood' of people, who heard a sermon of exhortation from the Pope.[72] In his Sermon VIII, for the First Sunday after Epiphany, Innocent stresses that in this place, too, the mother of Christ is also to be found.[73] At this newly established liturgical station of the Veronica he speaks of the Virgin finding her Son, whose effigy, on being carried around the hospital, encouraged the faithful sick and pilgrims to be amazed at his glory.[74]

Although processions had become so important, Innocent was aware of the necessity of stimulating in small groups of significant people the true importance of Christ's message. The Uronica and the Veronica, sparklingly impressive as they were when seen either by candlelight or sunlight, also possessed a solemn and more contemplative dimension when seen in

[65] *PL* 217, cols 581–6.

[66] Ibid., col. 584: 'Quia vero ad diluculum poenitentiae surgit, respiciat auroram, deprecetur Mariam, ut ipsa per filium cor ejus ad satisfactionem illuminet.'

[67] Grisar, *Sancta Sanctorum*, pp. 56–7.

[68] Kitzinger, 'A Virgin's face', pp. 16–17.

[69] Volbach, 'Il Cristo di Sutri', pp. 104–16.

[70] Kitzinger, 'A Virgin's face', p. 12, n. 46.

[71] *PL* 215, cols 1270–1; A. Albani, *Collectionis bullarum sacrosanctae basilicae Vaticanae*, 3 vols (Rome, 1747–54), 1, pp. 89–90.

[72] *Gesta Innocentii PP III*, *PL* 214, cols xvii–ccxxvi, esp. cols cc–cciii and cci, 'in qua populus illic confluit'.

[73] *PL* 217, cols 345–50.

[74] *Origins of the Liturgy*, pp. 102–3, 460.

their normal locations. The Uronica, by virtue of its position above the altar in the papal chapel of St Laurence at the Lateran, was confined in a very small space. When Mass was celebrated there by the Pope and the seven cardinal-bishops, there was room for no other, and the spiritual awareness of the ceremony in the presence of the image must have provided a religious experience of considerable intensity.[75] The fine decorative work on Innocent's silver cover, perhaps inspired by his reading of Ado of Vienne's *Martyrology*,[76] would have acted as a valuable aid to their meditation. The Easter *ordo* of Cencio Camerarius, in use in Innocent's day, tells how, when the image was opened, the Pope kissed its feet and repeated three times 'Surrexit Dominus de Sepulcro, alleluia', to which the response came back 'Qui pro nobis perpendit in ligno, alleluia.'[77] The cardinal-bishops then kissed Christ's feet, and each received in turn a kiss from the Pope. The ceremony was repeated at all the feasts of the Virgin.

The Veronica was not used in the same way, for at St Peter's Innocent wished to concentrate on the *confessio* or tomb of the Apostle to add a further dimension to the message he wished to convey. At this, the focal point of the basilica, he had a splendid new golden-bronze protective screen made, decorated with small human figures.[78] In antique and rustic capitals mixed with uncials, a one-line inscription identifies Innocent as the patron.[79] His inspiration for the *confessio* may well have come from his readings of the *Liber Pontificalis*.[80] The decoration is there well attested when Sixtus III (432–40) accepted from the Emperor Valentinian a gold image with twelve portals, twelve Apostles, and the Saviour, decorated with the most precious stones, and which was placed over the tomb.[81] Leo III (795–816) inaugurated the disposition later followed by Innocent by inserting a golden grille or *ruga* with a door to give access to the tomb.[82] Leo IV (847–55) renewed the decoration of Sixtus III, destroyed by the Saracens in 846, with a silver *tabula* showing the Saviour enthroned with

[75] *Origins of the Liturgy*, p. 93.

[76] Ado of Vienne, *Vetus Romanum Martyrologium*, *PL* 123, cols 143–82; Van Dijk, *Origins*, pp. 126–8, 226–7, 493–8.

[77] *PL* 78, col. 1077; Grisar, *Sancta Sanctorum*, pp. 50–1.

[78] Gautier, 'La Clôture Émaillée', pp. 237–42.

[79] Ibid., p. 238. + TERCIVS HOC MUNVS DANS INNOCENTIVS +.

[80] On the *confessio* see E. Kirschbaum, *Les fouilles de Saint-Pierre de Rome* (Paris, 1961); *Descriptio Vaticanae*, pp. 375–442.

[81] *Book of Pontiffs*, pp. 35–7, esp. p. 36.

[82] *Liber Pontificalis*, 2, p. 1.

precious gems on his head while, on his right hand, cherubim held the images of the Apostles.[83] Leo IV also seems to have had an altar frontal made in gold and enamel, which Boso claimed was destroyed in 1130 by the antipope Anacletus.[84] Innocent was not only inspired by these decorative precedents when he arranged for the new decoration of the *confessio*, but also took pains to replace the damaged Carolingian enamels with similar work executed by craftsmen from Limoges.[85] His protective screen is simple in the extreme and highly functional. Thirty-eight bars, each a finger's width, are bisected by one horizontal bar, on which is incised the bronze-caster's name, 'OBERT.A.G.'.[86]

Innocent's exquisite and religiously significant small works were designed to impart the message to those important visitors to Rome in November 1215, the 1,200 archbishops, metropolitans, bishops, and abbots attending the Council,[87] but he also took the opportunity to restore the decaying apse-mosaic of St Peter's, which would be visible to all.[88] This mosaic not only claimed equality for St Peter's, now 'the Mother of All Churches', but also revealed the Christian religion in its historical perspective. Innocent's significant alterations showed the importance of the Church and the symbolic purpose of the Eucharist, where the Blood of the Lamb, flowing into the chalice, was for the salvation of all. Such a message, complicated in design, but simple in purpose, was typical of the inspirational approach of Innocent III and deserves further attention elsewhere. His love of street theatre and his feeling for the city of Rome came together spectacularly in the entertainments considered suitable for the delegates to the Lateran Council—the consecration of S. Maria in Trastevere on Sunday 15 November and the Mass in St Peter's on 18 November.[89] Here we have a privileged glimpse of the lights, the music, the trumpets, and the razzmatazz on

[83] Ibid., p. 114.

[84] Ibid., p. 380.

[85] Gautier, 'Observations préliminaires', pp. 43–79.

[86] Gautier, 'La Clôture Émaillée', pp. 238–42.

[87] Ibid., pp. 242–6.

[88] *Gesta*, col. ccv, 'absidam ejusdem basilicae fecit restauri mosibus, quod erat ex magna parte consumptum.' Cf. J. Ruysschaert, 'Le tableau Mariotti de la mosaïque absidale de l'ancien S. Pierre', *Pontificia Accademia Romana di Archeologia, Rendiconti*, 40 (1967–8), pp. 295–317.

[89] S. Kuttner and A. Garcia y Garcia, 'A new eyewitness account of the Fourth Lateran Council', *Traditio*, 20 (1964), pp. 115–78; D. Kinney, *Santa Maria in Trastevere from its Founding to 1215* (Michigan, 1975), pp. 337–9.

which all great impresarios flourish.[90] Innocent III, that much-neglected patron of the small-scale work, merely added the religiosity!

Queen Mary and Westfield College,
University of London

[90] Bolton, 'Show with a meaning', pp. 61–4.

FRIARS, PATRONS, AND WORKSHOPS AT THE BASILICA DEL SANTO, PADUA*

by LOUISE BOURDUA

FEW incidents in the life of St Francis strike the art historian more than his demolition of the newly constructed chapter-hall in Assisi. As the date of a chapter at S. Maria della Portiuncula was fast approaching and there was no accommodation for the large number of friars expected, the people of Assisi built a house to shelter the incoming friars. Coming across this structure, Francis became so irritated that he climbed the roof and threw down tiles and rafters, and was only stopped when knights interfered and the municipality argued that the building belonged to them.[1] Ironically, this same man had answered God's call and had repaired the ruined churches of S. Damiano, St Peter, and S. Maria della Portiuncula in Assisi.[2]

Francis' negative attitude to new buildings, books, and property in general is indeed puzzling when one looks at any Franciscan church, especially S. Francesco at Assisi, burial-place of the saint from 1230. Whilst the opinions of Francis on the subject are relatively well known, it is worth asking what the rest of the Order thought; what precise role did the conventual branch of the Franciscans play in the development of the arts in Italy?[3] Assisi would seem to be the logical place to begin, but the basilica is ridden with problems of dating and attribution. These are so enormous, and current critical opinion so confused, that we must turn elsewhere for answers. The second most important Franciscan church of the Order, the Basilica of St Anthony of Padua, provides a great

* The material in this paper has been drawn from my forthcoming Ph.D. thesis on Franciscan patronage of the arts in the Veneto (University of Warwick). I wish to thank the Social Sciences and Humanities Research Council of Canada, the Gladys Krieble Delmas Foundation, and the British School at Rome for their generous support of my research.

[1] Thomas of Celano, *Vita Secunda*, ch. 27, *Analecta Franciscana*, 10 (Quaracchi, 1926–41), p. 166; *Speculum*, ch. 7, *Le Speculum perfectionis ou Mémoires de Frère Léon sur la Seconde Partie de la Vie de Saint Francois d'Assise*, 1, texte latin, British Society of Franciscan Studies, 33, ed. P. Sabatier (Manchester, 1928), pp. 21–3; *Scripta Leonis, Rufini, et Angeli Sociorum S. Francisci*, ch. 11, ed. R. B. Brooke (Oxford, 1970), pp. 106–7.

[2] Celano, *Vita Prima*, chs 8, 9, pp. 16–18.

[3] R. B. Brooke, *Early Franciscan Government* (Cambridge, 1959); M. D. Lambert, *Franciscan Poverty. The Doctrine of the Absolute Poverty of Christ and the Apostles in the Franciscan Order, 1210–1323* (London, 1961).

opportunity to set up a control for the development of Franciscan patronage.[4]

The basilica, begun immediately after the canonization of St Anthony of Padua in 1232, provides an ideal case-study of Franciscan patronage during the thirteenth and fourteenth centuries.[5] The Santo, as it is casually known, emulated the mother church at Assisi in both scale and lavishness of decoration. The fourteenth century in particular was marked by a succession of elaborate decorative programmes, both sculptural and two-dimensional.[6] Its excellent documentation makes the Santo of Padua an ideal place to begin an investigation of the complex relationship between friars, patrons, and workshops.

The building and decoration of the Santo, which spans many centuries, was the product of efforts by the commune, common people, nobles, confraternities, and the friars themselves. The decision to build a large basilica worthy of enshrining the body of St Anthony was taken soon after his canonization on 30 May 1232. The initial building project was probably funded by alms offered at his tomb. Miracles had occurred in Padua from the day of his death on 13 June 1231; the sick who touched his tomb were freed from illness, and even the multitude who remained outside the door regained their health in the square.[7] These miracles aroused the devotion of the people who came in great numbers from all regions. They marched towards the small church of S. Maria Mater Domini (where his body lay) in long processions, carrying great candles, which had to be trimmed upon entrance for fear of fire.[8] A larger church was definitely needed. Indulgences encouraged further donations. Pope Alexander IV conceded an attractive indulgence valid for six years, from 1256 to 1263.[9]

4 A very useful guide to the vast body of critical discussion exists in P. Scarpellini, *Fra'Ludovico da Pietralunga: Descrizione della Basilica di S. Francesco e di altri santuari di Assisi* (Treviso, 1982).

5 The standard work on the basilica is B. Gonzati, *La Basilica di Sant' Antonio di Padova*, 2 vols (Padua, 1852); for all documentation see A. Sartori, *Archivio Sartori: Documenti di Storia e Arte Francescane*, 1, ed. G. Luisetti (Padua, 1983) [hereafter *ArSartori*].

6 G. Lorenzoni, ed., *L'edificio del Santo di Padova* (Vicenza, 1981) [hereafter *L'edificio*]; G. Lorenzoni, ed., *Le Sculture del Santo di Padova* (Vicenza, 1984); C. Semenzato, ed., *Le Pitture del Santo di Padova* (Vicenza, 1984) provide useful introduction, although incomplete.

7 Anonymus O. Min., *Vita prima beati Antonii vel 'Assidua'*, in V. Gamboso, ed., *Fonti agiografiche antoniane* (Padua, 1981) [hereafter *Assidua*], ch. 25, 2–3, pp. 402–5.

8 *Assidua*, ch. 26, 11–14, pp. 410–11.

9 Published by Gonzati, *La Basilica*, 1, doc. 10, p. x. It is not known whether or not the Santo derived finance from cemeterial fees for the land around the basilica; burials occur at an early date. For these procedures in Britain see K. Wood-Legh, *Perpetual Chantries in Britain* (Cambridge, 1965).

Indeed, by this date a first version of the Santo was ready for the translation of the body of Anthony. The commune's special relationship with the friars prompted alterations to the existing fabric; 4,000 lire were donated annually to the project, and this financed the construction of a transept, ambulatory, gallery, radial chapels, and two campaniles.[10] The final result as it appears today is quite different from the initial original intention, a single nave church reminiscent of the upper church of S. Francesco, Assisi.[11]

The decoration of the church is better documented than the actual fabric. The ensemble as it appears today is the result of separate commissions, not a single, unified programme. Each family, individual, or confraternity exchanged building, decoration, and endowment of chapels for burial privileges and the celebration of Masses. Endowments, like the immortality of the soul, were meant to be perpetual; this, in turn, ensured the security and prosperity of the convent.

When lay patrons wished to build a chapel they provided all the equipment necessary to celebrate Mass: an altar, chalice with paten, a missal and its cushion, some sort of altar frontal (*paramento*), and vestments for the celebrant. This pattern is repeatedly observed in wills, as early as 1285, when Ailice, widow of Giovanni Mauro, wished to found an altar dedicated to S. Prosdocimo.[12] This continues well into the fourteenth century with the Lançaroto, Turchetto, Zabarella, Lupi, and Conti families.[13] Furthermore, surviving inventories describe the objects more precisely, and it is evident from these that the family coat of arms or emblem was placed on each one of the objects, save the paten or a minor vestment.[14] Thus there was no way of mistaking the identity of the patron of the chapel; the officiating priest sported the donor's emblem on his pluvial, read from a lectern displaying the patron's arms, was surrounded by painted or sculpted shields on the walls or entrance arch of the chapel.[15]

[10] M. Salvatori, 'Costruzione della basilica dall'origine al secolo XIV', in *L'edificio*, pp. 31–81, esp. p. 67.

[11] M. Salvatori, 'Nacque "francescane" la seconda basilica del Santo', *Il Santo*, 17 (1977), pp. 307–21, at p. 318.

[12] *ArSartori*, p. 557, no. 1.

[13] Lançaroto documents and objects in *ArSartori*, pp. 773, 777, no. 13, 782; Turchetto on pp. 565, nos 2, 4, 566, nos 5–8, 777, no. 6; Zabarella on pp. 554, nos 2, 4, 774, 781.

[14] The objects provided by the Lupi family were published along with their costs in A. Sartori, 'Nota su Altichiero', *Il Santo*, 3 (1963), pp. 291–326, doc. 12; reprinted in *ArSartori*, pp. 471–2, no. 106; for the Conti inventory see L. Guidaldi, 'Documenti', *Il Santo*, 1 (1928–9), pp. 358–64.

[15] 'Item dui camissi, dui amitti, II manipuli, una stuola, dui cordoni . . . forniti de cendale rosso a la sua arma . . . un palio de zendalo azuro, con uno compaso in meço eun lovo e con una

Before a chapel could be built, an altar dedicated, or a family tomb placed in the Santo, certain procedures had to be followed. One did not simply send in the builders. Some sort of permission first had to be obtained from the local chapter of friars. The documented cases of the Negri, Turchetti, and Lupi families make this clear. Sometime before 29 October 1364, Gerardo Negri requested the right to maintain the chapel and altar of the *Madonna Mora*.[16] The friars meeting at a general chapter refused his request for burial in the chapel, possibly because of the proximity to the tomb of St Anthony, situated in the adjacent chapel. Authorization to sculpt or paint the family's emblem on the walls of the chapel was however granted in return for an endowment.[17] Seven years later, and without any explanation, the chapter decided to allow the patron one tomb in the chapel in a specified location, next to the pillar on the left side of the chapel.[18] Interestingly, the Confraternity of St Anthony, which shared the chapel, still retained the right to celebrate Masses and hold services on the premises, but its members were forbidden to bury their dead there.[19]

Another chapel, dedicated to St Francis (now the entrance corridor to the chapel of the Treasury) was conceded and assigned to Francesco Turchetto during the local chapter meeting of 8 December 1378. The concession document minutely recorded the chapel's position and dedication, 'beyond the high altar, the fifth chapel after the sacristy'.[20] The chapel's maintenance was the responsibility of the Turchetto family and was to remain in their possession in perpetuity or until the money ran out. Indeed, in the Turchetto case no other persons or associations could have Masses celebrated at the altar. Burial rights were granted to the family as was permission to paint or sculpt the family's emblem.[21]

---

franca bianco e vermiglia . . . duo lectorilia de ligno, cum lupis . . . duae tobaleae a lectorile, cum arma lupi . . .' and many more in *ArSartori*, pp. 471–2, no. 106.

16 M. Ganguzza Billanovich, 'Per la storia religiosa ed edilizia della basilica antoniana: la capella della Madonna Mora e dell'Arca in un nuovo documento del XIV secolo', *Il Santo*, 19 (1979), pp. 67–79.

17 Ibid., p. 77: '. . . quod nullus de domo dicti domini Gerardi propter presentem concessionem et assignationem possit nec debeat infra dictam cappellam facere sepulturam aut facturam seu novitatem aliquam infra vel circa cappellam sine consensu voluntate et licencia sepedicti capituli Sancti Antonii conventus fratrum minorum de Padua. Possint autem in dicta cappella vel extra sua insignia vel arma sculpiri facere et depingi.'

18 Ibid., p. 78.

19 Ibid., p. 79: '. . . quod nullus de fratalea antedicta possit unquam in huiusmodi cappella aliquam sepulturam habere aut aliquod ius ibidem preter sibi supra reservatum pretendere.'

20 *Ar Sartori*, p. 565, no. 4.

21 Ibid., p. 565, no. 4.

The documentation suggests that families were primarily concerned with the assurances of Masses said for the benefit of their souls, whilst the friars were preoccupied with endowment formalities. Little attention is paid to visual decoration. It seems strange at first that none of the numerous proceedings that survive deal with pictorial decoration. One sole exception at the Santo, in 1403, shows the Minister Provincial demanding that an agreement be reached between the Confraternity of St Anthony and a friar to determine 'picturas ornamenta reparationes et queque fienda in dicta capella'.[22]

Once the initial promise of Mass in return for cash, land, rent income, animal or food stocks was granted, there was still work to be done. The privilege had to be confirmed a number of times, by various authorities, such as the provincial chapter and even the Minister General himself. The Negri and Turchetto families followed this procedure, the latter still obtaining reconfirmation in 1444, sixty-six years after the initial grant.[23]

Two surviving chapels commissioned by members of the Lupi di Soragna family provide a case-study of the rapport between friars, patrons, and artists. The chapel of St James Major (rededicated to St Felix in 1503) and the oratory of St George are amongst the best documented and preserved in fourteenth-century Italy.[24] The chapel of St JamesMajor occupies a strategic location in the south transept of the basilica, directly opposite the chapel of St Anthony. It was first contracted on 12 February 1372, to replace an earlier chapel with an altar dedicated to St Michael, was then frescoed by the painter Altichiero and his workshop, and completed by 1379, whilst minor payments for liturgical furnishings continued until 1382.[25] Bonifacio Lupi, soldier and diplomat, contracted the architect, while his spouse, Caterina di Staggia, appears to have supervised the work and certainly paid the bills.

The oratory of St George, a free-standing chapel situated on the piazza a little to the right of the basilica, was commissioned by Raimondino

[22] Ibid., p. 540, no. 70.

[23] Ibid., p. 566, no. 7.

[24] The patronage of these chapels has received scant attention save the following: C. Cenci,'Bonifacio Lupi di Soragna e i Frati Minori', *AFH*, 57 (1964), pp. 90–109; Sartori, 'Altichiero'; A. Sartori, 'La cappella di S. Giacomo al Santo', *Il Santo*, 6 (1966), pp. 267–359; M. D. Edwards, 'The tomb of Raimondino de'Lupi, its form and its meaning', *Konsthistorisk tidskrift*, 52 (1983), pp. 95–105.

[25] For payment sequence see Sartori, 'Altichiero', pp. 305–26; Sartori, 'S. Giacomo', pp. 303–7; for a complete edition of documents see *ArSartori*, pp. 456–75; on the building progression of the chapels see R. Simon, 'Altichiero versus Avanzo', *Papers of the British School at Rome*, 45, ns 32 (1977), pp. 252–71.

Lupi, cousin of Bonifacio, and himself a *condottiero*. The foundation was first recorded in November 1377; the building itself was completed by 3 May 1378, whilst its painted decoration was finished by 30 May 1384. Raimondino did not live to see the completed cycle, as he died on 30 November 1379; it was left to his cousin and nephews to bring the project to its successful completion.[26]

The focal point of the decoration of the chapel of St James by Altichiero and his workshop is the back wall. There, a large Crucifixion has been turned into a gigantic triptych through the clever use of the engaged wall columns.[27] It is flanked by two scenes from the life of Christ: an Entombment and a Resurrection, each positioned immediately above hanging wall-tombs, a theme of hope for the benefit of those buried there. The upper registers of this wall and the others are taken up by scenes from the life of the titular saint, James of Compostela. St James was not only of importance for the pilgrimage function of the basilica, but dear to the Lupi family, who bore the same name as Queen Lupa of Spain, who had been converted by the posthumous miracles of James.[28]

The oratory of St George has a more elaborate programme. A Coronation of the Virgin, populated by a consort of musical angels, occupies the top half of the altar wall, with a massive Crucifixion below. Episodes from the infancy of Christ are depicted on the opposite wall, while the side walls feature scenes from the lives of Saints George, Lucy, and Catherine of Alexandria. The cycle is not particularly Franciscan, save the Coronation of the Virgin Mary, a theme often present in the Order's churches. The choice of the dedication of the oratory and the subject-matter of the cycle reflect the patron's own choice: Raimondino Lupi had previously endowed and dedicated a hospital in Mantua to Saints Lucy and Catherine,[29] while St George is the patron of knights, the ideal choice for a family of soldiers.

In both the documentation and the decoration of these two chapels, the absence of extensive Franciscan iconography is striking, if not disturbing; in the chapel of St James the four Franciscan saints (Clare, Anthony,

[26] As is inscribed on his tomb: see Sartori, 'Altichiero', p. 309.

[27] Julian Gardner kindly pointed the coincidence of this Crucifixion and those in the Upper and Lower Churches at Assisi. The Crucifixion in the Santo was meant to be seen by pilgrims, as this chapel, directly opposite St Anthony's, performed a pilgrimage role.

[28] Jacques de Voragine, *La légende dorée*, tr. J.-B. M. Roze (Paris, 1967), pp. 479–85.

[29] As is evident from his will dated 11 May 1372, published in part by Sartori, 'Altichiero', pp. 309–11, doc. 9.

Francis, and Louis of Toulouse) appear only as busts. Two or three similar medallions are found in the oratory of St George.[30]

It could be argued that it would have been superfluous to place representations of Franciscans here, as the Santo is quite clearly a Franciscan church, but their invisibility in both the decoration and the documentation ought to give us pause for thought. Could this invisibility possibly be a consequence of the negligible role the friars played in the individual artistic commissions?

Take the Lupi commissions, for example: the first document, the building contract, was drawn up by a leading humanist, Lombardo della Seta, between Bonifacio Lupi and Andriolo de' Santi, architect and sculptor. Witnessing the contract were four civilians and no Franciscans.[31] The contract, written in sophisticated architectural jargon, was minutely detailed and provided step-by-step instructions to be followed. It listed models to be imitated, in particular, the opposing chapel of St Anthony and the nearby chapter-hall, but also focused on secular buildings, namely, the recently refurbished workshop of the humanist Lombardo della Seta.[32] The minds behind this commission were probably many; one could easily imagine the friars expressing a wish for continuity, to match the new chapel with its surroundings. However, that the Franciscans should be keen to imitate the latest experiments in domestic architecture is rather unlikely.

The payment records available for this chapel span ten years. They are equally revealing, for they make no mention of friars, not even as intermediaries. All steps are carried out by lay-persons. The initial payments are made via Domenico della Seta (20 February 1372 to 21 July 1374), already encountered as one of the witnesses in the building contract.[33] Then Coradin Lovo, a nephew of Raimondino Lupi, acts as

[30] These include either Saints Francis or Anthony of Padua, on a decorative band on the left wall, and St Clare holding a lily, both unpublished.

[31] These witnesses are 'Lombardo di Iacopo da Seta ... Domenego de Q. de ser Iacopo de la Seta ... Zoane de Q. de messer Pavino di Sbughi da Ferrara ... Pacino di messer Apardo di Donati da Fiorenca': cf. Sartori, 'Altichiero', pp. 311–14; repr. in *ArSartori*, pp. 456–8.

[32] *ArSartori*, p. 457, no. 9: 'Ancora per fatura e lavoratura de V archi de pietra biancha e pietra forte de Vesentina e de soa pietra, i quali deno essere volti sopra le sopradette colone da la parte de nançi de la deta capella, e deno essere lavorati a soaçe e cornixe seguitando quelmodo ch'è in certi volti che sono in uno bancho il quale è nela staçone di Domenicho e di Lombardo a mano drita a l'entrata ...'. For a more detailed discussion of these models see my forthcoming Ph.D. thesis, University of Warwick.

[33] *ArSartori*, p. 458, no. 2.

intermediate between the patrons and the craftsmen (until July 1375). And, finally, Domenico resumes his task (1380–1).[34]

When Raimondino Lupi deals with artists he does not seek to involve the Franciscans. Whereas in the project for the chapel of St James the initial building contract survives, the oratory of St George has preserved its concluding painting contracts.[35] These documents refer to parts of the initial painting contract, drawn between Altichiero and the patron, an arrangement which took place before Raimondino's death on 30 November 1379. Again, there is no mention of friars' involvement. In the concluding acts of 1384 we find Bonifacio Lupi, having taken over his cousin's role, satisfied with Altichiero's work at the oratory, and vice versa. Even though we are lacking the complete set of documents, the evidence seems to be against the Franciscans taking an active role in artistic commissions.

Yet the Order is involved with the patrons. We find Bonifacio Lupi in contact with the Franciscan Order on a number of occasions, through his procurator Andrea da Codagnelli.[36] However, the surviving correspondence deals with spiritual matters, the establishment of the chantry, the endowment proceedings, and the reconfirmation of privileges over the years. The earliest documented exchange between the two parties occurs half-way through the construction of the chapel of St James, on 19 October 1376. Gathered at the local chapter, the Paduan friars approve Lupi's request for the celebration of three Masses daily in return for 104 gold ducats.[37] The initial contact, that is to say, the permission sought and received to send in the builders, has not yet been traced. Could it perhaps have been a verbal exchange?

Having obtained assurance of Masses at the local level, Bonifacio Lupi turned to the provincial ministry and obtained confirmation of privileges on 3 May 1378, during the provincial chapter of Franciscans meeting at Padua.[38] This document again makes no mention of building, paintings, nor tomb, although by this stage the painting of the life of St James Major is under way. It is during the same chapter meeting that we first learn that

[34] *ArSartori*, pp. 458–9, no. 2.

[35] Ibid., p. 463, nos 67–8.

[36] During a local chapter on 19 October 1376; a provincial meeting on 3 May 1378; a general chapter on 4 June 1384; in a letter from Martino da Rivarolo, Minister General, to Bonifacio, dated 20 August 1385. The final exchange between the new Minister, Enrico Alfieri da Asti, and Lupi occurs on 30 August 1389. See Cenci, 'Bonifacio Lupi', pp. 99–109 for excerpts of documents; for a thorough account of the rapport see my forthcoming Ph.D. thesis.

[37] *ArSartori*, p. 472, no. 107.

[38] Ibid., pp. 472–3, no. 109.

Raimondino Lupi has also obtained ratification of earlier conventions granted at the local level for his Santo commission.[39]

The mechanisms of patronage at the Basilica del Santo are indeed thought-provoking. How do we account for the slight participation in the arts by the Franciscans? Why are there so few Franciscan images in the Santo?[40] Where, then, can Franciscan images be found in this city, if not in the Order's own major church? The scope of this paper has only permitted suggestions.

One possible answer to the first question might be found in the Order's history at the time, a period of increasing moral and spiritual decline.[41] Could it be simply that the Franciscans were too concerned with their own internal problems to bother with what went up on the walls?[42] Or perhaps because of the heated debate on poverty and property the Franciscans preferred not to be involved in further debates, such as artistic ones? Or better, since the commissioning of architecture, sculpture, and painting was so complicated in the first place, the friars might have judged it wise not to intervene.

As for the second query, it would not be correct to say that the Santo possesses no Franciscan imagery. Its chapter-hall decoration, painted around the turn of the fourteenth century, survives in a more or less precarious state, but includes a Stigmatization of St Francis, the martyrdom of Franciscan missionaries, and a row of six niches which contain representations of the Order's saints.[43] This room, which seems to have been of restricted access to the public, was reserved for the daily chapter. Thus it would be appropriate to find scenes of missionary zeal and self-sacrifice in this private zone.[44]

[39] Ibid., p.856, no. 1.

[40] Interestingly, there is an early parallel with the Upper Church of St Francis at Assisi. Although dedicated to St Francis, it had the Apocalypse/St Michael, Virgin, and St Peter cycles in the transepts and apse, in addition to two Crucifixions. Although Franciscans appear in the south transept next to the throne where Mary sits with Christ, beneath the angels who swing censers before the altar, and Francis weeps at the foot of Christ crucified, St Francis played a minor role there initially. I am grateful to Julian Gardner for bringing the following to my attention.

[41] J. Moorman, *A History of the Franciscan Order from its Origins to the Year 1517* (Oxford, 1968), pp. 339–62.

[42] Orvieto Cathedral was having similar problems forbidding unauthorized persons putting up paintings without official permission, see J. Gardner, 'The Cappellone di San Nicola at Tolentino: Some functions of a fourteenth-century fresco cycle', in W. Tronzo, ed., *Italian Church Decoration of the Middle Ages and Early Renaissance. Functions, Forms and Regional Traditions* (Bologna, 1989), pp. 101–7, at p. 115.

[43] For a recent discussion of the paintings see F. d'Arcais, 'La presenza di Giotto al Santo', in Semenzato, ed., *Le Pitture*, pp. 3–13.

[44] For the function of this building and comparative material, cf. J. Gardner, 'Andrea

Devotional images of an ex-voto character are dispersed around the basilica and its cloisters. These usually consist of an enthroned Madonna and Child, flanked by Franciscan saints who present the kneeling donors.[45] These painted lunettes were an essential feature of the hanging wall-tomb in the Veneto, and there are many parallels in Dominican and Augustinian churches.[46]

Elsewhere in the city a cycle depicting the life of St Louis of Toulouse was commissioned in Padua towards the end of the fourteenth century. It may come as a surprise to find that its original location was the church of S. Benedetto, a female Benedictine foundation. What seems to be an odd location at first makes perfect sense once we learn that the patron, Fina Buzzacarini, who was specially devoted to Louis of Toulouse, chose to patronize the nunnery in which her sister Anna was abbess.[47]

The case of the Basilica del Santo is not a *unicum*. Neighbouring Franciscan churches either show the same disregard for Franciscan images, and opt for decoration that appears to be dictated by the patrons' or artists' fancy.[48] Guglielmo Castelbarco (d. 1320) key patron in the building and initial decoration of S. Fermo Maggiore, Verona, presents a model of his church. But kneeling on the right side of the triumphal arch of this Franciscan church, he has usurped the rightful place of the Virgin Annunciate, who is now relegated to the back of the choir.

The friars of Padua, whether actively involved in image-making or contemplatively inactive, none the less gave artists and patrons the opportunity to express their devotion and pride in visual terms. Their role in the development of painting in Italy during the fourteenth century cannot be

Bonauito and the chapterhouse frescoes in Santa Maria Novella', *Art History*, 2 (1979), pp. 107–38.

45 Examples include the Conti family tomb in the Belludi chapel and the Lavellongo and Vigonza tombs in the vestibule off the south door.

46 The tombs of Ubertino and Jacopo Carrara in the Eremitani church in Padua are two outside examples.

47 The paintings were destroyed during the Second World War: S. Bettini, *Giusto de'Menabuoi e l'arte del Trecento* (Padua, 1944), p. 138.

48 Santa Maria Gloriosa dei Frari, Venice, and S. Francesco, Treviso, never seem to have had cycles of painting. Both churches of S. Francesco, at Udine and Cividale, show no unified programme; the same goes for S. Francesco, Mantua. The upper church of S. Fermo Maggiore is the exception, with cycles narrating the life of St Francis and St Louis of Toulouse. This seems to have been the product of collected efforts by the guardian, Fra Daniele Gusmerio, and a layman, Guglielmo Castelbarco.

undermined. Thus it could be said that the Order continued to walk in Francis' footsteps as he, in thought at least, always leapt from one picture to the next.[49]

University of Aberdeen

[49] Lambert, *Franciscan Poverty*, p. 33.

PATRONS AND MINDERS: THE INTRUSION OF THE SECULAR INTO SACRED SPACES IN THE LATE MIDDLE AGES

by ANDREW MARTINDALE

FROM the twelfth century onwards it became common for sacred spaces—that is, churches—to be invaded by objects and imagery which are often surprising and bizarre and which, in their secularity, have little to do with the fundamental teachings of Christianity. Many of these objects are familiar, some less familiar; and the topic seems appropriate for a 'generalist' audience of ecclesiastical history specialists. It should be said at once that this secularity seems to reach a peak around the middle of the fourteenth century, to be followed by a slow and somewhat irregular retreat; but since the entire sequence of events is accompanied by an almost complete silence in the written sources, the reasons for what was happening remain largely speculative. I shall return to this point.

Perhaps the best way into the problem is to state the orthodox view about the significance of the fabric of a church building. There are several texts which inform us about this, one of the most explicit being a passage from the book called *De diversis artibus*, written about 1140 by a monk called Theophilus.[1] The treatise is divided into three parts; and at the end of the preface to book iii Theophilus takes by the hand the apprentice, whom in his imagination he is instructing, and leads him into the church which together they are embellishing. This is what he says:

> Animated, dearest son, by these supporting virtues, you have approached the House of God with confidence and have adorned it with so much beauty; you have embellished the ceilings and walls with varied work in different colours and have, in some measure, shown to beholders the paradise of God.... For the human eye is not able to consider on what work first to fix its gaze; if it beholds the ceilings they glow like brocades; if it considers the walls they are a kind of paradise; if it regards the profusion of light from the windows, it marvels at the inestimable beauty of the glass and the

[1] See *Theophilus, De diversis artibus*, ed. C. R. Dodwell (London, 1961), pp. 63–4, for the passage quoted. There is some consensus that 'Theophilus' was the pen-name for a monastic goldsmith called Roger of Helmershausen.

> infinitely rich and various workmanship. But if, perchance, the faithful soul observes the representation of the Lord's Passion, it is stung by compassion. If it sees how many torments the saints endured in their bodies and what rewards of eternal life they have received, it eagerly embraces the observance of a better life. If it beholds how great are the joys of heaven and how great the torments in the infernal flames, it is animated by the hope of its good deeds and is shaken with fear by reflection on its sins.

Theophilus twice uses the word 'paradise'; and he is describing what he sees as a visionary experience in which anyone who goes into a church is lifted up to a clearer perception of the truths of the Christian faith. The fabric of the building and its embellishment become the metaphors for the institution and what it stands for; the building of the church becomes also a glimpse of heaven.

Theophilus was representative of the 'orthodox' approach to the significance of a church building. There is no reason to doubt that the silent contemplation of a Theophilus-like church interior moved some to silent rapture—there is the experience recounted by Abbot Suger of how he was transported to a higher spiritual world by the contemplation of the jewels of Saint-Denis.[2] But for the less visionary, more prosaic—but nevertheless thoughtful—persons, there was a long stream of analytical writing stretching from Honorius of Autun, about 1150,[3] to William Durandus in the late thirteenth century.[4] This offered, in William's words, historic, allegoric, tropologic, and anagogic interpretations of almost everything visible. It really was not possible to stand in a church and look in any direction without finding some detail of architecture, some image or indeed some ceremony which did not inform one about the Church as an institution, of the means to salvation which she afforded, and of the vision of heaven beyond.

It is still possible to savour something of this approach. Naturally one is hampered by problems of survival; but visitors to the Sainte-Chapelle, Paris, can still experience an interior whose content, dating from the 1240s, would have been entirely congenial to Honorius and Theophilus a

[2] For the text of Suger see E. Panofsky, *Abbot Suger on the Abbey Church of St-Denis and Its Art Treasures*, 2nd edn (Princeton, 1979). This episode is to be found on pp. 64–5.

[3] See particularly the *Gemma animae*, *PL* 172, cols 541–738. The comments on the parts of the church are to be found in book i.

[4] Gullielmus Durandus, *Rationale seu enchyridion divinorum officiorum*, ed. B. de Locatellis (Lyons, 1512): see particularly book i, *De ecclesia et eius partibus*.

century earlier. Although the detailed complexities of this vast sculptural and pictorial display are hard to unravel, there is no doubt about its general implications. Entering by the west portal, Theophilus' 'beholder' is at once surrounded by stories from the Old Testament—the Creation, the Fall, Joshua and Exodus, Gideon and David. He proceeds 'through' the Old Testament towards the altar, which is dominated by the history of the redemption of mankind through the birth and Passion of Christ. This, in turn, is flanked by the stories of the two Saints John, the last prophet and the first witness; and by windows devoted to the prophecies of Isaiah, Jeremiah, and Ezekiel.[5] Round the walls against the vaulting shafts stand figures of the Twelve Apostles, a reminder of the observation of both Honorius and William that we should see in the columns of the church the great ecclesiastical leaders who sustain the Church.[6] In the spandrels of the arcading flutter angels; and in the quatrefoils are pictured the lives of saints.[7]

It is possible to savour the completeness of this experience, though stylistically in an entirely different way, in the Arena Chapel at Padua.[8] This was built and decorated about 1305, some sixty years after St Louis' Sainte-Chapelle. Here again the kernel of the message is the life and Passion of Christ, though here it is surrounded by the birth, death, and Assumption of the Virgin, to whom the chapel is dedicated. On the west wall is a vision of the Last Judgement; and lower down along the north and south walls are arranged the Virtues and Vices—to follow the words of Theophilus, the faithful soul is animated by the hope of its good deeds and shaken by reflection on its sins. The whole scheme is simpler than the one at Paris, but the building is much smaller; and although the Arena Chapel was also in some sense a palace chapel (it was adjacent to the palace of the Scrovegni family), it was also a parish church. Naturally not all parishioners can hope to have their churches painted by Giotto; but in its

[5] The iconography of the glass is described in M. Aubert, L. Grodecki, J. Lafond, and J. Verrier, *Les vitraux de Notre-Dame et de la Sainte Chapelle de Paris* (Paris, 1959).

[6] According to Honorius, *Gemma animae*, i, ch. 131, *De columnis ecclesiae*, the columns symbolized the bishops. Durandus, *Rationale*, i, ch. 27, likened them to bishops and doctors, expanding the theme thus: 'Bases columnarum sunt apostolici episcopi universalis ecclesiae machinam supportantes. Capita columnarum sunt mentes episcoporum et doctorum.' Suger thought of the main columns surrounding the high altar at Saint-Denis as the Twelve Apostles: Panofsky, *Abbot Suger*, pp. 104–5.

[7] On these see R. Branner, 'The painted medallions in the Sainte Chapelle in Paris', *Transactions of the American Philosophical Society*, 58, pt 2 (1968), pp. 3–42.

[8] For an account of the Arena Chapel, see J. White, *European Art and Architecture 1250–1400*, 2nd edn (Harmondsworth, 1987), pp. 309–32.

own way it illustrates the general point with which this paper began—that for those with ears to hear and eyes to see, a church in its building and decoration provided direct access to the experience, mystical and intellectual, of the great truths of the Christian faith and of the means to salvation. The building provided a commentary on the institution. It held out the vision and promise of heaven. This was—and indeed probably still is—a good orthodox viewpoint.

There was a problem which is not at all referred to by the writers already mentioned. Churches tended to become dumps—repositories of memories, associations, and, often, objects. This is indeed a common expectation today; and some of these objects, such as, for instance, the Hereford *mappa mundi*, will still offer perfectly proper theological messages which can be contained within the 'orthodox' framework. We are on less certain ground when it comes to John Calvin's throne exhibited in the cathedral of Geneva; or the sword of Henry V, which used to sit rather casually on the document presses in the muniment room of Westminster Abbey.[9] Today this type of intrusion is probably taken for granted, even though it is possible to see that the messages which these objects send out are almost entirely particular and retrospective and in no sense eschatological. In the Middle Ages, however, the view that these associations and objects might legitimately form a focus of attention in an ecclesiastical setting was new; and it is of some interest to pause and to ask what happened—and why?

From the purist's point of view, undoubtedly the most offensive intrusions stemmed from a desire to draw attention to particular family connections and to particular founders. That this was considered necessary and desirable had not always been the case. It is extremely unlikely that William the Pious, Duke of Aquitaine, was commemorated at Cluny, which he founded in 910.[10] Rather more is known about the arrangements at Speyer Cathedral, which was rebuilt by Conrad II and Henry IV during the course of the eleventh century.[11] They certainly regarded it as the burial-place of their own family; and it is still possible to see in the twentieth-century *Kaisergruft* the resting-places of Conrad and his wife, Gisela, of Henry III, of Henry IV and his wife, Bertha, and of Henry V. Yet in the eleventh century, the bodies were laid out in the space

[9] It has now regrettably been tidied away into the museum in the Undercroft.

[10] He appears to have died and been buried at St Julien de Brioude. See M. Marrier, *Biblioteca Cluniacensis* (Macon, 1614, repr. 1915), col. 1617.

[11] See H. E. Kubach and W. Haas, *Der Dom zu Speyer* (Munich, 1972). Textband, pp. 923ff. for the Salian burials.

immediately before the nave altar and the choir.[12] They appear to have had no monuments, unless indeed the inscribed tops of their sarcophagi served as such. There are many detailed uncertainties here. The early medieval churches at Cluny have been destroyed; and Speyer Cathedral was disastrously mutilated by the armies of Louis XIV in 1689. It seems clear, however, that in the early Middle Ages, and certainly in the tenth and eleventh centuries, 'commemoration' meant not monuments and material embellishments but prayers, anniversaries, and obits; and this comes in strong contrast to the position reached by the sixteenth century.

The church at Brou (plate 1) provides a dramatic illustration of this point. Brou was founded as a house of Augustinians from Lombardy in 1506 by Margaret of Austria, daughter of the Emperor Maximilian.[13] She was the widow of Philibert le Beau of Savoy, who had died prematurely in

Plate 1 Brou, Church of St Nicholas of Tolentino, view of choir (photo: Author).

[12] Ibid., p. 925. The original position of the burials is reasonably clear from excavations. The six Salian burials were all in stone sarcophagi. Although the original floor level is not completely clear, the authors concluded that the sarcophagi were sunk in the floor 'zum Teil herausragend, zum Teil bundig legend.'

[13] V. Nodet, *L'église de Brou* (Paris, n.d.); F. Baudron, *Brou, l'église et le monastère* (Paris, 1951).

1504. The church was built and embellished between 1506 and 1532; and it is instantly apparent that by this date the sufficiency of verbal commemoration in the course of the conventual liturgy had been replaced by an approach which was materially far more ostentatious and possessive.

The choir at Brou contains three enormous and magnificent monuments. Philibert, the dead husband, lies in the centre. His mother, Margaret of Bourbon, Duchess of Savoy, lies on the south; Margaret of Austria herself lies on the north. These monuments dominate the centre of the conventual choir; and heraldry and inscription proclaim the identity of their subjects. They are, however, surrounded by an extraordinarily dense concentration of reminders of the lineage of Margaret and her late husband. Margaret's grandfather on her mother's side was Charles the Bold of Burgundy; and the *batons noueux* of Burgundy feature prominently in the carved decoration. But the most eye-catching reminders of the earthly status of Margaret and Philibert lie in the east windows. Of the five windows, four are almost entirely devoted to the heraldic celebration of their genealogical descent.[14] Shields for the more remote ancestors (such as St Louis) are ranged along the top, the more recent marriage alliances being found along the bottom. It is extremely splendid.

This symbolic presence of the founding families was not, however, the end of the story. Margaret's own personal presence was intended to be felt. This was not limited to the frequent appearance of her motto 'Fortune, Infortune, Forte Une' and to the pervasive presence of marguerites. She made architectural arrangements to enable her to attend the liturgical celebrations in the choir at Brou at her will and pleasure. The *pulpitum* at Brou is not what it seems. Customarily in the Middle Ages it was a singing gallery where the well-endowed might expect to place an organ. At Brou it forms part of an overhead passageway leading from lodgings on the south side of the church via the south transept to a two-storeyed oratory on the north side of the church—each storey being complete with seating and a fireplace, and from each of which it is possible to see the place where the high altar was set. Sadly Margaret never visited her foundation—the latter part of her life was spent as regent of the Netherlands, first for her

[14] See *Corpus vitrearum. France—Recensement III. Les vitraux de Bourgogne, Franche-Comté et Rhône-Alpes* (Paris, 1986), pp. 247–53, for an account of the glazing at Brou and a bibliography. The heraldry emphasizes particularly the ruling houses of France, Austria, Bohemia, Bavaria, Savoy, and Burgundy; also the family of Bourbon.

father, Maximilian, and then for her nephew Charles V. However, had she ever again become resident at Brou, the conventual devotions would in a very direct sense have been under her supervision.

The imagery of Brou is by no means exclusively dynastic and personal. The choir-stalls are decorated with Old and New Testament figures and reliefs. There are stained-glass representations of the post-Resurrection appearances of Christ and also of the Assumption of the Virgin. The chapel next to Margaret's oratories has a magnificent stone retable dedicated to scenes from the life of the Virgin. The pervasive heraldry and emblems, however, remain coupled touchingly with the repetition of the initials 'P' and 'M'. At Brou one is left with the strongest possible sense of personal commemoration, personal ownership, and, indeed, personal memories. It requires something of an effort of will in this sort of setting to say the psalm which begins 'Non nobis, Domine . . .'.

The idea that a church might be a parade-ground for displays which had little to do with the salvation of mankind or the celestial vision is indeed considerably older than Brou. What is perhaps surprising is that it appears initially to have been given considerable impetus by developments originating within the church establishment. A religious house might indeed belong to God; but it was a practice of the very greatest antiquity to believe that it also belonged to its saint—for instance, to Edmund, Martial, or Mark. In the twelfth century, however, there appears a development by which almost any distinguished layman connected with the history of the establishment might be given a monument—starting naturally with the supposed founder. In plotting this development, one is greatly hindered by the enormous destructions on the Continent. In England, however, where these objects tend to survive more completely than elsewhere, there is a strong impression that most abbeys by the time of the Dissolution had on display a founder's monument. Malmesbury still has a fifteenth-century monument to King Athelstan (tenth century). Gloucester has a sixteenth-century monument to King Osric (seventh century). Tewkesbury has a late fourteenth-century monument to Robert Fitzhamon (d. 1107). Westminster has an early fourteenth-century monument to Sæbert, King of the East Saxons (seventh century). Glastonbury, of course, had King Arthur and Queen Guinevere, translated to a new monument before the high altar in the reign of Edward I.

It will be remembered, however, that curiosity about Arthur began in 1172, during a visit from Henry II, and that the bodies were first moved into the church from the graveyard in the reign of Richard I.[15] However, one of the most striking English examples of this retrospection is even earlier; for in 1158, Bishop Henry of Blois collected together all the bones of the pre-Conquest kings and bishops buried in the cathedral and deposited them in six chests, which he set round the monastic choir. Though they have had a hard history, boxes and bones are apparently still there, now hidden within new chests provided by Bishop Fox in the early sixteenth century (plate 2).[16]

It would be convenient to assume that in the twelfth century this historical and retrospective attitude was an English preoccupation. Certainly the interest in history, curiosities, antiquities, and people finds an answering resonance in the writings of Geoffrey of Monmouth, William of Malmesbury, and Gerald of Wales. Yet already, about 1160–70, there were monuments in the abbey of St Germain des Près, in Paris, to Childebert (d. 558), Chilperic (d. 584), and to Fredegund (d. 596);[17] and one of the strangest of these monuments was that in the church of St Pharaon at Meaux to Ogier the Dane (plate 3). From its appearance, this seems to have been made about 1180.[18] Ogier was a fictitious companion of Charlemagne whose legend appears around this time. At the end of an eventful life, he was supposed to have returned to the north of France with his companion, Benedict, to seek a monastery to which they might both retire. The legend recounts how he chose St Pharaon because he was impressed by the attentiveness of the monks at their devotions. Unfortunately the tomb was totally destroyed at the French Revolution; but earlier accounts also show that the sword of Ogier was displayed to interested viewers.[19]

[15] It is generally supposed that the first exhumation of Arthur and Guinevere happened in 1172, during Henry II's return from Ireland. The main twelfth-century source for the whole history is Gerald of Wales, who described in detail the second exhumation in 1190 or 1191. On the problem of the dating and significance of these episodes see R. Barber, *The Figure of Arthur* (London, 1972), pp. 126–33.

[16] See A. Martindale, *Heroes, Ancestors, Relatives and the Birth of the Portrait* (The Hague, 1988), p. 13, for an account of the Winchester chests and a bibliography.

[17] See A. Erlande-Brandenburg, *Le roi est mort* (Paris, 1975), pp. 135–40.

[18] On the surviving sculpture see W. Sauerländer, *Gothic Sculpture in France 1140–1270* (London, 1972), pp. 396–7. On the legend of Ogier, see J. Bédier, *Les légendes épiques. Recherches sur la formation des Chansons de Gestes* (Paris, 1917), pp. 297ff.

[19] Ibid. The sword is already mentioned in the twelfth century. By the time of Montaigne, Benedict's sword was also on display. For a complete account, see D. Toussaints du Plessis, *Histoire de l'église de Meaux*, 2 vols (Paris, 1731), 1, ch. 88. By that date, both swords—one large and one small—were in the treasury, the monument itself being decorated with painted representations. Other swords are still visible, notably that of Roland at Roccamadour; and that of S. Galgano at the monastery of that name (near Siena). The sword and shield

[*cont. on p. 152*]

Plate 2 Winchester Cathedral, choir screen, showing the chests containing the bones of the pre-Conquest kings, queens, and bishops formerly interred in the cathedral (photo: Author).

Plate 3 Tomb of Ogier the Dane, formerly in the Abbey Church of St Pharon, Meaux (destroyed at the French Revolution).

From this it is clear that already by 1200 many ecclesiastical institutions were enriching their churches with reminders of a secular past. The tendency gathered momentum. Around 1220–30, the church of Ste Geneviève, Paris, installed an effigy to Clovis (d. 511);[20] and probably the most famous and complete of all these operations was the mass reorganization of the Merovingian and Carolingian tombs in Saint-Denis during the 1260s, during which a very large number of retrospective monuments was produced.[21] However, as can be seen in the case of Naumburg, these commemorations did not always take that form. The west choir at Naum-

supposedly carried before Edward III during his French campaigns and still on view in Westminster Abbey (see J. Dart, *Westmonasterium, or the History and Antiquities of the Abbey Church of St Peters Westminster*, 2 vols (London, 1742), I, p. 42) belong to the same general family.

20 See Sauerländer, *Gothic Sculpture*, p. 460.

21 Erlande-Brandenburg, *Le roi est mort*, pp. 81–3.

burg was built during the 1240s.[22] It is therefore contemporary with the Sainte-Chapelle at Paris. Here, too, the shafts supporting the vaults are decorated with standing figures. Yet whereas at the Sainte-Chapelle the patron adopted the orthodox approach and the chapel is apparently sustained by the figures of Apostles, the Naumburg figures are secular; and it may with some confidence be said that they are members of the family of the Counts of Meissen, who were instrumental in establishing the see at Naumburg in the early eleventh century. Here, therefore, it seems that the secular world has taken over the job of the Apostles or bishops; and it certainly dominates all activity in the choir.

Cathedrals, it must be said, on the whole avoided this sort of secular tagging—and for obvious reasons. It is rare that a cathedral can be said to have a founder, except in the sense of its first bishop; and on the whole it was the canonical successors of that first bishop who remained the visible lords of the establishment. Where the secular world is much in evidence, there is normally some special reason to do with the circumstances in which the see came into existence. Thus the west choir of Naumburg belongs to the family which procured the removal of the see from Zeitz to Naumburg in 1028 and became in a perfectly acceptable sense its *primi fundatores*. In a less aggressive way, the cathedral at Bamberg displays figures almost certainly of Henry II and Queen Kunigunde, who founded the see in 1007.[23] Palermo Cathedral was once dominated on its south-east side by a series of monuments which branded it a Norman and Staufen building.[24] Prague Cathedral, promoted to metropolitan status in 1342 under Charles IV, is still very much a Luxembourg building.[25] But, for the most part, cathedrals remained the preserve principally of bishops; and it

22 See W. Sauerländer, 'Die Naumberger Stifterfiguren: Rückblick und Fragen', in R. Hausherr and C. Väterlein, eds, *Die Zeit der Staufer*, 5 vols (Stuttgart, 1977), 5, pp. 169–245.

23 Queen Kunigunde had been canonized in 1201. For the figures on the Adam Portal, see J. Baum, *German Cathedrals* (London, 1956), pp. 20–2 and plates 47–50.

24 See J. Deér, *The Dynastic Porphyry Tombs of the Norman Period in Sicily* (Cambridge, Mass., 1959), pp. 86–9.

25 The rebuilding of Prague Cathedral (up to the east wall of the transepts) lasted from 1344 to 1385. The eastern chapels contain the posthumous memorials to six Premyslid ancestors of Charles's mother, Elizabeth (commissioned in 1376–7). Charles himself features as a painted donor figure in the chapel of St Wenceslas. The triforium gallery contains twenty-one busts, including Charles himself, his mother and father, his four wives, his two brothers, and his son and daughter-in-law. Doubtless the medieval glass, of which none survives, would have contained its due quota of late fourteenth-century heraldry. On the style of the building, see E. Bachmann and H. Bachmann, in K. Swoboda, ed., *Gotik in Böhmen* (Munich, 1969), respectively pp. 99–102 and pp. 124–7. For a comprehensive photographic record and further discussion, see A. Legner, ed., *Die Parler und der schöne Stil 1350–1400* (catalogue), 4 vols (Cologne, 1978–80), 2, pp. 650–3, 655–62.

is of episcopal monuments that one is most conscious in churches such as Lincoln, Salisbury, or Exeter.[26]

The developments of which Brou represents an advanced stage had begun already in the eleventh century, being a convergence of a number of different elements. Fundamental was the apparent belief that for the great men of secular society, burial-places were a matter for private choice; and that the most efficacious way of facing one's future in the hereafter was to enlist and to pay for one's own body of monks or canons. This point of view was clearly reinforced by the formulation of the doctrine of Purgatory; but both Speyer and the two great Norman abbeys at Caen testify to its currency in the eleventh century. The somewhat unpredictable nature of these choices is well exemplified in the case of the post-Conquest kings of England. Henry I was buried at Reading, Stephen at Faversham, Henry II and Richard I at Fontevrault, John at Worcester. Moreover, even at their most extensive, these burial churches were seldom seen as more than the focus of tiny family groupings. Westminster Abbey was initially the burial-place of Henry III, his son Edward and daughter-in-law Eleanor of Castile, and of his half-brother's family, the de Valences.[27] St Louis' foundation at Royaumont seems to have been intended to fulfil a similar function, even though Louis himself was eventually buried in Saint-Denis.[28] Margaret of Austria's foundation at Brou for herself, her husband, and her mother-in-law follows the same pattern. The virtues of individuality were in a sense built into the system.

Not surprisingly, it was on the quasi-private institutions that the presence of the secular world was most firmly imprinted. Already in the twelfth century, there was a feeling that mortal remains should receive monuments as well as prayers—as indeed has been seen in the case of Ogier the Dane; and, to shorten a complicated story, by the second half of the thirteenth century there was almost universal agreement throughout

[26] It should not be supposed that bishops in their patronage remained faceless office-holders. The choir vaults of Norwich Cathedral are extensively decorated on all the principal bosses with golden wells (they were built by Bishop Goldwell, 1472–99); and the nave vaults are supported on corbels showing a recumbent deer (they were built by Bishop Lyhart, 1445–72).

[27] William de Valence (d. 1296) was the half-brother of Henry III through Isabella of Angoulême. William had three children—John, Margaret, and Aymer—all of whom were originally buried in the circle of the presbytery. William's monument was subsequently moved out into the chapel of St Edmnd.

[28] See H. Goüin, *L'abbaye de Royaumont* (Paris, 1967). Louis' brother Philippe 'Dagobert' (d. 1235), his daughter Blanche (died in infancy, 1243), his son Jean (died, also in infancy, 1248) and his eldest son and heir Louis (d. 1260) were all buried at Royaumont. The process by which Louis himself was attracted towards burial at Saint-Denis is not clear.

Europe that human remains were most fittingly commemorated by a recumbent figure of the dead person.[29] The aim was almost certainly to suggest the continued presence of the person in question; and, by way of example, the Angevin monuments at Fontevrault do exactly this in an astonishingly casual and immediate way. We are apparently asked to believe that the dead people have just been carried on their beds into the church. Moreover, there must be some doubt whether they are indeed dead, since Eleanor of Aquitaine is reading a book (plate 4).[30]

It was not very long before this direct form of reminder also appears to have been thought insufficient. The question left unanswered seems to have been not so much 'Who was this person?' as 'What was this person?' Most of the major monuments of the later Middle Ages aim to supply this information. One means was heraldry—as in the stained glass of Brou. In many cases, however, these relationships were personified in the form of small figures now generically called 'weeper figures'. The term is misleading in that the notional relations never weep or show signs of sorrow. More commonly they strike graceful, even debonnaire, poses and are very smartly dressed (plate 5).[31] On the more elaborate monuments they would originally have been identifiable, either by coats of arms or inscriptions or both.

[29] By far the most comprehensive treatment of European tombs is K. Bauch, *Das mittelalterliche Grabbild. Figürliche Grabmäler des 11. bis 15 Jahrhunderts in Europa* (Berlin and New York, 1976). For an interesting examination of sepulchral effigies, their types and implications, see G. Schmidt, 'Die gotischen "gisants" und ihr Umfeld — Überlegungen zum Wirklichkeitsbezug spätmittelalterlicher Grabmäler', *Kunsthistoriker*, 4 (1987), pp. 65–72: and subsequently in *Skulptur und Grabmal des Spätmittelalters in Rom und Italien*, ed. J. Garmes and A. M. Romanini (Vienna, 1990), pp. 13–82; 'Typen und Bildmotive des Spätmittelalterlichen Monumentalgrabes', in which the author surveys (on a European scale) the typology of tombs and monuments.

[30] On the Angevin monuments, see Sauerländer, *Gothic Sculpture*, pp. 448–9. The effigies are dated by Sauerländer to the early thirteenth century. They belong to a very restricted group of effigies confined to the west of France. For other examples, see A. Martindale, 'The Knight on the bed of stones; a learned confusion of the fourteenth century?' *Journal of the British Archaeological Association*, 142 (1989), pp. 66–74; esp. p. 74, n. 26. To those effigies should be added that of Bishop Peter of Poitiers (d. 1135), formerly also at Fontevrault, but now known only in the water-colour of Gaignières (Oxford, Bodleian Library, Gough MSS, Gaignières, 14, fol. 230r). The monument from this group which survives *in situ* at Montbron still has in position under the effigy a 'leg', which increases the bedlike effect.

[31] The outstanding monument in this respect is that of John of Eltham, the brother of Edward III, who died in mysterious circumstances at Perth in 1337 and was buried at Westminster. The monument was originally set in the circle of the presbytery but seems to have been moved to make way for the tomb of Philippa of Hainault. Although much mutilated (it lost its canopy in the eighteenth century) the 'weeper' figures—all crowned and therefore notionally royal—are particularly attractive and striking in their costume and poses. The shields beneath them, now blank, would originally have been emblazoned.

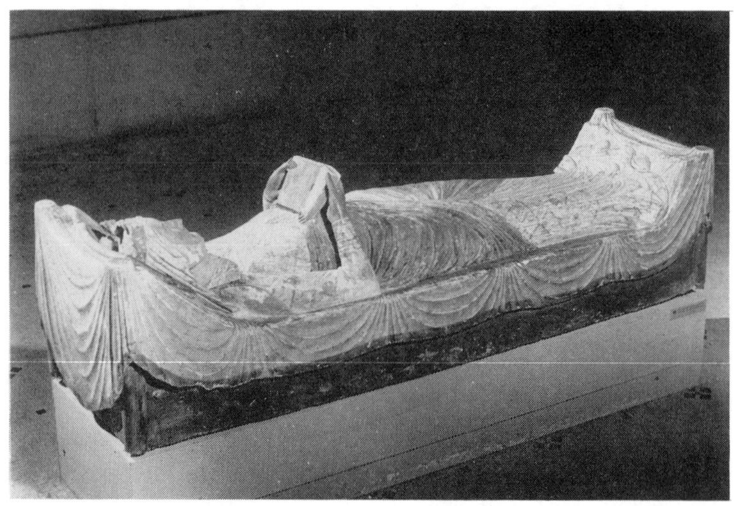

Plate 4 Effigy of Eleanor of Aquitaine, Abbey Church of Fontevrault (photo: Author).

Plate 5 Tomb of John of Eltham and Elevation of Tomb-chest (London, Westminster Abbey) (photo: Author).

One of the earliest monuments[32] to show what was possible was the tomb of Marie de Bourbon, Countess of Dreux (plates 6 and 7). It was formerly in the church of St Yved de Braine (near Rheims), the burial-place of the counts of Dreux and dukes of Brittany. Much of the church survives, but nothing remains of the numerous monuments, except what is recorded in the eighteenth-century water-colours of Robert Gaignières.[33] Marie de Bourbon appears to have had a tomb covered with copper plates. Round the base of her effigy were thirty-six figures, modelled in the copper and identified by inscription and also by heraldry (the colouring probably rendered in enamel). The genealogical links are of the most aristocratic and distinguished sort, embracing the kings of France, Sicily, and Navarre, and the dukes of Burgundy and Lorraine.

The tomb of Philippa of Hainault at Westminster once provided another elaborate display of family relationships. Erected in 1365–7 by the French court sculptor Jean de Liège, it presumably reflects the continental aristocratic practices already seen in the earlier monument to Marie de Bourbon. In the original figure programme,[34] Philippa's (continental) relations were ranged down the south side, her husband Edward's down the north. Five kings were set at her feet; and at her head were her husband, Edward; her eldest son, Edward the Black Prince, her father, William of Holland, her brother-in-law, the Emperor Louis of Bavaria, and King John of France.

One of the most elaborate monuments of this kind was that of Pope Clement VI at La Chaise-Dieu, in the Auvergne. Pierre Roger, it will be recalled, had entered the monastic order as a boy at La Chaise-Dieu; and after he became pope, in 1342, he demonstrated his affection for his mother house by, in effect, refounding it and rebuilding it.[35] Even today

[32] The enormous gaps in the evidence must again be stressed. Little is known about the iconography of the monuments of Philip Augustus, Louis VIII, and Louis IX (formerly in Saint-Denis); and the surviving monument of Henry III (Westminster Abbey) is in this context so eccentric as to be useless. For the Saint-Denis evidence see Erlande-Brandenburg, *Le roi est mort*, *passim*. An interesting monument to Thibaud III of Champagne (d. 1201, formerly in St Etienne, Troyes) is discussed by M. Bur, 'Les Comtes de Champagne et la "Normanitas"; sémiologie d'un tombeau', in R. Allen Brown, ed., *Proceedings of the Battle Conference of Anglo-Norman Studies*, 3 (1980), pp. 22–32. The sarcophagus was decorated with an arcade containing ten silver figures which in 1704 were still identifiable as members of the comital family. However, the question must arise whether this tomb was really datable to the early thirteenth century. Unfortunately there is no picture of it.

[33] Oxford, Bodleian Library, MS Gough Drawings, Gaignières, 1, fols 78, 79, 80.

[34] The original figure programme is given in Dart, *Westmonasterium*, 1, p. 41.

[35] On Clement VI, see D. Wood, *Clement VI. The Pontificate and Ideas of an Avignon Pope* (Cambridge, 1989), pp. 62–3.

TOMBEAU de cuivre esmaillé a costé droit du choeur de
l'Eglise de l'abbaye St Jued de Braine posé par moitié
en dedans du choeur, moitié en dehors, il est de MARIE
de BOURBON femme de JEAN I du nom Comte de Dreux
& de Braine, il est environné de petites figures, de tous ses
parens, dans des niches, & au dessus de chacune estoient
leurs armes dont il en reste encor quelques unes, & sur
les bords du tombeau leurs noms escrits en or, sur des

Plate 6 Tomb of Marie de Bourbon, formerly in the Church of St Yved de Braine (destroyed at the French Revolution). From the drawings of Robert Gaignières, now in Oxford, Bodleian Library, MS Gough Drawings, Gaignières 1, fol. 78.

Plate 7 Tomb of Marie de Bourbon, side elevation. From the drawings of Robert Gaignières, Oxford, Bodleian Library, MS Gough Drawings, Gaignières 1, fol. 79.

the visitor is greeted at every turn in church and cloister by Clement's arms; but the focus of this attention was certainly Clement's tomb in the centre of the monastic choir. The surviving monument is a mere fragment, having been the subject of a disastrous attack by the Huguenots in 1562. In particular, the side decoration, which would have resembled rather distantly that of the tomb of Philippa, has been reduced to a few detached fragments. However, it is known that originally there were forty-three figures round the sides, mainly representing Clement's close relatives.[36] Thus there were two uncles, one brother, one sister, seven

[36] The programme of figures is given in P.-R. Gaussin, *L'abbaye de la Chaise-Dieu 1043–1518* (Paris, 1962), pp. 431–2, n. 111. For the surviving fragments of figure sculpture, see F. Baron

nephews, nine nieces, five cousins, and a number of other persons married respectively to the nephews, nieces, and cousins. It is perhaps unnecessary to add that few of these people had remained 'nobodies' under Clement. Four were cardinals (one was the future Gregory XI), five were archbishops, nine were bishops. The secular world was also well represented by relatives who were lords in the area south of Limoges, whence Pierre Roger had originally come—Turenne, Ventadour, Chambon, and Comborn.

In selecting the relatives, the patron had various issues to address. One was the extent to which his or her choice should suggest territorial ramifications. Philippa's choice of weeper figures implied the presence of a greater Europe which should please even the most exacting Europeanists. The other obvious dimension was the chronological one. An interesting example of a monument devoted apparently entirely to ancestors still dominates the choir of the castle chapel of Neuchâtel, now in western Switzerland (plate 8). An inscription gives the date 1372 and announces that the monument was set up by Count Louis of Neuchâtel in memory of his family. It is, in fact, a very strange, composite affair, bringing together material of different fourteenth-century dates.[37] Although the paintwork is untrustworthy, the six male figures, if indeed retrospective, would take the family tree back into the twelfth century.

There is an example of this line of thought in England in the Benedictine abbey of Tewkesbury. Refounded in 1102 by Robert Fitzhamon, the abbey became closely associated with the Earldom of Gloucester and Tewkesbury Castle. In the early thirteenth century these had come by marriage to the de Clare family; and in the early fourteenth century the principal heiress was Eleanor de Clare, who married successively Hugh Despenser and William de la Zouche, dying in 1337. This abbreviated genealogy and attenuated history is necessary as a background to the stained glass still in the choir clerestorey of the abbey church. For in the windows overlooking the monks' choir, eight lights are devoted not to saints, but to Eleanor's two husbands and to her ancestors (plate 9);

---

in the exhibition catalogue *Les Fastes du Gothique* (Paris, 1981), item 47, pp. 101–2. Mlle Baron noted two fragments in Le Puy and a further two fragments (not illustrated) both still at La Chaise-Dieu. All four fragments were exhibited in (and illustrated in the catalogue of) the exhibition of Dijon in 1971. See P. Quarré, *Les Pleurants dans l'art du moyen âge en Europe* (Dijon, 1971), pp. 30–1 and plates VIII–IX.

[37] For a consideration of the monument, with bibliography, see Martindale, *Heroes*, p. 16.

Plate 8 Monument to the Family of Louis of Neuchâtel (Neuchâtel, Collégiale) (photo: Author).

Plate 9 One of the two windows commemorating the husbands and ancestors of Eleanor de Clare, Tewkesbury Abbey (photo: Author).

moreover, the six ancestors take the viewer back through two centuries to the foundation of the abbey.[38]

An alternative to the prospect of the past was the promise of the future—in the form of children. It might be supposed that as a theme this would be simple to interpret, but in practice this is not the case. Perhaps the earliest surviving monument with this particular emphasis is that of Edward III at Westminster (plate 10).[39] Edward died in 1377, but the monument seems only to have been completed some ten years later. There is no means of knowing how far the quirky, slightly morbid programme represents the old King's wishes. His twelve children were all shown, and six of the images survive, identified by heraldic shields. It will be instantly clear that they are raised up round the dead King as if they were all present and in full maturity. In fact, of the twelve, eight were already dead, two in infancy many years before. If Neuchâtel and Tewkesbury salute the past, it would be less than accurate to see this monument as saluting the future, though it may perhaps salute the fecundity of Philippa, who lies next door. The theme of 'children' was picked up in a less doleful way in the splendid tomb of Richard Beauchamp, Earl of Warwick—a monument which still survives in its chapel attached to the parish church. Beauchamp died in 1439; and his tomb with its extensive use of bronze was certainly influenced by the royal monuments at Westminster. The 'weepers' are identified by heraldic shields;[40] and they bring before us almost exclusively Richard's daughters by his own two marriages, together with their respective husbands. The theme of 'children' had, of course, a very long run, cropping up repeatedly on rather dismal late medieval brasses and Jacobethan monuments.

One final theme may be mentioned. It was also possible to move right away from the family and represent friends and associates. This was much less common but seems to be the message of the brass of Sir Hugh

[38] Martindale, *Heroes*, pp. 16–19.

[39] The names of the figures are given in Dart, *Westmonasterium*, p. 42. There is some reason to question the exact sequence of the original figures. The origins of this idea are likely to lie earlier. There were, for instance, standing statues of six of Louis IX's chidren set against the wall of the north choir aisle of the convent of Poissy. The only record of them is now a water-colour of Gaignières: Oxford, Bodleian Library, MS Gough Drawings, Gaignières, 2, fol. 31. Gaignières gave their names as Louis, Philippe, Jean, Ysabeau, Pierre, and Robert. The date of the sculptures and the logic of the choice are not entirely clear; but the figures were ranged almost chronologically, and the eldest, Louis, was perceptibly larger in size than the youngest, Robert.

[40] The details are given in W. Dugdale, *The Antiquities of Warwickshire Illustrated* (London, 1656), pp. 328–9.

Plate 10 Tomb of Edward III (London, Westminster Abbey) (photo: Author).

Hastings, who died in 1347. He still lies in the chancel of Elsing parish church (Norfolk), where his resting-place is marked by the fragments of one of the most sumptuous fourteenth-century brasses. Around his effigy were originally eight figures, of which five survive. All are in armour. None has any obvious family connection with Sir Hugh, and one is indeed King Edward III.[41] It seems likely, therefore, that Sir Hugh is here associated in death with companions-in-arms during the French wars.

The idea that churches might be places in which one celebrated and in a real sense exhibited one's family and associates had a long history; and this part of the essay may be concluded by noting two further outstanding sixteenth-century examples of the genre. One is a remarkable survival at Champigny-sur-Veude (near Saumur, south of the river Loire). Built by Louis I and II de Bourbon in the first half of the century, it still has its original glass of about 1555–60.[42] The windows contain three themes. The first is the Passion—the chapel is dedicated to the Holy Cross. The second is St Louis of France—the Bourbon family were descended from him. The third running round the lower part of the windows is the descent of the houses of Bourbon, Montpensier, Vendôme, and La Roche-sur-Yon. The ancestors of the sixteenth-century Bourbons were paired off, two-by-two, on either side of the church (plate 11); and in the east window, beneath the Crucifixion, stand St Louis and Margaret of Provence. This whole parade is in what might be called the High Medieval tradition and is reminiscent of the glass at Tewkesbury or the sculpture at Neuchâtel; though the aim of the genealogy is much more sharply focused—on St Louis.

The other sixteenth-century monument showing similar aspirations is the visionary memorial to the Emperor Maximilian at Innsbruck—'visionary' because much of it never existed, except in Maximilian's mind; and because what was completed came into existence in advance of any building to put it in.[43] In the absence of a building, Maximilian himself, when he died in 1519, was buried at Wiener Neustadt, and the Innsbruck monument remains a cenotaph. The tomb was intended to be surrounded by forty life-size, bronze figures. Of these, twenty-eight were eventually

[41] The surviving companions of Sir Hugh have been identified as Edward III, Thomas Beauchamp, Earl of Warwick, Henry, Earl of Lancaster, Ralph Lord Stafford, and Almeric Lord St Amand.

[42] See *Corpus Vitrearum. France—Recensement II. Les vitraux du centre et des pays de la Loire* (Paris, 1981), pp. 103–8, for description and bibliography.

[43] See V. Oberhammer, *Die Bronzestandbilder des Maximiliangrabmales in der Hofkirche zu Innsbruck* (Innsbruck, Vienna, and Munich, 1935).

Plate 11 Window from series commemorating the Life of Christ, the Life of St Louis, and the Lineage of the Bourbon Family. Visible, top to bottom, are the Road to Emmaus, the Battle of Mansourah, and Louis de Bourbon, Anne de Laval, Jean II de Bourbon, and Ysabeau de Beauvau (photo: Author).

completed. Of the twenty-eight, twenty-three represent the families of Maximilian and his wife, Margaret of Burgundy. Most of them are indeed Habsburgs, the earliest being the early thirteenth-century Count Albrecht. The late thirteenth-century emperor Rudolf is, of course, present. Beyond the family and kin, however, Maximilian's companions in death present an arresting appearance. They include Leopold the Saint, a twelfth-century margrave of Austria; Godfrey of Bouillon; Theodoric the Ostrogoth; Clovis; and Arthur. Other figures such as Julius Caesar, Charlemagne, and St Stephen of Hungary were intended to join them; and the whole group would have had something of the flavour of the upper reaches of the Luxembourg genealogy once at the castle of Karlstein (near Prague, *c.*1360).[44] These appear to be Christian worthies and heroes come to accompany the great Emperor in death—perhaps a massively inflated version of the companions of Sir Hugh Hastings at Elsing.[45]

It will be clear from this that, whether it be the sword of Ogier the Dane or the companions of Maximilian, churches during the Middle Ages came to be repositories of objects and ideas which are not accounted for in the pages of William Durandus. It is perhaps surprising that little or no reference was made to them in an age in which controversy certainly raged over various issues concerning the Church and poverty, the Church and austerity, and latterly the Church and imagery.[46] To the extent that one is dealing often with vainglory and pride, the Paradise of the Church had become tainted by the Fall; and some comment at least might be expected on the vanity and purposelessness of ostentatious human commemoration. Moreover, those whose lot it was to be surveyed apparently

[44] Some account of the Karlstein genealogy (with a bibliography) will be found in Martindale, *Heroes*, pp. 5–8.

[45] The earliest evidence (1528) distinguishes in fact between the 'pilder des stammes der fürsten' and the 'anderer pilder'. See Oberhammer, *Die Bronzestandbilder*, pp. 14ff.

[46] See particularly M. Aston, *Lollards and Reformers* (London, 1984), pp. 135–92. Especially 'silent' on the subject of commemoration and lay intrusion are the *Documents Illustrating the Activities of the General and Provincial Chapters of the English Black Monks 1215–1540*, ed. W. A. Pantin, 3 vols (London, 1931–7). There is, indeed, a well-known passage in Langland, *Piers Plowman*, ed. W. W. Skeat, 2 vols (Oxford, 1886, repr. 1969), lines 42–65, in which the poet criticizes the friars. The targets are the large churches, splendid cloisters, and, in particular, stained-glass windows in which the donors are recorded. The speaker, Lady Mede, offers to make all these things possible if the friar whom she is addressing will 'pardon' the lechery of the nobles who are providing the money—the implication being that the friars are conniving at gross sin in return for handsome contributions to the fabric fund. It will be perceived, however, that although Langland disapproved of the secular ostentation of the stained glass in particular, the burden of his complaint is not so much against the secularity itself as against the means by which he claimed it had been obtained.

in perpetuity by the ancestors of Eleanor de Clare or the relatives of Pierre Roger—and, at least in the short term, by Margaret of Austria herself—might well have felt that they were in the hands of minders as well as patrons.

There are many possible reasons to account for the silence. Those, so to speak, in the institutional firing-line may well have found themselves in a delicate position. It is unlikely that Eleanor de Clare was approached by a delegation of Tewkesbury monks saying that there was conventual feeling against a stained-glass window to Hugh Despenser; and if the Brou Augustinians, deprived of their *pulpitum*, had asked where they were supposed to put their organ, they would presumably have been told that this was what the emperor's daughter wanted and that they would have to make other arrangements. It must in any case have been realized early that, once generic categories of people such as 'ancestors' or 'forebears' were selected for special attention, some of the names which were singled out for attention were likely to be odd. Stigand, the last pre-Conquest bishop of Winchester, but also canonically deposed from the throne of Canterbury by a legatine council in 1070, was amongst those singled out for attention by Henry of Blois at Winchester in 1158.[47] More recently, many people must have been astonished by the modern stained-glass celebration of William Rufus in the south transept of Canterbury Cathedral. Yet institutions tend to cling tenaciously not merely to founders and benefactors, but also to those associated with dignity and office. Moreover, the theme is in part one of 'authority' through 'continuity'. It is standard Catholic doctrine that the efficacy of the sacerdotal succession is not impeded by the unworthiness of some of its members. Presumably, by extension, the force of secular continuity is not impeded by the questionable character of some of the human links in the chain.

In any case, the clergy were bound to pray for their benefactors; and by the late thirteenth century it was a common theological position that monuments were an *aide-mémoire* to such prayer. Centuries before, St Augustine had been severe on the subject of funeral pomp, pointing out that 'curatio funeris, conditio sepulturae, pompae exequiarum magis sunt vivorum solatia quam subsidia mortuorum.'[48] Yet Aquinas himself,

[47] There were political reasons for getting rid of Stigand; but the process was made easier by the fact that he had had his election to Canterbury confirmed by an anti-pope, Benedict X, and that he was considered to have held uncanonically two sees at once—that is, Winchester and Canterbury.

[48] *De civitate Dei*, bk i, ch. 12, *PL*, 41, col. 26. The passage continues: 'Si aliquid prodest impio sepultura pretiosa, oberit pio vilis aut nulla. Praeclaras exsequias in conspectu hominum

observing that it was praiseworthy to beautify a church, also commended the building of monuments because they incited men to pray for the souls of the departed;[49] and the 1292 synodal statutes of Bishop Gilbert of St Leofard of Chichester state clearly that those who do honour to the Church should themselves be honoured after death by a monument.[50] In general terms, therefore, there was sound official backing for much of what has been discussed above.

Nevertheless, it is of interest that by the late fourteenth century there were signs of retreat from some of the more extravagant positions adopted earlier. In England at least—where by far the largest concentration of evidence survives—images of the family which emphasized status and historic connections become less and less common after about 1400. Indeed, the Black Prince prescribed in his will of 1376 that his effigy in Canterbury Cathedral was to be surrounded simply by twelve shields—alternately of his own arms and of John of Bohemia's ostrich plumes.[51] Where 'weeper' figures continued to decorate a monument, the changing emphasis to children may also be significant. Emphasis on lineage is uneasily reminiscent of the Pharisee's cry, 'Lord, I thank thee that I am not as other men are.' But the Bible, especially the Book of Psalms, is full of references to children as being a sign of God's favour.[52] In this light, the monument might be seen as a form of thanksgiving.

Another pointer in the same direction may be the tendency to show the deceased kneeling. At Innsbruck, Maximilian, on the top of his memorial, kneels towards the altar. At Tewkesbury, Edward Despenser (d. 1375) also kneels on the top of his chantry chapel, facing towards the high altar (plate 12). Not many images of this sort survive;[53] but at the very least they

---

exhibuit purpurato illi diviti turba famulorum: sed multo clariores in conspectu domini ulceroso illi pauperi ministerium praebuit Angelorum, qui eum non extulerunt in marmoreum tumulum, sed in Abrahae gremium sustulerunt.'

49 *Summa Theologiae*, Editiones Paulinae (Rome, 1962), supplementum tertiae partis, qu. 71, art. xi, pp. 2626–7: 'Utrum cultus exequiarum defuncto prosit'.

50 F. M. Powicke and C. R. Cheney, *Councils and Synods with Other Documents Relating to the English Church*, 2 vols (Oxford, 1964), 2, p. 1117.

51 The text of the will relating to the monument is printed in R. Willis, *The Architectural History of Canterbury Cathedral* (London, 1845), pp. 131–2, note k.

52 For example, Psalm 127. 3, 'Lo, children are an heritage of the Lord and the fruit of the womb is his reward.'

53 A further example is to be found in the tomb, said to be of Hüglin von Schönegg (d. 1377–8) in St Leonhard, Basle. The recessed monument appears to go with the structure of the chapel (1362–9). Above the recess, set on a corbel but not in its original position, is an armed, kneeling figure, who bears the Schönegg arms: see F. Maurer, *Die Kunstdenkmäler des Kantons Basel-Stadt. Die Kirchen Kloster und Kapellen IV. Pt 2. St Katharina bis St Niklaus* (Basle, 1961), pp. 191,

show the prince or noble positively in an attitude of respect towards Christ and the Eucharist.

Moreover, by the fifteenth century some patrons were demanding that their tombs be almost ostentatiously humble. One example of this is the tomb of Isabel Despenser. She was the wife of the Richard Beauchamp, whose monument at Warwick was briefly alluded to above. Presumably, as a good Despenser, she was buried with her family at Tewkesbury. The chantry chapel still exists, but her effigy and tomb-chest do not seem to have been made. They were, however, described prospectively in her will.[54] Her effigy was to be made 'all naked with her hair cast backward'; and on the sides of her tomb-chest were to be 'poor men and women in their poor array with their heads in their hands'. The introduction of grief into the monument was not an invention of Isabel;[55] but the emphasis on the poverty of the mourners is a novelty.

Finally, in the late fourteenth century, the canon of tomb design was invaded by a totally new image—that of the corpse, cadaver, or *transi*. In its earliest surviving manifestations it is (or was) attached to monuments which were elaborate and ambitious. One was the tomb of the Cardinal Lagrange, once in the church of St Martial at Avignon. Lagrange was a distinguished ecclesiastic who had been adviser to Charles V and Bishop of Amiens. He died in 1402, but before his death had begun an enormous

---

245. See also the kneeling figure of Jean Porcher (*c.*1370) in the church of St Thibault at Joigny. Bauch, *Das mittelalterliche Grabbild*, who apparently did not know the Despenser and Porcher monuments, amalgamated all kneeling figures within the category of monument he called *epitaphs*. He disputed (p. 342, n. 410) that any of the figures could be in perpetual adoration of the Eucharist at the altar. However, there is little reason to doubt that the figure of Despenser is in its original position, and that he at least is in a posture of *ewige Anbetung*. To the same line of thought belongs the more famous figure of Philip the Bold of Burgundy, kneeling at the entrance to the chapel of Champmol, though he is in perpetual adoration of the Christ-child. The incorporation into a monument of an image of the dead person in an attitude of prayer is, of course, much older and probably thirteenth century. The point here is that in the late fourteenth century the image was 'extracted' and made a principal focus of attention.

[54] Quoted in Dugdale, *Antiquities of Warwickshire*, pp. 329–30.

[55] Already from the twelfth century there survive monuments—or evidence of monuments—in which the effigy of the dead person is accompanied by a representation of some part of the funeral rites. These images appear transferred to the sarcophagus in the monument of Louis of France (d. 1260) now in Saint-Denis but formerly in Royaumont (much restored). The explicit emphasis on mourning and grief is harder to trace in what survives. See particularly Quarré, *Les pleurants*. Early examples must be the monuments in Amiens Cathedral to Thomas of Savoy (d. 1333 or 1335–6) and Bishop Simon de Gonçon (d. 1325), each of which has a sarcophagus decorated exclusively with heavily cloaked and cowled 'weepers', some with their heads in their hands. Since there are no real distinctions in their clothing, they appear to be official (paid) mourners.

Plate 12 Edward Despenser from his Monument in Tewkesbury Abbey (photo: Author).

monument which celebrated, among much else, the Valois kings whom he had served. At the very foot of this towering mass of sculpture (the monument was about fifteen metres high) was a relief showing his corpse laid out, presented with no covering except a winding sheet (plate 13).[56]

There is a further monument, similar in date but very different in design, which is also distinguished by the introduction of a corpse. This is in the castle chapel at La Sarraz.[57] It is said to commemorate François de la Sarra, who died in 1363; but since it appears to be a reformed version of the 1371 monument at Neuchâtel, about thirty-five miles away, it seems likely that it was set up some years after François' death (plate 14). The tomb at La Sarraz is memorable for its treatment of the effigy, which is indeed a corpse infested with worms and toads. Now, meditation on the frailty of human flesh and on its eluctable tendency to putrefaction was by no means new in the late fourteenth century. There is a famous passage by Henry of Huntingdon on the distressing circumstances surrounding the interment of Henry I of England in 1135, in which he speaks of the 'horrible decay ... the loathsome state to which [Henry's] body was reduced'; and at the end he says, 'Learn to despise what so perishes and comes to nothing.'[58] But though the thoughts themselves were not new in the late fourteenth century, their intrusion into commemorative imagery was; and it seems possible that these various items collectively may represent the response to some implicit criticism—a toning-down of the extrovert celebration of secular status which appears to have reached a peak in the years around 1350.

There was, indeed, a further strand of thought which becomes increasingly prominent in the course of the fifteenth century. It emerges in one of the few contemporary comments on a tomb—a letter by an Italian, the humanist scholar Leonardo Bruni.[59] In about 1430 Bruni happened to meet on the road to Montepulciano the pieces of a monument intended to commemorate another humanist, Bartolommeo Aragazzi, who had recently died in 1429. Bruni recorded the incident and his reflections; and

[56] For the development of this image, see Bauch, *Das mittelalterliche Grabbild*, ch. 19, 'Bild des Leichnams'.

[57] The post-medieval inscription dedicates the monument to the 'pious memory' of François, lord of La Sarra who died in 1363. The chapel is said to have been consecrated in 1370. The armour appears to be later than that of the figures set on the monument at Neuchâtel. For further comment and bibliography see Martindale, *Heroes*, p. 41, n. 20.

[58] *The Chronicle of Henry of Huntingdon*, tr. and ed. T. Forrester (London, 1909), pp. 262–3 for the whole passage.

[59] The contents of the letter are discussed by R. Lightbown, *Donatello and Michelozzo* (London, 1980), pp. 128–33.

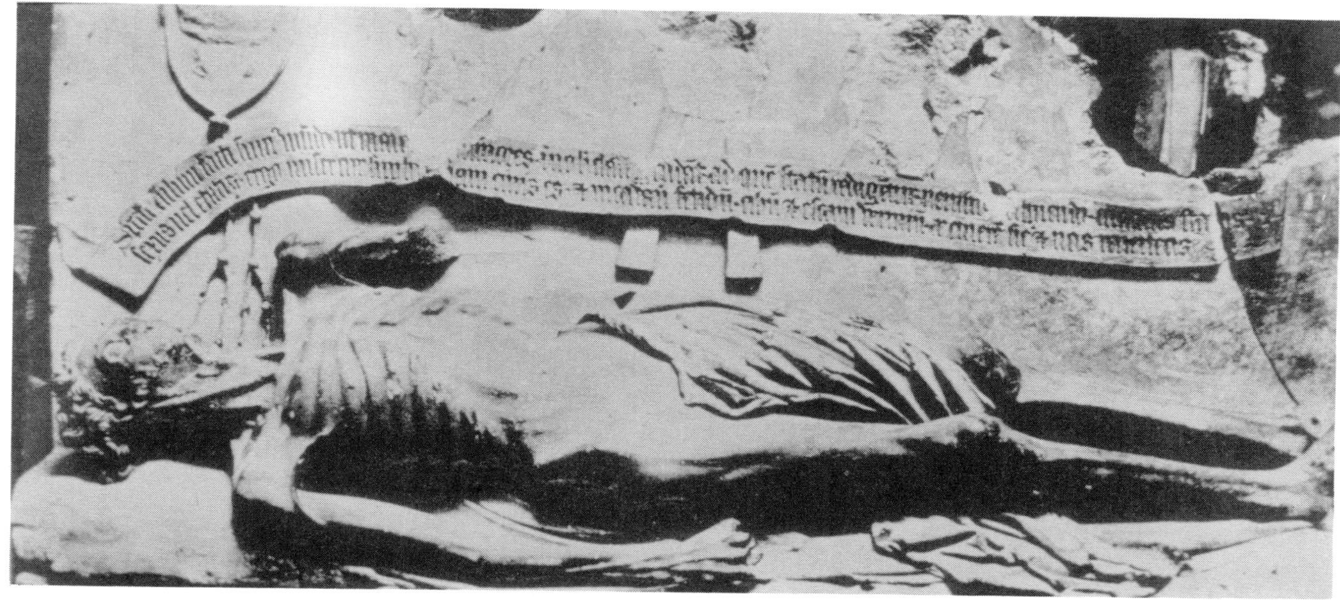

Plate 13 Fragment from the Tomb of Cardinal Lagrange, formerly in the Tomb of St Martial, Avignon (remains now in the Musée du Petit Palais, Avignon).

Plate 14 Monument to François de la Sarra, in the Castle Chapel of La Sarraz (photo: Author).

since he hated and despised Aragazzi, he spent some time casting aspersions on his intellectual achievements and on his parentage. The letter is nevertheless interesting for its assumptions. Monuments are appropriate for those of noble birth and distinguished achievements (according to Bruni, Aragazzi had been short on both). With that, most people in the thirteenth and fourteenth centuries would have been in agreement. Bruni, however, emphasizes the importance of achievement even to the extent of belittling that of monuments—'What is viler', he says, 'than to have one's tomb remembered, one's life forgotten?' Since the parish churches of England are full of monuments corresponding to this description, one can see what he meant. Moreover, others before Bruni had pondered with disfavour the prospect of oblivion, but had decided to attempt a remedy within the context of the monument. The problem was the choice of 'achievement'. One of the most bizarre choices must be the Peacock Feast of 1349, recorded on the brass of Robert Braunche (d. 1364).[60] In contrast stands the enormous monument of Bishop Guido Tarlati (d. 1327) in the north aisle of Arezzo Cathedral.[61] Originally dominating the high altar, the tomb has sixteen scenes in relief, illustrating for the most part the political and military exploits of the Bishop.

There were, however, other less aggressive and less explicit ways of alluding to the life of the dead person. The sarcophagus of Catherine of Habsburg (d. 1323) in S. Lorenzo, Naples, rests on the Virtues of Charity and Hope.[62] Faith, Hope, and Charity stand beneath the effigy of John XXII by Baldassare Cossa in the Baptistery at Florence (carved *c.*1425—see plate 15);[63] and this line of thought in effect opened up a new means

[60] See M. Clayton, *Victoria and Albert Museum. Catalogue of Rubbings of Brasses and Incised Slabs* (London, 1968), plate 39. The brass is in the church of St Margaret, King's Lynn.

[61] The monument is well characterized by White, *European Art*, pp. 447–9. Above the scenes in the central register, the Bishop is accompanied to his rest by a funeral ceremony. The top register is now empty, but Gert Kreytenberg has drawn attention to the possibility that this unusual memorial took as its model that of the Emperor Henry VII, once behind the high altar in Pisa Cathedral. See G. Kreytenberg, 'Das Grabmal von Kaiser Heinrich VII. in Pisa', *Mitteilungen des Kunsthistorischen Institutes in Florenz*, 28 (1984), pp. 34–64. Because of the constraints of time, little was said of Italy in the course of the lecture. However, these two tombs can be joined by the Angevin tombs in S. Chiara, Naples, the tomb of Bernabò Visconti, formerly in S. Eustorgio, Milan, and other monuments and frescos surviving or formerly in Verona and Padua as evidence of the increasing secularization with which the lecture was concerned.

[62] See J. Gardner, 'A princess among prelates: a fourteenth-century Neapolitan tomb and some northern relations, *Römisches Jahrbuch für Kunstgeschichte*, 23–4 (1988), pp. 31–60, for a discussion of the imagery. He points out that the sarcophagus of the slightly earlier monument to the Empress Margaret of Brabant at Genoa was supported on the theological Virtues.

[63] See Lightbown, *Donatello*, pp. 24–51.

Plate 15 Monument to Pope John XXII, Florence Baptistery (photo: Author).

towards characterizing the deceased person. It became increasingly common to suggest the person and his or her achievements via the symbols of the Virtues and of the Arts. The way was also open towards allegory. Further examination of that development lies beyond the scope of this paper. It had much to commend it, not least because of its flexibility and because of the subtlety with which it could be elaborated. Moreover, it introduced an intellectual dimension which had before been missing. It requires a mere herald to elucidate the monuments of Marie de Bourbon or Philippa of Hainault; but for the new fashion one increasingly needed a scholar often with a tortuous mind. The resulting programmes might have nothing to do with ancestors and little, indeed, to do with the intercession of saints. In a curiously Protestant way, they were much to do with the efficacy of deeds and actions.

While it is possible to observe and to analyse the changes outlined above, the reasons for change remain elusive, for there is little or no contemporary comment; and, to the extent that monuments were certainly matters of fashion, there is no real way into the conversations of those involved. Instead of indulging in further speculation, therefore, I shall reiterate the changes just discussed via what is in these terms a late example—the monument to Pope Julius II. It was originally designed and begun by Michelangelo in 1505 and is therefore of very much the same date as the church at Brou or the tomb of Maximilian. It was at least as visionary as this last; and, like it, it was never completed in its original form. The mid-sixteenth-century account by Michelangelo's friend Condivi gives some idea of the first plan.[64]

> I say briefly that this tomb was to have had four faces . . . All round about the outside were niches for statues and between niche and niche terminal figures. To these were bound other statues like prisoners . . . These figures represented the liberal arts and likewise Painting, Sculpture and Architecture each with her symbol so that they could be easily recognised—denoting by this that, like Pope Julius, all the virtues were the prisoners of Death, because they would never find such favour and nourishment as he gave them. Above these [on the cornice] were four great statues, one of [them] Moses. [NB, the others were also probably Prophets.] [At the upper level] were two angels supporting an *arca*. One appeared to be smiling as though he rejoiced that the soul of the pope had been received

[64] See C. Holroyd, tr. and ed., *Michael Angelo Buonarroti*, 2nd edn (London, 1911), pp. 28–9.

> amongst the blessed spirits, the other wept as if sad that the world had been deprived of such a man. [There were also to be further] subjects in *mezzo rilievo* to be cast in bronze, all appropriate in their stories and showing the acts of this great Pontiff.

It would be unhelpful to try to make this out to be a particularly humble monument. It is, however, interesting in the context of what has been discussed above. Its stress on grief, though appropriate, is not new—though here it is the Arts that grieve rather than Isabel Despenser's poor men and women. But in the new manner, it would have reminded the visitor of Julius's achievements as a patron of learning and the arts rather than his quite respectable della Rovere lineage and family. The figures surrounding Clement VI at La Chaise-Dieu seem in every sense a long way away. There was, moreover, one particular detail which removed it quite clearly from its medieval past and to which allusion has already been made. Although, according to Condivi, there were to have been more than forty figures, there is no mention of images of saints. Thus on the monument itself there would have been no allusion to their protection and intercession; and this goes some way to explaining why this general type of sepulchral iconography became popular in moderately Protestant countries. There would appear to be nothing in the Julius monument—apart, of course, from Julius himself—which would have been objectionable, for instance, to Lutherans. It is, of course, a matter of some irony that Julius's monument indirectly caused a great deal of trouble. Like that of Maximilian, it required a church to put it in. The plans for the tomb came to involve the rebuilding of St Peter's; and the activity attendant on funding that rebuilding produced some startling consequences which nobody had foreseen—but that is another story.

University of East Anglia

REWARDING DEVOTION: INDULGENCES AND THE PROMOTION OF IMAGES

by FLORA LEWIS

THE indulgence is one of the Church's mechanisms for encouraging pious practices which has generally had a bad press.[1] This paper is concerned with its use in the veneration of three images: the Veronica, the *arma Christi* or instruments of the Passion, and the Man of Sorrows with the indulgence referring to the Mass of St Gregory. It addresses in particular the circumstances of the original grant of indulgence (whether real or spurious) and the role played by the indulgences in the transmission of these images in devotional manuscripts in England.[2] The earliest of these indulgenced images, the Veronica, is also the most famous, and the one whose origin is most clearly attested.[3] The *Chronica maiora* of Matthew Paris tells how the Veronica suddenly reversed itself while being carried in procession in 1216. Innocent III responded by composing a prayer in its honour, with an associated indulgence of ten days for each time the prayer was recited. It is noteworthy that although Innocent's indulgence is commonly referred to as creating the new category of indulgenced image, the indulgence is attached to the prayer, and there is no suggestion that it was necessary to view the image. As is made clear in the *Chronica*, the addition of a representation of the image (plate 1) was prompted by the fervour of devotion: people did it for themselves. Thus two related, but not identical, impulses joined together to produce the indulgenced prayer to be said before the image, the model for all other indulgenced images. An early example of the prayer used as part of an exercise in devotional propaganda is found in the *Revelations* of Mechtild of Hackeborn. These normally followed the liturgical year, and on the day of the exposition of the relic she had a vision, aimed at arousing piety towards the image, in which she saw Christ in Majesty, with those who honoured the holy face with a special prayer approaching him,

[1] The standard work is N. Paulus, *Geschichte der Ablasses im Mittelalter*, 2 vols (Paderborn, 1922–3). A sympathetic account is N. Orme, 'Indulgences in the diocese of Exeter 1100–1536', *Reports and Transactions of the Devonian Association for the Advancement of Science*, 120 (1988), pp. 15–32. I owe this reference to Nicholas Kingwell.

[2] This paper is based on material from my thesis, 'Devotional Images and their dissemination in English manuscripts, *c.*1350–1470' (London Ph.D. thesis, 1989), where the manuscripts and their iconography are discussed in greater detail with a full bibliography.

[3] F. Lewis, 'The Veronica: image, legend and viewer', in W. Ormrod, ed., *England in the Thirteenth Century: Proceedings of the 1984 Harlaxton Symposium* (Woodbridge, 1985), pp. 100–6.

Plate 1 The Veronica (Cambridge, Corpus Christi College, MS 16, fol. 49v).

carrying their sins. They laid these at his feet, where they were transformed into jewels.[4]

The indulgences soon extended to the original. In 1289 Nicholas IV's indulgences for pilgrims to St Peter's placed particular emphasis on the Veronica,[5] and the spurious bull of Clement VI for the Jubilee of 1350 made seeing it a condition of gaining the Jubilee indulgence from all sins.[6] By the fourteenth century the relic was supposed to carry huge indul-

4 *De veneratione imaginis Christi*, *Liber Specialis Gratiae*, bk 1, ch. 10 = *Revelationes Gertrudianae ac Mechtildianae*, ed. L. Paquelin, 2 vols (Poitiers and Paris, 1875–7), 2, p. 31.

5 K. Gould, *The Psalter and Hours of Yolande of Soissons* (Cambridge, Mass., 1978), p. 85.

6 See H. Thurston, *The Holy Year of Jubilee* (New York, 1900), pp. 34–5, 58; J. A. Endres, 'Die Darstellung der Gregoriusmesse im Mittelalter', *Zeitschrift für christliche Kunst*, 30 (1917), p. 153.

gences, particularly for foreign pilgrims.[7] This, in turn, increased the interest in reproductions, with their smaller grants: much devotional practice in the later Middle Ages had a strongly imitative nature.

For the *arma Christi* the process of acquiring an indulgence is not so clearly recorded. But a certain amount can be deduced from the indulgence itself. The earliest indulgence, and the most influential for the English manuscripts, is first recorded on the Continent, in a devotional miscellany written in 1320 by John of St Trond, a monk of the Cistercian abbey of Villers, near Louvain.[8] The manuscript contains two images of the *arma Christi*. The first (on fol. 150r) includes a brief indulgence of forty days from Pope Leo, but the second (on fol. 152v: plate 2) has a much longer indulgence, which states that the various grants from St Peter and thirty other popes were confirmed in the council of Pope Innocent, who added four years and two hundred days.[9] Which Pope Innocent is not enumerated here. However, a Bohemian collection of devotional texts, written in 1312–14 by the Dominican friar Kolda, for Kunigunde, Abbess of St George's, Prague (Prague, National and University Library, MS XIV A.17), also focuses on the devotion to the *arma Christi*. Though it does not include an indulgence, Kolda writes (on fol. 2r) of 'arma redempcionis nostre que papa Innocentius explicavit' and (on fol. 5v) of how the devotion was approved by the pope 'in concilio Lugdunensi'.[10] Putting these together, it is clear that both refer to Innocent IV and the First Council of Lyons in 1245, and indeed a later fourteenth-century versification of the same indulgence also states that it was confirmed by Innocent IV at the Council of Lyons.[11] The authenticity of indulgence grants is notoriously

[7] See *The Stacions of Rome*, ed. F. J. Furnivall, *EETS*, os 25 (1867), pp. 1–2. For an untraced indulgence for the Veronica granted by Clement VI and dated from Avignon, 28 May 1350, see W. Grimm, 'Die Sage vom Ursprung der Christusbilder', in G. Heinrichs, ed., *Kleinere Schriften von Wilhelm Grimm*, 3 vols (Berlin, 1883), 3, p. 159.

[8] Brussels, Bibliothèque royale, MS 4459–70.

[9] Ibid., fol. 152v: 'Quicunque intuebitur hec arma domini nostri ihesu christi quibus nos redemit de peccata suis contritis habet tres annos a beato petro apostolo. Item a triginta summis pontificibus a quilibet centum dies. Item a viginti octo episcopis a quilibet xl dies. Item a domino leone papa xl dies. Item ab Innocencio papa qui in quodam concilio erat confirmans omnia predicta superaddidit quatuor annos et ducentos dies indulgencie. Item a Veronica xl dies. Item qui cotidie devota mente inspexerit nonquam mala morte peribit. Item mulieribus in partu laborantibus prestat optimum remedium.'

[10] See M. Evans, 'An illustrated fragment of Peraldus's *Summa* of Vice: Harleian MS.3244', *JWCI*, 45 (1982), p. 25, n. 75. The manuscript is published in facsimile by K. Stejskal and E. Urbánková, *Pásional Přemyslovny Kunhuty* (Prague, 1975).

[11] London, BL, MS Royal 6.E.VI, fol. 15v: 'Post hos Innocentius quartus papa decensius / Lugduno confirmanda ducentos dies addidit': noted by Evans, 'Illustrated fragment'. A later short prose indulgence, Cambridge, Corpus Christi College, MS 537, fol. 49v, also refers to a confirmation by Innocent at the Council of Lyons.

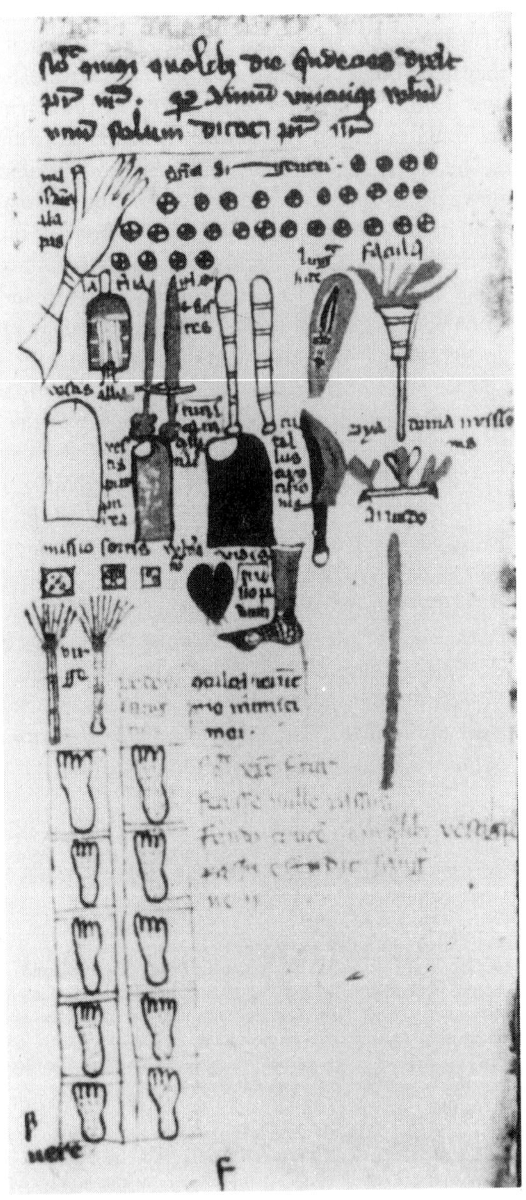

Plate 2 The *arma Christi* (Brussels, Bibliothèque royale, MS 4459–70, fol. 152v: photograph: Bibliothèque royale).

suspect, but the warning signals are excessive liberality of indulgence, combined with grantors of unusual antiquity and fame. The legitimate doubts we may have of St Peter's involvement in the Villers indulgence should not necessarily be extended to Pope Innocent.

The question remains: why would Innocent be interested in the *arma Christi*? Like the Veronica, the *arma Christi* were also thought to exist as actual relics. The two main points of transference of relics of Christ to the West were the sack of Constantinople in 1204 and the purchase of relics by St Louis for the Sainte-Chapelle from 1239 to 1246;[12] and papal support for the devotion at the 1245 Council may well be associated with Louis' Sainte-Chapelle relics. The Crown of Thorns was the chief prize of the treasury, but other relics were little less important: they included (as well as the inevitable portion of the True Cross) the lance, sponge, tunic, parts of the sepulchre and of the shroud, the *titulus* of the Cross, and a quantity of holy blood.[13] These were the last relics of the Passion to leave Constantinople before its recapture by the Greeks in 1261. It is also noteworthy that Innocent IV had taken the Sainte-Chapelle, with its relics, under his protection in a bull of 1243.[14] Thus, with the *arma Christi*, as with the Veronica, the public veneration of relics is paralleled by their private veneration, encouraged through grants of indulgence.

The third example, the indulgence of the Mass of St Gregory, is based on the same premise: that indulgences belong to images where the original has the status of a relic. The indulgence, which dates from around 1400 and is found in its fullest form in a group of English manuscripts (though there are also French and German examples) gives a lengthy account of the original circumstances of its granting.[15] One day, while Pope Gregory the Great was celebrating Mass in Rome, as he was about to consecrate the Host he had a vision of Christ 'in tali effigie sicut videtur hic depicta'.

[12] Comte de Riant, 'Des Depouilles religieuses enlevèes a Constantinople', *Memoires de la Société Nationale des Antiquaires de France*, 36 (1875), pp. 1–214.

[13] K. Gould, 'The sequences *De Sanctis Reliquiis* as Sainte-Chapelle inventories', *Medieval Studies*, 43 (1981), pp. 315–41.

[14] S. J. Morand, *Histoire de la Sainte-Chapelle Royale du Palais* (Paris, 1790), *pièces justificatives*, 2–3; for the bull see also Gould, 'Sequences', p. 316, n. 4.

[15] The German examples (not from manuscripts) were published by J. A. Endres, 'Die Darstellung der Gregoriusmesse im Mittelalter', *Zeitschrift für christliche Kunst*, 30 (1917), pp. 146–56. The English group are London, BL, MSS Addit. 33381, fol. 90r, and 37787, fol. 64v; Boulogne, Bibliothèque municipale, MS 93, fol. 9v; Bristol, Central Public Library, MS 14, fol. 10v; and Rennes, Bibliothèque municipale, MS 22, fol. 11v. London, BL, MS Addit. 18213, fol. 81r, though not of Sarum use, has strong English links: see N. J. Rogers, 'Books of Hours produced in the Low Countries for the English market in the fifteenth century' (Cambridge M.Litt. thesis, 1982), 1, pp. 118–19.

Because of the great compassion which he felt at the sight, the Pope then granted an indulgence to all those who said five Paternosters and five Ave Marias before this figure.[16] The accompanying images show Christ as the Man of Sorrows (plate 3).

Clearly, all this can be discounted on the literal level. Gregory was frequently employed to add weight to promises of indulgence, and the legend in which, as he was celebrating Mass, the Host turned to a bleeding finger to convince a sceptical woman probably inspired the later story. But the point of this story is not a eucharistic miracle, but the fostering of devotion to the image of the Man of Sorrows, an image by 1400 long introduced from Byzantium and widespread in Italy. So the difference between this image and the Veronica is that the image of the Man of Sorrows was not a relic, and there was no 'original', but the aim of the spurious indulgence and legend was to try to create a relic, and to authenticate this 'original', and thus downgrade all the other examples as mere copies.

This was, however, only partially successful, as is demonstrated by the difficulty of determining which 'relic' was being promoted. It is not that the indulgences omit identification; the problem is that they give too many. The most likely candidate is the late thirteenth-century mosaic given to the Carthusians at S. Croce in Gerusalemme, Rome, in 1385–6, identified by Bertelli, which was certainly being promoted as the 'source' later in the fifteenth century in the print produced by Israhel van Meckenem.[17] Most of the indulgences name the church where the event took place as 'perta cros', 'panta cros', 'porte-croix', or 'porta crucis'. But S. Croce was not the only contender, even if it probably was the source

[16] BL, MS Addit. 33381, fol. 20r: 'In illo tempore quo sanctus Gregorius erat in magna Roma presul, una die quando missam celebravit in ecclesia que vocatur Partacros, quando voluit consecrare corpus domini nostri, apparuit sibi dominus noster ihesus christi in tali effigie sicut videtur hic depicta. Et ex magna compassione quam habuit idem sanctus Gregorius quando vidit eum in tali figura, concessit omnibus illis qui ante istam figuram ponunt genua sua in terra dicendo cum devocione quinque Pater noster et quinque Ave maria omnes indulgencias que sunt in omnibus ecclesiis de Roma, que sunt xiiii milia annorum, et omnes istas indulgencias concessit dicta figura dicto sancto Gregorio. Et ultra hoc duodecim alii summi pontifices quilibet eorum concessit vi annos de indulgencia. Et adhuc xxx alii pontifices quilibet eorum concessit ducentos dies indulgencie. Similiter ultra hoc alii lxvi episcopi quilibet eorum concessit lx dies indulgencie. Summa omni indulgenciarum xxvi milia annorum et xxx dies de vera indulgencia.'

[17] C. Bertelli, 'The Image of Pity in Sancta Croce in Gerusalemme', in D. Fraser *et al.*, eds, *Essays in the History of Art presented to Rudolf Wittkower* (London, 1967), p. 54; E. Breitenbach, 'Israhel van Meckenem's Man of Sorrows', *Quarterly Journal of the Library of Congress*, 31 (1974), pp. 21–6. The print exists in three states, of which two are described as reproducing the vision of St Gregory, and one identifies the church.

Plate 3 Man of Sorrows (Boulogne, Bibliothèque municipale, MS 93, fol. 10r).

of the indulgence. It certainly never succeeded in cornering the market. Both the early French indulgences state that the church was the Pantheon.[18] The *Marvels of Rome* (1375) mentions the altar in S. Prisca where the image of the crucified Christ appeared to Gregory, an isolated early reference which may have been one of the sources from which the legend was developed.[19] Nicholas Muffel, who visited Rome in 1452, saw in S. Gregorio al Celio the chapel where Christ with the *arma Christi* appeared to Gregory.[20] The will made in 1519 by Anne Sulyard, daughter of the Suffolk judge Sir John Sulyard, gives directions for a pilgrimage to be made to Rome, including a visit to 'Cimitorium Calixti, the apparacion of Criste to Saincte Gregory'.[21] A guide to the churches of Rome written about 1475 for Margaret of York states that the vision occurred in the Basilica of S. Sebastiano.[22]

But the most telling reference is that by the Englishman William Brewyn in his guide to Rome, compiled around 1470. He does not mention the vision of St Gregory, but he does tell how in S. Croce there is 'a picture of our Saviour, which is called the image of divine pity . . . the aforesaid image of divine compassion has the head leaning upon the right shoulder, and the right hand clasped over the left'—showing that he is clearly talking about the Byzantine mosaic given to S. Croce. He continues: 'Also at the church of Saints Sebastian and Fabian there is another picture very much like this one; there are also many such pictures at Rome, though none quite so large as this one.'[23]

Here S. Croce merely has the biggest picture: evidently it also wanted to be known to have the best—the 'original'.[24] The Roman churches undoubtedly vied among themselves for possession of both relics and images: hence the proliferation of both. But it is doubtful whether this had much impact outside Rome, and the message of the indulgence was to say the prayers in veneration before any image of the Man of Sorrows. Whereas in the case of the Veronica people were conscious that the

[18] BL, MS Addit. 29433, fol. 107v, and Florence, Biblioteca Riccardiana, MS Ricc. 466, fol. 140r.

[19] R. Berliner, 'Arma Christi', *Münchner Jahrbuch der Bildenden Kunst*, 6 (1955), p. 132, n. 336.

[20] Bertelli, 'The Image of Pity', p. 50.

[21] C. Richmond, 'The Sulyard papers: the rewards of a small family archive', in D. Williams, ed., *England in the Fifteenth Century: Proceedings of the 1986 Harlaxton Symposium* (Woodbridge, 1987), p. 222.

[22] Sold Sotheby's 22 June 1982, lot 59.

[23] C. Woodruff, *A Fifteenth Century Guide-Book to the Principal Churches of Rome, compiled c.1470* (London, 1933), p. 57.

[24] The image is not large, but forms the centrepiece of an imposing reliquary triptych (see Bertelli, 'The Image of Pity', fig. 4).

original, the relic, was at St Peter's (and even so there were rival images), no single image of the Man of Sorrows achieved that status.

The first part of this paper has sought to move back from the manuscripts to the events which led to the creation of the indulgences for the original images and relics. At this point I want to return to the manuscripts and their copies of the images, from public to private veneration; veneration of a reproduction rather than an original relic or pseudo-relic.

In the complex process of transfer from public to private, three elements should at least be mentioned here. The first is concerned with the reproduction of images. As well as the movement from a single 'original' to representations in manuscripts of that original, there is also a parallel multiplication and dissemination of images and relics outside manuscripts; for example, when the future Urban IV sent the nuns of Montreuil a mandylion in 1249, exhorting them to receive it as the holy Veronica or the true image or likeness of it, or when St Louis and his successors sent gifts of *arma Christi* relics to favoured recipients throughout Europe: gifts which then became in turn the foci for public devotion.[25] The second is the role played by the *tabulae* displayed in churches. Such tables would list a variety of indulgences: those specifically available at the church, or for the saying of prayers (for example, *Ave verum corpus* at the elevation), for pious practices (for example, kneeling at the name of Jesus), and for regarding images (such as the *arma Christi*). These would then be copied: the above examples come from a fifteenth-century English Book of Hours, and the list is headed by a rubric saying that they are found 'in a table at Rome'.[26] Similar tables were found in English churches.[27] Finally, it is almost impossible to overstress the role of the religious, which is not confined to any one Order. We see this particularly in the manuscripts made for their own use, and by monks and friars for the use of nuns; but they are also the channel by which these images are introduced to the aristocratic laity. It is clear that the images of the Veronica and *arma Christi* were introduced via the manuscripts discussed above because of their promotion by the Church, in which indulgences played an important part. The indulgence of the Mass of St Gregory is a

[25] By the beginning of the fourteenth century Passion relics from the Sainte-Chapelle were held in France, Spain, Italy, Sicily, Scotland, Scandinavia, the Netherlands, and Bohemia. See Riant's tables, 'Des Depouilles religieuses', pp. 182–3.

[26] *Sotheby's Sale Catalogue*, 24 June 1980, lot 81.

[27] A rare surviving example is Oxford, Bodleian Library, MS lat. hist. a.2, from Glastonbury Abbey, which acted as a guidebook to the church, and included a list of the indulgences offered there.

different case in that the image was already known in manuscripts on the Continent, but, nevertheless, the 'copy-cat' indulgence was certainly a catalyst for the introduction of the image into English manuscripts, where the only early examples without the indulgence are initials in the Sherborne Missal (p. 200) and the Bohun Psalter and Hours (London, BL, MS Egerton 3277, fol. 114r). In the early examples the indulgences form clearly recognizable groups. During the late thirteenth and first half of the fourteenth centuries a very variable (but clearly related) indulgence in French was appended to the Veronica prayer, promising a larger pardon by Innocent.[28] The iconography of all three images is often extremely diverse, and it is the indulgence text (which also circulated separately, although it presupposes an available image) which can form the main link between manuscripts which otherwise appear to have little in common. Thus it is the indulgence of the Mass of St Gregory which links the group of early English examples of the Man of Sorrows, and in the case of the *arma Christi* the Villers version of the indulgence helps to bring together two groups of apparently unrelated manuscripts. The indulgence on folio 152v falls into two parts. The first gives the cumulative lists of indulgences and grantors: the twenty-eight bishops who each gave forty days, and so on. The second half gives a series of pardons for seeing the image each day for a week, a month, or a year.[29] The first part, recast into Latin verse (a process which probably took place on the Continent)[30] is found in London, BL, MS Addit. 33381, folio 177r, a devotional miscellany made for use at the Benedictine monastery of Ely, and also in *Omne bonum*, an encyclopaedia made by Jaques le Palmere for his own use,[31] while two other manuscripts, Boulogne, Bibliothèque municipale, MS 93, folio 8v, and Cambridge, Trinity College, MS O.30.10, folio 13r, both include the

[28] Oxford, Bodleian Library, MSS Laud. lat. 5, fol. 10r, and Douce 231, fol. 71r; London, Lambeth Palace Library, MS 36, fol. 5r; Cambridge, Sidney Sussex College, MS 36, fol. 35r; and Baltimore, Walters Art Gallery, MS 105, fol. 14v.

[29] Brussels, Bibliothèque royale, MS 4459–70, fol. 152v: 'Summa annorum indulgenciarum de veneracione armarum passionis ihesu christe trecentis sexaginta quinque diebus pro anno computatis extendit semper unum diem ad xviii annos et dimidium cum tribus diebus. Item pro ebdomadam centum et xix annos cum dimidio. Item pro mensem quingentos xviii annos cum duodecim septimanis. Item pro annum sex milia septingenti quinquaginta anni cum dimidio et tribus diebus.'

[30] For example, Paris, BN, MS lat. 10527. Though *Omne bonum* is slightly earlier it omits some lines of the rhyming couplets which are present in the Paris manuscript.

[31] London, BL, MS Royal 6.E.VI, fol.15v (see n. 6 above), and L. F. Sandler, 'Face to face with God: a pictorial image of the beatific vision', in W. Ormrod, ed., *England in the Fourteenth Century: Proceedings of the 1985 Harlaxton Symposium* (Woodbridge, 1986), pp. 224–35.

second part.[32] A further group of manuscripts, containing an illustrated poem in Middle English in honour of the *arma Christi*, incorporates the complete text, translated into Middle English verse.[33] Here the indulgence text serves to pinpoint clearly both the links between these manuscripts and the particular continental tradition to which they belong.

But during the fifteenth century—the heyday of manuscripts of private devotion (in quantity, if not in quality)—these indulgences are both rarer and more isolated. The French indulgences for the Veronica disappear, as does the Villers version of the *arma Christi* indulgence, though some less elaborate indulgences for both images are still found, and there are a few examples of the Mass of St Gregory text. But the most notable development in the fifteenth century is that, though this was a period when the market for devotional manuscripts in England was dominated by the supply of imported Flemish Books of Hours, virtually all the examples of these indulgences are found in English manuscripts.[34]

So, although I have emphasized the importance of the indulgence for the introduction of these images into England, finally I want to turn this on its head, and argue that for the wider dissemination of the imagery in devotional manuscripts in England the important factor is not the indulgence, but the presence of a devotional text. There are two main reasons for this. The first is primarily a matter of consumer preference. The development of the Book of Hours was itself part of a trend towards more elaborately structured devotions noticeable throughout the later Middle Ages. The usual 'Paters' and 'Aves' would remain suitable for the unlettered, but the owners of Books of Hours wanted the option of more sophisticated prayers. Even with the first indulgenced image, the Veronica, the indulgence was originally for saying Innocent's prayer, rather than for viewing the image,[35] and some of the early English

32 The only differing figures are the three days for daily viewing, missing in the English manuscripts, and the addition of an extra five years in the indulgence for twelve months' viewing.

33 IMEV no. 2577, printed in *Legends of the Holy Rood, Symbols of the Passion and Cross Poems*, ed. R. Morris, *EETS*, os 46 (1871). See also R. H. Robbins, 'The Arma Christi rolls', *Modern Language Review*, 34 (1939), pp. 415–21. The indulgences are found in four copies, including the two earliest manuscripts, Blairs College, MS 9, and Esopus, Mount St Alphonsus Seminary, MS 1.

34 The only exception is the Gregory indulgence in Manchester, John Rylands Library, MS 20, p. 16, which contains other unusual texts and images, suggesting that it was personally ordered. Indulgenced prayers are also quite frequent in English manuscripts, whereas in the imported Flemish Hours the only indulgenced prayer is the common *Deus qui hanc sacratissimam carnem*.

35 Laud MS lat. 5 specifies the circumstances of recital as before the Cross, and Sidney Sussex MS 36 as at the Elevation.

manuscripts also begin to combine the *arma Christi* with the hymn *Cruci, corone spinee*.[36]

The second, and more important, reason is not a matter of personal choice, but of what the producer makes available. The earlier English manuscripts were compiled by the owners (in the case of the religious) or personally commissioned, and we can fairly take them as a reflection of the owner's tastes. But the imported Flemish Books of Hours were often of a very standardized format, which gave much less leeway for individual choice.[37] The trade did attempt to provide books geared for the English market, but their standardization meant that a great deal hung on the original exemplars chosen for copy (which evidently did not include indulgences). However, this very standardization meant that if the images could find a place within such manuscripts, their dissemination was assured.[38] But to do this they had to function primarily as illustrations subordinate to a text, rather than as independent indulgenced images: a major transformation.

The Veronica was, of course, already accompanied by Innocent's prayer, and it also acquired two further hymns in its honour in the fourteenth century, *Ave facies praeclara* and the more popular *Salve sancta facies*.[39] Innocent's prayer does not seem to have circulated separately in the fifteenth century, but was appended to *Salve sancta facies*. The image does occur in the Flemish Books of Hours, sometimes finding a home in the *memoriae* of the saints, but remained very much an occasional element. The only place for the *arma Christi* in the imported Flemish Hours was as accessories for the figure of the Man of Sorrows (plate 4).[40] This last image was the only real success story, but not because of the indulgence. The Flemish Books of Hours recognized the importance of the image of the Man of Sorrows, whose dissemination on the Continent had never depended on the Mass of St Gregory indulgence. In the earliest imported

[36] Boulogne, MS 93, and Trinity College, MS O.3.10.

[37] See Rogers, 'Books of Hours'.

[38] In some ways the situation was reversed in the late fifteenth and early sixteenth centuries, where the printed Sarum Hours produced in France and England form a third group, differing in content from both the English and the French manuscript Hours. They have greater links with the English manuscripts in the extreme interest of some editions in indulgences, but this is mainly confined to indulgenced prayers, and their iconography owes much more to standardized combinations developed in French manuscript Hours.

[39] See S. Corbin, 'Les Offices de la sainte face', *Bulletin des Etudes Portugaises*, ns 11 (1947), pp. 37–8.

[40] They were found in English manuscripts, particularly the *arma Christi* rolls (see n. 33 above), but even there the new poem in their honour was the important element, and the indulgence was soon dropped.

Plate 4 Man of Sorrows (Liverpool University Library, MS Mayer 12009, fol. 242r).

Hours there are isolated instances of the image used to illustrate a variety of texts.[41] But the combination which became established (and was followed by many English manuscripts) was that of the Man of Sorrows with the newly introduced Psalms of the Passion, a text which became an important element of the Book of Hours.

The main legacy of the indulgence was the creation of a new image, showing the Mass taking place, with Gregory gazing at the Man of Sorrows (plate 5): a development which probably took place independently in France and Flanders. But though this image depended on the indulgence narrative, it followed precisely the same pattern in the imported Flemish Hours of abandoning the latter in favour of a devotional text. This was the 'Seven O's' of St Gregory, a set of invocations ascribed to the Pope beginning *O domine jhesu christe adoro te in cruce pendentem*, whose composition long antedates their connection with the image.[42] These prayers had never been considered important enough to merit illustration, so we do not find here the familiar pattern of experimental illustration followed by eventual standardization. The combination of prayers and image was made not because the prayers required illustration, but because the Mass of St Gregory required a devotional text, and the presumed authorship of the prayers explains their choice. The association was probably made first in France in the second half of the fifteenth century. Once established, the combination displaced earlier couplings of the image with various texts, and was advantageous for the spread of both text and image, particularly in France.[43]

This brief survey has moved from the indulgence as a way of honouring a relic and confirming its status to the indulgence as the impetus for the introduction of the imagery into devotional manuscripts, and finally has seen it supplanted in the transformation of an indulgenced image into a text illustration. In charting here the shifting patterns of indulgences and the promotion of images I have tried to point out some of the forces which underly the selection of texts and images—the raw materials of

[41] For example, *Omnibus consideratis*, London, BL, MS Sloane 2683; Penitential Psalms, Cambridge, University Library, MS Ii.6.2; Fifteen O's, Harvard College Library, MS Widener 2.

[42] For the Seven O's see S. Ringbom, *Icon to Narrative* (Abo, 1965), p. 25. They are printed in *Horae Eboracenses*, ed. C. Wordsworth = *SS*, 132 (1920), p. 81. The prayers occur in the Hours of Marguerite de Clisson, Paris, BN, MS lat.10528, fol. 23v, from the second half of the fourteenth century, headed 'Ceste oroison est bonne a dire devant le crucifix.'

[43] A similar pattern is seen in the printed books. The Man of Sorrows (with an indulgence shorter in text if not in liberality) had a new vogue as a separately circulating woodcut, which contributed to its introduction into printed books. The latter kept the indulgence, but again it became associated with a devotional text, the same Seven O's.

Plate 5 Mass of St Gregory (Cambridge, Emmanuel College Library, MS I.2.20, fol. 39v).

pious practice—in devotional manuscripts in England. In the origins of the indulgences and their early use to promote certain images we see the Church and its servants at work, but the circumstances of manuscript production were equally a force in the shaping of the piety of the laity.

ARISTOCRATIC AND POPULAR PIETY IN THE PATRONAGE OF MUSIC IN THE FIFTEENTH-CENTURY NETHERLANDS*

by ROGER BOWERS

IT has always been recognized that during the fifteenth century the vigorous and affluent commercial towns of the Low Countries served as centres of artistic excellence, especially in respect of painting and of manuscript production and illumination. That the region was no less fertile a generator of practitioners and composers of music—especially of music for the Church—has also long been appreciated. If for present purposes the Low Countries be defined—rather generously, perhaps—as the region coterminous with the compact area covered by the six dioceses of Thérouanne, Arras, Cambrai, Tournai, Liège, and Utrecht (see map), then it was an area if not packed with great cathedrals, yet certainly thickly populated with great collegiate churches, which sustained skilled choirs and offered a good living and high esteem to musicians who composed; the area also sustained a catholic and generous patron and consumer of artistic enterprise of all sorts, sacred and secular music included, namely, the House of the Valois Dukes of Burgundy and its Habsburg successors. From the end of the fourteenth century to the first half of the sixteenth, the region produced church musicians in such numbers that it became the principal area of recruitment for those princes of the south of Europe who were seeking the ablest men available to staff their household chapels. The Avignon popes of the 1380s and 1390s, the dukes of Rimini and Savoy, and the Roman popes of the mid-fifteenth century, and from the 1470s onwards the fiercely competitive dukes of Milan and Ferrara, the popes, cardinals, and bishops of the Curia, the king of Naples, the prominent families and churches of Florence and Venice, all alike recruited from the North; and though many of the ablest, like Ciconia, Dufay, Josquin, Isaac, and Tinctoris, were lured south to spend their lives in the sunshine, many more remained at home to maintain the Low Countries tradition.

* Music examples played during the course of the lecture were as follows: Gilles Binchois, *Agnus Dei* (à 3); Antoine Busnois, Mass *L'Homme armé* (*Sanctus*); Jacob Obrecht, *Salve crux, arbor vite*. All were performed on gramophone records by Pro Cantione Antiqua, directed by Bruno Turner.

Map Boundaries of the Dioceses of the Low Countries before 1559

Piety in the Patronage of Music

During the last fifty or sixty years, the manner of the cultivation and patronage of the music of the Church at several of the principal centres of excellence in this region has been studied in some detail. In particular, the earliest work on the music of the household chapel of the later Valois dukes of Burgundy and their Habsburg successors,[1] and of the Fraternity of Our Lady at 's-Hertogenbosch,[2] has recently been supplemented by a number of meticulous studies of the musical enterprise manifest in the major churches of Bruges,[3] Brussels,[4] Antwerp,[5] and Bergen op Zoom.[6] It seems, therefore, that a useful purpose might now be served by an attempt to draw together into a single synthesis certain of the various threads revealed by these discrete studies. Indeed, although primarily musicological both in intent and content, all these studies do happen to disclose certain commonalities concerning the high degree of lay and popular involvement in the support, encouragement, and cultivation of the music of orthodox devotion in the fifteenth and early sixteenth centuries in at least the southern Low Countries. These studies therefore possess a significance beyond their immediate objectives, in respect of the contribution which they are able to make towards the general recovery of some

[1] In outline at least, it is possible to trace a continuous history of the music of the household chapel of the dukes of Burgundy and of the archdukes of the Netherlands (and their regents) between 1364 and 1506 through the publications following: Craig Wright, *Music at the Court of Burgundy, 1364–1419: a Documentary History* (Henryville, 1979); Jeanne Marix, *Histoire de la musique et des musiciens de la cour de Bourgogne sous le règne de Philippe le Bon (1420–1467)* (Strasbourg, 1939); G. van Doorslaer, 'La chapelle musicale de Philippe le Beau', *Revue Belge d'Archéologie et d'Histoire de l'Art*, 4 (1934), pp. 21–57, 139–65. There is supplementary material for both the fifteenth and the early sixteenth centuries to be found in the following: Edmond vander Straeten, *La Musique aux Pays-Bas avant le xixe siècle*, 8 vols (Brussels, 1867–88; repr. New York, 1969), 7, pp. 94–261, *passim*; *Muziek aan het Hof van Margaretha van Oostrijk = Jaarboek van het Vlaamse Centrum voor Oude Muziek*, 3 (1987); G. G. Thompson, 'Music in the court records of Mary of Hungary', *Tijdschrift van de Vereniging voor Nederlandse Muziekgeschiedenis* [hereafter *TVNM*], 34 (1984), pp. 132–73.

[2] Albert Smijers, 'De Illustre Lieve Vrouwe Broederschap te 's-Hertogenbosch', *TVNM*, 11 (1923–5), pp. 187–210; 12 (1926–8), pp. 40–62, 115–67; 13 (1929–32), pp. 46–100, 181–237; 14 (1932–5), pp. 48–105; 16 (1940–6), pp. 63–106, 216; 17 (1955), pp. 195–230; continuation by M. A. Vente, ibid., 19 (1960–3), pp. 32–43, 163–72. Albert Smijers, 'Meerstemmige muziek van de Illustre Lieve Vrouwe Broederschap te 's-Hertogenbosch', *TVNM*, 16 (1940), pp. 1–30, and 'Music of the Illustrious Confraternity of Our Lady at 's-Hertogenbosch from 1330 to 1600', in Arthur Mendel, ed., *Papers read at the International Congress of Musicology, New York 1939* (New York, 1939), pp. 184–92.

[3] Reinhard Strohm, *Music in Late Medieval Bruges* (Oxford, 1985).

[4] Barbara Haggh, 'Music, Liturgy and Ceremony in Brussels, 1350–1500' (Illinois at Urbana-Champaign Ph.D. dissertation, 1988).

[5] Kristine Forney, 'Music, ritual and patronage at the church of Our Lady, Antwerp', *Early Music History* [hereafter *EMH*], 7 (1987), pp. 1–57.

[6] Rob Wegman, 'Music and musicians at the Guild of Our Lady in Bergen op Zoom, c.1470–1510', *EMH*, 9 (1989), pp. 175–249.

comprehension of the nature of popular devotion to orthodox religious practice in the period immediately preceding the Reformation. The scope and purpose of the present article, therefore, is severely circumscribed. It does not pretend to offer any new research as such; rather, I have endeavoured merely to draw from a collation and synthesis of the work of others certain inferences and conclusions that seem to have a significance in the broader historical view. I gladly acknowledge here the depth of my indebtedness to the labours and insights of the authors on whose work I draw, the extent of which will, I hope, be evident from the copiousness of the citations entered in the footnotes below.

The Church in the fifteenth century sustained more than one manner of rendering the music of the liturgical services, depending on the status of the occasion and the performing forces available. The fundamental music of the liturgy, performable whether only three or four were gathered together or a whole cathedral choir of some fifty or sixty voices, or anything in between, was the historic corpus of plainsong chant. In institutions where the performers were professionals (which excludes most monasteries, nunneries, and friaries, but includes the cathedral and principal collegiate churches), it was possible for the more important feast-days, and the more significant phases of the weightiest among the ordinary daily services of High Mass and the eight canonical Hours, to be especially distinguished by the substitution of polyphonic music for the authorized plainsong. Of the two forms of polyphony available, improvised and composed, it was the latter which carried greatest weight in elevating the character of any religious service, offered greatest esteem to its creators (the composers) and performers, and—not least—greatest satisfaction and prestige to the patrons who were paying for it.

The choirs of such collegiate churches and of the private chapels of aristocratic households included not only professional singing-men (both priestly and lay) but commonly, though not invariably, singing-boys of the choir as well. Until around the middle of the fifteenth century, polyphonic music was composed largely in three or four parts, for performance unaccompanied by any instrument; most commonly (perhaps exclusively), the medium was a small ensemble composed of the solo voices of singing-men performing one to a part, commonly (probably normally) excluding boys' voices (which latter were used only in plainsong). Around the middle of the century, however, the fortuitous but progressive simplification of the notation of polyphonic music made possible its teaching to a far higher proportion of the members of any choir, including even the chorister-boys. It was thus that there arose, from about the 1460s onwards, that special and extravagant panoply of sonic beauty that could be realized by the unaccompanied chorus of some twenty or thirty human voices singing in four, five, or six parts, all applied to the given texts of the Mass and Office, that wealthy patrons, lay no less than ecclesiastical, sought thenceforth to have added—for the good of their souls and of their credit in heaven—to the manner of worship in the churches and chapels which they undertook to support. It was natural enough that the Church itself should seek to exploit this newly-developed resource for enhancing its work, for deployment alongside, and in addition to, the many others already evolved to beautify the rendering of the liturgical service; the purpose of this paper is to suggest the very considerable extent to which the devout community of the laity likewise offered its resources to the same end.

* * *

Throughout the fifteenth century two choral establishments were recognized as pre-eminent in the Low Countries. One was the choir of the cathedral church of Cambrai;[7] the other, and the principal non-ecclesiastical patron of the music of the Church, was the choir of the household chapel of the Valois dukes of Burgundy and their successors. This latter enjoyed no permanent base; rather, it was peripatetic with the household, and thus—at least from the time of its re-establishment by Philip the Good in 1429—it functioned primarily in Brussels, Lille, and (later) Malines.

Philip the Bold (1363–1404) first inaugurated a plenary chapel for his household in 1384, and its personnel soon stabilized at around seventeen to twenty-one members. Of these, the majority were chaplains in priest's orders, supplemented by some three or four clerks in sub-priestly orders, all under a First Chaplain as general manager and overseer. Also among the chapel staff were three or four *sommeliers* (porters and general assistants); although these did not contribute to the music of the services, many were recruited for their potential to do so, and these duly succeeded in due course to vacant clerkships and eventually to chaplaincies.[8] In terms of

[7] See Craig Wright, 'Dufay at Cambrai: discoveries and revisions', *Journal of the American Musicological Society*, 28 (1975), pp. 163–229, esp. pp. 192–207, and 'Performance practices at the cathedral of Cambrai, 1475–1550', *Musical Quarterly*, 64 (1978), pp. 295–328; David Fallows, 'Cambrai', in Stanley Sadie, ed., *The New Grove Dictionary of Music and Musicians*, 20 vols (London, 1980), 3, pp. 641–2.

[8] Wright, *Music at the Court of Burgundy*, pp. 55–83, 138–58, 212–30.

musicianship, Philip was looking only for the best, as witness his opportunist recruitment for his own chapel of five of the members of the papal household chapel in Avignon on the death of Clement VII in 1394.[9] Philip's successor, Duke John the Fearless (1404–19), maintained a plenary chapel only between 1415 and 1419. It was as brilliant as it was short-lived; of its fifteen members (with four choristers, introduced in 1406) six were composers who have left surviving works.[10]

However, the headquarters of Philip I and John were mostly at Paris and Dijon; consequently the accomplishments of their household chapels are not really part of the history of music in the Low Countries. Nevertheless, they had established a commanding precedent for prodigality of recruitment and excellence of music which was followed by Philip the Good (1419–67) when he expanded his original, merely 'skeleton', chapel of a few chaplains and clerks and four to six choristers[11] to plenary status in 1429,[12] staffing it mostly from, and thereafter largely basing it in, his Low Countries territorial possessions. His chapel was maintained throughout his reign after 1429 at eighteen to twenty chaplains and clerks, with four *sommeliers*, but no chorister-boys.[13]

These dimensions were retained by Philip the Good's successor, Duke Charles the Bold (1467–77). His household ordinances of 1469 established

[9] Wright, *Music at the Court of Burgundy*, pp. 62–5.

[10] Ibid., pp. 84–110, 165–78, 231–4.

[11] Marix, *Histoire de la musique*, pp. 24, 61–2, 80, 127–8, 160–2, 164.

[12] The chronology and manner of Philip's restoration of the chapel cannot be determined precisely, since the necessary archival sources are missing for the period 1419–36. It appears (ibid., pp. 80–1) that as late as November and December 1428 the adult staff of the chapel was still of only 'skeleton' dimensions, numbering but five. However, in January 1430 the members of the chapel could be described as 'en grand nombre, des plus excellents en art de musique que l'on peust et seust eslire et trouver' (ibid., p. 28). Further, when one of the chapel staff, the chaplain Gilles Binchois, composed his four-part isorhythmic motet *Nove cantum melodie/Tanti gaude germinis/. . . Enixa meritis/Tenor* for the baptism on 18 January 1431 of Antoine, the short-lived, first-born son of Philip and his third wife, Isabella of Portugal, he set a text which called on the members of the chapel by name to welcome and honour the new-born, and the names—including his own—totalled nineteen: David Fallows, 'Binchois, Gilles', in Sadie, *New Grove Dictionary*, 2, pp. 709, 718; Jeanne Marix, *Les Musiciens de la Cour de Bourgogne au quinzième siècle (1420–67)* (Paris, 1937), pp. 212–17. Meanwhile, the boys of the chapel are not encountered again after 1428 (Marix, *Histoire de la musique*, pp. 61–2, 164). Consequently it appears that it was during 1429 that Philip the Good transformed his former skeleton chapel of a few chaplains, clerks, and boys into a musically fully professional but wholly adult chapel. As first disclosed in detail by the surviving household accounts of 1436 (ibid., p. 242), the chapel then consisted of the chief and sixteen chaplains and two clerks—totalling nineteen, as previously in Binchois' motet text of 1431.

[13] These statistics have been distilled from the lists of personnel printed in Marix, *Histoire de la musique*, pp. 242–63.

the personnel of the chapel at a Chief and twelve chaplains and six clerks (totalling eighteen professional singers) with five *sommeliers*. Of the chaplains, four priests were at any one time to be designated a pool for entablement as celebrants at the altar on non-festal days. This left fourteen singers to perform the polyphony, who were always to consist of four basses, three tenors, two countertenors and six *haultes voix*—probably singers of the type called in contemporary Italian sources *soverani*, namely, adult male sopranos.[14] After 1477 the chapel passed to Marie of Burgundy and thence to the Habsburg archdukes. Not surprisingly, the membership of the household chapel passed through a period of instability and contraction during the upheavals consequent upon the disputed succession to, and partition of, the late Burgundian territories; nevertheless, it quickly recovered thereafter, and during the rule of Philip the Fair (d. 1506) it stood at much its old dimensions, at a Chief Chaplain, some eighteen to twenty chaplains and clerks, and four *sommeliers*—but no boys.[15] Overall, in terms of simple numbers of staff, the household chapel of the Valois dukes and their successors compared roughly equally with those of the other kings and grandees of continental Western Europe of this period. It could not compare with the Chapel Royal of the kings of England; this, under Henry V in 1421–2, consisted of a dean, no fewer than thirty-two chaplains and clerks, and sixteen boys, and in 1448–9 under Henry VI, and again in 1465–6 under Edward IV, extended to a dean, thirty-six chaplains and clerks, and ten boys;[16] but then, probably no royal or aristocratic or ecclesiastical household chapel anywhere in continental Europe sought to emulate the extravagances of the English at this period.

Through the household chapel, the court of the dukes of Burgundy and their successors thus served as the principal single source of lay patronage for ecclesiastical music in the Low Countries in the fifteenth

[14] David Fallows, 'Specific information on the ensembles for composed polyphony, 1400–1474', in Stanley Boorman, ed., *Studies in the Performance of Late Mediaeval Music* (Cambridge, 1983), pp. 110–17, 145–59. The very high voice of the adult *soverano falsetto*, capable of sustaining a tessitura extending as a matter of course to around *e* a tenth above middle *c*, was apparently very rare; however, it appears that it was not until about the 1530s that the excess of demand over supply prompted the creation of its synthetic substitute, the *soverano castrato*.

[15] van Doorslaer, 'La chapelle musicale de Philippe le Beau', pp. 33–57, 139–65.

[16] PRO, MSS E 101/407/4, fols 21r, 36r,, 46r (1421–2); E 101/410/3, fols 30r–v (1448–9: 37 gentlemen listed; however, one—William Boston—was away on secondment to the chapel of King Henry's newly-founded King's College, Cambridge, as Master of the Choristers: PRO E 403/771, m. 11; Cambridge, King's College, Mundum Book I, fols 95r, 143r, 155r, and Commons Book I (1447–8), *passim*; PRO E 101/411/15, fols 16v–17r (1465–6).

century—just as it did also in respect of painting, secular literature, jewel-making, goldsmithery, tapestry-work, manuscript making and illuminating, and the other decorative and practical arts.[17] From 1384 until well into the sixteenth century, with only the two interruptions from 1404 until 1415 and from 1419 until 1429, the ruling (and, from the second quarter of the century, largely resident) lord of Flanders and its growing number of associated duchies and counties of the *Pays Bas* maintained a highly regarded and evidently commendably skilful body of chapel personnel consisting, with remarkable consistency through a period exceeding 130 years, of some seventeen to twenty professional singers, clerical and lay. However, only during the brief period 1406–28 were there any chorister-boys of the chapel;[18] normally, the staff was entirely adult.

The overt function of such a household chapel was twofold. Its routine duty was to accompany the duke and attend upon him within his household, and—*ad maiorem gloriam Dei* and for the good estate of the ducal family living and departed—to observe daily High Mass and the cycle of the Office in as honourable, decorous, and sumptuous a manner as possible, in the chapel of whatever palace, castle, or mansion the duke happened at that time to be residing. In this respect, the maintenance of a household chapel represented a due and proper expression of the natural and conventional piety of one of the greater late medieval magnates; it was no less, and (its lavishness notwithstanding) probably no great deal more, than what contemporary society would have expected.

This is not to deny the existence also of certain complementary objectives and motives. Alongside the execution of the conventional religious observance, the maintenance of a populous and ostentatious chapel personnel possessed also a political function and dimension. As well as serving as a means of advertising publicly its patron's orthodoxy and devotion to Holy Church, it provided a conduit for a conspicuous display of the duke's magnificence and wealth, so helping to establish his status in the eyes of those with whom he dealt in business both diplomatic and political; and in its execution of the religious ritual, it made manifest the resources in creative and executive talent that its employer was able to recruit and command to his personal service. Among such occasions of sumptuous and political ostentation were the periodic meetings of the

[17] For a concentrated survey, see Richard Vaughan, *Philip the Good* (London, 1970), pp. 150–60.

[18] Wright, *Music at the Court of Burgundy*, pp. 92–8; Marix, *Histoire de la musique*, pp. 61–2, 80, 127–8, 160–2, 164.

chivalric Order of the Golden Fleece, and also the *petit chapitre* of the Order held annually on the feast of St Andrew, the patron saint of the Valois dukes. It has indeed been suggested that particular musical works were in fact commissioned from prominent composers for performance by the chapel of the household on these occasions—for instance, the motet *Ut Phebi radiis* by Josquin des Pres.[19] It has also been suggested that the original impetus and inspiration for the composition of the Masses on the 'l'Homme armé' melody as *cantus firmus* may have lain in the commissioning of polyphonic settings of the Ordinary for performance at the grand High Mass, sung by the ducal chapel, which formed a high point among the ceremonies of each principal chapter meeting of the Order of the Golden Fleece.[20] It was by such means as these that the chapel of the household served to promote for its employer an image and aura of splendour and wealth, of diplomatic potency and political weight. There is, to be sure, some evidence that Philip the Good, and especially Duke Charles and Archduke Philip the Fair, took considerable personal pleasure in music;[21] probably, however, this was not among the first of their motives in maintaining a household chapel.

Primarily, the existence and activities of the ducal chapel manifested its employer's piety, and the orthodoxy of his adherence to contemporary conventions of religious practice. However, as a peripatetic body, it could not be expected to endeavour to observe the totality of the cycle of eight daily Offices as well as High Mass. According to the household ordinances of 1469, Vespers and Compline—the evening Offices—were observed every day; the remainder—Matins with Lauds, Prime, Terce, Sext, and None—were observed (in an immediate succession likely to take some two to three hours) just in Lent and in Advent, and on twenty-one specified feast-days. The principal observance each day, in addition to Vespers, was the High Mass, celebrated according to the use of the diocese

19 Jaap van Benthem, 'A waif, a wedding, and a worshipped child: Josquin's *Ut Phebi radiis* and the Order of the Golden Fleece', *TVNM*, 37 (1987), pp. 64–81; William Prizer, 'Music and ceremonial in the Low Countries: Philip the Fair and the Order of the Golden Fleece', *EMH*, 5 (1985), pp. 129–33.

20 Ibid., pp. 128–9, esp. n. 43; see also Alejandro Enrique Planchart, 'Guillaume Dufay's benefices and his relationship to the court of Burgundy', *EMH*, 8 (1988), pp. 159–60.

21 Charles the Bold was reported to have composed music himself, and also to have been an enthusiastic singer—his lack of a tuneful voice notwithstanding: Richard Vaughan, *Valois Burgundy* (London, 1975), pp. 168–9, and *Charles the Bold* (London, 1973), pp. 161–2; Judith Cohen, *The Six Anonymous l'Homme Armé Masses in Naples, Biblioteca Nazionale, MS VI E 40 = Musicological Studies and Documents*, 21 (n.p., 1968), pp. 62–71; van Doorslaer, 'La chapelle musicale de Philippe le Beau', pp. 36–7.

of Paris, and dignified daily with polyphonic as well as monodic music.[22] Philip the Good attended High Mass daily; however, he was not an early riser, and enjoyed a papal dispensation to hear Mass not in the morning but between two and three o'clock in the afternoon.[23] The chronicler Olivier de la Marche observed that Duke Charles likewise attended daily at solemn High Mass, and also at Vespers and Compline,[24] and an ordinance of 1500 recorded that the chapel's function was to observe daily High Mass, Vespers, and Compline, primarily in the presence of the Archduke, though otherwise if that be his pleasure.[25]

The Burgundian chroniclers were hardly unbiased, but their protestations of the high quality of the court chapel were probably not far wide of the mark.[26] Philip II attended the marriage of the son of the Duke of Savoy to Anne of Cyprus at Chambéry in 1434; Mass was sung by the Burgundian court chapel 'tant melodieusement que c'estoit belle chose a oyr: car, pour l'heure, on tenoit la chapelle du duc la meilleur du monde, du nombre qu'ilz estoient.'[27] In 1445 the duke's chapel performed Vespers in the presence of the members of the Order of the Golden Fleece in the church of St Jean, in Ghent, 'qui fut une de meilleures chappelles, des mieulx accordes, et en plus grand nombre de chappellains, que l'on sceut nulle part.'[28] The rewards which successive dukes and archdukes could offer to the singing-men, virtually all of whom were in priest's orders, clearly made the ducal chapel something of a cynosure. Pay was generous (twelve sous per day for chaplains, ten for clerks), and the duke's largesse in distributing to his singers the prebends of collegiate churches in his gift ensured that every one possessed not only substantial augmentation of his wages during his working life, but also tenured assurance of a pension and a comfortable retirement when advancing years caused his voice to fail. However, despite the rewards on offer, the peripatetic life did not appeal

[22] Fallows, 'Specific information on the ensembles for composed polyphony', pp. 147–8.

[23] Vaughan, *Philip the Good*, p. 128. A handsome manuscript copy of Jean Miélot's French translation ('Traité sur l'Oraison Dominicale') of the *Tractatus de Oratione Dominicali*, illuminated by Jean Tavernier (or a pupil), (Brussels, Bibliothèque royale, MS 9092, fol. 9r) is illustrated with a well-known illumination depicting Philip in attendance upon Mass performed by his chapel; it is reproduced in Robert Wangermee, *Flemish Music and Society in the Fifteenth and Sixteenth Centuries* (Brussels, 1968), p. 56, and Edmund Bowles, *Musikleben im 15. Jahrhundert* = *Musikgeschichte in Bildern*, 3 (Leipzig, 1977), p. 113 (plate 102).

[24] van Doorslaer, 'La chapelle musicale de Philippe le Beau', p. 25.

[25] Ibid., p. 45.

[26] As well as the two quotations following, see n. 12 above.

[27] Marix, *Histoire de la Musique*, p. 30, quoting the Chronicle of Jean le Fèvre, seigneur de Saint-Rémy.

[28] Ibid., p. 36, quoting Olivier de la Marche.

to all; the most celebrated composer of the mid-century period, Guillaume Dufay, centred the northern phases of his career on Cambrai Cathedral, and never became a member of the Burgundian court chapel, though his contacts with its members were close.[29] Nevertheless, Dufay was probably an exception. As has been seen, the chapel included, except for one brief period, no boys, and consequently it could not recruit *de gremio*. Even so, recruitment seems never to have been a problem; the chapel experienced no difficulty in obtaining established and experienced singers from all over the Low Countries. The antecedents of many are known, and the catchment area included the whole of the duke's northern estates.

The chapel offered its patronage especially to the composers of polyphonic music, for whom it provided a milieu in which their skills would be esteemed and appreciated, and an arena in which their creations could be assured of skilful and sympathetic performance. It is perhaps in this area that the ducal patronage of the music of the Church made its greatest contribution to the fifteenth-century enlargement of musical culture. Moreover, produced in so prominent a centre, these men's creations stood a better chance than most of circulating in their own time, and surviving into ours. Jean Tapissier, Jean Carmen, and Jean Franchois, members of the chapel of Philip I, and Nicolas Grenon, Master of the Choristers of the chapel of Duke John, have all left settings of movements from the Mass Ordinary and motets, preserved in manuscripts of the period *c.*1400–45.[30]

Contemporaries themselves were aware that the composers of the ducal chapel were not the least of its ornaments. In around 1438–42 one Martin le Franc completed his lengthy poem *Le Champion des dames*, dedicated to Philip the Good, at one point in which the hero, Franc Vouloir, explains that the end of the world is manifestly nigh; as evidence for the coming apocalypse he cites the way in which the arts (for instance, music, the visual arts, literature, chivalry itself) have been brought in contemporary days to unprecedented states of perfection:

> Tapissier, Carmen, Cesaris,
> N'a pas long temps sy bien chanterent
> Qu'ilz esbahirent tout Paris
> Et tous ceulx qui les frequenterent;

[29] Wright, 'Dufay at Cambrai', p. 185; Planchart, 'Guillaume Du Fay's benefices and his relationship to the court of Burgundy', pp. 135–40.

[30] Wright, *Music at the Court of Burgundy*, pp. 165–6, 168–71, 174–7. Wright creates circumstantial cases for adding Baude Cordier and Cassin Hullin as composers of sacred music employed by the first two Valois dukes, and discusses several other members of the ducal chapels who composed courtly song.

Mais onques jour ne deschanterent
En melodie de tel chois,
Ce m'ont dit ceulx qui les hanterent,
Que G. Du Fay et Binchois.

Car ilz ont nouvelle pratique
De faire frisque concordance
En haulte et en basse musique,
En fainte, en pause et en muance;
Et ont pris de la contenance
Angloise, et ensuy Dompstable—
Pour quoy merveilleuse plaisance
Rend leur chant joieux et notable.

> Not long ago, Tapissier, Carmen, and Cesaris sang so well that they astonished all Paris and everyone who attended upon them; but—so the people who heard them tell me—at no time did they make music, in melody and suchlike, as do G. DuFay and Binchois. For these possess a new practice, in music both learned and simple, of making elegant consonance through *ficta musica*, through phrase-structure and through melodic design. And they have taken on the English fashion, and have followed Dunstable, whereby a wondrous geniality renders their music radiant and arresting.[31]

Of the five continental composers singled out for special esteem by this client of Philip the Good, three (Tapissier, Carmen, and Binchois) were, or had been, members of the ducal chapel, and clearly were considered to be among its special ornaments. As well as the prolific Gilles Binchois, the chapels of Philip II and Charles included among their composers Philippe Foliot, Guillaume Ruby, and Antoine Busnois among those whose church music has survived; and if these are far outnumbered by chapel members now known for their composition only of courtly song,[32] then this circumstance is most probably less a reflection of contemporary priorities than simply of the very high proportion of *chansonniers* (song-books), and the relative paucity of ecclesiastical sources, among the surviving manuscripts of this period.

[31] David Fallows, 'The contenance angloise: English influence on continental composers of the fifteenth century', *Renaissance Studies*, 1 (1987), pp. 195–208. In offering this new translation of these well-known verses, I gladly acknowledge my debt to both the detail and the substance of Fallows's article, and also to the previous translation by Ernest Sanders quoted there.

[32] See Marix, *Histoire de la Musique*, pp. 223–41.

For the chapel of Philip the Fair, the survival pattern is the exact reverse, and it is possible to gain some true appreciation of the quality of the music of the archducal chapel from the surviving works of—as well as Antoine Busnois—Alexander Agricola, Nicolas Champion, Jerome de Clibano, Mabrianus de Orto, Gilles Reijngoot, Antoine Divitis, Pierre de la Rue, and Gaspar van Weerbeke.[33] From this later period a few manuscripts compiled for, and used by, the court chapel have had the good fortune to survive: Brussels, Bibliothèque royale, MS 5557, from the chapel of Charles the Bold, and Brussels, Bibliothèque royale, MS 9126, from that of Philip the Fair.[34] Some idea, perhaps, of the manner in which the celebration of High Mass was dignified on a daily basis in the chapels of Charles the Bold and Maximilian is provided by the setting by Antoine Busnois of the Ordinary of the Mass on the 'l'Homme armé' tune as *cantus firmus*. It is written for just the sort of four-part choir of adult male voices that was specified in Charles the Bold's household ordinances of 1469, made when Busnois was already a member of the court chapel.[35]

It is conventional to characterize the piety displayed by the several Valois dukes and their successors as 'conventional'. Certainly, the life and demeanour of none was distinguished by any special sanctity, and none exhibited conspicuous and pervasive habits of devotion or piety, or took express interest in matters theological or liturgical. Nevertheless, the fact that none exceeded conventional standards in matters of personal piety should not be interpreted as evidence of insincerity or indifference to the religious practice of their day; if they did no more than what was conventional, they did no less either.[36] There seems to be no good reason to doubt that it was as an overt manifestation and expression of genuine piety, sincerely embraced, that the successive dukes and archdukes undertook to

[33] van Doorslaer,'La chapelle musicale de Philippe le Beau', pp. 139–59. Except for Reijngoot, each of these composers is the subject of an article in Sadie, *New Grove Dictionary*.

[34] Facsimile edition of Brussels MS 5557: Rob Wegman, *A Choirbook of the Burgundian Court Chapel: Brussel, Koninklijke Bibliotheek, MS 5557* (Brussels, 1989); see also his 'New data concerning the origins and chronology of Brussels, Koninklijke Bibliotheek 5557', *TVNM*, 36 (1986), pp. 5–25. Inventory of Brussels, Bibliothèque royale, MS 9126: Charles van den Borren, 'Inventaire des manuscrits de musique polyphonique qui se trouvent en Belgique', *Acta Musicologica*, 5 (1933), pp. 70–1; Charles Hamm, Herbert Kellman, and Jerry Call, eds, *Census-Catalogue of Manuscript Sources of Polyphonic Music, 1400–1550*, 5 vols (Rome, 1979–88), 1, p. 94.

[35] Laurence Feininger, ed., *Antoine Busnois: Mass l'Homme armé= Monumenta Polyphoniae Liturgicae Sanctae Ecclesiae Romanae*, ser. I, 1, pt ii (Rome, 1948).

[36] Richard Vaughan, *Philip the Bold* (London, 1962), pp. 194, 197; *John the Fearless* (London, 1966), pp. 233; *Philip the Good*, pp. 128–30; *Charles the Bold*, pp. 161–2; *Valois Burgundy*, p. 185.

maintain and cultivate their household chapel of professional musicians, and thus to serve as the most efficacious of the lay patrons of the church music of their day.

* * *

This piety of the dukes and archdukes, and their consequent patronage of the music of the Church through their cultivation of the household chapel, constituted essentially private munificence towards a jointly religious and political end, and had little if any bearing upon the work of the Church at large among the people. And, in all probability, the other great territorial magnates of the Low Countries maintained chapels of the household for a like purpose: the bishops of Liège, Tournai, Utrecht, and Cambrai, the Wittelsbach counts of Hainault, Holland, and Zeeland, the dukes of Guelders, and such long-lived dowagers as Margaret, Duchess of Burgundy, widow of Charles the Bold. In comparison, the patronage of lesser lay landed families was wont to adopt a very much more public aspect, through devolvement upon not a private chapel, but a collegiate or parish church. Further, through association into religious fraternities, it was possible for any members of society—provided they possessed sufficient status and means to be accepted into membership—to make a contribution to the offering to the Almighty of a gift of devotion expressed through music.[37]

The rich musical life of the town of Bergen op Zoom presents a very good example of what could be achieved in a major provincial commercial entrepôt, in which the munificence of a single wealthy family established an example which lesser mortals could pool their resources to emulate. As a commercial town, Bergen developed late, and was thus served—even at the time of its greatest prosperity—by just a single parish church, St Gertrude; this church therefore enjoyed the considerable advantage of serving as the sole undisputed focus of the devotion of all the citizens. During the fifteenth century, lordship over the town and

[37] The fraternities mentioned below were pre-eminently associations of lay persons, and the nature of the enterprises and operations which they promoted manifested and responded to the preoccupations and priorities of lay society. Membership was, however, normally no less open to any member of the clergy, in his capacity just as a member of the community, who wished to further and be associated with the objectives of the fraternity—and in this respect, these organizations are, perhaps, better considered as 'popular' rather than quintessentially 'lay'.

seignury of Bergen op Zoom resided in the family of van Glijmes.[38] As the town's commercial fortunes, based on its twice-yearly fairs at Eastertide and Martinmas, rose in the early fifteenth century, the van Glijmes family and the town undertook in 1428 to devolve a substantial endowment upon St Gertrude's church, so as to raise it to collegiate status; this development finally received papal ratification in 1442, and between 1443 and 1470 Lord Jan II van Glijmes (1417–94) funded the total rebuilding of the church in a manner appropriate to its new status—in return for which generosity, collation to all the prebends was vested in him and his successors in perpetuity thereafter. Unfortunately no fifteenth-century accounts of the college seem to survive; however, it is known that by the 1460s its choral staff included a Master of the Choristers and a group of boys,[39] and there must also have been, ever since 1442, adult singers to observe the Office and attend upon the music of High Mass in the manner appropriate to, and inseparable from, the status of St Gertrude's as a collegiate church.[40]

As the rebuilding of the church neared completion in 1470, a Lady Chapel for worship of the Virgin Mary was built on the north side of the choir, and by 1470 Lord Jan van Glijmes and the city council had founded and established a Gild of Our Lady, to be a religious fraternity through which the devotion of the citizens to St Mary could be aggregated and channelled into ostentatiously and lavishly elevated acts of devotion. The membership of the fraternity became very large, ranging from some 750 to around 1,100. Members paid an entry-fine and an annual subscription, and made gifts and (especially) bequests to the gild, and from these resources the aldermen of the gild arranged for elaborate acts of devotion to the Virgin to be celebrated in the name, in the presence, and for the good of the souls of the paid-up membership, living and departed.

As well as occasional celebrations of the Mass in honour of the Virgin Mary, there was one principal devotion that took place daily. This was an extra-liturgical service added to the daily Office and called the 'Lof', consisting principally of a service of intercession addressed to the Blessed

[38] The lordship of Bergen was not raised to the status of a Margraviate of the Empire until 1533.

[39] Wegman, 'Music and musicians at the Guild of Our Lady in Bergen op Zoom', pp. 178–82. The college also maintained a master for its free Grammar School.

[40] A reference in 1474–5 to Herr Jan van Andehoven as 'canon and singing-man' (*canonic ende singer*) of Bergen appears to suggest that the adult department of the choir was, at least in part, staffed by the collation of the prebends upon men who were both prepared to reside, and also were able to serve no less as singing-men of the choir than as canons of the chapter: ibid., p. 187, n. 21.

Virgin, soliciting her good offices on behalf of the gild membership. The musical content of the 'Lof' (the term simply means 'praise') in a collegiate or parish church varied according to the resources of those founding and endowing it, but it began invariably with the performance of a sung text in honour of the Virgin Mary; this was commonly the *Salve regina*, from which in many places was derived an alternative title for the service, the 'Salve'. There followed prayers of intercession, and in some instances, further music; for example, from 1495 to 1496 at Bergen op Zoom, while the bells were being rung at the end of the 'Lof', *Ave Maria* was sung by the choirmaster and choristers.[41] On 24 December 1470, Lord Jan van Glijmes, the burgomasters (of the town), and the aldermen of the gild recorded that they had made agreement with the chapter of St Gertrude for the fraternity to enjoy the services of the choir of the collegiate church in the conduct of these devotions, and formulated (for their own records, which do survive) an ordinance decreeing the sums that the gild would pay to the singers in return. The 'Lof' was to be sung each evening by the Master of the Choristers, the boys, and five of the singing-men; the same singers were bound also to attend at and sing 'all the Masses of Our Lady', which probably extended to the usual weekly Lady Mass each Saturday, and High Mass on the six principal Marian feasts.[42]

At first the fraternity of Our Lady committed itself to a relatively modest budget for devotional services,[43] but at the end of 1474 the lavish patronage of Jan van Glijmes once again became evident. He and the city government transferred in perpetuity to the gild the profits of Bergen's two annual commercial fairs; the receipt of this grant immediately almost doubled its annual income with an infusion of cash extending to over

[41] Wegman, 'Music and musicians at the Guild of Our Lady in Bergen op Zoom', pp. 185, 217.

[42] Ibid., pp. 183–5, 219–20. The interpretation of this document offered here differs radically from that suggested by Wegman. He presents a scenario in which the gild employed a self-contained choir *of its own*, independent of that of the collegiate church, to whose members the modest payments made by the gild constituted their principal source of income. Wegman's own calculations (see, for example, p. 197) are themselves the best evidence of the implausibility of this scenario—especially his observation that, if he is right, 'even good singers or choirmasters in Brabant (particularly laymen) had to work very hard in order to earn more than unskilled hodmen in Antwerp.' Rather, it seems very clear from this document that the gild was contracting with the chapter to employ the existing singers of the choir of the collegiate church in work supplementary to their standing duties, for which an appropriate payment was made by the gild to each singer as merely a supplement to his prime stipend received from the college.

[43] Nevertheless, the gild paid the choirmaster and six, rather than five, singing-men until 1494: ibid., p. 214. The additional singers who participated on only an occasional and casual basis appear certain to have been simply other members of St Gertrude's choir.

15,000 groats of Brabant per year, and between 1480 and 1498 the revenue from the fairs nearly doubled again, finally reaching a thirty-year plateau (and all-time maximum) between 1498 and 1530. Suddenly the choir of the collegiate church of Bergen op Zoom had become one of the best funded such establishments anywhere in the Netherlands; indeed, by the early sixteenth century, the gild was spending over 25,000 groats per year on music in the Lady Chapel of St Gertrude's church, and the joint resources of the collegiate church and gild were able to attract to the town singers of high quality.

Through the endowment of first the collegiate church and then the gild, all this had been made possible largely by the patronage of one lay lord, Jan van Glijmes. The resources of the college sufficed, it appears, to maintain no fewer than some twelve or thirteen adult singers, plus a singer serving also as organist, with a *sangmeester*—Master of the Choristers—and an undetermined number of boys.[44] The collegiate choir is known to have made extensive use of polyphonic music on major feast-days, not least on St Anthony's Day, when the services were subsidized and sponsored by a second religious fraternity, the municipal Gild of St Anthony.[45] Meanwhile, the Gild of Our Lady was sponsoring the choir in respect of some 422 extra-curricular occasions per year, on probably all of which polyphony was used; this total evidently was comprised of 364 observances of the 'Lof', plus fifty-two weekly Lady Masses, and the six principal Marian High Masses.[46] The gild undertook considerable expenditure on the provision of music-books for use at its services,[47] and after 1498–9 concentrated its resources even more upon establishing a high quality of performance by paying considerably higher fees to a slightly smaller group of singers drawn from St Gertrude's choir. Among the musicians which the collegiate church and gild were able to attract and retain was Michiele Cramer, who in 1485 was content to decline an invitation to join the chapel of Archduke Maximilian so as to remain in Bergen instead.[48] Clais van Lyere was another; he did eventually join the

[44] Ibid., pp. 193–4.

[45] Ibid., pp. 182–3, 191.

[46] From the 1490s the boys and the *Sangmeester* were generally paid by the gild for 422 services per year, which gives the figure used here for the standard number of services (the 'Lof', of course, would not have been sung on Holy Saturday): ibid., pp. 191, 227–36. Prior to *c.*1491 there were apparently some additional services on offer, whereby conscientious singers could register up to 480 services per year.

[47] Ibid., pp. 195–6.

[48] Ibid., pp. 214–15, 239.

chapel of Philip the Fair.[49] Also in their employment were the composer Johannes Ghiselen, alias Verbonnet, newly returned in 1507 from Ferrara,[50] and the internationally renowned composer and musician Jacob Obrecht, who served as Master of the Choristers between 1480 and 1484, and returned as a singer during 1488 and from 1497 to 1498.[51] Among Obrecht's twenty-nine surviving Masses, five are based on Marian *cantus firmi* and are considered to belong among his earliest works, and thus may well have been written for the fraternity Masses at Bergen op Zoom.[52]

Very probably the model upon which the Gild of Our Lady at Bergen was constituted was the far older and more venerable Confraternity of Our Lady in the town of 's-Hertogenbosch, some forty miles to the east. Like Bergen, this town was served by a single parish church, St Janskerk, into the ennoblement of which the entirety of the reverence of the devout laity of the town was channelled. It appears that the St Janskerk was, for all its magnificence, a parish church possessing no collegiate endowments, and thus no ready-made body of clerks and boys to serve as a choir: in its sponsorship of music, therefore, its Gild of Our Lady was dependent just on the generosity of its bourgeois membership, since it was unaided by the munificence of any wealthy landed family comparable to that of the van Glijmes at Bergen. The gild's accomplishments in the patronage of the music of the services conducted under its auspices thus reveal what could be achieved just by the aggregated efforts of the more devout among the burgers of a prominent commercial town.

This gild had been founded in 1318, initially as a fraternity of townsmen and clergy committed to maintain and conduct on specified days services of worship of the Virgin Mary, in a chapel in one of the side aisles of the St Janskerk.[53] Almost from its very beginnings the gild did, of its own resources and in its own name, employ professional singers to dignify its services with polyphonic music; there are frequent and numerous payments for the copying of motets in the fourteenth century, and of a repertory more varied in the first half of the fifteenth, with a substantial extension and renewal between 1445 and 1449. The singers were

[49] Wegman, 'Music and musicians at the Guild of Our Lady in Bergen op Zoom', pp. 231–3, 244.

[50] Ibid., pp. 216, 245.

[51] Ibid., pp. 198–212.

[52] Edgar Sparks, 'Obrecht, Jacob' in Sadie, *New Grove Dictionary*, 13, pp. 482–3.

[53] This and the following paragraph have been drawn principally from Smijers, 'Music of the Illustrious Confraternity of Our Lady at 's-Hertogenbosch', pp. 184–92.

employed directly by the confraternity, not by the church; however, it has not yet proved possible to define in full what the duties of the singing-men were.

Throughout the fourteenth century, and on until 1435 or so, employment was extended by the gild to just a small ensemble of three solo adult voices, which would just have sufficed for the performance of most of the composed polyphony of the time. Thereafter resources became available to enable the gild to march with musical practice and fashion; by 1465 it was maintaining not just a small ensemble of soloists, but a small choir, of usually some eight adult voices, including a *sangmeester*, and a group of boys.[54] One of the singers, Nicholas de Clibano, was rewarded for composing and copying polyphonic settings of Marian antiphons in 1466.[55] After 1500 the choir consisted of between six and ten adults, some six to eight choristers, the *sangmeester*, and an organist; this added up to a substantial choir of some twenty voices, for the maintenance of which the confraternity was committed to raising the considerable sum of around 15,000 groats of Brabant per year.[56] In 1496 the gild commissioned the production of a sumptuous choir-book of polyphony from the well-known copyist Pierre Alamire,[57] to contain thirty-three sexterns of Masses, motets, and *Magnificats*. To this day, the Illustrious Confraternity—which still exists—preserves six of the choir-books prepared for it by Alamire and other copyists in the early sixteenth century;[58] their rich collection of Masses and motets, and Vespers antiphons, hymns, and *Magnificats*, indicates that its singers were capable of performing for the St Janskerk the full service of a collegiate church choir, and at around the turn of the sixteenth century its members included, as well as singers of a quality to be recruited from it to the archducal chapel, composers such as Nicholas de Clibano and his son Jerome, Mathieu Pipelare, and Nicolaus Craen.

* * *

54 For a possible reference to boys of the gild choir at 's-Hertogenbosch, see Wegman, 'Music and musicians at the Guild of Our Lady in Bergen op Zoom', p. 245.

55 Forney, 'Music, ritual and patronage at the church of Our Lady, Antwerp', p. 2.

56 Wegman, 'Music and musicians at the Guild of Our Lady at Bergen op Zoom', p. 188.

57 See Herbert Kellman, 'Alamire, Pierre', in Sadie, *New Grove Dictionary*, 1, pp. 192–3.

58 For a summary inventory of the contents, see Hamm, Kellman, and Call, eds, *Census Catalogue of Manuscript Sources of Polyphonic Music, 1400–1550*, 1, pp. 268–71; Albert Smijers, 'Meerstemmige muziek van de Illustre Lieve Vrouwe Broederschap te 's-Hertogenbosch', *TVNM*, 16 (1940), pp. 9–30.

For the town and city laity of the Low Countries, the existence of a profusion of collegiate churches—some seventy in the area covered by modern Belgium alone[59]—offered a particular opportunity for the expression of piety through the promotion of the beauty of music in the church. Many such churches were located in major cities sustaining a commercial life of great affluence: St Pierre of Lille, St Donatian of Bruges, and Our Lady of Bruges, Our Lady of Antwerp, Our Lady of Courtrai, St Martin of Ypres, St Pharaïlde of Ghent, and St Gudule of Brussels, to name but a very few. These all possessed, as well as chapter management and organization, their collegiate choirs, by whom the nine or ten services of the *opus Dei* had been performed daily throughout many centuries before the beginning of the fifteenth. In many instances these choral staffs were composed of a variety of ill-assorted and incohering components—bodies of staff simply accumulated, endowed, aggregated, and established piecemeal over several centuries,[60] with no objective in view other than the simple multiplication of bodies in the choir-stalls singing the plainsong of the *opus Dei*. For instance, at St Donatian of Bruges, the college was managed by a dean and chapter of thirty canons; by the end of the fifteenth century its very heterogeneous choir was staffed by some twenty-two *capellani de gremio chori*, ten vicars choral, eighteen *clerici installati*, a Master of the Choristers with the title of succentor, and eight boys—out of which collection of singers, some twelve of the *clerici installati*, the Master of the Choristers, and the eight boys undertook the performance of choral polyphony.[61] At Notre Dame in Antwerp, the department of the choral staff in the second half of the fifteenth century specializing in the singing of polyphony extended to the Master of the Choristers, an organ-player, twelve vicars choral, and ten to twelve boys.[62]

In churches such as these two, probably typical of all the major collegi-

[59] This figure is distilled from E. de Moreau, *Histoire de l'Eglise en Belgique*, 4 vols and 2 'Tomes complémentaires' (Brussels, 1946–8), Tome complémentaire 1, pp. 465–517. However, this total doubtless includes some number of minor or impoverished institutions which were in no position to endeavour to form a polyphonic choir.

[60] See especially the constitution of the choral force at the cathedral church of Notre Dame in Paris: Craig Wright, *Music and Ceremony at Notre Dame de Paris, 500–1500* (Cambridge, 1989), pp. 18–27. It may be observed that, with the single exception of Beverley Minster, English choral organization displayed far greater rationality and simplicity—a legacy, no doubt, of the intrusion of Norman powers of rationalization, simplification, and organization in the late eleventh and early twelfth centuries.

[61] Strohm, *Music in Late Medieval Bruges*, pp. 12–13, 25–6.

[62] Forney, 'Music, ritual and patronage at the church of Our Lady, Antwerp', p. 6; in the last decade of the fifteenth century the number of adult singers began to be increased towards eighteen: ibid., p. 17.

ate churches of the Low Countries, the opportunities for the cultivation of the composition and performance of polyphony that arose anyway in the normal sequence of observance of the liturgy in choir were much increased during the course of the fifteenth century by the patronage and sponsorship of the devout laity, both individually and as organized into confraternities. Doubtless these individuals did not see themselves as patrons of music; their objective was not the cultivation and encouragement of an art-form, but the augmentation of the store of merit in heaven that would be found on the Day of Judgement to have been aggregated to their account. Their means towards the accomplishment of this end was the enhancement of the splendour of divine worship on earth, and the pleading for the good offices and intercessory powers of the saints, and especially of St Mary the Virgin, in heaven. To this end, the temples of God were made ever more glorious by their gifts and offerings, in terms of images both painted and sculpted, of vestments, vessels, and other utensils for Mass, of the endowment of chaplaincies—and also, and certainly not least, the offering of the special beauty of the sound created by the polyphonic chorus in the course of sponsored religious services.

In these collegiate churches the polyphonic chorus already existed as part of the standing clerical staff, and performed in the normal course of at least the festal services. To this, the employment and sponsorship offered by the lay fraternities and individuals was essentially supplementary; nevertheless, it constituted in many instances a very substantial supplement, and it seems certain that without the popular patronage thus channelled into these churches, especially through the medium of the religious fraternities, the artistic (and spiritual) life of the Church would have been relatively much impoverished.

Commonest, and commonly the wealthiest, of all the fraternities were those of Our Lady. That of 's-Hertogenbosch, already mentioned, was founded as early as 1318; that of St Gudule, Brussels, was in existence by 1362. Many, however, were founded only in the second half of the fifteenth century, and those established in the major collegiate churches had as their particular objective the maintenance of a daily service of 'Lof' following Vespers, with polyphonic music performed—for a fee—by certain of the regular members of the choir, all for the good of the souls of the fraternity membership, many of whom, no doubt, turned up to attend. The Confraternity of St Mary in the church of Our Lady in Antwerp was founded in 1479, and its membership was allocated, and no doubt refurnished and beautified, a large chapel at the east end of the north nave aisle; it installed an organ of seventeen stops there in 1506–10.

Thenceforth much of the fraternity's resources were dedicated to the daily 'Lof', performed by an officiant, and by the Master of the Choristers, four adult singers and the organist, and all the boys. Each evening a polyphonic setting of *Salve regina* was to be sung, except in Eastertide, when (as usual) *Regina celi letare* was substituted. In the sixteenth century the gild is known to have had over one hundred members, including many of the more prominent bankers and merchants of the city.[63] Its sponsorship of polyphonic music was substantial. By the late fifteenth and early sixteenth centuries considerable sums of money were being expended by the collegiate chapter on the production of manuscripts of polyphony for the Office—*Magnificats*, responsories, and antiphons—and for High Mass; however, the Fraternity of Our Lady more than matched the chapter in its provision of volumes of motets—settings, that is, of Marian texts for the choir to use at the 'Lof'.[64]

While Our Lady's gild sponsored the daily 'Lof', another fraternity was active in sponsoring, for the good of the souls of its members, a weekly Mass. It is not known when the Fraternity of the Holy Sacrament was founded, but it was before 1446; to it was allocated the large chapel on the south side of the church, corresponding to that of Our Lady on the north. The Mass, established in 1506, was sung weekly, early on Thursday mornings; the gild paid for the services of priest, deacon, and subdeacon to celebrate, plus the Master of the Choristers, the twelve vicars choral, an organist, and all the boys, who were to sing the Mass largely in the same manner as they would sing High Mass in choir on principal (triplex) feasts. The complete Ordinary of the Mass, and from the Proper the Alleluia and the sequence (always *Ecce panis angelorum*), were sung in polyphony; so also was the hymn *Tantum ergo sacramentum* that was to be appended to the service following the Mass Proper.[65] By the early sixteenth century it is known that this Thursday Mass celebrated for the Holy Sacrament Gild was matched by a Friday Mass for the Holy Cross Gild, a Saturday Requiem Mass for the Gild of St Anthony, a Monday Mass of St Anthony for the same gild, a Tuesday Mass for the Gild of St Anne, and a Wednesday Mass for the Gild of the Circumcision—a complete weekly cycle of fraternity Masses, sponsored

[63] Forney, 'Music, ritual and patronage at the church of our Lady, Antwerp', pp. 4–5, 6, 9–11, 52–4. For a plan of the church, showing the location and dedications of the several chapels, see ibid., p. 5.

[64] Ibid., pp. 33–6.

[65] Ibid., pp. 5, 18–20.

by the laity, attended by the singers of the choir, duly rewarded for their services.[66]

For the daily Marian 'Lof' and the cycle of fraternity Masses in Our Lady's church, Antwerp, a great deal of polyphonic music must have been composed and consumed. Unfortunately no surviving manuscripts of music can for certain be assigned to this church as provenance,[67] though the accounts disclose the substantial quantities of music-copying that were commissioned. Around the turn of the sixteenth century three known composers occupied the office of Master of the Choristers in succession—Jacques Barbireau (*c.*1484–91), Jacob Obrecht (1492–8, 1500–1), and Jerome de Clibano (1499–1500). There is much in the output of Obrecht's middle years that would have served admirably certain of this church's daily requirement of polyphony; so, too, would Barbireau's Mass on a Marian responsory, *Virgo parens Christi*, as *cantus firmus*, and his motet *Osculetur me*, a text from the Song of Songs suitably sanitized by its specification for use in the Office upon the octave of the feast of the Nativity of the Blessed Virgin.[68]

* * *

It is through the work of Reinhard Strohm that it has recently become possible to appreciate the extent and the product of popular patronage of church music at all levels within a single city—that of Bruges, which, with Ghent and Antwerp, was one of the greatest of the Low Countries commercial towns. Large as the city was, with a population of some 30,000, the devotion of the citizens who dwelt within the walls was channelled into just the two collegiate churches of St Donatian and Our Lady, and four parish churches. St Donatian and Our Lady each had its own endowed choral body. Among the heterogeneous group of singers of St Donatian, the Master of the Choristers, some twelve of the *clerici installati*, and the eight boys sang polyphony in the second half of the fifteenth century. At Notre Dame there were, towards the end of the century, some twenty-four *capellani*, four vicars choral, at least fourteen *clerici installati*, a Master of the Choristers, and an undetermined number of boys; among

[66] Ibid., pp. 3–6, 9, 21–6. The Gild of St Anne had begun its existence as at least in some sense a trade gild, of the hosiers; its accounts have not survived, and it is not certain, though very likely, that the singers attended to raise this Mass, like the others, to polyphonic performance.

[67] For a reference to the discovery in Antwerp of fragmentary manuscript sources of music of this period which may have originated at the church of Our Lady, see ibid., p. 38 and n. 96.

[68] Ibid., pp. 32–44; Elly Kooiman, 'The biography of Jacob Barbireau (1455–91) reviewed', *TVNM*, 38 (1988), pp. 36–58.

all this body a certain nucleus was trained and competent to render polyphonic music.[69]

Lay endowment of the resources and opportunities for the performance of polyphonic music were lavished upon the singers of the Bruges churches by representatives of almost every social stratum—from princes of the land down to the neighbourhood hairdresser. For those with the greatest resources to deploy, such patronage could take a variety of forms, with a corresponding variety of objectives and intentions. At the very top of the scale, those sufficiently rich could effect a substantial and permanent augmentation of the trained choral force. Among the nobility, Jan van der Courtre devolved £600 a year on St Donatian in 1484 to augment the livings of the Master of the Choristers and six of the boys, and to enhance with polyphony the singing of the chapter Lady Mass every day.[70] Charles the Bold and his successors took the church of Our Lady under their special care; Marie of Burgundy opted to be buried there. Already in 1477 she had given an annual income of £72, so that on twelve principal feasts a Mass could be celebrated for her with polyphony; on her death, in 1482, she bequeathed an annual endowment of £108 to augment the livings of the Master of the Choristers and the organist, and to increase the number of choristers by four. In return, two Masses were performed daily for her soul, one a Lady Mass, the other of Requiem.[71] The city palace of the noble family of Gruuthuse stood immediately adjacent to Our Lady's church, and this family made numerous endowments to enhance the music of the services.[72]

Especially prominent among lay benefactors of this class was the merchant and *burgomeister* Louis Greffijnc, a parishioner of the city-centre parish of St Salvator. It seems probable that it was largely due to him that in the 1480s the existing musical personnel of this parish church was reorganized on collegiate lines, briefly, at least, under Antoine Busnois as Master of the Choristers. Moreover, in 1485 Greffijnc set up an endowment that guaranteed a steady supply of newly-composed music for three of the principal city churches. On the three days each year preceding the feast of the Ascension, the choirs of St Donatian, Our Lady, and St Salvator were to process, on successive days, to the suburban

[69] Strohm, *Music in Late Medieval Bruges*, pp. 12–13, 25–6, 43–5.

[70] Ibid., pp. 28, 36, 38.

[71] Ibid., pp. 48–9. This endowment recalls that made in 1425 by Philip the Good to the collegiate church of St Pierre of Lille, likewise augmenting by four the number of its choristers: ibid., pp. 22, 94.

[72] See ibid., pp. 42–3, 45.

churches of Holy Cross, St Catherine, and St Mary Magdalene, singing Mass in polyphony in each church on arrival; each of the three Masters of the Choristers involved was expressly required to compose a new Mass for this occasion each year. Before long, St Salvator had joined St Donatian and Our Lady as a third collegiate church for the city of Bruges. The draper Michiel van Hille provided much of the endowment necessary to sustain the choir at this level; his benefaction of 1496 provided a total revenue of £156 per year, in recognition of which the *sangmeester*, four boys, three adult singers, and an organ-player performed thenceforth every evening a Marian service of 'Lof' in the standard form. The church was finally raised to collegiate status in 1501.[73]

The city itself, in the persons of the *Burgomeesters*, played its part among benefactors of this scale and class, creating one of the most noteworthy of all benefactions for the musical life of the city. In 1480 it was agreed that thenceforth the city would pay to the chapter of St Donatian the very substantial sum of £730 per year (£2 per day) to have a daily 'Lof'—the 'Salve' service of praise to the Virgin—sung after Compline in St Donatian by the succentor (that is, the Master of the Choristers), the choristers, and an organist. It was not long before the city council's own professional musicians—instrumentalists, rather than singers—became involved as well, providing a milieu in which, for probably the first time anywhere, singers and instrumentalists could take the first steps towards the pooling of their respective resources and thus towards the creation of a totally new sound—sacred music accompanied by instruments.[74]

Nevertheless, in so supporting the work of Holy Church in this particular city, it could be said that the great, the good, and the merely very rich were doing no more than what was simply expected of persons in their position, and commanding their resources. More interesting in many ways were the contributions made by the men and women of less exalted—though in many instances by no means humble—station in life. Much of this activity, in Bruges as elsewhere, was channelled through the religious fraternities. The Confraternity of Our Lady in Our Lady's church was reorganized in 1428, and benefited much from the membership of members of the Gruuthuse family next door; it had a fraternity Lady Mass sung each Saturday from 1429.[75] In the same church, the Confraternity of the Three Saints, established in 1474 largely by the wealthy

[73] Ibid., pp. 52–5.
[74] Ibid., pp. 33, 39, 85–6, 144.
[75] Ibid., pp. 43, 45.

family of La Bie, sponsored the performance by the choir of Vespers motets on the feasts of Saints Mary Magdalene, Catherine, and Barbara. The Confraternity of Our Lady of the Snow, originating before 1450 as a religious fraternity for the gild of tailors, hugely expanded its membership in the 1470s so as to extend to several hundreds, and had its own chapel in Our Lady's church built in 1473. Here this fraternity had Mass and first and second Vespers celebrated with polyphony annually on its feast-day (5 August), and Mass on the octave, by the Master of the Choristers, boys, certain adult singers, and the organ; also at the expense of this fraternity, the boys and their Master, with some choirmen hired from St Donatian, performed a Marian 'Lof' or 'Salve' after Vespers every Sunday and on the Marian feasts.[76] In the parish church of St Salvator, the Confraternity of Our Lady of the Seven Sorrows subsidized the choir after 1492 to the extent of £228 per year for polyphonic renderings of the service music on their feast-day and numerous other days during the year.[77]

Meanwhile, many religious confraternities of the laity had their chapels and their community religious observances located not within the secular churches of Bruges, but within the churches of the monastic or mendicant houses—and were prepared to hire singers from the collegiate churches to sing the services with polyphony on their principal days. The Gild of St Luke in the Augustinian Abbey of St Bartholomew, the Fraternity of St Thomas of Canterbury (that is, the English Merchant Adventurers at prayer) in the Carmelite Friary, and the Confraternity of the Dry Tree ('Den Droghene Boome'—a symbol for the Immaculate Conception) based in the Franciscan friary, all hired singers—principally those of St Donatian—to dignify their special services.[78] The two hundred or so members of the Confraternity of the Dry Tree—aristocrats, merchants native and foreign, professional craftsmen, including painters, local and provincial grandees, and their wives and children—each paid a subscription of 24 shillings per year; out of this aggregated income, from as early as 1414, £78 per year was paid to certain of the singers of St Donatian to come to the church of the Franciscan friary and there sing High Mass for the fraternity in polyphony on all Sundays and high feasts—a clash of commitments (and of loyalties) for the singers which provoked plenty of acrimony and trouble between the fraternity and the chapter of St Donatian around the mid-century.[79]

[76] Strohm, *Music in Late Medieval Bruges*, pp. 47–8.

[77] Ibid., p. 56.

[78] Ibid., pp. 61–2, 63–4.

[79] Ibid., pp. 26–7, 70–2.

As well as acting through a confraternity, individuals could seek a more immediately personal way of furthering the saving power and work of Holy Church, by means of the endowment of the polyphonic performance of Mass on one particular day a year—usually the day of a saint personally special to the benefactor. In 1417, for instance, the Italian merchant Dino Rapondi endowed the chapter of St Donatian so that annually on the feast of St John *ante portam latinam* a Mass with polyphony should be sung by six of the church's singers in the chapel of St John within the collegiate church.[80] In 1470 Jean Meurin, *secretarius* to Charles the Bold, endowed a Mass to be sung in the same church with polyphony annually on the Thursday preceding Septuagesima.[81]

It has proved possible to identify some of the polyphony performed at, and presumably commissioned for, personal Masses of this kind. Among the less humble benefactors of this type were a wealthy merchant in furs, Donaes de Moor, and his wife, Adriaene. During the 1480s this couple endowed polyphonic Masses to be sung annually on the feast-days of their respective name-saints, Donatian and Adrian, in the parish church of St James; Strohm argues persuasively that it may well have been for this occasion that Obrecht was commissioned to compose his Mass *de Sancto Donatiano*.[82] Particularly detailed was the benefaction to the church of St Donatian of one Pierre Basin, who earned his living as a singing-man in the household chapel of Charles the Bold and Maximilian. In its final form, yielding £7 per year, this paid for one polyphonic Mass on the vigil of St Martin and another on the feast of the Translation, for motets following Vespers on both days and also on Martinmas Day itself, and also for a polyphonic votive antiphon (in sequence form) following Compline on the feast of the Translation—all to be performed by the Master of the Choristers, the boys, and certain of the adult singers. Strohm has suggested, with considerable persuasiveness, that it was for this observance that Obrecht composed his Mass *de Sancto Martino*, written on *cantus firmi* appropriate to St Martin; Obrecht served as succentor at St Donatian from 1485 to 1491, and between 1498 and 1500.[83] This Pierre Basin came of a Bruges family; from the humbler end of the social

[80] Ibid., p. 15. Such a practice was probably widespread; Wegman mentions the endowment of St Gertrude's church in Bergen in 1487 by a *wijntavernier*, Dierick de Clerck, for the regular singing of a Mass of the Name of Jesus: Wegman, 'Music and Musicians at the Guild of Our Lady in Bergen op Zoom', pp. 195–6.

[81] Strohm, *Music in Late Medieval Bruges*, pp. 36–7.

[82] Ibid., pp. 145–7.

[83] Ibid., pp. 38–41, 132, 144–8.

spectrum, his brother Jean, a barber in the city, and another brother, Adrien, endowed an annual Mass in polyphony in the chapel of St Adrian in St Donatian's church, to be sung by certain members of the choir on the feast-day of the saint.[84] Also at St Donatian, it was as a consequence of a private benefaction made in 1415 that chapter services on the feast of the Exaltation of the Holy Cross were raised to the status of a solemn feast—a benefaction which would have produced a need for motets on appropriate texts, including perhaps Obrecht's motet *Salve crux, arbor vite / O crux lignum triumphale*, a polytextual piece using texts drawn from sequences for that feast-day.[85]

There were other ways also in which particular individuals could opt to enhance the church services with polyphony. For instance, in 1434 the citizen Johannes Scateraers granted an income with which the singers of St Donatian could be rewarded for elevating the performance of *Salve regina* each Saturday from plainsong to polyphony.[86] Another possible procedure was for a benefactor to grant money so that the status of a given feast-day as observed at a particular church could be reclassified and raised, and all its services—especially High Mass—be performed with greater splendour. Around 1450–60, one Gilles Borlet granted to Our Lady's church income from which the feast of St Michael 'ad Monte Tumba' could be raised from modest status to that of a *festum principale*, its High Mass in choir being sung with polyphony and organ 'as on other principal feasts'. At much the same period two other benefactors, Gautier de Mandre and Antonius Brouc, similarly enhanced the festal services on the feasts of St Martin and St Michael.[87] At the humblest end of the scale, small personal endowments could serve to pay just for odd movements of Mass to be sung in polyphony on a specified day. For instance, the grant of Sijmon Coene in 1439 to the chapter of St Donatian covered the cost of having just the *Gloria* and *Credo* of the Ordinary, and a motet, sung in polyphony at High Mass once a year on the feast of Saints Simon and Jude to commemorate the feast of his name-saint.[88]

By the end of the fifteenth century the endowed and household ecclesiastical choirs of the Low Countries must have been producing and consuming prodigious quantities of composed music. Much of this activity, to be sure, arose in the natural course of the work of a collegiate

[84] Strohm, *Music in Late Medieval Bruges*, p. 49.
[85] Ibid., pp. 17–18, 145.
[86] Ibid., p. 23; for further examples, see ibid., p. 27.
[87] Ibid., pp. 46–7.
[88] Ibid., pp. 23, 117.

church; much also, however, arose primarily to satisfy the requirements of an evidently eager and generous exterior popular patronage. The accounts of the chapter of St Donatian, Bruges, reveal that for the 'official' chapter observances alone, in the thirty years between 1463 and 1492 a recorded minimum of ninety Masses, thirty-six *Magnificats*, and over a dozen other works were copied for the use of the choir[89]—and the archives of Our Lady, Antwerp, disclose how any one lay fraternity might very well match, or even exceed, the official chapter in its expenditure on music.[90] It seems extremely likely that it was this external patronage that gave rise to a high proportion of the opportunities and occasions for which many Netherlander composers of the first order—in particular, Obrecht, but not to overlook numerous lesser masters—wrote much of their surviving music.

* * *

Such a picture of extensive aristocratic and popular sponsorship of the music of the Church has something, I believe, to contribute to our appreciation of the nature and extent, and of the vigour, conviction, and sincerity, of popular piety in the Netherlands on the eve of the Reformation. It is also particularly illuminating to compare this aspect of religious life in the Low Countries with its counterpart in England; the differences are no less marked than the similarities, and are perhaps even more informative. For although the importance of the religious gilds and fraternities in maintaining professional choirs in major urban parish churches in England is evident and widespread by the early sixteenth century, any comparable involvement of local lay sponsorship in the conduct or augmentation of corporate worship in the collegiate and cathedral churches is virtually absent. The resources which in the southern Netherlands were dedicated to enlarging the work and enhancing the scope and professionalism of the local choir, appear in England to tend to have been devoted instead to the multiplication of non-corporate soul-masses, through the medium of either a perpetual or a temporary chantry, commonly located merely in the testator's parish church. In England, therefore, upon the emergence of an apparently cogent challenge to the efficacy of historic theological norms and to the liturgical practice founded upon them, there was little to tie any community in loyalty to its local great corporate

89 Ibid., pp. 29–31.

90 Forney, 'Music, ritual and patronage at the church of Our Lady, Antwerp', pp. 32–7.

church and to the fundamental premises underlying the liturgical life conducted within it. In a Low Countries town across the Channel, by contrast, important elements among the influential laity might well have forged for themselves a personal and almost proprietary involvement in the liturgical work of its local large corporate church in a way unknown in England, capable of inspiring a loyalty and devotion strong enough, perhaps, to be proof against the reception of novel ideas inimical to its liturgical spirit, and to the theology and the system of belief that inspired it. There is no scope in this article to develop this theme further; nevertheless, it is difficult not at least to wonder if there may not lie here some small but not insignificant contribution to our understanding of the reasons why at least the southern Netherlands remained Catholic in the century following the fifteenth, while in England a degree of Protestantism was able to establish itself in the towns, for eventual settlement on the kingdom as a whole.

Faculty of Music,
University of Cambridge

ART AND IDENTITY IN THE PARISH COMMUNITIES OF LATE MEDIEVAL KENT

by JUDY ANN FORD

HISTORIANS have long been aware that patronage is a crucial factor in interpreting the social meaning of art.[1] The late Middle Ages knew a variety of patrons, each employing art to communicate different sorts of concern: royal and aristocratic courts emphasized political messages, urban communes created governmental myths, cathedrals and monasteries gave expression to spiritual ideas—and all used art to convey notions of social identity. Recent investigations into the process of choosing and procuring works of art in these contexts have not only added perspective to formal art criticism, they have also deepened our understanding of the groups interested in the creation of art. One area in which questions of patronage could perhaps be better illuminated is the community of the parish. The parish served as the primary religious community for the majority of men and women for most of the Middle Ages. It was complex in composition, involving both laity and clergy, encompassing other religious associations, such as gilds, and including the devout and the indifferent, the orthodox and the dissenters.

The variety of religious, social, and political attitudes which flourished in parishes manifested itself in several ways, among which material culture was undoubtedly of great significance. The shape, size, and arrangement of the church building and the number, variety, and form of its goods and ornaments determined the parameters of religious ritual and other activity within the parish church. Medieval parishioners chose to fill their churches with what the modern eye calls 'art'; such as statues, stained glass, and objects of precious metal.[2] The art of parish churches certainly expressed notions of piety; thus an understanding of it might help to

[1] I would like to thank Andrew Butcher and Dr Maryanne Kowaleski for their help and encouragement.

[2] See J. Charles Cox, *English Church Fittings, Furniture and Accessories* (London, 1923); J. Charles Cox, *Churchwardens' Accounts* (London, 1919); and the handbook published by the National Association of Decorative and Fine Arts Societies, *Inside Churches* (London, 1989). For a discussion of the medieval definition of art, see Umberto Eco, *Art and Beauty in the Middle Ages*, tr. Hugh Bredin (New Haven and London, 1986); originally published as *Sviluppo dell'estetica medievale*, ed. Carlo Marzorati, in *Momenti e problemi di storia dell'estetica*, 1 (Milan, 1959).

illuminate religious beliefs and practices. Parochial art, moreover, was particularly rich in meaning, since the parish community was far more heterogeneous than other contemporary religious institutions, as the force which united its members was not voluntary, individual vocation, but a network of such diverse bonds as family, geography, and trade. Due to the complex social composition of its audience, parochial art must have been a tempting avenue through which notions of personal identity might be given voice.

The process by which works of art reached parish churches is documented in the annual accounts of churchwardens and in wills and testaments. Wills survive in great numbers from the fifteenth century, but good runs of churchwardens' accounts are rather rare before the mid-sixteenth century. Four parishes in Kent, however, have good surviving accounts, namely, Bethersden, Folkestone, Wye, and St Mary's, Sandwich.[3] This study is based primarily on these accounts and the wills of their communities, and on contemporary lists and inventories of church goods.[4]

Aside from aesthetic qualities, the art of medieval churches functioned essentially as an aid to spiritual practices and an embellishment of the tools of liturgical and sacramental rites. The preference for particular types of object to some extent reflected certain propensities in the piety of those involved in the process of selection. Although representations related to the cult of saints in wood, stone, and glass are most commonly

[3] Three of these accounts are in manuscript: Folkestone (1487–1530), in Canterbury Cathedral Library, U3/88/4/1; Wye (1515–30), in Wye Agricultural College, no reference number; and St Mary's, Sandwich (1444–1530, with gaps), CCL, U3/11/5/1. All three accounts continue well beyond 1530, which is the terminal date of this study. The fourth account has been printed: Francis R. Mercer, ed., 'Churchwardens accounts at Bethersden, 1515–1573', *The Kent Archaeological Society, Records Branch*, 5 (1928), pp. 1–165. There are other extant churchwardens' accounts for Kent; these four have been chosen partly for their quality and partly for the diversity of their communities: Bethersden was a rural village, Wye a market town, Folkestone a small urban seaside community, and Sandwich a Cinque Port.

[4] In the Archdeaconry Court of Canterbury and the Prerogative Court of Canterbury there are 674 wills proved for the inhabitants of Bethersden, Wye, Folkestone, and Sandwich from 1459 to 1530. Thirteen of the wills proved in the Prerogative Court of Canterbury were made by testators who lived elsewhere at the time their wills were written, but who made substantial donations to one of these four communities. Three of these communities had only one parish, but the town of Sandwich included the parishes of St Mary, St Peter, and St Clement, and the hospital of St Bartholomew. Among the lists and inventories, the two most important are the bede roll of St Mary's, Sandwich, CCL, U3/173/6/5; and the Inventories conducted during the reign of Edward VI, printed in M. E. C. Walcott, R. P. Coates, and W. A. Scott, eds, 'Inventories of parish church goods in Kent, A.D. 1552', *Archaeologia Cantiana*, 8 (1872), pp. 74–163; 9 (1874), pp. 266–84; 10 (1876), pp. 282–97; and 11 (1877), pp. 409–16.

associated with the art of medieval churches, the late medieval parochial documents of the four communities in question are all but silent on matters of statues, stained glass, and painting.[5] Churchwardens' accounts record the repairs of such objects, but they are often exasperatingly vague about descriptions.[6] An assessment of the role of representations of saints in these churches is complicated by the indiscriminate use of the word 'image'; it is often impossible to tell what was being repaired.[7] This tendency towards vagueness is present in records of painting as well; while the object painted is usually recorded, whether the painter was to create pictures or merely whitewash is almost never specified. Despite the evidence of repairs and maintenance, the churchwardens' accounts indicate no new purchases of such objects, while in all the wills examined only four bequests were made for windows, and none for the creation of statues or paintings.[8] Evidence of devotion to saints and their relics is not lacking in the wills, indeed, bequests were made for the refurbishing of saints' statues and for the repair of their reliquaries, while donations for saints' lights formed a part of the majority of testaments. Nevertheless, it is probable that by the fifteenth century most parish churches would have been amply equipped with these forms of art, making it less necessary to acquire new specimens.

Most of the bequests of art in the wills examined for these four communities had an association with the celebration of the Eucharist and the Crucifixion of Christ, that is, altar-cloths, chalices, crosses, and rood-lofts. This tendency is not surprising, since devotion to the Host and to the human life of Christ is known to have been particularly strong in the lay piety of the late Middle Ages. It is striking how parishioners found ways to

[5] It cannot be assumed that these findings would be equally applicable to all places. More local studies are necessary before any general conclusions may be reached.

[6] These sources show only one description of a stained-glass window: a design of the head of St Laurence. CCL, U3/11/5/1, 1517.

[7] Sometimes the record of repair or removal allows a distinction to be made: in Folkestone an image of St George, which acquired a cap and had a sword mended, was probably in wood, CCL, U3/88/4/1, 1508–9 and 1525–6; while in Bethersden a St Christopher which was 'blotted out' was certainly rendered in paint, Mercer, 'Bethersden', p. 85.

[8] It should be remembered that the written sources probably do not offer a complete account of all goods given to the church: while living parishioners may have made donations, gifts in kind may have gone unrecorded in the churchwardens' accounts. The only reference to such a gift in these accounts was the donation of a resurrection cloth to Folkestone, mentioned only because the wardens offered a small cash reward to the servant who delivered it. This donation is a special case since the donor, Lady Clinton, was a member of the family who held the Honour of Folkestone, CCL, U3/88/4/1, 1530–1. For a discussion of the possibility of unrecorded gifts, see Clive Burgess, '"By Quick and by Dead": wills and pious provision in late medieval Bristol', *EHR*, 142 (1987), pp. 873–58.

combine this devotional fashion with the cult of saints, as is evident from the examples of new cloth. Of the eighty-two donations towards objects of art made in the wills of these four communities, exactly half, that is, forty-one, were for cloths. Three of these named banner cloths, but without specifying an exact description or intended purpose.[9] Most bequests of cloth were much more explicit. Certain donations of cloth were associated unequivocally with crosses and the Eucharist, that is, three for cross cloths, two for housling cloths, and four for canopies. These last would be like the canopy of red silk which a parishioner of St Clement's, Sandwich, wished to have carried over the Sacrament during processions.[10] Most remaining donations were for altar-cloths. The consecrated altar, essential to the eucharistic celebration, became a special object of pious attention in the late Middle Ages, when devotion to the Host was strong. Its embellishment by hangings and cloths became a near-universal practice. These could take the form of quite humble table-cloths, but over them were usually laid rich and expensive frontals and super-frontals, made of silk, velvet, or cloth of gold, sometimes elaborately embroidered or decorated with silk fringes. In the case of altar-cloths, testators often specified not only their material, but also their placement. Of the thirty-three donations which named the altar intended, eleven were for the high altar and twelve for side altars. Parishioners may no longer have directed their attention to new statues, but they could choose to honour a favoured saint with a new altar-cloth, thereby combining a devotion to eucharistic celebration and a reverent identification with the chapel of a particular saint.[11]

Crosses, symbols of Christ's Crucifixion, not surprisingly attracted much attention in these late medieval parishes: after cloths, they were named most frequently by testators, that is, in thirteen of the eighty-two donations. The crosses named in parochial sources may, in fact, have been crucifixes, as the tendency to portray the dying Christ in a realistic or even exaggerated fashion was characteristic of late medieval art. Crosses had several uses: they were carried in procession on feast days, during funeral processions, and before the Sacrament; and for these occasions cross-staffs were made, which could be constructed either of precious metal, as many

[9] Banners were usually painted, and it is impossible to know their significance unless the image is known.

[10] Thomas Parys, PRC 17/7/51 (1495).

[11] This identification was strengthened in two cases when the testators requested burial before the altar to which they had bequeathed a cloth; Harry Grandame, PRC 17/12/512 (1515); and Sir Thomas Clerke, PRC 17/4/123 (1487).

of the crosses seem to have been, or of painted wood. While standing on an altar, a cross would be put into a stand called a foot, which was often constructed of precious metal.[12] Crosses might also be erected outside the church building, though these stone crosses were rarely acquired in these parishes in the later Middle Ages.

One very common use for a cross, in this case specifically a crucifix, was the adornment of a rood-loft, a beam or gallery between the chancel and the nave, whose function was to present the scene of the Crucifixion to spectators in the nave. Rood-lofts were themselves attractive objects for donors: nine of the eighty-two bequests under consideration were for their gilding. It is particularly in the setting of a rood-loft that the tendency to combine forms of piety may be seen; the crucifixes on them were normally accompanied by statues of Mary and St John, and it was not unusual for a crowd of saints to be portrayed around the Crucifixion scene. No descriptions survive for the rood-lofts of these parishes, but the best cross of St Mary's, Sandwich, certainly had an image of St John.[13] Crosses could also be engraved with saints' images; one of the donors from Bethersden, directing that a cross be constructed in a place called St Thomas croft, ordered that an 'ymagine in honore sancti Thome' be made upon it.[14] Thus, like altar-cloths, crosses were a manifestation of the popular piety of late medieval parish communities, indicating both general trends and particular choices.

Only eight of the donations under consideration concerned items of plate: two for chrismatories, two for paxes, and one each for candlesticks, a tabernacle, a thurible, and a chalice.[15] While churchwardens' accounts record some purchases of altar-cloths and fewer of crosses, the purchase of plate without a donor's bequest seems to have been quite rare, limited in these parishes to one purchase of great candlesticks and a handful of inexpensive paxes, pyxes, and cruets.[16] The infrequency of acquisition probably accurately reflects the limited number of items of plate

[12] The inventories of 1552 furnish many examples of the materials of crosses, staffs, and, in fact, all of the objects under consideration here. See Walcott, Coates, and Scott, 'Inventories'.

[13] CCL U3/11/5/1, 1496, the John of the Cross was mended; CCL U3/11/5/1, 1502, the St John of the Best Cross was new gilded and burnished.

[14] Roger Bromley, PRC 17/2/257 (1473).

[15] In addition to the donations mentioned in the text, there was one bequest for painting over the high altar, one for the covering of a font, and three for gravestones, making a total of eighty-two. Gravestones are an interesting form of art, but would perhaps be better considered in the context of funeral rites.

[16] CCL U3/11/5/1, undated account *c.*1497–1500.

possessed by parish churches.[17] The scarcity of these items may have been due to their expense, not to any disregard of their value; at least, they seem to occupy a place of prominence and to have been carefully enumerated in inventories.[18] Chalices tended to be the most valuable items of plate, although there were several exceptions. An example of a valuable chalice would be the one donated to St Clement's, Sandwich, by William Kenett in 1482; his will directed that a thirty-ounce silver goblet be given to the churchwardens to be turned into a chalice, to be kept there for ever, to the glory of God, Blessed Mary, and all the saints.[19] Notes of material and weight were common, but descriptios of visual appearance were rare, thus a consideration of the subtleties of late medieval church plate remains problematic; nevertheless, the chalices owned by these parishes were probably engraved with names and images.[20]

As the discussion thus far makes clear, a study of parish art from the perspective of written documentation has certain limitations, chiefly the inability to provide detailed descriptions of the works in question, yet such a study has compensations: this approach makes possible an analysis of the methods of acquisition. A parish church considered at any given moment is not the product of a single eye—far from it. All its parts were acquired, placed, and allowed to remain under the disparate eyes of the lay parish community, either by direct action or explicit or tacit consent. This was no less true of the works donated by individuals as it was of items bought from the common funds, for the parish community must either have approved of the overall propriety of any donation, or else recognized the authority of the patron to intrude his or her individual taste into the common fabric. Frequently, even in the case of individual donations, the lay parish organization was forced to become actively involved in the economic network for bequests to be realized; the object was brought in rather than merely handed over.

There were three ways in which a work of art could be acquired by a parish church: donation in kind, cash donation by a single party, and

[17] The inventories of 1552 show only a few large parishes possessing a substantial collection of plate, Walcott, Coates, and Scott, 'Inventories'.

[18] St Mary's bede roll: CCL, U3/173/6/5; the Fordwich inventory: CCL, U4, bundle 4; and an inventory in the parish of St Andrew's, Canterbury: Charles Cotton, ed., 'Churchwardens' accounts of the parish of St. Andrew, Canterbury', *Archaeologia Cantiana*, 32 (1917), pp. 204–11.

[19] William Kenett, PRC 17/3/479 (1482).

[20] Certainly the handbook published by the National Association of Decorative and Fine Arts Societies, *Inside Churches* (London, 1989), assumes that chalices were engraved, as all of its examples of chalices are engraved.

fund-raising from various sources by churchwardens. Of the eighty-two bequests under consideration, twenty-seven were donations in kind, twenty were individual projects, sixteen were donations to a parish collection, and nineteen were so worded as to make it unclear whether the object involved was to be bought collectively or not. Direct donation was the simplest method, the object passing from the owners to their executors to the wardens, or even from the owners to the wardens in the case of living donors. It was also the most limited in scope, usually confined to objects which had been part of the donor's household goods. Only two of the donations in kind were not of cloth: the silver goblet which William Kenett wished to be made into a chalice, and a chrismatory donated by Joan Kenett in 1474.[21] The cloth donated this way tended to be of the simplest kind: twenty-one of the twenty-five direct donations of cloth were plain boardcloths or of diaper. In these parishes art, even in the materialist sense of richly and decoratively rendered functional items, was rarely presented to the church ready-made.

Most works of art seem to have been provided by owners who bequeathed funds for specific items. Twenty of the bequests under consideration belong to this category, and while it is unlikely that all twenty would have come to fruition, the wording of the bede roll of St Mary's, Sandwich, indicates that most of the possessions listed there were donated in this manner.[22] The case of Master Richard Keynell illustrates a purchase of this sort. In 1461 the churchwardens of St Mary's recorded a receipt of £13 6*s.* 8*d.* from a bequest of their late vicar to be used to buy two silver basins and two silver cruets. The same account shows that £11 12*s.* was spent on the two basins, and 1*s.* of the parish fund was spent burnishing them. Two years later the wardens recorded that the money for the cruets was still in the parish chest, kept separately as Master Keynell's. The next year the accounts break off, so it cannot be known when the cruets were purchased.[23] However easily a bequest might be

[21] Joan Kenett, PRC 17/3/120 (1477); and William Kenet [*sic*], PRC 17/3/479 (1483).

[22] Only four donations in that list were recorded as having been given by the donor 'be hys lyf days': U3/173/6/5.

[23] I have found no will for Master William Keynell, so it is unclear how much time elapsed between the granting of the bequest and the receipt of the money by the churchwardens. St Mary's has no surviving accounts between 1464 and 1491, CCI, U3/11/5/1. Clergy form a very small part of the parochial community as viewed from the perspective of this documentation: only 8 of the 674 wills were for members of the clergy, and only two of these were art donors. The influence of the clergy as an independent force was probably quite weak in Kent during this time. See M. L. Zell, 'The personnel of the clergy in Kent in the Reformation period', *EHR*, 139 (1974), pp. 513–53.

fulfilled once the funds reached the hands of the churchwardens, the process of realizing funds from the testator's estate was likely to be slow and difficult and, in some cases, unsuccessful.

The wording of wills and testaments clearly indicates the complications which could be attached to a bequest of funds for a work of art. Twelve of the twenty bequests in this category were straightforward: the testators either bequeathed a specific sum for the purchase, or directed that the purchase be made while leaving the price unspecified. If the cash were readily available, the process should have been simple, but often testators included in their wills clauses that property be sold to meet their debts and bequests. Executors or relations who were unable or unwilling to meet the obligations of the will would have found themselves in dispute with the churchwardens, an actionable dispute, if the wardens proved determined to pursue the rights of the church.[24] The other testators left more complex bequests: one directed that a debt owed to her be collected and used to buy a chrismatory, three wished that their houses be sold, one his lands, one her moveables, one that his property be sold at his wife's death, and one left funding only residually.[25] This last was Thomas Parys, a carpenter of St Clement's, Sandwich, who in 1495 bequeathed that if both his sons died without legal heirs then, after his wife's decease, his two tenements were to be sold and half the money used to buy a red canopy, and for other deeds of charity. Even with the best intentions on all sides, such bequests would have involved the executors and wardens in complicated exchanges; difficulty, resistance, or even the passage of time would threaten their fulfilment, and completion would depend more upon local economic conditions and the energy and enthusiasm of those involved than upon the desire of the testator to make a donation. Two conclusions about patronage may be drawn: first, much of the art in parish churches, even if funded by an individual patron, was the product of exchanges involving many members of the community; and, second, the expressed intention to donate a work of art represented, on the part of the testator, not so much a desire to spend superfluous wealth as a wish to give a particular object, despite financial limitations.

[24] For examples see the bequests of Richard Dyar and John Stock's wife, unpaid in the accounts of St Mary's, Sandwich, from 1461 until the accounts break off in 1464; and the unpaid bequest of Simon Brerer's wife in the same accounts, 1446: CCL U3/11/5/1. These churchwardens' accounts show a great many unpaid bequests for purposes other than art.

[25] These were, in order mentioned: Alice Jancock, PRC 17/7/173 (1499); John Webbes, PCC 11/18/6 (1514); Elizabeth Iden, PRC 17/7/181 (1499); Agnes Warref, PRC 17/11/210 (1511); Laurence Blossem, PRC 17/3/244 (1479); Enswith Hall, PRC 17/14/318 (1517); William Brok, PRC 17/9/311 (1506); and Thomas Parys, PRC 17/7/51 (1495).

The third method of acquisition, a fund-raising campaign organized by the churchwardens, was also quite complex. Although this method was uncommon, it would have involved large segments of the parish community. In the accounts of St Mary's, Sandwich, there are records of two such campaigns, and wills indicate another three occasions, in times and places for which there are no surviving accounts. The wills also suggest an episode of fund-raising for which the surviving account shows no corresponding action, that is, for a covering for an altar in Folkestone.[26] The rood-loft gilding of St Mary's may be used to illustrate the process. In the account of 1508–9 a payment appears to a John Goson for the rood-loft gilding, and payments to him for that purpose appear in the subsequent two accounts. The account of 1509–10 has a list of fifty-five donations for this purpose; most are in pence, only nine in shillings, while the largest payment, namely eight shillings, is from a group called 'the Wives', who make their sole appearance in the account-book here. Although the list is not in strict order of valuation, most of the larger payments are listed first, and the warden's wife heads the list. The subsequent account also contains a list of donations. The donors named in these lists were probably living, since the three bequests made for the rood-loft about this time do not appear in them. Moreover, since these bequests do not appear at all in the account-book, they might not have been paid. Nevertheless, St Mary's rood-loft gilding shows these campaigns as large projects, involving many members of the community. The failure of any bequest made for a campaign for which there are surviving accounts to be paid sheds further doubt on the effectiveness of bequests for the purchase of art. Testators leaving money for collections made complicated bequests, as did those who directed funds to individual projects: of the sixteen in question, four

[26] The two instances in the churchwardens' accounts are: CCL, U3/11/5/1, undated account *c*.1497–1500, and 1508–11. There were other instances of parochial fund-raising, not related to works of art. Among the wills, seven relate to Bethersden's cross: German Glover, PRC 17/9/146 (1504); John Glover, PRC 17/9/89 (1504); Laurence Bresynden, PRC 17/8/171 (1500); John Brodestrete, PRC 17/8/132 (1501); John Bresynden, PRC 17/8/22 (1500); Christopher Wederden, PRC 17/9/58 (1504); and Thomas Wersele, PRC 17/8/122 (1501). Two wills relate to Bethersden's rood-loft: Laurence Blossom, PRC 17/3/244 (1479); and James Piers, PRC 17/4/60 (1484). Two wills relate to the gilding of St Bartholomew: Katherine Best, PRC 17/16/38 (1523) and Robert Marten, PRC 17/16/1 (1523). There are two bequests for the covering of an altar at Folkestone, but neither appears in the churchwardens' accounts, nor is there a mention of a covering bought about that time. The two testators were Robert Davy, PRC 17/12/331 (1514) and John Pargate, PRC 17/9/292 (1508).

directed that the money be raised from the sale of land upon their decease or that of a spouse.[27]

Considering the difficulties involved in bringing a bequest for the purchase of a work of art to fruition, one might ask why testators chose to make such bequests. The question of motivation has been much studied in the broader context of participation in religious ritual, and although a consensus has not been reached, certain answers might be put forward. Briefly, there are motives concerning community pride, others of social status, and a third group which might be called penitential.[28] Donations of works of art had a particular relevance to all three. Certainly such donations would have served to beautify the parish church, reflecting the wealth and honour of its community, thus increasing the esteem in which it might have been held by neighbours and travellers. The benefits derived from donations of works of art by those who sought to improve or amplify their social status, or shorten their time in purgatory, were more complex. Works of art offered a closer and more lasting identification of the donor with his or her pious act than did other acts of charity or more anonymous gifts to the fabric.[29] The most obvious way for this identification to be established was for the donor's name to be displayed on the object itself, as in William Brok's bequest to St Peter's, Sandwich, in 1506, of a chasuble, two copes, and a velvet embroidered altar-cloth, with angels or eagles of gold and 'a scripton uppon every of them to be made of my fadder name my moders and myn'.[30] Two chalices in a Fordwich inventory, also with their donors' names engraved upon them, show that William Brok was not alone in his choice.[31] Another method of establishing an identification of the donor with the donation was through the parish bede roll. This was a list of names and donations, sometimes with a valuation. There are several references to the use of the bede roll in the accounts of St Mary's, Sandwich; this parish paid its parish priest to read its bede roll out from the pulpit on Sundays. Such payments indicate that

[27] See n. 26 above. The testators were John Bresynden, Christopher Wederden, Laurence Blossom, and Thomas Wersele.

[28] The studies are too numerous to list here, but see especially P. W. Fleming, 'Charity, faith, and the gentry of Kent, 1422–1529', in A. J. Pollard, ed., *Property and Politics in Later Medieval English History* (London, 1984), and Clive Burgess, '"A fond thing vainly invented": an essay on Purgatory and pious motive in late medieval England', in Susan Wright, ed., *Parish, Church and People: Local Studies in Lay Religion, 1350–1750* (London, 1988), pp. 56–84.

[29] Of course, there were other acts of both formal and informal religion in which personal identity could be created or transformed, particularly funeral rites.

[30] William Brok, PRC 17/9/311 (1506).

[31] CCL, U4, bundle 4.

each week a more or less captive audience would be reminded, in English, to pray for those individuals whose generosity provided the parish with works of great cost, and presumably of beauty. To individuals wishing to attract approving public notice, either to proclaim social status or to inspire prayers for their souls, these methods of public identification of their names with a pious, charitable act must have been appealing.

It is worth noting that these methods of personal identification were created by parishioners over time. Since parish communities were fairly independent organizations before the changes made in local administration under Elizabeth, most activity concerning the material fabric of churches depended upon the initiative of their parishioners, and upon the customs they established. Some of this activity was directed towards obtaining costly works of art to attend upon the rites of religion, but it is well to remember that this need not have been so. Certain opinions had always existed amongst Christians which objected to the notion that divine worship was well served by the luxuries of the material world. The same parishioners who bequeathed silks and jewels to their parish churches also left money to support local houses of Franciscans, so the religious tradition available to them involved more than one approach to the proper relationship between material wealth and spiritual virtue. A parochial organization which encouraged donations of expensive items of art manifested distinct attitudes about worship, piety, worldly wealth, and social status. The employment of costly material in connection with those aspects of worship on which contemporaries placed a high value in a sense sanctified such an employment of wealth. The community which used these objects, guarded and inventoried them, may be said to have implicitly accepted the appropriateness of this sanctification. By actively involving the officers of the parish in the financial transactions of funding, the contact between these transactions and religious affairs was tacitly deemed appropriate. Furthermore, by instituting channels by which the donors would be publicly associated with these objects, approbation was extended beyond the object to the act of donation, ultimately to the donors themselves.

The parochial organization, in creating a channel by which the merits of a recognized act of pious generosity could be publicly conferred upon an individual, became an organization through which its members might establish their identity in the community. Not surprisingly, the group which tried to take advantage of this option was in some ways distinguished from the community at large in matters of wealth and gender. Although almost half of the testators who made bequests of works of art were of middling wealth, a comparison of this group with the whole set of testators from these communities shows that wealthy testators formed a somewhat larger percentage of donors of works of art than they did of the general population.[32] Nevertheless, the wealthiest testators examined here, namely the non-residents who proved their wills at the Prerogative Court of Canterbury, but who owned property or made bequests in these communities, did not donate works of art. As a rule they chose to scatter their bequests over a wide area, rather than make large donations to certain places.[33] Not surprisingly, those who made bequests of works of art were somewhat less likely to have children to be their heirs than were the greater population of testators, at least, they less frequently mentioned them in wills.[34]

Art donors were more likely to be male than female, yet the percentage of women who made bequests for works of art was twice as large as the percentage of women testators for the whole group.[35] This may indicate a particular piety, or perhaps a compensation for their relative lack of participation in the formal church organization. It is perhaps significant that the majority of women donors left bequests of the cheapest kind of cloth, indicating a possible lack of material possessions. Consequently, these women were excluded from the main avenues of public identification: these cloths had no embroidery and would not have been listed in bede rolls. Only those who recognized the cloth as a former possession of a particular individual would know the donor's identity. Nevertheless, the record of fund-raising for the gilding of the rood-loft in St Mary's, Sandwich, in 1509–10, demonstrates the active participation of wives, suggest-

[32] The 82 bequests under discussion were bequeathed by 69 testators. The figures here were obtained by comparing this group of 69 with the larger group of which it forms a subset, namely the 674 wills related to the 4 communities under consideration. The forgotten tithes mentioned in wills were taken as a rough index of wealth. 30 of the 69, or 43% of the art donors paid between 1*s.* and 5*s.* as forgotten tithes in their wills; I have taken this to be the middling range. Among the art donors, 4% paid between 5*s.* and 10*s.* of forgotten tithes as compared with 3% of the whole group; while 7% of the art donors paid 10*s.* or more of forgotten tithes as compared with only 3% of the whole group.

[33] These were John Payntour, PCC 11/6/12 (1473); James Goldwell, PCC 11/11/35 (1498); William Hopkyns, PCC 11/19/10 (1518); William Braybrok, PCC 11/6/7 (1472); John Pylbarough, PCC 11/20/6 (1520); John Heron, PCC 11/18/15 (1515); Christopher Hillis, PCC 11/23/7 (1528). Perhaps they had enough disposable wealth to have made such donations during their life. See the examples of Lady Clinton, n. 8 above.

[34] Of the art donors, 45% mentioned no children in their wills, as compared with 33% of the larger group. For this category only male, non-clerical testators were considered.

[35] Of the 69 art donors, 23 were women, that is, 33%, while only 15% of the larger group were women.

ing that women may have played a significant, although not formally rewarded, part in the processes of obtaining art for parish churches.

Perhaps the most remarkable tendency evident among those who included bequests for works of art is that they were more likely than the general population to have made bequests for services generally associated with traditional practices of piety, that is, special services at their burial and month's mind, and days or months of Masses said on their behalf after death.[36] This tendency suggests that there may have been something of a common religious outlook in this group, not different from others in the community necessarily, but perhaps a stronger or more intense manifestation of ideas of piety which were more diffuse in the larger community. This tendency is especially significant because the gift of works of art not only helped the donors establish their personal identity, it allowed them to shape, in a broad way, the identity of the parish community. The objects donated to the parish church, however richly made or beautiful, were ultimately functional, and their function was to enable the parish to participate in specific acts of piety and worship. The form of piety expressed in these objects was traditional, associated with both the cult of saints and with the eucharistic enthusiasm of the late Middle Ages. It may be seen to stand in opposition to whatever strains of late Lollardy or early Protestantism might have existed in these parishes in the late fifteenth and early sixteenth centuries. Donors of works of art, by making choices about the physical material present in the church, surely hoped to ensure that their community remained in conformity with their own religious outlook.

Fordham University

[36] Among the art donors, 35% requested burial services, compared with 25% of the larger group; 30% requested month minds, compared with 22% of the larger group; and 50% requested Masses, compared with 30% of the larger group.

MEDIEVAL LITURGY AS THEATRE: THE PROPS

by R. N. SWANSON

IT may be debated how far the liturgy of the medieval Church (in particular the Mass) can be considered as 'drama', but its theatrical impact and organization are undeniable.[1] Staged within a distinct space, the principal act of the Church's worship had its own text and directions, which through contemplation and allegory summarized Christ's terrestrial experiences and various aspects of the Christian faith.[2] The Mass and other liturgical celebrations were events to be visualized, both externally and internally. It has been said of medieval plays that their

> fundamentally visual nature . . . so apparent to [a] medieval audience, often escapes the attention of modern scholars. The lines drawn between disciplines hinder easy access to methods that would enable readers to pass from a text to a visual reconstruction of it. Nonetheless the readers of dramatic texts need to visualize stage properties, costumes, and sets, and, when appropriate, to see beyond their literal meaning to their symbolic import. Further, readers must see gesture, placement, and interrelationship of actors, and understand how these visual elements contribute to the content.[3]

With little alteration, the same might be said of liturgical events.

Part of the problem of visualizing derives from a lack of descriptions. The liturgical books lay down the regulations, the buildings provide the

[1] The Mass as drama is accepted in O. B. Hardison, Jr., *Christian Rite and Christian Drama in the Middle Ages: Essays in the Origin and Early History of Modern Drama* (Baltimore, 1965), pp. 35–79, see esp. p. 79; see also pp. 23–4, against K. Young, *The Drama of the Medieval Church*, 2 vols (Oxford, 1933), 1, pp. 79–85, 110–11. Although denying the Mass as drama, Young concedes that its choreography and actions do recall 'the circumstances of the theatre', being replete with 'dramatic externalities' (p. 80).

[2] J. Wickham Legg, ed., *Tracts on the Mass = Henry Bradshaw Society*, 27 (London, 1904), pp. 19–29; [Friar Gararde], *The Interpretacyon and Sygnyfycacyon of the Masse* (London, 1532; *STC* 11549), sig. i.iir–i.iiiv, kiir–oiiiv; M. Aston, *Lollards and Reformers: Images and Literacy in Late Medieval Religion* (London, 1984), p. 123.

[3] P. Sheingorn, 'The visual language of drama: principles of composition', in M. G. Briscoe and J. C. Coldewey, eds., *Contexts for Early English Drama* (Bloomington and Indianapolis, 1989), p. 173.

ground-plan,[4] but the full theatrical impact of the medieval liturgical performance is almost impossible to envisage. Paintings give some indication, but their static nature precludes the emotionalism of presence which would have generated the response. The post-Reformation compiler of the *Rites of Durham* describes the richness of processions, and his emphases offer some corrective to approaches which would concentrate consideration of the Church and the arts solely on the disparate components of the full experience.[5]

The liturgical celebrations were clearly directed at an audience. On one level this was the congregation: the laity beyond the performance space. But while spectators, the laity were not the main addressees. The liturgy was primarily meant for God: any further audience was fortuitous. There were, obviously, times when the liturgy's drama did engage a wider audience, escaping from the enclosures and the private out into the public; but these were by definition special events, with their own rules and an augmented 'cast' comprising both laity and clergy.

The ceremonial features highlighted by the Durham author—the copes, the crosses, the banners, and the images—were clearly important in late medieval devotional practices. So, too, were the other ornaments required for worship, especially for the Mass: books, plate, and vestments. For the richness of the liturgical theatre of the medieval Church to be appreciated fully, they cannot be neglected. If the building is the physical theatre, and the music and texts provide the plot, then we also need to consider the props, without which no production could be considered complete.

* * *

Every ecclesiastical institution in England required such props, from the smallest chantry to the wealthiest cathedrals and religious houses. In some cases their 'theatrical' function might be apparent from their creation, for plate especially might well glister without being gold.[6] Throughout the country, and across the centuries, lists of the plate, vestments, and books

[4] P. Draper, 'Architecture and liturgy', in J. Alexander and P. Binski, eds, *The Age of Chivalry: Art in Plantagenet England, 1200–1400* (London, 1987) [hereafter *AC*], pp. 83–91.

[5] For example, J. T. Fowler, ed., *Rites of Durham = SS*, 107 (1902), pp. 105–8; for the totality of the liturgical experience see N. Coldstream, 'The kingdom of Heaven: the architectural setting', in *AC*, pp. 92–7, esp. p. 96.

[6] C. Oman, *English Church Plate, 597–1830* (London, 1957), pp. 12–13.

which served as aids to worship can be culled from a variety of sources.[7] For individual chantries there are private inventories prepared at the transfer between chaplains, or lists drawn up by cathedral and visitatorial authorities (as at York). Parish churches offered lists at visitations and other inquests (like those from the dean of Salisbury's jurisdiction in the early fifteenth century, and the inquest in Norfolk in 1368); their church-wardens prepared separate inventories for their own purposes (as at St Ewen, Bristol). Within the cathedrals, fabric-wardens, sacrists, and treasurers similarly maintained inventories which, as at Exeter in 1327 and 1506, or York in about 1510, could reach massive proportions. Collegiate churches (like St George's, Windsor) and religious houses also had their catalogues; while as growing numbers of laity organized their own private chapels, so they acquired collections of liturgical impedimenta typified in the inventories of the lawyer Thomas Kebell of 1500, or of the Duke of Norfolk in 1524.[8]

With the private chapels, and for individual founders of chantries, such accumulation was largely a matter of private purchase, possibly with only a short-term perspective. For the greater churches, however, acquisition could be more varied, with greater emphasis on gifts. Purchasers were not precluded: Ixworth Priory, for instance, seemingly developed a programmatic approach to treasures, reserving the profits from its appropriated parish of Downham for such purposes. Parish accounts survive for 1513–21; the profits in 1513–14 went towards commissioning

[7] I therefore deliberately omit consideration of many other aspects of ecclesiastical decoration which encouraged devotion, but were not involved in the routine, clerical, organized liturgy, like paintings, images, shrines, and personally-owned books of devotion.

[8] R. N. Swanson, 'Thomas Holme and his chantries', *York Historian*, 5 (1984), pp. 4–6; J. Raine, ed., *The Fabric Rolls of York Minster, with an Appendix of Illustrative Documents = SS*, 35 (1858), pp. 274–306; T. C. B. Timmins, ed., *The Register of John Chandler, Dean of Salisbury, 1404–17 = Wiltshire Record Society*, 39 (1983), pp. 50–72 (this includes some inventories of chantries); A. Watkin, ed., *Archdeaconry of Norwich: Inventory of Church Goods temp. Edward III = Norfolk Record Society*, 19, 2 vols (1947–8); B. R. Masters and E. Ralph, eds, *The Church Book of St Ewen's, Bristol, 1454–1584 = Publications of the Bristol and Gloucestershire Archaeological Society, Records Section*, 6 (1967), pp. 1–11; G. Oliver, *Lives of the Bishops of Exeter and a History of the Cathedral, with an Illustrative Appendix* (Exeter, 1861), pp. 301–76; Raine, *Fabric Rolls*, pp. 212–35 (cf. the inventory from the reign of Edward VI, ibid., pp. 306–13); M. F. Bond, ed., *The Inventories of St George's Chapel, Windsor Castle, 1384–1667* (Windsor, 1947), pp. 32–83, 102–21, 148–59, 166–79; M. E. C. Walcott, 'Inventory of St Mary's Benedictine nunnery, at Langley, co. Leicester, 1485', *Transactions of the Leicestershire Architectural and Archaeological Society*, 4 (1878), pp. 119–21; E. W. Ives, *The Common Lawyers of Pre-Reformation England* (Cambridge, 1983), pp. 436, 443–6; J. Ridgard, ed., *Medieval Framlingham: Select Documents, 1270–1524 = Suffolk Record Society*, 27 (1985), pp. 134, 148–53, 155. For a general consideration of inventories, restricted to plate, see Oman, *Church Plate*, pp. 16–34.

two vestments, in 1514–15 to the purchase of candelabra, in 1515–17 (two years) on buying a processional cross, and in 1517–18 towards a holy water stoup and 'stykk'.[9] Deliberate acquisition is also evident in contracts and accounts, such as that for making liturgical books for St George's Chapel, Windsor, in the 1380s.[10]

These ornaments have rarely received detailed attention. Discussion of the props of the liturgy-as-drama usually treat them exclusively as artefacts, as products of manufacture rather than adjuncts to worship.[11] Yet they do need to be placed in the context of the services and devotions to which they contributed.

A full consideration of the ornaments of the medieval Church would be impractical. To focus on one collection, to see how that was treated over the years, is more feasible. While some lists are relatively well known, the pre-Reformation possessions of Lichfield Cathedral have received less publicity. The fourteenth century provides a list of the cathedral's treasures in a sacrist's roll of 1345; for the fifteenth, three lists survive in differing formats, which altogether allow some consideration of the changing inventory over a century and more.[12]

The procedure whereby the dean and chapter of Lichfield supervised their collections can be partially reconstructed from entries in the chapter act-books. In 1405 the sacrist, Richard Stayndrop, and his guarantors entered into a bond of £600 for his responsibilities towards the orna-

[9] PRO, E101/517/27, fols 1v, 2v, 4r–v—besides other materials and costs of workmanship these ornaments accounted for 184¾ oz. of silver.

[10] Windsor, St George's Chapel Archives, XV.3.3, printed in J. H. Middleton, *Illuminated Manuscripts in Classical and Mediaeval Times: their Art and their Technique* (Cambridge, 1892), pp. 220–2. The date is provided by comparison with other material in the Windsor collection.

[11] For example, D. King, 'Embroidery and textiles', in *AC*, pp. 157–61; M. Campbell, 'Metalwork in England, *c.*1200–1400', in *AC*, pp. 162–8; A. Wathey, 'The production of books of liturgical polyphony', in J. Griffiths and D. Pearsall, eds, *Book Production and Publication in England, 1375–1475* (Cambridge, 1989), pp. 143–61. A general study of the production of non-choral liturgical texts is lacking; for the present see comments in Wathey, 'Production of polyphony', p. 150; H. E. Bell, 'The price of books in medieval England', *The Library*, ser. 4, 17 (1936–7), pp. 312–32; and evidence cited elsewhere in this paper. Oman, *Church Plate*, pp. 3–126, deals with the Middle Ages, but while seeking to provide a context for the history of church plate, is mainly concerned with offering a species of catalogue of extant material (pp. 40–102).

[12] J. C. Cox, *Catalogue of the Muniments and Manuscript Books pertaining to the Dean and Chapter of Lichfield; Analysis of the Magnum Registrum Album; Catalogue of the Muniments of the Lichfield Vicars* = *Collections for a History of Staffordshire*, 6/ii (1886) [hereafter cited as 'Cox'], pp. 199–221; Shrewsbury Public Library, MS 2 [hereafter cited as 'SPL'], fols 91r–6r. I am grateful to Mr Douglas Johnson, of the Staffordshire *VCH*, for drawing my attention to this MS, and to Mr James Lawson of Shrewsbury School (who originally identified it) for his assistance.

ments. An indented inventory was drawn up, one copy being retained by the dean and chapter, and provision was made for an annual inspection.[13] Scattered notices throughout the chapter act-books indicate that this inspection did occur, beginning around Pentecost.[14] The roll of 1345 is the sole survivor of the original inventories. Presumably it would be annotated and amended at the inspections until a new list became necessary; it clearly was corrected for the sacristy visitation of 1346, with additions being somewhat haphazardly appended.

The fifteenth-century lists are different in character, but clearly within the same tradition. Two inventories are explicitly the results of sacristy visitations. As recorded, they were not separate documents, but entries in a chapter act-book, now known only from transcripts made in 1789.[15] The inclusion of such inventories makes this lost book quite different in character from those now extant; the possibility that further lists were included makes the loss all the more regrettable. The original occasionally baffled the transcriber, and it is not always possible to reconstruct the original wording from the squiggles he provides. The declared dates for the three lists are October 1433,[16] May 1445,[17] and 1450 or 1451 (of which 1451 is the more likely).[18] Sometimes donors cannot be reconciled with those dates, suggesting *ad hoc* additions, with changes of hand not noted in the transcriptions. The first list inventories the cathedral's jewels: it is short, and mainly provides a list of plate. Rather longer is the second list, the record of a sacristy visitation, mainly detailing relics, plate, and vestments. The final list also results from a visitation, detailing vestments and altar drapery, and listing the books in the sacrist's keeping. The appearance of the names of Bishop John Hales (d. 1493) in the 1445 list, and of John Redhill (probably the canon who was in office between 1452 and 1472) in that of 1451,[19] raises doubts about how far any of these lists is a valid cross-section of the cathedral's treasures at any particular point—

[13] Lichfield, Joint Record Office [hereafter LRJO], D30/I, fol. 70v. An indenture was provided for at Stayndrop's first appointment as sacrist in 1391 (ibid., fol. 29v); the 1405 arrangements presumably reflect a redrafting of the agreements.

[14] Oxford, Bodleian Library, MS Ashm. 794, fols 121v, 138r, 141v, 143v, 144r, 173v, 178v; LJRO, D30/I, fol. 95v; D30/III, fols 120v, 125r, 133v; D30/IV, fols 10v, 40r.

[15] These will receive further consideration in due course. They are parts of the lost chapter act-book from which other extracts are considered in R. N. Swanson, 'Lichfield chapter acts, 1433–61', *Collections for a History of Staffordshire*, ser. 4, 13 (1988), pp. 27–46.

[16] SPL, fol. 91r.

[17] SPL, fols 92r–4v.

[18] SPL, fols 94v–6r.

[19] SPL, fols 93v, 95v.

especially as it is impossible to date the numerous marginal and other notes which indicate losses. External evidence raises some doubts about the regularity of the up-dating of the lists. The will of James Langton (proved in December 1450) bequeathed a chasuble, which appears as his donation in the 1451 inventory.[20] He also left twenty marks to purchase two copes for the cathedral, which were to be embroidered with Langton's arms. These copes are not listed. Quite possibly they had not been presented when the 1451 list was originally composed; but their total absence when the gift of Bishop Hales is included is an oddity. Was the gift never made? Was the person responsible for recording subsequent donations slack in fulfilling his responsibilities? Or (perhaps the most likely solution) is the entry of Hales's gift the oddity, with the post-1451 donations being entered on later lists which no longer survive?[21]

None of these lists can be taken as a full record of Lichfield Cathedral's ornamental possessions at their respective dates. In 1345 one omission is clear, indeed glaring; but only from comparison with the later lists. Among the books detailed in 1345 are 'two most ancient books which are called the books of Blessed Chad'. That list's editors identified these as the St Chad's Gospels, surmising that that volume, 'when perfect, was probably a complete Gospellar; and the second volume mentioned in the inventory would most likely be an epistolar.'[22] The later lists disprove that supposition. In 1451 the 'two most ancient books' again appear; but the relic-list of 1445 identified something more explicitly named 'the book of St Chad', intended to be carried in processions.[23]

This scatter of lists for Lichfield is both instructive and useful. Changes can be noted; moreover, the records are complementary, and mutually enhancing. Where the same items appear in several lists, details can often be amplified. The 1345 list sometimes supplies names of donors not recorded later; while later inventories often give fuller descriptions. In 1445 the great cross, valued at £200 and weighing 39 oz., decorated with a variety of precious stones, is clearly that identified a century before as

[20] Swanson, 'Lichfield chapter acts', p. 41; SPL, fol. 95r.

[21] Some later acquisitions are entered in the act-books: LJRO, D30/II, fols 4r, 11v; D30/IV, fol. 27v.

[22] Cox, pp. 204, 211, 220, n. 64. A further complexity of the 1345 list is the record of donations by William de Bosco, who died as chancellor in 1329: J. Le Neve, *Fasti Ecclesiae Anglicanae, 1300–1541, x: Coventry and Lichfield Diocese*, ed. B. Jones (London, 1964), p. 9. In the chapter act-book he is recorded as bequeathing three books (Oxford, Bodleian Library, MS Ashm. 794, fol. 38v). None is associated with him in the 1345 list, which does name him as donor of a chalice and vestment (Cox, pp. 201, 203, 209–10).

[23] SPL, fols 96r, 94v.

given by Bishop Walter Langton.[24] Langton is similarly named in 1345 as the donor of a gold chalice, paten, and cruets valued at £80, which also appear in the later lists. There may be some confusion over precisely which was Langton's chalice, for the organization of the 1445 list suggests that it was of plain gold, whereas it was earlier described as ornamented with precious stones. If the chalice of 1345 was the ornamented chalice detailed in 1445, that description suggests that it fully justified its value:

> One gold chalice, having in the foot an image of the crucifix, and also decorated with sixty-four precious stones (that is, on the circumference with the image of the crucifix, in the first circle 6 large sapphires and 3 garnets therein, with 1 topaz above the head of the crucifix; next to the topaz in that circle 1 sapphire, 1 topaz, 1 small sapphire, 1 small topaz, and 1 sapphire. Item, in the third circle 3 small emeralds and 3 small garnets; and in the 4th circle 2 small emeralds and 2 small garnets; and in the 5th circle 8 small sapphires; and in the 6th circle 4 emeralds, 4 balasses; and in the 7th, 8 small sapphires. In the 8th circle, 2 small emeralds and 2 sapphires; and in the circumference at the foot of the chalice 15 small garnets and 6 sapphires).[25]

Such extremely full descriptions are not the norm, but, nevertheless, other items on these Lichfield lists are well described, vestments as well as plate. The 1345 list mentions 'one most precious cope, decorated with figures, the gift of Walter de Langedon'.[26] The 1445 inventory goes into greater detail:

> 1 precious gold cope, having images woven in on the gold, of the Nativity of Christ, and holy Epiphany, and the Purification of the Blessed Virgin Mary, and the Holy Innocents, and also with images of various prophets, the orphrey having an image of the resurrection and St Michael the Archangel, and one side with the arms of France, and a seraphim with the arms of England on the other side.[27]

The cope's full provenance is not given, but the note about the arms is suggestive, perhaps of some link with Langton's diplomatic activity in France under Edward I (but it might simply confirm his profiteering from his office-holding of the time).[28] Whether the cope should be considered

[24] Cox, pp. 200, 208; SPL, fol. 92r.
[25] Cox, pp. 201, 209; SPL, fols 92r–v.
[26] Cox, pp. 201–2, 209.
[27] SPL, fol. 93r.
[28] *DNB*, 11, pp. 570–3. For his exploitation of office-holding, M. Prestwich, *War, Politics, and*

a lost masterpiece of *opus Anglicanum* is not clear: it could equally be of French workmanship.

While Lichfield's pre-Reformation plate and vestments have all gone, some of the volumes listed in 1451 may still exist.[29] British Library, MS Harley 5249 is a processional donated to Lichfield by William Admondeston, a canon who died in 1432. He is not named as a book donor in 1451, yet possibly this volume was among the processionals entered then. Even more tantalizing is the volume now Shrewsbury School, MS VI. While not conclusively linked to Lichfield Cathedral, the circumstantial evidence is considerable. A collection of processional chants, the volume also includes the sole extant fragments of three liturgical plays, which correspond with those mentioned in Lichfield's cathedral statutes as the responsibility of the succentor (and so probably performed by the vicars choral). The full set probably required another two volumes for other parts to complete the plays. Like the Harley MS, this compilation is not immediately visible in the 1451 record; but may likewise have been among the processionals.[30]

* * *

All these impedimenta had functions: they made the celebration worthy of what was being celebrated. But how they were used, and attitudes towards them, could be complex. Levels of appreciation probably varied, to reflect differing perceptions of their role and utility within the liturgy-as-theatre and the liturgy-as-divine-celebration. Objects regularly used, but not for display, might receive much more utilitarian treatment than those serving a major liturgical role and more intimately connected with the holy. This is suggested by an account of the 1380s for liturgical books produced for the dean and canons of Windsor. The commissioned Gospel book, martyrology, and antiphoner used high-quality materials and absorbed considerable effort and investment. The bills totalled respect-

---

Finance under Edward I (London, 1972), pp. 152–3, 168; A. Beardwood, 'The trial of Walter Langton, bishop of Lichfield, 1307–1312', *Transactions of the American Philosophical Society*, ns 54/iii (Philadelphia, 1964).

29 This booklist is not to be identified as the cathedral library, of which details of the early seventeenth-century manuscript collections are provided in N. R. Ker, 'Patrick Young's catalogue of manuscripts of Lichfield cathedral', *Mediaeval and Renaissance Studies*, 2 (1950), pp. 151–9 (some of his identifications of survivals have now been rejected).

30 Le Neve, *Fasti*, p. 42; N. Davis, ed., *Non-cycle Plays and Fragments*, *EETS*, supplementary texts, 1 (1970), pp. xiv–xxii, 1–7, 124–33; S. Rankin, 'Shrewsbury School, Manuscript VI: a medieval part book?' *Proceedings of the Royal Musical Association*, 102 (1975–6), pp. 129–44.

ively 75*s.* 8*d.*, 28*s.* 4*d.*, and £7 7*s.* 11*d.* (the vellum for the last two included some from store, so real costs were higher). While less costly than the antiphoner, the Gospel book received particular attention, involving at least one trip to London, and work by a goldsmith. The three processionals used sheep vellum rather than calf, and cost much less—37*s.* 4*d.* all told.[31] The 1451 Lichfield book-list suggests a similar distinction. The missals are identified individually, as are the antiphoners, graduals, portiforia, and some psalters. The remaining psalters were simply bundled together ('15 psalters, of which 2 are glossed'), as were the five shortened pontificals, three ordinals, and twelve processionals.[32]

While care might be invested in production, an aesthetic concern with 'harmony' in the overall scheme of things is unlikely. The combination of styles, of colours, of architecture and ornaments, is hard to envisage. The rather eclectic nature of architectural developments, and the unplanned processes of acquisition reflected in the Lichfield inventories, argue against the existence or even need for 'harmony' in the stylistic organization of the liturgy-as-theatre—that contrasts which might jar twentieth-century susceptibilities would then have passed without comment.[33]

Precise definition of medieval attitudes towards this liturgical paraphernalia is virtually impossible; but some indications, and illustrations, can be extracted from the Lichfield material, especially the fifteenth-century lists. For one thing, very few of these treasures appear to reflect corporate purchases by the dean and chapter. In some instances they had assumed responsibility for repairs; but most of the vestments, books, and plate were received from individual donors. Some benefactors made massive gifts: the collection of vestments and ornaments given by Bishop Walter Langton is outstanding, but later bishops were almost equally generous. Indeed, almost every subsequent bishop appears as a donor, through to William Heyworth (1419–47). Thereafter, the mention of John Hales (1459–93) is obviously a later addition. The absence of William Booth and Reginald Boulers is thus highlighted, but it cannot be assumed that they gave nothing. Among other donors, canons

[31] Windsor, St George's Chapel Archives, XV.3.3; Middleton, *Illuminated Manuscripts*, pp. 220–3.

[32] SPL, fols 95v–6r. See also comments on book production for the chapel on London Bridge in C. P. Christianson, *Memorials of the Book Trade in Medieval London: the Archives of Old London Bridge = Manuscript Studies*, 3 (Woodbridge, 1987), pp. 14–17. The sheer functionalism of service-books perhaps accounts for the general lack of illustration: see K. L. Scott, 'Design, decoration, and illustration', in Griffiths and Pearsall, *Book Production*, pp. 33, 46, 48.

[33] Compare Sheingorn, 'Visual language of drama', p. 184.

of the cathedral naturally appear with great regularity; other named benefactors included chantry priests and lesser clerics among the cathedral establishment. Non-royal, lay donors are not obvious in the fifteenth century, but do appear in 1345. Royal gifts are specified in the lists of 1345, 1445, and 1451, being made by every king from Henry III to Edward III, several queens (most notably Eleanor of Castile), and by Henry VI and his wife.[34]

Perhaps the most striking feature of the Lichfield collection is that it was in constant flux. While inventories of ornaments have an intrinsic interest, they can too easily be seen in static isolation, and be transformed into a fully representative and unchanging statement of possessions. Yet just as medieval cathedrals were under almost constant reconstruction, so their internal ornamentation was ever being altered and renewed. The Lichfield inventories reflect changes over more than two centuries—between the pontificates of Meuland and Hales. These were both gains and losses: Bishop Roger Meuland is identified as a donor in 1345, but nothing is specifically allocated to him in the 1440s.[35] What is striking are the frequent notes of loss, damage, or decay: this was no static collection. These objects were used, and in being used suffered and needed repair or replacement.

The vestments offer one indication of the complexities in assessing attitudes towards these possessions. Clearly, as clothing reserved for special occasions, they served to separate the liturgical actors from the non-participants. But this was not their full function. Their decoration placed many vestments in the category of 'books for the unlearned', their depictions of saints and significant events in the lives of Christ and his mother matching similar portrayals in stone, glass, and wood.[36] In the Lichfield lists this would certainly apply to the cope given by Langton, already described, and to the cope decorated with pictures of the Trinity, the Annunciation, and the Coronation of the Virgin.[37] Other decoration, equally explicit but less pictorial, emphasized particular devotions—such as John Burghill's many gifts of vestments decorated with a crowned 'M',

[34] Cox, pp. 200–3, 208–10 (a gift bearing the arms of the king of Germany was probably made by Richard of Cornwall: ibid., pp. 204, 211); SPL, fols 93v, 95r.

[35] This may simply reflect defects in the fifteenth-century lists, which generally do not mention donors of the thirteenth and early fourteenth centuries.

[36] Compare Aston, *Lollards and Reformers*, pp. 183–5. Mass vestments also had a mystical meaning: Wickham Legg, *Tracts on the Mass*, p. 19; *The Interpretacyon and Sygnyfycacyon*, sig. i.iiv–i.iiir.

[37] SPL, fols 93r–v.

indicative of Marian devotion.[38] Nor can the donor's view of the gift's purpose be ignored: these vestments fitted into the gift-exchange economy of salvation. The giver was recognized as a benefactor, and in return would expect prayers for his soul.[39] Unfortunately the almost total loss of the Lichfield testamentary material prevents recovery of the conditions on which the gifts were made; besides, many donations were presumably made before death.[40] Inscriptions on some vestments named the donor, as with the copes given by John Cole and William Hall;[41] coats of arms did likewise. Many vestments described in Lichfield's fifteenth-century lists bore coats of arms, presumably precisely for that purpose. Generally the arms provided sufficient identification, although two black copes of satin bearing the French arms were further enhanced by crowned 'K's, perhaps to identify their donor as Katherine, daughter of King Charles VI of France and widow of King Henry V of England.[42]

Once given to the church, the status of these ornaments changed: they had to serve the functions imposed on them by their users as well as those expected by their donors. Here different sets of attitudes seem to come into play.

Just how assiduously Lichfield's dean and chapter cared for their possessions is irrecoverable. The sacristy visitations indicate some concern; but extant records give few concrete instances of maintenance, usually being content to remark that something is worn out, or damaged. Presumably, however, repairs were constantly under review, with mending and replacement being done if necessary. Presumably such concerns lay behind the new statute introduced by Bishop Heyworth in the 1420s, requiring part of the 100 marks paid by each incoming residentiary to be allocated toward the provision of ornaments and vestments.[43] Elsewhere, the precentors' rolls of St George's, Windsor, and those of the sacrists and feretrars of Durham Priory, provide lengthy catalogues of repairs to books, vestments, and plate. At Windsor, and probably elsewhere, the ornaments in regular use received most attention.[44] Sometimes, however,

[38] SPL, fols 93r–v, 94r, 95r, see also fols 94v (gift of William Hall), 95v.

[39] The demand for prayers might be stated explicitly on plate: Oman, *Church Plate*, pp. 55, nn. 2–3, 81, n. 1.

[40] This clearly applies to Langton: his will leaves very little explicitly to be retained by Lichfield: Beardwood, 'Trial of Langton', p. 40 (my interpretation differs from that given ibid., p. 39).

[41] SPL, fol. 93r.

[42] SPL, fol. 93v.

[43] W. Dugdale, *Monasticon Anglicanum*, ed. J. Caley, H. Ellis, and B. Bandinell, 6 vols in 8 (London, 1817–30), 6/iii, p. 1262.

[44] Bond, *Inventories of St George's*, pp. 5–8, 88–101, 122–45, 158–63; J. T. Fowler, ed., *Extracts*

these repairs—or with plate the replacement of lost stones—might well involve further donations.

While plate is quite likely to have been repaired, the maintenance of vestments and books posed different problems. Vestments would unavoidably wear out, so might books, which might also become obsolete through ritual developments or changing choral fashions.[45] Lichfield's surviving chapter act-books provide only one clear reference to vestment repairs, and none for books: such matters were generally left to the sacrist.[46] In August 1376 the chapter was shown five choir copes of gilded cloth, with four tunicles and other ornaments of those sets, together with a silk cope interwoven with gold which had been given by John Marreys (prebendary of Gaia Major, who died in 1375). The communar was loaned ten marks to pay for the workmanship and materials for the repairs of the unattributed vestments; but Marreys's executors were held liable for the repairs to his gift.[47] Presumably these were made, as in April 1385 the Marreys cope (unless he gave more than one) was among a collection of vestments lent to Bakewell Church.[48]

The extant inventories similarly provide little evidence of the maintenance of vestments. In the fifteenth-century lists there is just one mention of repairs (to the two copes given by St Thomas of Hereford with orphreys made by Queen Eleanor, for which the dean and chapter had purchased some new cloth of gold).[49] The dean and chapter are also explicitly credited with only a few purchases, although they were fairly spectacular. In 1445 they bought two cloths of gold of tissue to serve as altar-cloths on festival days; their other purchase (undated) comprised two copes, decorated with images of the Trinity on the breast, and on the back of one the Annunciation, and of the other the Coronation of the Virgin.[50] However, replacements may have been bought more frequently, even if only

---

from the Account Rolls of the Abbey of Durham, 2 = *SS*, 100 (1898), pp. 379–425, 441–82 *passim*.

[45] Christianson, *Memorials*, pp. 16–17; Wathey, 'Production of polyphony', pp. 144–5 (the physical characteristics of polyphonic material might also affect survival and retention: ibid., pp. 145–8).

[46] These responsibilities are implicit in the bond of 1405 (n. 13 above); see also the statutory definition of the sacrist's duties in H. Bradshaw and C. Wordsworth, eds, *Statutes of Lincoln Cathedral*, 2 vols in 3 (Cambridge, 1892–7), 2/i, pp. 18–20.

[47] Oxford, Bodleian Library, MS Ashm. 794, fol. 161v.

[48] LRJO, D30/I, fol. 3v.

[49] SPL, fols 93v, 94v.

[50] SPL, fol. 93v. Unfortunately, defective transcription in the second case has reduced the sum to gibberish.

from necessity. In March 1394 a chapter meeting imposed a contribution of a tenth on the prebendaries to meet a variety of needs, among them the replacement of worn-out choir copes. Unfortunately there is no identification of any consequent purchases.[51] This may have meant that the apparent wealth of the inventories was to some degree illusory. The state of the holdings certainly left much to be desired in the early sixteenth century. In 1528 four processionals were to be ordered, because there were none usable within the cathedral;[52] while the position regarding vestments was particularly dire. In 1523 the tradition of not wearing silk copes at the Purification (because of the dangers they faced from dripping wax) was at last terminated. In 1526, because the copes were worn out, with insufficient funds to provide replacements, Bishop Blythe decreed a tax of a fifth from prebendal incomes for five years for that purpose, and encouraged the prebendaries to make individual gifts. Nevertheless, identical complaints about the copes were made in 1531, and their use restricted by the chapter. Arrangements were also made for the repair of the service-books, similarly affected by age and daily use.[53]

A notable feature of the treatment of their treasures by the Lichfield dean and chapter is their willingness to lend them out. Several loans are documented in the 1345 list,[54] and loans of vestments and plate also appear intermittently in the chapter act-books.[55] Admittedly these are few (although the impression from the early list is that, cumulatively, a substantial part of the total might be outside the sacrist's control at any one time). Significantly, all the loans to churches were to places under the dean and chapter's jurisdiction, so that some oversight would be maintained. Nor were rights of ownership being tacitly given up: the right to recall the loans was expressly maintained. Supervision of loans to individuals could be more difficult: the 1345 list mentions the loan of a mitre to Bishop Roger de Meuland, who had died in 1295.[56] Nevertheless, willingness to lend suggests that these objects were not seen solely as valuables to be hoarded, but as the necessary adjuncts to divine service, valuable because they were used or available to be seen.

[51] LJRO, D30/I, fol. 39v.
[52] LJRO, D30/IV, fol. 54v (but this may refer to possessions of the vicars choral, rather than the sacrist's responsibilities).
[53] Dugdale, *Monasticon*, 6/iii, p. 1265; LJRO, D30/III, fols. 138v–9r, D30/IV, fols 75v–6r.
[54] Cox, pp. 205–6, 212–13.
[55] LJRO, D30/I, fols 1v, 3v.
[56] Cox, pp. 206, 212. The editors postulate that he had been buried in the mitre (ibid., p. 221, n. 79).

This may be confirmed by other dealings with the ornaments: the plate could be pawned, and might even be recycled. Again instances are rare, but at least three times between 1390 and 1430 Lichfield's chapter act-books record that a chalice was pawned; while in the 1433 jewel list the sacrist had pawned a chalice and a cope clasp for 6 marks.[57] More strikingly, in 1530 the chapter had pawned jewels to cover a loan of £100 made to King Henry VIII.[58] Lichfield provides no clear instance of the reworking of plate (there is one possible but unclear exception); but accounts of Lynn Priory for 1521–2 do. In that year the making of two new chalices required 12 oz. of new silver, plus that from the old chalices.[59]

Given the willingness to lend, and pawn, and the wear of usage, the constant fluctuation in the treasure-holdings is hardly surprising. Plate would probably last longer than vestments and books, but jewels would still become dislodged, metal broken.[60] Most losses would be accidental; but not all. In dire emergency plate might have to be disposed of, as Lynn Priory surrendered some of its plate to provide for a loan to Henry VIII in 1511–12.[61] Deliberate alienation through theft might also occur. Churches and images, for all their sanctity, were not inviolable. Lichfield offers no direct evidence of thefts, but other churches do. Numerous criminous clerks were arraigned on charges of theft from churches—and these are only cases which led to arrests: there must have been many others.[62] That cathedrals were not immune was dramatically demonstrated by the theft of the reliquary containing the head of St Hugh from Lincoln in 1364.[63]

While there were losses, there were replacements. The Lichfield lists suggest that these were usually provided by further donors. This indicates

57 LJRO, D30/I, fols 23v, 115r, 136r; SPL, fol. 91r.

58 LJRO, D30/IV, fol. 64r.

59 Norwich, Norfolk Record Office, DCN 2/1/82 (account for 13–14 Henry VIII). The possible exception in the Lichfield inventories occurs at SPL, fol. 91r.

60 See comment of Oman, *Church Plate*, p. 21.

61 Norwich, Norfolk Record Office, DCN 2/1/82 (account for 2–3 Henry VIII).

62 M. Archer, ed., *The Register of Bishop Philip Repingdon, 1405–1419*, 3 = *Lincoln Record Society*, 74 (1982), nos 154, 509, 538; R. N. Swanson, ed., *The Register of John Catterick, Bishop of Coventry and Lichfield, 1415–19* = *Canterbury and York Society*, 72 (London, 1990), nos 200–1. See also the miraculous recovery of stolen church property in P. Grosjean, ed., *Henrici VI Angliae regis miracula postuma ex codice Musei Britanici Regio 13.c.VIII* = *Subsidia hagiographica*, 22 (Brussels, 1935), pp. 150–2. The comments on security in Oman, *Church Plate*, pp. 35–7, strike me as rather optimistic.

63 E. Venables, 'The shrine and head of St Hugh of Lincoln', *Archaeological Journal*, 50 (1893), pp. 48–50.

a cyclical pattern: old materials wear out, new donors offer new gifts. This arrangement probably applies to most major secular churches and religious houses; but for parish churches and chantries, the pattern might be slightly different. Old chantries would decline, as endowments decayed and possessions wore out or were put to other uses. New chantries might be established, with their own vestments and ornaments, as separate entities. Even if only short-term foundations, they would have to be provided for in a fitting manner, perhaps with their own vestments and plate, which might eventually pass to parish use (if there was an immediate superfluity, some of the goods might be used elsewhere in the church right from the start).[64] In any event, these chantries and their ornaments would contribute to the overall beauty of holiness within the parish church, making their own contribution to the liturgy's theatrical impact.

* * *

The Lichfield treasures provide a focus for attention; but only the lists now survive. As the definition of holiness changed at the Reformation, so the treasures originally gathered to emphasize and complement the beauties of the supplanted definition of holiness were considered superfluous, and removed.[65] In this, Lichfield was not alone: the destruction of England's pre-Reformation ecclesiastical ornaments is almost total.[66] While it lasted, the investment of wealth, workmanship, and emotion in ornaments for liturgical purposes was functional, in a double sense: they decorated the House of God in an appropriate manner, provided for the proper celebration of the divine Office, and encouraged devotion by offering a route to contemplation and instruction; donations were also meritorious acts, functional in the sense of acquiring merit with God. While adding to the beauty of holiness, and contributing towards the theatrical aspects of the liturgy, the devotional function, the increase of holiness, must not be overlooked.

University of Birmingham

[64] For example, Swanson, 'Thomas Holme and his chantries', p. 6. See also C. Burgess, '"For the increase of divine service": chantries in the parish in late medieval Bristol', *JEH*, 36 (1985), pp. 62–4.

[65] *V.C.H. A History of the County of Stafford*, iii (Oxford, 1974), p. 168.

[66] M. Campbell, 'Metalwork', p. 162. For the fate of plate at the Reformation, Oman, *Church Plate*, pp. 113–26.

JOHN MARBECK AND *THE BOOKE OF COMMON PRAIER NOTED*

by KENNETH W. T. CARLETON

THE liturgical section of *The New English Hymnal* contains musical settings for both eucharistic orders of the Church of England's *Alternative Service Book 1980*. The modern-language service, Rite A, is provided with a newly-composed congregational setting in speech rhythm. The texts of Rite B use the traditional language of the Book of Common Prayer, and are given a musical setting taken from *The Booke of Common Praier Noted* by John Marbeck, published in 1550. An accompaniment is added, and the text is adapted where the original is no longer accurate. Its inclusion in this new hymn-book is evidence of the popularity which Marbeck's setting has enjoyed for more than a hundred years. Its rediscovery took place in the nineteenth century through the influence of the Tractarians and their successors, who sought to revive traditional liturgical practices such as the singing of plainsong during worship. *The Booke of Common Praier Noted* is a musical setting of parts of the first English Prayer Book, which had been promulgated in 1549. The appearance of a second Prayer Book in 1552 rendered Marbeck's work obsolete, as the new book expresses a different attitude towards music in worship. The 1549 Prayer Book encourages singing in many of the services, not least the Office of Holy Communion. The clerks, singing-men usually in minor orders, are expected to take a full part, and the normal eucharistic celebration is one which is sung virtually throughout. The Offices in the 1552 Book contain very few references to singing, and the clerks are nowhere mentioned. The only direction for singing any part of the order for Holy Communion is found at the end, when 'Glory be to God on high' may be said or sung. A rubric at Morning Prayer allows for the singing of the lessons in that service and at Evening Prayer, as well as the Epistle and Gospel at Holy Communion, so that the people may hear them more clearly. It is possible that the retention of this reference to singing from the first Prayer Book may have been an oversight, as the rubric is situated away from the main body of the service.

Vernacular liturgy came late to the English language compared to its continental counterparts. One of the first attempts of the sixteenth-century reformers to provide public worship in the language of the people was made by Thomas Müntzer. As parish priest of Allstedt from Easter

1523 to August 1524, Müntzer provided simplified, reformed, German services for his people, which drew enthusiastic support from the surrounding region. For the sake of the weak in conscience, he retained the plainsong melodies familiar to his flock, adapting them to suit his vernacular texts. Despite their often florid and extended musical form, with long passages of notes sung to a single syllable, Müntzer was none the less convinced of the importance of understanding the text used in worship. The 1523 *Deutzsch Kirchenampt*, German Church Service Book, proclaims itself as a reformed order,

> which takes away the covering treacherously devised to conceal the Light of the world, which now shines forth again through these hymns and godly psalms; for the edification and growth of the Christian people and in accordance with the unchangeable will of God, but destroying the bombastic ceremonies of the godless.[1]

The book contains five orders for Morning and Evening Prayer, based around the old Matins, Lauds, and Vespers, and heavily dependent upon those Offices for structure and content. Replacing the complex calendar of feasts and commemorations with five services, Müntzer is able to provide a simple framework for daily public prayer throughout the year. The reformed German Mass followed in 1524. Its publication was supported financially by the Allstedt Council, as it had been decided that not only the vernacular text, but also the music for the Mass should be provided. Müntzer's texts are fitted to the plainsong melodies of the old Latin rite. The *Deutsch euangelisch Messze* retains the structure of the Roman Mass, and presents five orders of service for use throughout the whole year, reflecting the practice adopted for the Offices. The Bible is to be read in its entirety, rather than just the selected portions which were used in the later medieval rites. The first service is for the season of Advent, taken to run from All Saints' Day[2] to the birth of Christ. The second is for use from Christmas to the Presentation,[3] the third from that feast to Easter, the fourth for the season to Pentecost, and the fifth from Pentecost to All Saints'.

[1] P. Matheson, ed., *Collected Letters and Writings of Thomas Müntzer* (Edinburgh, 1988) [hereafter Matheson], p. 166.

[2] Matheson gives All Souls' Day; the reading in the German original is *allerheilgentag*, and the editor's footnote reads '1 November'. See G. Franz, ed., *Thomas Müntzers Schriften und Briefe* (Gütersloh, 1968), p. 162.

[3] 2 February.

> In this way Christ will be explained to us through the holy spirit within us, through the testimony about how he was foretold by the prophets, how he was born, died, and rose again, who with his father and the same holy spirit rules eternally and makes us his pupils.[4]

The five orders of service and five Masses are only models, however. It is for the local pastor to amend, lengthen, or shorten them according to need. Far from attempting to impose uniformity of practice, Müntzer provides for a considerable amount of flexibility and openness to the Holy Spirit who dwells within the elect.

The first published vernacular liturgy of the Reformation, then, retains many of the features of the Roman rite which it replaced. The need for the communication of the Word of God to the people is met by a simplification of the structure of worship, the elimination of much that is not scriptural, and the importance given to the reading of the Bible. The music with which this worship is accompanied draws on the familiar notes of the old liturgy, adding to them new German words. Choral music of the type beloved of the late Middle Ages, in which the text is almost completely lost to the ear through elaborate polyphony, is here eliminated. The danger with using plainsong melodies of the type retained at Allstedt is that their very nature tends to obscure the text they accompany. Anything which gets in the way of the clear understanding of what is sung is anathema to the majority of reformers. The ideal musical setting consists of a single note to each syllable of text for perfect clarity. The first working out of this principle in a reformed liturgy in the vernacular may be found in Martin Luther's *Deudsche Messe* of 1525.

Luther's first reformed liturgy was the *Formula missae et communionis pro ecclesia Vuittembergensi*, published in 1523. It is a revision of the Latin Mass, paying detailed attention to the canon, retaining 'only that which is good and holy' and repudiating 'everything that smacks of sacrifice'.[5] The full text of the liturgy is not given, the work being a step-by-step account and rationale of the Evangelical Mass then in use at Wittenberg. It should be noted that the only parts of this service not in Latin are the sermon and a few hymns. A German translation made by Paul Speratus appeared in print in Wittenberg the following year. Luther was quite content to retain Latin in the liturgy. Aside from Müntzer's work mentioned above,

[4] Matheson, p. 168.

[5] *Luther's Works*, American edition 55 vols (Philadelphia, 1958–67) [hereafter *LW*], 53, *Liturgy and Hymns*, ed. U. S. Leupold (1965), p. 26.

vernacular services had been held in Basle and Pfortzheim since 1522, with other orders being introduced in Reutlingen, Wertheim, Königsberg, and Strasbourg during 1524. However, this profusion tended to lead to confusion, and Luther came under some pressure from his friends to provide his own German liturgy. Unlike his former colleague Andreas Karlstadt, who insisted on the use of German, he did not consider it to be essential. In the treatise *Against the Heavenly Prophets* (1524), he writes:

> I am happy the mass now is held among the Germans in German. But to make a necessity of this, as if it had to be so, is again too much. . . . I would gladly have a German mass today. I am also occupied with it. But I would like it to have a true German character. For to translate the Latin text and retain the Latin tone or notes has my sanction, thought it doesn't sound polished or well done. Both the text and notes, accent, melody, and manner of rendering ought to grow out of the true mother tongue and inflection, otherwise all of it becomes an imitation, in the manner of the apes.[6]

Luther clearly wished to avoid the mistakes which he believed Müntzer to have made, to which he clearly but indirectly refers in this passage. His vernacular liturgy was first used in Wittenberg towards the end of 1525, and appeared in print early in 1526 under the title *Deudsche Messe und Ordnung Gottisdiensts*. It was not his intention to impose uniformity, either of order or of language. In the preface he expressly states that he does not wish the use of Latin to be discontinued, and the vernacular services are not meant to abrogate or change the *Formula missae*. Latin should be retained for the sake of the young. The present work, the German Mass and Order of Service, is for the sake of unlearned lay folk; the didactic elements of public worship must be able to be understood by all, believers and non-believers alike. The 1528 *Instructions for the Visitors of Parish Pastors in Electoral Saxony*, drawn up by Philip Melanchthon, but endorsed by Luther, recognize a diversity of language in practice:

> Some sing the mass in German, some in Latin, either of which is permissible. It would be reasonable and useful if we used German where most of the people do not understand Latin. Then the people would better understand what is sung or read.[7]

[6] *LW*, 40, *Church and Ministry*, II, ed. C. Bergendoff (1958), p. 141.
[7] Ibid., p. 300.

Music forms an integral part of Luther's *Deudsche Messe*. His concern with an appropriate musical setting for German words led him to call upon the Elector of Saxony to send the two leading musicians of his chapel, Conrad Rupsch and Johann Walter, to Wittenberg for consultation. Much of the Ordinary of the Mass is replaced by metrical hymn-singing, the texts based on the Latin originals which they replace. For example, the Creed, sung after the Gospel, is the metrical hymn 'Wyr glauben all an eynen Gott'; it is recommended that the German *Agnus Dei*, 'Christe, du Lamm Gottes', or another hymn be sung during the administration of the cup. The *Sanctus* is a metrical paraphrase of Isaiah 6. 1–4, the prophet's vision of God enthroned amongst the angelic host which preceded his call, the text and music both by Luther himself. The more usual *Sanctus*, derived from the Book of Revelation, is replaced by this. It accompanies the Elevation of the Host, which Luther retained for the sake of weak consciences and 'because it goes well with the German Sanctus and signifies that Christ has commanded us to remember him.'[8] Chants for the Introit, Epistle, and Gospel are given, with worked-out examples. Traditional plainsong psalm tones are adapted to the inflections of the German language.

The music in Luther's *Deudsche Messe* is in traditional German 'hobnail' notation throughout, with only two basic note lengths. It is mensural—with measured, fixed time-values—unlike plainsong, which is flexible, adapting its note lengths to natural speech rhythms. This distinction is important, not least because the use of fixed time-values became characteristic of the style of congregational singing encouraged in many reformed liturgies.

John Calvin's first published liturgical work, *Aulcuns pseaumes et cantiques mys en chant* (1539) was an interim measure, supplying music for his congregation of French exiles at Strasbourg, and was soon followed by a complete service-book, derived almost word for word from the German service then in use in the city. It contains several metrical psalms in French for congregational singing, the text and music by Clément Marot. The psalm-settings make use of four note-lengths, in order to allow the music to reflect the natural rhythms of the text. Calvin's later liturgies, *La Forme des prieres* of 1542 and 1545 for the church at Geneva, and a 1545 edition of the same work for his old Strasbourg congregation, are simplified forms of his first liturgy. Music in these services is solely in the form of the metrical psalm. The liturgical choir has no place, the singing being an action of the whole Church as it exercises its priestly function.

[8] *LW*, 53, p. 82.

In England, the Latin liturgy remained almost untouched up to the death of Henry VIII. Whatever the late King's political attitudes may have been, in matters of worship he was essentially conservative. The accession of Edward VI in January 1547 opened up the possibility of widespread change in public worship. Of prime concern was the introduction of English into all the services of the Church. The first English Litany had been published in 1544, a compilation by Thomas Cranmer, drawn from the Sarum Processional, Luther's Litany, the liturgy of the Greek Orthodox Church, and some original material. Cranmer provides it with a musical setting heavily influenced by his own knowledge of the plainsong of the Sarum Processional. Each syllable of the text is set to a single note; the notation implies a variety of note-lengths, and is identical to that used subsequently for *The Booke of Common Praier Noted*. If the time-values set out in the later work are applied to the Litany, then it becomes apparent that Cranmer's work attempts to match the natural rhythms and inflections of the English language. Before becoming Archbishop of Canterbury, Cranmer had experienced Lutheran worship at first hand, and the adaptation of psalm tones to the vernacular, with careful regard to natural rhythms and inflections, is as characteristic of Luther's work as it is of Cranmer's Litany. With the publication of the First Book of Common Prayer in 1549, the English Church received its first complete reformed liturgy in the vernacular. Unlike its continental counterparts, it contains complete texts for the celebration of daily and occasional offices throughout the year, as well as for the celebration of the Eucharist. The Act of Uniformity which authorized the Prayer Book is quite specific in its aim to provide a single use for the whole realm, to replace the diversity of Latin uses in existence. It may also be that it tacitly aimed to replace unauthorized vernacular liturgies which were being used experimentally in St Paul's Cathedral, in London, and elsewhere.

The 1549 Book of Common Prayer contains a number of directions for singing, and the assistance of a choral body of clerks or singing-men is taken as a norm, though provision is made for establishments and occasions where none is available. Most of the musical directions are to be found in the order for Holy Communion, where the clerks have a significant role. They are directed to sing the Introit, the English *Kyries*, the *Gloria*, Creed, *Sanctus*, and *Agnus Dei*, along with sentences at the Offertory and post Communion, and a number of responses. Where there are no clerks, the priest is directed to say their part. The Epistle and Gospel may be sung, as also a number of the priest's prayers. At both Matins and Evensong, the psalms and canticles may be sung, and the lessons chanted.

The clerks also have a role in the Solemnization of Matrimony, and in the order for the Burial of the Dead. They would also presumably sing at the celebration of Holy Communion when there is a burial, for which proper texts are supplied. No music accompanies the text in the book itself, a variation from the general practice of continental reformers. The need for suitable music was met in 1550 by the publication by the King's printer, Richard Grafton, of *The Booke of Common Praier Noted* by John Marbeck.

Marbeck[9] spent his life as a musician of the Royal Free Chapel of St George at Windsor. He was organist of that foundation by 1542, and may have been one of the singing-men before being appointed organist.[10] He supplicated for the degree of Bachelor of Music at Oxford in 1549, but it is not known whether he was admitted to the degree, as records for the period are incomplete.[11] In the same year that *The Booke of Common Praier Noted* was published, Marbeck also produced a Concordance of the Bible. In the dedicatory preface to King Edward VI he refers to his own lack of education, calling himself

> one of your highnes moste poore Subiectes, destitute bothe of learnyng and eloquence, yea, and suche a one as in mane neuer tasted the swetnes of learned Letters, but altogether brought vp in your highnes College at Wyndsore, in the study of Musike and playing on Organs, wherein I consumed vainly the greatest part of my life . . .[12]

His work on a concordance had begun several years earlier, though it had been interrupted by his arrest and prosecution under the Act of Six Articles in 1543. Marbeck and three other Windsor men, Robert Testwood, Henry Filmer, and Anthony Peerson, were arrested 'for certain books and writings found in their houses against the Six Articles',[13] tried, and condemned to death. The charge against Marbeck was that he had copied out a work of Calvin, probably *De fugiendis impiorum illicitis*

[9] His name is variously spelt Marbeck(e), Merbeck(e), etc.; the form adopted here is that which was most commonly found in his later publications, though in *The Booke of Common Praier Noted*, it is found in the form 'John Merbecke'.

[10] R. A. Leaver, *John Marbeck = Courtenay Library of Reformation Classics*, 9 (Oxford, 1978), p. 25.

[11] Ibid., p. 34. Also see A. Wood, *Fasti Oxonienses*, 1 (London, 1815), col. 130.

[12] John Marbeck, *A Concordance, that is to saie, a worke wherein by the ordre of the letters of the A.B.C. ye maie redely finde any worde conteigned in the whole Bible, so often as it is there expressed or mencioned* (London, 1550) [hereafter *Concordance*].

[13] J. Foxe, *Acts and Monuments*, ed. G.Townsend and S. R. Cattley, 8 vols (London, 1837–41) [hereafter Foxe, *Acts*].

sacris, et puritate Christianae religionis observanda (Basle, 1537), allegedly written

> against thesame sixe articles, and this my concordance was not one of the least matters, that then thei alleged, to aggrauate the cause of my trouble: but thesame tyme was my greate worke, emong other, taken from me and utterly lost, whiche (beside my labor) I had spent no small tyme in.[14]

After a considerable spell in prison, and a number of lengthy interviews, Marbeck and his three companions were sentenced to death for heresy. Although his companions were executed, Marbeck received the King's pardon and was set free.[15] He had then to compile the work anew, and was eventually able to have it published by Richard Grafton after he had re-written and shortened it on the printer's instructions. Aside from the *Concordance*, Marbeck wrote five other theological works which survive, *The lyues of holy Sainctes* (1574), *The Holie Historie of King Dauid* (1579), *A Booke of Notes and Common Places* (1581), *Examples drawen out of holy Scripture* (1582), and a *Dialogue betweene youth and old age* (1584?). No musical works of his other than *The Booke of Common Praier Noted* were published, unless we include *The Holie Historie of King Dauid*, a versification of the story of David, from I Samuel 16 through to I Kings 2, which Marbeck may have intended for singing. The dedication suggests that such versifications of Scripture should replace 'filthy, fonde, and vnsauery songs, bookes, and fancies farre vnfit and ill beseeming the eies of baptized Christians.'[16] Other than the *Concordance*, all Marbeck's theological works were published some years after the Elizabethan settlement. Their contents shed some light on his apparent abandonment of musical composition for the church service. Under the heading 'Music', in *A Booke of Notes and Common Places*, he included two passages from Calvin which argue against the use of instrumental music in worship, and one from Peter Martyr on Augustine warning against paying too much heed to the sound and not enough to the meaning of the text.[17] On singing he cited various authorities from the Fathers, and a number of quotations from marginal notes extracted from various editions of the English Bible, which support the view that the style of singing

[14] *Concordance*, preface.
[15] Foxe, *Acts*, p. 491.
[16] John Marbeck, *The Holie Historie of King Dauid* (London, 1579).
[17] John Marbeck, *A Booke of Notes and Common Places* (London, 1581), pp. 754–6.

commended in Scripture is an inward melody of the heart, praising the Lord in mind rather than in voice. Prick-song (singing in parts) and descant (adding a counter-melody to a given tune) were brought into the Church by Pope Vitalian (657–72) 'to delight the vain, foolish, and idle ears of fond and fantasticall men'.[18] It might well be surmised that Marbeck had come to the position of Calvin on church music, that only unaccompanied monophony was acceptable for Christian worship. It is quite possible that he had held this view for some years, perhaps even before *The Booke of Common Praier Noted* was made obsolete by the publication of the second Prayer Book in 1552.

Marbeck's express intention in *The Booke of Common Praier Noted* is to provide 'so muche of the Order of Common prayer as is to be song in Churches'.[19] The notation used throughout is the same as that found in Cranmer's 1544 Litany, and the note-lengths are clearly defined. Four sorts of notes are used: a breve, the longest note then in common use in measured time; a semibreve, represented by a square note, worth half the time-value of a breve; a minim, half the length of a semibreve; and the close, used only at the end of a verse. In addition, a dot may be added to the square note, increasing its length by half.[20] One of the characteristic features of Marbeck's setting is its frequent use of the dotted semibreve and minim to set particular rhythms of English speech. The book contains musical settings of all parts of the 1549 Prayer Book which may be sung, or directions for their singing, except the Litany, a setting for which was, of course, already in circulation. The music for Matins and Evensong have their roots in plainsong originals, with which Marbeck was thoroughly familiar from daily usage. Some resemble their models more closely than others, though in all cases they are adapted to the natural rhythm and cadence of the English language. At Matins, the opening of *Venite exultemus* is given, with the instruction that the rest of the psalms are to be sung in a similar fashion. In all cases, the principle of one note to each syllable of text is strictly adhered to. The order for the Communion includes music for all those sections where singing by priest or clerks is specified in the Prayer Book. In addition, the whole of the action from 'The Lorde be with you . . . Lift up your heartes' to 'The peace of the

[18] Ibid., pp. 1015–20.

[19] John Marbeck, *The Booke of Common Praier Noted* (London, 1550), Sig. A.ii.

[20] Ibid., 'In this booke . . . are vsed only these iiij sortes of notes, . . . The first note is a strene note and is a breue. The second a square note, and is a semy breue. The iii. a pycke and is a mynymme. And when there is a prycke by the square note, that prycke is halfe as muche as the note that goeth before it. The iiii is a close, and is only vsed at the end of a verse.'

Lorde be alwaye with you' is set to music, taking in the Preface, the Prayer for the Church, Institution Narrative, and Prayer of Oblation. Where the clerks are not singing, the priest's part is set to a monotone. Marbeck's text supplies an 'Amen' to the end of the Prayer of Intercession for the whole state of Christ's Church, separating it from the Institution Narrative and Prayer of Oblation. The Prayer Book text, by omitting the 'Amen' at that point, provides a single, continuous prayer from the dialogue before the Preface to the end of the Prayer of Oblation. This creates a single consecration prayer, in which is included the intercessory Prayer of the Church. Intercession had an important place in the medieval Canon of the Mass, as it was the opinion of many theologians that the heart of the sacrifice of the Mass was in the words of consecration, and that intercession associated with that sacrifice more closely would be more efficacious. By inserting his 'Amen', Marbeck takes intercession out of the Prayer of Consecration and breaks down further any vestigial notions of sacrifice implicit in the rite, which were wholly excised in the 1552 revision. The General Confession, Comfortable Words and other preparation for Communion are not set; presumably they are to be spoken. The clerks sing the *Agnus Dei* at Communion time, followed by the post-Communion Sentences. The final Prayer of Thanksgiving is also intoned, though whether the Blessing is similarly sung is not clear.

The parts of the Burial Service which may be sung by the clerks are set by Marbeck, as is the priest's commendation at the graveside. The psalms are set to the same tone as for the Introit at Holy Communion and the daily offices. The celebration of Holy Communion when there is a burial is provided with a setting of the proper Introit and Collect, and with special settings of the *Kyrie*, *Sanctus*, and *Agnus Dei*.

The special quality of Marbeck's work may best be seen in those parts of *The Booke of Common Praier Noted* which are most free from plainsong models. In his settings of *Gloria* and Creed, the natural rhythms of the English language are carried in a melody which is imbued with the spirit of plainsong. When Luther compiled his *Deudsche Messe*, he was free to use whatever texts he chose for congregational singing. Marbeck was constrained within set translations of Latin originals in which ease of singing was not the first consideration. He was also required to meet a particular need, that of the clerks, taking their place in public worship.Though Marbeck had never experienced Lutheran worship at first hand, he was clearly aware of the principles behind Cranmer's Litany. Certain similarities may be noticed between Marbeck's book and Luther's work; each syllable of text is set to a single note; the melodic lines are sung in unison and without accompaniment; the rhythm of the music reflects the natural rhythms of the words, though it is precisely notated. Where Luther sets a text to plainsong tones, his settings are on the whole more elaborate, though it is here that some of the closest resemblances are to be found. The main difference is that Luther's style went on to become the foundation of a whole style of liturgical music, and the source for much which is great in Protestant Church music. Marbeck's work was very quickly made obsolete and lay virtually unused for centuries. When rediscovered, its measured, rhythmical nature was largely set aside or ignored in favour of its surface resemblance to plainsong, which was in reality only one of its sources. If justice is to be done to Marbeck's achievement, it is important that the use to which it is put today truly reflects the spirit of fidelity to the language in which it was written, and care is taken to treat it as much more than an experiment in the adaptation of plainsong to the vernacular. Rather, it should be seen as a unique hybrid between traditional melodic style and rhythmic innovation which has remained unequalled for four centuries.

King's College London

THE *BISHOPS' BIBLE* ILLUSTRATIONS

by MARGARET ASTON

THE illustrations in the *Bishops' Bible* have received more attention from art historians than from historians, though their story—which turns out to have been remarkably complicated—calls for the skills of both disciplines. The tale, which I can only outline here, throws interesting light on the state of the arts and art censorship in the early Elizabethan Church, at a time when there was much interrelationship between England and continental artists and craftsmen.[1]

First, a brief reminder of the history of this Bible. The *Bishops' Bible* was the brain-child of Archbishop Parker. The exact date of its conception cannot be determined. The idea had probably been in the air for some time, for Richard Cox, Bishop of Ely, recommended a scriptural revision to William Cecil in January 1562. The work was put in hand before the end of 1565, when some of the fifteen individuals (all but three members of the hierarchy) to whom the Archbishop parcelled out set books of the Great Bible for textual revision went to work on their copy. Bishop Parkhurst of Norwich had received his allocated portion of the Apocrypha before Christmas 1565, and Edwin Sandys must have worked fast on the Books of Kings and Chronicles, as he was able to return his corrections and marginal notes to Parker by 6 February 1566. He sent an accompanying letter advising the Archbishop to make sure the text was thoroughly corrected—something that would need time—so that 'the adversaries can have no occasion to quarrel with it.'[2]

Time was certainly taken. In November 1566 the process of correction was still going on. Archbishop Parker wrote to Cecil suggesting he might

1 Only after the delivery of this paper did I learn, thanks to the kind help of Elizabeth M. Ingram, that the main facts of this story had already been published by Colin Clair, 'The Bishops' Bible 1568', *Gutenberg Jahrbuch* (1962), pp. 287–90. However, as my (inadvertently independent) findings extend as well as confirm Clair's, I hope this article may give more notice to what now seems like a joint discovery. My thanks also go to Alan Jesson for all the work involved in giving me access to heavy folios in the British and Foreign Bible Society's collection; and to David Freedberg and Sergiusz Michalski, whose help on other topics contributed unwittingly to this piece.

2 *Correspondence of Matthew Parker*, ed. J. Bruce and T. T. Perowne, *PS* (1853), pp. 248, 256–7, 265 (cited at p. 257); *CalSPD, 1547–1580*, pp. 192, 239; V. J. K. Brook, *A Life of Archbishop Parker* (Oxford, 1962), pp. 179–80, 246–9; A. W. Pollard, ed., *Records of the English Bible* (Oxford, 1911), pp. 28–33, 287; B. F. Westcott, *A General View of the History of the English Bible* (London, 1905), pp. 95–102, 230–44.

care to look over an Epistle, so that he could be regarded as a 'builder' a well as patron of the work. On 22 September 1568, when Parker was ailing, the substance of the book was complete, though 'some ornaments were still lacking. But two weeks later, on 5 October 1568, a copy of the book was ready for presentation to Queen Elizabeth (specially bound perhaps by the Archbishop's own binder). Parker was still unwell, and had to ask Cecil to do the honours for him and to put in the necessary words for the printing licence and for Richard Jugge's rights over the edition.[3]

The book that emerged was a grandiose production, outstanding among Tudor Bibles. 'In typography and illustration', wrote A. S. Herbert 'this is perhaps the most sumptuous in the long series of folio English Bibles.' Its folio format was integral to the design. The *Bishops' Bible* was planned to succeed the Henrician Great Bible, many copies of which (the preface explained) had become 'so wasted', and Cranmer's preface to that work continued to be reprinted in the new version. This was essentially a church Bible, intended for the lectern and public use. Though there were half a dozen quarto editions of the new Bible between 1569 and 1584, it was the ten folio editions that were important and which concern us here.

Parker gave his own account of the new Bible in his 'Matthaeus'—the final section of his *De Antiquitate Britannicae Ecclesiae* on his tenure of the see of Canterbury. The Archbishop makes clear that the new, large-type edition was prepared in order to take the place of existing church Bibles since these were now worn out. Parker indicates his satisfaction with the emended text, which finally appeared in such 'elegant type', after this considerable collaborative effort. He says nothing about the illustrations though these must have added to the 'great and long . . . pains and study that Strype supposed the Bible to have occasioned.[5]

[3] *Parker Correspondence*, pp. 290, 334–7; cf. pp. 425–6, 468, for Parker's bookbinders. Parker sent Cecil a list of the revisers and the books they had worked on (their initials were printed in the text—'to make them more diligent'); Pollard, *Records*, pp. 30–1, 293. The Archbishop's prefaces to the Bible and the New Testament asked readers not to be offended by the 'diversitie of translatours'. On the copy of the 1568 Bible (*STC* 2099) in the Folger Shakespeare Library, Washington, which appears to have been a specially bound presentation copy for Elizabeth, see J. N. King, *Tudor Royal Iconography* (Princeton, 1989), pp. 107–8.

[4] A. S. Herbert, *Historical Catalogue of Printed Editions of the English Bible* (London, 1968), p. 70 *The holie Bible* (1568), sig.* 2v. See *STC*, I, pp. 87–9, nos 2099 *et seq*., for the various editions. The last folio appeared in 1595.

[5] Matthew Parker, *De Antiquitate Britannicae Ecclesiae* (London, 1572[–1574]), BL G 11757, from the unnumbered pages at the end of the 'Matthaeus'; 'Cumque sacrorum bibliorum Anglicana aeditio, quae in singulis ecclesiis ex statuto collocanda fuit, iam prope deleta defecisset . . .' The 'Matthaeus' (on which see Brook, *Parker*, p. 2, n. 2) was only included in some copies of the *De Antiquitate*; it was not in BL C 24 b 8, printed with illuminated vellum title-pages for presentation to Elizabeth. Strype, *Parker*, 2, p. 212, 3, p. 306.

What was the relationship between the *Bishops' Bible* and the Geneva Bible? Though the latter already existed in folio (1562), it was as the compact, well-produced quarto 'with moste profitable annotations' that the Genevan version gained immediate popularity after its first appearance in 1560.[6] But it was not printed in England. In March 1566 John Bodley (who had had a hand in the Geneva printing, and already held a seven-year licence for an English edition) applied for a twelve-year privilege for issuing the Geneva Bible. Parker and Grindal were not against this, and sent their approval to Cecil. Ostensibly, they did not see a conflict with the Bible they were working on.

> For thoughe one other speciall bible for the churches be meant by us to be set forthe as convenient tyme and leysor hereafter will permytte: yet shall it nothing hindre but rather do moche good to have diversitie of translacions and readinges.[7]

Despite these words, it seems that the privilege was not granted. The second edition of the Geneva Bible was again printed in Geneva, in 1569 or 1570. Not until after Parker's death was a folio edition of this version printed in England. Then, between 1576 and the end of Elizabeth's reign, the Geneva Bible romped home in the numerous editions printed by Christopher Barker, as England's household Bible. Parker had effectively suppressed the Geneva Bible. Tolerance towards a variety of readings was prejudiced by the Genevan annotations, and the Archbishop expressly laid down as one of the five rules for his editors that they should 'make no bitter notis uppon any text.'[8]

The lavish and high quality of its illustration is one of the features of Parker's version that distinguished it sharply from that of Geneva. Contemporaries give us virtually no help in assessing these pictures. John Strype was the first to describe the composition of the *Bishops' Bible*, but his report of the 'many ornamental cuts and instructive pictures, dispersed up and down the book', is misleading, since it forms part of an account of the 1572 edition which (though he failed to say so) was critically different from that of 1568. Notice, however, his phrase

[6] *STC*, 1, p. 87, no. 2093.

[7] Pollard, *Records*, pp. 284–6 (cited at p. 286).

[8] Pollard, *Records*, p. 297, cf. p. 295 for Parker on Bibles with 'diverse preiudicall notis'; P. Collinson, *The Elizabethan Puritan Movement* (London, 1967), pp. 164–5. The treatment of the Geneva version was an 'olde ulcer' in the 1572 Second Admonition to Parliament; W. H. Frere and C. E. Douglas, eds, *Puritan Manifestoes* (London, 1907), pp. 83–4.

'instructive pictures', suggesting the ability of illustrations to teach, alongside the text.[9]

Leaving aside an assortment of maps and tables, the illustrations to the 1568 *Bishops' Bible* are of two distinct kinds. First, there are the engraved title-pages, clearly custom-made for the new book. Secondly, there is the series of woodcuts, completely different in style, illustrating the text and scattered through the biblical books. The former have already been described by Arthur Hind and others, and need not long detain us.

Three rather finely-executed copper engravings appear at the start of three out of the five parts into which the Bible is divided. All are portraits. While it is no surprise to find Queen Elizabeth, with supporting figures of Faith and Charity, embellishing the general title-page, it was a novel feature to place two leading courtiers in positions of prominence in the body of the text. Both flank Old Testament books. Robert Dudley, the Earl of Leicester, stands martially equipped on the title-page to Part II, flatteringly juxtaposed to Joshua, the heroic conqueror of Canaan. Part III, which opens with the Book of Psalms, shows the standing figure of William Cecil, with one hand on a very large capital 'B', for the start of Psalm 1 ('Blessed is the man that walketh not in the counsell of the ungodly') while his other hand holds 'the Book of Psalms ... as being his great delight'—as Strype put it.[10]

Hind, following Sidney Colvin, assigned all three engravings to Franciscus Hogenberg. The grounds for this are purely stylistic, since there is no authenticating evidence, and we have to depend on comparison with other known work, in particular the 1569 engraving of the new Royal Exchange in London. Whatever weight we give to this ascription (and stylistically it seems convincing enough), we should notice, first, that there were no English craftsmen of sufficient calibre to be attributed with engraved work of this quality, and, second, that among the continental workmen known to have been in Parker's employment not long after this was Remigius Hogenberg, brother of Franciscus.[11]

This extraordinary combination of secular tribute and scriptural

[9] Strype, *Parker*, 2, pp. 212–24 (cited at p. 220); cf. 1, pp. 414–17.

[10] Strype, *Parker*, 2, p. 214. On these engravings see S. Colvin, *Early Engraving and Engravers in England (1545–1695)* (London, 1905), pp. 19–26; A. M. Hind, *Engraving in England in the Sixteenth and Seventeenth Centuries*, 3 vols (Cambridge, 1952–64), 1, pp. 64–5, 68–9, plates 33, 36. King, *Iconography*, pp. 105–7, sees Elizabeth as personifying Hope.

[11] Hind, *Engraving*, 1, p. 65: 'In 1563 there were no English engravers to approach; ... so the Archbishop had of necessity to appeal to the foreigner with his command of craft ...'; on Remigius Hogenberg, pp. 12–13, 64–6, 72–8.

ornament did not last. Already in the next folio edition of 1572 William Cecil was severed from the Psalmist's 'Blessed', and relegated to the free-standing dignity of the Part III title-page. His elevation as Lord Burghley in February 1571 gave his letter 'B' an additional personal attribute that might well have grated on tender consciences. The plate was reworked to remove this initial from his grasp, though traces of it are still just detectable. Then, all three portraits disappear. In the editions of the *Bishops' Bible* from 1574 onwards, Elizabeth no longer appears, any more than Leicester or Burghley. This change can be no accident, given the conviction of some contemporary purists that portraiture was an inherently idolatrous art. If, as Sidney Colvin suggested, objectors caused Burghley's removal from his Davidian position in the Psalms, it is altogether probable that similar pressures finally excised all the portraits, including the Queen's.[12]

Less notice has been given to the long series of woodcuts, totalling 124, that ornament Parker's 1568 text, though these are striking. Each scene measures about three by four and a half inches, and the permutating sequence of eight ornamental frames, in which they are placed, much enhances the effect of these illustrations.[13] These prints, quite different in style from the portrait pages, made a great contribution to the appearance of the first *Bishops' Bible*. What are we to make, then, of the fact that in the second, the 1572 edition, they have gone? This edition, which had a revised text of the New Testament and a new layout, carried a new set of illustrations, larger, fewer in number, and by a different hand. Why did Archbishop Parker find it necessary or desirable effectively to start again? Did the redesigning of the pictures, as well as the changes of text, account for the unusually long gap between the first and second editions—unlike the cluster that appeared between 1572 and 1578?

In the first place we might wonder whether the change of illustrations resulted from puritanical censorship. We know the view of some of the censors, for the Second Admonition to Parliament in 1572 included an acid comment on pictures in the 1568 *Bishops' Bible*.

[12] Colvin, *Early Engraving*, p. 21, n. 1. Colvin and Hind (following Strype) both assume that the 'B' in Psalms complimented Burghley in 1568, though (as Clair pointed out) this was well before he acquired the title. On fears of portraiture see M. G. Winkler, 'A Divided Heart: Idolatry and the portraiture of Hans Asper', *Sixteenth Century Journal*, 18 (1987), pp. 213–30. Another problem, with similar outcome, was the secularity of Jugge's initial letters, with scenes from Ovid's *Metamorphoses*; Herbert, *Historical Catalogue*, pp. 71, 76; Clair, 'Bishops' Bible', pp. 288, 289.

[13] Herbert, *Historical Catalogue*, p. 71, for the count of blocks; my count of frames (on occasion used upside down). This total does not include maps, on which see C. Delano Smith, 'Maps as Art *and* Science: Maps in Sixteenth Century Bibles', *Imago Mundi*, 42 (1990), pp. 65–83.

> . . . in their last great Bible in the first edition of it, such a sight of blasphemous pictures of God the father, as what they deserve for it, I will referre them to none other judge then their owne note uppon the 15 verse of the fourth of Deuteronomie . . .[14]

namely, when the Lord spoke from the fire in Mount Horeb, 'ye sawe no maner of image'; to which Bishop Alley's note read: 'Meaning that plagues hang over them that wold make any image to represent God by.'[15] Was Archbishop Parker forced to recognize this plaguey judgement? He was certainly conscious of the criticism, as we shall see in a moment. But that it was the main reason for commissioning new pictures for the second edition is doubtful.

The woodcuts illustrating Parker's first edition were borrowed wholesale from a foreign source. Not much detective work is needed to identify it, since many of the cuts bear the initials 'VS', in the well-known monogram of a very well-known artist and illustrator, Virgil Solis (1514–62).[16] Among the works that brought Solis fame was a long series of Bible illustrations which first appeared in 1560 (plate 1). The *Biblische Figuren des Alten und Newen Testaments, gantz künstlich gerissen*, by the 'world-renowned' Virgil Solis of Nuremberg, was printed in Frankfurt by a consortium—David Zöpfel, Johann Rasch, and Sigmund Feyerabend, the last of whom was himself a painter and engraver, as well as publisher, who outlived Solis and died in Frankfurt in 1590. At the same time the publishers brought out an edition of Luther's German Bible illustrated with these woodcuts. Both books were highly successful, and the Virgil Solis picture-series, which eschewed Lutheran polemics for textual fidelity, was so influential that it has been described as starting a new epoch in Bible illustration.[17]

The *Biblische Figuren* was an octavo book, which carried on the tradition of Holbein's *Icones*. It consists of a total of 147 woodcuts, 102 to the

[14] *Puritan Manifestoes*, p. 118.

[15] *The holie Bible* (1568), pt 1, fol. 110r, marginal note (h).

[16] After making the observations that follow I found that T. H. Darlow and H. F. Moule, *Historical Catalogue of the Printed Editions of Holy Scripture*, 2 vols (London, 1903–11), 2, p. 497, had noted the resemblance between the illustrations in the *Catholische Bibell* (Cologne, 1575) and those in the 1568 *Bishops' Bible*.

[17] Philipp Schmidt, *Die Illustration der Lutherbibel 1522–1700* (Basle, 1962), pp. 236–44 (p. 236 on the significance of a picture-series by one master illustrating the whole Bible text); H. Reinitzer, *Biblia deutsch: Luthers Bibelübersetzung und ihre Tradition* (Wolfenbüttel, 1983), pp. 240–3, no. 147; E. von Ubisch, *Virgil Solis und seine Biblischen Illustrationen* (Leipzig, 1889); I. O'Dell-Franke, *Kupferstiche und Radierungen aus der Werkstatt des Virgil Solis* (Wiesbaden, 1977), pp. 3–4, 14–17; *Allgemeines Lexikon der Bildenden Künstler*, 31, pp. 248–53.

Plate 1(a) Creation of Eve in Johann Dietenberger's German Bible, *Biblia* (Mainz, 1534).
Plates 1(b) and (c) Woodcuts from Virgil Solis, *Biblische Figuren* (Frankfurt, 1560).

Old Testament and 45 to the New, each accompanied by explanatory lines paraphrasing the text that is pictured, given in four lines apiece of Latin and German. We can see the book as an updated print-version of a *Biblia pauperum*—a Scripture book for the unlettered. The preface invites us to do precisely this. Referring to the woodcuts accompanying the Bible edition, it announces that the picture-series was to serve those Christians who were unable to read the text, and were here being offered the Bible figures as 'ein Leyen Bibell'—a layman's book.[18] It is a measure of how close Lutherans remained to Catholics in their tolerance of images that a few years later, in another publication of this kind, Feyerabend cited the famous letter of Pope Gregory the Great that lay behind the entire

[18] *Biblische Figuren* (Frankfurt-on-Main, 1560), sig. A2v: 'Zuletst auch umb der einfeltigen Christen willen, so die schrifft nicht lesen können, und dannoch lust unnd lieb darzu haben, denen werden diese Figuren ohn zweifel auch als ein Leyen Bibell sein.' Of course, the form is quite different from the *Biblia pauperum* proper, the typology of which, as Avril Henry shows in her edition, *Biblia pauperum* (Aldershot, 1987), pp. 17–18, was more suited to meditation than teaching the unlearned.

medieval theory of teaching through images, and which was anathema to Reformed churchmen. This defence of the illiterate learning through pictures as the *litteratura laicorum* (echoed in Strype's phrase, 'instructive pictures'), appears in the preface to *Neuwe Biblische Figuren dess Alten und Neuwen Testaments*, a new picture-Bible published by Feyerabend and others in 1564, with woodcuts by Johann Bocksberger and Jost Amman.[19]

Virgil Solis's Bible woodcuts were reissued by Feyerabend in several editions after the first of 1560. The illustrated Bible was reprinted four times in the 1560s, and the *Biblische Figuren* in both 1562 and 1565. The 1562 book had a larger format, and besides now placing elaborate ornamental frames round each scriptural scene, the total series of cuts was greatly increased by many additions to the New Testament series. It is interesting to notice, in the context of this continuing lay-books tradition, that—rather like a Gospel harmony—these Gospel illustrations follow a narrative sequence, not the order of the scriptural texts. The publishing history of Sigmund Feyerabend's editions of Virgil Solis shows that the woodcuts had certainly found a successful market. Why was it, then, that his last edition of these illustrations was in 1566, and that from the later 1560s onwards he was using the Bockberger series?[20]

The answer to this question seems to be that Feyerabend lost control of the wood-blocks of the popular Virgil Solis designs. In 1563 one of his partners, David Zöpfel, sold half the series to a Strasbourg printer, but owing to Zöpfel's death, it was a printer of Jena and Frankfurt who finally bought the blocks. Feyerabend had to have some new blocks made for his 1565 edition of the *Biblische Figuren*, and it seems that during the last twenty-four years of his life he never again printed the original Solis woodcuts.[21]

The scene now shifts to Cologne. It was natural, given the success of Virgil Solis's designs, and the technical skills of continental wood-engravers, that the Bible figures should be copied. They were. In 1564 the Cologne publishing house of Quentell brought out a new folio edition of

[19] Reinitzer, *Biblia deutsch*, pp. 244–6, no. 149; Schmidt, *Lutherbibel*, pp. 245–62. On the Gregorian theory in England see A. E. Nichols, 'Books-for-Laymen: the demise of a commonplace', *Church History*, 56 (1987), pp. 457–73.

[20] Reinitzer, *Biblia Deutsch*, p. 240; Ubisch, *Virgil Solis*, pp. 54–70; Schmidt, *Lutherbibel*, p. 485, conveniently lists editions. There were two more Feyerabend Bible editions with the Solis cuts after Sigmund's death (1590), in 1595 and 1606. See *Allgemeines Lexikon der Bildenden Künstler*, 11, pp. 523–4, on Feyerabend and the possibility (considered also by Reinitzer, p. 244, and O'Dell-Franke, pp. 21–2) that the monogram 'SF' which appears in the 1564 *Neuwe Biblische Figuren* is his.

[21] Ubisch, *Virgil Solis*, pp. 68–71.

the influential German Bible translation of Johan Dietenberger (1475–1534). This very long-lasting version was the first Catholic translation of the whole Bible to appear in the Reformation, and the earliest of its many editions, which came out in 1534, made no disguise of its anti-heretical stance. It took the Lutherans to task—by name—in its annotations, including, for instance, those on Exodus 20 and Deuteronomy 4, where Jews, heretics, and 'bildsturmer' were berated for believing that Scripture forbade all imagery in churches.[22]

The 1564 edition of the *Catholische Bibel* was profusely illustrated (as the title-page claimed) 'with figures of handsome appearance'—mostly Virgil Solis's designs. However, these were copies, very close and exact copies, of the original blocks. In addition to the 'VS' monogram of the originals, they carry some new monograms, including an unidentified 'SHF'. Apart from these changes of signature, there were one or two iconographic alterations, including the tactful insertion of a flower as a prelapsarian fig-leaf for Adam, and a different position for the apple as it passed, under the entwined serpent, between Eve and Adam.[23]

Still further to complicate matters, another Cologne publisher had access to copies of Virgil Solis's *Biblische Figuren*. In 1565 the heirs of Arnold Birckmann brought out an illustrated folio edition of the Dutch Bible version that had been made by Nicolas van Winghe and first published at Louvain in 1548. Another edition followed in 1566, also with these illustrations, which were called in the title 'beautiful new figures'.[24] Here, too, we see the Lutheran picture-series being issued in a Catholic Bible.

It is now time to return to Archbishop Parker's 1568 Bible. The woodcuts illustrating the first *Bishops' Bible* were none other than the copies of the Solis cuts that had been used by the Cologne publishers. They bear the same monograms, and appear (with minor variations) in the same

[22] *Catholische Bibel* (Cologne, heirs of J. Quentell and G. Calenius, 1564), fols 45v, 101r–v; these annotations were in the 1534 Dietenberger *Biblia* (Mainz), fols 36v–37r, 83v. On this Bible version see Reinitzer, *Biblia Deutsch*, pp. 203–5, no. 117; *CHB*, 3, pp. 108–9, 346.

[23] Ubisch, *Virgil Solis*, pp. 78–85 (pp. 79–81, lists the monograms in the original and the copied series). On the 'SHF' monogram see G. K. Nagler, *Die Monogrammisten . . . aller Schulen*, 5 vols (Munich, 1858–79), 5, p. 2, no. 9.

[24] *Den Bibel Inhoudende het oude ende nieuwe Testament . . . Met schoonen nieuwen figueren verschiert* (Cologne, 1566). There were many editions of this version following (like Birckmann's) the revised 1553 Louvain text; Darlow and Moule, *Historical Catalogue*, 2, p. 303; *CHB*, 3, p. 123. The Birckmann firm of Cologne had business links in Antwerp and London; L. Febvre and H.-J. Martin, *The Coming of the Book* (London, 1976), p. 189; E. J. Worman, *Alien Members of the Book-Trade during the Tudor Period* (London, 1906), pp. 3–5.

sequence in the text. They also have the same ornamental frames—though the permutations vary—that had been used with the Solis cuts since the 1562 *Biblische Figuren*. Some of these blocks had already reached Parker's printer when the production of the new Bible was still in its early stages. In 1566 Richard Jugge brought out his revised edition of Tyndale's New Testament, and among its numerous illustrations were twenty-one of the Solis sequence (fifteen in Revelation), which appear here without their frames.[25]

It can be proved that the same wood-blocks were used in sequence in the 1566 Birckmann Dutch Bible, in the 1568 English *Bishops' Bible*, and then, having returned to the Continent, in an Antwerp Vulgate of 1570–1, and a German Bible of 1571. The blocks were back in Cologne once more, serving Quentell's 1571 edition of the *Catholische Bibell*, having in the meantime produced illustrations for the *Biblia ad vetustissima exemplaria* that was printed in Antwerp shortly before that for the heirs of Jan Steels. In 1570 the Antwerp printer (Tavernier) had to make do, for the first sixty folios of his text, with a single plain surround as substitute for the set of ornate frames, which evidently came back from London (as they apparently went there) in a separate consignment from the blocks with the biblical scenes. But the Solis frames turned up in time to be used in Steels's Vulgate from the Book of Joshua onwards. Tiny tell-tale details, such as a damaged corner, or an intermittent line along an edge of the cut, show the identity of the picture blocks used in all these different Bibles, and sometimes a new chip hints at the hazards of this English journey.[26]

Most of the woodcut series made this cross-Channel foray unchanged, and no doubt the access to a ready-made sequence of plates added considerably to the ease of production for Archbishop Parker in 1568. However, some of the blocks were carefully altered to suit the confessional demands of the Elizabethan Church, and these changes offer conclusive evidence of this pictorial journey. They also throw light on the remark in the 1572 Admonition that I have already quoted.[27]

25 *The Newe Testament of our Saviour Iesus Christe* (London, 1566?); *STC* 2873; Herbert, *Historical Catalogue*, p. 68. The book includes a miscellany of illustrations.

26 It was Colin Clair ('Bishops Bible') who noticed the Antwerp Vulgate's place in this jigsaw. The *Biblia ad vetustissima exemplaria nunc recens castigata* (Antwerp, widow and heirs of Jan Steels) has dates 1570 on title-page and 1571 for colophon. The cut used, fols 39r and 46r, for Leviticus 24 and Numbers 15 shows a chip off one corner that was intact in 1568.

27 What follows is based on a comparison of the British and Foreign Bible Society's copies (in the University Library, Cambridge) of the four Bibles. For an example of a damaged block (inside the frame) with corner and lower edge chipped, see one in Rev. 6; *The holie Bible* (1568), pt V, fol. 146.

In several conspicuous places, woodcuts from the Virgil Solis series were doctored for the *Bishops' Bible*. Prints that included large depictions of God were reworked. The offending section was cut out, a plug of new wood deftly inserted into the block, and a wood-engraver filled the sometimes awkward space with the tetragrammaton, and whatever else might be needed to make good the picture. The first two illustrations in Genesis, chapters 1 and 2, were both altered in this way, removing the dominating figure of the Creator both from the Creation, and from the scene in which Eve is drawn from Adam's side. In the first example, though the Hebrew letters occupy a disproportionately large amount of the picture space, there is very little, apart from a remaining outline of the Creator's mantle, to reveal the change. The second seems to give the game away at once. A startled Eve (with what looks like a double face and disjointed arm) gazes surprisingly towards a hare and a small tree, placed on a hill that slides away into folds of drapery (plate 2).[28] Whoever cut this replacement definitely lacked the skills of Virgil Solis and 'SHF'.

If any doubts remain that these were censored images, remade for the benefit of the English Bible, we find further evidence in the Vulgate and *Catholische Bibell* of 1570–1. For here the blocks have been changed back. The creating God is once more *in situ*, put back where he belonged by a certainly expert hand, guided by an eye which must have had a copy of the original woodcut to follow as precisely as possible. In both the Genesis woodcuts there are some very small differences that show how the craftsman, despite his evident expertise, has varied from the original: the shape of the Creator's left hand and face, or the lack of a star, minute details which are only to be detected by close comparison of the two versions. Also—more of a giveaway—there are the just visible hair-line seams marking the join in the block (plate 3).[29]

The removal of the figure of God, envisaged as cloaked and bearded ancient, was in line with accepted Reformed thinking, that had long been in the making in England. The hazards of allowing bodily representations 'of the Father of heaven' into churches had already been pointed out in the 1530s, and Cranmer's *Catechism* attacked portrayal of the first person of the Trinity as 'an olde man with a long hore berd'. Such inhibitions were canonized in Calvin's *Institution*. 'We must be warned', he wrote, 'that the

[28] *Den Bibel* (1566), fols 1r, 2r; *The holie Bible* (1568), fols 1r, 2r. For illustrations of the Creation cuts see Clair, 'Bishops' Bible', p. 289.

[29] *Biblia* (1570), fol. 1r–v, *Catholische Bibell* (1571), fols 1r, 2r. For the technique of altering a block by 'plugging' (with examples) see D. P. Bliss, *A History of Wood-Engraving* (London, 1928), p. 4; Henry, ed., *Biblia pauperum*, p. 22.

Plate 2 (a) Creation of Eve: *Den Bibel*, heirs of A. Birkmann (Cologne, 1565). Note Adam's fig-leaf flower.

Plate 2 (b) Creation of Eve, altered for the first edition of the *Bishops' Bible*, *The holie Bible*, Richard Jugge (London, 1568).

Plate 3 (a) Creation of Eve with God replaced (note line of seam in block above Adam, and missing star behind God's head): *Biblia*, heirs of J. Steels (Antwerp, 1570–1).

Plate 3 (b) Creation of Eve. The altered block reunited with ornamental frame as used in Cologne editions of Dietenberger's Bible in the 1570s: *Catholische Bibell*, heirs of J. Quentell (Cologne, 1575).

invisible Father is to be sought solely in the image of Christ.' And again: 'We believe it wrong that God should be represented by a visible appearance, because he himself has forbidden it and it cannot be done without some defacing of his glory.'[30]

The framers of the 1572 Admonition certainly had much dogmatic support for the view that pictures of God the Father were reprehensible. Plenty of Trinitarian imagery had already been defaced or removed in England by this date. In 1561 one of Parker's revisers, Bishop Parkhurst of Norwich (whose stint was Ecclesiasticus to Maccabees), had issued orders for church walls, copes, banners, and books to be cleared of depictions 'of the Blessed Trinity or of the Father (of whom there can be no image made)'. The same year, one of the 11 Articles authorized by the bishops at Lambeth provided that the clergy should subscribe and teach twice-yearly that they 'utterly disallow . . . all kind of expressing God invisible in the form of an old man'.[31]

However, there were limits to Archbishop Parker's pedantic zeal—or perhaps it was simply a question of time running out. At all events, the process of 'purifying' the Bible pictures he had so conveniently come by was by no means thorough, or complete. A number of illustrations remain in the 1568 Bible that still contained small depictions of God in the objectionable form of the regal old man conveying his will to the earth beneath from an aura of clouds—in the iconographic convention that Virgil Solis perpetuated. Among the examples of this not too many pages into Genesis is the scene illustrating Jacob's dream, with the Lord at the top of the ladder on which angels are ascending and descending.[32]

Of course, the depiction of visionary or dream appearances could be seen as belonging to a different category. One of the key texts for this problematical imaging was the first chapter of Ezekiel, containing the vision of the four cherubim, with its reference to 'the facion of a throne' above the firmament, and on the throne 'the similitude of a man'. Even

[30] *Formularies of Faith*, ed. C. Lloyd (Oxford, 1825), p. 135; *A Catechism set forth by Thomas Cranmer*, ed. D. G. Selwyn (Appleford, 1978), pp. 19–21, cited at p. 21; John Calvin, *Institutes of the Christian Religion*, ed. J. T. McNeill, tr. F. L. Battles = *Library of Christian Classics*, 20–1 (Philadelphia, 1961), pp. 112, 544; I.xi.12; III.ii.1. See also D. Freedberg, *The Power of Images* (Chicago, 1989), p. 427.

[31] *Visitation Articles and Injunctions of the Period of the Reformation*, ed. W. H. Frere and W. M. Kennedy, 3 vols = *Alcuin Club Collns*, 14–16 (London, 1910), 3, pp. 90 (no. 32), 104 (no. 36); C. Hardwick, *A History of the Articles of Religion* (London, 1876), p. 359; W. P. Haugaard, *Elizabeth and the English Reformation* (Cambridge, 1968), pp. 239–42.

[32] *The holie Bible* (1568), fol. 18v. There are other similar depictions in Gen. 4, 7, 9, Exod. 16, Josh. 6, and elsewhere. See also Clair, 'Bishops' Bible', p. 288.

the Geneva Bible allowed an illustration of the Vision of Ezekiel, justified in the preface on the grounds that

> whereas certeyne places in the bookes of Moses, of the Kings and Ezekiel semed so darke that by no description thei colde be made easie to the simple reader, we have so set them forthe with figures and notes for the ful declaration thereof, that thei which can not by iudgement, being holpen by the annotations noted by the lettres a b c. &c. atteyn thereunto, yet by the perspective, and as it were by the eye may sufficiently knowe the true meaning of all suche places.[33]

The understanding of the eye here gained a loophole, but the Ezekiel cut noticeably makes much more of the cherubim than the diminutive throne (marked 'T'), 'which was set upon the firmament', 'where ('V') sate like the appearance of a man [*sic*]' (plate 4).

The reforming taboo on any representation of God came to be accepted as applying firmly to Bible illustrations, as much as to other imagery, witness William Perkins in 1601.'Hence it follows, that when the history of the bible is painted or pictured, as in some of our bibles it is, there are no images of God described, but only such visible appearances as (sometime) were signes of the presence of God, are expressed.' The tetragrammaton came to take the place of anthopomorphic ancients in the clouds.[34]

Virgil Solis, like his medieval predecessors, found no difficulty about representing the godhead in Ezekiel's vision on exactly the same lines as (for instance) the Lord sending a plague of boils on the land of Egypt. The likeness of the man is here the familiar regal figure with orb and sceptre, and his throne the conventionalized furling cloud-edge, signifying the heavenly kingdom. This would not do for the English bishops. Here too they saw to it that the picture of God was replaced by the tetragrammaton. And here again the image was changed back to its original form in the Catholic Bibles of Antwerp and Cologne. Once more there are tiny telltale variations: in the jovial expression on God's face; the lines of the halo round his head; and the addition of a cross on the top of his mitre (plate 5).[35]

[33] *The Bible and Holy Scriptures* (Geneva, 1560), 'To the Reader', and fol. 333v; Pollard, *Records*, pp. 282–3. Ezek. 1. 26; 'and upon the similitude of the throne was by appearance, as the similitude of a man above upon it.'

[34] W. Perkins, *A Warning against the Idolatrie of the Last Times* (Cambridge, 1601), p. 21, cf. pp. 107, 162.

[35] *Den Bibel* (1566), pt 2, fol. 64r; *The holie Bible* (1568), pt 3, fol. 139r; *Biblia* (1570), fol. 271v; *Catholische Bibell* (1571), fol. 441v.

Ezekiél.

vnto him that the citie ſhulde moſte certeinly be deſtroied, & the people grieuouſly tormẽted by Gods plagues, inſomuche that thei that remained ſhulde be broght into cruel bondage. And leſt the godlie ſhulde diſpaire in theſe great troubles, he aſſureth them that God wil deliuer his Church at his time appointed, and alſo deſtroie their enemies which ether afflicted them or reioyced in their miſeries. The effect of the one and the other ſhulde chiefly be performed vnder Chriſt, of whome in this boke are many notable promiſes, and in whome the glorie of the new Temple ſhulde perfectly be reſtored. He prophecied theſe things in Caldea at the ſame time that Ieremiáh prophecied in Iudáh, and there began in the fiſt yere of Ioiachins captiuitie.

a After that ÿ boke of the Law was founde, which was the eightenth yere of the reigne of Ioſiáh, ſo that fiue & twentie yeres after this boke was founde, Ieconiáh was led awaie captiue with Ezekiél & manie of ÿ people who the firſt yere after ſawe theſe viſions.

b Which was a part of Euphrates, ſo called.

c That is, notable, and excellent viſions, ſo that it might be knowen, it was no natural dreame but came of God.

CHAP. I.

1 The time wherein Ezekiél prophecied and in what place. 3 His kinred. 15 The viſion of the foure beaſtes. 26 The viſion of the throne.

IT came to paſſe in the a thirtieth yere in the fourth *moneth*, *and* in the fift *day* of the moneth (as I was amõg the captiues by the riuer b Chebár) that ÿ heauens were opened and I ſawe viſions of c God.

2 In the fift *daye* of the moneth (which was
the fift yere of King Ioiachins captiuitie)
3 The worde of the Lord came vnto Ezekiél the Prieſt, the ſonne of Buzí, in the
land of the Caldeans, by ÿ riuer Chebár,
where the d hãd of the Lord was vpõ him.
4 And I loked, & beholde, e a whirlewinde
came out of the North, a great cloude &
a fyre wrapped about it, and a brightnes
was about it, and in the middes thereof, *to
wit*, in the middes of the fyre *came out* as the
likenes of g ambre.

d That is, the Spirit of prophecie, as chap 3, 22 and 37, 1.

e By this diuerſitie of wordes he ſignifieth ÿ fearful iudgement of God, and the great afflictions, that ſhulde come vpon Ieruſalem

g Or, pale yelow.

THE VISION OF EZEKIEL.

A. The whirlwinde that came out of the North, or Aquilon.
B. The great cloude.
C. The fyre wrapped about it.
D. The brightnes about it.
E. The likenes of amber, or the pale colour.
F. The forme of the foure beaſtes.
G. Their fete like calues fete.
H. Hands comming out from vnder their wings.
I. K L M. The facion of the foure faces of euerie beaſt.
N. Their wings ioyned one to another.
O. Their two wings, which couered their bodies.
P. Fyre running among the beaſtes.
Q. Wheles hauing euerie one foure faces.
R. The rings of the wheles which were ful of eyes.
S. The firmament like vnto chryſtal.
T. The throne, which was ſet vpon the firmament,
V. Where ſate like the appearance of a man.
X. The appearance of amber aboue, and benethe the man.
Y. The fyre about him.
Z. The brightnes of fyre like the raine bowe.

Midi, or the South.

f Which were ÿ foure Cherubims ÿ repreſented ÿ glorie of God, as Chap. 3, 23.

5 Alſo out of the middes thereof *came* the
likenes of foure beaſts, f and this was their
forme: they had the appearance of a man,
6 And euerie one had foure faces, and euerie one had foure wings.
7 And their fete *were* ſtreight fete, and the

ſole

Plate 4 The Vision of Ezekiel in the Geneva Bible: *The Bible and Holy Scriptures* (Geneva, 1560).

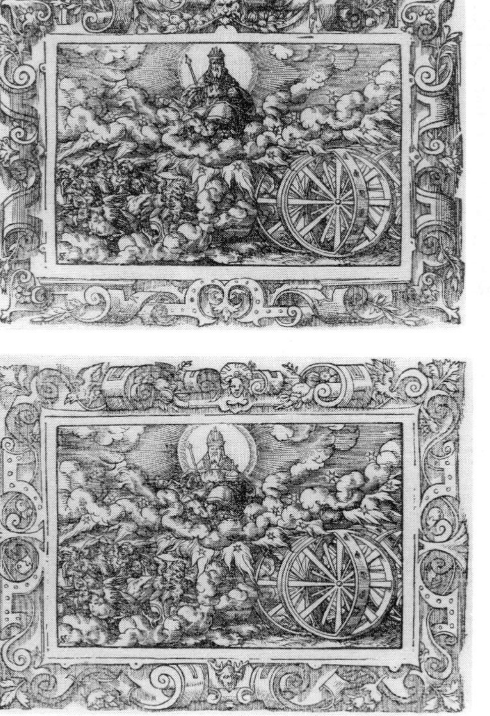

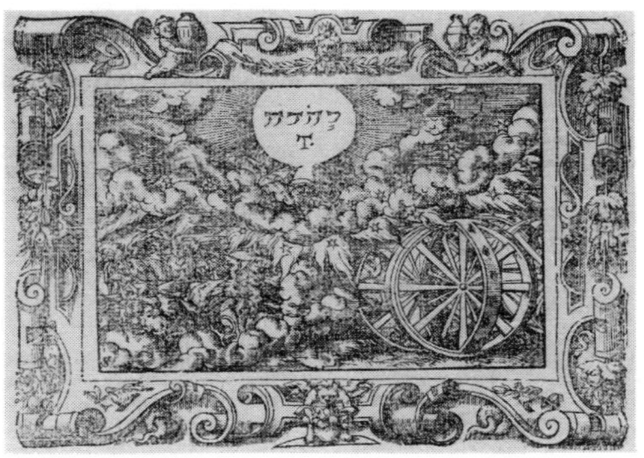

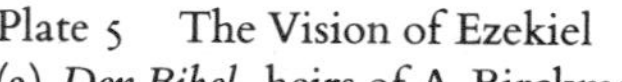

Plate 5 The Vision of Ezekiel
(a) *Den Bibel*, heirs of A. Birckmann (Cologne, 1566).
(b) *The holie Bible*, R. Jugge (London, 1568).
(c) *Biblia*, heirs of J. Steels (Antwerp, 1570–1). Note in (c) changes in God's mitre and sceptre and in the hatching of his halo.

These examples of iconographic changes in the 1568 Bible's borrowed wood-blocks show that Parker and his bishops were fully aware of the need to emend the Lutheran and Catholic images they had temporarily gained access to. Others thought they had not gone nearly far enough—though these critics can scarcely have known the source of the images they took exception to. In the second, 1572 edition of the *Bishops' Bible* the Solis designs have disappeared and been replaced by a completely different set of woodcuts. Fewer in number, and quite different in style, these composite scenes are placed at the opening of the biblical books they illustrate, with tags to identify the chapters depicted. Was this change a further result of the censuring process?

While this had some bearing, it may not be the only, or foremost, explanation. For if these new composite cuts are set beside the 1568 illustrations, we find that the earlier sequence is closely followed in these small scenes. The same subjects, in the same order, are depicted as in the first *Bishops' Bible*, and in some instances there seems to be clear evidence of iconographic dependence. It is almost as if an expert wood-engraver had been set to work to produce a less ambitious series of illustrations, taking the picture-series of 1568 as his model. The 1572 illustrations, though much reduced in number (but larger in size), do not avoid the imagery of 1568. All that they do by way of emendation is to eliminate all those remaining delineations (however small) of God, replacing them in each case with the tetragrammaton. This is clearly visible, for instance, in the cut at the beginning of Genesis, which has a total of four such symbolic representations.[36]

Why, then, did Archbishop Parker go to all the trouble and expense and delay of commissioning a new set of woodcuts for the second edition of his Bible? The likely answer is that he (like Feyerabend before him) lost control of the blocks. They had come to him from Cologne, and they went back there. They may already have been on their way when, in 1569, Richard Jugge printed the first quarto edition of the *Bishops' Bible* with a new illustration to Genesis—with tetragrammaton in place of God.[37] Was the whole series of Solis Bible pictures, with their ornamental frames, on some kind of loan or hire? Was there some objection to making more

[36] *The holie Bible* (1572), fol. 1r. The scene of the flood at the centre top of this illustration omits the divinity in the sky depicted in the 1568 Bible's woodcut (fol. 5v).

[37] *The holie bible* (London, 1569), pt 1, fol. 1r; *STC* 2105; Herbert, *Historical Catalogue*, p. 72, no. 126. This cut of Adam naming the creatures was later used in the folio Bibles (with a frame of multiple scenes), but in the quarto it was the only illustration.

changes to the blocks? Had they been brought by an immigrant who decided not to stay in England?

One possible candidate (though it would be unwise to limit the field, given the numbers of artists who came to England at this time of persecution in the Low Countries) is Franciscus Hogenberg, who fled from the Netherlands, being among the Protestants proscribed by the Duke of Alva. Cologne became Hogenberg's home for the rest of his life. He was there in 1570 (and married a woman of Cologne after the death of his first wife). It seems likely he was also there before his visit to England.[38] Possibly Hogenberg, as well as contributing the title-pages to Parker's Bible, was the intermediary who secured the wood-blocks that had been used in the 1566 Dutch Bible printed in Cologne, and who, for reasons unknown, returned them to that city (after their stop-over in Antwerp) to adorn the Quentell German Bible in 1571.

What is certain is that the illustrations in the first *Bishops' Bible* were on an outing between two Catholic Bibles. The adaptations that were made to enable the woodcuts to suit their Protestant context show reforming censors at work. Ten years after the wolves came padding back from Geneva, the English Church took over, with relatively slight alteration, a woodcut picture Bible series of Lutheran origin that proved acceptable for repeated Catholic use. Had the wolves known this they would surely have bayed louder than they did about the 'blasphemous pictures' that outraged them. As it was, they still had some effect on the appearance of Archbishop Parker's grand design.

[38] Hind, *Engraving*, 1, pp. 64, 67; *Allgemeines Lexikon der Bildenden Künstler*, 17, pp. 306–7.

THE SILENT COMMUNITY: EARLY PURITANS AND THE PATRONAGE OF THE ARTS

by BRETT USHER

> To Mr Thomas Neale and his wife, my loving son and daughter, for a poor token of remembrance, a pair of great French candlesticks and one great brass pot . . . a fair table of walnut tree standing in the great parlour . . . two pieces of Arras wrought in pictures with silk and gold, six tapestry cushions and the bedstead of walnut tree wherein I used to lie at Warnford . . . To Joan Knight, daughter of my son Mr John Knight, my diamond ring of gold and a pair of bracelets of gold which were given unto me by my . . . husband.

THE lady who in 1596 made these and many other lavish bequests[1] was Anne, Mrs William Neale, once the pious wife of Richard Culverwell, Mercer, who during the 1570s and early 1580s had, with great circumspection, financed the religious campaigns of John Field from his house in St Martin Vintry.[2] Whilst it is, of course, possible that as Mrs Neale the lady wore more jewellery than she had done as Mrs Culverwell, the first bequest quoted was specifically drawn from two schedules of goods, total value £169 12*s.* 8*d.*, 'remaining in the house of Richard Culverwell, deceased, in Thames Street near the Three Cranes in the Vintry'. A good illustration, if any were needed, that in the earliest days of radical Protestantism deep and practical piety was not apparently incompatible with—amongst other things—a certain worldly ostentation.

Amongst those other things was the whole panoply of popular culture inherited from the age-old traditions of religious drama and strolling minstrels. Professor Collinson has recently pointed out, with his usual vividness, that in its infancy,

> Protestantism embraced the cultural forms which already existed and employed them for its own purposes, both instructively and as

[1] PRO, PCC PROB 11/91 (4 Lewyn).

[2] All Bancroft and his agents ever ascertained was that 'they use to make collection of money for their brethren that travel for them beyond the seas, and the money gathered is commonly delivered to one Field, a preacher in the City, and one Culverwell in Thames Street': Albert Peel, ed., *Tracts Ascribed to Richard Bancroft* (Cambridge, 1953), p. 12.

> polemical weapons against its opponents . . . The first generation and perhaps the second too entertained little hostility towards plays. Nor, for that matter, were they opposed to other cultural forms such as popular music and pictures, at least not *per se* . . . The essential point is that early Protestantism was troubled by these cultural media as potential vehicles of false religion, not as inherently false and deceptive. There was hostility to mendacious art but not to art itself.[3]

Well and good: in the first years of Elizabeth, Protestantism displayed no fundamental hostility to the arts. But were they actively *encouraged*? Did these proto-Puritans actually *want* music and painting? Did they patronize and protect artists? Or were they cynically exploiting 'popular culture' for their own purposes until they felt strong enough to display their true colours and banish it from the New Jerusalem?

The evidence at our disposal for investigating the ramifications of early Elizabethan patronage of the arts is scanty and inconclusive, tantalizingly suggestive and virtually untapped. Just as we still do not know what arcane processes of consultation raised a particular Elizabethan cleric to the episcopal bench, whilst ensuring that another was saddled for life with a Welsh deanery, so we have very little inkling indeed of the mechanics of advancement in the much more obscure areas of music, literature, architecture, and painting. Were poets, painters, and composers raised to eminence or consigned to oblivion merely as their politico-religious views pleased or displeased their patrons, potential or actual?

At the very highest level of achievement, obviously not. It was Holbein's flattering portrait of Anne of Cleves which reduced Thomas Cromwell to his final extremity, and yet, of course, it was Cromwell who went to the block and not Holbein. A few years earlier John Taverner, composer of eight breath-takingly beautiful Masses, was excused his heresy by Cardinal Wolsey on the grounds that he was 'only a musician'.[4] In spite of the fact that he was still being arraigned as a recusant by the officials of the Bishop of London in the last months of Elizabeth's reign and beyond,[5] William Byrd had long been *persona grata* at Court and composed music for the Churches of England and Rome with equal inspiration.

We like to imagine that artistic worth is above politics, and in an

[3] Patrick Collinson, *The Birthpangs of Protestant England* (London, 1988), pp. 98, 102.

[4] *DNB*: Taverner, John (*fl.* 1530).

[5] London, Greater London Record Office [hereafter GLRO], DL/C/303, p. 369; W. H. Hale, *Precedents and Proceedings in Criminal Causes* (London, 1847), p. 228.

old-fashioned, liberal kind of way we applaud the fact that a Holbein or a Byrd was able, like a Lark Ascending, to side-step the petty intrigues of the time. If, however, we try to examine the careers of lesser artists, it is instantly apparent that survival, let alone success, must have depended upon an ability to minister to the religious and political sensibilities of would-be patrons. So, to reframe the original question: in the wake of the second and final triumph of Protestantism in England, was patronage of the arts left entirely to those to whom its ascendancy was but a secondary consideration? Or did the triumphant Protestants themselves play an important and positive role in the course of artistic events?

This piling-up of question-marks speaks for itself: we simply do not know. In our present state of knowledge, all we can do is to examine our scanty evidence more carefully, and I therefore propose to consider the handful of threads which the Culverwell family, prime though stealthy movers within the Godly Community of early Elizabethan London, have left for our consideration.

* * *

The Culverwells hailed originally from Somerset, but during the reign of Edward VI the true founder of the dynasty, Nicholas, who had begun his married life in Wells, established himself in London.[6] He had married Elizabeth Joyce, kinswoman to George Barne, also a native of Wells and one of the most successful merchant princes of his day: alderman of London from 1542, Lord Mayor at the time of Edward VI's death in 1553, and a founder member of the Russia Company in 1555. Barne's younger daughter, Mrs Anne Carleill, was in 1564 to take as her second husband the young Francis Walsingham.[7] By means of this transitory connection

[6] His descendants believed that Nicholas's father was one William Culverwell of 'Bomley', Middlesex: *Lincolnshire Pedigrees*, Harleian Society (London, 1902), I, p. 285; but this is almost certainly one of those family legends which bedevil genealogical research. All the Culverwell wills refer to family and friends around Taunton and Wells, and Nicholas's eldest son, Samuel, stated at the time of his ordination in 1578 that he was born in Wells (London, Guildhall Library [hereafter GL], MS 9535/2, fol. 4v). Samuel was 27 at the time, so was born probably in 1551.

[7] Kinship is established by comparing legatees in Barne's will PRO, PCC PROB 11/40 (13 Noodes) with those in various Culverwell wills; but the bald statement that Elizabeth was Barne's niece, found in the genealogical tree appended to the Introduction to Nathaniel Culverwell's *An Elegant and Learned Discourse of the Light of Nature*, ed. Robert A. Greene and Hugh MacCallum (Toronto, 1971) is not thus substantiated; for Barne's career, T. S. Willan, *The Muscovy Merchants of 1555* (Manchester, 1953), p. 78; for his family connections, Rachel Lloyd, *Elizabethan Adventurer: a Life of Christopher Carleill* (London, 1974), ch. 1.

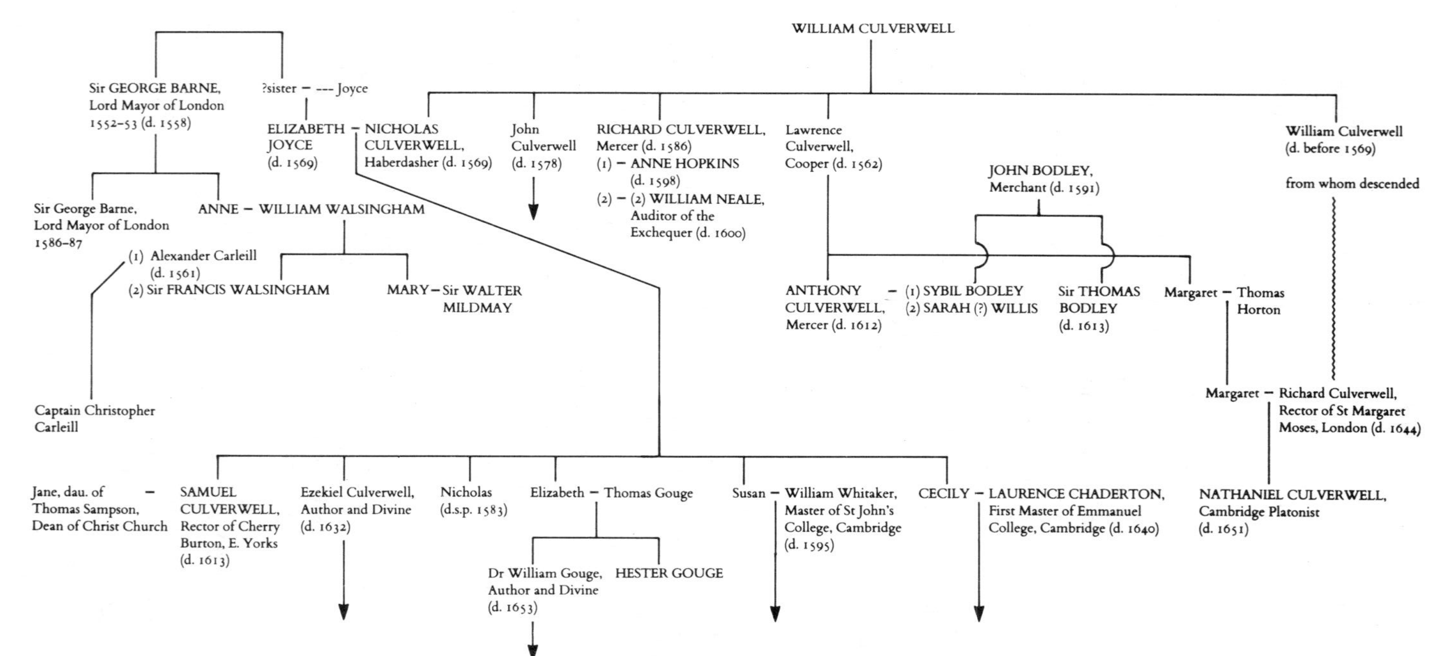

Table 1 The Culverwell Marriages, *c.* 1540–90 (capitals denote persons mentioned in the text and footnotes)

(the marriage ended in Anne's death within a year), the Culverwells were in time to find themselves in close proximity to the very fount of Elizabethan patronage: Walsingham's sister Mary married Walter Mildmay, the future Chancellor of the Exchequer.

Perhaps Culverwell served a full apprenticeship under Barne before marrying into the family. At any rate, he received the freedom of the Merchant Haberdashers on 12 July 1549, 'Mr Alderman Barnes' being his sponsor.[8] By the beginning of Elizabeth's reign he had acquired full London citizenship and had settled in the parish of St Martin Vintry with his growing family.[9] There is no evidence to suggest that in the interim he had fled from Marian London, either by going abroad or by retiring to the West Country. But it is as a friend and patron of the returning Marian exiles that he first emerges on to the public stage, and we have it on the authority of Laurence Humphrey that Nicholas and Elizabeth played host to John Jewel (a Devon man) for several weeks after his arrival home in March 1559.[10] They also quickly established a lasting friendship with the family of John Bodley (another Devon man), an adherent of Somerset who had helped to finance the suppression of the Western Rebellion of 1549, gone abroad with a large entourage under Mary, established a printing office in Geneva, and returned home to gain Elizabeth's patent for the exclusive production of the Geneva Bible in England.[11]

At the beginning of the new reign, the Genevan exiles were virtually a distinct sect within the early Elizabethan Church, their loyalty to each other and to their ideals imposing a 'tight internal discipline'.[12] The subsequent history of the Culverwells nevertheless confirms that they were accepted unreservedly by the Genevans, and became the major

[8] London, GL, MS 15,857, vol. 1, fol. 90r.

[9] *CPR (1558–60)*, p. 202.

[10] Laurence Humphrey, *Ioannis Ivelli Angli Episcopi Sarisburiensis vita et mors . . .* (London, 1573), p. 99. Humphrey actually says six months, but this hardly fits with Jewel's known movements as a Royal Commissioner in the autumn of 1559.

[11] C. H. Garrett, *The Marian Exiles* (Cambridge, 1938), pp. 92–4. John Bodley was one of the four overseers of Nicholas's will in 1569: PRO, PCC PROB 11/52 (7 Lyon), and one of the two overseers of Richard Culverwell's in 1584: PRO, PCC PROB 11/69 (9 Windsor). Elizabeth Culverwell, 'reposing my only and special confidence in him', appointed Bodley her sole executor in 1589 in preference to either of her surviving sons: London, GL, MS 9171/17, fols 262r–4r; and PRO, PCC PROB 11/75 (9 Drury). His daughter Sybil married Anthony Culverwell, nephew of Nicholas and Richard, and his own will of 1591 grants privileges to Anthony which were not extended to any of his other sons-in-law: PRO, PCC PROB 11/75 (90 Saintberbe).

[12] Patrick Collinson, *The Letters of Thomas Wood, Puritan, 1566–1577*, *BIHR*, special supplement no. 5 (1960), p. ix.

financial force behind the Puritan campaigns of the next twenty-five years.

Nicholas Culverwell's rise to prominence amongst the Godly Community was rapid, spectacular, and complete. But on 26 October 1569, probably in his mid-forties, he died.[13] His will, made four days earlier, with the young John Field as one of the witnesses, is a fascinating document for many reasons. For our present purposes, however, attention must be drawn to one of the several clauses bequeathing his substantial property: his wife, Elizabeth, received, amongst much else, two messuages within the parish of St Martin Vintry 'now occupied by my brother Richard Culverwell and John Cosen, musician'. Does this isolated reference provide us with an insight into the system of patronage exploited by early Elizabethan musicians? And who, anyway, was 'John Cosen'?

* * *

When, in October 1530, an unknown printer brought out the baldly-titled *XX Songes*, he was opening up an entirely new field in English music: the production of anthologies for secular, domestic use. Between that date and the publication of Byrd's *Psalms, Sonnets and Songs* of 1588, a further fifteen such song-books had made their sporadic appearance,[14] and the most striking fact about them is their heavy stress upon music for private devotions.

How so? Specifically because the more radical of the exiles brought home with them not only the Geneva Bible, but also a fully-fledged tradition of metrical psalm-singing.[15] Thomas Sternhold's *Certayne Psalms* of 1549, containing nineteen translations into English verse, seems to have struck a definite chord, for after Sternhold's death John Hopkins, an Oxford graduate,[16] brought out a new edition, adding a further eighteen translations by Sternhold and seven of his own. Frequently reprinted in the 1550s, this collection was the one preferred by the Genevan exiles:[17]

[13] PRO, PCC PROB 11/52 (7 Lyon); *CPR* (*1569–72*), no. 2416.

[14] Peter Le Huray, *Music and the Reformation in England 1549–1660* (London, 1967), pp. 370, 403–5.

[15] For background see Kenneth W. T. Carleton, 'John Marbeck and *The Booke of Common Praier Noted*', p. 259 above.

[16] And probably the man of these names ordained deacon in November 1551 and priest in May 1552 by Ridley: of St Bridget's, London, where he has lived 4 years; born, Wednesbury, Staffs.; aged 30: GL MS 9535/1, fols 9v, 11r, transcribed in W. H. Frere, *The Marian Reaction* (London, 1896), pp. 200, 204.

[17] Others circulated, such as Robert Crowley's *The Psalter of David Newly Translated into English Metre*, also dating from 1549.

their edition of 1556, including seven further psalm-translations and a metrical version of the Ten Commandments by William Whittingham, became an integral part of Knox's *Form of Prayers and Ministration of the Sacraments*. Expanded versions continued to appear, culminating in John Day's edition of 1562: at last the exiles had agreed upon translations of all 150 psalms, with a final attribution of 43 to Sternhold and 56 to Hopkins. The remainder bear the initials of Whittingham, Thomas Norton, John Pullan, Robert Wisdom, Thomas Bastard, John Markant, and William Kethe.[18]

William Kethe was a particular friend of John Bodley—both were natives of Exeter—and in the summer of 1557 the two men assisted the beleaguered congregation of Wesel, travelling with them widely through Savoy and Switzerland before sanctuary was found in Aarau.[19] Among Kethe's contributions to Day's metrical psalms was the only one that has passed into the collective subconscious of the English-speaking nations, 'All people that on earth do dwell', the Old Hundredth.[20]

Most of the dirge-like English tunes which the exiles took abroad with them were gradually dropped in favour either of French melodies, which they had learnt to adapt to their purposes, or else (to judge from later scathing references) of popular English ballad-tunes of the day. This amounts to a deliberate and shrewd tactic. They quickly realized something that Noel Coward, four hundred years later, knew by instinct: 'How potent cheap music is.'[21] Or, as Ponet reminded John Bale in Frankfurt, 'The ploughman's whistle is no vain instrument.'[22] It would be difficult otherwise to account for the rapidity with which psalm-singing spread from parish to parish in the London of 1559.[23]

But, of course, as the reign wore on, psalm-singing ceased to be a novelty and became the norm. The rising generation had no need to exploit popularity, laying the emphasis instead upon *suitability*, and accordingly more decorous settings began to appear. Since after about 1570 only cathedrals, chapels royal, and collegiate churches were in a position to support choirs, these settings must have been intended primarily for domestic use. A growing body of workaday musicians,

18 Nicholas Temperley, 'Psalms, Metrical; III. England', in Stanley Sadie, ed., *New Grove Dictionary of Music and Musicians* (London, 1980), 15, pp. 358–9; *DNB*: Hopkins, John (d. 1570).

19 Garrett, *Marian Exiles*, pp. 93, 204.

20 *DNB*: Kethe, Williams (d. 1608?).

21 Noel Coward, *Private Lives*, Act 1.

22 Collinson, *Birthpangs of Protestant England*, p. 103.

23 Temperley, 'Psalms, Metrical', pp. 360–1.

therefore, will have looked towards the Godly, and London's Godly Community in particular, for patronage and security.

What the Godly Community wanted, having astutely capitalized on the first flush of enthusiasm for (unison) communal psalm-singing, was a body of decent and comely versions which could be used without a blush at all times and in all places. There was, however, to be no question of dry intoning: these were outpourings of thankfulness and joy. John Day, who acquired from Elizabeth the exclusive right to print the Psalms (just as John Bodley acquired the exclusive right to print the Geneva Bible), used a quotation from St James on the title-page: 'If any man be afflicted, let him pray: and if any be merry, let him sing psalms.'[24] Even Arthur Dente, a Plain Man if ever there was one, went out of his way at the end of the reign to insist that 'songs of joy after great victories, are of great antiquity in the church.'[25] The inference is clear: the Protestant should rejoice constantly at the continuing victory of the True Faith over the iniquities of Rome.

The first harmonized 'Sternhold and Hopkins', published by John Day in 1563, was specifically described as being 'for the increase of virtue and abolishing of other vain and trifling ballads'.[26] More than half of its four-part harmonizations (81 out of 141) were provided by William Parson(s), probably the man of those names who had been resident composer, copyist, and perhaps organist of Wells Cathedral between 1550 and 1560, when references to him there cease. In view of his major contribution to the project, it is possible that he was brought in by Day in an editorial capacity[27]—and that, perhaps, on the recommendation of those two Wells-based families, the Barnes and the Culverwells.

Another composer used by Day was the otherwise unknown 'N. Southerton'. The Sothertons, a prolific Norwich clan, were related by marriage to the Bodleys, and George Sotherton, Merchant Taylor and later MP for London, was appointed one of the four overseers of the will of Richard Culverwell in 1584.[28] 'N.', most musical of Sothertons, was

[24] This is the wording in the (unharmonized) edition of *The Whole Book of Psalms*. . . of 1583 (Dr Williams's Library copy, shelfmark 5601.H.2).

[25] Arthur Dente, *The Ruin of Rome: or, an Exposition upon the Whole Revelation* (London, 1603), p. 162.

[26] Le Huray, *Music and the Reformation*, p. 376.

[27] Philippe Oboussier, 'Parsons, William (*fl.* 1545–63)', *New Grove Dictionary*, 14, pp. 249–50.

[28] Will of Alice Prestwood, John Bodley's mother: PRO, PCC PROB 11/42A (34 Wells); will of George Sotherton: PRO, PROB 11/119 (48 Fenner); will of Richard Culverwell: PRO, PROB 11/69 (9 Windsor). *The House of Commons 1558–1603*, ed. P. W. Hasler (London, 1981), p. 418.

probably George's cousin Nowell, long a subordinate of Sir Walter Mildmay at the Exchequer, who in 1572, as Clerk of the Extracts, received an *ex gratia* payment on the authority of Burghley and Mildmay for special diligence in his office.[29] He was undoubtedly of a pious disposition, was a West Country MP in three late Elizabethan parliaments (possibly as a protégé of Burghley), and made his will in 1608 as 'Baron of the Exchequer, of St Botolph without Aldersgate'. His 'loving kinsman' George Sotherton (son of the MP for London) was appointed sole overseer.[30]

The music books published in the twenty years after Day's harmonized 'Sternhold and Hopkins' were few and far between, and on the whole primitive. None challenged the continuing popularity of Day's venture. But in 1585 one John Cosyn published *Music of Six and Five Parts: Made upon the Common Tunes used in Singing of the Psalms*, a more ambitious attempt to turn the established unison tunes into respectable part-songs for the recreation of Godly households.

Nothing definite has previously been discovered about Cosyn (counted by Thomas Whythorne amongst the famous musicians of his time[31]) before his emergence into print in 1585. But there must be a strong suspicion that he is the same John Cosyn who was known to the Crawley family of Elmdon and Wendon Lofts, Essex. The substantial landowner Thomas Crawley, who made his will on 22 May 1559, left small bequests to his servant, Katherine Cosyn, to Reynold Cosyn, servant to his son-in-law, and to Reynold Cosyn's brother John (40 shillings and a cow, no less). Another Thomas Crawley, 'cousin and next heir apparent' of this man, was a Marian exile who must have died within days of his return home, for his will—an instructive document that mentions no fewer than six fellow exiles—was dated 5 February 1559 and names 'my cousin Francis Walsingham' as one of the three executors.[32]

The Essex John Cosyn, then, may well have been personally known to Francis Walsingham at an early date. But is he the same John Cosyn who

29 *HMC Laing* (London, 1914), I, p. 24.

30 PRO, PCC PROB 11/115 (38 Wingfield); *The House of Commons 1558–1603*, ed. Hasler, pp. 418–19.

31 *The Autobiography of Thomas Whythorne*, ed. James Osborn (Oxford, 1961), appendix III.

32 PRO, PCC PROB 11/42B (15 Chaynay and 47 Chaynay); abstracted without preambles in F. G. Emmison, *Elizabethan Life: Wills of Essex Gentry and Merchants* (Chelmsford, 1978), pp. 72–3. Garrett, *Marian Exiles*, p. 137, assumed that the Thomas who died in May was the exile, but a comparison of the two wills, and that of the Thomas who died in February with the Inquisition of 1556: D. M. Loades, 'The Essex Inquisitions of 1556', *BIHR*, 35 (1962), p. 93, places identification beyond a doubt. But it should be noted that Loades (p. 89) nevertheless accepts Garrett's assumption that the exile was the Thomas who died in May.

was imprisoned in the Counter, Newgate (no professional status mentioned), for defaulting on rent for a property in Islington in December 1561?[33] Even in those days it was a short journey from Elmdon to Islington. Did the Elmdon Cosyn make that journey after the death of his Crawley patrons and fall quickly into debt? And did the Culverwells then bail him out and set him up in the Vintry where 'John Cosen, musician' was occupying a property owned by Nicholas Culverwell in 1569?

It is a possible scenario. But the more important question is whether 'John Cosen, musician' lived in the Vintry at the grace and favour of his Culverwell landlord, or in some official capacity. Whilst no parish records or churchwardens' accounts survive for St Martin Vintry before the seventeenth century, fragmentary evidence gleaned from other sources suggests that there was a solid tradition of music-making in Thames Street from Henrician times. Thomas Munday had been sexton and musician at St Mary at Hill, further down the river towards the Tower, from 1527 until 1558; his son William, a prolific and important composer, is known to have been at St Martin Vintry in 1547, and in 1548 became parish clerk[34] at St Mary at Hill, where a choir of six or seven men survived the official dissolution of the choir school that same year. Thus he may well have written the three services and the *Te Deum* for men's voices which survive (whole or in part) for this particular Thames-side chorale.[35] More significantly, perhaps, William Munday later published psalm-settings in a style which seems to derive directly from John Cosyn.[36]

All in all, it is not impossible that Cosyn officiated as parish clerk at St Martin Vintry during the 1560s and began turning out the psalm-settings which he eventually published in 1585. Certainly he was a Godly man who disapproved of the secularizing tendencies of the burgeoning Golden Age:

> Howsoever the abuse of music may be great, when it is made an instrument to feed vain delights, or to nourish and entertain superstitious devotion, yet the right use thereof is commanded in singing Psalms and making melody to God in our hearts. Therefore . . . as by

[33] PRO, REQ 2 75/36. The name is given as 'Cousin' in the indictment, but one of the documents is endorsed 'John Cosyn' in an excellent hand.

[34] For the musical duties of the parish clerk, see Nicholas Temperley, 'Parish clerk', *New Grove Dictionary*, 14, p. 226.

[35] Gilbert Blount and Robert Reeve, 'Munday, William (b. *c.*1529; d. London, probably before 12 Oct. 1591)', *New Grove Dictionary*, 12, pp. 779–80; Le Huray, *Music and the Reformation*, pp. 211–13.

[36] Ibid., p. 380.

> the grace of God I labour to avoid the former, so have I been careful in my profession to further the second.[37]

He goes on to record that he had been 'encouraged by some' to publish his settings 'for the private use and comfort of the godly, in place of many other songs neither tending to the praise of God, nor containing anything fit for Christian ears . . . [and] *for the furtherance of godly exercises*.'[38] Here, surely, he explains completely his presence in St Martin Vintry sixteen years earlier. Whether privately or officially, the Culverwells had made a point of supporting a composer who was prepared to produce the kind of music desired by the Godly Community. Although they did not, of course, receive the dedication of the book when it finally appeared, Cosyn naturally chose a 'patron of Godliness', and one to whom

> I have now a long time specially been devote [*sic*] . . . as one most joyful to hear both of your singular zeal for the truth and of your manifold actions to advance the same . . . [M]y trust is that the least thing tending to the praise of God and furtherance of piety are not little to Your Honour.

The paragon whom Cosyn addresses is Francis Walsingham.[39]

* * *

Nicholas Hilliard also had cause to be grateful to Francis Walsingham, but his first protector was John Bodley. Son of the Protestant Exeter goldsmith, Richard Hilliard, an associate of John Bodley in financing the suppression of the Western Rebellion of 1549, young Nicholas was a member of the Bodley entourage which was accepted at Geneva on 8 May 1558.[40] He returned to England to be groomed as a court painter. On

[37] John Cosyn, *Music of Six and Five Parts* (London, 1585), preface, sig. A2; Ernest H. Meyer, *English Chamber Music* (London, 1946), pp. 114–15. The use of the phrase *in my profession* is surely significant. It would suggest that a growing number of composers were beginning to assume that their professional competence placed them in a position to expect *independent patronage* from persons willing to *pay* for the kind of music they wished to hear performed.

[38] Cosyn, *Music of Six and Five Parts*, sig. A2. My italics.

[39] Little else can be said of Cosyn. He is usually assumed to be the 'one Cosen' employed by the Kytson family of Hengrave Hall during 1575: John Buxton, *Elizabethan Taste* (London, 1963), p. 189. For the remaining facts see Suzi Jeans, 'Cosyn, John (bur. Camberwell 5 Feb 1608/9)', *New Grove Dictionary*, 4, p. 827; Le Huray, *Music and the Reformation*, p. 379.

[40] Mary Edmond, *Hilliard and Oliver* (London, 1983), pp. 25–7; Roy Strong, *Artists of the Tudor Court* (London, 1983), p. 58, and *The English Renaissance Miniature*, rev. edn (London, 1984), p. 66. The two authors, preparing for publication at precisely the same time, never refer to

technical grounds it is likely that he was trained in the art of limning by Lavina Teerlinc, and in that of painting on panel by the unidentified Master of the Countess of Warwick. This man may have been the Frenchman Nicholas Lizard, who in November 1554 had been appointed Serjeant Painter to the Crown.[41] As will appear, the Culverwells were intimately acquainted with at least one member of the Lizard family.

That the Bodleys gave any financial support to Hilliard over the ensuing years cannot be shown. Reckless and spendthrift, he pursued a brilliant artistic career beneath the shadow of permanent financial embarrassment and lived to see his father-in-law cut him out of his will.[42] Prudent and puritanical, the Bodleys may well have decided early on that it was safer to keep him supplied with commissions rather than with cash. His fine miniature of Sir Thomas Bodley, executed in 1598, nevertheless indicates that their friendship remained intact forty years after they had spent their youth together in Geneva.[43] In the interim he had risen to the top of his profession and could solicit patronage from the most exalted quarters: he seems to have been working for Leicester as early as 1571, and by 1587 he could look to Burghley and Mildmay as personal sureties when no one else would come forward, Walsingham having apparently acted as intermediary in securing him the reversion of certain leases.[44] Between those dates, in 1584, Hilliard had produced 'the most splendid illumination of the decade', the charter for Sir Walter Mildmay's new Cambridge college, Emmanuel.[45]

Whilst this commission doubtless owed something to Mildmay's 'known support',[46] the Bodley–Culverwell connection is an equally tangible link. Since the death of Nicholas Culverwell, in 1569, the family's

---

each other in print, and for details of Hilliard's early life Sir Roy constantly cites Erna Auerbach, *Nicholas Hilliard* (London, 1961), pp. 1–10. But it should be pointed out here that Auerbach never mentions John Bodley, the Marian exile or even (an extraordinary lapse) Miss Garrett, who opined (*Marian Exiles*, p. 183) that there was nothing either to prove or to disprove identification of the Genevan Nicholas Hilliard with the painter. For the available facts about Hilliard's career and private life Edmond has now provided chapter and verse and should henceforth be quoted in preference to Auerbach. Yet, in her turn, she makes no reference to the Emmanuel charter, upon which Sir Roy lays so much emphasis (see below).

[41] Strong, *English Renaissance Miniature*, p. 68, *Artists of the Tudor Court*, pp. 60–1; Erna Auerbach, *Tudor Artists* (London, 1954), p. 146; Edmond, *Hilliard and Oliver*, pp. 29–30. For the extant works of the Master of the Countess of Warwick see Roy Strong, *The English Icon* (London, 1969), pp. 107–14.

[42] Edmond, *Hilliard and Oliver*, pp. 105–7.

[43] Strong, *Artists of the Tudor Court*, p. 60.

[44] Edmond, *Hilliard and Oliver*, pp. 50, 78; PRO, E/310/41/15, nos 511, 513, 515–27.

[45] Strong, *English Renaissance Miniature*, p. 89.

[46] Ibid.

financial interests had been controlled by his younger brother, Richard. During 1583, together with an old business associate, Robert Taylor, his nephew by marriage, Laurence Chaderton, and Mildmay himself, Richard Culverwell literally set about preparing the ground for the new foundation. After Taylor had received royal licence to transfer the site of the Black Friars in St Andrew's Street to Culverwell and Chaderton, a complicated series of transactions took place (five deeds associating Culverwell and Chaderton survive in the college archives), during which Culverwell received £550 for the site, conveyed to him on 12 June 1583 and subsequently re-conveyed to Mildmay. On the official foundation of Emmanuel the following year, Chaderton was appointed its first Master.[47]

During the few months of life left to him, Culverwell continued to take an active interest in the affairs of Emmanuel and is officially counted among its first important benefactors. He is credited with a gift of £200 and a large number (*multitudo*) of books, a handful of which still survive.[48] Within the generous scale of this visionary enterprise, involving the single-mindedness of Mildmay, the talents of Hilliard, and not only Culverwell's business acumen, but also a handsome portion of his apparently extensive library, it is surely not fanciful to see the seeds of that spectacular benefaction of the next generation—Sir Thomas Bodley's foundation of one of the world's greatest academic institutions.[49]

* * *

At any rate, it is instructive that within Mildmay's scheme for a Puritan seminary a place could be found for utilizing the skills of the greatest painter of the age. There is further evidence that neither the Culverwells

[47] Vivienne Lake, 'Richard Culverwell: *Res tuas age*' (typescript deposited in Emmanuel College Archives, box COL. 9.3; copy kindly supplied to me by the author); H. C. Porter, *Reformation and Reaction in Tudor Cambridge* (Cambridge, 1958), p. 239; Royal Commission on Historical Manuscripts, *The City of Cambridge* (London, 1959), 1, p. 61.

[48] Lake, 'Richard Culverwell'. Seven volumes belonging to Richard, uniformly bound, still survive at Emmanuel, and another came to light as recently as 1985 with the inscription, *Ex Dono Annae Culverwell*: Emmanuel College Archives, COL. 20.1; Frank Stubbings, *A Brief History of Emmanuel College Library* (Cambridge, 1981), pp. 1–2; S. Bush and C. J. Rasmussen, *The Library of Emmanuel College Cambridge, 1584–1637* (Cambridge, 1986), p. 22 and fig. 14, and for details of the books, pp. 97, 145, 149, 155, 171, 174. (My thanks are due to Dr Frank Stubbings, formerly Librarian of the College, for supplying information and full references.)

[49] For the circumstances surrounding the foundation of the Bodleian, see Frederick S. Boas, 'Sir Thomas Bodley and his Library', in *Queen Elizabeth in Drama and Related Studies* (London, 1950), pp. 122–40.

nor the Chadertons bore any obvious hostility towards painters or painting. In 1589 Elizabeth Culverwell, widow of Nicholas, bequeathed to her daughter Cecily, Mrs Laurence Chaderton, four messuages in Stepney, one of them occupied by 'Thomas Lysard, painter'. To her granddaughter Hester Gouge she left a quantity of household stuff including 'my painted cloths' in the possession of 'goodman Lysarde the painter'.[50]

The records are silent about Thomas Lysard(e), and I suggest that Elizabeth's notary actually wrote, or meant to write, *Lewes* Lysard(e). Nicholas Lizard, the Serjeant Painter, named five sons in his will—William, John, Nicholas, Lewes, and Henry.[51] All except Henry are known to have followed in their father's footsteps, and whilst only John was certainly dead by 1589, young Nicholas and William disappear from the records during the early 1570s.[52] The survivor appears to have been Lewes: apparently taking precedence over the then Serjeant Painter, George Gower, he 'and his company painters' were responsible for the ceiling of the Banqueting House at Westminster 'upon the canvas' in 1586.[53] This brings us to within months of Elizabeth's will, with its 'painted cloths'. Thus, whilst it is possible that 'Thomas' was a Lizard of the third generation, it is surely more likely that he is one of those scribal errors in which, particularly with regard to proper names, will registers notoriously abound. The name, moreover, is unusual, 'Thomas' would be an understandable substitution for a poorly-written 'Lewes' by an over-hasty clerk of the Prerogative Court.

* * *

Fragmentary though the evidence necessarily is, there are reasonable grounds for suggesting that, if the Culverwells are typical, the Godly Community of London, far from eschewing domestic music-making and the visual arts, was actively promoting them well beyond the currently proposed cut-off point between Puritan complacency and Puritan intransigence in these matters, Professor Collinson's 'critical year' of 1580.[54]

[50] For Elizabeth's will, see n. 11 above. For a discussion of the precise definition of painted cloths, Susan Foister, 'Paintings and other works of art in sixteenth-century English inventories', *Burlington Magazine*, 123 (1981), p. 274.

[51] PRO, PCC PROB 11/53 (18 Holney).

[52] Auerbach, *Tudor Artists*, pp. 174–5.

[53] James Lees-Milne, *Tudor Renaissance* (London, 1951), p. 84. Auerbach, *Tudor Artists*, p. 174, lists no reference to Lewes later than 1581.

[54] Collinson, *Birthpangs of Protestant England*, p. 112.

It is, moreover, striking how often the names of Walsingham and Mildmay, those Puritan brethren-in-law, crop up. I would suggest that they stood at the centre of an unofficial 'Puritan' patronage system: when Walsingham and others managed to bend the royal ear, Mildmay was in a position to call the *official* patronage system into play on their protégés' behalf. The elision between public and 'private' roles will have been at one and the same time simple (to the initiated) and bewildering (to the outsider). Like Sir Joseph Porter, both men could evidently reckon up their cousins in dozens, and both received practical support (and doubtless almost daily advice) from an important sector of the Godly Community linked to them by ties of marriage, friendship, and identity of aim. The present essay has attempted to chart only a tiny fraction of the pressures—political, ideological, and genealogical—to which they must have been constantly subjected. Clearly there is much scope for further research in this area for, with such a man as Mildmay at its head, the Exchequer was inevitably staffed with a goodly assortment of Godly men. That is why I have proposed Nowell Sotherton, a future baron, as the otherwise obscure 'N. Southerton', composer.[55]

With the proposition—one that will need to be rigorously scrutinized—that the Exchequer was a powerful source of Puritan patronage, both official and unofficial, it is thus possible to bring this brief argument full circle. When Anne Culverwell married William Neale, in 1596, he had been one of the seven Auditors of the Exchequer for over a quarter of a century. By 1574 at the latest he had purchased Mildmay's mansion in Smithfield and in the course of time became a personal friend: he was the first to witness Mildmay's will in 1589.[56]

When it came to his own will-making in 1600, William Neale eschewed all ostentation in typically puritanical terms:

> My body I leave to the earth, whereof it came, to be buried where it shall please God to call me; which because it was sometime the Temple of the Holy Ghost, I desire may be performed in decent order according to my calling, without respect of pomp or worldly glory.[57]

Sir Walter Mildmay's tomb is one of the glories of St Bartholomew, Smithfield, but no slab or plaque commemorates William, Anne, or

[55] See above, pp. 294–5.

[56] *CPR (1563–6)*, no. 933; (1569–72), no. 2216; E. A. Webb, *The Records of St Bartholomew's Priory and of the Church and Parish of St Bartholomew the Great, West Smithfield*, 2 vols (Oxford, 1921), 1, p. 551; 2, pp. 137, 271, 523.

[57] PRO, PCC PROB 11/98 (81 Wooddall).

William's heir, Sir Thomas Neale. The marble monuments, like the fulsome dedications, were the particular preserve of those who by birth or by choice were the *identifiable* wielders of power. More sober benefactors like the Culverwells, the Bodleys, and the Neales did not want the one and did not expect the other. No Elizabethan Culverwell or Bodley apparently desired or sought aldermanic status.[58] Confident of inward spiritual grace, they had no need of outward visible signs: they used their influence and exercised their formidable economic power in more subterranean, and perhaps much more subtle, ways. As patrons, they were happy to take a back seat, secure in the knowledge that they were in reality driving the bus. Their function was to provide the day-to-day means of living tolerably without receiving public recognition of the fact in return. But on those occasions when Puritan musicians and painters, let alone Puritan divines, heaped paeans of praise upon a Leicester, a Warwick, a Walsingham, or a Mildmay, they undoubtedly did so mindful of the active ideological and economic support which such notables expected as their due from the Godly but—as in so many other areas of their activities—Silent Community.

[58] Neither family is indexed in A. B. Beaven, *The Aldermen of the City of London*, 2 vols (London, 1913); Richard Culverwell is by implication dismissed as a 'Ruler' in Frank Freeman Foster's *The Politics of Stability: a Portrait of the Rulers in Elizabethan London* (London, 1977), p. 169.

Colour plate 1 Encaustic icon with Bust of Christ, Monastery of St Catherine, Mount Sinai (by permission of Princeton University Press).

Colour plate 2 Late Fourteenth–Early Fifteenth-century Icon Illustrating the 'Triumph of Orthodoxy' (843) (National Icon Collection 18, by courtesy of the Trustees of the British Musem).

Colour plate 3 The Four Evangelists, Aachen Gospels (*c*.800–814) (Aachen, Minster Treasury).

Colour plate 4 Christ Victorious Trampling on the Beasts, and Scenes from the Life of Christ: Ivory Book-cover, Charlemagne Court School (*c.*800) (Oxford, Bodleian Library, MS Douce 176).

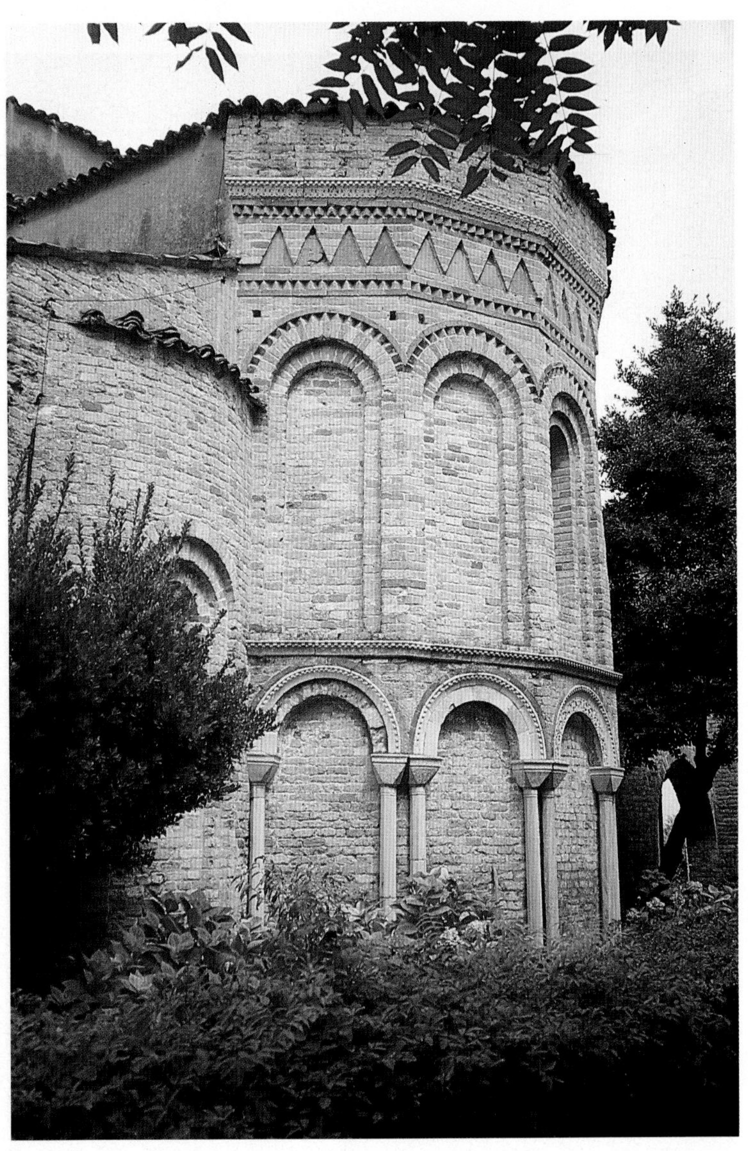

Colour plate 5 Basilica of Santa Fosca, Torcello (photo: Clyde Binfield).

Colour plate 6 Pulpit of Union Chapel, Islington, photographed in 1990 (photo: Clyde Binfield).

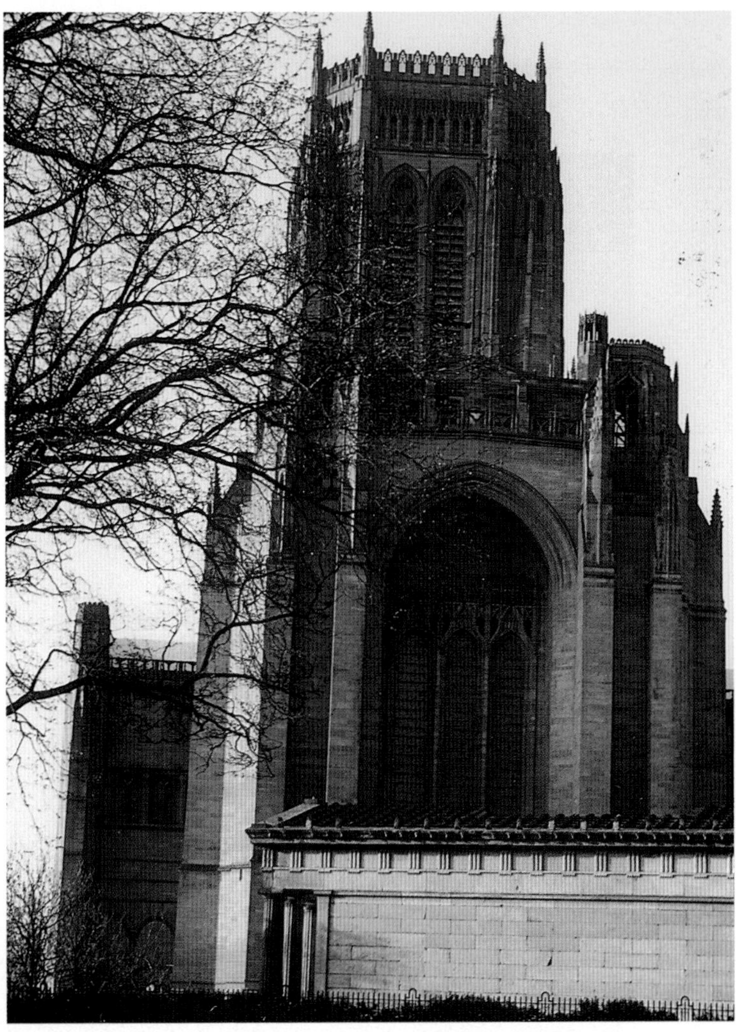

Colour plate 7 The Anglican Cathedral, Liverpool, Exterior from the West (photo: John Nelson Tarn).

Colour plate 8 The Metropolitan Cathedral, Liverpool, Exterior from the South (photo: John Nelson Tarn).

HOLINESS IN BEAUTY? ROMAN CATHOLICS, ARMINIANS, AND THE AESTHETICS OF RELIGION IN EARLY CAROLINE ENGLAND

by KEITH A. NEWMAN

THIS paper is more concerned with posing questions than attempting to provide answers. I am principally interested in trying to establish whether there was a connection between the English Arminians' emphasis on ritual and the beautification of churches in the 1620s and 1630s and the perception at the time that Roman Catholicism was gaining ground, especially in London and at the court.[1] It has long been known that Charles I's court was considered by contemporaries to have been rife with Catholic activity. Likewise, the embassy chapels in London provided a focus for Protestant discontent as a result of their attracting considerable congregations of English Catholics. The 1620s also saw the Arminian faction within the Church of England grow in influence, acquiring the patronage of the Duke of Buckingham and of King Charles himself.[2] As has been demonstrated by Nicholas Tyacke, for example,[3] this faction was very much orientated towards the court, and gained power by working within this milieu under the leadership of Laud and Neile. However, I am not concerned here with the politics of the Arminian rise to control of the Church of England hierarchy, but rather with their interest in ceremonial worship, their endeavour to place liturgy rather than the sermon at the centre of services. Was a leading Arminian such as John Cosin, for instance, reacting to what amounted to a Roman initiative? Furthermore, one needs to ask what part aesthetics played in attracting and retaining the allegiance of Catholics to what was, after all, an illegal form of worship. Even if they no longer faced the likelihood of physical martyrdom, financial penalties were severe, and the threat of

[1] P. Lake, 'Anti-Popery: the Structure of a Prejudice', in R. Cust and A. Hughes, eds, *Conflict in Early Stuart England* (London, 1989), pp. 72–106.

[2] The York House Conference of 1626 marks an important stage in the process. For a contemporary account see John Cosin's 'Sum and Substance', in *The Works of John Cosin*, 2 (Oxford, 1845), pp. 17–83.

[3] Nicholas Tyacke, *Anti-Calvinists. The Rise of English Arminianism* (Oxford, 1987).

imprisonment remained for priests and laity alike.[4] Yet some twenty per cent of the titular nobility and many ordinary folk remained loyal to Rome. May not the very nature of Catholic worship provide a clue to explain this phenomenon? Clearly this is an extremely wide subject which the time and space available does not permit me to explore in depth on this occasion. Therefore, I propose to focus on two specific areas: what attracted crowds of Londoners to the Catholic worship offered by the embassy chapels; and on one aspect of the Arminian response, namely the field of devotional literature. I shall examine John Cosin's *A Collection of Private Devotions . . . Called the Hours of Prayer* (1627)[5] in the context of its being a reply to popular Catholic devotional books of the period, such as the *Officium Beatae Mariae Virginis*,[6] commonly known as the *Primer*. Thus I shall address issues connected with both public and private devotions.

Evidence of the impact of contemporary Catholic practice upon a wide variety of people can be found by examining reactions to the ceremonies and settings offered by the Catholic chapels of seventeenth-century London. On Palm Sunday 1613, for instance, according to examinations conducted before John King, Bishop of London, numerous Catholics resorted to the Spanish ambassador's residence, then in the Barbican. Apparently some 600 persons were reported to have processed with palms. While estimates of numbers by eyewitnesses are notoriously inaccurate we may safely assume attendance was high, despite the criminal nature of such an activity for Englishmen and women. One Robert Wise, a weaver, described hearing Mass, where he 'had a bough of hallowed box delivered unto him by ye priest as likewise there was unto divers others which bough he brought away with him. . . .' Robert Baxter spoke of 'sundrie ladyes and gentlewomen' being present, and indicated that three Masses were said on solemn days at the ambassador's house. This episode shows that traditional Catholic ceremonies were being maintained in London, something of their popularity with a core of Jacobean Catholics, and the concern felt by the secular and ecclesiastical authorities. Clearly, the emotional appeal of attending outweighed the risk of doing so in many minds.

Some ten years later, there occurred the Blackfriars Accident, or

[4] K. J. Lindley, 'The lay Catholics of England in the reign of Charles I', *JEH*, 22 (1971), pp. 199–221.

[5] Cosin, *Works*, 2, pp. 85–332.

[6] For a detailed study see J. M. Blom, *The Post-Tridentine English Primer = Catholic Record Society Monograph Series*, 3 (1982).

[7] *Catholic Record Society*, *Miscellanea VII*, 9 (London, 1911), pp. 121–6.

Doleful Vespers, on Sunday 26 October 1623, at the residence of Count de Tillières, the French Ambassador.[8] Though this is a well-known incident, it is interesting to note that around 300 persons had crowded into a room to hear Father Robert Drury, S.J., and Father William Whittingham, S.J., say Mass and preach. Moreover, the list of victims killed when the floor collapsed, as recorded by the coroner's jury, does give a useful, if not necessarily scientifically accurate, guide to the social status of English Catholics. Of 101 names given, only two, Lady Webb and Lady Blackstone's daughter, are titled, while of the men whose occupation is recorded, we have Morris Beucresse, an apothecary; Mr Knuckle, a painter, as was John Brabant; a pewterer from Fancy Street; and Mr Staker and John Netlan, both tailors. It may well be that the desire to seek out the elaborate forms of service associated with the embassy chapels was by no means restricted to court circles or the gentry.

There is evidence, however, that it was during the reign of Charles I rather than James I that these chapels were most influential, both in terms of the actual numbers hearing Mass, and of their provoking Protestant fears and government wrath. On 22 February 1625, for instance, Henry Montagu, 1st Earl of Manchester, the Lord President, wrote on behalf of the Council to the Bishop of Durham—the French ambassador's residence now occupied part of Durham House in the Strand—demanding that action be taken since there was 'daily resort of multitudes of Englishe subjects of more than one hundred at once to Masse' at the embassy chapel.[9] The Bishop promptly ordered that English Catholics be detained, though the constables were instructed 'to make no disturbance or trouble' inside the residence. Unfortunately the Ambassador was not so reluctant to disturb the peace, and allowed armed followers to attack the pursuivants and constables with swords. Brawls were commonplace outside the chapels, sadly, but this incident is perhaps indicative of the determination of English Catholics to worship there, and of the importance assigned by foreign ambassadors to their role in providing a haven of sorts where Mass might be heard accompanied by the trappings of the Tridentine rite unavailable to those outside the protection of diplomatic immunity.

This situation reached its apex in the 1630s, one may argue, in the context of the Spanish embassy. In this respect, Juan de Necolalde cuts a fascinating figure. He was the Spanish representative in London for some

[8] H. Foley, ed., *Records of the English Province of the Society of Jesus* (London, 1875), 1, pp. 76–8.
[9] *Catholic Record Society, Miscellanea*, 1 (London, 1905), pp. 92–5.

six years, from June 1631, and appears to have been determined to set the standard, as it were, amongst the Catholic ambassadors. He spent approximately £1,600 of state funds, plus additional amounts from his own pocket, 'for altar plate, decorations, and paintings'.[10] King Philip supported this effort, despite a warning from Charles I that he looked upon such activities with disfavour. Indeed, the Spanish King was moved to write to Necolalde of the chapel and its work, '. . . this is so important, and is God's cause; I will consider this the first and highest service that you could do for me. . . .'[11]

The ornate quality of setting and ceremonial alike is exemplified by the Holy Week celebrations of 1635. On Good Friday, for instance, Necolalde installed 'a painted monument' in the chapel, depicting the Passion, and even arranged a procession of cross- and candle-bearers, twenty priests and choristers, and sixteen hooded flagellants, which circled the embassy gardens. This was not, one suspects, an everyday sight in Clerkenwell at the time. Furthermore, having noted the presence of courtiers at his services, he caused the chapel to be divided by railings, so that they could arrive and depart by a separate door. It was in this Easter Week that he visited the chapels of French Ambassador Pougny, in St Bartholomew Street, and of the Venetian, Correr, which he condemned for their comparative paucity of decoration. The mantlings of white paper on the French altar he deemed insufficient to the occasion, while a mere four candles on the Venetian altar attracted his scorn, as did the paintings borrowed from a Flemish painter to decorate the sanctuary in the French chapel. At this time he also inspected Henrietta Maria's oratory in Somerset House—not to be confused with the splendid chapel then under construction—where he discovered an altar replete with a diamond crown and wax statues of Christ, Mary, and St John. Having introduced a similar monument or sepulchre into his own chapel four years previously, he now claimed that others 'had been obliged to do it, whether it be to compete or follow after.'[12] Whether he saw, or what he thought of, the Queen's chapel at Somerset House when completed I have not been able to discover, but there François Dieussart created a mechanical oval paradise forty feet high, ornamented with prophets and supported by

[10] Albert J. Loomie, 'London's Spanish chapel before and after the Civil War', *Recusant History*, 18 (1988), pp. 402–17.

[11] Ibid., p. 405.

[12] Ibid.

pillars, to display the Holy Sacrament, while behind the high altar were ranked seven rows of clouds and two hundred angels.[13]

To state that Necolalde's chapel—'a royal chapel which lacks nothing' in his words—was an example of ecclesiastical one-upmanship, and part of the political attempt to bolster the English Catholics' hispanophile tendencies deprecated by Charles and Henrietta Maria alike, is not a charge without foundation. However, just as Cosin, for example, commissioned at Durham a sumptuous baptismal font, adorned with painted images of Christ, John the Baptist, and the Four Evangelists,[14] drawing upon himself Puritan ire in 1627 and 1628, for what he considered a valid religious purpose, so, too, did Nicolalde's munificence serve to meet a need amongst those who found the post-Reformation austerity of the Church of England unfulfilling in an aesthetic sense. In other words, there were those in early Caroline England, Catholic and Protestant, who sought to use art as a servant of the Church, who wished to revive an element of the visual in worship.

I shall now consider the question of the reaction of the Arminian faction within the Church of England to the perceived growth in the Catholic threat, and how that response was couched in a renewed emphasis on the use of the literary and visual arts in worship. Innovation, of course, was anathema to the early modern mind. The notion of being responsible for change was often used as a means to attack one's opponents in religious controversies. Just as Laud was condemned by Puritans such as Prynne[15] for introducing Romish innovations, so the English Arminians argued that it was they who were the true conservators of the Church of England. It is interesting to note that Cosin wrote in the Preface to his *Hours of Prayer* that those

> who accuse us here in ENGLAND to have set up a *new Church* . . . to have taken away all the religious exercises and prayers of our forefathers, to have despised all the old ceremonies, and cast behind us the blessed Sacraments of Christ's Catholic Church . . .[16]

were unable 'to understand us what we are'. In this passage he was, I believe, working towards a dual end. Whilst well aware of the enmity his

[13] Thomas Birch, *The Court and Time of Charles I*, 2 (London, 1849), pp. 310f.
[14] John Cosin, *Correspondence*, ed. George Ornsby, 1 (Durham, 1869), p. 168.
[15] See, for example, William Prynne, *A Briefe Survay and Censure of Mr Cozens His Couzening Devotions* (London, 1628).
[16] Cosin, *Works*, 2, pp. 90–1.

book might arouse amongst the broad Calvinist consensus within the Church of England, as well as the Puritans, he was also trying to counter Roman attempts to seek converts. That this was the case is indicated by the book's genesis. King Charles, having been made aware of the presence at court of numerous Roman devotional works, requested Cosin 'to prepare a book . . . as like to their pocket offices as he could.'[17]

The popularity of the *Primer*, for instance, seems undoubted. Fifteen editions, in a number of variants, are known to have been produced between the publication of Richard Verstegen's first English translation of the post-Tridentine *Officium Beatae Mariae Virginis*, in 1599, and 1633.[18] If, as J. M. Blom suggests, the average print run was 1,500 copies, then some 22,500 books may well have been produced during this period. Furthermore, there were also twenty-seven editions of the *Manual of Godly Prayers* between 1583 and 1637. Even allowing for seizures, losses through careless handling and ageing, and books lost in transit from the Continent, where the bulk were printed, it would appear that the number of Catholic devotional works circulating in England was considerable. Hence, I would suggest, the need seen by men like Cosin to produce a Church of England alternative. His efforts, however, were misunderstood not only by Prynne and his ilk: Rome, too, considered the Arminians ripe for conversion. Laud was even offered a cardinal's hat should he consent to be received into the Roman Church.[19] There is, though, little or no evidence that these men did intend to defect from their allegiance to the Church of England. Cosin, for example, during his Parisian exile between 1643 and 1660, 'remained steady and unmoved in the profession of the protestant religion.'[20]

The important question, to my mind, is not so much what this faction within the Church of England did—or sought to do—but rather why they should apparently court unpopularity with so many of their fellow countrymen. Arminian emphasis on ritual, liturgy, and church embellishment, is well known. So, too, are the Laudian reforms of the 1630s designed, for instance, to move the focus of worship from the pulpit to the altar. However, their motivation for so doing remains, I think, less clear. Merely to dismiss Archbishops Laud and Neile, Bishops Wren and Juxon, and John Cosin, amongst many others, as power-hungry bureau-

[17] Blom, *Primer*, p. 162.
[18] Ibid., pp. 43–4.
[19] H. Trevor-Roper, *Catholics, Arminians, and Puritans* (London, 1987).
[20] Cosin, *Works*, 1, p. xvii.

crats, intent on obtaining and retaining preferment through producing a form of worship pleasing to the King, does not, I believe, help us to understand what seems to have been a desire to return the Church of England to a pattern of worship through the soul, the body, and the 'worldly goods' we are blessed with, to use Lancelot Andrewes's description.[21] Certainly the desire to enforce uniformity of worship, too, formed a part of the Laudian package, but perhaps that also may be seen in terms of a response to the influence of Roman post-Tridentine authoritarianism, an attempt to fight clerical discipline with discipline, and beauty in worship with beauty.

Let us return to Cosin's *Hours of Prayer*. Though the author clearly states that his words were 'taken out of the holy scriptures, the ancient fathers, and the divine service of our own Church', the formula he adopted is assuredly more akin to traditional Roman usages. He included, for example, prayers before and after the receiving of the Blessed Sacrament, 'divers forms of devout and penitent Confessions', and 'a devout manner to receive Absolution', as well as noting amongst the major festivals of the Church those of the Purification of the Virgin Mary and the Annunciation.[22] Likewise the purpose of a private devotional work differs markedly from that of the Book of Common Prayer. At the heart of the Protestant approach to divine service was the desire that the congregation be able to participate fully in the act of worship. Roman Catholics, on the other hand, most definitely heard Mass, obtaining spiritual sustenance from reading the private devotions in works such as the *Primer* or the *Manual*, while the priest celebrated the holy sacrifice. Furthermore, guidance or teaching, according to the Protestant model, was drawn largely from the sermon. I am, of course, discussing at this stage ideal rather than actual standards of worship, since we have a considerable body of evidence indicating, as in churchwarden's presentments, for instance, that orderliness was not necessarily an attribute of worship in early seventeenth-century England. Moreover, as Keith Thomas has demonstrated, there is some doubt as to whether popular attitudes to religion were notably Christian at all.[23] Again, according to Christopher Haigh's persuasive arguments, the Reformation itself was by no means the instant, overnight accomplishment indicated by the Whig historiographical tradition.[24]

21 Lancelot Andrewes, *Ninety-Six Sermons*, 1 (Oxford, 1841), p. 262.
22 Cosin, *Works*, 2, p. 332.
23 Keith Thomas, *Religion and the Decline of Magic* (London, 1971).
24 C. Haigh, 'From Monopoly to Minority', *TRHS*, ser. 5, 31 (1981), pp. 129f.

This being the case, or at least part of the case, we may well ask a number of valid questions concerning the impact of the aesthetic appeal of both Roman and Arminian approaches to the practice of religion in the period I am discussing. The importance of church embellishment and ritual could have had a wider appeal to a spectrum of members of the Church of England than has generally been acknowledged hitherto. Lengthy sermons built around the learned exposition of scriptural texts may well have appealed to the literate Godly; the rest of the community might have found that process dull, even off-putting. This being so, the existence of a substantial and committed Catholic minority would have been all the more worrying; and therefore provided a compelling reason for the Arminians to attach importance to aesthetics as a further means, together with legal coercion, of combating the Roman threat.

A book of devotions, like the *Primer* or Cosin's *Hours of Prayer*, offered the gift of familiarity to the user, a fixed mark upon which to meditate. This could not be provided by sermonizing or discussion amongst the Godly, at least not for those who sought spiritual fulfilment through emotion and ritual as well as in an intellectual sense. It was this need, I would suggest, that Cosin was seeking to meet in a literary sense, reacting in part to his perception of the activities of the regular and secular priests of the Mission to England. That the English Roman Catholic Church in the late 1620s was riven by internal dissent over the attempt to exercise episcopal jurisdiction by Dr Richard Smith, Bishop of Chalcedon, does not matter. What was important was the belief amongst Protestants that Roman Catholicism was growing in strength. This apparent threat was made visible in London by the embassy chapels. While in the regions Catholicism had largely retreated into the manor house,[25] in the capital the chapels maintained by the Catholic powers were a potent reminder that organized Catholicism remained an international force. Furthermore, the Queen's chapels served as an *aide-mémoire* that the court itself hosted, through Henrietta Maria and her retinue, an ornate, baroque Catholicism.

Of course, the courtiers of Jacobean and early Caroline England were surrounded by pomp and splendour in their secular lives, whether in state ceremonial or masques, for example; and Charles I was renowned as one of Europe's leading art collectors. If the services of baroque art could be harnessed for the propaganda purposes of a burgeoning if inept absolut-

[25] John Bossy, *The English Catholic Community 1570–1850* (London, 1975): see particularly chs 6 and 7.

ism, as instanced by those van Dyck portraits which transmogrified the mild-mannered, dwarfish king into an armoured paladin, could that same art not be adapted to the service of the Church of England? Again, the architectural surroundings of the court, exemplified by Inigo Jones's Banqueting Hall, represented the antithesis of the dour setting for much of the worship in the mainstream Church of England. It seems hardly surprising to me that elements of this court would have found the Calvinist emphasis on the Word, and antipathy to religious ceremonial, uninspiring. The Arminian tendency, which found fruition in the Laudian reforms of the 1630s, being attuned to this milieu, may well have been influenced by a desire to fulfil this want.

Lancelot Andrewes, in controversy with Cardinal Perron, expressed some caution over the use of images in church, but by no means discounted their utility: 'To have a story painted, for memory's sake, we hold it not unlawful, but that it might be well enough done, if the Church found it not inconvenient for her children.'[26] In this attitude we find a development of Hooker's ideas on the necessity for an element of beauty in liturgical worship. Moreover, if adornment in the Church's services is merely *adiaphora*, then the way is opened to utilize embellishment for the edification of worshippers. Counter-Reformation Catholicism also took a wary attitude to the use of art in church. The decree of the twenty-fifth session of the Council of Trent was careful to guard against Protestant charges of idolatry, stating of images, '. . . the honour which is shown them is referred to the prototypes which they represent, so that by means of the images . . . we adore Christ and venerate the saints whose likeness they bear.'[27] Furthermore, the Council condemned 'any unusual image unless it has been approved by the bishop.'

In an English context, perhaps one of the most eloquent attacks on Puritan iconoclasm came from John Donne, who stated, 'Woe unto such peremptory abhorrers of pictures . . . as had rather throw down a church than let a picture stand.'[28] He also wrote:

> that where there is a frequent preaching there is no *necessity* of pictures; but will not every man add this, that if the true use of pictures be preached unto them, there is *no danger* of an abuse; and so,

[26] Lancelot Andrewes, *Two Answers to Cardinal Perron and Other Miscellaneous Works* (Oxford, 1854), pp. 21–3.

[27] H. J. Schroeder, ed., *Canons and Decrees of the Council of Trent* (St Louis, 1941), pp. 216–17.

[28] John Philips, *The Reformation of Images: Destruction of Art in England, 1535–1660* (Los Angeles, 1973), p. 150.

> as *remembrances* of that which hath been taught in the pulpit they may be retained.[29]

Thus we see an echo of Tridentine willingness to use art, provided that such a use should not be misunderstood either by the faithful or by opponents of the faith. It seems to me that at the centre of Arminian endeavours to introduce into the Church of England outward as well as inward worship of God was the desire to show those in danger of falling into the snares of Rome, as it were, that the prospective convert need travel no further than the local parish church in order to see that art and ritual might add a dimension to worship.

In conclusion, I would like to emphasize the importance of the embassy chapels, and especially that of Spain under Necolalde and his successors, Onate and de Cardenas, in lending a higher profile than would otherwise have been possible to the ornate worship introduced during the baroque phase of the Catholic Reformation in Europe. In Albert Loomie's words, these chapels 'allowed people who were without the gentry's privileges to partake of the full resources of the Counter Reformation's devotions.'[30] They may also have served, however, to increase the determination of the Laudians to provide an answer, through the Church of England, to those who sought more elaborate forms of worship which engaged the senses as well as the intellect. Likewise, though, in capturing the interest of the King and leading courtiers, in filling the heartfelt need of some Englishmen and women for a Church in which art was joined with the Word in the service of God, lay also the beginnings of the downfall of a faction which became too greatly associated with the excesses of Charles I's personal rule, as well as being tainted in the minds of a majority with Romish pictures. When many Englishmen began to see little difference between the decoration and ritual in the Queen's Roman Catholic chapel and the King's Church of England chapel, the seeds of conflict were indeed sown. Art may be used to create an illusion of reality. Unfortunately the Laudian innovations, created in part to counter Rome, merely helped to foster belief in a largely illusory popish plot which served to undermine all that the Archbishop strove to achieve. Holiness may well be seen in beauty, but in the context of early Caroline England too many influential men saw not the holiness but a mirage of popery therein.

West Sussex Institute of Higher Education

[29] Philips, *The Reformation of Images*, p. 150.
[30] Albert J. Loomie, 'Spanish chapel', p. 415.

ICONOCLASM, ICONOGRAPHY, AND THE ALTAR IN THE ENGLISH CIVIL WAR*

by JACQUELINE EALES

ON 16 January 1641 Anna Temple wrote from Broughton, Oxfordshire, to her daughter in Sussex:

> God is exceeding good to us every way, both body and souls, and hath done wonderful things among us already, and gives us hope of more, and that we shall see idolatry and superstition rooted out; and God's ordinances set up in the purity and power of them. Altars begin to go down apace and rails in many places, and yours must follow if it be not down already. Let us labour to be thankful and continue our prayers, hold up our hands that Israel may prevail.[1]

Her letter testifies to the acute tensions that had been created at parish level by the official drive to reintroduce the railed altar, which had taken place during the reign of Charles I. Arguments about the altar policy were intimately connected with the wider ideological debates about religion and politics which brought the nation to civil war in 1642. Conflict over the altar thus contributed to the local divisions which preceded the outbreak of the war and had important implications for the stability of the early Stuart state.

The change from the movable communion table brought into the body of the church for the administration of the Sacrament to the fixed altar at the east end of the church, with its association with the Catholic Mass, was the most intrusive alteration to parish practice that had taken place during the 1620s and 1630s. Opposition to the altar sprang not simply from a desire to uphold custom: it was linked to a nexus of religious and political

* The initial research for this paper was undertaken during my tenure of a 1988–9 British Academy Thank Offering to Britain Fellowship. I am grateful to the trustees of the Thank Offering Fund and to the Fellows of the British Academy for their support for my work.

I would like to thank Andrew Foster and Peter Lake for commenting on an earlier draft of this paper. I am also indebted to Judith Maltby for allowing me to make use of her unpublished paper '"Contentiousnesse in a Feaste of Charity": The Altar Controversy in the Church of England, 1547–1640', and to Sheila Hingley and the staff of Canterbury Cathedral Library for their help with printed sources.

[1] East Sussex County Record Office, MS Dunn 51/54. For the general subject of English iconoclasm see J. Phillips, *The Reformation of Images: Destruction of Art in England, 1535–1660* (Los Angeles, 1973); M. Aston, *England's Iconoclasts: Laws Against Images* (Oxford, 1988).

objections. For Protestants, the Mass and the theology of transubstantiation represented idolatry, and the introduction of the altar was widely interpreted as the first step towards reconciliation with Rome.[2] Beyond this lay a range of arguments that equated Catholicism with ecclesiastical and political tyranny. Religious imagery and its symbolic significance were thus central elements in the ideological debates of the mid-seventeenth century. On one side the Crown and its advisers were alarmed by what they perceived as a Puritan threat to political order and hierarchy; on the other side the Crown's critics feared that traditional English liberties, including right religion, were being sacrificed in pursuit of Catholic-inspired authoritarian rule. Thus the royal chaplain, Peter Heylyn, wrote his tract in favour of the altar in 1637 as an antidote to the dispersal of principles of 'faction, schism and disobedience', while William Prynne joined battle against the altar in the same year and argued that 'the Jesuits, priests and some English prelates' have 'been guilty of many hundred treasons, conspiracies and rebellions against your majesty's royal progenitors, as our historians and writers witness'. 'Puritans', he maintained, had been made 'odious to your majesty', but they were 'the only men that keep both your crown and religion safe'.[3]

A petition to the Long Parliament from Nottinghamshire, printed in 1641, clearly demonstrates the impact that the altar made on the hostile beholder. The petition complained of the

> preferring the communion table to the east end of the chancel, turning it to the posture and name of an altar, advancing it with new steps to it, railing it in, with single or double rails; placing a canopy over it, tapers by it, crucifixes, or other superstitious images upon, over, or about it, appropriating peculiar parts of service to it.[4]

The revival of church art, which took place in the 1620s and 1630s, was spearheaded by the King and the Court and was endorsed by the religious

[2] See, for example, M. Newcomen, *The Craft and Cruelty of the Churches Adversaries Discovered in a Sermon Preached at St Margaret's in Westminster, before the Honourable House of Commons Assembled in Parliament November 5 1642* (London, 1643), pp. 37–8.

[3] P. Heylyn, *Antidotum Lincolniense. Or an Answer to a Book Entitled, the Holy Table Name, and thing*, 1st edn (London, 1637), sig. A2r. Heylyn was writing in reply to an anonymous tract by Bishop Williams entitled *The Holy Table, Name and Thing*, published in 1637. William Prynne, *A Quench-Coal or a Brief Disquisition and Inquiry in what Place of the Church or Chancel the Lord's Table ought to be Situated, Especially when the Sacrament is Administered* (Amsterdam, 1637), p. 14.

[4] *A Petition Presented to the Parliament from the County of Nottingham. Complaining of Grievances under the Ecclesiastical government by Archbishops, Bishops, etc arising from the Inconveniences in that form or Constitution of Government, and praying the removal of the same Inconveniences* (London, 1641), pp. 12–13.

grouping headed by Archbishops Neile and Laud, who were widely dubbed 'Arminians' by contemporaries.[5] Works created by skilled craftsmen in the two decades before the Civil War were used in cathedrals, churches, and private chapels primarily for the beautification of altars. While some patrons were undoubtedly consciously following the fashions of the Court, others were aesthetically attracted by the devotional appeal of religious imagery. The physician Sir Thomas Browne represented this latter sensibility when he wrote in the first authorized edition of his *Religio Medici* of 1643, 'I should violate my own arm rather than a church, nor willingly deface the memory of saint or martyr. At the sight of a cross or crucifix I can dispense with my hat, but scarce with the thought and memory of my saviour.'[6] The erection of altars and their adornment with hangings, church plate, Bibles, and prayer books, often bearing religious images which had been largely outlawed in the English Church since the Elizabethan Reformation, had, however, a profoundly disturbing effect on that section of society which Patrick Collinson has described as 'iconophobic'—opposed to 'false and idolatrous art'.[7] Much of the art-work of this period was thus to disappear during the crisis of civil war: church plate was melted down in order to mint coin to pay for the parliamentarian war effort, textiles in the form of altar-hangings and vestments were destroyed, and any precious metals or jewels on them were also used to raise cash for Parliament. Stained-glass windows and carved altar-rails were to suffer at the hands of iconoclasts.[8] Although much has been lost, manuscript and printed accounts do survive which describe individual altars and their decorations. These descriptions illustrate the anxieties created by the symbolism of the altar and by the iconography of its associated decorations; but before surveying some examples it is necessary to consider the context of the altar controversy, in order to appreciate fully the hostility which the railed altar provoked and the ways in which that hostility was linked to other areas of ideological debate in early Stuart England.

[5] R. Lightbown, 'Charles I and the Art of the Goldsmith', in A. MacGregor, ed., *The Late King's Goods: Collections, Possessions and Patronage of Charles I in the Light of the Commonwealth Sale Inventories* (Oxford, 1989), pp. 244–54.

[6] T. Browne, *Religio Medici* (np, 1643), p. 5. The two previous editions of 1642 were both unauthorized by the author.

[7] P. Collinson, *From Iconoclasm to Iconophobia: the Cultural Impact of the Second English Reformation = University of Reading, Stenton Lecture* (1985), pp. 22–9.

[8] See, for example, the papers of the Long Parliament Committee for the destruction of monuments of idolatry and superstition, chaired by Sir Robert Harley, BL, MS Add. 70005, fols 107r–35r.

The Elizabethan Injunctions of 1559 were widely interpreted as providing for the 'holy table' to be placed at the east end of the church and to be brought into the chancel at Communion. It was not until the issue of the canons of 1640 that the alternative practice of railing the altar at the east end of the church was clarified as the official usage.[9] The fixed altar had, however, been retained by Elizabeth and by the early Stuarts in the royal chapels, and in 1617 altars had been introduced at Gloucester Cathedral by William Laud and in Durham Cathedral by Francis Burgoyne.[10] The House of Commons first expressed corporate alarm about this process in 1629. The resolutions on religion drawn up by a subcommittee of the House in that year denounced the

> bold and unwarranted introducing, practising and defending of sundry new ceremonies and laying of injunctions upon men by governors of the Church and others, without authority, in conformity to the Church of Rome; as, for example, in some places erecting of altars, in others changing the usual and prescribed manner of placing the communion table and setting it at the upper end of the chancel, north and south, in imitation of the High Altar, by which they also call it and adorn it with candlesticks, which by the Injunctions 1 Eliz., were to be taken away.[11]

This declaration was directed at the former Bishop of Durham, Richard Neile, who was attacked in the Commons for encouraging such innovations at Durham and for introducing similar alterations at Winchester, where he had been elected bishop at the end of 1627.[12] Neile was an influential patron who numbered William Laud, Bishop of London, and Richard Montagu, Bishop of Chichester, amongst his numerous protégés. All three men had been singled out in former Parliaments as members of an Arminian faction, 'that being', as the 1628 Parliamentary Remonstrance averred, 'but a cunning way to bring in popery.' At the heart of the hostility towards the Arminians was the conviction that they rejected the Calvinist theology of double and absolute predestination, which held that each individual was predestined either to hell or salvation and earthly

[9] J. P. Kenyon, *The Stuart Constitution: Documents and Commentary* (Cambridge, 1966), pp. 170–1.

[10] N. Tyacke, *Anti-Calvinists: the Rise of English Arminianism c.1590–1640* (Oxford, 1987), pp. 116–17.

[11] S. R. Gardiner, *The Constitutional Documents of the Puritan Revolution, 1625–1660*, 3rd edn rev. (Oxford, 1968), p. 80.

[12] W. Notestein and F. H. Relf, eds, *Commons Debates for 1629* (Minneapolis, 1921), pp. 144, 203–4.

behaviour could not alter this ultimate fate. The altar controversy was a crucial element in this debate, for to many contemporaries the railed and decorated altar constituted a visible representation of the Arminian assault on Calvinist theology. As Nicholas Tyacke has noted, there was a theological 'rationale at work here—eucharistic grace versus that of absolute predestination'.[13]

From 1633 onwards there was a steady official drive towards the conversion of communion tables to the altar position, following the Privy Council ruling in favour of the dean and chapter of St Paul's Cathedral, who had ordered that the communion table of St Gregory's, a nearby parish church, should be 'placed altar-wise' at the upper end of the chancel 'in such manner as it standeth in the said cathedral and mother church, (as also in all other cathedrals and in his Majesty's own chapel)'.[14] As Archbishop of York, Neile had approved the move at parish level some months earlier in 1633, while in the southern province in the following year Archbishop Laud instructed his Vicar General, Nathaniel Brent, to enforce the positioning of the communion table against the wall at the east end of the chancel in his metropolitical visitations. Individual bishops enthusiastically pursued this policy, Bishops Goodman at Gloucester, Wren at Norwich, and Piers at Bath and Wells being amongst the most rigorous enforcers.[15] The altar policy was, of course, both controversial and widely unpopular, and rigorous enforcement would certainly explain why the issue of the altar was given such prominence in petitions and other complaints at the start of the Long Parliament from certain areas. Some local disputes had already achieved national notoriety in the late 1620s and early 1630s, and these cases had contributed to making the altar policy a contentious and nationally debated issue. The altar dispute at Grantham in 1627, for example, provoked a series of pamphlets during the 1630s, which brought the whole issue of the altar into public prominence, while the St Gregory's case of 1633 was seen as a national test case, since it was heard by the Privy Council. In Somerset the churchwardens of

13 Tyacke, *Anti-Calvinists*, p. 84.

14 P. Heylyn, *A Coal from the Altar, or an Answer to a Letter not long since written to the Vicar of Grantham against the placing of the Communion Table at the East End of the Chancel* (London, 1636), pp. 64–6.

15 A. Foster, 'Church Policies of the 1630s', in Richard Cust and Ann Hughes, eds, *Conflict in Early Stuart England* (Harlow, 1989), p. 204; Tyacke, *Anti-Calvinists*, pp. 202–8. Recent research on the implementation of the altar policy suggests that by 1640 its acceptance was extensive, indeed almost universal, in many areas: J. Davies, 'The Growth and Implementation of Laudianism with Special Reference to the Southern Province' (Oxford, D.Phil. thesis, 1987), pp. 214–64.

Beckington made their own local dispute of wider consequence by appealing to the Court of Arches against the Bishop.[16]

The erection of railed altars was undoubtedly a source of widespread and intense local conflict, which has been little studied. Well before the outbreak of the Civil War the laity were provoked into taking action against the offending symbolism of the railed altar. In Essex the troopers raised to fight against the Scots in 1640 tore down parish rails in the months of July and August, while John Rous, the incumbent of a Suffolk parish, noted in his diary that before the meeting of the Long Parliament in November 1640, 'Many rails were pulled downe . . . at Ipswich, Sudbury, Marlowe, Bucks: the organs too.'[17] The Long Parliament received a mass of evidence which illustrates the active role taken by parishioners, and also the violence which often accompanied local disputes about the altar. In June 1641 Oliver Whitby, the curate of St Olave's, Southwark, petitioned Parliament because his parishioners had threatened to drag him around the church by the ears if he would not administer the Sacrament to them sitting, instead of at the railed altar. In the same month the parson, churchwardens, and inhabitants of St Thomas the Apostle, in the ward of Vintry, London, complained that when they had gone to the church to take the Protestation Oath, a group led by one John Blackwell, His Majesty's grocer, had struck the churchwardens, pulled down the altar rails with great violence and burnt them, and threatened to burn the parson, too, if he wore his surplice.[18] Once civil war had started, parliamentarian troops were particularly active in throwing down rails and other church images, often spurred on by the sermons of their chaplains. An account written in 1642 by Nehemiah Wharton, a recruit in Denzil Holles's regiment of foot, reveals the destruction which took place in a three-day period on 9, 10, and 11 August on their march from London to Worcester. At Acton 'the soldiers got into the church, defaced the ancient and sacred glased pictures and burned the holy rails.' The next day, 'Mr Love gave us a famous sermon', and 'the soldiers brought the holy rails from Chiswick and burned them.' On the third day, 'at Hillingdon . . . the rails being gone, we got the surplice' to make handkerchiefs, and 'one of our soldiers wore it to Uxbridge.' As a finale, the rails of

[16] Tyacke, *Anti-Calvinists*, pp. 199–200, 204.

[17] W. Hunt, *The Puritan Moment: The Coming of Revolution in an English County* = *Harvard Historical Studies*, 102 (Cambridge, Mass., 1983), pp. 285–6; M. A. E. Green, ed., *Diary of John Rous Incumbent of Santon Downham, Suffolk from 1625 to 1642* = *Publications of the Camden Society*, os 66 (1856), p. 99; cited in Aston, *England's Iconoclasts*, p. 83.

[18] *HMC*, Fourth Report, Manuscripts of the House of Lords (London, 1874), pp. 74, 80.

Uxbridge and the service book were burned, and 'Mr Harding gave us a worthy sermon.'[19]

Popular action of this kind obviously helped to arouse royalist feelings based on a revulsion for disorder. An anonymous author, writing in 1641 against 'the pulling down of communion tables by divers rash and misguided people', argued that 'God's word doth not allow or countenance mutinies, unlawful assemblies, or rebellions against Government, pulling the sword of justice out of the magistrate's hand, and using it, or rather abusing it, as we please.'[20] Similarly, members of the Long Parliament did not generally endorse spontaneous destruction of church images, and they pursued various official measures to abolish altars. In January 1641 the Commons ordered that commissions should be sent into the counties to demolish all altars and superstitious or idolatrous images, and Alderman Pennington introduced a bill with the same intent into the Commons on 5 February. Neither initiative was generally effective, and in September 1641 the Commons issued an order calling on churchwardens to destroy altars and other religious images. The response to this order was undoubtedly patchy, not least perhaps because it was issued on the authority of the Commons alone, a constitutional sticking-point which would later become a key element in the royalist attack on Parliament.[21] In 1643 the Commons appointed a committee for the destruction of monuments of superstition and idolatry, which was chaired by Sir Robert Harley, and which drew up the ordinance of August 1643, again aimed at the destruction of altars. Once more the response to this order was varied, and in 1645 the Commons ordered Harley's committee to ensure that this and a subsequent ordinance were being carried out. The combination of uncontrollable enthusiasm in some areas and refusal to comply with the ordinances in others further illustrates how divided people were over the issue of the altar.

The origins of this division can be traced to the early years of Charles I's reign and were closely associated with the royal family and the Court. The theatricality, the sensual seduction and apparent idolatry centred on the altar were nowhere more evident in England than in the chapel at Somerset House used by the Catholic Queen Henrietta Maria.

19 PRO SP16/491/119.

20 I. W., *Certain Affirmations in Defence of the Pulling Down of Communion Rails, by Divers Rash and Misguided People, Judiciously and Religiously Answered by a Gentleman of Worth* (London, 1641), p. 3.

21 For this constitutional point see Jacqueline Eales, *Puritans and Roundheads: the Harleys of Brampton Bryan and the Outbreak of the English Civil War* (Cambridge, 1990), pp. 130–5.

A much later account penned by Father Cyprien, one of the Queen's Capuchin friars, gives a detailed account of the first Mass held at the chapel on 10 December 1636, when elaborate machinery made by the French sculptor François Dieussart was employed 'to exhibit the holy sacrament and to give it a more majestic appearance. It represented in oval a paradise of glory, about forty feet in height.' The techniques employed by Dieussart were borrowed from contemporary masque staging, and

> Behind the altar was seen a paraclete, raised above seven ranges of clouds, in which were figures of archangels, of cherubim, of seraphim, to the number of two hundred, some adoring the holy sacrament, others singing and playing on all sorts of musical instruments, the whole painted and placed according to the rules of perspective . . . those who sung being in fact concealed and not seen by anybody; thus eye and ear found at the same time gratification in this contrivance of piety and skill.[22]

The chapel was to become a focus for religious protest in the capital, and in May 1640 the Southwark apprentices threatened to pull it down because it was a house of 'popery'.[23] Amerigo Salvetti, the Tuscan ambassador, recorded in his despatches that in 1643 a mob burnt all the vestments and pictures in the chapel, the most costly being a Rubens altarpiece, which they first smashed with halberds.[24] This assault represented the triumph of the war party in taking more drastic measures against religious images. It coincided with the nomination of Harley's committee at the end of March 1643, and was part of a concerted parliamentarian assault on the royal chapels and on images in 'any public or open place in or about the cities of London and Westminster'. The destruction which took place under the direction of Harley and his committee was seen as a direct attack on monarchy, and the royalist news book, *Mercurius Aulicus*, in describing the destruction of the altar and stained glass at the chapel royal at Whitehall noted that 'Kings and Queens, as well as apostles,

[22] T. Birch, *The Court and Times of Charles I*, 2 (London, 1849), pp. 311–13; see also Erica Veevers, *Images of Love and Religion: Queen Henrietta Maria and Court Entertainments* (Cambridge, 1989), pp. 165–8.

[23] PRO SP16/453/96. In November 1642 and again in the following March the House of Commons ordered that the 'monuments of idolatry' in the chapel should be demolished, *Commons Journals*, II, 843, 1001, III, 27.

[24] BL, MS Add. 27962 K, fol. 84r–v: I am grateful to Michelle Brown of the British Library Western Manuscripts Department for her assistance with this latter reference.

fathers, martyrs, confessors, are counted monuments of vanity and superstition.'[25]

From its inception the debate about the altar had been firmly linked to issues of authority and obedience to the Crown. In the public debates of the 1630s advocates of the altar thus interpreted obedience to the altar policy as a prerequisite for order in the secular and religious spheres. The centrality of obedience was clearly expressed in Charles I's summation during the St Gregory's case, which was published by Peter Heylyn in 1636. The order of the dean and chapter concerning St Gregory's had been challenged by five parishioners, who based their arguments on the claim that the Book of Common Prayer and the eighty-second canon of 1604 'do give permission to place the communion table, where it may stand with most fitness and convenience'. When the case came before the Privy Council, the King upheld the 'act of the said ordinarie' and

> was also pleased to observe that; that if those few parishioners might have their wills, the difference thereby from the foresaid cathedral mother church, by which all other churches depending thereon ought to be guided, would be the more notorious and give more subject of discourse and disputes that might be spared . . . likewise, for so much as concerning the liberty given by the said common book, or canon, for placing the communion table in any church or chapel with most convenience, that liberty is not so to be understood, as if it were ever left to the discretion of the parish, much less to the particular fancy of any humerous person, but to the judgment of the ordinary, to whose place and function it doth properly belong.[26]

The dire consequences of disobedience were eagerly described by Charles's supporters in the subsequent pamphleteering on the altar of the late 1630s. Peter Heylyn argued that

> should we all be so affected, as to demurre at the commands of our superiors, in matters of exterior order and publicke government, till we are satisfied in the grounds and reasons of their commandments; or should we fly of from our duty, at sight of every new devise, that is offered to us: we should soon find a speedie dissolution of Church and State.

[25] *Commons Journals*, III, 57, 63; *Mercurius Aulicus* (16–22 June 1644), p. 1040.
[26] Heylyn, *A Coal from the Altar*, pp. 64–6.

A year later John Pocklington attacked

> this ferocious and pregnant plebiscite, that what is by law, custom, prescription, or prerogative royal appointed, and settled, shall not be allowed, or practised by the men of some incorporation, or other, before it be maintained *rationibus cogentibus*. Let this principal be granted, behold what a spectacle I shall present to you withal.

As a consequence, said Pocklington, not only would the authority of the Church be overthrown, but also its theological foundations would be called into question and ultimately 'the power of Kings and Monarchs with their crowns and dignities, with their laws, ordinances and prerogatives be shaken, nay racketed up and down.' Such advocates of the altar argued that it had been used in the primitive Church and was endorsed by the Church Fathers, that railing the altar prevented the prophanation of the Lord's Table, and encouraged the congregation to regard it with 'reverence and respect'. Pocklington concluded that this was 'so holy and godly a purpose, and so fully comformable to the beauty and awful Majesty that the houses of God were in the primitive church.'[27]

The opponents of the altar tried to demonstrate that the altar had not been used in the early Church, but was a later accretion and they interpreted this policy as evidence of Catholic infiltration of the Church and State. In *A Quench-Coale*, published in 1637, William Prynne argued, 'Now all things are, except Latin service, prepared for the mass in many churches.'[28] Not only did the altar symbolically represent an alien theology, but the adornment of the altar was a further visual and iconographic reinforcement of links with Catholicism. Prynne also complained of 'altar clothes, tapers, basins and other Romish furniture' on the altar. Altar-hangings had a particularly dramatic effect, and individual items attracted specifically adverse comments, perhaps because their iconographic messages were more visible to the congregation than the images on smaller items of altar furniture, such as chalices or covered Bibles. At the start of the Long Parliament, William Voyle, a Shropshire curate, demanded that the communion table should not 'have a cloth or covering of any sort upon it hanging down within a foot & an half of the ground. (A fashion not liked for the gaudiness of it & because it helps to assemble an

[27] Heylyn, *A Coal from the Altar*, p. 2; J. Pocklington, *Altare Christianum: or, The Dead Vicar's Plea. Wherein the Vicar of Gr*[*antham*] *being dead, yet speaketh, and pleadeth out of Antiquity, against him that hath broken down his Altar* (London, 1637), pp. 148–9, 146.

[28] Prynne, *A Quench-Coal*, pp. 5, 70.

altar).'[29] The visual and iconographic impact of altar-hangings were considered by Bishop Williams's committee of divines in 1641, who noted the recent innovations 'in making canopies over the altar so-called with traverses and curtains on each side and before it', and 'in advancing crucifixes and images upon the para front, or altar cloth so called'.[30]

The fragile nature of embroidered textiles has in most cases robbed us of visual evidence of the deliberately provocative images which were being reintroduced in the 1630s, but in some cases descriptions of altar-hangings have survived, which serve to illustrate the sense of outrage and offence that they engendered. In 1644 a Kentish minister, Richard Culmer, described the altar in Canterbury Cathedral, 'dressed after the romish fashion with candlesticks and tapers etc, for which altar they have lately provided a most idolatrous costly GLORY-CLOTH or Back-Cloth.'

> That Glory [he continued] is the shame of their cathedral, is made of very rich embroidery of gold and silver, the name Jehovah on the top in Gold upon a cloth of silver, and below it a semicircle of gold, and from thence glorious rays and clouds, and gleams and points of rays, direct and waved, stream downwards upon the altar, as if Jehovah (God himself) were there present in glory, in that cathedral at the altar, and therefore to usher in the breaden God of Rome and idolatry.[31]

At the trial of Archbishop Laud in 1644 testimony was heard about the altar decoration in his private chapel at Lambeth Palace, where

> he had much superstitious Romish furniture never used in his predecessor's days, as namely, two great silver candlesticks, with tapers in them, besides basins and other silver vessels (with a costly common prayer book; standing on the altar, which as some say had a crucifix

[29] The Book of Common Prayer called for 'the table at the communion time' to have 'a fair white linen cloth upon it', while the canons of 1604 ordered that the communion table 'be covered, in time of divine service, with a carpet of silk or other decent stuff, thought meet by the ordinary of the place . . . and with a fair linen cloth at the time of ministration': Edward Cardwell, *Synodalia: A Collection of Articles of Religion, Canons and Proceedings of Convocations in the Province of Canterbury from the Year 1547 to the Year 1717*, I (Oxford, 1842), p. 293.

[30] Prynne, *A Quench-Coal*, p. 70; BL, MS Add. 70002, fol. 365v; *A Copy of the Proceedings of Some Worthy and Learned Divines, appointed by the Lords to meet at The Bishop of Lincoln's in Westminster Touching Innovations in the Doctrine and Discipline of the Church of England* (London, 1641), p. 4.

[31] R. Culmer, *Cathedral News from Canterbury: shewing, the Canterburian Cathedral to be in an Abbey-Like, Corrupt, and Rotten Condition* (London, 1644), pp. 2, 6.

> on the bosses) with the picture of Christ receiving his last supper with his disciples in a piece of Arras, hanging just behind the midst of the altar and a crucifix in the window directly over it.

The imagery of the Last Supper further emphasized the Eucharist as a font of grace. The Archbishop was also accused by Sir Henry Mildmay of introducing 'a rich large crucifix, embroidered with gold and silver, in a fair piece of Arras' over the altar in the royal chapel at Whitehall. According to Mildmay, 'This gross notorious innovation gave great scandal and general offence to many well-affected courtiers, who spake much against it and to himself in particular, who openly complained of it to the King, and spake to the Archbishop himself about it; yet it continued there sundry passion weeks.' In his defence the Archbishop asserted that the arras depicting the Last Supper 'was fit for that place and occasion', and that 'such images and representations were lawful, approved by all the Lutheran churches, yea by Master Calvin himself, for an historical use', and cited Calvin's *Institutes* as evidence of this. As for the hanging at Whitehall, Laud denied responsibility and said that Bishop Wren was dean of the chapel royal when the crucifix was set up.[32]

Similar, but obviously less lavish, hangings were also to be found in parish churches. In Hertfordshire John Mountford introduced a carpet on the altar bearing 'the Jesuit's badge' in his parish church at Anstie, and in Yelden, Bedfordshire, John Pocklington 'placed a cross in a cloth behind the altar, called the altar cross'. It was not only the clergy who promoted such decorations. At St Giles in the Fields 'the ornaments of the holy table, the silk curtains, carpet, covering, books and much plate' were all the 'pious gift' of Lady Alice Dudley, who also 'bestowed the screen'. They were intended for the 'decency of God's service and well accepted of by the parishioners'; thus the incumbent, Dr Haywood, 'had no reason to refute them'.[33] Amongst Lady Dudley's gifts were a 'rich green velvet cloth' for the back of the altar, with the letters 'IHS' embroidered in gold: 'very costly handsome rails, to guard the altar or Lord's table from profane abuses', and communion plate 'of all sorts in silver and gilt, for that sacred use, which is as large and rich as any in the city and suburbs.' Apart from

[32] W. Prynne, *Canterburies Doom* (London, 1646), pp. 62, 67–8, 466, 474, 463.

[33] *The Petition and Articles Exhibited in Parliament against John Pocklington Doctor in Divinity Parson of Yelden in Bedfordshire* (London, 1641), p. 1; *An Answer to a lawless Pamphlet entitled the Petition and Articles Exhibited in Parliament against Doctor Haywood, late Chaplain to the Bishop of Canterbury* (London, 1641), p. 15.

the plate and a bell, all of these ornaments at St Giles were sold during the Civil War when they were 'counted superstitious and popish'.[34]

It was the active role taken by the laity that made the altar policy such a vital issue in the process of polarization that ultimately led to civil war, for laymen were involved at parish level on both sides of the altar controversy in the 1630s. In Montgomery on Easter Day in 1637, for example, Richard Griffith of Sutton, a leading local Puritan gentleman and one of the bailiffs of the town, publicly refused to take Communion at the rails 'wherewith the communion table' was 'altarwise newly engirt'. Griffith, his daughter, and a servant kneeled at the 'usual place in the chancel' until Communion was over, and then Griffith informed the minister, Dr Coote, that he wished to receive Communion in 'the ancient usual place' and asked why Coote made him 'a gazing stock to the congregation'. The minister retaliated by accusing his antagonist of 'hardness of heart, pride and rebellion', but proceeded to administer Communion to the group.

The case was known locally, and an account of the dispute written by the curate of Montgomery is to be found in the private papers of Sir Robert Harley, of Herefordshire, who had long been regarded as one of the leading Godly gentlemen in the Welsh border areas, and who was to prove an active opponent of the altar policy during the course of the Long Parliament.[35] Harley's opposition to the altar fully illustrates the hostility that this policy had aroused and the determined efforts that were made in the 1640s to reverse it. In 1638 Harley, his rector, and schoolmaster were themselves under investigation for their Puritan practices at Brampton Bryan, where 'the communion table is not railed in there, nor in divers parishes thereabouts, furthermore the communion table is brought down out of the chancel into the body of the church (every communion day) by common and ordinary fellows.'[36]

At the start of the Long Parliament Harley took the initiative in proposing that the communion table in St Margaret's parish church at Westminster should be removed from the east end and replaced in the chancel; his demand was supported by Sir John Wray and by Denzil Holles.[37] In his capacity as senior knight for Herefordshire, Harley also

[34] R. Boreman, *A Mirror of Christianity and a Miracle of Charity, or a True and Exact Narrative of the Life and Death of the most Virtuous Lady, Alice Duchess Dudley* (London, 1669), pp. 22–4.

[35] BL MS Add. 70002, fol. 138r; *Commons Journals*, III, 57. For Harley, see Eales, *Puritans and Roundheads*, *passim*.

[36] PRO SP16/381/92.

[37] W. Notestein, ed., *The Journal of Sir Simonds D'Ewes From the Beginning of the Long Parliament to the Opening of the Trial of the Earl of Strafford* (New Haven, 1923), pp. 43, 46.

received numerous complaints about altars from individuals throughout the Welsh border areas and the west Midlands. One of the most detailed of these is the case of Leominster, in Herefordshire, which again illustrates the involvement of the laity at parish level, although in this instance Wallop Brabazon, a local JP and churchwarden, was acting in defence of the altar. Furthermore, in Leominster the altar policy reinforced religious conflict which was already present in the town, and which would help to divide local opinions at the outbreak of the Civil War. In December 1640 John Tombes, vicar of Leominster, complained to Harley about the actions of Brabazon, who in 1635 in his capacity as churchwarden had turned the communion table at Leominster altar-wise. Behind this conflict lay two totally opposite religious and cultural tempers. Tombes's letter itemized a series of charges against Brabazon, who had refused to pay tithes, sending the money instead directly to the bishop, had forced an organist on the parish at the charge of £10 per annum, and in his capacity as a justice had licensed an alehouse and a bowling alley, 'whereby', alleged Tombes, 'the people of this town are much corrupted in their manners.' Brabazon also kept company with excommunicated papists and himself 'comes not to the communion above once a year'. A petition drawn up at about the same time amplified these points and added that Brabazon had also 'been a forward man in urging the payment of the ship money'.[38]

Brabazon's support for the railed altar may have originated partly from a desire to oppose Tombes, but he may also have seen his actions more positively, as an expression of obedience. The desire to conform was strong and explains why Puritan nonconformity created such powerful tensions in early seventeenth-century society, and also why there was support for and acceptance of the altar policy in some parishes. The hostility between Brabazon and Tombes rumbled on for another two years. In May 1641 Tombes again wrote to Harley and complained that in Easter week Brabazon 'as a man enraged' had accused Tombes of 'grievous crimes for turning the communion table from the altar situation, for disusing the ceremonies, and threatening me for so doing'. Brabazon had some support in the local community, and Tombes observed that 'as the cathedral men seek to sting me, so the common people exclaim much against me, which moves me little.' It comes as little surprise to learn that in 1642 Tombes was an ardent supporter of Parliament, whilst his old antagonist, Brabazon, was an active Royalist.[39]

[38] BL, MS Add. 70002, fol. 344r; MS Add. 70086/73.

The railed altar and the history of its destruction thus stand at the centre of a debate which was not purely aesthetic or religious in scope, but which also held wider political implications. Earlier episodes of iconoclasm in the Tudor period had been aimed at surviving Catholic images, but the later assault of the 1640s was qualitatively different in that it was geared to eliminating church decorations that had been introduced by the current, ostensibly Protestant, regime.[40] Historians have, however, interpreted the iconoclasm of the 1640s as a throw-back to the early days of the Reformation, as an interesting cultural phenomenon, triggered primarily as a response to the Arminian stress on church ornamentation and ceremonial in the previous decade, which was ultimately peripheral to the main issues at stake between Crown and Parliament.[41] In fact, the altar- and image-breaking of this later period was specifically linked to a broad spectrum of secular and religious tensions that had intensified under the rule of Charles I. Conflict over the altar centred on what were perceived to be correct forms of liturgy, ritual, and church decoration, but it also dovetailed with arguments about obedience to the Crown. The iconoclasm of the Civil War years was indeed the product of a century of teaching against images, yet it was also and significantly, in terms of Civil War studies, the culmination of an ideological debate which had been sharply defined during the reign of Charles I and which, for contemporaries, demonstrated the indissoluble links between the maintenance of true religion and the exercise of power within the State.

Hollins College, London

---

39 BL, MS Add. 70003, fol. 99r.

40 The accusation that the secular and religious authorities in England had encouraged idolatry was particularly inflammatory, for its logical end lay in the tenets of resistance theory, see C. Dow, *Innovations Unjustly Charged Upon the Present Church and State or an Answer to the most Material Passages of a Libellous Pamphlet made by Mr Henry Burton, and Entitled An Apology of an Appeal etc.* (London, 1637), pp. 140–1, 191. One of the most famous resistance tracts, John Ponet's *Treatise of Politique Power*, first published in 1556, and which argued forcefully for the overthrow of idolatrous rulers, was reprinted in 1642: John Ponet, *A Short Treatise of Politique Power; and of the true Obedience which Subjects owe Kings, and other Civil Governors*, 1st edn (Strasbourg, 1556), repr. (London, 1642). I am grateful to Johann Somerville for his help with this reference.

41 See, for example, Aston, *England's Iconoclasts*, p. 93.

BAROQUE IN THE HYMN-BOOK

by DONALD DAVIE

'BAROQUE' is a word that has never yet been thoroughly acclimatized among us. To most English-speakers, I think, the word still smacks of something pretentious and affected—if not, indeed, of special pleading. At best it denotes a category that we may learn about and agree to trust so long as we are dutiful tourists in Italy or perhaps Poland, which we can thankfully discard when we get back to native soil.

To this, however, there is at least one notable exception: amateurs and historians of English architecture long ago domesticated 'baroque' to designate, if not Christopher Wren's St Paul's, certainly Seaton Damerel, Blenheim, Castle Howard—the great country seats designed by Sir John Vanbrugh. I take it that the only firm and reputable sense for 'baroque' in English relates it to these buildings, or to a few others of their kind; hence, that those of us who talk of 'baroque' in other contexts are, whether we know it or not, exploring an analogy that we claim to find between our experience of architecture and our experience in other areas. If this is so, none of us has been so comfortable with the arrangement as our musicologists, among whom 'baroque' has found a home not much less comfortable than it has with historians of architecture. Indeed, if I were in this paper to explore the *music* of the English congregational hymn, I should probably go unchallenged if I discovered the musical baroque in the figured and elaborate tunes, often derived from Purcell or Handel, that the Wesley brothers obliged their choirs to master. However, my more contestable and presumptuous purpose is to discover 'the baroque' in the *language* of certain hymns, irrespective of the music they were sung to.

This takes me into the territory of the literary historians, among whom, I soon find, 'baroque' is a house-guest altogether less welcome than among historians of architecture or of music. For instance, in *A Dictionary of Modern Critical Terms*, wherein literary criticism clearly shoulders ahead of criticism of any other art, we read of 'baroque' that it is:

> a term denoting a distinctive style deeply characteristic of the seventeenth century, long since firmly established for critics of art and

> music, whose usefulness for literary critics must still be regarded as problematic and controversial.[1]

Our authority here is Michael Hollington, who writes on 'the baroque' under the direction of his general editor, Roger Fowler. Art historians, Hollington tells us, 'generally now agree to regard the Baroque as the third Renaissance style, setting in around 1600, with its centre in Rome and its quintessential representative in Bernini, and with important Catholic and post-tridentine tendencies'; whereas 'Musicologists associate the Baroque with the advent of Monteverdi, the birth of operatic recitative and the *concertante* style, and with figured bass.'[2] The carry-over of this concept into the history of poetry is, Hollington warns us again, fraught with difficulty: John Donne's poetry, for instance, though it has been called 'baroque', should more properly be called 'mannerist'—Mannerism being a mode or style lately isolated by art historians to denote what happened between High Renaissance and Baroque, or between Michelangelo and Bernini. Moreover, there is current, it seems, an expression, 'Contemporary Baroque', which has been used to herd under one umbrella such contemporary story-tellers as John Barth, Irish Murdoch, and Günther Grass. Michael Hollington will have none of this: 'The best Baroque art—the work of Bernini, Rembrandt, Milton, Monteverdi and Bach—is of a different order of intensity and coherent grandeur altogether, and one should not readily assume its recurrence.'[3] With that adoption of Milton into the company of Bernini and Rembrandt, Monteverdi and Bach, Hollington nevertheless seems to have conceded, despite his misgivings, that the term 'baroque' may be, and perhaps must be, applied to some poetry in English. And that is the window of opportunity that I must try to exploit.

Milton, of course, figures in our hymn-books, or in some of them. Of his nineteen versions of various psalms,[4] as many as seven have been in habitual use, though mostly by Unitarians. It is hard to see what in any of these can be called, or needs to be called, 'baroque'. A quite different case is Milton's 'Hymn on the Morning of Christ's Nativity', which may indeed be called, so far as I understand the matter, a grand baroque composition. However, out of this elaborate structure only a few brief

[1] Michael Hollington, 'The Baroque', in Roger Fowler, ed., *A Dictionary of Modern Critical Terms*, rev. edn (London, 1978), p. 20.

[2] Ibid., p. 21.

[3] Ibid., p. 22.

[4] John Milton, *Psalms in English and Latin* (London, 1673).

centos have come into common congregational use; notably, from the introductory four stanzas, the nativity hymn: 'This is the month, and this the happy morn.' Milton's poem as a whole isn't for congregational use; it is one of those 'Hymns to the Gods' that were, along with encomia on virtuous men, reluctantly approved by suspicious ancient pagans like Plato. That kind of hymn, still quite vigorously alive among us as a poetic genre, has nothing in common with the congregational hymn which, itself a poetic genre, can be understood and assessed only in the context of communal worship.

Even more marginal to our hymnology are two greatly gifted poets whose lives overlapped with Milton's. One is Richard Crashaw (?1613–49). Crashaw's importance is obvious if we remember Hollington's remark that the baroque of Bernini had 'important Catholic and post-tridentine tendencies.' Other scholars have pushed this perception so far as to claim that the *baroque* came into being deliberately as the propaganda arm, through the arts, of the Counter-Reformation. And the papist Crashaw is by common consent the greatest, if not quite the only, voice of the Counter-Reformation in our poetry. However, we read in John Julian's magisterial *Dictionary of Hymnology* that Crashaw's hymns 'belong more to the hymns of Latin origin, and are useless in their present shape.'[5] That was a hundred years ago, and in liturgical as in other matters we have changed our minds about what is useless and what isn't. However, I'm not aware that Romanists have been at pains to adapt Crashaw's hymns to congregational use. And if not, they may have been well advised. So the case of George Herbert suggests. Of Herbert's poems, the following appear, drastically altered, in British and American hymn-books: 'Let all the world in every corner sing'; 'My stock lies dead, and no increase'; 'Throw away thy rod'; 'Sweet day, so cool, so calm'; and 'Teach me, my God, and King'. This may seem a respectable tally until we recall that Herbert's *The Temple* (1633)[6] has been recognized, through generation after generation (and by unbelievers as well as believers), as the most brilliant and affecting collection of devotional lyrics in the language. In the light of that consensus we must surely be struck by how stubbornly Herbert's texts have resisted being adapted for congregational use, even when the would-be adapter was as dogged and intelligent as John Wesley. The same is true of other seventeenth-century masters like Henry Vaughan and Robert Herrick, some of whose verses have a ghostly

[5] John Julian, *Dictionary of Hymnology* (London, 1892), p. 348.
[6] George Herbert, *The Temple* (Cambridge, 1633).

presence, as it were, in the margins of our hymn-books. The lesson to be drawn from all these cases is, I suggest, that the gulf between the devotional lyric and the congregational hymn yawns very wide. They are two distinct genres; and the difference between them is neither arbitrary nor pedantic. Nowadays, as at any date in the past, a person may speak in poetry either for his or her unrepeatable idiosyncrasy, or else for what he or she has in common with humankind. Theologically, what he or she can share with others (not statistically nor demographically but *really*) must count for more than what cannot be thus shared. Of course, the shareable common ground may at times shrink to the point in common estimation where only a courageously declared idiosyncrasy—George Herbert's or Gerard Manley Hopkins's—can widen it again. But in principle the devotional lyric and the congregational hymn differ irreconcilably; and the poet who prescribed the ground-rules for the latter genre was the Nonconformist minister Isaac Watts (1674–1748), who accordingly is the hero of this discourse, as of others on related topics that I have delivered in recent years.

No hymn by Watts—not even 'Our God, our help in ages past' —is better known or more loved than 'When I survey the wondrous Cross':

When I survey the wondrous cross
On which the Prince of glory dy'd,
My richest gain I count but loss,
And pour contempt on all my pride.

Forbid it, Lord, that I should boast,
Save in the death of Christ, my God:
—All the vain things that charm me most
I sacrifice them to his blood.

See from his head, his hands, his feet,
Sorrow and love flow mingled down!
Did e'er such love and sorrow meet
Or thorns compose so rich a crown!

His dying crimson, like a robe,
Spreads o'er his body on the tree;
—Then am I dead to all the globe,
And all the globe is dead to me.

Were the whole realm of nature mine,
That were a present far too small;
Love so amazing, so divine,
Demands my soul, my life, my all.[7]

The word is 'survey'; not 'behold' nor 'discern', not 'observe' nor 'perceive'. 'Survey' is the word also at the start of Johnson's *Vanity of Human Wishes* (1749):

Let Observation with extensive view
Survey mankind from China to Peru . . .[8]

The distrustful wag who translated this as 'Let observation with extensive observation observe' had not allowed for the nicety of Johnson the lexicographer. And in Watts's usage, too, the rightness of 'survey' can be appreciated only if we consult the dictionary. The *Oxford English Dictionary* gives under 'survey':

> To look at from, or as from, a height or commanding position; to take a broad, general, or comprehensive view of; to view or examine in its whole extent. *b*, *fig.* To take a comprehensive mental view of; to consider or contemplate as a whole.

Ever since George Whitefield in 1757 the fourth stanza has habitually been omitted, and the reason for that seems to have everything to do with 'survey' understood too loosely.

For one sees the point of the excision well enough: Watts's 'crimson . . . robe' quite flagrantly refuses to consider the pus and the sweat, the scab and the coagulation and the stink; not to speak of the thronging multitude, its jeerings and gawkings, its horse-laughs or worse. But 'survey' has signalled in advance that these actualities will be ignored: the Crucifixion is to be looked at 'from, or as from, a height or commanding position', from which the sweat cannot be smelt, the horse-laughs cannot be heard.

So it is also in the Scripture that Watts is working from: 'But God forbid that I should glory, save in the Crosse of our Lord Jesus Christ, by

[7] *The Psalms, Hymns and Spiritual Songs of the Rev. Isaac Watts, D.D.* (Boston, 1853), p. 478.
[8] Samuel Johnson, *The Vanity of Human Wishes* (London, 1749), lines 1, 2.

whom the world is crucified unto me, and I unto the world.'[9] Paul cannot be expostulating to the back-sliding Galatians that he 'glories in' the stink and the scab and the horse-laughs; the outlandish English construction, 'crucified unto' (not 'for' nor 'by', but 'unto') could doubtless be explained to us by a student of Pauline Greek. Lacking such help, we can only suppose that by Paul, as by Watts keeping the faith centuries later, the Crucifixion is seen, is 'surveyed', across a vast aesthetic and conceptual distance. A poetics that distrusts, and indeed cannot explain, aesthetic distance falls in with an evangelical piety that distrusts and cannot explain conceptual distance. Both of them—the poetics and the piety—want to 'rub our noses in it'; whereas both Paul and Watts are determined we shall do no such thing. A poetics of 'immediacy' cannot, any more than a theology of 'immediacy', find room for either of them.

To press this home we can consider an admirable treatment of the Crucifixion by a modern poet—W. H. Auden's in 'The Shield of Achilles':

> Barbed wire enclosed an arbitrary spot
>   Where bored officials lounged (one cracked a joke)
> And sentries sweated, for the day was hot:
>   A crowd of ordinary decent folk
>   Watched from without and neither moved nor spoke
> As three pale figures were led forth and bound
> To three posts driven upright in the ground.
>
> The mass and majesty of this world, all
>   That carries weight and always weighs the same
> Lay in the hands of others; they were small
>   And could not hope for help and no help came:
>   What their foes liked to do was done, their shame
> Was all the worst could wish; they lost their pride
> And died as men before their bodies died.[10]

Auden's treatment of the Crucifixion is sharp and moving. It may even be thought by some readers superior to Watts's treatment. But let no one suppose that it is more *immediate*. If recent literary theory, so largely frivolous and self-promoting, has been useful in any way at all, it has been by underlining the fact, never denied but constantly evaded, that nothing comes to us through art except as *mediated* through art; that 'the imme-

[9] Gal. 6. 14.

[10] W. H. Auden, 'The Shield of Achilles' in *Collected Poems*, ed. E. Mendelson (London, 1976), p. 454.

diate' is accordingly in art a will-o'-the-wisp, an *ignis fatuus* that recedes before us however far we go. In art, whether verbal or non-verbal, everything is mediated—through the medium that is that art's special conveyance. The nearer art comes to 'the particulars', the more it is prey to the contingent, including the historically contingent. Thus Auden's poem of 1952 is already dated. What we have learned since then of the attitude of a television public towards atrocities suggests that 'neither moved nor spoke' is quite inaccurate; the image we need, on the contrary, is of motor cars crawling bumper to bumper through a tail-back of many miles, chivvied indeed by traffic police, but leniently because they are impelled by what is thought to be 'natural curiosity', and in any case each car-full represents a 'family outing'. Accordingly Auden's treatment of the Crucifixion is seen to be as stylized, as far from immediate, as Watts's. And indeed Auden, alluding rather plainly to politically enforced 'judicial murders' of the 1930s and 1940s, seems to have recognized this and provided for it.

Yet Watts's poem is still disconcerting. For the stanza that we suppress seems strikingly and quite uncharacteristically disjointed. What, after all, is the point in time that is defined by 'Then', at the start of its third line? The only way to make sense of it is to relate it back—in defiance of all the punctuation of intervening verses—to the first word of the poem, 'When'. On this showing, it is only when the survey is completed—when it is, as it must aim to be, comprehensive—that we can be (temporarily, no doubt) 'dead to all the globe', 'crucified . . . unto the world'.

Very interesting from this point of view is the word 'compose' in line 12: 'Or thorns compose so rich a crown'. In Watts's day 'composure' and 'composition' lay very close together; Philip Doddridge spoke of his hymns as his 'composures'. And for us, too, the common root must be allowed its force. We may well be shocked at the notion that any one should regard the Crucifixion composedly, with composure; yet the dictionary (once again) compels us to recognize that the attainment of such composure is one necessary aspect of making a satisfactory artistic composition that has the Crucifixion for its subject. What the dictionary inescapably documents as the attitude of our ancestors on this excruciating topic is borne out by testimonies and speculations in modern aesthetics which maintain, with impressive logic, that the atrociousness of such a subject (the event supposedly recorded) is always, *and must be*, dissolved away entirely into the delicious felicities of the medium—into Annibale Carracci's colours and contours and brush-strokes, into Watts's choice diction, his cadences, his rhymes. This perception is the source of the not uncommon protestation that modern atrocities signalled by names like Auschwitz must be declared off limits to artists—since to regard Auschwitz with composure is humanly inexcusable. Yet artists continue trying to comprehend Auschwitz in their art, just as they continue trying to comprehend that prototype (for Christians) of all atrocities, the Crucifixion of God made man. If we are honest with ourselves, it is precisely the atrociousness that grips us and spellbinds us—a less atrocious subject would not hold our attention so rapt.

If we agree to that, we are faced with a range of alternatives, none appealing, some appalling. One of the least appealing explanations is that we exult in art, we triumph in it vicariously, when we see it making beauty out of what is most brutal and squalid. It would be rash to deny that there are—and not just in modern times—artists and connoisseurs of whom this is a true account. The trouble with it is, obviously, that it gives the aesthete and even the artist a vested interest in the brutal and the perverted; in preserving and perpetuating them, since they present our arts with their most challenging occasions. A less ignominious explanation—so it will seem to some, though by no means to all—is that we value these atrocious occasions for the challenge they pose not to our sensibility but to our understanding, not to our art-making but to our conceptualizing. To *understand* these occasions, and even the necessity of them, is different from surmounting and domesticating them. An artist like Watts—and there were relatively many of them in his era, as we shall see—can do the second thing, can seem to 'prettify'; but he can also do the first thing, simultaneously and by the same means. When that happens, art is seen to be, along with much else, an *intellectual* achievement. And that is what we can see Watts achieving; but only if we fly in the face of many generations, and insist on restoring to the poem its fourth stanza.

There remains the problem of the disjointedness, not to say the grammatical disorder. For us to relate the 'Then' of the fifteenth line back to the 'When' of the first, we have to consider most of the intervening lines as a distraught parenthesis. And Watts's practice elsewhere (he, the logician!) gives us no warrant for such a manœuvre. He of all poets is least likely to have embraced the modern heresy of 'imitative form', according to which the poet expresses distraction (his being distraught) by writing distractedly.

The best solution comes from considering more closely his scriptural source. Paul's Epistle to the Galatians is one of the most impassioned and personal texts in the New Testament. For Galatians 6. 11 *The New Oxford Annotated Bible* gives: 'See with what large letters I am writing to you with my own hand.' And the editors comment that this is 'bitterly satirical'.[11] Certainly it seems that in this letter Paul is bitter; wounded and disappointed, and fighting back. So 'God forbid that I should glory, save in the Crosse of our Lord Jesus Christ' is not a pious commonplace, but fighting talk, from one with his back to the wall. Watts expects us, or some of us, to bring that scriptural context to bear—so as to hear in his asseveration not imperturbable assurance but, on the contrary, desperation. What else, indeed, what but desperation, could have provoked from him those exclamatory lines that subsequent generations have found indigestible?

His dying crimson, like a robe,
Spreads o'er his body on the tree;
—Then am I dead to all the globe,
And all the globe is dead to me.

The 'tree' is as remote from the pegged together baulks of timber as 'dying crimson, like a robe' is from the blood coagulated or trickling. Both usages, if we attend to them, confirm that the purpose of the verses, their desperate endeavour, is to raise the atrocious occurrence to the level of a concept, a level on which it can be comprehended, with hard-won composure. After all it is only 'in the abstract' that the Cross (any cross) can be conceived of as a 'tree'. Yet the antiquity of the trope suggests that such abstracting, such conceptualizing, was familiar and sought after through many centuries before Isaac Watts. And yet this is an enterprise so alien, if not to modern poetry, then to commentators on that poetry, that for these verses to have survived at all into modern memory, however imperfectly, seems not much short of miraculous.

'Aesthetic distance' is a formulation that was sufficiently bandied about, not many years ago. But 'conceptual distance' is something newfangled, which cannot be justified by established usage. And indeed it is only an awkward device for obviating or postponing the one right word: 'idealize'. Watts *idealizes* the Crucifixion, not in the sense that he prettifies it or denies its monstrousness, but in the sense, etymologically correct, that he raises the monstrosity to the level of *idea*. As we have seen, he signals that such is his intention when he announces that he 'surveys' the Cross, not beholds it in his imagination, still less vicariously experiences it. Such idealizing, in that strict sense, was common in his generation and

[11] *The New Oxford Annotated Bible*, ed. H. G. May and B. M. Matzger (Oxford, 1962, 1973), p. 1415.

through several before him. Annibale Carracci of Bologna (1560–1609) painted St Lucy presenting her eyes to the Blessed Virgin; and in his painting the objects that St Lucy proffers on a salver are as far from blood-bespattered blobs of jelly as Watts's 'crimson robe' is from the actuality of what Jesus looked like as he hung on the Cross.[12] The trouble that we have in making this connection derives from our preconception that the *baroque*, a vehicle of the Roman Counter-Reformation, could not have been available to an heir of Cromwellian Puritanism like Watts. But the evidence to the contrary is there, in Watts's poems; and if one looks for external evidence, it's to be found in the documented fact of Watts's indebtedness to 'the Christian Horace', the Polish Jesuit writing in Latin, Matthew Casimire Sarbiewski (1595–1640). Odd as it must seem, the idealizing and yet sensuously saturated art of the Counter-Reformation found one of its finest expressions in English in a sacred poem by a Nonconformist pastor.

In its disjointedness, whether artfully intended or (more probably, we may think) forced on the poet by the ardour of his meditations, 'When I survey the wondrous cross' seems to stand alone. If this poem is baroque, the greater number of Watts's hymns may be called 'Palladian'. This is a term borrowed from the history of architecture, and reasonably so, for architecture is the only one of the arts in which, for the English, the term 'baroque' can go unquestioned. The difference, in the English architecture of Watts's lifetime, between the baroque of Sir John Vanbrugh and the Palladianism of Lord Burlington, uncovers a tension within and beneath what literary history too indifferently and equably recognizes as 'Augustan'. If 'When I survey . . .' is on its small scale a literary analogue to Vanbrugh's Castle Howard (1699–1726), more of Watts's hymns correspond to William Kent's Chiswick House for Burlington, built (*c.*1725) to the specifications of Andrea Palladio in his *Quattro Libri dell' Architettura* (1570). The difference is between an art of calculated disproportion and even disjunction, and an art which eschews such devices as too sensational.

Without being fanciful, 'Palladian' is what we may call, for instance, a much less exciting yet estimable treatment of the Crucifixion, in *Hymns and Spiritual Songs*:

12 Since the legend of St Lucy rather obviously derives from a pun on her name (Lucy—*lux*—light), Carracci's picture, like other compositions on the same theme, can be seen as controverting in advance the vaunts to be made by, and on behalf of, 'the Enlightenment'.

Deceiv'd by subtle snares of hell,
Adam, our head, our father, fell!
When Satan, in the serpent hid,
Propos'd the fruit that God forbid.

Death was the threat'ning; death began
To take possession of the man;
His unborn race receiv'd the wound,
And heavy curses smote the ground.

But Satan found a worse reward;
Thus saith the vengeance of the Lord,
'Let everlasting hatred be
Betwixt the woman's Seed and thee.

The woman's Seed shall be my Son;
He shall destroy what thou hast done:—
Shall break thy head, and only feel
Thy malice raging at his heel.'

He spake—and bade four thousand years
Roll on; at length his Son appears:
Angels with joy descend to earth,
And sing the young Redeemer's birth.

Lo, by the sons of hell he dies;
But, as he hung 'twixt earth and skies,
He gave their prince a fatal blow,
And triumph'd o'er the powers below.[13]

This is a narrative poem. And since in Palladian aesthetics proportion is very nearly all in all, it is worth noting what the proportion is in Watts's narrative between the Old Testament and the New. He gives four stanzas to the Old Testament, two to the New. This is plainly at odds with the account of Christian faith thrown out by a modern commentator: 'There's the high line, the religious line which goes from the birth of Christ to the hypothetical return of that same Christ, with the time-space in between these events seen as a vale of tears, a testing period.'[14] Watts sees the birth of Christ not as the beginning of the Christian narrative but as its culmination, in a real sense its end. Thus when the modern commentator declares, 'This line is still a locus of belief, but no longer a locus

[13] *Psalms, Hymns and Spiritual Songs*, p. 107.

[14] Kenneth White, 'Notes from an Outpost', *London Review of Books*, 6 July 1989.

of live thought', we may agree with him, observing, however, that the belief in question is certainly not Christian.

An incidental felicity in these lines is what, in lines 15–16, Watts makes of what seems incurably primitive in Genesis 3. 15, where God, cursing the serpent, ordains: 'And I will put enmitie between thee and the woman, and between thy seed and her seed: it shal bruise thy head, and thou shalt bruise his heele.' Watts's 'Thy malice raging at his heel' elucidates, though not conclusively yet plausibly, what is meant by the licence given to the serpent to 'bruise'. (A snake in the grass, a venomous attack, a bruising encounter—primitive or not, the fable is now sunk to a level in our language and imagination too deep to be rooted out.) However, what makes this poem memorable is its last quatrain. The fatal blow that the dying Christ gives to Satan is metaphysical, obviously; and there is a metaphysical sense in which the God-man in his death throes (though earlier also) is 'hung 'twixt earth and skies'; but what vividly clinches the stanza and the whole poem is that, as seen from ground-level, the figure on the Cross is *physically* a hanging silhouette against the sky. That touch of physicality in what has been a metaphysical drama strikes home very powerfully. But there is nothing baroque about it. The touch comes just where a rationally-proportioned art would prescribe—as the climax, even (as in a good joke) 'the pay-off'. And the atrociousness is nearer being acknowledged in 'his dying crimson, like a robe' than in 'hung 'twixt earth and skies'. (Certainly the first locution is the more decorative. But what it decorates is, and is offered as, monstrous. English speakers have to learn from Italian, Iberian, and Latin-American art that 'decorative' need not mean 'unfeeling'.)

Often Watts's Palladianism served him much less well. In another Crucifixion hymn, 'Infinite grief! amazing woe!' we read:

> Oh, the sharp pangs of smarting pain
>   My dear Redeemer bore,
> When knotty whips, and ragged thorns
>   His sacred body tore!
>
> But knotty whips and ragged thorns
>   In vain do I excuse,
> In vain I blame the Roman bands,
>   And the more spiteful Jews.
>
> 'Twere you, my sins, my cruel sins,
>   His chief tormentors were;
> Each of my crimes became a nail,
>   And unbelief the spear.[15]

Leaving aside the prejudice against Jews (who are, after all, no sooner accused than they are exonerated), we surely and rightly feel rebellious at the all too elegant turn and re-turn on 'knotty whips and ragged thorns'. It is not any allegiance to an anachronistic and in any case untenable aesthetic of 'immediacy' that makes us protest: 'Has he ever imagined what it is like to be whipped? And if what a whiplash does is called a smart, must there not be another word for what is painfully done by thorns bound round the temples?' The neatness of the return on 'knotty whips and ragged thorns' is bought at too steep a price. It is true that self-advertising elegance of this sort is valued differently in different ages; that Watts's age valued it probably too highly, as our period almost certainly rates it too low. But in any age there has to be a point at which order, harmony, composure are bought too dearly at the expense of fellow-feeling with torment and suffering. Watts, we may well think, too often did not accurately estimate the price that he was paying. 'When I survey the wondrous cross' represents one moment when he knew the price that was asked of him, and refused to pay it. By refusing that bargain he moved outside the orbit of contemporaries like John Byrom or Joseph Addison.

'Baroque' has been invoked to vindicate other usages in English eighteenth-century hymnody. Thus Robert Brittain, admirable pioneer in appreciating the hymns of Christopher Smart (certainly congregational in intent, though never sung by any congregation), decided forty years ago that 'His art is the art of the baroque . . .'. I believe, on the contrary, and think I can show, that Smart's art is quite precisely rococo—an artistic mode distinct from the baroque though related to it, which was practised in the England of the 1750s in circles that Smart can be shown to have frequented. More challenging, and stretching still further that seventeenth-century context which Michael Hollington insists on, is Vincent Newey's finding the baroque in an untypical Olney hymn by William Cowper in the 1780s:

> There is a fountain filled with blood
>   Drawn from Emmanuel's veins;
> And sinners, plunged beneath that flood,
>   Lose all their guilty stains.
>
> The dying thief rejoiced to see
>   That fountain in his day;
> And there have I, as vile as he.
>   Washed all my sins away.

---

[15] *Psalms, Hymns and Spiritual Songs*, II, p. 95.

Dear dying Lamb, thy precious blood
  Shall never lose its power,
Till all the ransomed church of God
  Be saved, to sin no more.

E'er since, by faith, I saw the stream
  Thy flowing wounds supply,
Redeeming love has been my theme,
  And shall be till I die . . .[16]

Though I admire Newey's bold defence of this as 'a fine hymn—in an idiom that is alien to us',[17] I cannot accept that in this case the alien idiom is *baroque*. We must beware, surely, of finding the baroque wherever we come across blood-boltered imagery. There may be ways of saving evangelical hymns like this from the charge of 'morbidity', but *baroque* I think is not a way of doing so. For Cowper's invocation of the saving and cleansing blood is surely quite different from, and much less controlled than, Watts's use of the same trope.

Accordingly, though I maintain that the baroque was briefly domesticated by the English imagination, and that that domestication is recorded in our hymn-books, what in saying so I try to recall from history is indeed a very brief chapter in the development of the English religious as well as poetic sensibility. It isn't true that the English sensibility recoiled from the baroque always, and refused to entertain it; it was entertained right enough, but only for a few years. To think so is after all to bring our literary history into line with the history of our architecture, where Vanbrugh's baroque had only a brief flowering before being overtaken and quenched by the more congenial Palladianism of Lord Burlington. In the work and life of Isaac Watts we see both the flowering and the quenching. And that is only one of the ways in which Watts, along with the hymn-books that he pioneered and made for a time a vehicle of serious poetic endeavour (by Charles Wesley, Smart, John Newton, Cowper), registers the movements of European consciousness more accurately than a poet of genius like Pope, who just because of his genius was unassimilable and idiosyncratic.

[16] William Cowper, *Political Works*, ed. W. Benham. The Globe Edition (London and New York, 1889), p. 28.

[17] Vincent Newey, *Cowper's Poetry. A Critical Study and Reassessment* (Liverpool, 1982), p. 296.

ART AND SCIENCE: OR BACH AS AN EXPOSITOR OF THE BIBLE

by W. R. WARD

FOR a long time before dramatic recent events it has been clear that the German Democratic Republic has been in the position, embarrassing to a Marxist system, of having nothing generally marketable left except (to use the jargon) 'superstructure'. The Luther celebrations conveniently bolstered the implicit claim of the GDR to embody Saxony's long-delayed revenge upon Prussia; still more conveniently, they paid handsomely. Even the Francke celebrations probably paid their way, ruinous though his Orphan House has been allowed to become. When I was in Halle, a hard-pressed government had removed the statue of Handel (originally paid for in part by English subscriptions) for head-to-foot embellishment in gold leaf, and a Handel Festival office in the town was manned throughout the year. Bach is still more crucial, both to the republic's need to pay its way and to the competition with the Federal Republic for the possession of the national tradition. There is no counterpart in Britain to the strength of the Passion-music tradition in East Germany. The celebrations which reach their peak in Easter Week at St Thomas's, Leipzig, are like a cross between Wembley and Wimbledon here, the difference being that the black market in tickets is organized by the State for its own benefit. If Bach research in East Germany, based either on musicology or the Church, has remained an industry of overwhelming amplitude and technical complexity, the State has had its own Bach-research collective located in Leipzig, dedicated among other things to establishing the relation between Bach and the Enlightenment, that first chapter in the Marxist history of human liberation. Now that a good proportion of the population of the GDR seems bent on liberation by leaving the republic or sinking it, the moment seems ripe to take note for non-specialist readers of some of what has been achieved there in recent years.

The old image of Bach as the Fifth Evangelist has been effectively undermined by the musicologists and is not, I think, to be restored by the enormous effort put in over the years by the bibliographers (one notable one being English)[1] on what are called Bach's 'Spiritual Books' or

[1] Robin A. Leaver, *Bachs theologische Bibliothek. Eine kritische Bibliographie* (Neuhausen and Stuttgart, 1983).

'theological library'. A word is in order on each of these points. Bach's career is only to be understood in the light of his descent from an old musical family in the technical sense of that word. His forbears were town-pipers, professional fiddlers, musicians to councils and courts, who pursued their trade as artisans and were appropriately unionized in guilds. The organists, too, emerged from these trades, and were distinct from the academically trained *Kantors* (or precentors) who studied music as a science in a liberal arts course at the university, obtained the qualification to teach in Latin schools, and could unite school and church service. This distinction was beginning to disappear as organists rose in status with the increased significance of instrumental music, and the rise of spiritual recitals from which the cantata developed. Eventually the distinction between *Kantor* and organist disappeared, but although it was bridged by Bach, it remained in full force in his lifetime.

Bach himself followed the family pattern in detail, becoming by a process of apprenticeship a practical violinist and organist, developing as an autodidact into the leading virtuoso of his day, and then maturing into a composer. Not only was a theoretical education at a university beyond his means, even the few months' study he enjoyed at Lübeck under Buxtehude would now be thought very informal, a matter of listening, discussing, making music of his own. The kind of musician Bach was and conceived himself to be was brought out by the fact that right through his earlier appointments he was in demand not only as a virtuoso performer, but as an adviser on the mechanical construction of organs. Moreover, his first major appointment as *Kammermusicus* and court organist to Duke Wilhelm Ernst in Weimar (1709–18), illustrated his merit as a musical jack of all trades. As *Kammermusicus* he had to pick up the latest fashions in Italian orchestral music, and did so largely from the works of Vivaldi. Bach indeed undertook to transcribe Vivaldi for the organ, a work which was characteristic of the lifelong interest of the honest journeyman in musical forms and techniques for their own sake. As *Kammermusicus* he performed with the ducal orchestra on the violin and harpsichord, often directing the orchestra in the place of the ageing kapellmeister. Given his double-barrelled appointment, the organ could not be neglected, but it may be significant that his youthful intention of creating 'a regulated church-music to the honour of God'[2]—that is, a year's plan for liturgical music, attained only 45 of the planned 164 pieces, and the title had a ring of the artisan rather than the liturgical mystic: *Little Organ-book, in which*

[2] *Bach-Dokumente*, 4 vols (Leipzig and Kassel, 1963–79), 1, p. 19.

the aspiring organist is introduced to the execution of a chorale of any kind, and also to qualifying himself in pedal study, for in the chorales to be found in it the pedal is treated quite compulsorily. To the sole honour of God in the highest and for the instruction of one's neighbour. Bach became adept in this period at the cantata form, but here again there might be no clear distinction between liturgical and non-liturgical music. Cantata no. 61, we are told, is in the instrumental form of a French overture, and secular orchestral work is included.[3]

The Weimar experience, however, bears on the story in another way. Bach did not receive the recognition which was his due, for Drese, the kapellmeister, was succeeded on his death by his son. Bach got himself another appointment as court kapellmeister at Anhalt-Köthen in 1717, and such was the ill odour in Weimar that he had to do a month in gaol before he could leave to take up the new job. In the age of the baroque to be the director of a court orchestra, even of a small court like that at Anhalt-Köthen, was the summit of the ambition of a working musician such as we have seen Bach to be. This no doubt is why he took it, notwithstanding that it included no responsibilities towards the Lutheran liturgy, since the prince and his territory adhered to the Reformed faith. Equally he displayed unparalleled creativity in orchestral and chamber music; and in the family way, too. He married his second wife, and embarked on a family of thirteen, of whom many died, though two became composers of note. He seems, however, to have been upset by the remarriage of his prince to a woman of narrow musical interests, and began to look for another appointment. This he found in 1723, as *Kantor* of St Thomas's, Leipzig.

Quite apart from the fact that in the original competition Bach was placed third to Telemann and Graupner, the kapellmeister to the Landgrave of Hesse, and finally received the appointment on very humiliating terms, the appointment itself was a professional step backwards, and was felt by Bach to be so.[4] What made it tolerable was that the Prince of Anhalt-Köthen allowed him to keep his title on a non-resident basis, and he continued to use it in signatures ahead of his Leipzig titles.[5] Again for four years he displayed immense creativity, writing new cantatas Sunday by Sunday, and both the St John and the St Matthew Passions. Then the

[3] For this biographical material see the brief study by the doyen of Bach research, Walter Blankenburg, 'Johann Sebastian Bach', in M. Greschat, ed., *Orthodoxie und Pietismus = Gestalten der Kirchengeschichte*, 7 (Stuttgart, 1982), pp. 301, 304–5.

[4] *Bach-Dokumente*, 1, p. 67.

[5] Ibid., 1, p. 53.

creativity slackened, he went in for secular concerts in the Zimmermann coffee house, and eventually more court compositions for the king of Poland. He did in this final period gather together a great deal of what he had done for music in general from the *Goldberg Variations* to the second part of the *Well-tempered Klavier* and the *Art of Fugue*; but here Bach spoke as an autonomous though not emancipated artist addressing the possibilities and limits of his art. In these years he hardly appears as a figure in church history, and when he died in 1750 he was already old-fashioned and about to go out of fashion altogether. Given the disappointments with which he began at St Thomas's and the way he wound up there, Bach might have derived a wry satisfaction from the stained-glass window introduced on the south front by a nineteenth-century superintendent who helped to found the Gustav-Adolf Verein, that fog-horn of the Protestant interest; in three panels this depicts him in a rake's progress between Luther and Gustavus Adolphus.[6] An honest workman, after all, should be able to turn his hand to anything.

It has frequently been thought that a view of this kind, not to mention any Marxist attempt to claim Bach for the Enlightenment, might be nullified by appeal to what is called Bach's theological library. This was, in fact, not a library at all, still less a library catalogue, but chapter 12 of a posthumous assessment of Bach's property, which was discovered in legal archives in Leipzig in 1870. It is headed 'To Spiritual Books' and puts a rather low valuation on fifty-two short titles running to eighty-one volumes.[7] With enormous labour the great bulk of these short titles have been identified with a high degree of certainty. They include two sets of Luther and are mostly of an old Lutheran character, but include Francke, Spener, and Rambach, from the Pietist side, and, in Josephus, a non-theological text much used by church historians. The material thus identified is not without significance for assessing Bach's religious position, but is virtually useless for instant application. For it is quite clear that a list of books which contains none of the Latin works which would be in a scholar's library, and none of the devotional works, especially English devotional works, which a Protestant German bourgeois family would have, and, above all, the list of a professional musician which contains not a single title in that field, is not a library at all, but the sorry remnant that was left when Bach's sons had rifled all they wanted. And the

[6] There is a colour reproduction of this window in Martin Petzoldt and Joachim Petri, *Johann Sebastian Bach. Ehre sei dir Gott gesungen* ([East] Berlin and Göttingen, 1988), pp. 168–70.

[7] This list has been most recently reprinted in *Pietismus und Neuzeit*, 12 (1986), pp. 180–1.

valuer was right to put a low assessment on this rump, because he knew no one else wanted them. For in the middle of the century the same change in taste which carried Bach's music into oblivion, dealt dramatic execution to the demand for the literature of Lutheran Orthodoxy.[8]

All, however, is not lost. There remain the questions of whether anything can be inferred from Bach's musical use of biblical texts, what a correspondent of Goethe referred to as his 'absolutely barmy German church-texts',[9] or from his own informal exegesis in the shape of his marginal notes to his Calov Bible, a treasure, preserved, appropriately or otherwise, in the library of that Middle Western fortress of pure Lutheranism, the Concordia Seminary, St Louis, USA. The first question requires a lengthy working-out on paper which is neither appropriate nor possible in a conference communication, and the interested inquirer is best referred for it to the researches of Elke Axmacher.[10] One or two of his examples, however, cast light on our point. A particularly 'barmy text' appears in Cantata BWV 161:

> Komm, du süsse Todesstunde,
> Da mein Geist,
> Honig speist
> Aus des Löwen Munde.

Messrs Tate and Lyle have ensured that at least no English listeners will fail to grasp the reference to Samson's riddle in Judges 14. 8, 14. But what has this to do with death? Eighteenth-century hearers were presumed to be familiar with a sermon on this passage in Heinrich Müller's *Evangelischer Hertzens-Spiegel* (1st edn, 1679):

> When Samson found honey in the lion, he propounded this riddle . . . Sweetness proceeded from the terrible. What is more terrible than death when it breaks bones like a lion? How Isaiah complains of this (Isa. 38: 13). Yet a Christian finds honey in the lion and comfort in death.

[8] On all this see Johannes Wallmann, 'Johann Sebastian Bach und die "Geistlichen Bücher" seiner Bibliothek', *Pietismus und Neuzeit*, 12 (1986), pp. 162–81.

[9] *Briefwechsel zwischen Goethe und Zelter*, ed. L. Geiger (Leipzig, n.d. [1902]), 2, p. 468.

[10] Elke Axmacher, *'Aus Liebe will mein Heyland sterben'. Untersuchungen zum Wandel des Passionsverständnisses im frühen 18. Jahrhundert* (Neuhausen and Stuttgart, 1984), 'Die Deutung der Passion Jesu im Text der Matthaus-Passion von J. S. Bach', *Luther*, 56 (1985), pp. 49–69, 'Ein Quellenfund zum Text der Matthäus-Passion', *Bach-Jahrbuch*, 64 (1978), pp. 49–69, 'Bachs Kantaten in auslegungsgeschichtlicher Sicht', Martin Petzoldt, ed., *Bach als Ausleger der Bibel. Theologische und musikwissenschaftliche Studien zum Werk Johann Sebastian Bachs* ([East] Berlin and Göttingen, 1985), pp. 15–32.

The cantatas stand in a tradition, well-established since the early Church and especially since the Reformation, of poetry based on the lectionary and especially upon the Sunday Gospels, the object of which is to produce not a metrical version of the Scripture, but an exegesis with a contemporary application. Thus, for example, in the cantata BWV 23 the poet appropriates to himself the cry of the blind man in Luke 18. 38, 'Jesus, thou Son of David, have mercy on me.'

Du wahrer Gott und Davids Sohn,
Der du von Ewigkeit in der Entfernung schon
Mein Herzeleid und mein Leibespein
Umständlich angesehn, erbarm dich mein.

And blindness is interpreted as spiritual darkness, much as, in many passages, tears of suffering are interpreted as the water at the wedding in Cana transformed by the act of Jesus into the wine of joy.[11] These exegetical procedures had, of course, an ancient lineage in the fourfold sense of Scripture in which alongside the *sensus litteralis* (or *historicus*) there were various applications of the *sensus spiritualis* (or *mysticus*) to the Church and its dogmatic history, to the conditions of individual believers, and to metaphysical and eschatological secrets.[12] And as the same exegetical procedures were widely employed in the lectionary sermons, those sermons were the great reservoir of motifs employed by the cantata poets. By the same token, Bach's works, and especially the cantatas, are full of passages from the Old Testament, and especially from the Psalms and the Song of Solomon, which are taken not as prophesying what was realized in the New Testament, but as representing the New Testament itself, exactly as in Handel's *Messiah* the bulk of the saving events of the birth, death, and Resurrection of Christ are proclaimed with Old Testament passages.[13] This Christianized Old Testament was one of the presuppositions of the exegesis which Bach inherited and his text-writers used.

Of course, in the same way as the cantata texts were not just metrical versions of the Scriptures, they were not just metrical versions of lectionary sermons. They enjoyed a life of their own, and in Bach's time underwent a development which ended in their breaking away not only from the text of the biblical passages, but also from the old spiritual, allegorical,

[11] On the above see Axmacher, 'Bachs Kantaten', pp. 15–16.
[12] See G. Ebeling's article 'Hermeneutik', in *RGG*, 3, cols 249–50.
[13] Helene Werthemann, *Die Bedeutung der alttestamentlichen Historien in Johann Sebastian Bachs Kantaten* (Basle, 1959), pp. 1–5.

tropological, and anagogical exegesis. This may be illustrated by the parable of the unjust steward (Luke 16. 1–9), the Gospel lesson for the Ninth Sunday after Trinity. This story, in which the steward, threatened with dismissal for poor performance, secured his retreat by writing down the obligations of his master's debtors, had, of course always posed problems for the exegetes, not least in the Lord's commendation of the steward's cunning and his injunction, 'Make to yourselves friends of the mammon of unrighteousness.' Most of the sermons dealt with this by saying that what was commended was not the dishonesty of the unjust steward, but the speed and skill with which he dealt with his plight; it was the part of the Christian to repent in good time before the judgement, and to give the same attention to his eternal salvation as the children of this world give to their temporal interests. Müller, however, applies the plans of the unjust steward tropologically to the Christian. If the unjust steward would not dig or beg, but live on the property of others, Müller's advice to his congregation is: 'O my heart, begin to dig, beg and provide for yourself with the substance of others.' Here digging signifies searching the depths of conscience till tears of penitence arise, begging is seeking forgiveness for sin or debt, and the Christian provides for himself with the substance of others when he lays hold of the work of Christ, of his blood as the redemption for sin.

When Solomon Franck came to use this passage for Bach (in BWV 168) he followed the main lines of this exegesis. Great emphasis is laid on the idea of judgement, but whereas the traditional preaching had acquired a Christological motif by allegorizing the intentions of the steward, Franck presents the death of Jesus as the judgement suffered representatively which frees men from the death sentence. A part is also played by the idea of the blood of Jesus as a ransom for sin. And being skilled in the use of an exegetical tradition as a source of verbal images he can get away from the preaching tradition of expounding the passage sentence by sentence or even word by word. He also uses the Passion theme to give the cantata a more powerful eschatological twist than did the sermons:

> Stärk mich mit deinem Freudengeist,
> Heil mir mit deinem Wunden,
> Wasch mich mit deinem Todesschweiss,
> In meiner letzten Stunden;
> Und nimm mich einst, wenn dir's gefällt,
> In wahrem Glauben von der Welt
> Zu deinen Auserwählten.

Yet when Picander, by this time Bach's 'house poet',[14] came to work over the same passage in 1728–9, comparison shows how close to Orthodoxy Franck still was. He does not take over the Christological interpretation of the passage, and so the problem of sin loses the weight which it had in Müller and Franck. The closing chorale is on a different level altogether:

> Lass mich mit jedermann
> In Fried und Freundschaft leben,
> So weit es christlich ist.
> Willt du mir etwas geben,
> An Reichtum, Gut und Geld,
> So gib auch diess dabey,
> Dass von unrechtem Gut
> Nichts untermenget sey.

Here Picander's cantata reveals already the thought of the early Enlightenment.[15]

Bach was, of course, a good Lutheran, who not merely communicated regularly, but also coupled this with regular confession at a time when this was going out of fashion; though the hot sacramentarians of the late twentieth century might not be impressed with a regularity which consisted of twice a year. But he seems to have consulted his confessors on the choice of Scripture passages for his liturgical music, and they were of the Orthodox party.[16] Moreover, as a matter of musical theory Bach was prepared to affirm the good old ecclesiastical doctrine of the thorough-bass.

> The thorough-bass is the most perfect foundation of music, which is played with both hands in such a way that the left hand plays the prescribed notes, the right adds the consonants and dissonants, so that it is a pleasing harmony to the honour of God and the permissible delight of the spirit, and should, like all music—and this is the be-all and end-all of the thorough-bass—be solely to the honour of God and the recreation of the spirit; where this is not observed, it is not

[14] Friedrich Blume, *Syntagma Musicologicum II*, ed. A. A. Abert and M. Rulinke (Kassel, Basle, Tours, and London, 1973), p. 192.

[15] Axmacher, 'Bachs Kantaten', pp. 17–23. Cf. Winfried Zeller, 'Tradition und Exegese. Johann Sebastian Bach und Martin Schallings Lied, "Herzlich lieb hab ich dir, o Herr"', in Petzoldt, *Bach als Ausleger*, pp. 151–76.

[16] M. Petzoldt, 'Christian Wiese d. A. und Christoph Wolle — zwrei Leipziger Beichtvater Bachs, Vertreter zweier auslegungsgeschichtlicher Abschritte der ausgehenden lutherischen Orthodoxie', in Petzoldt, ed., *Bach als Ausleger*, pp. 109–29.

> actually music, but a diabolical bawling and lack of expression [Geplärr und Geleier].[17]

This is not the utterance of an autonomous or emancipated musician; but emancipation of a sort was creeping in by another door.

The author of the libretto of the *St John Passion* is not known, but has often been thought to be Bach himself. Be this as it may, the piece makes substantial use of six pieces of the Passion by B. H. Brockes (1712–13), but is more Orthodox than Brockes to the extent that it does not use Brockes's dramatic methods to make the Passion a contemporary event. What is contemporary about the Passion is comprised in its eternally valid results of reconciliation, redemption, and discipleship. Bach brings this out by separating the Passion narrative from reflection upon it. In the *St Matthew Passion*, Bach's text was provided by Picander on the basis of the sermons by Heinrich Müller, who, as we have seen, was much drawn on in the cantatas. The conclusion of Axmacher's careful comparison of the texts of the three Passions is that they reveal the steady dissolution of the Anselmian doctrine of reconciliation as it had been held in early Protestantism. The reasons for this were both intellectual and existential. Difficulty in accepting the paradox that God punished the innocent Christ led gradually to the elimination of the idea of punishment from the understanding of the Passion. As God disappeared from the story in this sense, the sufferings of Christ and human consciousness of sin were both more intensely represented. If the action of God was to be replaced by Jesus' sacrificial love for man, there was inevitably a concern that that love must be capable of being experienced or, in other words, made accessible to feeling.[18] A generation after Bach's death, in the age of sensibility, feeling could take a leading role, and one of the objects of liturgical music might be to balance or even offset the effects of rationalist preaching. This is not a situation which Bach himself contemplated; but the solvents applied to Orthodoxy by Pietism and revival were not absent even from the *St Matthew Passion*.

This, of course, is not enough for the Marxist critics who, objecting

[17] Quoted in Walter Blankenburg, 'Johann Sebastian Bach und die Aufklärung' in Walter Blankenburg, ed., *Johann Sebastian Bach = Wege der Forschung*, 170 (Darmstadt, 1970), pp. 100–10, at p. 103 [repr. from *Bach Gedenkschaft* (Freiburg im Breisgau and Zurich, 1950), pp. 25–34]. For a brief introduction to the thorough-bass see the article 'Figured bass', in Percy A. Scholes, *The Oxford Companion to Music*, 8th edn (London, 1950), pp. 317–18.

[18] Axmacher, *'Aus liebe will mein Heyland sterben'*, pp. 149, 152–61, 204–8.

quite reasonably to the blanket application of the term 'baroque',[19] and exaggerating the progress of the bourgeoisie in music patronage,[20] claim 'to set free the core of the new in Bach's creativity'.[21] But at the bottom the crude appeal to politics has to do duty for the refining of concepts or the weighing of evidence. As E. H. Meyer put it in a discussion,

> If the word baroque is used for Bach and Handel, there is the danger they will be heard out of the great central area of the music today to be performed for the masses of men. For us, Bach and Handel are also the greatest masters immediately before the *classics* . . .[22]

A socialist state competing for the national tradition cannot say otherwise; but the appeal to politics will do nothing to define how deeply Bach was rooted in Lutheran Orthodoxy nor the ways in which he reveals the disintegration of that system of doctrine, still less will it explain why there was no contact between Bach and Gottsched, the *aufklärerisch* professor of poetry in Leipzig, and himself an energetic composer of texts for music.

Bach's own annotations to his Calov Bible assume the pre-critical realism common to his age and embody a mixture of genuine personal piety, of pride in the religious and liturgical function of music, with doubtless an edge against the Reformed who did not see things in the same way, and in his office to provide it. Thus, for example, on Genesis 26. 33[23] Calov, like many versions of the Authorized Version, has a note saying that the word Beersheba means 'well of the oath', and adds that a well had been given the same name in Erfurt. Bach's comment is 'N.B. There is a village of that name about an hour from Erfurt.' The Bible, even Beersheba, was very much Bach's native land.[24] On I Chronicles 25, in which David and the captains of the host separated, many to 'prophesy with harps, with psalteries, and with cymbals', he notes, 'This chapter is the true founda-

19 For a non-Marxist argument to the same effect see Ulrich Siegele, 'Bachs Ort in Orthodoxie und Aufklärung', *Musik und Kirche*, 51 (1981), pp. 3–14.

20 As Werner Neumann harshly put it in a public discussion, the innumerable dedications and addresses of homage to princes and nobility by Bach and his contemporaries would be odd garb for an anti-feudal, anti-absolutist emancipation movement. *Johann Sebastian Bach und die Aufklärung* ed. for the Forschungskollektiv 'Johann Sebastian Bach' by Reinhard Szeskus (Leipzig, 1982), p. 131.

21 Ibid., 4, pp. 8–9.

22 Walter Blankenburg, 'Die Bach-forschung seit etwa 1965', *Acta Musicologica*, 55 (1983), pp. 39–40. Cf. his 'Aufklärungsauslegung der Bibel in Leipzig zur Zeit Bachs. Zu Johann Christoph Gottscheds Homiletik', in Petzoldt, ed., *Bach als Ausleger*, pp. 97–108.

23 'And he called [the well] Sheba: therefore the name of the city is Beer-sheba unto this day.'

24 The texts are usefully assembled and commented on in Petzold and Petri, *Johann Sebastian Bach*, pp. 18–21, 44–7, 8–11, 86–8, 104–7, 120–3, 136–8.

tion of all church music pleasing to God'; more convincingly perhaps, on the great chorus of choral and instrumental music which accompanied the dedication of Solomon's temple, 'In devotional music God is always present with his grace.' I Chronicles 28. 21, in which David instructs Solomon how to set up the temple, refers in the Authorized Version to the 'courses of the priests and Levites' and 'to all manner of workmanship', but in the Luther version refers to the offices of the priests and to all the other officers. This to Bach is evidence that his office as organist or *Kantor* is equivalent in its sphere to that of the pastoral office in its sphere: 'N.B. A glorious proof that alongside the other institutions of the liturgy music was also specially ordained by the spirit of God through David.' On Exodus 15. 20, in which 'Miriam the prophetess . . . took a timbrel in her hand; and all the women went out after her with timbrels and with dances', Calov commented that this was not a new song, but a response or echo to the song which Moses and the men of Israel had sung before. To Bach this signified the element of dialogue in the liturgy: 'N.B. The first anticipation of two choirs making music to the honour of God.' And there are two entries of a more personal nature. On the sacramental level, Leviticus 17. 11, 'The life of the flesh is in the blood', is silently underlined. And the elaborate marginal transcription of Mark 10. 29–30, 'There is no man that hath left house, or brethren, or sisters, or father, or mother, or wife, or children, or lands for my sake and the gospel's but he shall receive an hundredfold now in this time', speaks volumes for the piety of a man who lost four brothers and sisters in infancy or childhood, and two more later, a mother when he was nine, and a father at ten; and who was himself widowed at the age of 35, having lost four of the seven children of his first marriage, and was in due course to lose seven of the thirteen of his second marriage at a very early age. The reward he notes for losses for the Gospel's sake is not that of eternal life in the world to come, but that of recompense 'an hundredfold now'. This was the response of a man of faith.

CONTEMPORARY ECCLESIASTICAL REACTIONS TO HOME'S *DOUGLAS*

by HENRY R. SEFTON

IT is not entirely clear whether the man in the gallery who cried out, 'Whaur's yer Willie Shakespeare noo?' was being facetious, but the audiences both in Edinburgh and in London gave the tragedy *Douglas* by John Home an enthusiastic reception.[1] The Reverend Alexander Carlyle, better known as Jupiter Carlyle from his fine appearance, noted in his *Anecdotes and Characters*:

> The Play had unbounded Success for a Great Many Nights in Edin[r] and was attended by all the Literati, and most of the Judges, who except one or two had not been in use to attend the Theatre. The Town in Gen[l] was in an uproar of Exultation, that a Scotchman had written a Tragedy of the First Rate and that its Merit was first Submitted to their Judgment.[2]

But the author of *Douglas* was not only a Scotsman. He was also a clergyman, minister of the parish of Athelstaneford in East Lothian, and so the Presbytery of Edinburgh took note of the play which received its first performance within its bounds on 14 December 1756. Three weeks later it issued an *Admonition and Exhortation* against stage plays and players which was ordered to be read in every church within the bounds immediately after divine service on 30 January 1757. The Reverend Thomas Whyte, minister at Liberton and therefore a member of the Presbytery of Edinburgh, was accused before the Presbytery of having attended the playhouse. He admitted the charge, but pleaded by way of alleviation that he had gone to the playhouse only once and had endeavoured to conceal himself in a corner to avoid giving offence. He expressed deep sorrow for what he had done and undertook to be more circumspect for the future. In view of all this, the Presbytery suspended him from duty from 12 January to 2 February.[3]

Having dealt with their own erring brother the Presbytery decided that

[1] McDonald Emslie, 'Home's Douglas and Wully Shakespeare', *Studies in Scottish Literature*, 2 (1964), pp. 128–9.
[2] Alexander Carlyle, *Anecdotes and Characters of the Times*, ed. J. Kinsley (London, 1973), p. 58.
[3] N. Morren, *Annals of the General Assembly 1752–66* (Edinburgh, 1840), pp. 112–16.

something must be done about the other ministers who had attended the playhouse. Letters were therefore sent to the Presbyteries of Haddington, Ayr, Earlston, Chirnside Duns, and Dalkeith, informing them that ministers under their jurisdiction had been present in the playhouse at the head of the Canongate while a tragedy called *Douglas* was acted. This conduct was described as extremely offensive and as interrupting the Presbytery's endeavours for suppressing stage plays.

The Presbytery of Duns did not welcome this zeal on the part of the Presbytery of Edinburgh and described the Edinburgh letter as 'an unconstitutional attempt of one presbytery to anticipate the judgment and regulate the conduct of another'. The Duns letter also pointed out that some members of the Presbytery of Edinburgh had attended the playhouse when on business for the Church of Scotland in London. The letter from Duns concludes:

> You must, however, excuse us, when we say that your intermeddling in the manner you have done with the conduct of our brethren, who have hitherto been eminently useful in our bounds, hath a natural tendency, and will undoubtedly, unless guarded against by the utmost prudence and caution on our part, greatly mar and obstruct those valuable ends you seem to have in view.

The Presbytery of Duns did, however, rebuke the two ministers concerned, as did the Presbytery of Chirnside. The Presbyteries of Ayr and Earlston accepted apologies from the accused brethren and let the matter rest.

The Presbytery of Haddington, which was Home's own presbytery, did attempt on several occasions to consider his conduct, but was frustrated by the playwright's absence in London, arranging for the production of *Douglas* there, and finally by his resignation of his charge of Athelstaneford.[4]

The Presbytery of Dalkeith took their duties much more seriously than did the other presbyteries, and the minister of Inveresk, Alexander Carlyle, was cited to appear on 1 March 1757. In his *Anecdotes and Characters* Carlyle states that he had not attended the playhouse either on the first or second nights of the performance of *Douglas*, because he was well aware that all the fanatics and some other enemies would be on the watch and would make all the advantage they possibly could against him. But six or seven clergymen from the Merse who were friends of the

[4] Morren, *Annals*, pp. 116–22.

author had attended and reproached him for his cowardice. As a result of upbraidings by the author himself and some female friends of his, Carlyle had gone on the third night and drew on himself 'all the Clamour of Tongues and Violence of Prosecution'.[5] The treatment given to Carlyle is in marked contrast to the lenience with which the other offenders were dealt. A formal libel was drawn up against him in which he was charged with associating himself or familiarly keeping company with the players, persons who by their profession and in the eye of the law were of bad fame, with attending the rehearsal of the tragedy of *Douglas* and assisting or directing the players on that occasion, and appearing openly in the playhouse in the Canongate within a few miles of his own parish. He was further charged with having taken possession of a box in the playhouse in a disorderly way, or forcibly turning some gentlemen out of it, and there witnessing the representation of the tragedy of *Douglas*. It was alleged that the tragedy tended to encourage the monstrous crime of suicide and contained such dreadful oaths or expressions and mock prayers, as were so offensive to the audience that they were struck out or varied in later presentations. When the 'proof' or supporting evidence of the libel was laid before the Presbytery on 3 May it was deposed that one of the characters swore 'by him that died on the accursed tree', and that another said, 'No priest! No priest! I'll risk eternal fire.'[6] Neither of these appears in the printed versions of the play, though the villain on one occasion says, 'By the most blessed cross, you much amaze me.'[7] In Act IV one of the speeches of the heroine, Lady Randolph, might be construed as a prayer:

> O thou all righteous and eternal King!
> Who father of the fatherless art call'd
> Protect my sons![8]

After hearing the proof, the Presbytery decided that Mr Carlyle's offence deserved a higher censure than a rebuke, and that a censure inflicted by the highest authority would have greatest weight and be followed with the most salutary effects, and so they referred the whole matter to the Synod of Lothian and Tweeddale, the next superior court, which was due to meet the following week.

Carlyle had more friends in the Synod than he had in his own

[5] Carlyle, *Anecdotes*, p. 159.
[6] Morren, *Annals*, pp. 122–7.
[7] John Home, *Douglas*, ed. G. D. Parker (Edinburgh, 1972), p. 40.
[8] Ibid., p. 59.

Presbytery and the Synod's finding was as critical of the Presbytery of Dalkeith as it was of Carlyle. It would have been better if the Presbytery had proceeded by way of privy censure or brotherly conference, rather than by the libel procedure. But the Synod also declared their high displeasure with Mr Carlyle for the step he had taken in going to the theatre, and strictly enjoined him to abstain therefrom in time coming. The Presbytery appealed the case to the General Assembly of 1757, which considered the matter on 24 May and upheld the Synod's sentence by 117 votes to 39.[9]

Why was Carlyle pursued with such vigour through the various courts of the Church? Carlyle was in no doubt that it was due to the machinations of two men, Robert Dundas of Arniston, then Lord Advocate, and the Reverend Patrick Cuming, Professor of Ecclesiastical History in the University of Edinburgh.[10] Dundas's quarrel was not so much with Carlyle as with Lord Milton, one of the judges of the Court of Session,[11] who had encouraged John Home to have *Douglas* performed. Cuming, however, seems to have had a strong dislike of Carlyle and his friends John Home and William Robertson.[12] Robertson was too prudent to attend the playhouse, and Home was beyond his reach, and so Carlyle was the obvious target. Carlyle indeed alleges that Cuming helped to draw up the libel against him.[13]

In his *Anecdotes and Characters* Carlyle also acknowledges the help of a secret friend who sent him two anonymous letters offering him good advice. Carlyle's father recognized the handwriting as being that of a former fellow student, the Reverend Robert Wallace, minister of the New North Church in Edinburgh, and was in consequence prevented from wavering in support of his son.[14] Carlyle might have been equally surprised had he known that Wallace had also written a pamphlet in connection with the *Douglas* controversy.[15] It must surely be a matter of regret that Wallace did not see fit to publish his *Address to the Reverend the Clergy of the Church of Scotland . . . on occasion of composing, acting & publishing the Tragedy called Douglass*, for it is both witty and entertaining. Rarely has

[9] Morren, *Annals*, pp. 127–9.

[10] Carlyle, *Anecdotes*, pp. 159, 161; Morren, *Annals*, p. 124.

[11] George Brunton and David Haig, *Historical Account of the Senators of the College of Justice* (Edinburgh, 1832), pp. 498–9, 523–5.

[12] Carlyle, *Anecdotes*, p. 159.

[13] Ibid., p. 162.

[14] Ibid., p. 161.

[15] University of Edinburgh, Laing MS II 620².

the bubble of the presbyterial pomposity been more effectively pricked than it is by Wallace in his answer to the *Admonition and Exhortation* of the Presbytery of Edinburgh.

Wallace says that he will treat the *Admonition* with all due respect, unlike the writers of lampoons in verse and prose, but phrase by phrase he demolishes its wild generalizations about the decline of religion, the open profanation of the Lord's Day, the contempt of public worship, and the growing luxury and levity of the present age. If all this is true, it is partly the fault of the clergy themselves, and they would be better employed in denouncing obvious vices, such as gluttony, drunkenness, and debauchery, than in deploring a growing luxury, which is not only a natural consequence of the growing wealth of the country, but is necessary for promoting industry and the support of the poor. The *Admonition* claims that the Christian Church had always regarded stage plays and players as prejudicial to the interests of religion and morality. Wallace denies that there has been this unanimity of opinion and points out that the Westminster Larger Catechism in its answer to the question on the Seventh Commandment says that by it all lascivious stage plays are forbidden. It may therefore be supposed that other sorts of plays are not forbidden. Quoting Alexander Petrie[16] as his authority, Wallace remarks that the General Assembly of 1574 had enacted that

> no comedies nor tragedies or such playes should be made on any history of Canonicall Scripture nor on the Sabbath day: If any Minister be the writer of such a play he shall be deprived of his ministry: as for playes of another subject they also should be examined before they be propounded publickly.

From this it can be inferred that the General Assembly then supposed that good plays might be written both by the clergy and the laity and might be performed in the theatre.

Wallace also attacks an equally pompous statement which had been issued by the Presbytery of Glasgow on 2 February 1757. Anyone reading the Glasgow statement who did not know what the clergy were like might conclude that it referred to some terrible calamity and would be surprised on reading further to discover

> that these dreadfull events amounted to no more than, as their narrative acquaints us, that one 'who is a minister of the Church of

16 Alexander Petrie, *A Compendious History of the Catholic Church from the year 600 until the year 1600* (The Hague, 1662), p. 385.

> Scotland (strange, a minister of the Church of Scotland, it had not been so great a wonder had he been a minister of the Church of England but what did this minister of the Church of Scotland? He) did himself write and compose a stage play intitled the Tragedy of Douglas.' Strange did he? Ay he did, nay 'and got it to be acted on the theatre att Edinburgh & that he & severall other ministers of this Church were present & some of them oftener than once att the acting of the said play before a numerous audience.' Assure yourselves Gentlemen, however much the Presbytery of Glasgow or any of you be affected with this which is called 'a new and strange appearance' by such solemnity about a trifle they have exposed themselves to a world of Ridicule. We of the Laity[17] . . . will think the nation very happy if no more dreadful vice or calamity shall ever be heard of.

Having roundly condemned the effusions of both presbyteries, Wallace declares that he is actually on their side of the controversy. He was inclined to believe that the legislature acted very wisely in 1737 in not allowing a playhouse in Edinburgh. Edinburgh was too little a place to support a company of good actors for the stage:

> There is not a sufficient number of rich & Genteel company for this purpose. Either the stage must sink or the greatest part of the good company must go too often for their fortunes & spend too much of their time and for this reason I never took any share in supporting the playhouse in this place.

Wallace's *Address* was never published and exists only in manuscript. A note written on the title-page on 15 September 1764 says that it was intended to be published in 1757 and 'may be published att any time when such events happen', but gives no hint why it was not published. The main point of the *Address* is to moderate the zeal of the prosecuting presbyteries, especially Dalkeith, but it seems that Wallace decided it would be better to encourage Carlyle in private than come out into the open with another pamphlet. This was not the only occasion when Wallace's prudence overcame his zeal. His papers include unpublished pamphlets on the Porteous riots,[18] on the intended prosecution of David Hume and Lord Kames,[19] and other controversies.

In spite of his circumspection, there is some evidence that Wallace as

[17] The *Address* is supposedly 'by a layman of their Communion'.

[18] Laing MS II 620[4].

[19] Laing MS II 972.

well as Carlyle suffered as a result of the *Douglas* controversy. Dundas of Arniston made things difficult for the Reverend Thomas Turnbull, the minister of nearby Borthwick, who was Wallace's brother-in-law and had supported Carlyle before the Presbytery of Dalkeith. He also blocked the progress of Wallace's son George in his career as an advocate.[20] When Carlyle was named as a preacher before the General Assembly of 1760 two dissents were entered against him, and in 1789 he failed to be elected in a bitter struggle for the Principal Clerkship of the Assembly.[21]

Many years later, when Carlyle as a very old man was writing his *Anecdotes and Characters*, in 1803, he gave his reflections on the part he had played in the Douglas controversy and observed that of the many exertions he and his friends had made for the credit and interest of the clergy of the Church of Scotland none was more meritorious or of better effect than this. It was of great importance that a distinction should be made between artificial virtues and vices formed by ignorance and superstition and real ones. Without this the rising liberality of young scholars would have been checked, and those of better birth and more ingenious minds prevented from entering the clerical profession.[22]

King's College,
University of Aberdeen

[20] Carlyle, *Anecdotes*, p. 161.
[21] Morren, *Annals*, p. 124.
[22] Carlyle, *Anecdotes*, p. 164.

GILLOWS' FURNISHINGS FOR CATHOLIC CHAPELS, 1750–1800

by LINDSAY BOYNTON

WHEN Catholic Emancipation came at last in 1829 it was the culmination of half a century's agitation. The first landmark was the Relief Act of 1778, which repealed most of the penal legislation of the 1690s, and the second was the Act of 1791, which, in effect, removed penal restraint on Catholic worship in England.[1] Of course, both the anti-Catholic hysteria of the Gordon Riots which followed the 1778 Act and the repression after the rebellions of 1715 and '45 have remained vivid in the national memory. On the other hand, we ought to recall how Defoe observed that Durham was full of Catholics, 'who live peaceably and disturb nobody, and nobody them; for we . . . saw them going as publickly to mass as the Dissenters did on other days to their meeting-house.'[2] After the death of the Old Pretender in 1766 the Pope recognized George III *de facto* and ordered the Catholic Church to pay no royal honours to 'Charles III'.[3] The penal laws on church-going were now only lightly enforced and then usually at the behest of informers, until the 1778 Act frustrated them, since it was no longer illegal for a priest to say Mass. Thomas Weld of Lulworth Castle (the head of probably the richest Catholic family in the kingdom[4]) maintained six chaplains in different houses;[5] his ability to do so must have been helped by the fact that the Lulworth estate had not paid the double land tax, for which it was theoretically liable, since 1725.[6] Mr Weld deliberately flouted the remaining archaic laws by building a handsome chapel in his grounds ('truly elegant,—a Pantheon in miniature,—and ornamented with immense expense and richness', said Fanny Burney).[7] This was in 1785–7, when it was still illegal to do so. The story that he had sought permission from the King, who gave it on condition that the

[1] See, in particular, John Bossy, *The English Catholic Community* (London, 1978), pp. 295, 330; Bryan Little, *Catholic Churches since 1623* (London, 1966).

[2] Daniel Defoe, *A Tour through England and Wales* (Everyman edn, nd), 2, p. 249, cited in Little, *Catholic Churches*, p. 30.

[3] Little, *Catholic Churches*, p. 28.

[4] J. C. H. Aveling, *The Handle and the Axe* (London, 1976), p. 314.

[5] Joan Berkeley, *Lulworth and the Welds* (Gillingham, Dorset, 1971), p. 161.

[6] Ibid., p. 181.

[7] *Diary and Letters of Madame d'Arblay*, ed. by her niece, Charlotte Barrett (London, nd), 3, p. 201.

chapel should look like a mausoleum, is much later and, if true, would have constituted an extraordinary reversion to the royal dispensing power. It is true, however, that Mr Weld intended the visit of George III to confer respectability: 'I think the King's seeing the Chapel in that publick manner might be a kind of sanction to it.'[8]

In recent months I have visited eighteenth-century Catholic chapels as far afield as Hazlewood Castle and Holme upon Spalding Moor in Yorkshire, West Grinstead in Sussex, and Hornby in Lancashire, which owns a tabernacle inlaid with the Sacred Monogram and festoons of wheat-ears that may confidently be attributed to Gillow, and a bureau writing-table that is assuredly by Gillow. Not all such chapels have a Gillow connection, of course: that of the Bar Convent in York (where several of the Gillow girls were educated) apparently does not, and St Peter's in Winchester certainly does not. My purpose here is not to survey the whole scene of Catholic chapels in eighteenth-century England, however, but to demonstrate the involvement of the firm of Gillows, of Lancaster and London, above all in their altar furnishings.

The Gillow family came from the heartland of English Catholicism in the Fylde. If Lancashire sent more students to the priesthood when it was dangerous to do so than all the rest of England, the Fylde sent more than the rest of Lancashire put together.[9] The Gillows themselves had a long tradition of sending members of the family into the religious life. When Robert Gillow (1704–72) founded a dynasty of furniture manufacturers in Lancaster about 1730, to be continued and expanded in London by his sons and grandsons, it was natural that Catholic families should be prominent among their clients and inevitable that such families would commission altars and tabernacles.

Private altars were available in Gillows' London shop,[10] although they were 'disguised' as domestic furniture. Sir John Lawson of Brough Hall bought one consisting of a large mahogany box with a hinged lid (a cross inlaid on its underside so that it showed when the lid was up) and a fall-front supported by brass quadrants.[11] Usually a bookcase or a secretaire-bookcase was the preferred form.[12] William Glendonwyn's is particularly

[8] Berkeley, *Lulworth*, p. 169.

[9] Bishop Bilsborrow, quoted in F. O. Blundell, *Old Catholic Lancashire*, 3 vols (London, 1925–44), 2, p. 148.

[10] Westminster City Libraries, Archives Department (Victoria branch) [hereafter W: the Gillow archive is numbered 344, which is to be understood before all citations], 95/622,649; 96/1128.

[11] W 16/1183; 96/963, April 1793.

[12] As bookcase: Mrs Butler: W 17/1805; with arched pediment, Gillows London, 10 July 1790.

interesting since it was of the bookcase type with a segmental pediment and dentil cornice (both classical features), but a Gothic interior decorated in white and gold, the columns and mouldings gilt, enclosed by doors (not shown on the sketch) with wire panels and green silk curtains (plate 1).[13]

Most of Gillows' altars, however, were not of this kind, but more ambitious affairs, destined for chapels both public and private. Although the chapels might be Gothic, the altars and tabernacles were invariably classical.[14] This was not because Gillows lacked expertise in Gothic: among their designs in that style the screen for the France chapel at St Michael's-on-Wyre of 1798 was in a passable thirteenth-century idiom. No, their fidelity to classical detail even in a Gothic context was in line with established practice in the early Gothic Revival,[15] the distinguishing feature in Gillows' case being their 'Roman' altars.[16]

Gillows were commissioned to furnish several public chapels. As early as 1759 the firm made an altar-piece for Singleton Chapel, with an open pediment 'wherein we intend to place a Busto of the B: Virgin'. Richard Gillow asked his cousin James to find one in London (such as he had seen there) for two or three shillings and sixteen inches high. He also mentioned that his clients wanted a picture eight feet high to place over the altar, 'but as they're unwilling to lay out money perhaps a good print

[13] W 95/649; 14/100–105. William Glendonwyn of Glendonwyn, near Carlingwark, Kirkudbrightshire.

[14] A tabernacle dated February 1809 still retained a classical outline, but with Gothic touches, e.g. cusping round the Sacred Monogram and crocketed pinnacles above classical columns: W 99/1855. Compare an altar of 1791 with almost baroque curved ends and 'IHS' within a heart on the front, tabernacle with dome, cross and candlesticks, supplied to John Giffard, Nerquis, near Mold, W 95/973; 172/337. See also a tabernacle supplied 1 May 1773 for £7 17*s.* 6*d.*, with carved columns, part gilt, ogee dome, gilt ball and cross, enclosed by doors, with two drawers, sent to the London shop, W 4/55; an altar frame and tabernacle (inlaid steps, wheat-ear motif, dome with grapes, spandrels with cherubs, carved and gilt dove, carved capitals, door to be inlaid in London), 23 Sept. 1782, W 8/399; cf. door of tabernacle to be inlaid in London for Mr James Farrer, Chancery Lane, W 8/395; tabernacle with fluted columns, hipped pediment, for The Revd Dr Rigby, 8 Dec. 1794, £5, W 17/1822; altar, tabernacle and steps, with purplewood columns, carved and gilt bases and capitals, and four candlesticks, to the London shop for Johnson, 18 gns, W 18/2290; tabernacle and steps, with two purplewood columns, gilt capitals and bases burnished, pediment, Tuscan cornice, lined with rose silk, inlaid door, gilt and burnished mouldings, £6 10*s.* 0*d.*, for The Revd Mr Baines of Garstang, W 19/2687; supplied to the London shop for Mr Weeble: altar and tabernacle, W 8/307; six carved gilt candlesticks for same, W 8/310 (15 Apr. 1782 and 22 Apr. 1782); inlaid altar and tabernacle like Weeble's for Mrs Hennage, 20 May 1782, W 8/327.

[15] Michael McCarthy, *The Origins of the Gothic Revival* (London, 1987), p. 165.

[16] For example, 'a handsome mahogany Roman altar with Tabernacle and steps, inlaid and varnished' for Sir William Gerard in 1796, W 19/2440–55; cf. the frontispiece to Bossy, *English Catholic Community*.

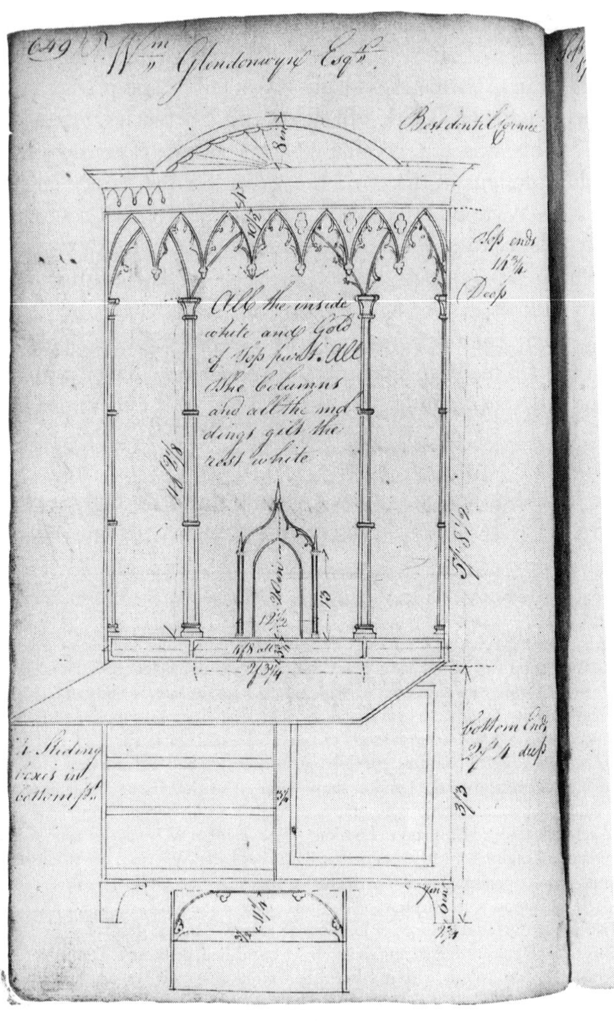

Plate 1 Private Altar for William Glendowyn, 1790 (Westminster City Library).

of Our Saviour's Crucifixion or some striking part of His Passion would come nearer their price.'[17] In Lancaster itself a priest had ventured to settle about 1730 in St Leonardsgate, then on the outskirts. The first chapel was a so-called barn, variously described as below or behind the house. Following the arrival of a new priest, the Revd Dr John Rigby, in 1784 this was renovated. Gillows carved a swag of husks as a pattern for the stonemason Richard Fisher, and fixed a tabernacle 'in the room upstairs'. During the 1790s the firm supplied Dr Rigby with a prayer-stool, altar-stool, and two cushions, four large candlesticks, a carved and gilt cross and tabernacle, and a circular japanned flower-stand.[18] The old chapel was in turn superseded by a new and larger building in Dalton Square, erected between 1797 and 1799. The largest subscribers were the Worswicks (a banking family), and their cousins the Gillows, who were also generous with gifts of vestments and other adornments. Gillows bought the old chapel and used it as a furniture warehouse, nicknamed 'The Temple' by their men.[19]

Greenwich was among the first missions to take advantage of the 1791 Act, launching an appeal for funds in 1792 and leasing land in 1795. The patron who paid for the building was James Taylor, a young and wealthy man: he gave himself a private entrance from his garden in Park Place (on the north side of Greenwich Park) and erected tribunes either side of the altar which were reserved for his household—a stylish variant on the manorial pew or chapel in the Established Church, with late baroque overtones.[20] Gillows supplied a tabernacle and steps (drawn at full size and presumably designed by Thomas Romney, cousin of the artist George Romney), with four cabled columns and carved capitals, a dome above supported by four Corinthian columns and carved capitals, mostly gilt; the interior was lined with white silk; the whole cost £24 3*s.* 0*d.* The four large candlesticks were gilded by Thomas Dobson, who agreed to find all materials, including the brass pans and nozzles, to pay for turning, and to execute the carving and gilding in oil gold (plate 2).[21]

So far I have dealt mainly with the firm's Lancaster branch, which was

[17] W 163/118.

[18] R. N. Billington and J. Brownbill, *St Peter's Lancaster* (London, 1910), p. 85 and *passim*; *VCH Lancashire*, 8 (1914), p. 47; W 9/1092,968–9,1000,1039,1041.

[19] Billington and Brownbill, *St Peter's*, pp. 85, 214–15, 217.

[20] The Revd E. G. Dunn, 'The Return of Catholicism to East Greenwich', *Transactions of the Greenwich and Lewisham Antiquarian Society*, 7 (1961–3), pp. 160ff.

[21] W 97/1149,1154,1184; Romney had drawn a design for an altar and tabernacle in 1791: W 95/793.

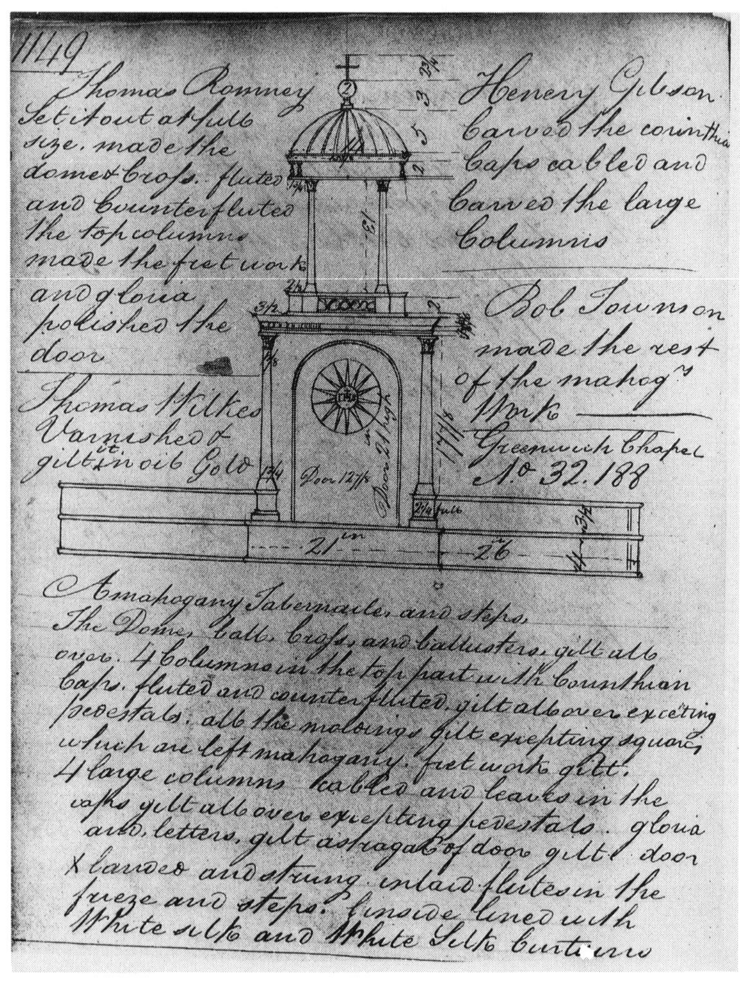

1149
Thomas Romney
Set it out at full
size. made the
domes Cross. fluted
and Counterfluted
the top columns
made the fret work
and gloria
polished the
door
Thomas Wilkes
Varnished &
gilt in oil Gold
Henery Gibson
Carved the corinthian
Caps cabled and
Carved the large
Columns
Bob Townson
made the rest
of the mahog^y
Work
Greenwich Chapel
No 32.188
Door 21 high
Door 12 7/8
A mahogany Tabernacle and steps
The Dome, ball, Cross, and ballusters, gilt all
over. 4 Columns in the top part with Corinthian
Caps. fluted and counterfluted. gilt all over excepting
pedestals. all the moldings gilt excepting squares
which are left mahogany. fret work gilt.
4 large columns cabled and leaves in the
caps gilt all over excepting pedestals. gloria
and letters gilt astragal of door gilt. door
& banded and strung. inlaid flutes in the
freeze and steps. Inside lined with
White silk and White Silk buttons

Plate 2 Tabernacle and Cupola for Greenwich Chapel, 1795 (Westminster City Library).

founded by Robert Gillow I (1704–72). This was now managed by his eldest son Richard I (1733–1811). The London branch was run by his brother Robert II (1747–95) at 176 Oxford Street (on part of Selfridge's site), assisted by his nephews (sons of Richard I): Robert III, George, and Richard II. Robert and George leased 11–12 North Audley Street from the Grosvenor Estate in 1793: a pair of grand early Georgian houses joined as one, with a gallery, or Great Room, running across both on the garden side. This was, and is, decorated with medallion heads of Popes Clement IX and X, which the previous occupant Earl Ligonier—as staunch a Protestant as the Gillows were Catholics—would certainly not have countenanced.[22] The Gillows must surely have installed these heads, and there is every probability that they used the gallery as their chapel. The third brother of this third generation, Richard II, lived firstly at 18 Upper Seymour Street. He spent part of every summer at a house in Prospect Place, Margate, where he had Mass said privately from about 1793.[23] In 1801 six members of the Gillow family subscribed towards a chapel in Margate, which was built over the next three years.[24] Having moved his London residence to Kensington (first to Little Holland House, then, in 1812, to Bute House), Richard II was the prime mover in erecting the first Catholic chapel in London since the Reformation (apart from royal and embassy chapels)—St Mary's, Holland Street, forerunner of Our Lady of Victories.[25]

Private chapels, once hidden in the the attic regions, gradually shifted to more accessible locations. The trend is nicely exemplified at Mapledurham in Oxfordshire, where the chapel was on the second floor when John Loveday visited the house in 1733: note that although 'hidden', he had no trouble in seeing its pictures as a connoisseur rather than a worshipper.[26] The Blount family took advantage of the 1791 Act to build a

22 *Survey of London*, 39, *The Grosvenor Estate in Mayfair*, part i (London, 1977), p. 101.

23 B. W. Kelly, *Historical Notes on English Catholic Missions* (London, 1907), p. 270, citing Joseph Gillow, *A Literary and Biographical History, or Bibliographical Dictionary of the English Catholics* [London, 1885–1902], 2, p. 484. Gillow's dictionary is to be used with caution, especially where his own family is concerned.

24 'Mr [Richard] Gillow, Lancaster, £5; Mr Robert Gillow, Lancaster, £2 2.0.; Miss Gillow, Lancaster, [illegible]; Mr George Gillow, London, £10; Mrs Gillow, Margate, £10; Mr Richard Gillow, London, £5 5. 0.' These extracts from a MS book at Thanet Central Library, Margate, were kindly supplied by Father Corcoran.

25 Not St Mary Abbots as in Gillow, *Dictionary of English Catholics*, 2, p. 484; he also regularly confuses Richard Gillow I of Lancaster with his son Richard II of London. The history of this church is given accurately in *Survey of London*, 37, *Northern Kensington* (London, 1973), p. 68. See also Kelly, *Historical Notes*, p. 233: 'Mr Gillow and some friends contributed £500 . . .'.

26 Sarah Markham, *John Loveday of Caversham, 1711–1789* (Wilton, 1984), p. 164.

chapel that projected from the house without actually being separate; in accordance with the Act it had neither steeple nor bell.[27] The interior of the chapel (dedicated in 1797) is in a delightful Gothic style, but the Gillow altar and tabernacle are predictably classical.[28]

Mapledurham's chapel has obvious stylistic affinities with those at Milton Manor (completed 1773; from the exterior apparently an ordinary room on the first floor) and at Stonor Park. Nearby East Hendred House should also be mentioned, for though its fabric dates from the thirteenth century, it was adorned with a Gillow tabernacle at much the same time as the other houses, where Gillows were also responsible for the altars and their ornaments. None of this was coincidence. At Mapledurham and Stonor there were important family connections between the Blounts and the Stonors; Bryant Barrett of Milton took as his second wife Winifred Eyston of East Hendred. Barrett was a customer of Gillows' London branch; there were ties of friendship as well as business between Gillows, Blounts, and Stonors. The earliest link appears to be Gillows' involvement with work on Gothicizing the hall and chapel at Stonor in 1757–9. Charles Stonor (1737–81) married Mary, daughter of Michael Blount of Mapledurham, who was on friendly terms with Robert Gillow, Senior. Blount's younger brother, Henry Tichborne Blount, acted briefly as Gillows' agent in London before they set up their own business there. Later he became president of Douai College, where Robert Gillow's youngest son, John, was a student: it was he who ordered from the family firm the fine writing-table as a gift for Mr Stonor which is still at Stonor.[29] Robert Gillow's eldest son, Richard I, was an 'intimate friend' of Henry Blundell of Ince, whose daughter Catherine married Charles Stonor's son Thomas, and who gave the altar and painted glass when the chapel at Stonor was largely remodelled by Gillows in the late 1790s.[30] I give this as one instance of the convoluted links that ramified among Catholic families at this

27 Richard Williams, *Mapledurham House* (Mapledurham, 1977), p. 7.

28 The altars at Milton and Mapledurham have or had in common sets of painted frontals for the various liturgical seasons: at Milton these are still stored in a 'cupboard' which opens at the side of the altar; at Mapledurham one has strayed to the Hall. Evidence for Gillows' responsibility at Mapledurham is in Michael Blount's letterbook now at Stonor (information kindly given by the Hon. Georgina Stonor). See also n. 29 below.

29 The Gillow bills and letters at Stonor are, with the rest of the extensive archive there, presently closed under the trust established by the will of the late Sherman Stonor, 6th Lord Camoys, and will remain closed for some years to come. I am indebted to Georgina Stonor for the information on which this section is based.

30 *Passages from the Diaries of Mrs Philip Lybbe Powys*, ed. Emily J. Climenson (London, 1899), pp. 345–6; *Stonor* [guidebook, nd], pp. 14–15.

time, when frequent intermarriage, and ties of trust, and of trusteeship, were an essential part of their social fabric.

Another Oxfordshire house with a direct link to Gillows in Lancaster was Britwell Prior, which was inherited from the Simeons by Thomas Weld, younger brother of Edward Weld of Stonyhurst and Lulworth. He visited Britwell in 1771 and soon after went to live there for a few years before he succeeded his brother in 1775.[31] In 1771, the year of his majority, he ordered a 'very neat altar for the Chapel' (an elegant oval room), 'with mahogany ends, & curious front or Antependium, inlaid, carved, & gilt', and 'a very neat Tabernacle & steps with a Dome, all curiously inlaid & gilt; also a neat Temple upon the Dome, carved & gilt', accompanied by six handsome carved and gilt candlesticks, plus four more the next year.[32]

Thomas Weld's elder brother Edward was the earliest-known patron of Gillows in this context. In 1770 they supplied his house at Stonyhurst with a 'large & handsome tomb altar of curious wood and workmanship with carving, gilding and inlaying, also a cupboard within with doors . . . 2 neat mahogany pedestals, 1 for each side the altar, a little inlaid' for £44 8*s*. 6*d*., plus £1 underpaid.[33] Six large and handsome mahogany candlesticks, part gilt and 'curiously neat' at 38*s*. each, followed in April;[34] and in September 'a very neat mahogany tabernacle with a variety of carving and gilding about it, a Rich Temple upon it, and a large double pedestal to place it and the candlesticks upon' for £21.[35] The altar, described some years later as a 'masterpiece', does not survive, but the tabernacle and pedestals do (plate 3).[36] Richard Gillow I suggested fitting up the chapel in Passion Week, since the Lancaster Assizes fell in Holy Week, and then he could not possibly leave home,[37] because so much business was done while the town was thronged.

All this emphasis on 'neat', 'curious', and 'handsome' work suggests

[31] For the correct succession [cf. Mrs Bryan Stapleton, *A History of the Post-Reformation Catholic Missions in Oxfordshire* (London, 1906), and Biddy O'Sullivan, *The Two Britwells* (privately printed, Britwell Salome, 1969), p. 61, which introduce an extra generation, making Thomas Weld-Simeon succeeded Sir E. Simeon in 1768, whereas he did not survive his uncle], see Berkeley, *Lulworth*, p. 127.

[32] W 22/304; 3/154; 3/320.

[33] W 22/210, 220.

[34] W 22/156.

[35] W 22/189.

[36] [Father T. G. Holt, S.J.,] 'Church Furniture for Stonyhurst in 1770', *The Stonyhurst Magazine*, 35, no. 433 (Oct. 1966), pp. 25–6.

[37] W 166/112; altar fixed Oct. 1771: 3/344; 22/431.

Plate 3 Tabernacle and Pedestals for Stonyhurst, 1770 (Stonyhurst College).

that Gillows lavished particular care on these items. Stonyhurst was an influential house in its locality, and its altar was admired: but one neighbour who liked it could not afford to emulate it and inquired if Gillows could supply a plainer and cheaper set of candlesticks. Indeed they could, came the reply, for half the labour and half the cost, 'that would look sufficiently neat for Chappels in a common way'.[38] Gillows did supply some less expensive altar fittings.[39] One commission that tells us something about problems and solutions was for The Revd Lawrence Hadley, O.S.B., of Brindle, Lancashire. Richard Gillow I was anxious to hurry the work along in time for Easter 1800: he even put the work in different hands in the hope of getting it finished for Passion Week, since it was obviously inconvenient to have workmen in the chapel during Holy Week; there was no gilder in Lancaster who could undertake the delicate gilding of the monstrance—these were always sent to London; and in the capital Richard Gillow's sons were so far unable to find four suitable figures for the niches.[40] Mr Hadley's commission included an altar, tabernacle, cupola, and two oval cupboards, a stool, reading-desk, and mahogany tripod candlestand with gilt capitals. The tabernacle was lined with white silk lutestring; it had two curtains for the door, fringed with yellow, and neat, ornamental blue sarcanet drapery for the 'Temple'. There were six candlesticks and six sham tin candles. The base or drum of the cupola was carved with wheat-heads and other motifs, and gilded. The oval cupboards were veneered with the usual mahogany, purplewood, and holly; less usual were the limewood capitals and bases, and the maple used in the astragals of the dome.[41] Almost a year later Gillows wrote that they had finished Mr Hadley's crucifix at last: it had been a tedious job to gild the ivory figure without spoiling it, and part of the work had to be done in London. At the same time they supplied 'an elegant Gilt Cross, with 3 carved Cherubs, a Carv'd Globe to place it in with a Serpent twisted round it', all gilt in burnished gold.[42]

The pulpits made by Gillows were also classical in style. In 1778 they supplied Mr Butler of Hornby with a neat mahogany pulpit, having a

[38] W 166/75.

[39] For example, W 8/307,310 (Mr Weeble); 8/327 (Mrs Hennage); 17/1753 (Walsh Porter); 17/1822 (The Revd Dr T. Rigby).

[40] W 174/44; also 29–30, 159, 175, 320–1, 331; 98/1562–1575.

[41] W 98/1575 a–f.

[42] W 174/201v,196. None of these ornaments is known to survive, but the handsome church (1796) at Brindle St Joseph's does. It was restored in 1986–7 under the leadership of Father Thomas Loughlin, O.S.B., to whom I am indebted for this information.

curved front inlaid with a dove, for £7 5*s.* 8*d.*[43] A deal pulpit cost a mere 35*s.*[44] Much more expensive was an oak pulpit made in 1783, which had a fluted frieze and cornice, a back with fluted pilasters, bases, and capitals, also fluted pilasters on the enclosed part, which was supported on a pillar and approached by steps and handrails of turned balusters—in other words, a 'wine-glass' pulpit, which cost £33 8*s.* 0¼*d.*[45] A mahogany pulpit made in 1801 for The Revd Mr Barrow of Garstang had a purplewood longband; its principal ornament, engraved by Monsieur Mangenot, was the Holy Lamb on a white holly ground. William Barrow was responsible for the greater part of the work, which took four weeks and four days and required the light of four pounds of candles. 'Duke' (Marmaduke) Ball bored the feet for wheels. All this cost £14 2*s.* 0½*d.*, which would have been more had not the client provided an old panel of his own for the side that did not show (plate 4).[46]

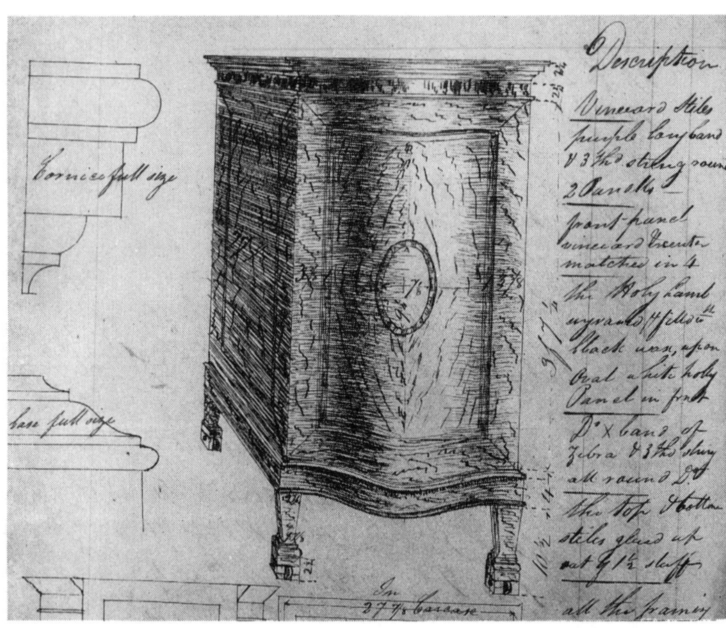

Plate 4 Pulpit for The Revd Mr Barrow, 1801 (Westminster City Library).

[43] W 169/118.
[44] W 8/623.
[45] W 8/678.
[46] W 98/1667.

I have digressed from the chapels in the larger houses and I must now return to them, for it is inevitably these which are most interesting and for which some designs survive, if not the furnishings themselves.[47] I cite three examples. Sir William Stanley ordered an altar for his new house, Hooton Hall, in 1777, only to be informed by Gillows that while it would be completed as soon as possible, 'it is a sort of work that cannot be executed so well if hurried.'[48] The altar and its accompaniments were dispatched some ten weeks later: the altar-piece of the Ionic Order (not indicated in the design, plate 5) had pilasters, capitals, and carved ornaments for the frieze and pediment gilt in burnished gold; below was 'a neat tomb altar' of mahogany, banded and strung, inlaid with various colours and ornaments, and a satinwood tabernacle with an inlaid dome top; all the ornaments were carved and gilt in London.[49] The basic cost to the firm was £34 9*s.* 1½*d.*, their charge to Sir William £52 7*s.* 6*d.*, which means a profit of about fifty per cent.[50] Second, Basil Fitzherbert had a chapel at Swynnerton Hall, which was enriched in 1788 with a Gillow altar inlaid with purplewood, tulipwood, and kingwood. Its inlaid panel came from London, and the tabernacle door was also inlaid there—another example of co-operation between the two ends of the Gillow empire (plate 6). The basic cost was £24, the charge £31 10*s.* 0*d.*, so that Gillows made about thirty per cent on this job.[51] Lastly, Tixall Hall near Lichfield was the seat of another leading Catholic family, the Cliffords. Thomas Clifford's altar was ordered in London but, as often, made in Lancaster in 1795. Its panel, of finest mahogany, was inlaid with a white oval in the centre; the pilasters were of solid purplewood, and tulipwood was used for inlaid bands. The mouldings, capitals, flutes in pilasters, letters, and Gloria were gilt and burnished (plate 7). The basic cost was £10 7*s.* 10¼*d.*, the charge £15 15*s.* 0*d.*,[52] so that Gillows' profit was again about fifty per cent. This was distinctly higher than their more normal twenty-five per cent, and it looks as though they stung these clients—either because the work was out of the ordinary (not very convincing since the firm kept a stock of altar designs ready[53]) or, I fear, because they were rich.

[47] Cf. Sir William Gerard: pedestal and cross supplied, ivory crucifix repaired, W 9/974, 170/580, dated 21 and 29 Dec. 1784; gilt cross for top of tabernacle and gilt image on metal sent from London for the Dowager Lady Gerard, 19/2654.

[48] W 171/189.

[49] W 71/2061; 94/109; 171/213.

[50] W 171/213; 11/2601; 94/109.

[51] W 12/2601; 94/230.

[52] W 18/2102; 97/1184.

[53] Cf. Gillows to James Maxwell, of Kirkconnell, near Dumfries: they had showed several altar designs to Frederick Maxwell, W 173/27.

Plate 5 A Tomb Altar for Sir William Stanley, 1787 (Westminster City Library).

Plate 6 Antepodium, Step, and Tabernacle for Basil Fitzherbert, 1788 (Westminster City Library).

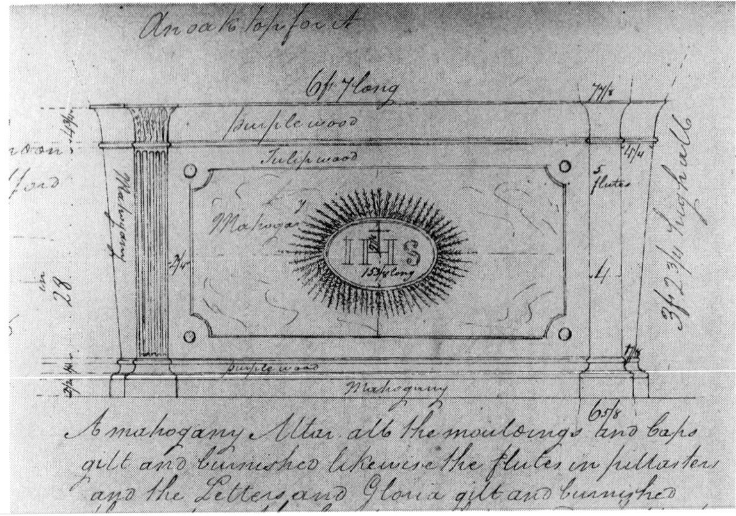

Plate 7 Altar for Thomas Clifford, 1795 (Westminster City Library).

As I indicated at the beginning, this topic has grown (and is still expanding) from the objects that Gillows produced to the chapels for which they were designed to the families who worshipped in them. Such is the nature of research. There are many questions either unanswered or only partly solved. In conclusion I return to the chapel at East Hendred. It is one of the rare instances in this country (others are at Stonor and Hazlewood Castle) where Catholic worship has never ceased. It is gratifying to record that its owner has recently rescued from a store-room a number of carved items which evidently form part of a design based on classical architecture: they include a tabernacle as well as a shelf supported on console brackets. I think it is now superfluous to mention the name of the maker,[54] but I end by remarking that after Gillows had 'left trade' and

[54] Mr J. Eyston informed me that his brother has Gillow bills at East Hendred, but I have not seen them. I am indebted to many people who have kindly helped me in the preparation of this article, especially the Hon. Georgina Stonor, Mr J. and Lady Anne Eyston, Mr T. Eyston, the late Mrs Marjorie Mockler, The Revd Geoffrey Scott, O.S.B., the archivist at the Westminster City Library Archives Department (Victoria branch), Miss M. Swarbrick and her colleagues; and to the authorities at Stonyhurst College for help and for permission to reproduce plate 3.

established themselves as landowners at Leighton Hall (which, of course, has a chapel and altar) one of their descendants married into the Eystons of East Hendred. Thus the story has in a sense come full circle.

Queen Mary and Westfield College,
University of London

VICTORIAN FEMINISM AND CATHOLIC ART: THE CASE OF MRS JAMESON[1]

by SHERIDAN GILLEY

'NOW Church History', wrote John Henry Newman in 1843, 'is made up of these three elements—miracles, monkery, Popery',[2] so that anyone sympathetic to the subject must sympathize with these. Much the same, however, could be said of Christian art. The young Southey on a visit to Madrid stood incredulous before a series of paintings depicting the life of St Francis. 'I do not remember ever to have been so greatly astonished', he recalled. '"Do they really believe all this, Sir?" said I to my companion. "Yes, and a great deal more of the same kind", was the reply.'[3] The paradox was that works of genius served the ends of a drivelling superstition, a dilemma resolved in the 1830s by the young Augustus Pugin, who decided that the creation of decent Christian architecture presupposed the profession of Catholic Christianity. The old Protestant hostility to graven images was in part a revulsion from that idolatrous popish veneration of the Virgin and saints which had inspired frescos, statues, and altar-pieces in churches and monasteries throughout Catholic Europe; but what on earth did a modern educated Protestant make of the endless Madonnas, monks, and miracles adorning the buildings which he was expected as a man of cultivation to admire? At the very least, he required a sympathetic instruction in the meaning of the iconography before his eyes, and some guidance about its relation to the rest of what he believed. The great intermediary in this process was Ruskin; but there was at least one other interpreter of Catholic art celebrated in her day, Mrs Anna Brownell Jameson, whose most popular works, *Sacred and Legendary Art*,[4] *Legends of the Monastic Orders*,[5] and *Legends of the Madonna*,[6] told the Englishman what he could safely think and feel amid the alien aesthetic allurements of Catholicism.

[1] I wish to thank Dr A. L. Sanders of Birkbeck College, London, and Dr C. J. Wright of the British Library for their assistance with the writing of this paper.

[2] Newman to J. R. Hope, 6 Nov. 1843 [Francis Bacchus, ed.], *Correspondence of John Henry Newman with John Keble and Others 1839–1845* (London, 1917), p. 282.

[3] Robert Southey, *Vindiciae Ecclesiae Anglicanae Letters to Charles Butler, Esq. comprising Essays on the Romish Religion and Vindicating the Book of the Church* (London, 1826), p. 8.

[4] See n. 27 below.

[5] See n. 29 below.

[6] See n. 31 below.

I approach Mrs Jameson in fear and trembling, as I can only imagine that she has been the subject of a big American biography, given that her life story is such a text-book case for study by feminist historians.[7] She was born in 1794, in Dublin, the oldest child of the Irish nationalist artist Denis Brownell Murphy, who had the good luck to be in England in 1798 and so escape hanging or worse in the English suppression of the first modern Irish revolution. The family was celebrated but impecunious; at sixteen, the young Anna was already a bread-winner as governess to the daughter of the Marquis of Winchester. Her father was financially embarrassed by the death of his patroness the Princess Charlotte, whose executor, Leopold of Belgium, declined to pay him for the miniatures which he had painted from Lely and others for the Princess of 'The Beauties of the Court of Charles II'; and it may have been partly money that prevented Anna's marriage to a promising young Irish barrister, Robert Jameson, as, nursing a broken heart, she set off as a governess on her first Italian tour.

On her travels she wrote *A Lady's Diary*, reissued as the *Diary of an Ennuyée*,[8] which was the first work to make her famous. It conveyed a strong confessional sense of her private suffering, and she concluded it in the best romantic manner with her own death and burial in the graveyard of the Capuchin monastery at Autun. In 1825 she married Jameson, who quickly showed her the sort of husband he meant to be by deserting her for an evening with friends on the Sunday after his wedding. In 1829 he became puisne judge in Dominica, leaving Anna in England. Her visit to Goethe's family in Weimar in 1833 introduced her to the flower of German culture and made her its interpreter in her own country,[9] just as her husband journeyed west to Toronto, where he was in time to become Chancellor, Speaker, and Attorney-General of Upper Canada. Anna made the effort to live with him there in 1836, as she recorded in her three-volume work *Winter Studies and Summer Rambles in Canada*,[10] which also

[7] The main sources for her life are Gerardine Macpherson, *Memoirs of the Life of Anna Jameson* (London, 1878); Mrs Steuart Erskine, *Anna Jameson: Letters and Friendships (1812–1860)* (London, 1915); G. H. Needler, *Letters of Anna Jameson to Ottilie von Goethe* (Oxford, 1939); Harriet Martineau, 'Mrs Jameson', in *Biographical Sketches* (London, 1869); Bessie Rayner Parkes, *Vignettes: Twelve Biographical Sketches* (London, 1866); Bessie Rayner Belloc, 'In Rome with Mrs. Jameson', in *In a Walled Garden* (London, 1895), pp. 67–77; and *DNB*.

[8] *Diary of an Ennuyée* (London, 1826).

[9] Mrs Jameson, *Sketches of Germany Art—Literature—Character* (Frankfurt, 1837); *Visits and Sketches at Home and Abroad*, 2 vols (London, 1839). She also translated Princess Amelia of Saxony's *Social Life in Germany* (London, 1840).

[10] *Winter Studies and Summer Rambles in Canada*, 3 vols (London, 1838).

describes her brave journey to the wigwams of the Chippawa and Ottawa Indians. 'I can promise you', she wrote to Goethe's daughter-in-law Ottilie,

> an Indian Hunter, six feet high and very prettily tattoed, one side of his face covered with red paint and the other painted with soot and oil,—will you have him? You must know how to skin a Buffalo in five minutes, and cut him up, *artistement*, and how to knock a dog on the head and put him, half dead, into a pot for a stew . . . And if your Indian is dissatisfied, he will not kick you above six times a day and then sell you to his comrade for a gun or a Brass kettle . . . on the whole good husbands and faithful lovers are not *more* common in savage than in civilized life.[11]

In the end Anna decided that in some ways Indian women were better off than their European sisters; at least Indian men did not falsely claim to be civilized and Christian. In 1838 she returned to Europe and lived apart from her husband till his death. Jameson was a correct, cold man, and acquiesced in their separation; in the end he turned to drink, and in 1850 lost his post through alcoholic incompetence. Until his last years he gave Anna an allowance, but even that ceased when he was pensioned off, and he left his money to another married woman.

Thus Anna spent her life husbandless, and her early books were about women. She followed up the ennuyée's diary with a volume on *The Loves of the Poets*,[12] and two volumes of *Memoirs of Celebrated Female Sovereigns*.[13] Her best volume in this vein is *Characteristics of Women* from Shakespeare,[14] which brings out both her talent for clear and simple story-telling and her wide and generous sympathies. She supported her father by writing the letterpress when his miniatures of the Caroline beauties were published at small profit to himself;[15] and after his stroke, in 1834, she was the sole support of her mother and unmarried sisters, and her writing was their main working means of livelihood.

It was also, however, the product of a pattern of friendships, especially with female friends with unsatisfactory husbands. Anna's two deepest associations were with Ottilie von Goethe and with Lady Byron. I need

[11] Anna Jameson to Ottilie von Goethe, 18 Jan. 1837, in Needler, *Letters*, p. 73.
[12] *The Loves of the Poets* (London, 1829).
[13] *Memoirs of Celebrated Female Sovereigns*, 2 vols (London, 1831).
[14] *Characteristics of Women, Moral, Poetical, and Historical* (London, 1832).
[15] *Beauties of the Court of King Charles the Second: a Series of Portraits* (London, 1833).

not reflect on Byron's character as a husband, while Ottilie's husband died of dissipation; and it was Anna who later cared for Ottilie in Vienna, where Ottilie bore the illegitimate son of a young Englishman, Charles Sterling, who deserted her for the ministry of the Church of England. One of the deepest distresses of Anna's life was to be the loss of the love of Lady Byron, who turned on her in a rage, it seems, when Anna had become the repository of the confidences of Byron's sad and scandalous daughter Ada. Other lady friends included the writer actress Fanny Kemble, who divorced her American husband, and Harriet Martineau, whose fiancé died insane and who, like Anna, had to support herself by her writing. Anna's own romantic nature was only reinforced by her sufferings, and she accompanied the Brownings on part of their honeymoon. Her last great friendship was with her niece Gerardine, who was her secretary and fellow-artist in her studies in Italy; but, to her sorrow, Gerardine married a headstrong and ultimately unsuccessful Scots artist, Robert Macpherson. Anna's own last years were relieved by a government pension secured for her by Thackeray, and she died in 1860, a martyr to art, of pneumonia contracted from walking through the snow to the British Museum. The widowed and impoverished Gerardine wrote Anna's biography in Rome while dying of rheumatic heart disease. The final note to the volume is by yet another doughty Victorian lady-writer, Mrs Oliphant.

It is, therefore, hardly surprising, given Anna's need to work as breadwinner with other women in a world of unsatisfactory men, that in her own day she was widely condemned as a wild feminist and a disgrace to her sex.'Though greatly admired and respected', sniffed Samuel Carter Hall, 'she was one of the few exceptions I have met with as regards Irishwomen—not made to be loved.' '"The Beauties of the Court of Charles II"', continued Hall, 'was not a seemly introduction to a literary career in the case of a woman', and Mrs Jameson was a precursor of those 'strong-minded' sister-soldiers of women's rights, 'who wrangle at public meetings, and annually assail Parliament, so to alter their accustomed legal and natural rights as to place woman in all ways on what they term an equality with man.'[16] The judgement is not unexpected, but it is surprisingly echoed by the bluestocking Miss Martineau, who, rather unkindly, considered Anna vain and given to 'craving for society and its luxuries'.[17]

[16] S. C. Hall, F.S.A., *Retrospect of a Long Life: from 1815 to 1883*, 2 vols (London, 1883), 2, pp. 171–2.

[17] Martineau, 'Mrs Jameson', p. 434.

Anna's feminism, however, was of a very moderate sort: her manifesto on the equality of the sexes claims to be founded on the Gospel of Christ, and insists on the 'virtue, self-control and purity of heart and person required from man and woman equally'—in short, her feminism was a protest against a double moral standard, against 'all conventional laws and all relations and constraints between the two sexes which . . . let loose the passions of the one sex to prey on the other . . . depraving and degrading both.' 'Marriage', she wrote, is 'the holiest . . . of all human institutions', but its obligations are equally binding on both partners. It is not clear that she believed in divorce, which was not legally available to her in any case, and she also thought that 'the ordering of domestic life' was the 'sacred province' of women, who were rightly excluded by 'the infirmities and duties which maternity entails' from any part in government or politics.[18] When she turned her pen to the subject of women's rights, it was to the defence of a special sphere for women's work, especially for the spread of sisterhoods of Charity.[19] It was this moderate feminism which enlarged her sympathies towards Catholicism, for though she was no friend to enclosed nunneries, the sisterhoods gave women valuable work to perform and allowed a degree of feminine autonomy from male control. Catholics were also kind to her: there is a pleasing vignette of the Fathers of an Irish Dominican priory regaling her with whisky-punch and electing her their Reverend Mother.[20] In her last years her closest friends included such strong-minded feminist women, who were to become converts to Rome, as the writer Bessie Parkes, later mother of Hilaire Belloc,[21] and the poetess Adelaide Anne Procter, now best remembered as the inventor of Arthur Sullivan's Lost Chord.[22] Anna denied the existence of distinctly feminine virtues, but she did admit the existence of feminine attributes, and it was the strongly feminine streak in Catholic devotion and piety that informs and pervades her interpretation of Catholic art.

These sympathies were only slowly acquired. Her own religious upbringing was liberal: her later admiration was for Unitarian divines like Dr Channing, and she never addressed herself to the truth of dogmatic or controversial theology. Her insight into Catholicism came on her first

[18] Needler, *Letters*, pp. 233–4.
[19] *Sisters of Charity, Catholic and Protestant, Abroad and at Home* (London, 1855); also *The Communion of Labour: A Second Lecture on the Social Employments of Women* (London, 1856).
[20] Erskine, *Anna Jameson*, p. 252.
[21] Rayner Parkes, *Vignettes*; Rayner Belloc, 'In Rome with Mrs. Jameson'.
[22] See *The Complete Works of Adelaide A. Procter with an Introduction by Charles Dickens* (London, 1905).

Italian tour, from a visit to a miraculous Madonna, 'decorated with a real blue silk gown spangled with tinsel stars'. Anna's indignation was turned to warmth by a woman who brought her little boy to the image to teach him his Ave Maria, and to leave an offering in a box marked 'for the bashful poor'. 'The simple piety of this woman, though mistaken in its object' wrote Anna, 'appeared to me respectable, and the Virgin, in her sky-blue brocade and gilt tiara, no longer an object to ridicule. I returned home rejoicing in kinder, gentler, happier thoughts.'[23] It is this spirit that suffuses Anna's books on *Sacred and Legendary Art*. She is not too worried about the historic truth or otherwise of the 'miracles, monkery, Popery' of her subject; rather, they encompass a vast range of human experience much of which calls forth the deepest sympathy, especially the sympathies most accessible and natural to women.

Thus the volumes are pervaded by a religious spirit, in spite of the authoress's claim to be writing from an artistic rather than a religious point of view. As the daughter of an artist, Anna might have been supposed to take a burning interest in technique. She was a competent copyist, and she and her niece filled her volumes with line-drawings of the paintings described in the text. Her earliest purely artistic work included her now historically important guidebook to the London picture galleries.[24] Again, her volumes on the Italian artists show a professional interest in art history as such,[25] and she was one of the earliest to propagate a taste in England for Italian and German primitives. Writing before the discussion of technique became common, however, she shows very little interest in aesthetics, which is what may lie behind Ruskin's remark that she knew 'as much about art as the cat'.[26]

Rather, she built on a sort of lower criticism of instruction on the actual content of the painting. Thus the Introduction to the first volume of *Sacred and Legendary Art* distinguishes devotional from historical subjects, as the '*sacra conversazione*' from miracles and martyrdoms, and explains the association of saints with other saints in art, and with particular institutions, families, and places, with a long list of just such local patrons. It then surveys the meaning of a range of Christian symbols variously depicted: the nimbus, fish, cross, lamb, pelican, dragon, lion,

[23] Macpherson, *Memoirs*, pp. 34–5.

[24] *A Handbook to the Public Galleries of Art in and near London* (London, 1842).

[25] *Memoirs of the early Italian Painters, and of the Progress of Painting in Italy*, 2 vols (London, 1845).

[26] Ruskin to John James Ruskin, 28 Sept. 1845, Harold I. Shapiro, *Ruskin in Italy: Letters to his Parents 1845* (Oxford, 1972), p. 216; cited in Francis Haskell, *Rediscoveries in Art: Some Aspects of Taste,Fashion and Collecting in England and France* (London, 1976), p. 106.

hind, peacock, crown, sword, arrows, poniard, cauldron, pincers and shears, wheels, fire, bell, shell, skull, anvil, palm, standard, olive, dove, lily, flaming heart, book, church, scourge, chalice, ship, anchor, lantern; then the sacred associations of particular colours. The text of the volume proper passes from the legends, attributes, and characteristic depiction of the angels and archangels, through the Four Evangelists, the Twelve Apostles, which conclude on the portrayal of Judas, and the four Latin and five Greek Doctors of the Church, and the stories of St Mary Magdalene, St Martha, St Lazarus, St Maximin, St Marcella, St Mary of Egypt, Mary the Penitent, St Thais, and St Pelagia. The second volume surveys the patron saints of Christendom, virgin patronesses, early martyrs, Greek martyrs, Latin and Roman martyrs, then martyrs of Tuscany, Lombardy, Spain, and France, early bishops, hermit saints, and warriors. Their stories are told with skill and sympathy, with a survey of the principal paintings depicting them. The reader primarily learns the religious meaning of the picture through its wealth of distinctive forms and symbols, how to distinguish the cherubim from the seraphim, why St Jerome has a lion, which saints floated across land and sea on what, why an old lady, Mark's mother, might appear in the Last Supper, or why the Emperor Trajan should have been delivered from hell-fire. Indeed, on this level the volumes are still very useful, if you cannot get beyond the name of the fourth archangel, or wonder what Lazarus had to do with Provence, or why St Barbara should appear on cannon and suits of armour: the lesson being one in a complex religious symbolism which seemed exotic, colourful, and new in the Protestant England of Victoria.

Anna's real interest, however, was in the spiritual meaning of this material: that the symbolic language of the Catholic centuries contained the teaching of

> a literature ... which asserted and kept alive in the hearts of men those pure principles of Christianity ... in which peace was represented as better than war, and sufferance more dignified than resistance: which exhibited poverty and toil as honourable, and charity as the first of virtues; which held up to imitation and emulation self-sacrifice in the cause of good, and contempt of death for conscience' sake; a literature in which the tenderness, the chastity, the heroism of woman, played a conspicuous part; which distinctly protested against slavery, against violence, against impurity in word and deed; which refreshed the fevered and darkened spirit with images of moral beauty and truth; revealed bright glimpses of a

> land, where 'the wicked cease from troubling,' and brought down the angels of God with shining wings and bearing crowns of glory, to do battle with the demons of darkness, to catch the fleeting soul of the triumphant martyr, and carry it at once into a paradise of eternal blessedness and peace![27]

Peace, blessedness, sufferance, poverty, toil, charity, self-sacrifice, the tenderness, the chastity, the heroism of woman, suggest the personal qualities that Anna found in Catholic art, perhaps not least because so much of it depicted women anyway. Even the story of St Peter devotes a page to the Roman legend of his daughter Petronilla. The virtues extolled are generally of a gentle, abnegatory, contemplative kind, as if in protest against the values of a brute, male, Protestant industrial world.

Saintly women are as common in the annals of the religious life, but in Anna's third *Sacred and Legendary* volume, on the monastic orders, she had a stronger antipathy to overcome. 'There is a *reality* in these monkish personages which puts them beyond the reach of poetry, and that reality is sometimes horrible', she wrote to Ottilie. 'Neither are the pictures so pleasing, and you must remember that the whole subject I have treated *artistically*, with reference to art and not with reference to Religion or morals.'[28] This is not strictly true, because the authoress was essentially concerned to explain the art in terms of the religion that inspired it. She begins unpromisingly enough: 'Monachism is not the consecration of the beautiful, even in idea; it is the apotheosis of deformity and suffering ... Pain is pain; ugliness is ugliness; the quaint is not the graceful.' Too many monastic pictures are concerned only with the glory of the order, seeming to some to serve a 'selfish palpable purpose' associated with 'the depravation of the priestly character, the tyranny of rulers, and the ignorance of the people'. Yet Anna's overall judgement is far more positive. The pictures of the Cistercians, Vallombrosians, Camaldolesi 'are especially characterised by an air of settled peace, of abstract quietude'. The Franciscans inspired that 'Mystic school in poetry and painting ... which so strangely combined the spiritual with the sensual, and the beautiful with the terrible, and the tender with the inexorable; which first found utterance in the works of Dante and of the ancient painters of Tuscany and Umbria.'[29]

[27] *Sacred and Legendary Art*, 2 vols (London, 1848), 10th edn (London, 1890), 1, p. 5.

[28] Anna Jameson to Ottilie von Goethe, 2 June 1849, Needler, *Letters*, p. 167.

[29] *Legends of the Monastic Orders, as represented in the Fine Arts* (London, 1850), pp. xviii–xxii.

> To this we may add another and a stronger claim on our respect and moral sympathies. The protection and the better education given to women in these early communities; the venerable and distinguished rank assigned to them when, as governesses of their Order, they became in a manner dignitaries of the Church; the introduction of their beautiful and saintly effigies, clothed with all the insignia of sanctity and authority, into the decoration of places of worship and books of devotion—did more, perhaps, for the general cause of womanhood than all the boasted institutions of chivalry.[30]

It is, however, in the fourth volume in the series on the *Legends of the Madonna* that Anna's enthusiasm for her subject attains its most fervent expression, and its most feminist as well. Again, she begins by insisting that her plan is 'purely artistic'; but her real concern is for the inner meaning of the legends, above all

> that, in spite of errors, exaggerations, abuses, this worship did comprehend certain great elemental truths interwoven with our human nature ... Everywhere it seems to have found in the human heart some deep sympathy—deeper far than mere theological doctrine could reach—ready to accept it; and in every land the ground prepared for it in some already dominant idea of a mother-Goddess, chaste, beautiful, and benign ... Others will have it that these scattered, dim, mistaken—often gross and perverted—ideas which were afterwards gathered into the pure, dignified, tender image of the Madonna, were but as the voice of a mighty prophecy, sounded through all the generations of men, even from the beginning of time, of the coming moral regeneration, and complete and harmonious development of the whole human race, by the establishment, on a higher basis, of what has been called the 'feminine element' in society. And let me at least speak for myself. In the perpetual iteration of that beautiful image of THE WOMAN highly blessed—*there*, where others saw only pictures or statues, I have seen this great hope standing like a spirit beside the visible form: in the fervent worship once universally given to that gracious presence, I have beheld an acknowledgement of a higher as well as gentler power than that of the strong hand and the might that makes the right,—and in every earnest votary one who, as he knelt, was in this sense pious beyond

[30] Ibid., p. xx.

> the reach of his own thought, and 'devout beyond the meaning of his will.'[31]

Anna's ideal was only fully realized in the Sistine Madonna, 'the transfigured woman, at once completely human and completely divine, an abstraction of power, purity, and love . . .'.[32] The reader is shown the Virgin's praises in the words of Dante and Chaucer, Petrarch and Wordsworth, and even in an imaginatively interpreted piece of Shelley, and then proceeds to consider her symbols, sun, moon and star, lily, rose, enclosed garden, tower, temple, city, gate, and cedar; and so to her pictures under their innumerable titles, as the Virgin Glorious, enthroned and crowned, as the Virgin of Mercy, the Mater Dolorosa, and the Immaculate Conception, and with all the permutations and combinations of her attendant saints. Only then do we contemplate the details of her background and historic life on earth from the marriage of her parents, her conception and nativity, presentation and betrothal, annunciation, visitation, childbearing and flight into Egypt, her presence at the Temple and at the Cross and Pentecost, and so on, to her Assumption and her Coronation once again. The underlying tone is one of agnostic reverence, recalling the teaching of Miss Martineau's master, Auguste Comte, that while Catholicism was scientifically untrue, it was true in a deeper sense as the model for Comte's own Religion of Humanity, in which mankind itself would be worshipped under the form of the ideal woman, the combination of Beatrice, Laura, and the Blessed Mary.

Anna did not live to write more than a portion of the crown of the series, *The History of Our Lord*, which was completed on a more severely chronological model by Lady Eastlake, who began with the fall of Lucifer and moved through all the types of Christ as patriarch, prophet, king, and priest in the Old Testament.[33] Like the Virgin, Our Lord is described in lovely flowing prose, but I must not claim more for my authoress than she is worth: 'There was no philosophy in all this', wrote Harriet Martineau of Anna's *Characteristics of Women*, 'but only fancy and feeling'.[34] Perhaps, remembering Miss Martineau's grim utilitarian philosophy, we may be grateful for its absence in Anna. 'Out of the fulness of my own heart and

[31] *Legends of the Madonna, as represented in the Fine Arts* (London, 1852), 5th edn (London, 1872), pp. xviii–xix.

[32] Ibid., p. xlii.

[33] *The History of Our Lord as exemplified in works of art: with that of his types . . . Continued and completed by Lady Eastlake* (London, 1864).

[34] Martineau, 'Mrs Jameson', p. 432.

soul have I written it',[35] she said of one of her books, so justifying Miss Martineau's charge that she was so 'prepossessed by personal griefs and rendered liable to dwell on the scenery of human passions in one direction till it became magnified beyond all reason.'[36] Yet that is surely characteristically Victorian, the appropriation of Catholic art to an end not Catholic. Rather, Anna's Catholic sympathies had an obvious role in that deepening of humanitarian sentiment which, as in Dickens, still claimed a general religious sanction; and that sanction in Dickens, as in Anna, might be called Unitarian. It is not always to our taste. As Wilde said, a man would have to have a heart of stone not to laugh at the death of Little Nell; and many moderns find distressing the more overtly religious expression of the same sort of sentiment in a gentle Jesus meek and mild or in the Marian effusions of Fr Faber. I hope that I have done justice to Anna's lively spirit. Where she was surely right was in only finding art interesting when it points to something beyond itself.

University of Durham

[35] Cited in ibid.
[36] Ibid., p. 433.

HENRY STYLEMAN LE STRANGE: TRACTARIAN, ARTIST, SQUIRE

by W. M. JACOB

THE life of Henry Styleman le Strange illustrates a number of significant factors in the development of the Tractarian Movement and its relationship with the arts. He was a devout layman who wished to advance the practice of Tractarian worship and spirituality. He did this by encouraging Tractarian worship in the churches on his estates and by appointing Tractarian clergy to livings of which he was patron.. He was himself a distinguished amateur artist and architect, who was modestly influential in the nineteenth-century ideal for exploring the interrelationship between the self-dedication of the artist to moral and religious truth, and Christian art. This can be seen in his own artistic work, in the tower and nave roofs at Ely Cathedral, and his collaborations with other architects, notably Butterfield. As important as his own work is his influence as a patron, not merely in restoring churches on his estate or in the development of a seaside resort, but in the pattern that emerges of his friends and acquaintances also commissioning his favoured architect.

Le Strange was born in 1815 and, like his forebears, was educated at Eton and Christ Church. It was presumably as an undergraduate at Christ Church in the mid-1830s that he became acquainted with Tractarianism. For a sensitive youth of his background it must have been a most emotionally attractive expression of Christianity. Through his grandmother he was descended from what nineteenth-century guide books described as 'the distinguished family of Le Strange', who claimed their descent, through the eleventh-century Roland le Strange, from 'the original Saxon possessors of the soil'.[1] The parish church was full of medieval monuments to his ancestors. Among his ancestors was the royalist Sir Hamon l'Estrange, who had impetuously and ineffectually seized King's Lynn for the King in 1644. His early eighteenth-century forebears had been Nonjurors.[2] Fortunately perhaps for him, the male line had expired on the Grand Tour in 1734, and so the ancient but ramshackle mansion at Hunstanton had not been rebuilt in a Palladian style and had been left to be restored to its Tudor and rustic Jacobean glory by Henry le Strange in 1838.

[1] William White, *History, Gazeteer and Directory of Norfolk* (Sheffield, 1864), p. 998.

[2] G. M. Yould, 'Two Non jurors', *Norfolk Archaeology*, 25 (1972), pp. 364–81.

His medievalizing and romantic nature is indicated by his assumption by royal licence in 1839 of his grandmother's family name of le Strange, in addition to his father's less distinguished surname of Styleman, and his removal from the comfortable late seventeenth-century Snettisham Hall, which the Stylemans had built, to the more romantic Hunstanton Hall. His successful petition to the House of Lords in 1839 to be declared coheir of the barony of Camoys, and again in 1841 to be declared coheir of the barony of Hastings, is probably further evidence of his medievalizing tendencies.[3] Fortunately, perhaps, because his origins were authentically knightly and medieval, he was not as ambitious in his personal building projects as some of his contemporaries, for example, Charles Tennyson d'Eyncourt, who built the vast Bayons Manor in the 1830s to the ruin of his family fortune.[4] Le Strange's architectural ambitions were clearly restrained by his straitened financial circumstances. For years on end he economized by living in rented houses in London and not bringing his family and household to Hunstanton. Lengthy stays in Brussels and Paris were also undertaken to reduce household expenditure. The estate was very heavily mortgaged. Soon after le Strange's death his son, in 1865, put the Snettisham estate on the market in an attempt to pay off the mortgages held on the estate by Gurney's Bank. When the Snettisham estate was eventually sold in 1871 for £110,000 it failed to raise enough to pay off all the mortgages.[5]

Le Strange's deeply religious character emerges in a letter the distinguished architect William Butterfield wrote to the *Guardian*, rebuking the editor for the brief notice of his death. Butterfield noted that

> in his great humility and modesty he himself would wish me to be silent ... His deep and earnest religious character entirely accepted the Church movement of the last 30 years so far as it was loyal to the English Church. But it seemed a simple impossibility for him to go along with it when it failed in that respect. He would gladly have restored to her much that she had possessed in the earlier ages of her history, and was deeply sensible of the defects of the two centuries and more which preceded the Reformation.[6]

[3] *DNB*, 33.

[4] Mark Girouard, *The Victorian Country House* (London, 1979), pp. 103–9.

[5] Norfolk and Norwich Record office [hereafter NNRO], le Strange (Hunstanton) Supplementary Deposit, in a tin trunk containing diaries, 1850–1900. Diaries, 1865–71.

[6] The *Guardian*, 6 Aug. 1862.

There is no evidence about le Strange's early spiritual development. His diaries only survive from 1850. However, from 1848 there was a programme of restoration at the parish church by the gates of his newly restored hall. In 1848 an anonymous benefactor, who must have been le Strange, gave £100 to be offered at the Christmas offertory and applied to the restoration of the porch and the interior of the church. In January 1849 a new south door 'covered with iron scroll work facsimile of the antique' was hung. In November 1849 the same anonymous benefactor offered £200 towards the restoration and decoration of the interior of the church.[7] The following year, in March 1850, le Strange notes in his diary, 'Bullen and Forester begin to sing the Gregorian chants very well'; and on 31 March, Easter Day, he notes '*Te Deum* and Easter Anthems chanted to the Gregorian tones'. On Low Sunday *Venite* and *Magnificat* were chanted for the first time, and he notes that the day after Low Sunday was kept as his wife's birthday, which had fallen during Lent and could not then be observed properly. The following week he expressed hopes that a daily service would be established.[8]

He was also concerned for the restoration of other churches on his estate. In 1852 he consulted Butterfield about drawing up plans for the restoration of Snettisham church and was busy securing a faculty for the work. Correct fittings were a matter of considerable concern. He was much involved in discussion about the design for an altar-cloth at Hunstanton and in 1855 presented candlesticks for the use of the altar there.[9] He subsequently designed and gave a brass lectern (which he had hoped would be exhibited at the Paris Exhibition of 1855), about which the incumbent recorded a significant anecdote.

> I was helping him [le Strange] to unpack a brass lectern after his own design.... A lady who was looking on asked me to translate the Latin inscription round the base. I read off 'To God and the Church of the Blessed Virgin Mary at Hunstanton in memory of mercies received this lectern is given by H S le S'. 'Stop', said my friend, 'I never said given, we can none of us give to God, we are all beggars in his sight'. I ought to have read 'dedicated'.[10]

Le Strange was a frequenter of advanced Tractarian churches. In May 1852 he notes that he attended St Thomas's, Oxford, 'where the service is

[7] St Mary's Church, Old Hunstanton, Parish Chest, Vestry Minute Book, 1848–71.
[8] NNRO, le Strange Diaries, 1850.
[9] St Mary's Church, Old Hunstanton, Vestry Minute Book.
[10] The *Guardian*, 27 Aug. 1862.

properly performed with Gregorian chants and intoned.'[11] A year later he might have heard William Morris and Burne-Jones singing in the choir.[12] In London he normally attended the Margaret Chapel, which was an early centre for ritualism, and which from 1847 had a complete musical Mass.[13] He was much consulted by Butterfield over the designs and building of All Saints, Margaret Street, which replaced the Margaret Chapel.[14] When Hunstanton church was eventually reopened after the lengthy restoration, in 1857, le Stange arranged for men to sit on one side of the nave and women on the other, as at All Saints, Margaret Street,[15] and in 1862 he appointed a former curate of All Saints to Ringstead, one of the parishes on his Norfolk estate of which he was patron.[16] At his funeral there was full Tractarian ceremonial, a pall was lent from All Saints, Margaret Street, and the clergy of the parish were in 'surplices, hoods, stoles and caps. . . . The service in the church and at the grave was monotoned by the priest, the responses being made by the excellent village choir. All felt that a kind landlord, a liberal patron, a considerate master and, above all, a devout and consistent churchman had been taken from them.'[17]

He was obviously concerned not merely with pious ceremonial. He devoted his energies and architectural skills not merely to church restoration and the restoration of his house, but also to building schools for the National Society in which the Catechism would be taught as well as the three Rs in the villages on his Norfolk estate. In 1847 he designed and built a girls' school at Hunstanton.[18] In 1851 he was engaged in designing and building a school at Ringstead,[19] which was opened in 1852 with fifty-nine children, and was inspected by Bishop Hinde of Norwich when he visited Ringstead to consecrate an extension of the churchyard, for which occasion le Strange had written a hymn to be sung to the tune of St Michael.[20] In 1854 he made drawings for a school of which he was a trustee at Brancaster, a neighbouring village.[21] He had also begun discus-

[11] NNRO, le Strange Diaries, 1852.
[12] Peter F. Anson, *Fashions in Church Furnishings 1840–1940* (London, 1965), p. 96.
[13] B. F. L. Clarke, *Church Builders of the Nineteenth Century*, 2nd edn (London, 1969), p. 119.
[14] NNRO, le Strange Diaries, 1850–7.
[15] Le Strange Diaries, 1857.
[16] Le Strange Diaries, 1862, and *Crockford's Clerical Directory*, 1863.
[17] The *Guardian*, 13 Aug. 1862.
[18] White, *History*, p. 999.
[19] Le Strange Diaries, 1851.
[20] Ibid., 1852.
[21] Ibid., 1854.

sions about establishing an agricultural college and choristers' college at Hunstanton in 1851, but these came to nothing.[22]

In many ways le Strange seems rather like the hero of one of Charlotte Yonge's novels, which were being written at precisely this time.[23] Like one of her heroes, he has 'a serious ascetic temper'; he is just and fair in dealing with his tenants; he is devout and holy and much concerned to maintain the rights of the Church; above all, he died in his prime. However, he has greater significance for the Church and the Arts than a model Tractarian squire who got his labourers and tenants to sing plainsong and meticulously restored the churches on his estate. He was himself an artist of some ability and distinction, and he exemplified the ideal of much nineteenth-century artistic theory that sincerity of sentiment, genuineness of religious feeling, should be the criterion for judging art, and that the self-dedication of the artist to moral and religious truth, to honesty and humility of labour, would be demonstrated in the quality of the work produced.

The idea was first promoted by Alex-François Rio in his *De la Poesie Chretienne*, published in 1836, and translated into English as *The Poetry of Christian Art* in 1854. However, the ideas were already being propounded in English by Lord Lindsay in his influential three-volume *Sketches of the History of Christian Art*, published in 1847,[24] and earlier Pugin had quoted Rio extensively in the second edition of his *Contrasts*, in 1841.[25] Rio believed that the artist must be moved by an inner sympathy with his subject. He believed that artists must first be good Christians and secondly labour at drawing. He, like Pugin, believed that the restoration of the glories of medieval art depended on the restoration of medieval faith. Rio's book gave an impulse to a new seriousness in art that sought to pierce beyond the outer forms of picturesque medievalism to the inner feelings of the Middle Ages in order to understand how it had wrought its miracles of art. He emphasized the significance of early medieval manuscripts for medieval art and for the development of a truly Christian art.

Surprisingly, in view of the extensive interest in all things medieval in the first half of the nineteenth century and its deep effect on architecture,

22 Ibid., 1851.

23 *The Heir of Redclyffe*, her first novel, was published in 1853: see Georgina Battiscombe, *Charlotte Mary Yonge* (London, 1943), pp. 73ff.

24 R. W. Lightbown, 'The Inspiration of Christian Art', in Sarah Macready and F. H. Thompson, eds, *Influences in Christian Art and Architecture*, Occasional Paper, The Society of Antiquaries, ns 7 (London, 1985), pp. 6–37.

25 Phoebe Stanton, *Pugin* (London, 1971), p. 87.

literature, politics, and social action,[26] there was little interest in medieval painting. In fact, as a result of the activities of church restorers, it was probably a period of wholesale destruction of medieval mural paintings, when plaster was stripped off church walls and tympana were ripped out of chancel arches. Even when the Royal Commission appointed by Peel in 1841 'to take into consideration the Promotion of the Fine Arts of this Country in Connection with the rebuilding of the Houses of Parliament' appointed a Select Committee on the Fine Arts, which recommended that the Houses of Parliament should be decorated with several series of large historical subjects, no suggestion was made that the paintings should be in the same style as the architecture of the Houses, that is, in a medieval style. It seems to have been assumed without question that they should follow the modern German version of Raphaelesque Italian.[27]

Butterfield, who himself exemplified the ascetic and devout Tractarian who expressed his faith in his church designs,[28] saw le Strange as a pioneer in this area.

> He delighted in all Christian art and made it the chief occupation of the best period of his life. Few knew as he did the treasures of religious painting which the British Museum, the University libraries and other such places possess in their manuscripts. None I imagine have ever so extensively, patiently or accurately copied them or have so entered into their spirit. His time was not wasted in indiscriminate admiration, but was reserved mainly for the works of the eleventh, twelfth, and thirteenth centuries, when Scripture and not legends formed the subject matter of manuscript illustrations, and where religious art was in some degree worthy of its subject. In addition to such work he also studied anatomical and other drawing. He took full advantage of all the aids that modern science affords. Whatever he undertook in life he did patiently and thoroughly, always aiming at perfection. He would seize and sift and examine everything which bore upon the pursuit he had chosen. He was bent upon more than a mere revival of medieval painting. He felt especially that there was something to be worked out for painting in connection with archi-

[26] For discussions of this influence see Alice Chandler, *A Dream of Order. The Medieval Ideal in Nineteenth Century Literature* (London, 1971), and Mark Girouard, *The Return to Camelot: Chivalry and the English Gentleman* (London, 1981).

[27] John Steegman, *Victorian Taste: A Study of the Arts and Architecture from 1830–1870*, repr. (London, 1970), pp. 130–5.

[28] Paul Thompson, *William Butterfield* (London, 1971), pp. 27–39.

tecture which had scarcely ever been consistently done and he hoped to unite the two arts in a real harmony of principle.[29]

How Butterfield and le Strange first met is not clear; perhaps it had been through the proposal to rebuild the Margaret Chapel, perhaps through the Ecclesiological Society, of which Butterfield had been a member since 1844, and to the committee of which le Strange was elected in 1851.[30] It would certainly seem that it was through his membership of the Ecclesiological Society that Butterfield had built up a network of aristocratic and genteel Tractarian patrons, Beresford Hope, the Marchioness of Lothian, Henry Wilberforce, George Frederick Boyle, subsequently Earl of Glasgow, the Coleridges, and Sir William Heathcote. Le Strange would have been at home with any of these, but he never mentions any of them in his diary. Perhaps for financial reasons he seems to have led a very modest social life. However, it is clear from his diary that le Strange regarded Butterfield as a close friend, and there was obviously mutual respect as artist and architect between them. He consulted Butterfield about the details of the restoration of Hunstanton and Snettisham churches, as well as about the major project of painting the tower and the nave ceilings at Ely. Butterfield also commissioned le Strange, whom he regarded as being able to respond to an architectural situation, to paint the east wall of St Alban's, Holborn.[31] Le Strange even recommended a carpenter on his Hunstanton estate, whom he had taught to draw, as an assistant to Butterfield,[32] and presumably it was le Strange who introduced his cousin, Frederick Preedy, a Worcester architect, to Butterfield, which resulted in their collaboration in a number of projects, not merely those sponsored by le Strange.[33]

That le Strange did, as Butterfield suggests, spend much time copying drawings from medieval manuscripts is clear from his diary. From at least 1852 le Strange was working on his cartoons for the tower ceiling at Ely.[34] He was working on it throughout 1853, much of the earlier part of which he spent in France, presumably for financial reasons. In the autumn he was studying in Brussels and was visiting the Bibliothèque nationale,

[29] W. Butterfield, a letter to the *Guardian*, 6 Aug. 1862.
[30] Thompson, *Butterfield*, p. 44, and le Strange Diaries, 1851.
[31] Thompson, *Butterfield*, p. 459.
[32] Ibid., p. 65, and le Strange Diaries, 1852.
[33] Thompson, *Butterfield*, pp. 347, 417, and Gordon Barnes, *Frederick Preedy* (Evesham, 1984).
[34] Le Strange Diaries, 1852, the first diary entry referring to work at Ely is for 23 July 1852, 'Called on Butterfield and went to talk over the matter of the execution of the Ely ceiling with Castell of South Molton Street by his suggestion.'

there to copy manuscripts. On 31 January 1854 he noted, 'I have now completed the design for Ely tower ceiling except the inscription and border.'[35] The whole 'fair drawing' was finished by 8 February, and in March he showed it to Butterfield and Edward Sparke, one of the Ely residentiaries, whom he notes was 'delighted' with it, and then took it to Ely to show the dean, whom he notes 'was entirely satisfied with my design'. During the spring of 1855 he is again in Brussels, copying manuscripts and taking lessons in painting with oils from Monsieur Krolikowski. From Brussels he went to visit the Exhibition of Beaux Arts in Paris in May. During the summer he began work on the tower ceiling at Ely, arranging for Castell of South Molton Street to work with him. On 2 August he notes he had finished the cartoon for the centre figure of the ceiling and that he had used 144 yards of paper for the cartoons. On 9 August preparations were being made for commencing the colouring of the figures, and on 11 September he notes that the principal figures were finished.[36]

During the autumn he returned to Brussels and began work on a new project, new tracery and stained glass for the east window of Snettisham church on his estate, which was finished in May 1856. In July he visited the dean of Ely, whom he notes is now 'anxious for me to give designs both for St Catherine's Chapel and the nave roof painting'. The commission is accepted, and in October he is 'drawing at the British Museum for nave ceiling at Ely', and, later in the month, 'with Butterfield at British Museum drawing'. What is most surprising is that there is no mention in the diaries of the architect who was actually responsible for the restoration of Ely Cathedral, until 15 October 1857, when le Strange noted, 'Called on Scott the Architect about Ely nave ceiling.'[37] Work continued on the nave ceiling throughout the summer of 1858. During the actual painting le Strange stayed at the Deanery, and in June 1858 one of his fellow guests was Bishop Philpotts,[38] who 'complimented me on my work'. Work continued on the Ely ceiling throughout 1859 and 1860, interrupted by a visit to Highnam, in Gloucestershire, to stay with Gambier Parry, another gentleman artist, who had commissioned Butterfield's pupil Henry Woodyer to rebuild the parish church on his estate. Gambier Parry had made a study of the technique used by the Italian painters of the

[35] Le Strange Diaries, 1853.
[36] Ibid., 1855.
[37] Ibid., 1857 and Nikolaus Pevsner, *Cambridgeshire*, 2nd edn (London, 1970), p. 342.
[38] Le Strange Diaries, 1858.

fourteenth and fifteenth centuries, and invented 'spirit fresco', suitable for wall painting in the English climate.[39] At this stage Gambier Parry was painting a doom over the chancel arch 'in colours prepared in wax'.[40] The following month, March 1860, le Strange's forces at Ely were augmented by 'Mr Holmes of the British Museum', who 'arrived to help with drawings'. By mid-May 1861 the first six bays of the nave roof at Ely were completed.

Through his work at Ely le Strange seems to have established a reputation as an architectural artist. In May 1859 he read a paper on 'Colour in union with architecture' at the Architectural Congress in Cambridge. Later in the year 'Wailes the glass painter' visited Ely to see and discuss his work. In March 1862 he was appointed a member of the Royal Commission on Fine Arts, appointed to investigate and report on the condition of the recently painted frescos in the Houses of Parliament.[41]

Butterfield also commissioned le Strange to paint the east wall of St Alban's, Holborn, which he regarded as, up to then, one of his most important buildings, both because of its site in one of the poorest districts of London, where it could bring the benefits of worship to the poor and deprived, and as marking an important stage in his own stylistic development.[42] He believed that le Strange was the only painter who could respond adequately to an architectural context.[43] From early 1860 he was in consultation with Butterfield about the reredos and east wall for his new church, and at an early stage le Strange brought Frederick Preedy into the discussions, which was fortunate, because when le Strange died suddenly, in July 1862, Preedy was able to continue with the project. Throughout the winter and the spring they were working together on the cartoons for a set of ten paintings, beginning with the Annunciation and ending with the Day of Pentecost. Of this work Butterfield thought highly. 'For his co-operation with me in that church I must ever feel most grateful to him. It was the crowning act of a long friendship, and it testified to a most real sympathy between us: but his work was done from higher motives than mere friendships.'[44]

[39] David Verey, *Gloucestershire: The Vale and the Forest of Dean* (London, 1970), pp. 269–70: Gambier Perry took over the painting of the nave ceiling at Ely after le Strange's death in 1862.

[40] Le Strange Diaries, 1860.

[41] Le Strange Diaries, 1862, and the *Guardian*, 6 Aug. 1862.

[42] Thompson, *Butterfield*, pp. 38–9, 97.

[43] Ibid., p. 459.

[44] The *Guardian*, 6 Aug. 1862. The work was executed by Preedy after le Strange's death. When le Strange's son attended Morning Service there in 1873 he noted that the design seemed

In addition to his activities as an artist, le Strange tried his hand as a developer. Presumably his main motive for this was to increase the income from his Norfolk estate and to raise capital to pay off some of the mortgages with which the estate was encumbered. From 1850 onwards he was preoccupied with the development of that part of Hunstanton that faced the Wash, where the beach sloped gently down into the sea, and where, although it was on the east coast, the sun set over the sea. From the start he involved Butterfield in this venture. It is clear that he saw it as more than a financial venture. He was concerned for it as an aesthetic enterprise, and for him aesthetic implied Christian. Perhaps he envisaged that a Tractarian landowner and a Tractarian architect would produce a Tractarian resort.

This venture was Butterfield's only practical experience of town planning.[45] His plan was for a strictly-controlled picturesque, with a series of irregular triangular greens with a medieval cross, removed from the old village, forming a focus above the pier, and a church at the apex of the greens. In the midst of drawing the cartoons for Ely, le Strange was negotiating for the promotion of a Lynn and Hunstanton railway to bring visitors to his resort and with builders and developers for sites.[46] He was also concerned about drawing up model leases which would not only protect his financial interests, but prevent the construction of such undesirable buildings as public houses and Nonconformist places of worship.[47] Le Strange personally, with Butterfield, marked out the streets and the plots, and he spent much time with Butterfield discussing plans and designs for first- and third-class houses which Butterfield was designing for him. He noted, ten days before his death, that three houses on the Green were then being built, and that the station was finished.[48]

Not only were three of the churches on his estate very extensively restored during his lifetime in a distinctly Tractarian manner,[49] but he had a hand in the restoration of the churches of his neighbours and friends. He recommended Preedy as an architect to his friend Henry Coldham at Anmer when he, as patron and landowner, restored his parish

---

faded and injured by damp (le Strange Diaries, 1873), and it was eventually replaced by a reredos by Garner: Anson, *Church Furnishings*, p. 139.

45 Thompson, *Butterfield*, p. 319.

46 Le Strange Diaries, 1853, 1854, 1856.

47 Le Strange Diaries, 1861.

48 Le Strange Diaries, 1862.

49 Old Hunstanton, Snettisham, and Ringstead. Eventually Preedy worked on all the churches on the estate. Heacham, Holme next the Sea, Thornham, and Sedgeford: see Barnes, *Preedy*.

church in 1856. He commented on the restoration of the chancel at Ingoldisthorpe by the rector. He designed the font for his friend William Pratt, the rector of Harpley.[50] Through his friendship with the Sparkes, le Strange had probably been given the commission to paint the Ely ceilings, for Edward Bowyer Sparke was a canon residentiary of Ely.[51] He had also been presented to the living of Feltwell by his redoubtable father, and in April and May 1859 le Strange was busy at Feltwell St Mary with Preedy taking measurements for a new aisle, which was completed in 1861.[52] It was also probably le Strange's connection with the Sparkes that ensured Preedy a commission to restore Bale and Gunthorpe churches extensively in 1862 and 1863 and probably to rebuild Gunthorpe Hall for The Revd John Sparke, who was patron, rector, and lord of the manor. In the course of his career Preedy restored another eight churches for le Strange's neighbours in west and north Norfolk.[53]

In le Strange's life we see a vivid illustration not only of Tractarianism and the principles of the Ecclesiological Society being defused through the example of a landowner among the parishes on his estate and amongst his friends and neighbours. We also see an example of a Christian and Tractarian artist who was moved by an inner sympathy with his subject, who had sought to rediscover the principles of medieval illustrations, which had been produced by men of faith, in order to fulfil Rio's and Pugin's expectation that beautiful churches would be built by men who held the true faith and had beautiful characters and, through such buildings, would attract people to God.

Lincoln Theological College

[50] Le Strange Diaries, 1856.

[51] Of whom it was said that he was pleased when he secured a stall for his eldest son, but when he secured another for his second son, he was so pleased he gave a ball at the Palace to celebrate. It was also said that people could find their way across the Fens at night because of the number of little Sparkes planted at intervals in the livings of the diocese: S. C. Carpenter, *Church and People 1789–1889* (London, 1933), p. 57, n. 1.

[52] Le Strange Diaries, 1859, and Barnes, *Preedy*, p. 22.

[53] Barnes, *Preedy*, p. 22.

THE VICTORIAN REVIVAL OF PLAINSONG IN ENGLISH: ITS USAGE UNDER TRACTARIANS AND RITUALISTS

by WALTER HILLSMAN

THE revival of plainsong in mid-nineteenth-century English parish churches constituted one of the most distinctive developments in church music of the period. Even a brief study of the subject affords valuable insights into church musical usage and its interweaving with changes in musical taste and churchmanship.

The revival involved only the simpler forms of plainsong, all to English words: versicles and responses, recitation tones for psalms and canticles, hymns, and simple settings of the Ordinary of the Mass, like the *Missa de Angelis* and Marbeck's Communion Service. (The latter, incidentally, was regarded by most Victorians as plainsong, although it was actually a mixture of adapted plainsong and original plainsong-like music.) The music of the more elaborate and typical plainsong repertoire, such as antiphons and propers, did not feature in Anglican usage until very late in the nineteenth century, and then mostly in religious communities.[1]

I BACKGROUND

Although Tractarians were not able to cite much evidence for the use after 1559 of simple plainsong like that in Marbeck's 1550 *Booke of Common Praier Noted*, they did think that continuing use of it was certain in the late sixteenth and early seventeenth centuries, in view of brief comments by figures like Hooker,[2] and probable after the Restoration, given publications like those of Lowe and Playford in 1661 and 1703[3]—publications which contained recitation tones. They regarded plainsong

[1] W. Hillsman, 'Trends and aims in Anglican church music 1870–1906 in relation to developments in churchmanship' (Oxford D.Phil. thesis, 1985), pp. 33, 35, 290, 359.

[2] 'On the Gregorian Tones for the Psalms', *Parish Choir*, no. 22 (Oct. 1847), p. 158.

[3] [W. Dyce, ed.], *The Order of Daily Service, the Litany, and Order of the Administration of the Holy Communion, with Plain-Tune, according to the use of the United Church of England and Ireland* (London, 1843), Editor's preface, [p. 10]. Dyce refers to the following publications: E. Lowe, *A Short Direction for the Performance of Cathedrall Service* (London, 1661); J. Playford, *A Breefe Introduction to the Skill of Music*, 15th edn (London, 1703).

as having then lain dormant in Anglicanism until the early Victorian years.[4]

Some eighteenth-century musicians and churchmen were kept aware of plainsong when they travelled to the Continent[5] or visited London embassy chapels. Others knew it as an object of antiquarian curiosity in publications of Burney and Hawkins.[6] In the late eighteenth century, the stage was set for the revival of plainsong in Anglican use by the Romantic Movement, with its frequent focus on the remote past, and by the revival of older music, particularly of the Tudor period, in publications and public concerts.[7]

The impetus for the revival, however, came after 1833 from clergy and musical dilettanti fired with the zeal of the Oxford Movement. These reformers were faced with services which were blatantly far from devout: rural west-gallery male and female musicians flirting with each other and ignoring the clergy, town charity children who shrieked, congregations prevented by both types of choir and by parish clerks from singing anything but metrical psalms before and after services. Not surprisingly, reformers decided to take drastic action. They swept away the old choirs, established surpliced men and boys in chancel stalls, and promoted plainsong and Tudor choral music. Tractarians shared credit for establishing surpliced choirs with moderate High Churchmen, like Walter Hook at Leeds Parish Church,[8] but stood virtually alone in championing plainsong.

II THE SPREAD OF PLAINSONG

Tractarian success in promoting plainsong was impressive. Walter Kerr Hamilton introduced it first at St Peter's-in-the-East, Oxford, in 1839.[9] Three years later Thomas Helmore began using plainsong alternately with Anglican chant in daily services at St Mark's College, Chelsea.[10] By 1843 Frederick Oakley was establishing plainsong at Margaret Chapel, Margaret Street, London (the forerunner of All Saints' Church).[11] The

[4] 'On the Gregorian Tones for the Psalms', p. 158.
[5] B. Rainbow, *The Choral Revival in the Anglican Church 1839–1872* (London, 1970), p. 21.
[6] 'X', 'On Modern Mutilations of the Gregorian Psalm Tones', *Parish Choir*, no. 13 (Feb. 1847), p. 103.
[7] N. Temperley, *The Music of the English Parish Church*, 2 vols (Cambridge, 1979), 1, p. 245.
[8] Rainbow, *Choral Revival*, p. 26.
[9] Temperley, *Music of the English Parish Church*, 1, p. 255.
[10] Rainbow, *Choral Revival*, p. 57.
[11] Ibid., p. 20.

next year, W. J. E. Bennett was causing plainchant to be used at the new St Paul's Church, Knightsbridge.[12] St Andrew's, Wells Street (near Margaret Street), maintained Gregorians for a few years after its 1847 consecration.[13] St Barnabas, Pimlico, gave plainsong a prominent role from its 1850 consecration.[14] St Matthias, Stoke Newington, also used plainchant, most probably from 1853, when it opened.[15]

By 1869 Mackeson's *Guide to the Churches of London* was listing 49 out of 620 churches (or 7.9 per cent) as using Gregorian tones, either exclusively or in alternation with Anglican chants. (As statistics of plainsong use were frequently based on what type of psalm chant was used, much of the discussion of plainsong in this paper centres on Gregorian psalms rather than other types of plainsong repertoire.) In the peak year of 1875, Mackeson's figures had risen to 152 out of 786, or 19.3 per cent.[16] In the early 1870s annual festival services of the London Gregorian Choral Association at St Paul's Cathedral often involved about a thousand singers.[17]

The provinces did not lag too far behind. At mid-century, *The Parish Choir* recorded Gregorian use at churches in Brighton, Leeds, Maidstone, Oxford, Wantage, Draycot (Staffordshire), and at several churches in Bristol. By the mid-1870s, 18 per cent of Bristol churches were using it to some extent.[18] Advances in the late 1850s and early 1860s were fostered in part by plainsong use at several diocesan choral festivals, for example, at Ely and Southwell from 1859, and Canterbury in 1861.[19]

III SOURCES

One factor facilitating the spread of plainsong was the limited number of sources available, and thus the relative lack of conflicting systems of pointing (compared to Anglican chant). Several of these call for comment.

The 1839 *Collection of Psalm and Hymn Tunes, Chants, and other Music, as Sung in . . . St. Peter's in the East Oxford* [*sic*] was mostly a collection of

[12] Ibid., pp. 148–50.
[13] Ibid., pp. 169–70.
[14] Ibid., pp. 154–6.
[15] Ibid., pp. 185–7.
[16] C. Mackeson, *A Guide to the Churches of London and its Suburbs for 1879* (London, 1879), p. 162.
[17] Hillsman, 'Trends and aims', pp. 155–6, 179.
[18] 'Bristol and Clifton Churches', *Church Times*, 15 (19 Oct. 1877), p. 591.
[19] 'The Ely Choir Festival', *The Ecclesiologist*, 20 (1859), p. 373; 'The Second Choir Festival at Southwell Minster', ibid., p. 189; 'First Festival of Parochial Choirs in Canterbury Cathedral', ibid., 23 (1861), pp. 210–11.

metrical psalm and hymn tunes, without words. It did, however, contain harmonized versions of the Gregorian psalm tones, again without words.[20]

More important were William Dyce's 1843 edition of Marbeck's *Booke of Common Praier Noted*, issued as *The Daily Service*, and Dyce's publication the same year called *The Psalter, or Psalms of David, Pointed as they are to be sung or said in churches*. The first volume heralded the beginning of the movement which produced many editions of Marbeck's Communion Service, and which eventually established that Service as the most widely sung in Anglicanism. (Although hard for us to imagine today, this Communion Service was apparently never sung by congregations before 1843, and only rarely by choirs.) Both volumes also made some Anglicans aware of the possibility of singing Prayer Book psalms and canticles to Gregorian tones. In that both brought words and music within two covers, they helped singers more than the 1839 collection. For canticles, the *Daily Service* printed syllables under every note, but only in first verses.[21] *The Psalter* printed texts and tones in different parts of the publication; the former were unpointed, despite the full title. In these respects the volumes were still less than ideal for the early Victorians, who needed very clear guidance on how to match syllables to unfamiliar tones.

Oakley and his organist, Richard Redhead, met choir and congregational needs in their 1843 *Laudes diurnae*, the first complete Anglican Psalter pointed and set to Gregorian tones, intended for use at Margaret Chapel. In this publication, every note of a cadence (except for the final note) was fitted to one syllable of text, regardless of the accentual result:

Example 1 (from Redhead, *Laudes diurnae*, sig. 1 [p. 1])

[20] A. R. Reinagle, *A Collection of Psalm and Hymn Tunes, Chants, and other Music, as Sung in the Parish Church of St. Peter's in the East Oxford* (London, [1839]), pp. 113–17.

[21] For example, [Dyce, ed.], *The Order of Daily Service*, sig. F 1ʳ.

Oakley defended this less than satisfactory procedure by claiming that it forced singers to sing deliberately and prevented them from gabbling.[22]

Helmore's 1849 *Psalter Noted* quickly became *the* plainsong Psalter for Anglican use and was never really superseded before the end of the century. Its layout, with a separate note printed for each syllable, left no singer in doubt about its intentions.[23] Helmore's 1850 *Manual of Plainsong*, comprising the *Canticles Noted, A Brief Directory of Plain Song*, and three appendices, also assumed enormous importance.

Example 2 (from Helmore, *Psalter Noted*, p. 155)

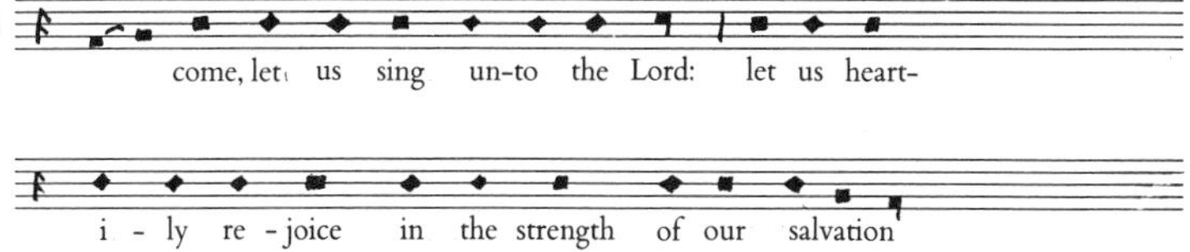

IV TRACTARIAN IDEALS IN PROMOTING PLAINSONG

Even more crucial factors than sources, for the success of the plainsong movement, were the dogmatism, determination, and drive of the leaders. These characteristics shine through the pages of their prefaces to the above works, through articles in the *Ecclesiologist* (1842–68), and through letters and articles in the *Parish Choir* (1846–51).

Tractarians' dogmatic insistence on plainsong stemmed in great measure from several of their most important liturgical ideals and theological tenets. First, they sought to restore to worship a feeling of other-wordliness and mystery. Plainsong, to at least one *Parish Choir* correspondent, did not merely *convey* such a feeling, it positively *excited* 'the most powerful emotions of reverence and awe' in those who heard it. The need to make services more devout seemed to Tractarians to require slow performance of plainsong.[24]

[22] For Example 1, see R. Redhead, *Laudes diurnae: the Psalter and Canticles in the Morning and Evening Service of the Church of England: Set and Pointed to the Gregorian Tones* (London, 1843), sig. 1 [p. 1]; for Oakley's defence: ibid., preface, [p. 20].

[23] For never superseded, see Rainbow, *Choral Revival*, p. 86; and Temperley, *Music of the English Parish Church*, 1, p. 261; for Example 2: T. Helmore, *The Psalter Noted* (London, 1849), p. 155.

[24] For 'powerful emotions', see 'X', 'An Apology for Plain Chant', *Parish Choir*, no. 22 (Oct. 1847), p. 82; for slow: 'Ecclesiastical Music', *Ecclesiologist*, 10 (1850), p. 215.

Secondly, Tractarians sought to encourage not just an undirected atmosphere of wonder and awe, but an atmosphere which made worship feel like the central activity of the Christian Church, that ancient and divinely-founded institution which, by its very nature, was set apart from secular society and culture. Plainsong to Tractarians was uniquely Christian[25] and capable of intensifying feelings in the faithful of identification with the Church of the ages. Tractarian writers incessantly rehearsed the evidence for what might be termed plainsong's claim to Apostolic Succession: its survival through Playford, Lowe, and Marbeck, back to its use by the undivided medieval Church, and, still further, to St Gregory, St Ambrose, and the early Church itself.[26] The sight of its square- and diamond-shaped notation—distinct from modern crotchets and quavers—was supposed to be acceptable to worshippers as part of Christian historical tradition.[27] The sound of ancient plainsong even allowed those worshippers to experience what Horton Davies terms 'the thrill of sacred tradition'.[28]

Thirdly, Tractarian attention to the authority of the Church and her rubrics tied in with references to plainsong as the only 'authorized' or 'ordered' music of the Anglican Church.[29]

Fourthly, Tractarians sought to restore a sense of objectivity in worship. Liturgy, to be sure, had to excite emotions, but those emotions were ideally supposed to unite members of the body of the Church in worship toward God, and not to allow individual Christians to dwell on personal feelings.[30] The singing of medieval hymns, and the recitation to ancient musical formulae of liturgical texts of the Offices and Eucharist, were to Tractarians sufficiently removed from the more pietistic of Evangelical hymns.

Fifthly, Tractarians exalted what to them probably seemed like a logical extension of objectivity in worship, namely manliness. They held

[25] T. Helmore, *Accompanying Harmonies to the Brief Directory of the Plain Song, as used in Morning and Evening Prayer, Litany, and Holy Communion* (London, 1853), preface, p. vi.

[26] Ibid., Preface, pp. iv, v; T. Helmore, *Plain Song* (London, [1878]), pp. 48, 61–2; 'X', 'On the Gregorian Tones, and their adaptation to English Psalmody', *Parish Choir*, no. 11 (Dec. 1846), pp. 85–6.

[27] T. Helmore, 'On Hymnody', *Ecclesiologist*, 12 (1851), p. 177.

[28] H. Davies, *Worship and Theology in England from Watts and Wesley to Maurice, 1690–1850* (Princeton and Oxford, 1961), p. 254.

[29] For 'authorized', see [W. Dyce, ed.], *The Psalter, or Psalms of David, Pointed as they are to be sung or said in Churches* (London, 1843), Appendix, [p. 4]; for 'ordered': Helmore, *Plain Song*, p. 48.

[30] Temperley, *Music of the English Parish Church*, 1, p. 252; Davies, *Worship and Theology*, pp. 258, 265.

plainsong to be manly, and its ideal executants to be men. Oakley urged users of his *Laudes diurnae* not to pronounce their words

> in a mincing and effeminate tone of voice, but giving out the accents of the Holy Ghost in a manly strain and spirit. Men should chant like men, not like women, aping the wantonness of the stage with shrill and affected voices.[31]

By all accounts, most mid-century plainsong performances demonstrated the least attractive and most exaggerated aspects of masculinity. They were not just bold, but hammered (as were contemporary continental performances). They were even condemned by plainsong opponents as barbarous, and supporters admitted the truth of this.[32]

Finally, Tractarians insisted on congregational participation in liturgical music, partly in order to encourage in the faithful a sense of the corporate nature of the Church. Plainsong, by its supposed simplicity and its limited melodic range (compared to Anglican chant), was the most obvious means of effecting participation. If participation by all social classes in congregations was to be achieved, some lack of polish or even some barbarity was, according to Tractarians, inevitable.[33]

Tractarian determination to *use* plainsong as a means of achieving liturgical and didactic ends, in spite of the crudities of mid-century editions and performances, revealed an anti-artistic side to their nature. Nathaniel Woodard reflected this attitude when he said that he preferred Gregorians 'not on aesthetical, but on religious grounds'.[34]

V DECLINE UNDER THE RITUALISTS

Plainsong, as we have seen, advanced steadily in Anglican usage, in spite of its unpopularity with a majority of churchgoers and most professional musicians. Both categories of people found it too severe and simple, and its performances too barbarous. Evangelicals objected to it as just another manifestation of creeping popery in the Established Church. Even as late as 1882, the *Rock* gave it a rating of 59° on its

[31] Redhead, *Laudes diurnae*, preface, [p. 19].

[32] For hammered, see Hillsman, 'Trends and aims', p. 38; for continental: W. Hillsman, 'Instrumental Accompaniment of Plain-Chant in France from the late 18th Century', *Galpin Society Journal*, 33 (1980), p. 13; for barbarous: 'X', 'Practical Hints on Congregational Psalmody. No. III', *Parish Choir*, no. 19 (July 1847), p. 153.

[33] 'X', 'Practical Hints', p. 153.

[34] J. Otter, *Nathaniel Woodard: A Memoir of his Life* (London, 1925), p. 178.

Centigrade Ritualometer—a higher mark than any other feature of Anglican musical innovations.[35]

Objections on grounds of mere distaste or popery, however, proved insufficient to reverse the success of plainsong; more serious social, musical, and religious grounds were necessary. On the social front, a growing number of Anglican churchgoers at mid-century were becoming upwardly mobile and wanting to distance themselves from less respectable Dissenting traditions like hearty hymn singing.[36] These churchgoers, along with most choir singers, were also becoming more musically educated and sensitive, and less tolerant of the inartistic character of plainsong performances. They came to want the 'warmer', more elaborate, Victorian repertoire of foundations like the Temple Church. This is reflected from the mid-1860s in the 'warmer' trend in the repertoire of diocesan choral festivals.[37] In 1866, St Andrew's, Wells Street, which had been 'severe' in the 1840s, first performed a Gounod Mass setting liturgically—a notable occasion.[38] Significantly, this occurred the same year as J. M. Neale's death and near the time of the demise of the doctrinaire *Ecclesiologist*.

On the musical front, organists, who in any event disliked plainsong, were by the 1860s becoming more musically competent and were beginning to take over the leadership of church music from Tractarian clergy like Helmore.[39] Where plainsong was in use, organists and clergy began to water it down. In order to 'warm the severity' of unison Gregorians, organists began to elaborate their accompaniments to plainsong recitations with galloping scales and increasingly chromatic harmonies.[40] Clergy were allowing plainsong to be juxtaposed with modern, music-hall-type tunes for hymns, which in their dotted rhythms often resembled the 'Marseillaise'. This bizarre Anglican compromise, known as 'jigs and groans', became a frequent feature of services at places like St Alban's, Holborn.[41]

The decisive factor causing decline in plainsong use, however, was the abandonment in Ritualistic churches from around 1870 of congregational

[35] 'The Centigrade Ritualometer', *Rock*, no. 878 (12 May 1882), supplement, p. 360.

[36] Rainbow, *Choral Revival*, p. 266.

[37] Ibid., pp. 268, 274.

[38] J. D. Brown and S. S. Stratton, *British Musical Biography: A Dictionary of Musical Artists, Authors and Composers, born in Britain and its Colonies* (Birmingham, 1897), p. 26.

[39] Hillsman, 'Trends and aims', p. 133.

[40] Ibid., p. 225.

[41] Ibid., p. 85.

plainsong settings of the Ordinary of the Mass, in favour of elaborate continental Mass settings for choir, sometimes with orchestral accompaniment. At St Alban's, Holborn, for instance, elaborate music by Haydn, Mozart, Weber, Schubert, and Schumann became a frequent feature of Sunday High Celebrations.[42] Recent developments in the High Church movement provided background for this change, and Ritualistic persecutions played the role of catalyst. On the former front, 'advanced' High Churchmen had for several years been coming to value the more exotic externals of worship as means of teaching their doctrine to ordinary lay people. Ritualists began to measure their Catholicity by the contemporary practices of continental Roman Catholics, unlike Tractarians, who had sought security in the traditions of the undivided Church. Progressive clergy clearly demonstrated this shift in attitude when they decorated their churches with ornaments from France and Belgium.[43]

Sudden legal action restricting their use of vestments and ceremonial presented Ritualists with a challenge. They responded by introducing elaborate Mass music, thus ensuring that their doctrinal tenets would continue to receive obvious external expression. In noting this, the *Church Times* said:

> ... forcible suppression there [at Holborn] and elsewhere of the accessories to Christian worship, resulted in the natural desire to discover some other means whereby the worship of Almighty God might be rendered with some degree of dignity and impressiveness. Hence the substitution of the seven lamps continually burning before the altar for the two lighted tapers, and the employment in the great Service [meaning the Sunday High Mass] of far more elaborate music. Thus, in this respect, a new field was opened for Church musicians, and the results are daily seen in our midst.[44]

Ritualists showed great ingenuity in seizing straight away on elaborate music, as it enjoyed freedom from rubrical control and thus legal censure; incurred less hostility from conservative Evangelicals than plainsong (Ritualometer 47° versus 59°);[45] and raised little opposition from people in general. After all, as already noted, moderately 'High' places like Wells Street had been performing similar music for several years.

[42] Ibid., p. 10.
[43] Ibid., p. 83.
[44] [Misc.], *Church Times*, 9 (2 June 1871), p. 250.
[45] 'The Centigrade Ritualometer', p. 360.

Elaborate Mass settings spread quickly among Ritualistic churches. Critics claimed that they opened the floodgates of the Church to people who came simply to appreciate the aesthetic experience (for example, Walter Pater, who frequented Holborn in the 1870s). These aesthetes, it was argued, either took the place of the devout or annoyed them by their manners.[46] But the ability of elaborate settings to attract people to services began to weigh as heavily in the minds of Ritualistic clergy by the late 1870s as their usefulness in illustrating doctrine had in the early part of the decade.

Tractarian arguments that plainsong was the only 'authorized' or 'rubrically ordered' Anglican music began to sound very dated, particularly in view of the Ritualistic tendency to stretch or even ignore rubrics. It was no longer this liturgical music which excited churchmen; it was the more subjective religious music like anthems and oratorios which made an impact. At a performance of one of the Bach Passions at St Anne's, Soho, for example, the rector was seen to be sobbing 'unobtrusively'![47] Plainsong continued its decline until the 1890s, when, for instance, about ten per cent of churches in London and twelve per cent in the diocese of Peterborough were still using it to some extent.[48]

VI RESURGENCE

The second spring of plainsong around 1900 was due in large measure to the efforts of the Plainsong and Mediaeval Music Society (founded 1888), who were promoting English versions of the more scholarly editions of plainchant emanating from the Solesmes Abbey, along with Solesmes' lighter, faster, more graceful and artistic performing style. It was due as well to the influence of Percy Dearmer at St Mary the Virgin, Primrose Hill, who was restoring liturgical music to his congregation by means of plainsong, and arguing strongly from rubrics for an end to the liturgical chaos caused by the Ritualists.[49] Dearmer's influence spread far beyond Primrose Hill because of his contribution to many publications, including *The English Hymnal* of 1906.

[46] 'Summary', *Church Times*, 10 (21 June 1872), p. 283.

[47] J. H. Cardwell, *et al.*, *Men and Women of Soho Famous and Infamous.* [*1st Ser.*] *Actors, Authors, Dramatists, Entertainers and Engravers* (London, [1903]), p. 172.

[48] For London, see R. A. Turner, 'The Proposed new Gregorian Psalter', *Church Times*, 30 (26 Feb. 1892), p. 189; for Peterborough; [Misc.], *Musical Times*, 39 (1 Jan. 1898), p. 19.

[49] Hillsman, 'Trends and aims', pp. 107–11.

The pendulum in the story of plainsong in English had thus come full swing. Music and churchmanship were continuing to intertwine. Each influenced the other.

Faculty of Music,
University of Oxford

A CHAPEL AND ITS ARCHITECT: JAMES CUBITT AND UNION CHAPEL, ISLINGTON, 1874–1889* (*PRESIDENTIAL ADDRESS*)

by CLYDE BINFIELD

A NONCONFORMIST church is a place for drama, not mime or magic. It is a place for the production of the Word; for communication and for decision; for encounter, therefore, and crisis. It is a place for salvation. Its sole purpose is to promote the crisis of salvation and sustain its outworking in worship. When the question which must be asked of any building is asked of such a building—'Does it work?'—what is really asked is: 'How effectively does this meeting of client, architect, and craftsman house that historic crisis of man's salvation when God meets man and is recognized? Has this been especially a place for such a crisis?' This paper concentrates on one architect's role in this process. James Cubitt (1836–1912) was a Nonconformist architect twice over, since he happened to be a Nonconformist as well as an architect who worked consciously for an architecture of Nonconformity.

The vigour of Cubitt's works and words is equalled only by the reticence of his personal record. Here is a man who is one generation away from the solid, rural middle classes of farmers, millers, and almost-capitalists;

* In the preparation of this paper, and the larger study of which it forms a part, I have received particular help from Mr M. R. Alden, Mr E. Atkinson, Miss Jean Ayton (Manchester Central Library), The Revd D. Batten, Mr J. Bettley (RIBA Library), Dr H. Bowen, Mr J. H. Y. Briggs, Mr N. Burton, Mr R. Clarke, Mr D. Cubitt, Mr C. Dowse, Mrs R. Dunk, Dr Mary English, The Revd D. V. Fagan, Miss D. M. French, Mr N. Gibbs, Miss S. Groves (Northants Record Office), Miss J. Gyford, Mrs L. Hamilton (Stockport Central Library), Mrs K. Haslem (Glos Record Office), Dr Brenda Hough, Mr S. C. Humphry (Southwark Local Studies Library), Mr B. Jackson (Tyne and Wear Archives), Mr F. Keay, Mrs J. E.Kingscott (Nottingham County Library), Mr K. Kyffin, Ms S. Mackenzie (Hackney Archives Dept), Mrs S. Mills (Librarian, Regent's Park College, Oxford), Ms N. J. Mungeam, Mrs J. C. Powles (Librarian, Spurgeon's College), Mrs B. Reid (Loughton Central Library), The Revd H. A. Richardson, Dr T. Roberts (Archivist, University College of North Wales, Bangor), Dr S. Salter, Mr P. C. Saunders (Cambridgeshire Record Office, Huntingdon), The Revd Professor A. P. F. Sell, Mrs P. Sheldon (Newcastle Central Library), The Revd A. J. Spring, Mr A. A. Smith, Miss J. T. Smith (Essex Record Office), The Revd J. Tattersall, Mr B. Thomas (West Glamorgan County Library, Swansea), The Revd D. Tucker, Mr R. Wallington, Mrs R. Watson (Northants Record Office), Mr D. B. Weston, The Revd B. R. White, Mr C. Wilkins-Jones (Norwich Central Library), Mr David Wilkinson, Mr J. Trevor Williams, Mr R. Wilson, The Revd Dr Janet Wootton.

who is born into the fringes of the clerical intelligentsia, more country town than country; who then moves more firmly into the professions, settling in London to pursue a calling poised uncertainly between trade and art; who marries back into the rural middle classes and retreats to what is not yet quite a suburb. Here is a mental-art man about to turn gentleman, with a specialism in what has most formed him: chapel and education.

All Cubitts come from Norfolk. James's Cubitts came from Neatishead and Worstead in East Norfolk. Although no connection can be traced with the building Cubitts of Belgravia, he was the first cousin once removed of the first wife of Sir William Cubitt the engineer (1785–1861). He was born on 20 March 1836 in Ilford, the only son and elder child of The Revd James Cubitt, Baptist minister successively at Ilford, Stratford-upon-Avon, Bourton-on-the-Water, and Thrapston, and latterly tutor at Spurgeon's Pastors' College. He became an architect, working in the office of Isaac Charles Gilbert of Nottingham (1851–6), E. V. Elmslie of Great Malvern (1856–7), R. J. Twitchen, and W. W. Pocock of London (1857–62). Gilbert had Congregational connections, and Pocock was a Wesleyan. Each had a church or chapel specialism, and Pocock's masterwork was Spurgeon's Metropolitan Tabernacle (opened 1861), where Cubitt's parents and sister became members.

By 1863 he had set up on his own account in Camberwell, moving by 1868 to 26 Finsbury Place, where he became a partner of another of Isaac Gilbert's pupils, Henry Fuller (1832–72). Like Gilbert, Fuller had a Congregational background, with useful Manchester and London connections. Cubitt was at 2 Finsbury Pavement by 1875 and at 2 Broad Street Buildings, Liverpool Street, by 1881. There he remained until his death. Cubitt had two partners after Fuller: George Frederick Collinson (1867–1937) from 1891 to 1899 and Herbert J. Manchip from 1905 to 1912. In addition, there was a fruitful association (it seems not to have been a formal partnership) between 1884 and 1887 with J. M. Brydon (1840–1901). He became FRIBA in 1890.

In 1873 he married Fanny Comely (1851–75), the daughter of a prosperous Baptist Cotswold farmer. She died in childbirth, and he never remarried. By then his home was in Loughton, Essex, where his brother-in-law, W. H. Vivian (1846–89) was minister of the largely Baptist Union Church. He died at Loughton on 8 August 1912.

Cubitt's practice was mainly ecclesiastical: his entire church work was, in fact, chapel work, undertaken for Baptists, Congregationalists, the Countess of Huntingdon's Connexion, and the Presbyterian Church of Wales. This work included:

Rye Hill Baptist Church, Newcastle-upon-Tyne (1863–4);
Almshouses, schools, and orphanage at Newington Butts and Stockwell for the (Baptist) Metropolitan Tabernacle (1866–9);
Congregational Chapel, New Barnet (1872);
Emmanuel Congregational Church, Cambridge (1872–4);
Bourton-on-the-Water Baptist Church (1875–6);
Union Chapel (Congregational), Islington (1875–89);
Countess of Huntingdon's Church, St Helen's Road, Swansea (1876);
Morley Hall (Congregational), The Triangle, Hackney (1879);
Algernon Road Congregational Church, Lewisham (1881, 1887–8);
Church of the Redeemer (Baptist), Hagley Road, Birmingham (1882);
West Kensington Congregational Church (1884–7);
Haddon Hall (Baptist), Bermondsey (1884, rebuilt to same design on adjacent site 1901);
Westgate Road Baptist Church, Newcastle-upon-Tyne (1886);
Osborne Road Baptist Church, Jesmond, Newcastle-upon-Tyne (1887);
Welsh Presbyterian Church, Charing Cross Road, London (1887);
West Cliff Baptist Church, Bournemouth (1889–91);
Dulwich Grove Congregational Church (1889, 1901–2);
Congregational Mission Hall, Badingham, Suffolk (1894);
Infant schoolroom, Union Church, Loughton, Essex (1898);
Avenue Congregational Church, Southampton (1898);
Streatham Congregational Church (1901);
Tabernacl (Presbyterian Church of Wales), Bangor (1905).

Cubitt's secular work included a manse, later called Salcombe House, for Union Church, and Salcombe College, later known as Loughton School (1886), and Board Schools at Loughton (1888–1911), as well as at Leytonstone, Lewisham, Dulwich, and Urmston (Manchester). He exhibited five times at the Royal Academy on architectural subjects between 1883 and 1887, and he wrote pungently and persuasively on architectural matters, chiefly for *Building News*, between 1863 and 1912. The best of these articles he gathered into two widely-noticed books: *Church Design for Congregations: its Development and Possibilities* (London, 1870) and *A Popular Handbook of Nonconformist Church Building* (London, 1892). He also wrote *A Short Specification of Materials, Labour and Goods for Works Connected with Buildings* (London, 1911). In some ways, however, his most original piece was 'Wren's work and its lessons', *Contemporary Review*, 46 (July 1884), for here the high Goth, by annexing Wren to his cause, turned steadfastly and logically towards Arts and Crafts.

Plate 1 James Cubitt, 1836–1912 (Sheffield Central Library).

Plate 2 Morley Hall, The Triangle, Hackney, 1879 (London Borough of Hackney Archives Department).

Plate 3 Rye Hill Baptist Church, Elswick, Newcastle-upon-Tyne, 1863–1864 (Sheffield Central Library).

Plate 4 Cubitt's 'Design for Galleried Church' (illustrated in 1870) was most nearly realized in his Baptist Church of the Redeemer, Hagley Road, Birmingham, opened in 1882 and hailed as 'Architecture in the New Spirit'.

Plate 5 Osborne Road Baptist Church, Jesmond, Newcastle-upon-Tyne, opened in 1887

Plate 6 Welsh Presbyterian Church, Charing Cross Road, London, 1887–1888.

Plate 7 Streatham Congregational Church, 1901 (Sheffield Central Library).

Plate 8 Avenue Congregational Church, Southampton, 1898 (Sheffield Central Library).

II THE MASTERWORK

Union Chapel, Islington, was Cubitt's masterpiece. 'I see you have great works about', wrote E. A. Freeman, the medievalist, to Union's minister in January 1876. 'But I say to you, as I say to all denominations, why not build plain English? Surely I see a touch of Ruskinesque in your buildings?'[1] Union was built for that minister, Henry Allon. Allon was a man to know, editor, preacher, ecclesiastic and administrator, initiator and pastor.[2] He was a remarkable man, holding together a remarkable people—670 members by December 1875, 87 of them new since 1874: City men, aspiring businessmen, teachers, clerks, landladies, bankers, resting ministers, returned missionaries, widows. They included Asquith's mother and two of her brothers, one of them on the building committee. There were some paper-making Spicers, some Betjemanns, and the parents and sisters of Brooke, of Brooke Bond Tea. Canonbury, Highbury New Park, Aberdeen Park, Hillmarton Road were rich with Union's ample households.

The original Union Chapel, brick, but Portland-stone fronted, Ionic pillared and clock-cupolaed, was the centrepiece of a terrace of single pairs of semi-detached villas set back from the High Road near Highbury Corner.[3] As so often, the decision to rebuild was more evolution than conversion. It began in the Sunday school.

The stages of evolution are instructive.[4] They took between November 1869, when the deacons accepted the need for 'new school premises', and October 1874, when Lord Northampton's Mr Boodle agreed to a premium of £1,500 in return for extending Union's lease to ninety-nine years from Lady Day at the existing rent of £65. In between, the Highbury Young Men's Society had urged the introduction (or rather, the consideration of the introduction) of 'a liturgical element into public worship';[5] collections had been authorized for the new chapel at Cambridge, and a subcommittee reported on plans 'for sundry alterations', including 'certain plans which were considered but not finally decided upon'. The activists at this stage were two elderly brothers, Henry and William Revell Spicer, the

[1] Edward Augustus Freeman to Henry Allon, 13 Jan. 1876: A. Peel, ed., *Letters to a Victorian Editor* (London, 1929), p. 106.

[2] For Henry Allon (1818–92) see *DNB*.

[3] The architect is thought to be H. Leroux (1806); porticoed and enlarged 1839.

[4] Union Chapel Deacons' Meeting Minute Book [hereafter Deacons' Minutes], 22 Feb. 1869— Union Chapel MS in possession of Union Chapel, Islington.

[5] Ibid., 28 Feb. 1870. In its early years Union's worship had followed Prayer Book usage, but now a congregational meeting 'decided by a large majority that it was not advisable to introduce any liturgical change.'

papermen.[6] The key meetings were usually at Henry's house. By January 1872 the Rubicon had been crossed. It was agreed 'after a long and careful conversation' to go for complete rebuilding, provided that the site could be enlarged. That would mean negotiating with the Marquess of Northampton. Henry Spicer would look into it. The decision brought into the open some delicate questions about architects. Inevitably there were architects in Union's membership, notably Finch Hill, who had competed for the Metropolitan Tabernacle. The partnership of Lander and Bedells, whose principals worshipped at Park Chapel, up in Hornsey, had for some time exercised a watching brief over Union's premises; and there was 'Mr. Wagstaff who had been consulted professionally in the contemplated alterations'.[7]

The appropriate diplomacies followed. Wagstaff 'courteously stated he had no charges against the Treasurer in this matter', but Lander 'expressed surprise that, considering the professional services he had rendered in the former alterations of the Chapel, plans and estimates had been obtained from another surveyor. [He] did not dispute the right of the Deacons to take this step but felt it to be a reflection upon his former work.' Hastily the deacons explained that the plans to which Lander took exception were solely to show what *might* be done; any final decision would be based on 'plans anonymously sent in', including to be sure, 'plans from yourself in common with some other Gentlemen in the profession'.[8]

The decision had been taken, but the practice proved hard. Lord Northampton's agents, Boodle and Co., declined to sell the freehold or extend the lease. Briefly the deacons reverted to their old scheme of alteration, and for a while both plans of action were held in tandem. There were attempts to build on another site, but negotiations with the Dawes Estate on Highbury Crescent and the Great Northern Railway on Highbury Plain came to nothing. Worse yet, W. R. Spicer moved out of Highbury and down to Bickley. Only when the house to the south of the chapel came on to the market, and the tenant agreed to assign what remained of his lease for £300, was the situation transformed, for now the church owned the houses to either side of it. On 17 April 1874 church meeting determined to set up a full building committee. By mid-July Lord Northampton's Boodle had changed his tune.

6 William Revell Spicer (1805–85), Henry Spicer (1801–77), and Henry Spicer, Jr (1837–1915) of Spicer Brothers, New Bridge Street, Blackfriars. The younger Henry Spicer was Liberal MP for South Islington, 1885–6.

7 Deacons' Minutes, 29 Jan. 1872.

8 Ibid., 22 Jan. 1872; 29 Jan. 1872; 20 Oct. 1873; 21 Oct. 1873.

So far the deacons have held the stage, mediating among the professional men and from time to time testing the congregational temperature, but now that the way was open for public competition the key role was taken by Henry Allon.

At the turn of 1873 Allon's people gave him £1,200.[9] In return he furnished them with some notes on essentials for a new church from the minister's point of view. As his biographer put it, they were 'a fair illustration of Dr. Allon's high ideals of the mere machinery of worship'. In Henry Allon, Cubitt met his match.

An efficient Congregational chapel must meet two requirements. It must be good for preaching, and it must be good for congregational worship. Allon considered both.[10] A good preaching-house must allow each hearer to do just that: hear, without conscious effort. Consequently there must be no barrier between hearer and preacher, no intercepting lights, no lights at the wrong level, no internal supports. The shape of the building, and especially its roof, must be angled acoustically. The pulpit must be the right height and at the right distance from the worshipper in the front pew and the worshipper in the back pew alike. And there must be space for weddings.

So much for preaching. Worship meant prayer and praise. It meant extempore, that is to say unpredictable (but not unprepared) prayer.'The preacher may be loud in addressing an audience; he who prays cannot shout in addressing the Almighty.' 'Thus, except during singing, the congregation *through the entire service* are dependent upon hearing the words of the minister.'[11] What then of the singing? Here Union was at its most distinctive and Allon at his most insistent. At Union, wrote the Allon of *Allon and Gauntlett* and the *Congregational Psalmist*:[12]

> No hymn, chant, or anthem, is sung in which the congregation does not join. The idea, very largely realised in Union Chapel, is that the whole congregation shall sing from music-books in four-part harmony.
>
> The choir, technically so-called, is therefore only part of the singing congregation; its function is simply to lead it. It should therefore be in it, and of it—under no circumstances separated from it. It

[9] W. H. Harwood, *Henry Allon D.D. Pastor and Teacher* (London, 1894), pp. 54–5.

[10] Ibid., p. 56.

[11] Ibid., pp. 56–8.

[12] For Henry John Gauntlett (1805–76), organist at Union Chapel 1853–61, compiler with Allon of *The Congregational Psalmist* (London, 1856), see *DNB*.

should be felt in its lead and control of the congregational song, but not seen or even heard apart from it. Hence it should be so placed as to be part of the congregation.

Here, with a vengeance, was a consumer's plea for form to follow function. 'Our church buildings are for use, not for the realisation of conventional ideas.'

The competition was announced in 1874 and settled early in spring 1875. It was to cost £15,000. Seven firms, each with a Congregational specialism, were invited to compete.[13] In the assessor's order of merit they were James Cubitt, Lander and Bedells (who had enlarged Cheshunt College, Henry Allon's old college and special administrative concern), T. Roger Smith (a son of the manse and an expert on acoustics), T. and J. Steane (who were Coventry Congregationalists), Paull and Bickerdike (originally from Manchester, but with Welsh interests; they secured London Congregationalism's other big commission, Newman Hall's Christ Church, Westminster Bridge Road), T. Lewis Banks (since his father-in-law was John Curwen, founder of tonic-sol-fa, he could be presumed to know something about choral psalmody), and Finch Hill, who was a Union member. Alfred Waterhouse was the professional assessor.[14]

That was a measure of the competition's importance, for this was the decade of Waterhouse's most assured achievements—the great range of buildings for Owens' College in Manchester and Manchester's Town Hall, that essay in municipal thirteenth-century Gothic, suffused with the spirit of the present age; Balliol in Oxford and Caius in Cambridge; a palace near Chester for the Duke of Westminster and another in Liverpool for Lime Street Station. Waterhouse already had direct experience of Congregational chapel building in Manchester, notably at Rusholme (1863–4), which Henry Allon had opened. In the 1880s he went on to design two leading London chapels, Grosvenor Square's King's Weigh House and Hampstead's Lyndhurst Road. He was, therefore, genuinely conversant with congregational needs. Even so, the competition was not plain sailing.[15]

Each competitor took a motto: 'Torcello'; 'Off the Beaten Track'; 'Au

[13] R. H. Harper, *Victorian Architectural Competitions. An Index to British and Irish Architectural Competitions in 'The Builder' 1843–1900* (London, 1983), p. 100.

[14] For Alfred Waterhouse (1830–1905) see *DNB*.

[15] The following account is drawn from *Builder*, 3 April 1875, pp. 292–3; 10 April, p. 333; 17 April, p. 356.

Fait'; 'Hearing, Seeing, Breathing'; 'One Focus'; 'Faith'; 'Progress'. The torch was awarded to 'Torcello', but the trade press was severe about the way he and his fellow-competitors had gone about the matter, and by implication it criticized Waterhouse's handling of the business. The *Builder* was particularly severe. Each competitor had played ducks and drakes with the rules, and three had deliberately included features which could be omitted if funds dried up. Morally such features could form no part of any assessable designs, and yet they could have been the very features which most attracted notice. That was sharp practice.

Waterhouse was swift to defend himself. He had formed, he insisted, his own quite independent estimate of costs. He had found, taking 'the most favourable view possible', that five of the seven came out below his estimates. 'Torcello' was not one of those five, but since 'Torcello's' excess lay in his tower, and since Union's committee preferred 'Torcello' without his tower rather than any other design *with* its tower, they felt it entirely proper to give 'Torcello' their suffrage, 'particularly as it was left entirely to the option of the competitors whether to show a tower in their design or not.'

The one competitor who had kept within bounds exploded. 'Off the Beaten Track' (T. Lewis Banks) found Waterhouse's defence 'extraordinary', and his method of valuation left him speechless. He doubted 'Torcello's' integrity. And although he was sure that the building committee 'desired to do nothing but what is strictly honourable', he believed that the entire exercise had 'so far . . . been a signal failure'.

What then of these slippery designs for the most important chapel prize since Spurgeon's Tabernacle? The *Builder* looked carefully at them.

'Off the Beaten Track' was 'not off the beaten track in any marked degree'. It was in what 'may be called Romanesque, half modernised, half classicised'. Its interior promised well acoustically, 'but hardly has anything else to recommend it'.[16] The schools, however, were admirable. 'The idea which seems to be coming up a good deal at present of making the class-rooms above part of the schoolroom, with an open gallery or balcony of communication round, is here carried out.' That at least was carried out at Union: 'Torcello' adopted 'Off the Beaten Track's' schools.

'Au Fait' (Paull and Bickerdike) was 'of Italian Romanesque type, with "navy stripes", somewhat weakly though heavily treated; the terminations, or lanterns, of the campaniles are very questionable.' So was the

[16] *Builder*, 3 April 1875. The plan would appear to owe much to Banks's Whitehaven Congregational Church (1872).

entrance. The acoustics were inferior to 'Off the Beaten Track's'; the pulpit was 'less cribbed and confined than usual'; but the 'figures sketched on the seats . . . afford a rather sorry specimen of the kind of thing which draughtsmen take for wit.'[17]

'Hearing, Seeing, Breathing' (T. and J. Steane) was 'Italian treated Gothic-wise, in a manner which we have seen elsewhere'. The *Builder* found it a quiet design and suitable, though not 'interesting or captivating'. It, too, had a mean entrance and disingenuous campaniles—one full grown but the other cut short. The architects' explanation was that the campanile was 'the extracting shaft for ventilating the chapel'. The *Builder* dismissed this as 'a specimen of the inconsistencies into which architects fall when they try ostensibly to comply with, and really evade the conditions of a competition.'

As for 'One Focus' (T. Roger Smith), that 'perhaps emphasises a theory a little too much'; but the *Builder* was decidedly taken with it. 'One Focus' claimed 'to have arrived at a combination of the Greek theatre with the basilica'. It was in 'a variety of Romanesque, well-treated, richly but not heavily, with a small truncated tower at one flank, and the same design carried up on the other side with an octagon stage and a short circular spire.' The *Builder* found this 'architecturally very effective', even if the 'break from the square to the octagon' were 'harshly managed'; and it noted the 'adroit' proposal that the spired tower might be a private gift, 'so as to take it out of the limited amount to be expended'. But the real point about the chapel and its schools was their concentricity:

> the pulpit, near one end of the interior, is the centre from which all the lines of seats are struck, the nearest forming a complete circle round the pulpit, and the same curve carried back the whole extent of the area. The interior perspective sketch shows the circular line carried out everywhere, in the roof, the plan, the apse, and the large organ towering behind the pulpit and tribune; there is a certain degree of genius about the conception.[18]

There was little genius about 'Faith' (Lander and Bedells) or 'Progress' (Finch Hill). The former was of 'Romanesque type', the latter 'avowedly Gothic'. 'Faith' was encumbered with a companile, a barrel vault and draughts. 'The author has hardly studied ventilation philosophically.'[19]

[17] Ibid.
[18] Ibid.
[19] Ibid.

'Progress' had sent in some lovely drawings, but its details 'are quite below the mark, and the style ... seems made up of bits from various Gothic periods put together with little congruity.'[20] The *Builder*, which was otherwise most drawn to that architect's architect T. Roger Smith (whose drawings were 'admirably got up, and show the hand of a true architect in the union of practical consideration and good planning with architectural unity of effect'), reflected wryly that the selection was likeliest to fall 'on the roughest and least finished set of drawings'.

These were 'Torcello's'. Cubitt's plans showed every sign of hurry; his arrangements for class- and lecture-rooms were open to objection; his details needed refining; but the concept was satisfactory, and the plan as simple as it was practical. He had rejected Romanesque for 'Lancet Gothic of a French type ... the general effect ... solid, but somewhat bald and heavy'. But it would work:

> The plans, based on that of Sta Fosca, Torcello, will work admirably as a combination of architectural effectiveness with suitability for congregational worship, which, as we have often observed, is best served by an *area* rather than an *avenue*. The ground floor seats are arranged in concentric curves; the gallery front forms an octagon (with straight-lined seats), and the roof over takes the octagon form, with a small lantern at the apex. The galleries and centre part of the roof are carried on stone piers, of sufficient dimensions for satisfactory architectural effect, and the seats are so arranged that the piers scarcely obstruct any of them.

Here at last was Cubitt's opportunity to put his theories to the congregational test. Hurried or not, he took it.

The *Builder* was clear that the plan was based on Santa Fosca, the smaller of Torcello's two churches (colour plate 5). A later biographical notice was vaguer: 'planned somewhat on the lines of the ancient church at Torcello'.[21] How much should be read into that choice of name, 'Torcello'?

It was an odd name for a people's space in a London suburban hub. For Torcello was the Venice that failed, a town of 20,000, reduced to fewer than twenty families, flat on the lagoon's furthest isle. There are still two churches on its grass-grown piazza. Santa Maria Assunta is the cathedral, a

[20] *Builder*, 3 April 1875.

[21] C. Welch, ed., *London at the Opening of the Twentieth Century: Contemporary Biographies* (Brighton, 1905), p. 475.

severe and lofty basilica, the oldest in the lagoon, built between the ninth and eleventh centuries, enlivened by mosaics. Mary cradles the infant Jesus in her arms, a great figure rising in the apse over the Twelve Apostles, protecting them too. The second is Santa Fosca, an early eleventh-century octagon, squat and unadorned. Santa Fosca is pure mass in miniature, its octagon covered by a plain, wooden, domed roof.

Torcello, however, occasioned one of the most memorable set pieces in Ruskin's *Stones of Venice*.[22] Gazing from a 'rude brick campanile, of the commonest Lombardic type', Ruskin found 'one of the most notable scenes in this wide world of ours'. It spread from 'a waste of wild sea moor' and 'the paleness and roar of the Adriatic' to Venice, where 'rising out of the bright lake into which they gather . . . are a multitude of towers, dark and scattered among square-set shapes of clustered palaces, a long and irregular line fretting the southern sky.'

As for Torcello's own buildings, grouped by its piazza, 'they lie like a little company of ships becalmed on a far-away sea.' Santa Fosca's pillars are of pure Greek marble, with delicately sculptured capitals, but its roof is only the height of a cattle shed: 'Whatever sin it might have been which has on this spot been visited with so utter a desolation, it could not at least have been ambition.' The larger church, too, 'has evidently been built by men in flight and distress'. Ruskin was profoundly moved:

> I am not aware of any other early church in Italy which has this peculiar expression in so marked a degree; and it is so consistent with all that Christian architecture ought to express in every age (for the actual condition of the exiles who built the cathedral of Torcello is exactly typical of the spiritual condition which every Christian ought to recognise in himself, a state of homelessness or exile, except so far as he can make the Most High his habitation) that I would rather fix the mind of the reader on their general character than on the separate details, however interesting, of the architecture itself.

That must be the clue: the vanished history of the city working on the spirit of the childless, Protestant, widower; the idea of the cathedral; the shape of Santa Fosca and the influence of its own internal idea.[23] If this is accepted, then four elements might be translated from Torcello to Union Chapel.

[22] J. Ruskin, *The Stones of Venice* (London, 1853). I have used the Everyman edn, 2, pp. 10–24.

[23] The sceptical might find more of Santa Fosca in parts of Henry Fuller's Clapton Park Congregational Church (1872) than in Cubitt's Union, Islington.

The first is 'luminousness': 'the sunshine ... freely admitted into a church built by men in sorrow', who 'sought for comfort in their religion, for tangible hopes and promises, not for threatenings or mysteries', their minds fixed by mosaic on two great facts of their faith, 'the present mercy of Christ to His Church, and His future coming to judge the world'.

The second is the pulpit (colour plate 6). Ruskin had an appendix on 'Modern Pulpits'.[24] He quoted Bunsen as authority:

> that there can be no doubt that the bishop always preached or exhorted, in the primitive times, from this throne in the centre of the apse, the altar being always at the centre of the church, in the crossing of the transepts.

Torcello's pulpit was 'studiously plain'. Ruskin approved: 'When the form is kept simple, much loveliness of colour and costliness of work may be introduced, and yet the speaker not be thrown into the shade by them.' Its ornaments should be 'of a chaste, grave and noble kind'. Ruskin was tact itself: 'When the sermon is good we need not much concern ourselves about the form of the pulpit. But sermons cannot always be good.'

The third element is the pulpit's occupant:

> a man sent with a message to us, which it is a matter of life or death whether we hear or refuse; if we look upon him as set in charge over many spirits in danger of ruin, and having allowed to him but an hour or two in the seven days to speak to them; if we make some endeavour to conceive ... how precious these hours ought to be to him, a small vantage on the side of God after his flock have been exposed for six days together to the full weight of the world's temptation, and he has been forced to watch the thorn and the thistle springing in their hearts, and to see what wheat had been scattered there snatched from the wayside by this wild bird and the other, and at last, when breathless and weary with the week's labour they give him this interval of imperfect and languid hearing, he has but thirty minutes to get at the separate hearts of a thousand men, to convince them of all their weaknesses, to shame them for all their sins, to warn them of all their dangers, to try by this way and that to stir the hard fastenings of those doors where the Master himself has stood and knocked yet none opened, and to call at the openings of those dark streets where Wisdom herself hath stretched forth her hands and no man

[24] Ruskin, *Stones of Venice*, pp. 349–50.

> regarded—thirty minutes to raise the dead in—let us but once understand and feel this, and we shall look with changed eyes upon that frippery of gay furniture about the place from which the message of judgement must be delivered . . . we shall wish that his words may be simple . . . and the place from which he speaks like a marble rock in the desert, about which the people have gathered in their thirst.

There most certainly and most imperishably is the call for such a church as Henry Allon's Union Chapel. But a fourth element must be extracted from Torcello: the early Christian symbolism of the Church as a ship, with its bishop as pilot. Here was the essence of Torcello, as of that great galleon, Union Chapel:

> And if the stranger would yet learn in what spirit it was that the dominion of Venice was begun . . . let him ascend the highest tier of the stone ledges that sweep round the altar of Torcello, and then, looking as the pilot did of old along the marble ribs of the goodly temple-ship, let him repeople its veined deck with the shadows of its dead mariners, and strive to feel in himself the strength of heart that was kindled within them, when first, after the pillars of it had settled in the sand, and the roof of it had been closed against the angry sky that was still reddened by the fires of their homesteads—first, within the shelter of its knitted walls, amidst the murmur of the waste of the waves and the beating of the wings of the sea-birds round the rock that was strange to them—rose the ancient hymn, in the power of their gathered voices:
>
> THE SEA IS HIS, AND HE MADE IT:
> AND HIS HANDS PREPARED THE DRY LAND.

Union's evolution was an opera with several plots, in which the leading roles were played by minister and architect, with Mr Stone singing in Spicer's place for the deacons and building committee, Mr Boodle singing on for Lord Northampton and, of course , the builders, Messrs L. H. and R. Roberts of Rheidol Terrace, Islington.

The progress of Messrs Roberts was a necessary worry. In September 1876 Mr Stone was 'requested to put some pressure on the builders with a view to hasten the completion of the works'.[25] Two months later Stone was 'requested to write Mr. Cubitt desiring him to urge Messrs. Roberts to hasten the works'.[26] In May 1877, 'Mr. Stone was requested to remonstrate

[25] Deacons' Minutes, 29 Sept. 1876.
[26] Ibid., 30 Nov. 1876.

with Messrs. Roberts on the slow progress of the Buildings.'[27] A sharper worry came in May 1876:

> Mr. Stone reported that the house no 20 Compton Terrace had been purchased for the purposes of a Refuge for fallen women and possibly a kind of Lock Hospital, also that there was a strong feeling against such an institution being brought into such a prominent position and thereby injuring the property adjoining it. Mr. Stone reported that he had called on Mr. Boodle to make inquiries, was unable to see him but received a message from him to the effect that he (Mr. Boodle) 'thought it a very commendable object'.
>
> After some conversation it was felt that as a Christian church all philanthropic efforts claimed our sympathies but that the bringing of such an Institution into so public and prominent a position was very undesirable and would be a serious injury to the adjoining properties. It was agreed that we could not take any combined action in the matter, but it was hoped that individual influence or interference by the parochial authorities would lead to the selection of some other site for the proposed institution.[28]

The chief excitement remained the building itself. In February 1876 the deacons had 'some conversation on the merits of certain materials proposed for the interior of Union Chapel'.[29] A week later Richard Stone wrote carefully to Cubitt:

> Dear Sir,
>
> The red brick (of whatever tone) seems to go very heavily with many of our friends. Can you relieve it in any way where there is a mass?
>
> The thought has occurred to me (it may not be worth much) that there must be a large mass of the colour in the gallery under the Tower facing the pulpit. The spot where you spoke of using a different tone of coloured [*sic*] in the brick in lieu of a dado—
>
> Could you not in this spot, instead of taking the bricks of a different colour up to a string course, or whatever marks the line, use the gothic pattern dado—making the course [?tops] run in a straight line, just as you intended the bricks to run—and could not two or three small gothic blind windows or arches be made above the shafts etc being of stone—would this be a relief to the mass of colour?

[27] Deacons' Minutes, 28 May 1877.
[28] Ibid., 31 May 1876.
[29] Ibid., 28 Feb. 1876.

> It has also been suggested that if the walls must be red toned brick, then *all* the arches should be rendered in stone, and no brick mouldings used—Will you work out the cost of this? As this inside lining question has thrown us all at sea at present, but I hope we shall land safe.[30]

Union's deacons were persistent men. In March Stone wrote again:

> The Committee were unanimous in recommending stone for the principal arches, and Terra Cotta or Brick for the minor arches—Notwithstanding this decision of the Committee, there is so strong a feeling against bricks of a red tone that it is more than probable a compromise of some sort will be necessary.
>
> It has struck me, why not have the Coalville bricks, and have them washed with a Silicate and so bring them up to the desired uniform tone of colour—As Silicate does not look like paint, I think such a plan might solve the difficulty, and any tone of colour might be used.[31]

Four days later he attacked again in his firm, polite way, on two fronts. Dr Allon was worried about the lights, 'which as a preacher he thinks a great deal of'. And they were all still worried about the heaviness of the interior:

> Could you possibly procure a sufficient number of Bressingham Bricks, of the *right tone* of colour, so as to show a good body of them together . . . ? Say by Friday . . .? . . .Could you give me the relative proportions of brick and stone in the interior supposing the arches to be of stone as suggested by the subcommittee. Would you also give the relative proportions of surfaces—of stone as proposed, Red Bricks and Terra Cotta, supposing the latter to be used in the Octagon.

Stone threw in a thought of his own. Why not fill the spandrels of the gallery front with terra cotta bricks? 'What do you think of these ideas?'[32]

A week later deacon Bolton 'reported visits made to inspect Church interiors and lengthened discussion took place on the relative cost and merits of brick and stone . . .';[33] and for the rest of that year discussion

[30] Richard Stone to James Cubitt, 7 March 1876: Union Chapel Letter Book 1875– ; Union Chapel MS [hereafter Letter Book].

[31] Ibid., 16 March 1876.

[32] Ibid., 20 March 1876.

[33] Deacons' Minutes, 27 March 1876.

concentrated on the facing of the gallery front, the appearance of the lecture-room, and ventilation.

Richard Stone, Union's unsung hero, pressed and cajoled his way. In June, August, and November he urged Cubitt to produce his designs for the gallery. In May he considered the lecture-room roof:

> The Committee much prefer your *first* design, but it is suggested that it might be made more ornamental if the straight struts of the side were removed, and *circular* used instead. I have marked it in pencil.[34]

In September it was the walls:

> I thought if you wd consider the propriety of breaking the large dead flat surface of the wall opposite the window—It makes a noble room, and it is desirable that it shd be as complete as possible.[35]

In October it was the stained glass:

> Will you ask the artist to send three or four alternative designs for the Windows. The Committee are very anxious about these, and would be obliged by yr pressing this on as fast as you can.[36]

There was an afternoon meeting in November with Dr Allon 'at the back entrance of Dr. Parker's Church' to examine Dr Parker's pulpit.[37] There were such domestic concerns as oak furniture and Turkey carpets for the vestries or Jennings Patent Wash Basin and Urinal for the minister's lavatory. And there was the organ. Cubitt's view was that the entire chancel end should be used for that, so Allon sought Dr Stainer's advice. The decision to go for a new Willis organ (cost £1,100) was taken by late July. In early July, and not a moment too soon, the deacons had pondered the running costs of their new premises. On the basis that average pew rents would amount to £1,700, a third could be allocated to incidentals and the rest to Dr Allon. His stipend of over £1,100 was perhaps four times that of the average urban Congregational minister.

Somehow Richard Stone maintained friendly relations with the

34 Richard Stone to James Cubitt, 23 May 1876: Letter Book.

35 Ibid., 26 Sept. 1876.

36 Ibid., 25 Oct. 1876.

37 R. Stone to J. Cubitt, 6 Nov. 1876: Letter Book. The City Temple (Mawson and Lockwood: 1874) was Congregationalism's City counterweight to the Baptist Metropolitan Tabernacle. It, too, was classical, but its façade was Wren, a domeless St Paul's perhaps. Its famous Ruskinian 'Great White Pulpit' was the gift of the Corporation of London. Joseph Parker was its minister 1869–1902.

architect, worrying over Cubitt's health in April 1876 and reproaching himself for thoughtlessness in December: 'I must apologise for not asking you to come round with me and take some supper—as you were so late. I thought of it when it was too late—please take the will for the deed.'[38]

It was to be a dozen years before such concerns faded away. The building committee was dissolved in March 1880, but Stone's responsibilities were perennial. In December 1880, for example, it was 'agreed that the proposed eight chandeliers for the church should be of the inexpensive kind, as it was hoped that before long the electric lighting would be adopted.'[39] By August 1881 that had happened. 'Mr. Stone was authorized to dispose of the removed Gasoliers.' It was hoped to dispose of them in 'the Australian market'; and 'Mr. Stone was requested to have one or two (if necessary) Electric bells placed in the pulpit, one to communicate with the Organist, the other with Mr. Stone's pew, as attendant deacon.'[40]

That September saw a move to clear the debt and complete the church. The year 1881 was the jubilee year of the national Congregational Union, and Henry Allon was to be its chairman. Consequently twenty to thirty of Union's solider men met at a Spicer house to consider completing the tower in celebration, which meant £5,000. In February 1882 Cubitt submitted plans for that. It was not completed, however, until 1889, and the debt was not cleared until December 1891. Henry Allon died in 1893.

'Torcello's' church remains Allon's memorial and Cubitt's triumph. It is an intelligent mystery of largeness of parts, interplay of shapes and shades, counterpoint of arch and column (plates 9 and 10). There is life and rich, restrained colour. There is colour in the windows, the brick, the glazed tiles. There is life in the rhythm of the pews, in the promise of trumpeters perched high in the arcade above the pulpit, in the invisible organ's music. The combined best advice of the College of Organists and the Institute of Architects was for a lofty space above the top of the organ pipes.[41] Cubitt responded by devoting the whole of the 'chancel' end of his church to the organ, concealing console and pipes alike behind the central pulpit, grilles, and arcading, so that the sound might 'develop itself and . . . pass into the church'. As the architect thus liberated his church's best space, so the new organist, Fountain Meen, would liberate its best music, unseen yet unimpeded, while Henry Allon, duly visible, carefully

[38] Letter Book, 6 Dec. 1876.

[39] Deacons' Minutes, 2 Dec. 1880.

[40] Ibid., 1 Aug. 1881.

[41] J. Cubitt, *A Popular Handbook of Nonconformist Church Building* (London, 1892), pp. 67–8.

Plate 9 Interior of Union Chapel, Islington, 1875–1889.

Plate 10 Union Chapel, Islington, 1875–1889. Interior, looking to the south wall and south-east corner (Greater London Photograph Library).

focused, yet cut properly to size, would liberate the Word; and the space and the sound and the preacher in his pulpit and his people in their pews would unite in worship. It would be Union.

Cubitt's Union passes the prime architectural test. It works. It demonstrates Christianity's twin genius for individualizing faith and for holding it in collectivity. No individual can escape in this building made for choral endeavour in four-part harmony. This very Protestant place for listeners to Word (or music) is no place for those who prefer the sidelines. The moment you are seated in it you are on the preacher's sight-line. Wherever you sit, there is nothing between you and the preacher, you alone and the preacher alone. In the body of the church or at the side in the gallery you and he share the open arena. Even at the back of the tower gallery you are your own centre, with the pulpit still the focal point, you and the preacher in it, though from the tower the drama of the great church space is now seen from behind a proscenium arch. Seen from the tower, Union has become a theatre of eternity, with the pulpit centre stage above the table, ready for some apostolic Henry Irving. Or, to correct the metaphor, from the tower the whole church space has become a chancel, the priests' part wherein all are priests, people's Gothic for a Protestant people.

So much for the person in the pew. How is it from the pulpit? It is a carved and marbled pulpit, each corner peopled by a Reformer's head; and it is a pulpit, not a rostrum, although it is large enough to offer room for thought and good effect, since the honest preacher is an actor. The view from the pulpit is of a symphony of pews when empty and of heads when full, held intelligently together, body, soul, and voice, by the building. This individualizing, Protestant, space is thus also a very gathering, Catholic space. It is truly Congregational.

The acoustics are good. The ground floor of this octagon is in fact almost square, and a strong voice can fill it. The articulation must be precise, the delivery full and slow. Nothing must be left to chance. It is a building which makes sense of elocution. As for music, whether organ or oratorio, the impact is magic. Since nothing 'musical' is visible, neither organist nor pipes, when the organ plays the whole building is liquefied in sound, as in a cathedral, and there is no distraction.

Union is thus a consolidated rhythm. The pews are raked, their raking hardly apparent from the pulpit, varyingly so from the body of the church. They provide their own rhythm. So, too, with the walls. In this building, as in a good sermon, there are no awkward afterthoughts. The red brick, the stone dressing, the marbling of the frieze, the polished granite for the slender pillars between the great piers of hard Yorkshire stone, the wood panels of the ceiling are all as intended. The ornament, like the colour and the texture, is intelligent too: the dado, punctuated by wooden uprights which turn out to be ventilation shafts; then the ring of encaustic tiles above the dado; then the polished marbles of the gallery frieze, gently catching the light, very gently gleaming to provide a band of life around the auditorium.

Protestant churches, being places for Word proclaimed and Word received, are often assumed to be static places. They are for sitting and listening. Union is a fine place for sitting, but listening is a complex process, at once a relationship and a movement; and the keynote of Union is rich and stately movement. It is a great chorale of a church. Each corner invites exploration, and once explored each corner makes sense. The wooden ceiling springs from the corners of the brick and stone walls rather than squats four square on them. The pulpit, backed by its arcaded grille, is uplifted rather than dwarfed by the tier of Romanesque arches above that grille, each arch awaiting its trumpeter, a pride of nine all told. Little angels, now removed, flew among the grilles behind the pulpit, and a fugue of angels still flies, one in each section, in the rose window above the arcades.

And then at night there is the quintet of five-light electroliers, each throwing its pool of light, making more sense from the gallery than from the body of the church. Perhaps that is when the footloose clerks or the girls in service or the sermon-tasting students came, slipping into odd corners, only to be spotlit by the Word.

There is even movement implicit in the memorial which comes closest to being the holy relic that any cathedral should have. Fixed above the door through which the preacher must pass on his way from vestry to pulpit is a piece of pilgrim's Plymouth rock, given by the Pilgrim Society of America in 1883. As to that sort of thing, Henry Allon had set the tone in his stone-laying sermon:

> The only sanctity with which we would invest this place is the sanctity of holy service and association. In every high and holy sense we consecrate these buildings to whatever may tend to God's great glory—to a special service rather than to a special sanctity.[42]

By the time of its completion Union had cost nearer £50,000 than the specified £15,000.[43] It was opened in the presence of Mr Gladstone,

[42] Harwood, *Henry Allon*, p. 59.
[43] Ibid., p. 68. Emmanuel Church, Cambridge, cost £14–£16,000.

Plate 11 Union Chapel, Islington, 1875–1889.

speaking to one observer of 'absolute congregational worship', generally felt to be one of the remarkable buildings of the age and listed by the *Builder* as one of the past half-century's sixty-eight most notable examples of British architecture (plate 11).[44] While some might see it as a great snail of a building, those who know it better will recognize such a ship as Ruskin had pictured for the faith which built Torçello. And its people, like Torcello's, have largely gone, although careful visitors come out to it from Venice.

University of Sheffield

[44] Harwood, *Henry Allon*, pp. 61, 68. H. W. Brewer's sixty-eight 'Notable Examples', 1842–92, included Union Chapel and Christ Church, Westminster Bridge Road. *Builder*, 1 Jan. 1943, p. 17.

MAKING CATHOLIC SPACES: WOMEN, DECOR, AND DEVOTION IN THE ENGLISH CATHOLIC CHURCH, 1840–1900*

by SUSAN O'BRIEN

I

> Nanda took in her surroundings . . . At the end of the corridor stood a statue of Our Lord in white robes wearing a red, thorn-circled heart on his breast like an order. The bent head with its pale brown hair and beard was girlish and gentle; the brass halo had been polished till it winked and reflected each flicker of the little glass lamp that burned on the pedestal . . . At the end of the passage hung a large oil painting of Our Lord, showing his five wounds . . . Between the lines [of desks] stood a statue of Our Lady, supported on each side by angels with folded wings and flying girdles. Nanda thought it was a privilege to be near so holy company. Her desk was empty but for a small picture of the Sacred Heart gummed inside the lid. . . . 'I never thought there were so many holy pictures in the world,' she thought to herself. Every room she had entered since she had arrived at the Convent of the Five Wounds had had its picture or statue.[1]

A NEW and distinctively Catholic environment was created in England between 1840 and 1900 by two generations of Roman Catholics, and Antonia White's faithful, if fictional, description of a turn-of-the-century Catholic boarding-school is but a fully-developed specimen of the genre. Although English Catholicism had undergone expansion in the later eighteenth and early nineteenth centuries, and the number of Catholic places of worship had increased markedly, it was only after 1840 that there were changes in the physical setting and visual display of Catholicism. They paralleled and reflected changes in devotional life, institutional organization, and clerical-lay relations, as well as the general shift in style and taste away from

* I am grateful for the financial support given to me by the Nuffield Foundation and for the help so willingly given by the archivists of the religious congregations whose archives have been used in this essay.

[1] Antonia White, *Frost in May*, Virago Press edn (London, 1983), pp. 15–23.

Plate 1 Statue of the Sacred Heart in the Catholic Church of St Gregory the Great, Cheltenham. A typical example of the genre, second half of the nineteenth century (photo: Author, by kind permission of The Very Revd Fr Tim Kelly, O.S.B.).

Plate 2 Statue of Virgin and Child in the Catholic Church of St Gregory the Great, Cheltenham (photo: Author, by kind permission of The Very Revd Fr Tim Kelly, O.S.B.).

neo-classicism.[2] The expanding and re-established Church was to become Romanized, aggressive, and exclusive, confident of its wares in the competitive market-place for souls, and concerned to create an identity for its people.[3] One element in the process of creating a Catholic identity was that of the everyday visual and physical environment—a distinctive Catholic space. By the end of the nineteenth century a Roman Catholic space, whether it was church or home, school or convent, was recognizable to insiders and outsiders through the images and artefacts on display. Because of the power and distinctiveness of these artefacts, writer Antonia White could rely on them to transport her recently converted heroine Nanda, and the reader, into a Catholic sub-culture. Although the influence of Pugin and Victorian Gothic was general, making Nonconformists, Anglicans, and Catholics participants in the same general aesthetic shifts, and even though Protestants came to share some of the images previously shunned as Catholic, the clustering and conjunction of particular visual images by Catholics was none the less unmistakable.[4] The range and type of decor was common to all Catholic spaces, regardless of the status of their patrons, and played a crucial part in the self-identity of Catholics in England and in the transformation of English Catholicism.

The urgency with which some Victorian English Catholics set about transforming the practice of their faith has been well documented.[5] Change was political and structural, devotional and doctrinal, and the end result was to erode many of the differences which had developed between the practice of Catholicism in England and on the Continent.[6] The transformation had a pronounced visual dimension which was implicit in the widespread adoption of devotions such as the Sacred Hearts of Jesus and Mary, the Rosary, the Blessed Sacrament, and the Way of the Cross. In addition, there were visual repercussions in the renewed emphasis on

[2] For a general survey see J. Derek Holmes, *More Roman than Rome: English Catholicism in the Nineteenth Century* (London, 1978).

[3] Gerard Connolly, 'The transubstantiation of myth: towards a new popular history of nineteenth-century Catholicism in England', *JEH*, 35 (1984), pp. 78–104.

[4] For an analysis of the general shift away from neo-classicism towards the Gothic in the Methodist, Congregational, and Presbyterian, as well as the Established Church, see H. Davies, *Worship and Theology in England: from Newman to Martineau, 1850–1900* (London, 1962).

[5] See, for example, Holmes, *More Roman than Rome* and Richard J. Schiefen, *Nicholas Wiseman and the Transformation of English Catholicism* (Shepherdstown, W. Va., 1984). On Ireland, which in turn had an impact on English Catholicism, see the seminal work of Emmet Larkin, 'The Devotional Revolution in Ireland, 1850–75', *AHR*, 78 (1972), pp. 625–52.

[6] Such a comparison of the pre-1850 and post-1850 English Church is one of the main underpinnings of John Bossy's *The English Catholic Community, 1570–1850* (London, 1975).

traditional doctrines such as the Real Presence, and in the promulgation of new doctrines such as the Immaculate Conception. It seemed inevitable to many contemporaries that a re-emergent English Catholic church would, and should, look different from the classical and 'Garden of the Soul' Catholicism of eighteenth-century England. However, there was no consensus about a new style for English Catholicism, and the subject roused passions to the highest levels.[7] Fierce though debates were during the 1840s and 1850s between supporters of the Gothic and proponents of the Roman, it seems reasonable to suggest that, by the end of the century, for most Catholics the differences between the two camps was of little importance compared with the significance of the common devotions, the atmosphere, and features of all Catholic churches: elaborated altars; the flickering of candles; the use of bright colours; and the multiplicity of images in stone, glass, wood, fabric, and paint in which the emphasis was on compassion, gentleness, pity, and sorrow.[8] Whether Gothic or Roman, from the perspective of the ordinary Catholic the effect seems to have been very similar.[9]

In so far as the creation of Catholic spaces was part of the Gothic revival and of Victorian Gothic architecture and furnishings, it has been the subject of considerable study by architectural historians and ecclesiologists.[10] Controversies between supporters of the baroque or rococo and of the Gothic have likewise taken their place in the narrative history of the

[7] See, for example, E. Norman, *The English Catholic Church in the Nineteenth Century* (Oxford, 1984), pp. 234–43.

[8] For a different view or emphasis see ibid.

[9] For example, Franciscan Father Gomair Peeters wrote in 1874 of the changes he had made to the Franciscan church in Glasgow, 'Our chapel was so wretched and miserable looking that I could not stand it any longer, and I took it into my head to change, to alter, to renew nearly everything, to make it at least a little more becoming place for our Lord . . . Every one here is highly delighted with the change and improvement, it looks a little like heaven; no one thought that it was possible to make it so nice and beautiful, and I am sure it will inspire a little more devotion, help the people to pray better and carry off their hearts towards heaven': Letters of Father Gomair Peeters, O.S.F., to Alice Ingham, privately printed by the Franciscan Missionary Sisters of Saint Joseph as *The Preparation Period 1870–1880* (np, 1983), pp. 42–3 [hereafter FMSJ Letters]. One of the clearest statements from a parishioner about the achievement of the hoped for effect is from an American source, Ann Taves, *The Household of Faith: Roman Catholic Devotions in Mid-Nineteenth-Century America* (Indiana, 1986), p. 124. As Taves makes clear, there are good grounds for seeing the transformation of Catholicism in England and the USA as parallel phenomena. See also S. Gilley, 'Vulgar piety and the Brompton Oratory, 1850–1860', in R. Swift and S. Gilley, eds, *The Irish in the Victorian City* (London, 1985), pp. 255–66.

[10] See, for example, Peter F. Anson, *Fashions in Church Furnishings 1840–1940* (London, 1960); Basil F. Clarke, *Church Builders of the Nineteenth Century. A Study of the Gothic Revival in England*, repr. (London, 1969).

nineteenth-century Church. More recent historians, notably Sheridan Gilley and Ann Taves, have integrated an appreciation of Catholic environments into their understanding of nineteenth-century Catholicism.[11] Their work, with its emphasis on the meaning and significance of Catholic experiences, and the relationship between popular beliefs and practices, has done much to bridge the gap between the old institutional histories, on the one hand, and the histories of art and architecture, on the other. However, the subject has by no means been exhausted. My particular emphasis in this paper is on the content of interiors rather than the construction of buildings, the ornamental and decorative rather than the structural, and on the emphemeral as much as the permanent. In this brief exploration I want to do two things: to provide examples of the practical processes by which a Catholic visual world was made by others than professionals or experts; and, in what is a refinement and elaboration of the first point, to show that it was an aspect of Catholic public life in which women were highly active.

II

As a preliminary to discussion of women's involvement in the making of Catholic spaces, I would like to make some more general observations about women, decor, and religion. Writing of Anglican church interiors in the second volume of *The Victorian Church*, Owen Chadwick drew a parallel between the Victorian drawing-room and the church. Both, he noted, manifested a taste for elaborate furniture, 'clutter', 'little ornaments', and colour.[12] In this suggestive, if undeveloped, comment Chadwick implied that the 'taste of the middle-class housewife' somehow influenced the furnishing of churches. Of the process by which this influence was exerted he simply writes: 'It was natural that religious sentiment should desire to ornament churches in conformity with the better taste of the generation.'[13] Chadwick seems to see a female hand at work in the creation of church interiors, but his assumption is not supported by any

[11] For example, Gilley, 'Brompton Oratory'; Taves, 'Household of Faith'; Sheridan Gilley, 'Heretic London, Holy Poverty and the Irish poor, 1830–1870', *Downside Review*, 89 (1971), pp. 64–89; 'The Catholic Faith of the Irish Slums: London, 1840–70', in H. J. Dyos and M. Wolff, eds, *The Victorian City: Images and Reality* (London, 1973), 2, pp. 837–53; and 'The Roman Catholic Church and the nineteenth-century Irish Diaspora', *JEH*, 35, 2 (1984), pp. 188–207.

[12] O. Chadwick, *The Victorian Church* (London, 1970), 2, p. 310.

[13] Ibid.

evidence of women's active involvement. It is possible that what he saw as a womanly touch was, in fact, the emphasis on detail and the decorative that was so integral to contemporary taste, and has been associated with femininity by historians of the aesthetic, even where it was generated by men.[14] The simple appearance of a 'feminine' or even 'domestic' style does not thereby guarantee that women have been actively involved, but Chadwick reminds us of the possibility. Moreover, as Chadwick's comparison of church and drawing-room implies, church interiors may have occupied an unusual place within the Victorian discourse of separate spheres. The classification of places and spaces as either private, and therefore familial and appropriate for women, or public and inappropriate for women, was a significant aspect of separate-spheres ideology. Yet churches do not fit readily into such polarized categories.[15] For much of the nineteenth century they were unique as public places in which the presence of respectable girls and women was encouraged and expected, and this may have had implications for the style and content of church decor in general to which historians should be alert. These general observations about mainstream cultural practices are of relevance, both as context and as contrast, to the picture of female activity which emerges from a study of the making of Catholic spaces in nineteenth-century England.

During the 1840s and 1850s, when, for good reason, many Catholics urged a cautious approach to the advancement of the Church, highly visible changes were none the less introduced by advocates of a 'new' English Catholicism. For pioneers, changes to the appearance of Catholic places of worship was not simply a matter of style and good taste but rather of theology, of the proper practice of the faith, and of evangelization. Margaret Hallahan, for example, who as founder of a Third Order of Dominicans worked in Coventry and Stoke during the early 1840s, took most seriously the connections between doctrine and decor:

> We went yesterday to the chapel at Stoke, and oh, my Sisters! I cannot tell you what I have felt since! A total want of all things! Our Lord and God in a *pewter* ciborium, gilt a little on the inside! and not one

[14] For a general survey and a bibliography, see N. Schor, *Reading in Detail: Aesthetics and the Feminine* (New York, 1987). An example, relevant to this discussion, of the connections made between the 'feminine' and the 'decadent' is to be found throughout E. A. Roulin, O.S.B., *Vestments and Vesture: a Manual of Liturgical Art* (London, 1931).

[15] The literature on 'separate spheres' discourse and ideology is considerable. For a recent survey and critique of the literature see, Linda Kerber, 'Separate spheres, female worlds and a woman's place: the rhetoric of women's history', *AHR*, 75 (1988), pp. 9–39.

> decent thing in the place. How can we expect the people to be converted? they have nothing to attract them; and how can they believe us when we instruct them in the Real Presence? They may well doubt the faith of Catholics—the Lord of heaven and earth in *pewter* for the love of us, and His creatures using silver for the meanest purposes![16]

She approached Coventry as mission country, establishing the first Rosary circle there in 1842 for factory workers. High on her list of priorities was the purchase and use of a school altar, a triptych, a statue of the Virgin, and other ornaments which she saw as essential to proper devotion. Fund-raising for their purchase, and collective use of these objects were keys to bonding between Catholics in Coventry, as they were to be to all Catholics throughout the century.[17]

In this period of flux the introduction of new objects, images, and arte-facts was a highly public act, and often a controversial one. Yet it does not seem to have been thought improper for women, either lay or religious, to pioneer in this way. The Hon. Laura Petre, for example, erected the first public statue to Mary in England, according to her biographer, who tells how 'from her earliest years [she] had been remarkable in her devotion to Our Blessed Lady', and therefore 'it was only a natural outcome of this feeling which made her desire to place a statue of the Queen of Heaven in the chapel at Selby and in the church at Chelsea.' However, 'when she unfolded her project to Father Sisk [priest at Chelsea], delighted as he was with her idea, his prudence at once took alarm.' Laura Petre persisted and was given financial and moral support by other women, including the Countess of Talbot and the Duchess of Braganza.[18] As this example shows, elite women could and did take a lead in promoting particular aspects of church interiors, even against the advice of clergy. In Bristol, where she went after Coventry, Margaret Hallahan was perceived by the Vicar General, The Revd Dr Hendren, as 'a very daring woman' because she

[16] *Life of Mother Margaret Mary Hallahan* (London, 1869), p. 200.

[17] Ibid., p. 73. An example of the communal side of Catholic interior decorating is given in the correspondence between the Franciscan Father Gomair Peeters and Alice Ingham. Gomair writes of his redecoration and furnishing of the church in Glasgow, FMSJ Letters 30G/A, p. 43: 'How shall I pay for all that? Providence will assist me; the children of Mary have promised me to pay and collect for our Blessed Lady's altar; those who are called *Patrick* pay for St Patrick's altar; the brothers and sisters of the third order have promised me to pay for what is more particularly referring to our dear Lord, the Tabernacle, Lamp etc etc; one lady of Manchester has sent me all the silk, satin etc for the throne, veils, linings of the tabernacle, besides a big box of splendid flowers, and so I hope to get through it.'

[18] A. M. Clarke, *Life of the Hon. Mrs Edward Petre* (London, 1899), pp. 100–1.

pioneered devotions to Mary. In order to do so, she introduced the first statues of the Virgin to be seen in public in Bristol. Unlike Laura Petre, Margaret Hallahan was poor (she had been in service before she entered the religious life), and her methods reflect ingenuity and energy rather than wealth, although they show the same kind of commitment and insistence. One of the Dominican sisters described how, in 1847,

> She . . . sent over to Ireland for an image of Our Lady to be publicly exposed during the month, for which she paid £3. She also induced an artist in Bristol to make a mould from Deger's well-known statue, and paid him £16 for doing so, no inconsiderable amount considering the then straitened circumstances of the Community. From this mould a vast number of very small statues were cast, as have since become very common, though at the time they were quite a novelty, and so many were sold that the artist realised a handsome profit.[19]

Her efforts, which clearly found popular support, were not always welcomed by the more powerful long-standing members of the Clifton mission chapel. On one occasion they took advantage of her absence in Belgium to remove the statue of the Virgin, only to find that they had more than met their match in Mother Hallahan. 'I have been in many passions on Our Lady's account', she wrote of this incident, 'and when they turned her out of the chapel, I told them *they* might stay away if they liked, but that Our Lady should never be turned out.'[20] There was nothing discreet or 'domestic' about the manner in which either Laura Petre or Margaret Hallahan behaved in relation to church decoration during the 1840s.

This was true on an even grander scale of the work undertaken by Mother Cornelia Connelly in restoring the Bishop's Palace at Mayfield, Sussex, during the 1860s. The ruined palace was bought by the Duchess of Leeds in 1863 and given to Cornelia Connelly and her Society of the Holy Child Jesus in the same year, on condition that it was restored. The palace was regarded as an ancient Catholic shrine, desecrated at the Reformation, but now returned to Catholic hands by Providence as a sign of the conversion of England. It was a considerable responsibility, but one which Cornelia Connelly seemed to embrace willingly. Her first action was to employ Edward Welby Pugin as architect, and her second to embark on a massive fund-raising campaign. Holy Child Jesus nuns were sent

[19] *Life of Mother Margaret Mary Hallahan*, p. 147.
[20] Ibid., p. 158.

throughout the country and to the Continent on begging tours, while their supporters ran bazaars and raffles.[21] Once the building work was completed and the synod hall had been turned into a church, Cornelia Connelly was solely responsible for its furnishing and decoration. She was a keen practitioner as well as patron of church art, and completed oil paintings of Our Lady of Sorrows and of St Ignatius. At various times a professional gold worker, silk embroiderer, and point lace-maker were employed to teach their skills to the community. According to the community historian, 'The nuns were especially successful in painting statues, which were something of a novelty in England at that time.' Mother Connelly thought they could improve on the design of these statues and hired a Mr Regali from London to teach them to make statues. This experiment was not successful, however, since the nuns 'lacked the strength to do more than 2′ high ones', although carpentry was not beyond them, and Cornelia Connelly made at least one set of Stations of the Cross.[22] Convents and convent churches, of which Mayfield was one of the most spectacular and public examples, gave many Catholic women, both lay and religious, the opportunity to exercise aesthetic and devotional preferences, and thereby to play an active part in the transformation of the English Catholic Church during the middle decades of the nineteenth century.

Although patronage of the Virgin Mary, in her many manifestations, was common to all classes and both sexes during the nineteenth century, there is some evidence for suggesting, tentatively at this stage, that women played a disproportionate role in promoting devotion to female saints through donations of statues, pictures, and stained glass. Laura Petre endowed a stained-glass window showing St Juliana in the Phillips de Lisle chapel; the young women who followed Margaret Hallahan in the early 1840s contributed a medallion of Our Lady of Dolours for a window in the new church of the Most Holy Sacrament and St Osburn, Coventry; Cornelia Connelly promoted devotion to St Walburga and her healing oil, and to St Theophilia; the Faithful Companions of Jesus promoted the cult of St Philomena, which was encouraged by Popes Gregory XVI and Pius IX; and the cult of Mater Admirabilis started with a mural painted by a Sacred Heart nun and was propagated via copies of the mural.[23]

[21] See *The Life of Cornelia Connelly, 1809–1879* by a member of the Society (London, 1922), pp. 356–67.

[22] *Life of Cornelia Connelly*, p. 197, and Mayfield, Archives of the Society of the Holy Child Jesus [hereafter SHCJ], D60, MS Sacristy Journal, St Leonards, 1862–1888, 4.

[23] *Life of the Hon. Mrs Edward Petre*, p. 137; *Life of Mother Margaret Mary Hallahan*, p. 83; SHCJ

A more systematic study of devotions and patronage in nineteenth-century England is necessary before the suggestion made here about gender could be developed further, but at the very least it seems that Catholic devotions gave plenty of scope for the valorization of women and of 'feminine' attributes in both women and men.

III

More typical of women's involvement were the decorations and displays mounted for the high points of the liturgical year. Easily overlooked because of their temporary and ephemeral nature, these decorations were none the less integral to Catholicism by the end of the century. As with the introduction of images and artefacts, women took part in the establishment and institutionalization of special decorations at Christmas, Easter, Corpus Christi, and during the month of May. It seems likely, for example, that the 'traditional' Christmas crib was first seen in many English towns at the local convent, or in the school run by Catholic sisters. The first crib on public display in Bristol was the work of the Dominican nuns, those in Middlesborough, Isleworth, and Paisley were introduced by the Faithful Companions of Jesus, in York by the Institute of the Blessed Virgin Mary, and in Plymouth by the Notre Dame Sisters.[24] The nuns were well aware of the evangelizing potential of the cribs, particularly where children were concerned. In Plymouth, for example, 'The sisters became an object of much curiosity to the inhabitants of Plymouth, especially at Christmas time, when a crib which they arranged in one of the classrooms drew great numbers to see the "waxworks" or "Moses in the bulrushes" as Protestants termed the crib.'[25] The crib in the Holy Child Chapel at St Leonards in 1854 also attracted crowds to see 'A natural grotto made by our dear Reverend Mother—a rocky, rough cavern in perfect imitation of nature, the front of which represented a ruinous arch, with moss and ivy creeping over, or hanging in slight festoons around it. . . .the whole scene lighted by a lamp concealed in a fissure of the rock.'[26]

Archives, D60 MS Sacristy Journals; FCJ Archives MS Annals; Margaret Williams, *The Society of the Sacred Heart* (London, 1978), p. 54; Taves, *Household of Faith*, pp. 99–100; and John Morris, S.J., ed., *The Life of Mother Henrietta Kerr* (Roehampton, 1892), p. 283.

[24] *Life of Mother Margaret Mary Hallahan*, p. 190; Broadstairs, Kent, Archives of the Faithful Companions of Jesus, MS typescript House History of Paisley and of Middlesborough; *Life of the Hon. Edward Petre*, p. 186 for Notre Dame in Plymouth.

[25] *Life of the Hon. Mrs Edward Petre*, p. 186.

[26] SHCJ Archives, D60, MS Sacristy Journal, St Leonards, 2, p. 50.

Four years later the crib was re-rendered as a wintry scene, replete with frostwork and icicles, 'a flock of sheep and a company of rejoicing angels.'[27] At Easter there were sepulchres and altars of repose to create and decorate. Laura Petre and her sister-in-law, Lady Julia Howard, made it their job to 'adorn the Altar of Repose . . . with the costliest exotics from Costessy Hall', while at the other end of the social spectrum Margaret Hallahan built a Sepulchre at Coventry 'with very poor materials', before which the people watched 'with unwearied ardour and one poor man, who kept a rag shop in the town, remained before it the entire night standing all the time.'[28] From 1854, on 8 December, children in all the schools run by the Faithful Companions of Jesus held vigil in specially dressed class-rooms for the feast of the Immaculate Conception, such as the one in Salford in 1886, in which 'Our Lady's altar was adorned with [silver] foliage from floor to ceiling so that the statue of our heavenly Queen seemed as in the midst of a grove of dazzling whiteness lightened by a great number of lamps and candles.'[29]

Processions were also events whose visual success, or lack of it, could be decided by women's needles and their dressing and grooming of the participants. In the 1840s and 1850s, and even later in some places, processions were innovative activities for the Catholic community and were part of the process by which Catholic identity was formed.[30] Preparations for the 1868 Whitsun processions in Preston, for example, began in the New Year when the convent received a 'formidable order of needlework—15 processional banners for St Augustine's parish.'[31] Cardinal Manning's visit to Middlesborough in 1878 to consecrate the new cathedral church of St Mary's was the occasion of much needlework and female labour. Hundreds of garlands, scarves, and cloaks, and four banners were made for the confraternities.[32] The sodalities appeared for the first time in special uniforms, all distinguished by different-coloured wreaths and sashes. Processions, like other aspects of Catholic popular art, lent themselves to commercialization, but there continued to be a strong element of the amateur and home-made about many decorations throughout the century.

A rare record of these liturgical 'happenings' is to be found in the

[27] SHCJ Archives, MS Sacristy Journal, St Leonards, 3, p. 123.

[28] *Life of the Hon. Mrs Edward Petre*, p. 133; *Life of Mother Margaret Mary Hallahan*, p. 77.

[29] FCJ Archives, MS Annals 1886, Salford, Box 27, p. 34.

[30] *Life of Cornelia Connelly*, p. 200; *Life of Mother Margaret Mary Hallahan*, p. 189.

[31] FCJ Archives, typed House History of Lark Hill.

[32] FCJ Archives, typed House History of Middlesborough.

Plate 3 Altar dressed for Corpus Christi Procession in the Convent Garden, 1916. There were usually five or six altars in the garden for this occasion (Archives of the Society of Holy Child Jesus, Mayfield).

sacristy journals of the Holy Child Jesus Chapel in St Leonards. For the forty years between 1848 and 1888 there are detailed descriptions of altar dressings, church decoration, processions, and the transformation of the convent garden into a grand stage for ceremonials. Almost everything used was handworked by the community, present and former pupils, and women friends of the convent. In 1858, for example, at Christmas, they were given 'a white Antependium with Our Blessed Lady's Monogram worked in gold on Blue Velvet'; at Easter the community held a

> Procession to Our Lady of Miracles in which were carried two new Banners, one painted and the other worked by Our Mother. The first represented St Walburga full length carrying her bottle of Sacred Oil . . . the second was especially worked for Our Lady of Miracles. It was sky blue turkish Cashmere bordered with silk lace and fringe. . . .

In June they built five altars in the garden and a Calvary; and at the annual feast for the Reverend Mother, gifts for the altar worked by the school and community were presented to her, including a clothing carpet, tabernacle veil of moire antique embroidered; a sanctuary rug embroidered by junior children, a cushion, a point lace alb, and a Pugin altar-cloth.[33] Such gifts made it possible to dress altars richly and differently for every feast celebrated in the chapel. The devotions and the decorations worked hand in hand to create a considerable impact, and in surroundings like these postulants were clothed, novices professed, the younger children of the schools admitted to the Confraternity of the Holy Angels, and the older ones to the Sodality of the Children of Mary.

Behind the effects which attracted congregations on special occasions, and those which could be taken for granted throughout the year, lay the everyday work of sewing, cleaning, and laundering, which was almost certainly undertaken by women. Despite the convention that women should not go into the sanctuary, it seems likely that many sacristans were women.[34] Certainly where there were nuns in a parish they were likely to fulfil this duty and to dress the high altar as well as side altars.[35] All of these activities were totally in accord with a range of feminine duties, including sewing and embroidering; making decorations; the placing of objects for effect; flower arrangement; cleaning and polishing, and laundering. Most dioceses had sewing guilds to provide altar linen and vestments. In Shrewsbury diocese, for example, one was founded by Lady Mostyn and the Misses Sankey and met regularly at the Convent of the Faithful Companions of Jesus in Birkenhead.[36] Up and down the country women of all social classes were organized into societies and confraternities, such as the Children of Mary and, like many other Victorian women, they spent a good deal of their time sewing as they listened to edifying readings or talks.[37]

[33] SHCJ Archives, D60, MS Sacristy Journal, St Leonards, 4.

[34] For example, Father Gomair Peeters writing to Alice Ingham of Rochdale, FMSJ Letters, 30 G/A, p. 53: 'To give up dressing the altar, has been an awful temptation: oh no! dear Alice, never give up that glorious work, I say . . . let it be your greatest joy and glory and happiness, and when dressing and cleaning the altar with true love and devotion, remember that our dear Lord is dressing your heart and cleaning it from its daily imperfections.'

[35] Laura Petre, as Sister Mary of St Francis ND, records as exceptional that Canon Drinkwater, parish priest of Battersea where Notre Dame had a convent, '. . . would never yield to a sacristan the honour of decorating the altar': *Life of Hon. Mrs Edward Petre*, p. 192.

[36] FCJ Archives, typed MS House History Holt Hill (written *c*.1930).

[37] For example, see records of the Children of Mary of the Religious Society of the Sacred Heart, first established during the 1850s. MSS held at the Society's Archive, Convent of the Sacred Heart, Roehampton.

IV

This paper began with Nanda Gray's response to the considerable physical impact which her new convent boarding-school made on her: the statues and pictures, the smell of polish, and the flicker of candles beneath red glass. It was an unmistakably Catholic and wholly female space. No other church or denomination in nineteenth-century England offered women anything like the opportunities afforded in the Catholic Church to create physical settings for worship and prayer, catechism and education. Three factors can be identified as promoting such opportunities, although it was their conjunction which was unique. First, and most obviously, the existence of a separate and identifiable female world in the convents meant that there were many buildings and spaces over which women exercised an unusual degree of control. As we have seen, they felt justified in spending time and money on creating the right kind of devotional settings. Convents, and especially those from France and Belgium, should be seen, therefore, as providing early examples and teachers of Catholic decor in nineteenth-century England. Secondly, because the English Catholic Church in the mid-nineteenth century was newly restored and established, impoverished, and growing rapidly, priests and bishops were open to offers of assistance. There were simply more opportunities for anyone who wanted to be actively involved, including women. Benefactors were always welcomed, but so was the experience of women who were versed in the ways of Catholic Europe, and the time of those prepared to sew, make, or arrange liturgical items. Thirdly, Catholic re-establishment in England coincided with the wholesale promotion of devotional practices within the international Church. It coincided, therefore, with an emphasis on the material culture of Catholicism, the objects of collective and individual devotional practices. Devotional and liturgical objects had to be made or bought, arranged, cleaned and cared for—tasks which fitted easily into Victorian definitions of domestic femininity.

Perhaps with all these elements in focus, historians may be able to add a fresh dimension—that of the material world of Christian piety—to their exploration of the feminization of religion in the nineteenth century. There are several aspects, for example, the role of female benefactors, which have been no more than broached in this essay, and others, such as the aesthetic criticisms of the 'feminine' in Catholic liturgical art, which have been set aside.[38] A gendered approach to questions of agency, content, and style in Victorian church decor is overdue.

Anglia Polytechnic, Cambridge

[38] A thorough analysis of the gendered language used by experts in liturgical art is well beyond the scope of this essay. However, it is worth noting the connections made between 'poor taste' and feminine work throughout Dom Roulin's manual, *Fashions in Church Furnishings*. See, for example, pp. 18, 33, 37, and 225. Roulin's position is that of a reformer bent on discriminating between the good, the bad, and the downright ugly in liturgical art. It is implicit and explicit in his writing that women (as amateurs) have been responsible for much liturgical art in the previous generations.

MUSIC AND RELIGION IN THE FIRST WORLD WAR

by STUART MEWS

'LISTENING to instrumental music has really become the only form of worship which is still possible to us.' These words, said to have been uttered by a distinguished Oxford philosopher, were quoted by Hastings Rashdall, then an Oxford theologian but later Dean of Carlisle, when he preached in Hereford Cathedral in connection with the Three Choirs Festival in 1912.[1] Rashdall rejected the substitution of aesthetic appreciation in the concert hall for Christian worship because, he contended, it did not evoke any practical response. That he should have felt it necessary to stress this difference was in itself evidence of the strength of the view he was repudiating. It was also a significant comment on the secularization of the English academic profession and perhaps of a wider section of the middle class. It is a reminder, too, of suggestions made by scholars of history, sociology, and anthropology that there are significant connections and similarities between the development and social functions of music and religion. H. G. Koenigsberger has argued that the decline of religion left an emotional void in Western Europe which came increasingly to be filled primarily by music.[2] David Martin points out that both music and religion serve similar purposes, 'such as orgiastic stimulation, group solidarity, martial sentiment'.[3] J. S. Eades begins with the view that both 'artistic performance and religious ritual may be symbolic expressions of solidarities which can be used for political ends.'[4]

Rashdall's warning might also be taken as a comment on the quality of the services in many churches at the time, both those which were for a variety of social and cultural reasons slowly losing support, but also those

[1] Oxford, Pusey House, Hastings Rashdall MS, sermon T.221.

[2] H. G. Koenigsberger, 'Music and Religion in Modern European History', in H. G. Koenigsberger and J. H. Elliott, eds, *The Diversity of History* (London, 1973), pp. 35–78. See also George Whitfield Andrews, 'Music as an expression of religious feeling', *Musical Quarterly*, 2 (1916), pp. 331f. Sir Adrian Boult, 'Preface' to R. W. S. Mendl, *The Divine Quest in Music* (London, 1957), p. ix.

[3] David Martin, *Tracts against the Times* (London, 1973), pp. 171f.; *The Religious and the Secular* (London, 1969), pp. 79–99; 'Music and religion: ambivalence towards the "Aesthetic"'; *Religion*, 14 (1984), pp. 269–94.

[4] J. S. Eades, 'Dimensions of meaning: Western music and the anthropological study of

which attempted to combat this decline by expanding the musical part of the service. That this was at all possible was due to the extraordinary revitalization of musical life in late Victorian society. At the inauguration of the Royal College of Music in 1882 W. E. Gladstone had said of church music fifty years before, 'I cannot use any epithet weaker than one that may perhaps shock the meeting.'[5] But this situation had gradually changed. What Helen Mellor has called 'the passion for music' began in socio-religious circles.[6] The sight-singing 'mania' was immensely boosted by the German political refugee, ex-Catholic priest, and temperance advocate Joseph Mainzer, who began to hold singing classes in London in 1841. His message that choirs were more wholesome than pubs for working people was made more realistic when a Congregationalist minister John Curwen popularized the tonic sol-fa method of sight-reading.[7] The result was a vast increase in choral singing and a more widespread appreciation of high musical standards.

Though music-making received encouragement from religious groups, it could not be controlled by them. Relations between composer and divine, organist and priest, were always fragile, and never more so than at the turn of the century, when higher professional standards and status created the possibility of resentment when their respective spheres overlapped. Ralph Vaughan Williams was dismissed as organist of a church in South Lambeth in 1897 because he refused to take Communion.[8] Soon after his arrival at St Margaret's, Westminster, in 1900 Hensley Henson got rid of the organist because he feared that musical showmanship was eclipsing the sermon.[9] J. G. Simpson lectured Henry Thompson, music critic of the *Yorkshire Post*, in 1908, after being criticized in the paper for a comment in a sermon in Leeds Parish Church about the inappropriateness of Brahm's *German Requiem* to the season of Advent. 'What I dislike', he wrote, 'is the unintelligent conclusion that, because Brahms has got something to do with Death, and because Spohr calls itself the Last Judgment, that therefore they must be appropriate to this season.

---

symbolism', in J. Davis, ed., *Religious Organization and Religious Experience = ASA Monograph*, 31 (London, 1982), p. 195.

[5] *The Times*, 1 March 1882.

[6] H. E. Mellor, *Leisure and the Changing City, 1870–1914* (London, 1976), p. 219.

[7] Joseph Mainzer, *Music and Education* (London and Edinburgh, 1848); William J. Gatens, *Victorian Cathedral Music in Theory and Practice* (Cambridge, 1986).

[8] Michael Kennedy, 'The Unknown Vaughan Williams', *Proceedings of the Royal Music Association*, 99 (1972), p. 34.

[9] H. Hensley Henson, *Retrospect of an Unimportant Life* (Oxford, 1942), p. 131.

I do not mean to say that you are unintelligent! But I am afraid that the choice of music "in choirs and places where they sing" often is.'[10]

Concern about the role of music in worship went beyond the Church of England. In 1904 the Pope issued the encyclical *De motu proprio* aimed at pruning severely the efflorescence of banal and turgid music in the Catholic Church and restoring those qualities of 'holiness, beauty and universality' which were thought to find their most appropriate musical expression in the Gregorian chant.[11] In England, Pius X's reforms had already been anticipated at Westminster Cathedral by Richard Terry, who in his writings and performance demonstrated that plainsong music 'need not be cold, unrhythmic, and lifeless'. 'At Westminster', commented an attender at a Holy Week service in 1915, 'the music lived, like the faces of old burghers in a masterpiece of Rembrandt, or the dark, beady eye of a Rubens portrait.'[12]

The First World War, as Professor John Sommerville has pointed out, 'does seem to have been something of a turning-point' in the development of religious themes in music. The war, he maintains, 'forms a divide between a period of a somewhat frivolous religious reference, and one of a more austere and introspective tone.'[13] His article focuses mainly on post-war compositions by internationally-known musicians. This article looks at some of the more immediate responses of mainly lesser mortals who found themselves crossing the boundaries between music and religion between 1914 and 1918.

The outbreak of war presented a challenge to both the religious and musical worlds. For musicians the immediate practical effect was to disrupt concert programmes and deplete audiences and orchestras. To meet this situation a Committee for Music in War Time was formed, though its primary function was more accurately revealed in June 1915 when it amalgamated with the Professional Classes War Relief Fund. The Musicians' section retained its separate identity under the chairmanship of Sir Hubert Parry and included on its committee most of the illustrious names in British music: Edward Elgar, Henry Wood, C. V. Stanford,

[10] Leeds, Brotherton Library, MS 361/241, J. G. Simpson–H. T. Thompson, 4 Dec. 1908.

[11] '*Motu Proprio* of Pope Pius X on Sacred Music', in Nicolas Slominski, ed., *Music since 1900*, 4th edn (London, 1971), pp. 1285–9; Anthony Milner, 'Music in a vernacular Catholic liturgy', *Proceedings of the Royal Music Association*, 91 (1964), p. 27.

[12] Joseph W. Hathaway, 'Modern Church Music', *Music Student*, April 1915, p. 105; R. R. Terry, *Our Church Music* (London, 1901); *Catholic Church Music* (London, 1907).

[13] C. John Sommerville, 'The religious music of the twentieth and twenty-first centuries', *Religion*, 14 (1984), p. 247.

Walford Davies, Frederick Bridge, and Vaughan Williams. Its object was to 'develop schemes for the employment of people in the musical world during the war, and to deal with cases of distress'. In the first six months, from January to June 1915, 176 concerts had been given in hospitals, 89 in army camps, and 124 in clubs, schools, and other places. Commanding officers, chaplains, and hospital matrons were all agreed on the inspiring and elevating effects of the concerts upon recruits in training, and the fillip they gave to soldiers and sailors convalescing after being wounded in action.[14]

Rudyard Kipling was the chief speaker at a meeting at the Mansion House on 27 January 1915 to promote the formation of bands as recruiting agents. His description of the social function of the band was very similar to that which, two years before, the French sociologist Emile Durkheim had ascribed to religion. The band, said Kipling, 'revives memories, it quickens associations, it opens and unites the hearts of men more surely than any other appeal ... the magic and the compelling power are there to make men's souls realize certain truths which their minds might doubt.' Kipling went on to argue that the best expression of the 'soul of the battalion' was often to be found in the band, which provided a 'common means of expressing and interpreting the thoughts and feelings of the battalion'.[15] It was not difficult, recalled John Rogan, bandmaster of the Coldstream Guards, 'to get a man to *give his life* for his country by appealing to his heart through his national airs'.[16] It was even easier to use band concerts to persuade businessmen in the city to invest in War Loan.

In June 1915, a month in which the whole nation was being goaded into making greater efforts to concentrate all the nation's latent powers on the defeat of the enemy, *The Times* weighed in with an article on 'The Mobilization of Music'.[17] It was no coincidence that this slogan was being used at exactly the same time as the Bishop of London. A. F. Winnington Ingram, was calling for the mobilization of the nation's spiritual resources in a 'holy war'.[18] The *Times* article drew a letter from Walford Davies, organist at the Temple Church, on 'the vital uses of music in wartime'. He had been told by a man on leave after eight months in the trenches that 'fragments of familiar music come as the greatest help in hard times.'

[14] *Musical Times*, 1 July 1915, pp. 393f.
[15] Ibid., 1 March 1915, p. 147.
[16] John Mackenzie-Rogan, *Fifty Years of Army Music* (London, 1926), p. 185.
[17] *The Times*, 12 June 1915.
[18] Stuart Mews, 'Spiritual mobilization in the First World War', *Theology* (1971), pp. 258–64.

What was needed for the troops, Davies claimed, was 'a little first-rate music' and songs that can be easily remembered.[19]

The First World War produced an abundance of songs which could be sung. As well as the quasi-religious sentimentality of Ivor Novello's 'Roses of Picardy' and 'Keep the Home Fires Burning', there was the use of well-known hymn tunes for rough rhymes of a blasphemous character. Samuel Sebastian Wesley's tune *Aurelia*, which usually accompanied 'The Church's one foundation' now had a new set of words, 'We are Fred Karno's army', while the tune used for 'What a friend we have in Jesus' had an even more obscene version. Protests to the Archbishop of Canterbury were of little avail, for he could not think of any way in which he could censor the soldiers' songs.[20] This desecration or secularization of the music of the Church was in some instances a case of the wheel turning full circle. Henry Hall, the well-known band leader of the inter-war years, had no knowledge of popular music until he served in the Army. He had been brought up in the Salvation Army and worked with his father in the Music Department at Salvation Army headquarters. The effect of military service was to broaden his horizons and sever him from his religious roots. As the only pianist in his company, he was soon being called upon to improvise ragtime tunes, and responded by converting Salvation Army tunes into popular hits. The theme tune for his wireless programme was called 'Here's to the next time', but had been composed as a Salvation Army march before the war.[21] So the wheel turned full circle. General Booth had taken the devil's best tunes and baptized them, and within ten years of the founder's death, his tunes were in turn being handed back to Mammon.

Concerts at army bases were immensely popular. Soldiers, whose lives alternated between brutality, exhaustion, and boredom relished good music and poetry. At first the actress Lena Ashwell had had every obstacle put in her path when she attempted to take concert parties to the front. Indeed, the Army, which thought they were engaged in a war of movement, had even less time for performers than for chaplains; and at first not much time for them either. Only by pulling royal strings were concert parties allowed out,[22] and only then under the unlikely umbrella of the YMCA, an organization which before 1914 was associated with narrow

[19] *The Times*, 17 June 1915.
[20] E. D. Mackerness, *A Social History of English Music* (London, 1964), p. 140.
[21] Henry Hall, *Here's to the Next Time* (London, 1955), p. 31.
[22] Lena Ashwell, *Myself a Player* (London, 1936), p. 195.

evangelical attitudes.[23] Lena Ashwell imagined that most of the YMCA leaders looked upon the theatre, 'which they had never entered, as the front door of Hell where painted females devoured the souls of the righteous'.[24] 'To them we are a class of terribly wicked people who drink champagne all day long, and lie on sofas, receiving bouquets from rows of admirers.'[25] She amused herself by conjuring up the fantasies of YMCA staff, who probably 'expected us to land in France in tights, with peroxide hair, and altogether to be a difficult thing for a religious organisation to camouflage.'[26]

The concert parties organized by Lena Ashwell usually consisted of a soprano, contralto, tenor, baritone or bass, instrumentalist, entertainer, and accompanist. She found an increasing demand for depth. 'We all sing rot at first and end by finding they have better taste', recorded Madelaine O'Connor, a singer and lecturer, who worked for the YMCA at the base in Rouen.[27] She urged Lena Ashwell to recite 'something good'. Lena responded by offering 'Abou Ben Adhem' and Elizabethan love lyrics, and 'was very much astonished at the deep interest and very real response of the men'.[28] 'In a crowded hut or tent filled with smoke and packed to suffocation', she recalled, 'one felt the hunger of the souls of men, the aching, wondering query in their hearts.'[29]

Good music was even more evocative than fine poetry. 'We suffered a good deal from want of music', wrote Canon J. O. Hanney, after being chaplain at a base in France.[30] Lena Ashwell considered that of all the singers who went out with her concert parties, the most appreciated was Gervase Elwes.[31] In June 1917 he sang at a rest camp at Equihen in terrific heat: 'I shall never forget the experience as long as I live', he wrote home, 'never have I sung to such an audience.'[32] The night before the legendary T. B. Hardy left the base for the firing line he was overcome by a tenor singing in a concert. He later explained that he left after the song because

[23] Clyde Binfield, *George Williams and the Y.M.C.A. A Study in Victorian Social Attitudes* (London, 1973), ch. 14.

[24] Ashwell, *Myself a Player*, pp. 197f.

[25] Lena Ashwell, *Modern Troubadours. A Record of the Concerts in France* (Copenhagen, 1922), p. 7.

[26] Ibid., p. 7.

[27] Ibid., p. 15.

[28] Ibid., p. 14.

[29] Ibid., p. 12.

[30] George A. Birmingham (pseudonym for James O. Hanney), *A Padre in France* (London, n.d.), p. 73.

[31] Ashwell, *Myself a Player*, p. 206.

[32] Winifred Elwes and Richard Elwes, *Gervase Elwes. The Story of his Life* (London, 1935), p. 249.

he wanted to keep the memory of it in his mind when he was in the line.[33] 'Next to religion', commented J. O. Hanney, '. . . music is probably the most powerful means we have of spiritual treatment.'[34]

In her eagerness to legitimize the stage and concert-hall, Lena Ashwell probably exaggerated both the narrow-mindedness of YMCA staff and the spiritual appeal of performers. After three months of war, Sir Herbert Lewis, the deeply devout Liberal MP for Flintshire, made his own enquiries. 'The theatrical people had been contending that the men were getting tired of the YMCA sing songs and wanted some more exciting entertainments which only theatrical people could supply.' Investigations 'convinced me that all YMCA tents were full to overflowing every night.'[35] Nevertheless, Arthur Burroughs, YMCA lecturer at Rouen, and a future bishop, was probably correct when he stated in 1916 that 'religious meetings were never anything like so popular as concerts.'[36] This inevitably led to friction, and an attempt by the YMCA to take over the concerts. This Lena Ashwell defiantly resisted.[37] But in wanting to take control the YMCA was recognizing the power of the performing arts, and in doing so overcoming in the minds of its members a barrier which had long existed. 'So many of those working with the YMCA', according to Lena Ashwell, 'who had never been to a play' took to them 'like ducks to water', and went on to become enthusiasts for 'sound and wholesome recreations for the people'.[38]

As the months passed, it became obvious that the war was going to last longer than anyone imagined. An antipathy to all things German now began to pervade the nation. Pulpit and press thundered against the poisoned products of German *Kultur*, and in the summer of 1915, when the rumours of German atrocities appeared to have been authenticated by the Bryce Report and the message rubbed home by the sinking of the *Lusitania*, there came demands for the boycotting of German music. In the House of Commons, Sir Arthur Markham raised what he considered to be the scandal of the inclusion by Sir Henry Wood of German music in his Promenade Concerts.[39] Sir Walter Parratt, Master of the King's

[33] Ashwell, *Modern Troubadours*, p. 134. For a recent interpretation of this amazing man: David Raw, *'It's Only Me' A Life of the Reverend Theodore Bayley Hardy, V.C., D.S.O., M.C. 1863–1918* (Gatebeck, 1988).

[34] Birmingham, *Padre*, p. 77.

[35] Plas Penucha (courtesy of Mrs K. Idwal Jones), MS Diary of Sir Herbert Lewis, 14 Nov. 1914.

[36] E. A. Burroughs, *The Valley of Decision* (London, 1916), p. 197.

[37] Ashwell, *Modern Troubadours*, p. 132.

[38] Ibid.,p. 7.

[39] *PD*, LXX, col. 2326, *Musical Times*, 1 Sept. 1915.

Musick, and organist of St George's Chapel, Windsor, tried hard to show the absurdity of the demand for the boycott of all German music. To do so would mean expurgating many of the most popular tunes used in English churches. He refused to believe that Cruger's seventeenth-century tune *Nun danket*, associated with 'Now thank we all our God', would be readily discarded. 'In all my musical activities', wrote Parratt, 'I have taken no notice of the war. Music is cosmopolitan.'[40] Such Olympian detachment, however, shocked those who held that musicians should be involved in the national struggle. Both in London and the provinces, festivals of British music were being mounted, and towards the end of 1915 vigorous protests were made at the use of foreign music at funerals of the famous. Sir Charles Stanford wrote to *The Times* objecting to the use of Russian music at the memorial service for Lord Roberts at St Margaret's, Westminster. His former pupil, Martin Shaw, organist at St Mary's, Primrose Hill, protested in *The Church Times* against the selection of music by foreign composers at the memorial service for Edith Cavell in St Paul's Cathedral.[41]

The war gave a tremendous boost to those like Martin Shaw, who had long wished to liberate British composers from European and especially German influence. In August 1916 Shaw interrupted his honeymoon to lecture on 'The Church and National Music' at the Welsh Church Music Conference in Aberystwyth.[42] An ardent patriot, who compensated for his rejection for military service by drilling the choirboys at St Mary's, Primrose Hill,[43] he began by asserting that the Germans had already won their cultural war against England. The average child's life, he said, began by associating Christmas with the German Santa Claus; his first school was directly copied from Germany and called a *Kindergarten*. He was taught 'almost exclusively' at school both to sing and play German tunes until he married to the strains of Mendelssohn and Wagner. If he achieved eminence, his death would be honoured with a German dead march.

'Now the Germans', asserted Shaw, 'are a very thorough nation.' He considered it likely that they had all along been planning not only a war of weapons against England, but also a war of ideas. 'I mean the insidious force that conquers us mentally and undoubtedly is part of that system of "peaceful penetration" which the Germans have been organizing in the

[40] Sir Walter Parratt, 'Our German Church Music', *Monthly Musical Record*, 1 July 1916.
[41] *The Times*, 16 Nov., *Church Times*, 19 Nov., *Musical Times*, 1 Dec. 1915.
[42] Martin Shaw, *Up to Now* (Oxford, 1929), p. 132.
[43] Ibid., p. 123.

British Isles for many years.' Having detected the presence of these subversive influences, Shaw summoned the Church to react. In the struggle for freedom of mind and spirit, he believed that the Church had a vital part to play because he claimed that the Church was the only remaining stronghold of national music.

> The true music of the people of these islands is to be found not in the streets or music halls—there it is debased beyond recognition; not on the concert platform, the public school, the home—there it is either alien or full of that sloppy sentimentality which we would be the first to condemn in actual life; no, the true music of the people can only be found in the church, and that too rarely.

The academies and colleges of music had in Shaw's view surrendered, but although 'Germanism', by which he meant the influence of Handel and Mendelssohn, might predominate, it had not entirely driven the native idiom from English Church music. Now that the war had revealed the true state of things to everyone, he challenged organists and clergy to take a deliberate decision to expunge foreign elements in music and to follow the French, and even more the Russians, in drawing nourishment from the native tradition instead of 'filching fruit from our neighbour's garden'.[44]

This onslaught on the alleged German cultural capture of church music did not come solely from the Anglican Martin Shaw. Indeed, the most savage attack of all came from the Roman Catholic Richard Terry, Director of Music at Westminster Cathedral. Terry had been for years the leading English champion of the restoration of plainsong and a strong advocate of the revival of Tudor music. The war provided him with an excellent opportunity to promote his enthusiasms. Germany, he claimed in August 1915, had captured the Catholic church music market 'to her commercial profit and to our artistic degradation'. His indictment was directed towards the Cecilian Movement as it developed after the death of Franz Witt in 1888. Terry conceded that a debt was owed to the Germans, particularly Carl Proske of Ratisbon, who had begun in 1830 to collect and score large quantities of beautiful but neglected music. 'The old ideals of church music—dignity, sobriety and liturgical fitness were revived', Terry admitted. 'But that was before 1870—before Germany turned from

[44] Martin Shaw, 'The Church and National Music', *Musical Opinion and Music Trade Review*, Nov. 1916, pp. 91–2.

greatness in search of bigness, before she forsook idealism for commercialism.' Under Dr F. Habl, Director of the Ratisbon School of Sacred Music, vast quantities of dull, monotonous, uninspired 'Cecilian' music poured from the press. 'As usual', commented Terry, 'John Bull fell an easy victim to Teutonic wiles.' Branches of the Cecilian Society were established in England, Ireland, and the United States, 'with the richest results' for the pockets of the German publisher. The consequence was 'the abiding presence in Church music circles of an aggressive Potsdam party'. Cecilian church music reform was, in Terry's view, 'nothing more than a trade, a trade masquerading in the name of Religion and Art'. Germany's mission since 1870, he concluded 'has been to supply foreign nations with the cheapest shoddy they would put up with, and her Cecilian wares are the cheapest shoddy that ever debased the name of music.'[45]

Terry's diatribe provoked a lively correspondence in *The Tablet*, in which his knuckles were soundly rapped by protagonists of Cecilian music, such as Canon Henry Parkinson, of Oscott College, and James Britten, the lay Catholic Truth Society apologist.[46] Both objected to the manipulation of prejudices aroused by the war to influence judgements which should be made on grounds of scholarship and taste. Nor did they take kindly to being described as 'the Potsdam party' of the English church musical world.

Martin Shaw and Richard Terry had causes to plead, and were perhaps no more than the most strident representatives of a trend, but perhaps their vigorous campaigning in the war years played some small part in creating a greater readiness for the characteristic 'English' style of music which became popular in the 1920s and 1930s. But in their zeal to promote their cause it really was not necessary to be so fanatically anti-German. Musicians had no need to be more patriotic than the Government.

On 5 August 1914, the day after the British declaration of war, the Foreign Secretary, Sir Edward Grey, wrote to the singer Campbell McInnes, 'I love Handel's music and it does me good. Europe is in the most terrible trouble it has ever known in civilised times and no one can say what will be left at the end. But Handel's music will survive.'[47] Later in the war, Grey returned to the same theme:

[45] R. R. Terry, 'Sidelights on German Art: The great church-music imposture', *Musical Times*, 1 Aug. 1915.

[46] *The Tablet*, 14, 22 Aug., 4 Sept. 1915. Terry replied in *Musical Times*, 1 Dec. 1915.

[47] G. M. Trevelyan, *Grey of Falloden* (London, 1948), p. 159.

> I think it is a good and wholesome check upon the horror cast by war to think of the things that even the war cannot shake or alter. Great music loses none of its power, but it must be great like the 'Messiah' or a Beethoven symphony. I am sure these things have the eternal in them.[48]

University of Lancaster

[48] Ibid., p. 342.

BRITISH CHURCHES AND THE CINEMA IN THE 1930s

by G. I. T. MACHIN

WITH the possible exception of the 'wireless', the cinema was the most popular form of entertainment in Britain from the 1920s to the 1950s, when attendances began to decline and cinemas to close because of the competing power of television. On the eve of the Second World War, television was still in struggling infancy, while the number of cinemas had grown from some 3,000 in 1914 to about 5,000 in 1939, some of the recent ones having been built on a palatial scale.[1] The introduction of sound films in 1929 enhanced the cinema's popularity, and by 1939 annual attendances exceeded 1,500 million. Still higher figures were reached for a few years from 1945.[2]

Rising real wages and decreasing hours of work in the inter-war years, and to some extent the high unemployment, fuelled ever-expanding forms of leisure, led by the cinema.[3] Testimonies to the social importance of films were endless. The novelist John Buchan said in the House of Commons in 1932 that 'the film is by far the greatest educative power in the country today . . . it has an incalculable effect upon the growth of taste and the training of every class and of every age.'[4] So great was confidence in the cinema in the 1930s that one of its champions declared that 'the cinema today is so perfect, so universal in its appeal that I doubt if television can stand up to it for a long time to come.'[5]

Could the churches stand up to it? Lenin wrote in 1917 that the cinema was the most important of the arts, and many Christians no doubt agreed. This paper will discuss the churches' concern with cinematic treatment of central features of religious teaching; their attitudes to the use of film for

[1] J. Walvin, *Leisure and Society, 1830–1950* (London, 1978), p. 133; S. G. Jones, *Workers at Play: a Social and Economic History of Leisure, 1918–39* (London, 1986), p. 44; J. Curran and V. Porter, eds, *British Cinema History* (London, 1983), p. 375. See also J. Richards, *The Age of the Dream Palace: Cinema and Society in Britain, 1930–9* (London, 1984).

[2] B. S. Rowntree and G. R. Lavers, *English Life and Leisure* (London, 1950), p. 228; Curran and Porter, *British Cinema History*, p. 372.

[3] Jones, *Workers at Play*, pp. 12–17; A. Aldgate, 'Comedy, class and containment: the British cinema in the 1930s', in Curran and Porter, *British Cinema History*, pp. 257–8.

[4] 29 June 1932; *Hansard's Parliamentary Debates*, 5th ser. [hereafter *PD*], cclxvii, col. 1836.

[5] Quoted A. Briggs, *A History of Broadcasting in Great Britain*, 3 vols (London, 1961–70), 1, p. 599.

carrying a Christian message; their worries about the general moral and cultural effects of such a widespread medium; and their doubts about the opening of cinemas on Sundays.

The forms in which God and Christ were depicted and referred to on the screen, and whether they should be represented there at all, were matters of concern in this period. Like the question of censorship in general, they were not matters on which any consensus existed among Christians. God, Satan, and Christ had been foremost characters in medieval morality plays, but since the Reformation, British theatre had excluded them. The Lord Chamberlain forbade their representation in public plays, and there was anxiety that films should not depart from this convention. In December 1936 the Home Secretary, Sir John Simon, was asked in the House of Commons whether he would forbid any portrayal of the Almighty on the screen 'in view of the anxiety which many sections of the British public feel'. Simon replied that the decision to exhibit a particular film belonged exclusively to the local licensing authorities and that he had no power in the matter.[6] The British Board of Film Censors, an unofficial body appointed by the film industry and formed in 1912, could only recommend whether a film should be shown; the decision whether or not to show it lay with the local authorities, though usually the Board's recommendation was accepted without further action.

'Improper references' to God on stage and screen had already worried the Pubic Morality Council, an organization founded in 1899 to improve the public moral state of London. This was, in effect, an inter-denominational Christian body, presided over by the Bishop of London, in which clergy and ministers had a large presence.[7] In 1930 a deputation from this Council to the President of the Board of Film Censors, Edward Shortt, urged the 'reverential treatment of the presentation of Sacred Rites'.[8] *Green Pastures*, a film based on a play of the same title about the religious attitudes of North American negroes, aroused controversy because it included biblical characters, including God in the form of an old negro pastor. The play was banned in 1930 after Archbishop Lang had written to the Lord Chamberlain, Lord Cromer, informing him that only a few members of a theatre audience in this country 'would have the imaginative insight to see the play from the point of view of a naïve and childlike negro, and that it would move the great majority either to

[6] *PD*, cccxvii, col. 1033.
[7] Public Morality Council, 30th Annual Report, 1929 (London, 1929).
[8] 31st Annual Report, 1930 (London, 1930), p. 11.

ridicule or to indignation.'[9] Cromer informed Lang in October 1930, in connection with another play, that the ban on such representations would be maintained.[10] But in 1936 a film version of *Green Pastures* was publicly shown after receiving the Board of Censors' endorsement. Three Congregational ministers at Preston protested that the film was 'sheer blasphemy' in a letter to their denominational newspaper, *The Christian World*, published on 3 December 1936. But a letter in this paper the following week declared both the play and the film to be 'fundamentally reverent', merely setting forth 'the negro's simple testimony to the God of Love'. Blasphemy could only lie in a dishonouring picture of God, which was not given in the film.[11]

Lang had now changed his attitude, and accepted the film. He refused a request by the Moderator of the Free Presbyterian Church of Scotland that he should persuade Lord Tyrell, President of the Board of Film Censors, to withdraw approval of the film. 'It has been a matter of surprise to His Grace', wrote Lang's chaplain, A. C. Don, to the Moderator, 'that so few objections to this film have been raised, even by devout Church-going people who have actually seen the film; indeed many clergy of all denominations have spoken warmly of the good that the film may do.'[12] Lang's tolerance was sorely tried, however, by a film licensed for public showing which mocked the coronation ceremony. Don wrote to Lord Tyrell in May 1937:

> His Grace cannot but think that it is singularly unfortunate that a film representing a burlesque of the Coronation Ceremony should have been released just at the time when multitudes of people are flocking to see the pictures of the actual Coronation Service. It would be, in the Archbishop's opinion, deplorable if the deep impression made by the Coronation Service as broadcast over the wireless and as represented in the Coronation films should be impaired by the fact that sometimes on the very same evening this travesty of the Coronation Ceremony is thrown upon the screen.[13]

[9] Lang to Cromer, 7 June 1930; London, Lambeth Palace Library, Archbishop Lang Papers [hereafter Lang Papers], 102, fol. 197.
[10] Cromer to Lang, 8 Oct. 1930, ibid., fol. 185.
[11] *The Christian World*,3 Dec. 1936, p. 7 (letter from The Revd P. H. Goodwin and others); 10 Dec. 1936, p. 8 (letter from C. F. Garden).
[12] The Revd A. C. Don to The Revd James McLeod (Moderator, Free Presbyterian Church of Scotland), 26 Jan. 1937, Lang Papers, 16, fol. 11.
[13] Don to Tyrell, 26 May 1937, ibid., fol. 81.

The late 1930s saw only a slight relaxation of opinion against the representation of sacred persons on film. It might have been thought that Christ would have been permitted more easily than God, as he had been so frequently depicted by painters. But in 1938 the London County Council refused, with Lang's approval, to license a film of Christ's life, *From the Manger to the Cross*, despite the fact that a silent version had been shown in the Albert Hall for twelve months in 1913. The trouble was partly that the film suffered from changes in fashion: the County Council considered that 'the figure of Christ is made to look ridiculous by out-of-date technique and exaggerated wigs and costumes.'[14] By 1939 the question of sacred portrayals on stage and screen was still a difficult matter which would be subject to further consideration and controversy.

The cinema was seen as a powerful means of assisting the propagation of Christianity. It was widely believed that the churches should use film for their own purposes. George Bell, who became Bishop of Chichester in 1929, not only appointed the first diocesan Director of Religious Drama, but authorized the first film service in an English cathedral in January 1938.[15] The Revd Albert Peel, later a chairman of the Congregational Union, wrote in 1936 that the Church should devote all her resources to the production and distribution of good films: 'the Church will be failing her Lord if she fails to baptize this magnificent instrument into the service of His kingdom.' The minister of Queen's Road Baptist Church, Coventry, The Revd Howard Ingli James, said at the annual meeting of his congregation in 1933 that the cinema was 'that great gift of God which we in our blindness have allowed to get into the devil's hands. We must capture it for Christ's kingdom.' The *Methodist Times and Leader* consistently advocated using the cinema for religious purposes. The Roman Catholic Church formed a special committee, presided over by a cardinal, to consider the use of film in religion as well as the social effects of the cinema.[16]

In the Church of England, Archbishop Lang, who according to his

[14] *Guardian* (Church of England newspaper), 1 Apr. 1938, p. 210. Cf. Lang to Major Nugent (Secretary to the Lord Chamberlain, Lord Clarendon), 22 Sept. 1938, copy, Lang Papers, 160, fol. 70; Don to Baron Guido Fuchs, 1 Oct. 1938, copy, ibid., fol. 74; Don to Major Nugent, 16 Dec. 1938, ibid., fol. 75.

[15] R. C. D. Jasper, *George Bell, Bishop of Chichester* (London, 1967), p. 121; *Guardian*, 7 Jan.1938, p. 3.

[16] A. Peel, *Thirty-five to Fifty* (London, 1938), pp. 147–8; C. Binfield, *Pastor and People—the Biography of a Baptist Church* (Coventry, 1984), p. 213; letter of S. J. Hart, *Methodist Times and Leader*, 14 Mar. 1935; Sir James Marchant Archbishop Lang, 3 Feb. 1933, Lang Papers, 14, fols 22–5.

chaplain had seen only about six films in his life, was nevertheless impressed by advice he received about the need for Church intervention in the cinema, and took much interest in the subject.[17] The Archbishops of Canterbury and York decided to establish a central council to consider the moral influence of films and to use them for religious ends. The suffragan Bishop of Croydon, Edward Woods (later Bishop of Lichfield), became chairman of this body, and the inaugural meeting of the Cinema Christian Council took place in March 1933. Woods informed the meeting that the expert help of several leaders of the film industry had been assured, including that of Mark Ostrer, head of British Gaumont, and John Maxwell, owner of the rival Associated British Picture Corporation. Members of the Council included several bishops and headmasters and the otherwise ill-assorted figures of Hewlett Johnson (the 'Red' Dean of Canterbury), the President of the Mothers' Union (Mrs Theodore Woods), and Harold Macmillan. The Council's general object was to promote 'the practical use and the development of the Cinema in the cause of religion, education, recreation and social welfare at home and in our Dominions and Colonies'. More specifically, the Council aimed to bring together 'representatives of all organisations interested in raising the moral and aesthetic standard of the cinema with a view to united action to secure the production and exhibition of better entertainment films on Sunday and week-day.'[18]

The Council petered out in less than a year, but attempts were made to revive it in 1935, this time on an undenominational basis. The Cinema Christian Council, with the same aims and the same chairman, was relaunched in July 1935, after a meeting at Lambeth Palace on 17 May. The enlarged Council had some forty members, including representative Nonconformists such as Scott Lidgett, Sidney Berry, and M. E. Aubrey. It was noted that some Roman Catholics attended the Council's third summer school in 1938.[19] But in 1937, to Lang's annoyance, a break-away Anglican group was started by The Revd Brian Hession of Aylesbury, called the Church of England Film Society; and an Anglo-Catholic film group (the Seven Years' Association, attached to the Church Union) was

[17] Marchant to Lang, 3 Feb. 1933, Lang Papers, 14, fol. 22; The Revd A. C. Don to Marchant, 14 Mar. 1935, ibid., 15, fols 43–4; Don to Lady Hurd, 16 Aug. 1937, ibid., 16, fol. 162.

[18] Draft statement of Bishop of Croydon, Mar. 1933, ibid., 14, fols 72–8; leaflet on Cinema Christian Council, 'private and confidential', ibid., 14, fols 82–3.

[19] Lang Papers, 15, 15 Apr., 17 May, and 15 July 1935, fols 60–1, 90–2, 109–10; *Guardian*, 17 June 1938, p. 393.

also active. In some other respects also the Cinema Christian Council's fortunes were disappointing.[20]

In 1939 the Council united with a similar body, the six-year-old Guilds of Light, and with the Religious Film Society (formed in 1934), whose treasurer and main financial supporter was J. Arthur Rank, the Methodist owner of the Rank Organization. The combined body was thenceforth known as the Christian Cinema and Religious Film Society, and worked closely with Religious Films Ltd.[21] The Society encouraged the use of films 'for education and for wholesome entertainment in connection with many church organizations, for example Mothers' Meetings, Girls' Friendly Societies, Guilds, Scouts, Guides, and so on.' In 1942 the Society stated that it had helped about 700 churches to install projectors, had arranged a series of films for use in religious services, and had built up a large film library managed by Religious Films Ltd. During the year 1941–2 it received 9,000 bookings for films, and it claimed to offer members much enlightenment for a minimum subscription of 10*s.* 6*d.* a year.[22]

The vexed question of opening cinemas on Sundays closely concerned the churches. The high Victorian Sunday had already been considerably eroded before Sunday cinemas were debated after the First World War, so public film shows on Sundays were not the flagship of a secularized Sabbath that they might otherwise have been. There was clearly no agreement on this question between denominations or within them. Lang admitted in a letter to Stanley Baldwin that he did not object to Sunday cinemas provided the films shown were 'really healthy' ones which would 'promote the civic, intellectual, moral, and religious life of the community'.[23] Bishop Woods thought cinemas should be opened on Sunday evenings to help to occupy the crowds of young people aimlessly filling the streets.[24] But many Christians were strongly against Sunday opening, especially in Wales and Scotland and in the smaller Nonconformist denominations. Numerous objections to Sunday opening were expressed

[20] The Revd A. C. Don to The Revd B. Hession, 20 July 1937, Lang Papers, 16, fol. 130; Don to Lady Hurd, 16 Aug. 1937, ibid., fol. 162; Don to Captain F. Hazle, 4 Nov. 1937, ibid., fols 179–80; The Revd B. Hession to Don, 8 Nov, 1937, ibid., fol. 183; *Church Times*, 7 and 21 Jan. 1938, pp. 3, 55.

[21] Letter of T. E. Marks, J. Arthur Rank *et al.*, in *Methodist Times and Leader*, 14 Mar. 1935; Lang Papers, 16, 14 June 1937, fols. 94–5; *The Christian Cinema and Religious Film Society*, undated leaflet, London, Lambeth Palace Library, Archbishop William Temple Papers, 24, fols 20–1.

[22] Undated leaflet, William Temple Papers, 24, fols 20–1.

[23] Lang to Stanley Baldwin, 3 Feb. 1933; Lang Papers, 14, fol. 21.

[24] Jones, *Workers at Play*, p. 176.

by church organizations and by some leading church figures. Hewlett Johnson, for example, opposed Sunday opening, believing that 'to multitudes of men and women who cross no Church threshold, Sunday itself is still a sacrament.'[25]

Since about 1900 local authorities had used their licensing powers to circumvent the Sunday Observance Act of 1780 and allowed Sunday cinema shows, especially in London, County Durham, West Yorkshire, and at seaside resorts. In January 1931, however, the High Court pronounced Sunday cinema shows illegal, and Parliament's aid was sought to prevent cinemas and other forms of entertainment on Sundays closing by October 1932. After several attempts a Sunday Entertainments Bill for England and Wales, easing Sunday cinema opening, was enacted in July 1932. The passing of this bill followed strenuous opposition on sabbatarian and other grounds, and the defeat of various amendments, such as that Wales should be excluded, that the opening hours should be restricted, and that only 'decent and clean' films should be allowed.[26] The Act legalized Sunday cinema opening where it was already common practice, and elsewhere provided a system of local option of the kind which had long been campaigned for over the sale of alcohol but had hardly succeeded. In areas where Sunday opening was proposed, polling of ratepayers would decide whether there would be opening or not. Some polls went against Sunday opening, others in favour. By 1934 it was estimated that nearly a quarter of cinemas in England and Wales opened on Sundays (including nearly all the ones in London), but only about seven per cent in Scotland and Wales.[27] In many areas Sunday opening did not occur until the later 1940s.

The opinion that if films were to be shown on Sundays they should be better ones was linked with concern about the low and possibly harmful quality of many films. Broadcasting, under the sway of Sir John Reith, won little but praise from the churches.[28] But there could not be the same confidence in the cinema, which was under no overall Christian control. The Church and Nation Committee of the Church of Scotland reported

[25] S. G. Jones, *The British Labour Movement and Film, 1918–39* (London, 1987), pp. 131–4.

[26] Ibid., pp. 116–18; Jones, *Workers at Play*, pp. 174–5; *PD*, cclxvi, cols 715–800, cclxvii, cols 1821–1984; debates in Lower House of Convocation of Canterbury, 19 Jan. 1933, and in Upper House, 24 Jan. 1934: *Chronicle of Convocation of Canterbury*, ix.3, pp. 165–206, ix.5, pp. 16–29; *Reports to the General Assembly of the Church of Scotland*, 1931, p. 546.

[27] Jones, *The British Labour Movement and Film*, p. 118.

[28] Briggs, *History of Broadcasting*, 2, pp. 227–39; *Universe*, 24 Dec. 1936, p. 12; Peel, *Thirty-five to Fifty*, p. 145.

to the General Assembly in 1931 that the cinema was a welcome counter-attraction to the public house, but could be a bad influence on the young through the suggestiveness and stress on materialistic values to be found in some films.[29]

Differing views about the damaging effects of the cinema were expressed in the Commons debates on the Sunday Entertainments Bill. 'The really vicious film is not very common', said John Buchan, Conservative MP for the Scottish Universities. 'What we have to complain of much more is silliness and vulgarity . . . [which] may be a real danger if it results in a general degradation of the public taste and a communal softening of the brain.' He wanted no stringent censorship, but agreed measures among film producers to 'allow quality to come to its own'.[30] Sir Charles Oman, a well-known historian, who was Conservative Member for Oxford University, flatly opposed the bill on the ground that 'children are the greatest patrons of the picture palaces and there is no doubt that the picture palace industry at present is very wickedly conducted.' The Board of Film Censors was merely a body appointed by the trade, and therefore could not be expected to reject many films: 'You cannot serve God and Mammon . . . much of the stuff that [the censors] do pass is so empty and rotten and so deleterious that I can only suppose that what they do not pass is absolute garbage.'[31] The fact that local authorities had the final say in the public showing of a film did little to increase his confidence: 'Is it likely . . . that a committee in some small rural district will be able to spend its whole time in seeing whether films to be produced locally are really moral and excellent and suitable for children?'[32] He referred to investigations conducted in Birmingham by a committee chaired by Sir Charles Grant Robertson, another well-known historian, who was Vice-Chancellor of Birmingham University. Robertson's committee, Oman emphasized, was 'not composed of fanatical ministers':

> It is composed of professors, doctors, schoolmasters, business men, men of leisure, all chosen for their intellectual powers and common sense, and all more or less men of the world. It is not . . . a body of fanatical clergy. Of the 285 films shown, the committee has held that 79 were in every respect objectionable, and of those 79 more than half were films licensed for children as well as for adults. You may

[29] *Reports to General Assembly of Church of Scotland*, 1931, pp. 552–5.
[30] *PD*, cclxvi, col. 743.
[31] Ibid., col. 763.
[32] Ibid., col. 764.

> guess what the films licensed for children were like from a few of their titles: 'The Compulsory Husband', 'One Mad Kiss', 'His Other Wife', and 'Too Hot for Paris'. That is the sort of stuff which, under this bill, can be shown to children in Birmingham on Sunday evenings.[33]

A further 81 films out of the 285, Oman continued, were considered to be not too harmful for adults but definitely unsuitable for children, on account of 'emphasis laid on drunkenness or sexuality', 'horrors and murder and unhealthy excitement', and 'the details of gambling, burglary and cardsharping'. *The House of Horror*, *The Godless Girl*, *The Man who was Girl-Crazy*, and *The Unkissed Man* fell into this category.[34]

On the other hand, George Lansbury, leader of the Labour Opposition and former President of the Church Socialist League, thought that cinemas should be praised for elevating the moral tone of the country. Oman, he said, had 'read out a lot of silly nonsense':

> When I was a boy the things to go to were—I will not use in this House the words by which they ought to be described—sinks of iniquity, in the East End of London, where you could go for twopence and see and hear the foulest things possible. No cinema comes within a thousand miles of them, and to talk as people talk today, as if we were living in an age of downright vice and crime is an insult to the intelligence of the people.[35]

A balanced view of the 1930s cinema might well be that an endless diet of triviality was provided, liberally spiced with vulgarity, but that possible moral corruption was a very small ingredient; and, of course, the question remains whether anyone of mature mind would be corrupted by films anyway. However, the generally low cultural level of such a habitual form of popular relaxation was a matter of concern to religious bodies. The Church of Scotland's Church and Nation Committee believed in 1932, partly on the evidence of the Birmingham figures, that 'the number of sordid, indecent and harmful films is very definitely on the increase', and that drastic action was needed to stem 'the tide of pollution'.[36] The Baptist Association of Great Britain urged in 1932 and 1933 that local authorities

[33] Ibid., col. 765.
[34] Ibid., cols 765–6.
[35] Ibid., cols 779–80.
[36] *Reports to General Assembly of Church of Scotland*, 1932, pp. 512–14.

should do more to reject films which were 'debasing or immorally suggestive'.[37]

Much of the supposed cultural dilution was ascribed to the American imports which formed the majority of films shown. But when a quota of twenty per cent was given to British-made films by the Cinematograph Films Act of 1927, the quality did not improve, as poor British films were rushed into production in order to fill up the quota.[38] The Anglican *Guardian* said in 1936: 'These "quota" films have done as much as the worst American productions to debase the moral and cultural standards of the cinema', and suggested that a 'quality test' be applied to quota films.[39] A leading object of the Cinema Christian Council was 'the raising of the moral and aesthetic standard of the cinema with a view to securing the production and exhibition of wholesome entertainment films.' By about 1942 the Council claimed that the quality of entertainment films had improved, and that 'a number which are of real value' were being shown.[40]

In 1950 Seebohm Rowntree and G. R. Lavers, whose views seem to have resembled those of the Cinema Christian Council, stated in their social survey *English Life and Leisure* that, out of 125 films seen, 14 per cent were of 'cultural or educational value', 47 per cent were 'reasonable entertainment', and a further 24 per cent were 'harmless but inane'. Twelve per cent, they believed, 'glorified false values' (they, and especially the American films amongst them, emphasized ostentatious luxury at the expense of 'plain living, hard work and unsophisticated pleasures'), but only 2.4 per cent were 'really objectionable' in that they stressed horror and cruelty. Altogether, they felt they could dismiss 'the view, not infrequently expressed by moralists and sociologists, that the cinema is a thoroughly undesirable influence';[41] but they were not, of course, dealing with the more pronounced permissiveness emerging by the late 1950s.

A different objection to the inter-war cinema was that the films shown lacked social and political criticism and therefore reinforced the dominant conservative consensus.[42] But this objection, though no doubt

[37] *Baptist Handbook*, 1933, p. 192; 1934, p. 195. Cf. Mrs Theodore Woods to Lang, 26 May 1933, Lang Papers, 14, fols 106–8.

[38] Curran and Porter, *British Cinema History*, pp. 65–8.

[39] *Guardian*, 4 Dec. 1936, p. 839.

[40] Undated leaflet, William Temple papers, 24, fols 20–1.

[41] Rowntree and Lavers, *English Life and Leisure*, pp. 237–41.

[42] Curran and Porter, *British Cinema History*, pp. 264–71; J. Richards and A. Aldgate, *Best of British: Cinema and Society, 1930–70* (Oxford, 1983), pp. 30–2.

shared by some Christians, did not enter the ambit of religious bodies concerned with the moral and cultural influence of the medium.

The assiduous cinema visiting of the Public Morality Council in the inter-war years (running parallel with its surveys of stage plays) appeared to give a general endorsement to Rowntree and Lavers's conclusion. The Council's cinema committee in 1929 expressed concern about films which concentrated on 'sex relations (viewed in the physical aspects), shootings, murders, fighting, thefts, and underworld scenes', to an extent out of proportion to 'the facts of human life'; but noted with pleasure the considerable proportion of films thought 'free from objection'. Among 617 films inspected that year by critics employed by the Council, a number were found to be morally dubious, a few, for example, 'treating marital infidelity as a matter of course'; and some were 'based on low life without any very strong tendency of an uplift character'.[43] The 1930 report said that fruitful consultations had taken place with the Board of Film Censors in an effort to suppress grossly sordid productions, but that 51 out of the 599 films seen were 'most unsatisfactory'. The Council's cinema committee welcomed a code issued by American film producers which aimed to uphold the sanctity of marriage and not to justify adultery; to ban obscenity, undue exposure, pointed profanity, and any reference to 'sex perversion'; and to ensure that 'ministers of religion in their character of ministers of religion should not be used as comic characters or as villains.'[44] By 1937 a marked tendency to improvement in accordance with the Council's views was recorded. In that year 756 films were seen, and elements in only 26 called for reproof.[45]

In the late 1930s the British cinema seemed not far removed from what the Public Morality Council deemed permissible, and probably the churches in general were satisfied that the cinema did not appear very menacing to moral convention and domestic stability. There remained, however, the question of more widespread opening of cinemas on Sundays. Moreover, though religious films were apparently flourishing and their use expanding, their future was somewhat problematic, not least because the secular cinema had developed levels of technique which would be difficult to emulate. Rowntree and Lavers stated that 'the religious films we were shown were so imperfect, artistically and technically, that they could not

[43] Public Morality Council, 30th Annual Report, 1929 (London, 1929), p. 18.
[44] 31st Annual Report, 1930 (London, 1930), pp. 11–18.
[45] 38th Annual Report, 1937 (London, 1937), pp. 21–2. Cf. 40th Annual Report, 1939 (London, 1939), p. 16.

conceivably have impressed favourably a generation that has become used to a high technical level in the cinema.'[46] The wider question of the moral influence of films became more acute when the churches were placed in the dilemma of deciding how far they could accept the libertarian tendencies of later twentieth-century Britain.

University of Dundee

[46] Rowntree and Lavers, *British Cinema History*, p. 253. Cf. *Guardian*, 7 Jan. 1938, p. 11; 11 Mar. 1938, p. 155; 17 June 1938, p. 393.

CHURCH ART AND CHURCH DISCIPLINE ROUND ABOUT 1939

by BRIAN TAYLOR

On 3 May 1939 Dr Francis Carolus Eeles, General Secretary of the Central Council of Churches, wrote to Dr John Victor Macmillan, second Bishop of the new diocese of Guildford.[1] He began by praising the Guildford Advisory Committee, 'one of the best in the country; its businesslike methods and its thoroughness leave nothing to be desired.' It was not one of the six on which Eeles himself served. He went on to speak about Guildford St Nicolas'.

> It occurs to me also that the coming of a new Rector might possibly be made the occasion of getting the services a little more definitely English. I understand that the church is supposed to have English ceremonial, I also understand that it is not as correctly done as it might be. The weight of Roman propaganda among English Anglo-Catholics is so great that a church in this position is always exposed to pressure in that direction, and it requires liturgical knowledge coupled with a good deal of firmness to withstand it.

The bishop himself was the patron of the living, and the new rector was instituted on 25 May, so the choice had already been made. Eeles was therefore asking that pressure should be put on him. He was also implying criticism of the rector who had left in January, Egbert de Grey Lucas, who had gone to be archdeacon of Durham and canon residentiary. Lucas was firmly in the Catholic tradition of the Church of England. At Oxford he was a founder member of the High Church Monday Club, with K. D. Mackenzie and S. L. Ollard, and with Nugent Hicks as the senior member,[2] and E. K. Talbot, later superior at Mirfield, was another friend. But, as his son writes, 'My father was very much *not* a Romaniser. He was privately critical of priests and parishes which were, and of many of the tenets and practices of the Roman Catholic Church.'[3] The archdeaconry had been vacant since the death in August 1938 of Bishop J. G. Gordon,

[1] Eeles to bishop of Guildford, Archives of the Council for the Care of Churches, file 'St Nicolas' Guildford'.

[2] Maurice Headlam, *Bishop and Friend* (London, n.d.), pp. 49–50.

[3] J. R. Lucas, his son, to the author, 31 May 1990, in a letter which expands on this, and explains the appointment to Durham.

who had held it with the canonry and the suffragan bishopric of Jarrow since 1932. The Bishop of Durham, Hensley Henson, knew that he was to resign on 1 February 1939, and he did not want the vacancy to be prolonged. He therefore asked his successor, A. T. P. Williams, to nominate whom he wanted, and Williams chose Lucas, a Wykehamist ten years older than himself, who had been missioner at St John's Rudmore, Portsea, the Winchester College mission, from 1908 to 1924, for over half of which Williams had been a master, then second master at the college. Neither Williams nor Henson would want a Romanizer in a senior position in the diocese of Durham. Eeles had the opportunity to get to know Lucas better, as he became chairman of the Durham Advisory Committee straight away, and held the post for most of his time in the north. The further career of Archdeacon Lucas does not concern us, nor do developments at St Nicolas', though we shall need to return to that church later.

English parish churches faced a crisis with the Ancient Monuments Consolidation Act, 1913. There was a fear that because of unwise restorations in the past, churches would pass under the control of the State. Archbishop Davidson promised that the Church of England would set up a responsible and workable system to assist the operation of faculty procedure. A committee was formed, consisting of Sir Lewis Dibdin, the Dean of Arches, and two diocesan chancellors, Sir Alfred Kempe and Sir Charles Chadwyck-Healey. They reported in July 1914, recommending that every diocese should have an advisory committee to assist the chancellor. This was acted on in 1916, though the committees did not become statutory bodies until 1938. In some dioceses war memorial committees were formed, the first being Bishop Gore's, in Oxford. Some of these developed into the basis of advisory committees, as they were given other work to do. This happened first at Truro. Then it was thought desirable to form a national body, and this met for the first time on 4 November 1921, in the Jerusalem Chamber, under the chairmanship of the Dean of Westminster, Bishop H. E. Ryle. Its first title was the Central Committee for the Protection of Churches. This name showed that churches were to be protected from unwise treatment. (Eugène Emmanuel Viollet-le-Duc is often mentioned in the literature of the time as a bogy, whose example in restoration must be avoided.) It also perhaps hinted that churches were to be protected from state control. The first report, *The Protection of Our English Churches*, appeared in 1923. By then thirty-one out of the thirty-eight English dioceses had advisory committees.[4] From the start the Secretary was F. C.

Eeles, with whom this paper began, and who remained in office until his death in 1954.[5] Of those thirty-one advisory committees, he was a member of no less than nine, all in the southern province.

Eeles was an enthusiastic ecclesiologist—not exactly from his school-days, for he never went to school, but from his childhood in London and Somerset, and then in Scotland. In 1916, as he was unfit for war service, he joined the staff of the Victoria and Albert Museum, and it was from there, in room 21, that the committee was run. It became the Central Council for Diocesan Advisory Committees for the Care of Churches in 1927, with the short title Central Faculties Council. However, in its reports it always called itself the Central Council for the Care of Churches.

From the time that he moved from Scotland to London, Eeles worshipped at St Mary's, Primrose Hill, and was associated with it for thirty-five years. He was a supporter of the English use movement of Percy Dearmer, the vicar when he arrived, and whose successors he also served, as lay reader, assistant parish clerk, and as sub-deacon at the Solemn Eucharist. He had an all-round admiration for Dearmer, extending further than the art and the arts of worship. In a lecture to the congregation of St Mary's when Dearmer was leaving, in 1915, Eeles said:

> I wonder if you know how many people, men and women, many of them far away from S. Mary's, sickened by the apathy of the Church to those social problems which cut down to the very roots of our life as a nation, have been saved to religion and to the Church by Dr. Dearmer? And how many more attached to the Church, who never thought Christianity had any message for them? . . . It is that wider catholicism, that has made S. Mary's what it is.[6]

However, it is worship and church art that we must turn to now. Eeles was a founder member of the Warham Guild, which Dearmer established in 1912 as a successor to the St Dunstan's Society, with the published object of 'the making of the ORNAMENTS of the CHURCH

---

[4] For the inception and development of the diocesan and central committees see the first and second reports 1923 and 1925; also Judith Scott, 'Who Cares? or the Red Door in London Wall', *Maintenance and Equipment News*, 12 (1970), no. 2, pp. 17–21, no. 3, pp. 15–19.

[5] For F. C. Eeles see Judith Scott, 'Francis Carolus Eeles', offprint from *Aberdeen University Studies*, 136 (1956), foreword to an article by Eeles on King's College Chapel.

[6] Quoted in Nan Dearmer, *The Life of Percy Dearmer* (London, 1940), pp. 199–200.

and the MINISTERS thereof according to the standard of the Ornaments Rubric, and under fair conditions of labour.' The guild's principles emphasized design and proportion rather than costliness of materials. A bishop could equip himself from a catalogue of about 1939 with a tapestry cope for £5 10*s.*, and a silk mitre for £2 12*s.* A silk chimere cost £6 15*s.*, and a nainsook rochet, complete with wristbands, £1 11*s.* (Piecrust frills were not allowed.) Pectoral crosses for bishops were not mentioned in the catalogue, but were tolerated by Eeles in a booklet that he wrote for the guild in 1925, *The Episcopal Ornaments: an Outline*.

It is clear that Dearmer's views influenced Eeles in his work for the Central Council, which steadily gave encouragement to the English medieval revival in Dearmer's British Museum adaptation, which was, of course, selective. In ceremonial, for example, the elevation of the Host at the Eucharist was disallowed in later editions of *The Parson's Handbook*, because it was forbidden by rubric in the 1549 Book of Common Prayer. The reports of the Central Council illustrate this influence, which had already for many years been promoted by the *English Churchman's Kalendar*, edited by J. Wickham Legg. Dearmer, however, was not the pioneer. The medieval renaissance of J. N. Comper had already begun, but Dearmer did not acknowledge that he owed anything to Comper, as Peter Anson pointed out.[7] Anthony Symondson has put it more strongly:

> Dearmer was a shameless plagiarist, and sham ... He never once referred to Comper's learned papers in the bibliography of his handbook, nor to his pioneering research into the history and significance of medieval ceremonial and the gothic altar: he simply adopted his conclusions, passing them off as his own.[8]

Comper was nobody's man, and could not be used as the symbol of a movement—not least because he outlived those who may have tried; but some who worked for him did find their way into the mainstream of English use design—Christopher Webb, the Roman Catholic W. Ellery Anderson, and W. H. Randoll Blacking.

In the first report of the Central Committee, the only architect to be named was indeed Comper, for his restoration of Rickmansworth church. There are a few photographs of new work, designs that Eeles approved of, but without identification of place or artist. One of the photographs is of

[7] Peter F. Anson, *Fashions in Church Furnishings 1840–1940* (London, 1960), p. 306.

[8] Anthony Symondson, *The Life and Work of Sir Ninian Comper 1864–1960* (London, 1988), p. 22.

the aumbry that Blacking designed for Guildford St Nicolas' in 1921. In the second report, published in 1925, there were further illustrations of modern work, all on the same lines, and including Blacking's altar for display at the British Empire Exhibition in 1924, complete with riddel curtains and hanging pyx. After that, illustrations were linked more with articles giving advice, and reports on the care of the fabric of churches, but not entirely. The frontispiece of number 3 (1928) is Blacking's altar, with ciborium, at St Andrew's, Hove. There are also pictures of the churches at Tyneham, Dorset, and Mullion, Cornwall, in the approved style. There is a page with a lectern, and samples of altar crosses and candlesticks. One set is a Warham Guild design,[9] so the others probably are too. Number 5 (1932) has as its frontispiece the reredos that Blacking designed for Porlock, in Somerset, and which Christopher Webb painted. Number 7 (1937) has a photograph of the restored St Martin's at Wareham, with a glimpse of the altar designed by Blacking, though it is not attributed. His high altar at Edington is praised but not illustrated; on the other hand, the altar in St Katharine's chapel in Sheffield Cathedral, by Blacking and Christopher Webb, is illustrated but not attributed, and is shown in its English use Lenten array.

The reports make it quite clear that Eeles was promoting a style of church furnishing which he hoped would become normal in the national Church. It will have been noticed that illustrations that have been mentioned have been mostly of West Country churches, and that Blacking's name has appeared repeatedly. The two had become friends, and their letters—'Dear Eeles', 'My dear Blacking'—indicate some degree of intimacy.[10] In the 1920s, mindful of his childhood, Eeles bought a holiday home at Alcombe, on the outskirts of Minehead. He began to write scholarly guidebooks to churches in the neighbourhood. These are descriptive—but also sometimes didactic. At Lynch, 'The altar reproduces as far as possible what must have been the ancient arrangements.' This had been done by Blacking, and the hangings had been made and given by Eeles's mother, who was head of the Royal School of Needlework.[11] At Tivington, 'The altar has been rearranged in a strictly English manner with an upper frontal or low dorsal surmounted by a simple triptych.'[12] The Porlock booklet contains what amounts to an excursus on the subject,

[9] *The Warham Guild Handbook* (London, [1932]), p. 73.
[10] Council for the Care of Churches, Blacking file.
[11] Francis C. Eeles, *The Church of All Saints Selworthy*, 4th edn (Taunton, 1944), p. 22.
[12] Ibid., p. 28n.

as well as describing Blacking's work.[13] Although he did not remain a member of the Bath and Wells Advisory Committee, Eeles had considerable influence, and brought a lot of work to Blacking. The Central Council reports mention his repairs at Bicknoller, Selworthy, and Porlock, and, in 1937, 'the remarkably fine bronze altar rails' that he had designed for St Mary Magdalen, Taunton. No doubt a search of faculty papers would disclose many commissions to add to those mentioned here. The Porlock booklet describes Blacking as 'one of the most distinguished architects of the present day . . . who very generously carried out the work below the normal cost', and a footnote lists other work that his friend had done in churches and cathedrals—almost in the style of a prospectus.[14] In 1937 Eeles moved from Alcombe to Dunster, to a larger house, Earlham, but not before Alcombe church was extended eastwards, to designs by Blacking, whose Lady Chapel was in true English style. When war broke out, the office of the Central Council was moved to Earlham, and plans to return to London were still being made when Eeles died, on 17 August 1954, the day before he was due to retire.

Captain William Henry Randoll Blacking began to practise as an architect in Guildford in 1919, after his war service, and stayed there until he moved to Salisbury in 1932. Christopher Webb worked with him in Guildford for a while, and they were both members of the congregation at St Nicolas'. A new rector had arrived in 1918, Lucas's predecessor, George Massey Wheeler, who steered the church in an English use direction—or perhaps I should now use a term that I shall return to later, the Sarum use. St Nicolas' had been in the tradition of the Catholic revival for a long time. A daily Eucharist began in 1885. The Guild of All Souls had a branch from 1883, and the Confraternity of the Blessed Sacrament a ward from 1884. Eucharistic vestments were in use by 1890, and copes by 1897. There were six candles behind the altar very early in the new century at the latest. Incense came later on. A photograph of choir and servers in the sacristy, taken in 1921, shows Blacking dressed in an alb and apparelled amice. While he was there he designed several things in addition to the aumbry mentioned above, including making the Lady Chapel more English, a statue of Our Lady, painted by Webb, and a new chapel of St George, formed in an aisle. Blacking's famous St Nicolas damask was designed and produced at this time, with its pattern of fans and pineapples. The advance of Sarum was not liked by everyone. Captain

[13] Francis C. Eeles, *The Church of St Dubricius Porlock* (Taunton, 1935), pp. 27–8.
[14] Ibid., p. 17.

Newcome Waymouth, for example, the National Secretary of the Guild of All Souls from 1920 to 1937, left money to the church on condition that it was not used to promote the English use.[15] Blacking married Waymouth's daughter, the *odium liturgicum* notwithstanding.

During his Guildford period, Blacking, as an architect, fell into the role of Eeles's standard-bearer in the campaign to promote the English use, and the revival of English medieval design. In a similar way, Martin Travers, who had also worked for Comper, but who later turned in a different direction, was the standard-bearer for the new baroque. But there was a difference. Travers did not share the faith of the Anglo-Catholics who employed him, and he was producing stage sets for the elaborate ceremonial of the Western rite as they reproduced it.[16] Work of this kind is never mentioned in the Central Council reports, but Travers is given credit for his stained glass, which will last longer than his furnishings.

Early in this century the distinction between Sarum and Western churches was mainly in ways of expression, not doctrine, and the origins went well back into the nineteenth century. Dom Anselm Hughes has a chapter in *The Rivers of the Flood* in which he summarizes this: 'Decline and Fall of the Sarum Empire'.[17] He correctly diagnoses the weakness in the Sarum school, or one part of it—its inevitable association with Percy Dearmer. A man of whom H. D. A. Major could write in an obituary in the *Modern Churchman*, 'He became increasingly impressed with the need for truth in religious teaching and the necessity of theological reform. It was that which led him to join the Modern Churchman's Union'[18]—such a man could not be trusted as a leader in the Catholic movement in the Church of England, nor would he want to be. Dearmer had an attractive personality, and was kept in the public eye by the causes he espoused, his numerous publications, and his broadcasting. He had an ability to get able people to work on his schemes, notably Ralph Vaughan Williams as musical editor of *The English Hymnal*, the book which almost all Anglo-Catholic churches used, even if not uncritically. This prominence meant that his growing 'unsoundness' could not be ignored: liberal theology, *Songs of Praise*, the Guild House, Maud Royden. If to be English implied associations with these and other deviations, then it was not surprising

[15] Brian Taylor, *The Lower Church* (Guildford, 1980), p. 45.

[16] For Travers, see J. S. Fairhead, 'Martin Travers ARCA (1886–1948)' (St Andrew's M.A. dissertation, 1983).

[17] Anselm Hughes, *The Rivers of the Flood* (London, 1961), ch. 5.

[18] *The Modern Churchman*, repr. 46 (1956), pp. 266–7.

that some took fright. Hughes lists some of the churches in London where a change was made from English to Western use: St Matthew's, Westminster, St Mary Magdalene's, Munster Square, St Cyprian's, Clarence Gate, St John's, Red Lion Square, St Columba's, Haggerston, The Ascension, Lavender Hill, St Agnes', Kennington.[19] Comper's St Cyprian's had been used by the Alcuin Club for photographing ceremonial. The arrival of six candlesticks on the altar caused the Club to go elsewhere, and for the second edition of *A Directory of Ceremonial*, part ii (1950), St Bartholomew's, Reading, was used, where Comper had succeeded Bodley as advisory architect in 1907.

I make the suggestion that Hughes did not detect an important distinction that had arisen among churches of the English medieval renaissance, which I define with the words 'English' and 'Sarum'. This is not an entirely arbitrary use of terms, for it was sometimes found, though not consistently. The English use, as promoted by Dearmer and Eeles, became associated with the Establishment. It was anti-Roman, and so medieval externals were used in a way that was at odds with the theology that the originals expressed. The course was set which led to the new canon B8, which permits eucharistic vestments, as an option, and states, 'The Church of England does not attach any particular doctrinal significance to the diversities of vesture permitted in this Canon, and the vesture worn ... is not to be understood as implying doctrines other than those now contained in the formularies of the Church of England.' When that canon was debated in the full synod of the Canterbury Convocation, Archbishop Fisher said, 'We do not mean anything doctrinal when we say that there are different uses.'[20]

The Sarum use, however, survived and flourished in places where doctrinal orthodoxy and Catholic principle were unimpeachable. It was not a protest or a political stance, rather it was a preferred style, a matter of aesthetic expression. You will often find, however, if you look at old photographs on sacristy walls, that these Sarum churches had outward signs of their orthodoxy, which made it plain that they were not erring in a liberal direction. I list three signs. You will see six candlesticks on the altar, and you will see that the priests wore birettas. The other sign was an action; genuflexion was preferred to the deep bow. A retired priest who has lived through much of this period wrote recently, 'The trouble is that if you don't genuflect many devout church people (and not only Church

[19] *The Rivers of the Flood*, p. 55.
[20] *Convocation of Canterbury Chronicle* (1958), p. 55.

Union ones) seem liable to suspect that your belief in the real presence is shaky.'[21] Such a church was St John's, Upper Norwood, where Comper worshipped. This style was also to be found in some parts of the mission field (to use the language of the time), for example, in the diocese of Labuan and Sarawak.[22]

Years passed, and the positions that had been taken up did not much change until after the Second World War; then other influences began to be felt. At Queen's College, Birmingham, a new chapel was dedicated on 2 May 1947, the altar being an unvested table on a chord of the apse. Straight away the Eucharist, on Sundays at least, was celebrated with the celebrant facing the people. Except for the mysterious survival at St Nonna's, Altarnum, in Cornwall, where they seem never to have done anything else, this appears to be the first known instance of the practice in England. The pioneering principal was J. O. Cobham, who was to succeed Lucas as archdeacon of Durham in 1953. I stayed at Queen's College for a weekend in July 1950, and wrote in my diary, 'The Eucharist, with the westward facing ceremonial is a little bewildering, but most impressive.' Cobham may have been the first cuckoo, but the spring was slow to come, and it was some years before the practice spread in the Roman Catholic and Established Churches. I did not see a westward-facing celebrant again until 16 August 1964, in St Alban's, Tokyo. As the custom became common, the revolution in church design and decoration, and in the ornaments of the church and of the ministers thereof, surely followed, and old rubrics lost their point and practicality.

Eeles died in 1954, and was buried close to his favourite church, Selworthy. He had served his cause faithfully, if unscrupulously, but perhaps that was how he conceived his task. Blacking died in 1958. As well as his other work, he left many churches, especially in Wiltshire and Dorset, with gracious furnishings that suit them very well. I do not believe that there is evidence that he was an ally in the campaign that Eeles maintained, and I doubt if he approved of his friend's opposition to Comper.[23] Blacking's daughter states unequivocally that his theology remained essentially Catholic, just as his loyalty to the Sarum use and his dislike of spikiness were unchanged.[24] Comper died in 1960, having

[21] J. Worsfold to the author, 16 June 1990.

[22] See illustrations in the *Chronicle* and annual reports of the Borneo Mission Association in the 1920s and 1930s.

[23] Anthony Symondson, *Sir Ninian Comper*, p. 24.

[24] Susan Worth in a conversation with the author, 13 July 1990.

enjoyed his knighthood for ten years, and his ashes were buried in Westminster Abbey. He was not defeated.

The Warham Guild wound down, and after being an aspect of Wippell-Mowbray for a few years, faded away at about the end of 1972. Even if its *Economy Leaflet* were still published, nowadays it would not easily compete with the bargains advertised in the annual lists of Vanpoulles's January sales.

The letter that we started with did not have the effect that Eeles hoped for. The new rector did not fall into line, and I do not know that the Bishop tried to persuade him to. The Sarum style continued much as it had. If Blacking were to return today, he would see much that he recognized, and some of what he designed. The servers still wear albs and apparelled amices, though the cope boys in sleeved rochets have no successors now. There are still six candlesticks behind the high altar, though not the brass ones of earlier years; they were replaced with a silver-plated set, designed by Stephen Dykes Bower. The priests and servers genuflect, though not so frequently as our predecessors did. And at the outdoor procession on Palm Sunday, the ultimate symbol of orthodoxy may be seen: the priest wears a biretta.

Guildford St Nicolas'

PATRICK MACGILL, 1890–1963: AN ALTERNATIVE VISION

by BERNARD ASPINWALL

'SOME attribute their pauper condition to a wrong disposition; others lay their misfortunes to a cruel fate; but it is evident that the passion for drink is at the bottom of ninety per cent of the vagrancy of England'[1] wrote Josiah Flynt, the brother of the American temperance campaigner Emma Willard.

Patrick Macgill, the navvy, in his thinly disguised autobiographical books, reveals a very different story:

> Christianity preaches contentment to the wage slaves and hob-nobs with the slave drivers; therefore the Church is the betrayer of the people. The Church soothes those who are robbed and never condemns the robber who is usually a pillar of Christianity. To me the industrial system is a great fraud and the Church which does not condemn it is unfaithful and unjust to the working people.[2]

His writings give a fascinating insight into Irish Catholicism, the fortunes of some of its adherents in Scotland, the attitudes of other religious bodies, and the limitations of the Social Gospel. A thoroughgoing social democrat, opposed to Fascism and the confessional State, and, unlike his contemporaries Belloc or Buchan, free from any anti-Semitic strains, he vigorously questions the male-dominated social order and celebrates the pilgrim Church.

His writing therefore differs markedly from earlier Catholic writers like Cardinals Newman and Wiseman.[3] His characters do not prove the comforting superiority of the Catholic way, as in Robert Hugh Benson, Mrs Wilfred Ward, or G. K. Chesterton.[4] Neither do they offer a rather

[1] Josiah Flynt, *Tramping With Tramps* (London, 1909), pp. 250 and 264. He died an alcoholic. His glossary is borne out by Macgill's characters. Glasgow was 'the best kip town we found' in his transatlantic travels. 'No Hoboland can ever be completely depopulated . . . As long as there are lazy people . . . criminals, drunkards and boys of *wanderlust*, Hoboland will have its place in our social geography and a jargon more or less exclusively its own.'

[2] See my 'Half-Slave, Half-Free: Patrick Macgill and the Catholic Church', *New Blackfriars*, 65 (1984), pp. 359–71. Owen Dudley Edwards, 'Patrick Magill and the making of a historical source', *InR*, 37 (1986), pp. 73–99 has a full list of his writings.

[3] Nicholas Wiseman, *Fabiola* (London, 1855); J. H. Newman, *Loss and Gain* (London, 1848).

[4] R. H. Benson, *Come Rack! Come Rope!* (London, 1912), new edn (London, 1959); Mrs

cosy clerical view, as in Canon Patrick Sheehan's writings.[5] A. J. Cronin, perhaps, in writing of the next, settled, generation of Irish Catholics in Scotland comes near, although the sectarian element dominates his social criticism.[6] Macgill is the first self-conscious, Catholic, working-class writer, the first realist, the first lay critic *within* the Church.

Patrick Macgill's is the creative art of the poor believer: 'I sing of them / The underworld, the great oppressed / Befooled of priest and king.'[7] Unlike contemporary middle-class investigators, he was born to that hard life: 'And we are brothers one and all / Some Day we'll know through Heaven's grace / And then the drudge will find a place / Beside the master of the hall.'[8] Like Chesterton's donkey, he would be recognized. In the trenches of Donegal, of Scottish construction sites, and the First World War he was a unique, authentic, working-class voice rather than a vehicle for ideological notions beloved of radical or socialist patrons.

Born in Glenties, Co. Donegal, Ireland, he was the first of eleven children. After brief, brutal schooling, he was hired out at Strabane, 'the slave market of the Lagan',[9] before going to the Scottish potato fields in 1905. His 'Slum Child' shows the harshness of those times: 'But often I pray when the / Night is gloomy / That God would send / In all His Mercy, from / Heaven to me, / One loving Friend.'[10] From there he drifted around, holding numerous labouring jobs, potato picking on Bute, tipster at Ayr races, labouring in Argyll, at Kinlochleven Dam, and on the Caledonian Railway. A self-taught, voracious reader, he read Montaigne while working on the railway. Not surprisingly Macgill found such a fractured youth dispiriting and inspiring. He joined the pre-war Glasgow Socialists, debated on Glasgow Green, and organized a disastrous strike. Through a second-hand Gorbals bookstore, he read numerous novels, but interestingly no Irish writers. He also read social and economic thinkers, like Adam Smith or Ruskin: 'Marx the more logical appealed to

---

W. Ward, *One Poor Scruple* (London, 1916); G. K. Chesterton, *The Father Brown Stories* (London, 1947). Unlike Belloc, Macgill mentions Jews twice as sellers of religious devotional aids, once as a moneylender, one group as war profiteers, and defends Jews against the Fascist-minded businessman. *The House at World's End* (London, 1935), pp. 126, 134; *The Rat Pit* (London, 1915), p. 292; *Carpenter of Orra* (London, 1925), pp. 26, 199.

[5] For example, *My New Curate* (London, 1901).

[6] For example, *Hatters Castle* (London, 1931); *A Song of Sixpence* (Boston, 1964).

[7] On the background see James E. Handley, *The Navvy in Scotland* (Cork, 1970); Dick Sullivan, *Navvyman* (London, 1983).

[8] 'A Navvy's Philosophy', in *Songs of The Dead End* (London, 1913), p. 24.

[9] *Black Baron* (London, 1928), p. 35.

[10] 'The Slum Child', in *Songs of the Dead End*, p. 36.

me least.'[11] A railway union activist, he began contributing to newspapers and published his first book, *Gleanings from A Navvy's Notebook* (1911). Within a year the *Daily Express* (London) signed him up before Dean Dalton employed him as a librarian at Windsor Castle. In 1914 his first novel, *Children of the Dead End*, sold 35,000 copies within a week of publication. Many more books followed, but immediately the First World War broke out he volunteered for the 2nd London Irish Battalion. Wounded at Loos, he was invalided home, but later returned to the front. In 1915 at St Mary's, Hampstead, he married the romantic novelist Margaret Gibbons, niece of Cardinal Gibbons of Baltimore, who was given away by C. E. Maurice, grandson of F. D. Maurice, the Christian Socialist.[12]

After the war Macgill continued writing novels invariably based upon his Donegal experience: his characters recur in several novels. In 1930 he and his family moved from Southend, England, to America, first to California and then, in 1941, to Miami, Florida. Unfortunately the Great Depression hit. His multiple sclerosis, changes in public reading tastes, the lecture circuit, and the failure of his wife's acting school forced very hard times upon his family. He died in November 1963.

Macgill's life was all of one piece. As a navvy and soldier he knew death in the midst of life—or life in the midst of death. His views therefore were sharply focused. Truth resided in Christian simplicity; all are brothers and sisters in Christ. Three things were vital for a full Christian life: the thin stream of the milk from the breast, the thin blade of corn, and the thin thread of wool—and brotherly love—a theme repeated in several novels.[13] He echoed the basic notions of Chesterton and Gill. The poor did not have real choices. 'The want of bread makes him [the poor man] a conscript'[14] in 'the imprisonment of the boots' for 'loveless labour'.[15] In his later novels, the Ballad Singer and the Carpenter of Orra are prophetic, Christ-like voices of conscience in post-war society; they regret 'The Gods are

[11] *Children of the Dead End* (London, 1914), p. 5.

[12] *Glasgow Herald* and London *Times*, 29 Nov. 1915. I am indebted to Macgill's twin daughters, Patricia McGowan and Chris Macgill for hospitality over the last ten years in Glasgow, Fall River, and Miami.

[13] *Songs of Donegal* (London, 1921), p. 25; *Carpenter of Orra*, pp. 230, 251; *The House at World's End*, pp. 217–18; and *Black Bonar*, p. 363.

[14] *Carpenter of Orra*, p. 216.

[15] *Children*, p. 173; *Songs of The Dead End*, p. 14, sustain E. P. Thompson's ideas of the changing rhythms in an industrial order: *The Making of the English Working Class*, repr. (New York, 1964).

dying, the Gods of Ancient Ireland—Wisdom, Truth, Courtesy and Simplicity.'[16]

In his works the Church has a negative image. Any critic of its unholy alliance with business was considered a 'Bolshevik' or 'atheist'. Money alone determined whether a boy or girl became a priest or nun: vocation seemed of little consequence. Macgill sharply criticized the Church's failure to focus on Christ, to identify with him and his suffering people and to deal with the pressing social problems of human existence amid its preoccupation with legalism, irrelevant devotions, and deference. Children catechized by rote did not comprehend the living faith. Significantly, the cruelly abused Norah threw her holy water and picture of the Virgin into the fire, but retained the crucifix. Macgill is very Christ-centred. But, in the final analysis, the Church remained like the crucifix in the shelled church, 'a symbol of something great and tragical overlooking the area of destruction and death.'[17] If all had sinned, none had a monopoly on virtue or vice.[18] But the rich and influential had a far greater responsibility. They had options.

In Macgill's experience the Church seemed aloof from the suffering faithful in the brutal conditions of Scottish industrial life.[19] Catholic Ireland left him unprepared for life in vermin-infested byres, where he might kill 1,500 rats in a season. With the exception of an Irish priest in the Glasgow slums, the clergy seemed uniformly 'class-' rather than 'Christ-'conscious: 'Its only God and the poor who helped the poor.'[20] Respectability and upholding the *status quo* took precedence in the Church commercial over Christian virtues. The Irish village priest is an appalling money-grubber.[21] His expensive life-style and tastes made considerable demands on his poor, deferential flock. Fr Devaney demanded £8 per family towards the cost of his new presbytery. Another priest loudly demanded more money at a funeral.[22]

[16] *The House at World's End*, p. 253.

[17] *The Red Horizon* (London, 1916), p. 160. Also *Glenmornan* repr. (London, 1983), pp. 21–2; *The Rat Pit*, p. 279.

[18] 'A Soldier's Prayer', in *The Diggers* (London, 1919), p. 97. Also in *Soldier Songs* (London, 1916), p. 115.

[19] 'The Faith of A Child', *Songs*, pp. 25–6; *The Rat Pit*, pp. 108, 265; *Glenmornan*, pp. 130, 214, 262, among many references.

[20] The Revd Nolan had served as chaplain to Moleskin Joe's battalion: *Moleskin Joe* (London, 1921) repr. (London, 1983), pp. 87, 92, 123.

[21] *The Rat Pit*, p. 30. Cf. Horace Plunkett, *Ireland in the New Century* (London, 1904), pp. 107, 115; L. Paul-Dubois, *Contemporary Ireland* (London, 1908), p. 477 on conspicuous clerical consumption.

[22] Also *The Rat Pit*, pp. 91–2.

However, Macgill softened a little in his later novel, *Maureen* (1920). The real charismatic, The Revd James McFadden of Gweedore, inspired a newly-ordained priest to abandon his sports and esoteric sermons for a real identification with his poor parishioners. In that way the message of Christ comes alive for him and them.[23]

But unquestioning submission to the *status quo* was not a Catholic monopoly. On the railway, Macgill found the Presbyterian workers prone to 'clergy-craft, psalm singing and hymn-hooting'. The railwaymen raised their hats to the overseers 'who controlled their starved bodies', and 'to the clergy who controlled their starved souls. They had no rational doctrine, no comprehension of a just God. To them God took on the form of a monstrous ganger who might be pacified by prayers instead of the usual dole of drink.'[24] He cites a Scottish minister who turned a dog on a dying labourer and his mate: the mate got six months while the minister 'got free for allowing a man to die at his own doorstep . . . It is not for the likes of you and me they work.'[25] Not surprisingly, an evangelical navvy missionary was unceremoniously sent packing from Kinlochleven:

> I have never heard of missions for the uplifting of M.P.s or the betterment of stock exchange gamblers; and these people need saving grace more than the untutored working men. But it is in the nature of things that piety should preach to poverty on its shortcomings and forget even wealth may have sins of its own.[26]

Outraged by such condescension, Macgill found lack of work or self-respect led to drunkenness: 'I became primaeval, animalised and brutish.'[27] Dehumanized at 18, he was a slave to his master, landlords, parents, and family. God, as Sarah, one of Macgill's many strong women characters, said, was obscured by 'conceit, falsehood, snobbery and class consciousness'.[28]

To fight for existence, for identity, for some principle became a way of life.[29] Or, as one of his characters, Lanty Hanlon, a businessman with a

[23] *Maureen* (London, 1920), pp. 70–8. The Revd James McFadden (1842–1917), a forceful parish priest, who enforced his will with a blackthorn stick. Also a defender of the evicted. In 1889 he was acquitted at his trial following the death of a policeman in an affray at an eviction. He wrote on land ownership: Boyle, *Dictionary of Irish Biography*.

[24] *Children*, p. 256.

[25] Ibid., pp. 246–7.

[26] Ibid., pp. 214, 257.

[27] Ibid., pp. 120, 80.

[28] *Glenmornan*, p. 31; *Carpenter*, p. 115. Also *The Rat Pit*, p. 31; *Children*, p. 110; *The Diggers*, p. 98.

[29] *Children*, p. 209.

leaning to socialism and drink, said, 'I'm lord as far as my fist can reach.'[30] Without a community sense of justice, formal law was 'like a briar that shelters sheep in a storm and keeps their wool in payment.'[31] Three things cursed the poor: 'The Gambling Den / The Whisky Bottle and the Lawyer's pen.'[32] A gentleman, as Macgill wrote in *Children of the Dead End*, was the monster who took six ears of every seven ears of corn from the peasant and had taken the money that might have saved his brother's life: 'on account of him I had now set out to the Calvary of Mid-Tyrone.'[33]

In the novels and poems, landowners and businessmen head an unChristian social order in which a Scottish manager declares: 'A conscience is rather a nuisance.'[34] Another, the gombeen man, Farley McKeown, dominates the Irish village. He gives £250 to the Church when the average parishioner can afford only 6*d.* or 1*s.* He benevolently provides employment at tiny sweated wages and then makes a further huge profit in England.[35] Where half the clergy were the sons of gombeen men, they use the pulpit to threaten the debtors of the gombeen man: the thinly disguised Macgill, Doalty Gallagher, says, 'If I'd my way with priests like those, I'd hang every man of them from the crosses of their own altars.'[36] The hapless Norah, abandoned in a Glagow slum, sends money to pay not only the priest and the landlord, but also the 'arch-scoundrel', gombeen man.[37]

In scorning privilege in British society, Macgill preached the same message in the trenches as on the construction site: liberation for mature Christian choices. As his Carpenter of Orra later said: 'All things great and good are simple and lie within easy reach',[38] but he tells the townsfolk: 'You are the poor, crying for freedom which means only the desire to run from one form of slavery to another, from the slavery of avarice to the slavery of opulence, superfluous desire and unholy gratification.'[39]

Macgill had few illusions about secular social revolution: he pitied 'those who think salvation is to be found in strikes, class war and bloody

[30] *Lanty Hanlon* (London, 1921) repr. (London, 1983), pp. 10–11.
[31] *Lanty Hanlon*, p. 18; *Songs of Donegal*, p. 24.
[32] *Songs of Donegal* (London, 1921), p. 33.
[33] *Children*, p. 30.
[34] *Carpenter*, p. 253; also pp. 55, 68, 75, 199.
[35] *The Rat Pit*, pp. 20–8; *Children*, p. 3.
[36] *Glenmornan*, p. 17.
[37] *The Rat Pit*, p. 273.
[38] *Carpenter*, p. 16.
[39] *Carpenter*, p. 42.

revolution'.[40] Externals might change: the simple unchanging basis of human nature remained. He said as much in his early 'Song of the Shovel': 'But some day you'll scatter the clay on grieving lady and lord / For yours is the cynical triumph over the sceptre and the sword.'[41] War, as his own novels suggest, only intensified the suffering of the poor and further delayed solutions in an ever more deeply divided community.

Although Macgill travelled far intellectually and spiritually, he never shook off his past. If he complained frequently about the burden of that heritage, he dwelt on his simple if short childhood in Glenties:

> Nothing seemed to be getting done. Tomorrow and tomorrow the same labour would be performed, the same energy would be expended and for all the strain and stress of toil, the people would be as poor at the end of the year as at the beginning. But they were happy enough. Petty cares and worries filled their day, and their years and their lives. Is not Life itself, for Glenmornan and for the world at large, a poor and petty business.[42]

In his childhood, the bartering economy still functioned: a teapot cost eighteen eggs.[43] Whatever its shortcomings, the community retained Christian hospitality, unlike 'modernised' Scotland where 'when idle I was not worth the shelter of the meanest roof of the whole community.'[44] An old, homeless Mayo man in Scotland sees his condition as callous Protestant rejection.[45] But in post-war Donegal, old Sally Garaty might work eighteen hours a day. In Glenties previously the poor were always aided: 'The fire is never out for the lone stranger.'[46] Now, like mainland Britain, it was a land of soulless isolation. Mrs Flaherty was 'a tight fisted woman who gave generously to God but stopped short at his creatures': greed 'put wrinkles in the soul as well as on the forehead'.[47]

The superstitious—and attractive—nature of Donegal's Celtic past frequently appears in Macgill's writing. Primitive rhythms often concealed deeper truths. His father would turn back if he met a red-haired woman on the road. Butter was left around the door lintels for

[40] *Carpenter*, p. 100.
[41] *Songs of The Dead End*, p. 16; *Carpenter*, p. 120.
[42] *Glenmornan*, p. 215.
[43] *Lanty Hanlon*, pp. 7–8.
[44] *Children*, p. 89; also pp. 93–4.
[45] Ibid., p. 77.
[46] *Black Bonar*, p. 12; *Glenmornan*, p. 25.
[47] *Black Boar*, pp. 52–3; *Lanty Hanlon*, pp. 202–3.

the fairies. On All Souls' Eve the villagers did not venture out for fear of the souls of the dead. At the same time Macgill recognized the 'taboos'[48] in such close-knit communities. However, it was humane, unlike urban industrial society, in which none would 'know a new day if the clocks did not chime'.[49] The burden of the past remained, but, as he said, life was for laughter: 'There was peace surely in old things, in dreams and longings, realised or unrealised.'[50]

As with his contemporary Chesterton, the land and the integrity it implied was sacred. In the novels the destructive tension between the grinding industrialism and the joys of nature persists. That is best seen when Roche, a brutal railway ganger, is killed by his own pick after killing a rabbit.[51] Macgill, confident that simple Christian joys would prevail, retained his youthful Catholicism: like all Romantics he found the *genius loci* irresistible. As Old Oiney said:

> For once ye're born in the faith, its always yours. It may be like a silver coin with rust all over, but all ye have to do is to scrape the rust off and ye find the coin as bright and white and shiny as ever . . . God is always waiting.[52]

The middle class coffined in four walls was 'aloof and austere in its seclusion'.[53] 'Progressive'-minded radicals like the bank clerk, Alec Morison, patronized the poor: 'He lived in middle class society, was cradled in its smug self conceit and nourished at the breasts of affectation.'[54] Sensitive and refined, he was the patronizing leader of the ignorant masses to a higher life: they were a race apart, who might have some goodness in their natures. 'These strange, half-savage people have a certain fascination for me.'[55] To Macgill, self-discipline was preferable to the godly commonwealth.[56] He was sceptical about the unco good slum rack-renter, Mrs Crawford of Hillhead, who motored to church every Sunday and campaigned for sanitary reform. As a tenant, an old prostitute, said, 'If the likes of her finds women like me and you goin' to hell, they try to rob us outright before Old Nick put his mits on our shoulders.'[57]

[48] *The House at World's End*, pp. 11, 202; *Glenmornan*, p. 23; *Carpenter*, pp. 203, 226.
[49] *The Rat Pit*, p. 272.
[50] *Black Bonar*, p. 384; *Lanty Hanlon*, p. 33; *Moleskin*, p. 371.
[51] *Children*, p. 145.
[52] *Glenmornan*, p. 200.
[53] *The Great Push*, p. vi; *Children*, p. 166.
[54] *The Rat Pit*, p. 160.
[55] Ibid., p. 154.
[56] *Tulliver's Mill* (London, 1934), p. 133.

Ireland was no better. The patronizing English 'sucked the marrow out iv our bones in the old days and now they come over here telling us how to keep in good health.'[58] The world would not be saved by the export of soccer or of Hampstead Garden Suburb.[59] Lanty Hanlon's co-operative farce,[60] and smug Socialist intellectuals in Scotland who attacked charity as a bribe 'paid to the maltreated to hold their tongues',[61] were repellent. Even at home Christian charity was limited.[62]

It was a world where judgements were made solely on external appearance, but the army and the navvy men could be self-governing universities of life. Able to initiate independent action, each was a fellowship of common endeavour, with a moral strength of a pilgrim church. That philosophy was epitomized in the unforgettable Moleskin Joe. A workhouse foundling, he soon learned the inhumanity of the work ethic, but won several decorations in the First World War: his country consisted in what lay beneath his finger nails. Undaunted, he tramped through life believing there was a Good Time coming, even if he did not live to see it: 'Let's live today if we can and tomorrow be damned.'[63] The open road of the future lay before them. That existentialist mentality breathed Christian freedom from artificial constraint, unholy powers, and pretension.

Macgill's realistic books on the First World War included *The Brown Brethren* (1917). Among comrades killed at the front were an ex-seminarian, who had tramped the world, and one who had fought in the Mexican Revolution.[64] Another tramp was a widely-read anarchist poacher.[65] Moleskin Joe claimed to be the Antichrist or Anarchist.[66] In both navvy and army camps men were bonded as they sang the authentic people's songs rather than commercial ragtime tunes. In the democratic army of war, men discovered their unity. In the commune of the trench, soldiers and workers were bonded as no other groups in society: 'He is a

57 *The Rat Pit*, p. 255.
58 *Glenmornan*, p. 105.
59 *Sid Puddiefoot* (London, 1926), p. 300.
60 *Lanty Hanlon*, pp. 180–1, 209.
61 *The Rat Pit*, p. 203; *Children*, p. 98.
62 *Lanty Hanlon*, p. 202.
63 *Children*, pp. 103, 149; *Moleskin*, p. 132.
64 *The Brown Brethren* (London, 1917), p. 19.
65 *Children*, p. 115. Maguire ironically was the then archbishop of Glasgow.
66 *Children*, p. 245. A Glasgow-born navvy, John Young, who was working with the Preston Gas Co. in 1914, volunteered, was wounded, gassed, and then won a VC and returned to die from his wounds in 1916. Information from Miss Kathleen Aspinwall, Preston.

Socialist in the highest sense of that much abused word.'[67] Indeed, 'There is romance, there is joy in the life of a soldier.'[68] If sceptical of the absolute purity of the allied cause, Macgill still remained conscious of the enemy's humanity:[69] its human cost was 'apt to be doubted by a man who came through a bayonet charge. The guilty secrecy of war is shrouded in lies and shielded by bloodstained swords.'[70]

After the war Macgill was disenchanted.[71] International conglomerates superseded the old capitalists. If sport, popular music, and the cinema distracted the masses and eroded their culture, the industrialists found that the independent-minded worker, bereft of pride in his job, frequently struck.[72]

Macgill despised patriotic businessmen: 'The rich deny themselves little.'[73] In the post-war novel, *Moleskin Joe*, only one of the forty-five men treated by the 'patriotic' contractor actually enlisted.[74] Likewise, in *The Carpenter of Orra*, Henry Martyn, an unprincipled tycoon, 'had a liking for military life and permitted himself the honour of being turned down several times during the Great War. But his action, the action of a middle aged patriot and mine-owner was a spur that goaded the younger men to action.'[75] He was later knighted in the 'good old days of patriotism and profiteering.'[76]

Similarly, in post-war Ireland, businessmen had few moral principles. The 'Holy Trinity' of shopkeepers in *The Glen of Carra* (1934) merely sought financial advantage in the Irish Civil War.[77] Macgill also saw the absurdity of both Fenianism and British Imperial power: the eviction of a blind old woman raised a basic Christian moral issue.[78] Money alone concerned the successor to Farley McKeown, Black Bonar, an Irish war profiteer: he neither supported Irish freedom nor his only child's desire to become a priest. At least England offered wages: 'In Bonar's kingdom the slaves worked without wages.'[79] Even the redeeming entrepreneur was

[67] *The Brown Brethren*, p. 167; *The Amateur Army*, pp. 15, 20–1.
[68] *The Red Horizon*, p. 306; *The Amateur*, p. 15.
[69] *The Diggers*, p. 60.
[70] *The Great Push*, p. vi.
[71] *Carpenter*, p. 251.
[72] Ibid., pp. 199, 221.
[73] *Moleskin Joe* (London, 1946), pp. 42, also pp. 14–47.
[74] *Moleskin*, p. 42; also pp. 14–47.
[75] *Carpenter*, pp. 56–7.
[76] Ibid., p. 57. The dying soldier's long outburst is on p. 26.
[77] *The Glen of Carra* (London, 1934), p. 137.
[78] Ibid., pp. 128–9, 230–57.
[79] *Black Bonar*, p. 200.

dangerous. The Irish-American millionaire might buy out exploiting landlords, but his values offered little improvement. In unleashing the competitive commercial elements, he would destroy the community.[80] To these divided, suspicious communities, the charismatic transcending Carpenter, who allegedly had 'neither a country, a religion nor a God', preached their common humanity.[81]

But perhaps the most striking aspect of Macgill's writings is his concern for woman. It intensified after his marriage and war service. The Glenties gombeen man, Farley McKeown, left £500,000 to the Church.[82] He had ignored his exhausted, barefoot women employees in the freezing cold, following a thirty-mile overnight walk to collect their pay of 1¼*d.* per pair of socks. Yet he feared the curse of an angry woman as much as the curse of a Catholic priest. But rather than assert themselves, repressed Irish Catholic women seemed to have a low self-perception: they felt so inferior to animals they tried to improve on nature.[83] As the elderly Oiney said:

> I dont know whits come over the glen girls nowadays. They puff out their bodies in a way God never intended them and think they are queens. But in the ould days yer hand could feel what the eye saw and ye were never disappointed . . . Now its hoodwinkin' us all the time.[84]

The woman may be a reproach to a male-dominated religious society; a persistent maternal or Virgin Mary presence; a symbol of exploited Ireland; or a vivid illustration of the defenceless nature of the poor as embodied in the feminine. 'But each time a woman falls, one man alone is responsible, the man is responsible for the first fall.'[85] Adam, a man, was the cause of original sin.

In Macgill's works wealthy women invariably appear unsympathetic dogmatists; bigoted authoritarians like Mrs Frith; amoral snobs like Mrs Wycherley;[86] or bitter, bigoted patriots like Lady Henry Martyn. Even the Catholic Mrs Bonar appears ludicrous: 'Hearing "God Save the King" for the first time, [she] thought it was a hymn and said a decade of the rosary on the head of it.'[87] The superficial Margaret Martyn later redeems her

80 Ibid., p. 363.
81 Ibid., pp. 162, 104.
82 *Black Bonar*, p. 53.
83 *Children*, p. 177.
84 *Glenmornan*, p. 189.
85 *Carpenter*, p. 258.
86 *Black Bonar*, pp. 229, 311. Also *Helen Spenser* (London, 1937), pp. 18, 38, 55, 75 (Mrs Frith).
87 *Black Bonar*, p. 130.

family and class in housing reform. To her imperialist mother, a German was more evil than the whole of mankind, and the white race alone was godly.[88] To such vacuous ladies, marriage was merely selling their daughter to the highest bidder. Love, to Macgill, was sacred; such marriage was not. Love in a loveless world was the Holy Grail.[89]

A 'good' marriage was too often the ultimate goal of the respectable. Potential partners were property rather than people. Eileen Kelly, who inherited a farm with twenty sheep and three cows was 'a good match'.[90] Another, later Mrs Bonar, with a farm, seven cows, and £350, found 'her marrying age commercially sound'.[91] Equally, men were reluctant to marry. Lanty Hanlon absolutely refused to marry before he was 40.[92] That episode endorses recent interpretations of Irish celibacy.[93]

Sexuality was heavily repressed from fear of the 'mortal sin of love'.[94] The Church was obsessed with the law rather than the spirit, the appearance rather than the substance. A kiss was considered the equivalent of Judas. Even a fraternal kiss was embarrassing. Courtship meant discussions with the girl's father over a bottle of whisky. A dozen bottles were sometimes needed to secure a suitable choice.[95] Marriage was but another property contract.

Modesty collapsed in the horrendous social conditions of Scotland: the grandeur of pure womanhood disintegrated. In squalid byres Macgill could not imagine love: 'It is only the rich and beautiful who can be amorous without being ridiculous.'[96] He defends cruelly abused Norah, as invariably he did the wronged woman.[97] Capitalist living and working conditions destroyed humanity:

> On my way upto the hills I had longed for things beyond my reach—wealth, comfort and the love of fair women. Now these things had

[88] *Carpenter*, pp. 40, 199.
[89] *Tulliver's Mill*, pp. 246–7.
[90] *Glenmornan*, p. 131; Carpenter, p. 165.
[91] *Black Bonar*, p. 52; *Glenmornan*, p. 31.
[92] *Black Bonar*, p. 136; *Lanty Hanlon*, p. 93.
[93] Cf. Robert E. Kennedy, Jr., *The Irish, Emigration, Marriage and Fertility* (Berkeley, 1973). Macgill may have been influenced by George Moore's fears of increased evils from procreation and reacting against the eugenics of Yeats. See *Herbert Howarth, The Irish Writers: Literature and Nationalism, 1880–1940* (New York, 1958), pp. 48–9, 81, 163.
[94] *The Rat Pit*, p. 183. Peter Gardella, *Innocent Ecstasy: How Christianity Gave America an Ethic of Sexual Pleasure* (New York, 1985), gives an excellent theological insight on Catholic sexual attitudes.
[95] *Children*, p. 12.
[96] *The Carpenter*, p. 7.
[97] *The Rat Pit*, pp. 125, 162, 176, 298.

> given place to an almost unchanging calm, an indifference towards women and an almost stoical outlook on things as they are.[98]

Short-term relationships between men and women were the norm in such dehumanized conditions. They might be resumed on some other site.

In this climate the illegitimate child was the worst if not the *only* sin in the community: Sheila Carroll fled from Glenties in shame.[99] She was later killed, symbolically in a Glasgow tram-car accident, a victim of the alliance of religion and industrial capitalism. Prostitution further emphasized woman's role as the victim of rapacious male capitalism, as in 'The Song of the Lost' and 'The Song of the Cigarette'.[100] 'Society sated with the labour of her hands, asked for her soul and society being stronger, had its demand gratified.'[101] Destructive capitalism had to produce more replacements for its heavy casualties.[102]

In this context, children were property rather than the expression of Christian love: 'New brothers and sisters were no pleasure to me.'[103] A child's death could have devastating effects on the family economy: the funeral, wake, and payment to the priest were expensive. Patrick Macgill himself had to be sent to the hiring fair to meet his dead brother's expenses.[104] Family relationships were economic. Parents wanted only the extra income from their working children. Such demands continued until marriage.

Even the serving girl, Maureen, faithful to her Church in the face of abuse, hardship, and a lusting, drunken master, remained at risk. Although a judge praises her exposure of the horrors of her employer's murderous baby farm, she is left homeless, unemployed, and barefoot.[105] Meticulous observance of the work ethic, or the same thing, Irish Catholic morality, brought no reward: 'A man can never sacrifice but a woman can,

[98] *Children*, p. 251.

[99] *The Rat Pit*, pp. 95, 4. John Ferguson, the dynamic Protestant Irish nationalist, was also killed by a Glasgow tram in 1905. See my 'Glasgow Trams and American Politics, 1894–1914', *ScHR*, 56 (1977), pp. 64–84.

[100] *Songs of The Dead End*, pp. 30, 33–5.

[101] *The Rat Pit*, p. 256. See also Khalid Kishlansky, *The Prostitute in Progressive Literature* (London, 1982); Mark Thomas Connelly, *The Response to Prostitution in the Progressive Era* (Chapel Hill, NC., 1982); David J. Pivar, *Purity Crusade: Sexual Morality and Social Control, 1868–1900* (Westport, Conn., 1973). Contemporaries like James Connolly, G. B. Shaw, Theodore Dreiser, and David Graham Phillips wrote on the subject.

[102] *Children*, p. 165.

[103] Ibid., p. 110; *Glenmornan*, p. 105.

[104] *Children*, pp. 110, 47. Also see *Glenmornan*, pp. 17, 194–5.

[105] *Maureen*, pp. 168–77.

and does ever and always.'[106] The male-dominated Church had failed to develop a social dimension in its teaching.

Education failed disastrously to awaken Christian conscience. Macgill was to thrash his bullying thug of a teacher.[107] In the glen the girls were badly educated: 'to learn to cook what God doesnt send us'.[108] Fear of the facts of life prevailed. Fear rather than understanding informed the pupils, who were ill prepared for harsh reality. Fear, debilitating fear, remained endemic: fear of emotion; of the priest, the gombeen man, the teacher; of others, of other faiths and the damage such fears caused. Creative praise could be a severe shock: the positive was invariably submerged.[109]

Fear on the battlefield released some constructive Christian sentiments. But fear of mixed marriages, mixed social gatherings and dinners permeated unhappy Ireland: they were dangerously destructive.[110] Popular pamphlets preyed upon minds already indoctrinated with the notion that love and men were evil.[111] As in James Joyce's *Portrait of the Artist as a Young Man*, creative moral choices were constantly repressed: Christian maturity was impossible. In this atmosphere Catholic and Protestant were agreed that the Irish needed stern, unfinching discipline.[112]

That simplistic solution was preferable to facing up to realities; the realities of Christian love; of self and community; of excuses and evasions. To the Glenties villagers, Mr Brogan was a businessman. In reality he shovelled manure on a Glasgow Corporation tip. Discovered, he bribed a villager £2 18*s*. 0*d*. to maintain his lie.[113] That evasion, for Macgill, went to the heart of Ireland. Better to hide behind class and sectarian myths than face human beings: 'Never talk to anyone with the blood of a rent collector in his veins.'[114] Any religion other than one's own was 'an infection, disease or pestilence that blighted by touch or breath'.[115] Intermarriage 'brought up a crop that would never be trusted'.[116] History was

[106] Margaret in *Carpenter*, p. 209. Also her 'Marriage is a sacrifice which the very saints will not make', p. 243.

[107] *The Rat Pit*, p. 56; *Children*, p. 15.

[108] *Glenmornan*, p. 124.

[109] Oiney in *Glenmornan*, p. 116; also *The Rat Pit*, pp. 122, 279.

[110] *Helen Spenser*, p. 75.

[111] *Black Bonar*, pp. 78–9.

[112] *Helen Spenser*, p. 26.

[113] *Maureen*, p. 23.

[114] *Helen Spenser*, p. 93.

[115] Ibid., p. 112.

[116] Ibid., p. 116.

essentially a lie: 'But in Ireland, as is the way of it, contradictions must be maintained and nonsense kept sacred.'[117]

Patrick Macgill was a precursor of modern Catholicism. He wanted honesty in the Church and State, an openness, a mature, adult, ecumenical outlook. He wanted a Christ-centred, firmly-grounded theology, together with an education which prepared its pupils for critical assessments of State and ecclesiastical institutions and persons. Christian social theology must confront unfettered economic power, capitalist or otherwise. Sceptical of ideological, especially violent, solutions and of the futile savagery of war, he urged peace through a dialogue based on the active equality of all men and women, regardless of colour, creed, and class. People took priority over property. He raised uncomfortable, and still largely unanswered, questions about Catholic thinking on marriage, single parents, children, and nurture. His was a pilgrim Church rather than a settled, comfortable, clericalized, authoritarian institution. 'Who has a settled home on the Road of Pilgrims?'[118] But, above all, he laid particular emphasis on the equality of women in society and in the Church. Like his Carpenter of Orra, Patrick Macgill was a most dangerous man.

University of Glasgow

[117] Ibid., p. 202.
[118] *Black Bonar*, p. 327.

HONESTY AND CONSECRATION: PAUL TILLICH'S CRITERIA FOR A RELIGIOUS ARCHITECTURE

by MARTIN DUDLEY

> In my early life [Paul Tillich told a conference of church architects in 1965], I wished to become an architect and only in my late teens the other desire, to become a philosophical theologian, was victorious. I decided to build in concepts and propositions instead of stone, iron, and glass. But building remains my passion, in clay and in thought, and as the relation of the medieval cathedrals to the scholastic systems shows, the two ways of building are not so far from each other. Both express an attitude to the meaning of life as a whole.[1]

TILLICH had not just chosen a convenient recollection of his childhood in the tiny east German town of Schönfliess to begin his lecture. Building, if not exactly architecture, was an early passion, and as he spent these early, impressionable years in a near-medieval environment of walls, turrets, and towers that centred on the fifteenth-century Gothic church served by his father, system and symmetry, cultural and sacramental shaped much of his later thinking. And having been faced with genuine Gothic, and knowing the spirituality and culture that brought it into being, he deplored all imitations and reproductions, which were, in his view, dishonest. Tillich chose theology, but he maintained a multi-disciplinary approach and attempted to relate 'all cultural realms to the religious center',[2] and to facilitate this he maintained close relationships with artists, poets, and writers from the time he went as a *Privatdozent* of theology at the University of Berlin in 1919 until he left Germany for America in 1933. That relationship then lapsed, and there are no further references to the visual arts and architecture until the early fifties. Yet he was clearly not unaware of developments before and after the Second World War.

[1] Tillich's writings specifically concerned with art and architecture have been gathered together in a book *On Art and Architecture* [hereafter *OAA*], ed. John and Jane Dillenberger (New York, 1989). They are: 'Theology and Architecture', pp. 188–98; 'On the Theology of Fine Art and Architecture', pp. 204–13; 'Contemporary Protestant Architecture', pp. 214–20; 'Honesty and Consecration in Art and Architecture', pp. 221–8. The opening quotation is on p. 221.

[2] *OAA*, p. 9.

EARLY MODERN ARCHITECTURE

There were three architects of particular note active in Germany in the late 1920s and early '30s: Otto Bartning, Dominikus Böhm, and Rudolf Schwarz.[3] In the Steel Church erected for the Pressa Ausstellung in Cologne in 1928, and resited in Essen after the exhibition closed, Bartning not only made radical use of undisguised steel, but was also concerned to establish a unified, uniting space for worship. He wanted to build 'a shrine of light, a luminous vessel'. It is an interesting point, to which we will return, that Lutherans at the time considered it Catholic! He followed it with the Round Church, also in Essen, in 1929–30, a dramatic, if ultimately unsuccessful, attempt to utilize a circular design centred on the font. Both of these were Lutheran churches. At the same time Böhm designed two Roman Catholic churches, one on the Isle of Norderney, the other at Cologne; the former revealing an affinity with Schwarz's work, the latter, an historical breakthrough, the first Catholic church of modern times to be circular. The altar is not within that circle but in a sanctuary coming off it. Although there is a greater sense of relatedness for the congregation, the sanctuary, and therefore the altar, do seem to be separated, floating in unreality. The church was much argued over and much attacked.

Corpus Christi Church at Aachen has been called the most important church of early modern architecture. Certainly Tillich refers directly to its architect, Rudolf Schwarz, and makes an oblique reference to the church itself in one of his addresses. It was built in 1930; a compact, high, rectangular hall, with a low side aisle. Internally it is all white, and absolutely calm and tranquil. A solemn emptiness prevails. Schwarz called it a room waiting for parishioners, accomplishing itself, becoming animate, a body, when people fill it with their prayers. The church offers itself simply as a vessel for worship, ethereal, like a tent. It has been spoken of as a great renunciation, the deliberate wish to have nothing which comes from asceticism. And in a sense we must see it as a first expression of those radical principles which governed the liturgical movement. Schwarz had previously worked in collaboration with the theologian and liturgist Romano Guardini on the chapel of Schloss Rothenfels-am-Main,

[3] Details of their work can be found in A. Henze and T. Filthaut, *Contemporary Church Art* (New York, 1956); Dom Urban Rapp, 'Modern Church Architecture', in V. Ryan, ed., *Studies in Pastoral Liturgy*, 2 (Dublin, 1963); R. Maguire and K. Murray, *Modern Churches of the World* (London and New York, 1965); R. Gieselmann, *Contemporary Church Architecture* (London, 1972), pp. 10–24.

the castle which was headquarters of the Catholic Youth Movement. It was a flexible, rectangular space, with pure white walls, deep windows, and a stone floor, able to be used for concerts, conferences, and festive occasions. For liturgical celebrations an altar was placed in the middle of one of the long sides, and the black cuboid stools, which were the only other furniture, were put around it on three sides. The celebrant, behind the altar, closed the circle.[4]

The rise of Hitler and the Nazis caught this early flowering of modern church design like a frost and brought it to a premature end. Even in the immediate post-war period it would be Switzerland, and then only the German-speaking part of Switzerland, that took up the work of these three architects and developed it further in an independent way. Much of the post-war reconstruction was, though not without merit, imitative rather than innovative.

TILLICH ON RELIGION AND ARCHITECTURE

Tillich produced four papers concerned with architecture, in 1955, 1961, 1962, and 1965. They can be put into context in two ways, in terms of architecture itself and in terms of his life and the development of his theology. The first paper was given in the year in which Le Corbusier's pilgrim church at Ronchamp was completed. It was the year he retired from Union Theological Seminary, where he had 'lived in a pseudo-Gothic seminary with a very large pseudo-Gothic church alongside'. He was well known and highly respected and went to be a professor at Harvard. He was preparing the second volume of his *Systematic Theology*. The fourth paper, two years after the Second Vatican Council canonized the principles of the liturgical movement and ratified their architectural expression, came in a year in which, to give but one example, Helmut Striffler was involved in building the Protestant Atonement Chapel at Dachau, a monument without monumentality, a sinuous form denying the deathly rectangularity of the camp. Tillich was now a professor at Chicago. It was two years since he completed the *Systematic Theology* and the year before his death at the age of 79.

Tillich was a cultivated intellectual with a passion for the arts. He drew on all aspects of Western culture, and not just philosophy and theology, in order to express his message, and his thought is very complex. This

[4] See the entry by F. Debuyst, 'Architectural Setting (Modern) and the Liturgical Movement', in J. G. Davies, ed., *A Dictionary of Liturgy and Worship*, 1st edn (London, 1972), pp. 30–41.

complexity is amplified by his ability to speak traditional religious language and to discuss traditional religious questions, including those that concern church buildings, their furnishings and use, and an equal fluency in what has been dubbed 'Tillichese',[5] the language of 'ultimate concern', 'the ground of our being' and 'new being', which employs clusters of terms and displays apparent but inconsequential inconsistencies. He was also an ordained minister of the Evangelical Church of the Prussian Union, but he was never a churchman. He had not attended church regularly since 1919. At Union, he attended chapel because he was expected to, and there he learned to enjoy the habit of common worship.[6]

PROTESTANT AND ROMAN CATHOLIC CHURCHES

Never a churchman, he was, however, clearly a *Protestant* philosopher and theologian. He saw essential differences between Catholic and Protestant approaches to the holy and to religious symbols, and in his papers he addressed the difference between Protestant and Catholic churches and what they express religiously. This difference relates to the building rather than to those who use it, for when a Catholic church—Romanesque, Gothic, Renaissance, or baroque—is used by Protestants, as happened frequently after the Reformation, there is a tension between the principles and needs of the Protestant congregation and the symbolic meaning embodied in the architecture of a genuine Catholic church. Tillich calls that early use of Catholic churches an emergency situation. If a new church is built, it is absurd, he says, 'to repeat intentionally and without necessity, an emergency situation of the past'.[7] In explaining the difference between Protestant and Catholic buildings, he speaks first in Tillichese and then in more traditional terms. A Protestant church building 'serves the congregation to hear the message of the New Being and to answer in prayer and praise.' And the two fundamental elements distinguishing a Protestant service are the predominance of the Word over the Sacrament and the predominance of the congregation over the liturgical leaders.[8] So, he prefers a central plan, as does Karl Barth, in which the members of the congregation can look at each other and in which the

[5] The expression appears to have been coined by Malcolm Diamond in *Contemporary Philosophy and Religious Thought* (New York, 1974), pp. 305–89.

[6] W. and M. Pauck, *Paul Tillich: His Life and Thought* (London, 1977), p. 228.

[7] *OAA*, p. 215.

[8] Ibid., p. 216.

minister is among the congregation.[9] And the altar—Tillich seems to have no difficulty with the word 'altar' and uses it synonymously with the liturgical 'table'—should not be removed, but preserve its tableness as the place of the sacramental meal. 'Churches that retain a central aisle', he declares, 'leading to a removed altar as the holiest place, separated from other parts of the building, are essentially un-Protestant.'[10]

In the work of Böhm, Bartning, and Schwartz we see the distinction between Catholic and Protestant buildings being overcome. Bartning's use of light in the Steel Church created an atmosphere—sacred, mystical—that was thought to be Catholic. Böhm's round space was criticized as Protestant. Schwarz again uses light, this time in an un-Catholic way. Tillich thought that the use of light was highly significant. 'The development of light in the churches is very interesting', he wrote.

> Slowly the daylight replaced the light that is broken through stained-glass windows. The daylight is not the outburst of Divine light but rational light by which one can read and the congregation can see one another. Broken light is mystical light and when in modern churches today the windows are tinted again I have a great sympathy for it.[11]

And again, justifying tinted windows, he wrote that

> Our deep understanding of the sacramental and its reception by the unconscious makes it possible for us, even in Protestant churches, to experience the miracle of refracted light and escape the one-sided dominance of white light, that is, dominance of the intellect.

Coloured light emphasizes instead the mystical element of religion and creates a numinous atmosphere. He favoured pure colours and geometric designs, and abhorred figured glass, whether it employed borrowed figures of the past or 'embellished naturalistic figures of the present'.[12] Other Catholic features—symbolic objects of all kinds—could become part of a Protestant building so long as they were elements of the architecture and not objects of veneration.[13]

[9] See Karl Barth, 'The architectural problem of Protestant places of worship', in A. Biéler, ed., *Architecture in Worship* (Edinburgh, 1965), pp. 92–3.

[10] *OAA*, p. 217.

[11] Ibid., p. 193.

[12] Ibid., p. 213.

[13] Ibid., p. 218.

TRADITION AND CREATIVITY

Another principle that Tillich enunciates is that of genuine creativity. 'Architecture excludes forms which are not born out of the creative situation and which are superimposed only out of artistic traditions.'[14] Consecration means the expression of the holy in the concreteness of a special religious tradition. So Catholic and Protestant churches will be consecrated places in different ways, and each will use the symbolic tradition appropriate to them. The artist and architect are commissioned to produce a building whose form and structure express that tradition. Where the symbolic matrix expresses something different, those who come to the building are confused and perhaps angry. But for the artist the demands of the principle of consecration are limited by the demands of the principle of honesty.[15] It is dishonest to deny the developing tradition and the possibility of radical protest against it by building imitations, pseudo-Romanesque and pseudo-Gothic. And this is so not because imitations are necessarily without merit—indeed, Tillich confessed that the pseudo-Gothic Riverside Church reminded him, internally at least, of genuine Gothic—but because imitation comes out of the scientific study of things done in the past. Imitative buildings are produced 'without the unconscious, symbol-creating side of the artistic process', and this is dishonest.[16] Honesty also eschews trimming, the adding of designs or features to make something beautiful. The beauty of a building must be in its structure and not in contingent additions.

THE FUNCTION OF A CHURCH BUILDING

It may seem a little late to consider what Tillich thought the function of a church was. Until now we have been involved in traditional questions, the shape and ordering of a building for Protestant worship, the relation of Word and Sacrament, pulpit and table. Only that line about a congregation hearing the message of the New Being and answering in prayer and praise suggested another theological agenda. Tillich held to a fundamental doctrine of two concepts of religion. The larger, basic concept is that of religion as the state of being driven by ultimate concern. The narrower, derivative concept is that of religion 'as the life of a social group which expresses a common ultimate concern, an experience of the holy, in

[14] *OAA*, p. 192.
[15] Paul Tillich, *Systematic Theology*, 3 (Digswell Place, 1964), p. 212.
[16] *OAA*, pp. 222–3.

symbols of myth and cult as well as in moral and social ways of life.'[17] Ultimate reality can be present, can be more accessibly present, in those things, philosophy, science, literature, visual arts, which are not religious in the second sense. The ostensibly religious can render not only the holy inaccessible, but it can become a reproach, a witness against humanity proclaiming human estrangement, showing the split between what humanity essentially is and what it actually is. Tillich's demands on churches and those who build them are, therefore, inevitably paradoxical. 'A church building is a building that both serves a purpose and is a symbol.'[18] When we consider its purposes, we may use traditional language. When we speak of its symbolic function, then we are at the heart of Tillich's thought because 'the language of faith is the language of symbols.'[19] The church is to be a place of consecration, 'where people feel able to contemplate the holy in the midst of secular life', and it is to be honestly and creatively expressive of the holy, which both transcends everything finite and is the creative ground of everything finite. Tillich affirms the validity of the variation that will take place even within the same religious tradition because the expression of the holy depends upon the religious group's relation to ultimate reality. There cannot be just one way to express the holy, and he goes out of his way to suggest the different ways in which it might be expressed, and yet, even as he tries so hard, he is ultimately unconvincing. His affirmation of the architect's important role is, like the opening 'In my early life I wished to become an architect', addressed to architects, and to church architects at that. He is being polite. He has asked whether churches are needed at all, whether they are not exclusive, divisive, strange, and esoteric, but he has not, ostensibly, pressed these questions to their logical, *theological* conclusion.

Emptiness, as we saw in the case of Schwarz's Corpus Christi, Aachen, was something to which some early modern architects aspired. Their desire sprang from a conviction that the church should not be a place of objective presence, but a place in which God was found when the community celebrated the liturgy. Tillich also wants 'sacred emptiness'. '. . . I am most satisfied', he says, 'by church interiors—if built today—in which holy emptiness is architecturally expressed; that is of course quite different from an empty church.'[20] The beauty of holiness is the beauty of

[17] Ibid., p. 225.
[18] Ibid., p. 211.
[19] Paul Tillich, *Dynamics of Faith* (New York, 1957), pp. 41–54; M. E. Johnson, 'The Place of Sacraments in the Theology of Paul Tillich', *Worship*, 63 (1989), pp. 17–31.
[20] *OAA*, p. 193.

emptiness. 'It's not an emptiness where we feel empty, but it is an emptiness where we feel that the empty space is filled with the presence of that which cannot be expressed in any finite form.'[21] But he also wants it to express the experience of 'the absent God'. This does not mean the negation of God, but rather that God has withdrawn 'in order to show us that our religious forms in all dimensions were largely lacking both in honesty and consecration.' Church buildings and liturgies are therefore to be about 'waiting' for the return of the hidden God. But one cannot help thinking that in saying this Tillich is really answering an earlier question and saying that we neither need nor want places of consecration called churches. He finds it hard to say so at a conference of church architects, but he seems to think that his criteria rule out the need for specifically religious architecture and that anywhere, or at least anywhere where secular architecture is a genuine expression of human creativity, will serve just as well. 'There is truth in every great work of art, namely the truth to express something; and if this art is dedicated to express our ultimate concern, then it should not be less but more honest than any other art.'[22] If it is honest in that way, then it is also consecrated and meets both his criteria.

St George in Owlsmoor

[21] *OAA*, p. 227.
[22] Ibid, p. 194.

'AESTHETE, IMPRESSARIO, AND INDOMITABLE PERSUADER': WALTER HUSSEY AT ST MATTHEW'S, NORTHAMPTON, AND CHICHESTER CATHEDRAL

by GARTH TURNER

UNTIL 1955, the setting of Walter Hussey's life was buildings by Victorian masters: St Matthew's, Northampton, built by Pearson's pupil Matthew Holding; Marlborough College, with buildings by a series of Goths; Butterfield's Keble; Street's Cuddesdon; Scott's St Mary Abbots, Kensington, and then St Matthew's, Northampton, again, succeeding his father as vicar. But if this was the tradition in which he grew up, his achievement was to protest against its continuation inside the Church, when art outside employed a new idiom.

Hussey always loved the arts. The first stirring came when—still at school—he was taken by his father to the Diaghilev Ballet at Covent Garden.[1] Anthony Blunt, John Betjeman, and Louis MacNeice were school contemporaries, but it is not clear that any was an early influence. His first enthusiasm was music, and at school and at Oxford he played the trombone, with, he said, more enthusiasm than talent.[2] Opera also claimed him, his first visit being to see *Tristan* at Covent Garden in 1931. Meanwhile an interest in other arts, especially painting and sculpture, was growing. In February 1932 he went to a production of *Romeo and Juliet*, by the Oxford University Dramatic Society. It led to his first artistic purchase: the design, bought for ten shillings, for Romeo's costume.[3]

His Kensington curacy marked a great advance in Hussey's appreciation of the visual arts; he began to visit the Royal Academy and occasionally the National Gallery, and 'gradually I found that the Academy was beginning to bore me. I started going more to the National Gallery and the Tate Gallery and the Bond Street Galleries, which dealt in contemporary art, were, somewhat to my surprise, beginning to interest me.'[4] This was the young clergyman who returned to his roots in 1937; he had a devotion

[1] *Northampton Chronicle*, 23 July 1977. Interview with Hussey.
[2] Walter Hussey, *Patron of Art* (London, 1985), pp. 3, 24 (hereafter Hussey).
[3] *The Fine Art Collections*, Pallant House Chichester, p. 5.
[4] Hussey, p. 3.

to the arts, the beginnings of a private collection, a sense of sadness that 'the arts had become divorced from the church' and 'a dream of the possibility of doing something about it'.[5]

He inherited a tradition. The church had a musical reputation, a fine Walker organ, and an annual celebration on 21 September. In 1943 it would be 50 years old, and 'that seemed a good occasion to try to bring the arts into the celebrations.'[6]

Hussey's programme was fivefold.[7] Easiest to achieve was a recital by a 'first-rate organist', George Thalben-Ball. A musical composition was more difficult; limited funds and his wish that the piece should 'reflect the spirit of the times' demanded a young composer. Pre-eminent was Walton, who declined. Then, impressed by a broadcast of *Sinfonia da Requiem*, Hussey wrote to Benjamin Britten. His letter evidently spoke of a bee in his bonnet about closer links between the arts and the Church, for Britten's reply confesses to the same 'bee'. *Rejoice in the Lamb* was the outcome, first performed by his church choir on St Matthew's Day 1943. Britten's fee was £25. His ambition for a musical composition was doubly fulfilled; the service began with a fanfare commissioned from Michael Tippett.

Hussey's acquaintance with Britten was a most fortunate one: *Rejoice in the Lamb* (soon broadcast) drew attention to him and St Matthew's, and his friendship with Britten led to others: with W. H. Auden, Kenneth Clark, Tippett, and Peter Pears, so enabling him to fulfil a third ambition—a recital by a 'really fine soloist'. Pears, accompanied by Britten, first sang in the church in 1943.

'A work of art-painting or sculpture' was a fourth ambition. Visiting an exhibition of pictures by war artists at the National Gallery in 1942, Hussey thought outstanding a set of pictures by Henry Moore, of whom he had never heard. Again he was fortunate. The Chelsea College of Art was evacuated to Northampton, and Moore was visiting Hussey's friend the principal the next week. So *Madonna and Child*, his first, and perhaps most controversial, commission, was conceived. The statue, unveiled in February 1944, cost £350. He was able to make this start, augmenting his reputation as an aesthete, because it was a gift to the church from his father.

Hussey's fifth ambition was 'a concert by a top orchestra and con-

[5] Hussey, p. 3.
[6] Ibid., p. 4.
[7] Ibid., chs 1, 2, 3, 6.

ductor'. Costs meant that, practically speaking, the BBC Symphony Orchestra was the only possibility. Achieving this outside broadcast, supported by the BBC music staff, Arthur Bliss and W. K. Stanton, resisted by the BBC administrators fearing precedent, and after an interview with the Controller, the chillingly unimpassioned B. E. Nicholls, is, if not Hussey's most enduring artistic memorial, evidence of his tenacity.

All of this was only a beginning. St Matthew's subsequently became a famous centre of the arts. Best known, and the only other major commission, was *Crucifixion*.[8] Hussey wanted to complement the sculpture in the north transept with a picture in the south. Characteristically, he was moving towards this before the carving was installed. Moore confirmed his judgement that Graham Sutherland—who also had work in the War Artists' Exhibition—was the most suitable artist, and introduced them. So another great work, controversial, but acclaimed by all the critics, was unveiled in 1946. It seems to have cost between £300 and £350—it is not clear that Sutherland charged a full fee. The money was raised partly by a box 'for the commissioning of works of art for the church', partly by a recital given free by Britten and Pears. Hussey was 'determined that none of the cost of works of art should fall on parish funds.'

While still a curate, he had heard Flagstadt's first performance in England.[9] 'It was overwhelming . . . *this* must be one of the great voices of the century.' In Northampton, 'The wild dream occurred to my mind of how wonderful it would be if it were ever possible to persuade Kirsten Flagstadt to sing in the church.' She sang in July 1947, and volunteered to return in July 1948. She accepted about one-third of her normal fee—Hussey guaranteed 100 guineas, the sum he predicted from admissions. It was one of Hussey's most audacious commissions. There were two successful literary commissions. W. H. Auden wrote a *Litany for St Matthew's Day* (1946). Hussey claims to have discussed this with Britten, together with the possibility of him setting suitable words;[10] but Britten seems to have been surprised by Auden's words: 'Wystan Auden has sent me direct already part of the St Matthew's anthem', he wrote, 'and it is very lovely . . . But Walter, you blighter, you never told me that it meant more homework for me! . . . Auden's stuff is desperately hard to set and can't be done overnight . . . you blighter!'[11] Britten never set the words—'how on

[8] Ibid., ch. 4.

[9] Ibid., ch. 2.

[10] Ibid., p. 83.

[11] Chichester, West Sussex Record Office, Hussey Papers, acc. 7365, Britten 26 Feb. 1946 (hereafter WSRO. All letters are to Hussey, writer and date noted).

earth does one set "their childish ows"!'[12] Three years later Norman Nicholson wrote a poem.[13] Auden asked that his fee should be 'a bit more than you can afford' and should be given to 'any fund for the relief of distress in Europe which does not intentionally exclude the Germans.' Hussey sent £25 to Oxfam. Nicholson received five guineas, and would have settled for three. Hussey liked to commission a musical composition for St Matthew's Day each year—among those who wrote for him were Malcolm Arnold, Lennox Berkeley, Gerald Finzi, and Edmund Rubbra.[14]

Such patronage brought controversy: the correspondence columns of the Northampton papers in 1944 and 1946 were storm centres—'You should have seen some of those we didn't print', a newspaper man said to him in 1944. Then, in 1949, Hussey was listening to the broadcast of the speeches at the Royal Academy Banquet, when he heard the President, Sir Alfred Munnings, say,'People were disgusted and angered . . . with this "Mother and child" in the church in Northampton'; and there was controversy again.[15]

If such controversy was unpleasant, the commissions brought him fame and acquaintance with people of influence. All his major commissions were reviewed in *The Times* and the *Sunday Times* and the *Manchester Guardian*, and in the more specialist journals; by 1946 all the London intelligentsia were aware of Hussey.[16] By then also composers—including Rubbra, Stanton, and Tippet—were sending copies of their works to Hussey, hoping for a performance, preferably at the festival.[17]

Through the arts Hussey met George Bell, who had used his position as Dean of Canterbury, and then as Bishop of Chichester, to further them. In 1943, Hussey, wanting an ecclesiastical opinion that would impress his Church Council, wrote to Bell—'the only bishop whom I knew of who was very interested in the arts and might be sympathetic.'[18] He had the opinions of Kenneth Clark and the critic Eric Newton. 'I am anxious also if possible to be able to put forward high and knowledgeable ecclesiastical commendation, I know of no one other than yourself who could do this.'[19] There was continuing contact, and Hussey invited

[12] Hussey, p. 83.
[13] Ibid., pp. 88ff.
[14] Full list in *Muse at St Matthew's* app. 1 (Northampton, *c.*1968).
[15] Hussey, pp. 67ff.
[16] So Professor R. H. Preston remarked to me.
[17] WSRO, Rubbra, 17 Dec. 1945, 6 May 1949; Stanton, 14 Sept. 1946; Tippett, 15 June 1943.
[18] Hussey, p. 18.
[19] Chichester; Bishop's Palace; Bishop of Chichester Hussey file. Hussey to Bell, 19 July 1943 (hereafter BC).

him to preach at the 1946 festival and dedicate Sutherland's *Crucifixion*.[20]

Bell was impressed; he wrote to Archbishop Fisher, 'I have preached at his festival and was immensely impressed by the quality of the man, and his great gift of carrying people with him, and by his admirable taste': so impressed that he had 'offered him the post of Treasurer of Chichester Cathedral, to be held with a parish in Brighton, with a view to his giving a lead in this diocese in this very field of religion and the arts.' In 1955 he was fighting off Fisher's candidate for the deanery of Chichester, and pressing Hussey's claims—his liturgical and musical standards, his desire for a closer relation between the Church and the arts, his pastoral gifts, his ability to link the cathedral and the city of Chichester, and the cathedral and the diocese.[21]

Bell won. 'How glad I am', he wrote to Hussey, 'that you whom I so much wanted to have a close association with this cathedral should have the best association of all as Dean!'[22] Hussey quotes this letter, but its full meaning is only clear when the offer of the treasurership is known. He also says, 'I had always felt that the most desirable job in the Church of England would be to be Dean of an ancient and beautiful cathedral, preferably'—the lover of galleries adds—'not too far from London.'

The deanery fell vacant twice during Bell's episcopate. In 1929 Bell's influence is to be assumed in the appointment of Arthur Stuart Duncan Jones, before whose time, 'the Cathedral services and the general ordering of the Cathedral life were very dull and flat. He really achieved a revolution.'[23] But it was a curious appointment for Bell to have endorsed: his own artistic taste could enthuse over Moore and Sutherland; Duncan Jones's was controlled by his commitment to the English use. Although undoubtedly a man of culture, well informed about music, art, and architecture, his tastes were backward looking, antiquarian, derivative, refined in the way that the later stages of the Gothic revival were refined. His architect at Chichester was W. H. Randoll Blacking, a disciple of Comper. His last artistic addition, the representational windows in the north nave aisle, are by Christopher Webb, another Comper pupil.

Such was the artistic inheritance of Hussey at Chichester.

After less than two years there, Hussey, writing at the time of Bell's

[20] Ibid., 3 April 1946.

[21] Ibid., Bell to Fisher, 2 Feb. 1955.

[22] Hussey, p. 99.

[23] BC, Bell to Fisher, 2 Feb. 1955.

retirement, said: 'I'm sad that none of the major projects for fostering the contemporary arts have come to completion while you are here. The affairs of a Cathedral, like the creations of real artists, seem to mature very slowly.'[24] But in his book he wrote:

> I knew that my reputation for introducing works of modern art into the church had gone before me and I had a feeling that there would be resistance to anything of that sort at Chichester . . . so for the first couple of years I kept a low profile, sensing the atmosphere and trying to get to know the people and to build up confidence.

He goes on to describe, as though it had been his first priority, the discussions which led to the re-placing of the Arundel screen.[25]

The letter to Bell is the more accurate. William Croome, then Chairman of the Cathedrals Advisory Commission, wrote to Robert Potter, who was to become the architect at Chichester:

> We were told that on appointment as Dean, Hussey at once applied to the RIBA to suggest to him a suitable architect. Whether he knew Blacking held the office, or never enquired, I have no idea. The RIBA (capable de tout in such matters as I sometimes feel) at once suggested Basil Spence.[26]

And as early as January 1956 Judith Scott, Secretary of the Central Council for the Care of Churches, had written to Croome, telling him that Spence had been in touch with her 'after a visit to Chichester Cathedral, where he had been invited to advise the Dean on general improvements', and specifically on the decoration of the Sherbourne screen, behind the high altar.[27]

At this early stage Hussey seems to have been uncertain which way to proceed, but determined to proceed in some direction. Croome's letter lists ideas Hussey had put to the Cathedrals Advisory Commission. They included the colouring of the Sherbourne screen, the removal of the nave pulpit, and the refurnishing of the St Mary Magdalen Chapel. Simultaneously his artist friends were thinking about the cathedral: Piper about glass, Moore about sculpture. Spence was working on designs for

[24] London, Lambeth Palace Library, Bell Papers, 204, doc. 203.

[25] Hussey, p. 100.

[26] London, Council for the Care of Churches, Cathedrals' Advisory Commission Chichester file, Croome to Potter, 13 March 1957 (hereafter CAC).

[27] Ibid., Scott to Croome, 18 Jan. 1956.

the Sherbourne screen, Frederick Etchells considering the Magdalen Chapel.[28]

The plan to recolour the Sherbourne screen was abandoned—partly perhaps because, as Croome wrote, 'Basil Spence went down, inspected, and was, we thought, a little daunted at this complete change from the Coventry manner',[29] partly because Hussey had doubts about Spence's proposals, partly because almost everyone—Hussey, the Cathedrals Advisory Commission, Spence—agreed the reredos should go. Almost everyone: but, as Hussey told Judith Scott, 'There is no question of being able to go to the Chapter again on the subject of removing the reredos . . . I am afraid that is exactly what they refuse to do.'[30]

Behind this capitular resistance probably lie the iron will and settled views of the then Archdeacon of Chichester, Lancelot Mason. If so, it is only the first of numerous occasions when he was to frustrate Hussey. The need for a fitting memorial to Bell and the recantation of Mason on this issue suddenly meant that the Arundel screen could be returned to the cathedral. So Hussey could write of that as his first achievement at Chichester, and with it of the satisfaction of another early ambition—the clearing of the front of the nave of 'clutter':[31] the corporation stalls, for which Robert Potter designed replacements, the Victorian lectern, relegated to the Lady Chapel, 'the large and somewhat elaborate' Victorian pulpit, concerning which he invoked the opinion of John Betjeman that he would 'find it difficult to say anything in favour of it'. In its place he put one which contrived to 'avoid looking like a pimple on the solid Norman pillar', yet did not interrupt the view east. Again, Potter supplied the solution, collaborating with Geoffrey Clarke, an artist working for the first time in the cathedral. Meanwhile the Magdalen chapel became the focus of attention. Its restoration was one of Hussey's early plans—it is on Croome's March 1957 list, when Frederick Etchells was said to be involved. Etchells was an improbable partner for Hussey, who seems quickly to have repented, for, still in practice, Etchells was surprised to learn from a letter circulated to the Friends of the Cathedral that he had retired on grounds of ill health.[32] At any rate, by early 1957 Potter was involved, and by the autumn was close to the treatment adopted—the clearance of all existing furnishings; a stone altar; behind, a

[28] Ibid., Croome to Potter, 13 March 1957.
[29] Ibid.
[30] Ibid., Hussey to Scott, 28 Jan. 1957.
[31] Hussey, pp. 101f.; cf. CAC, Potter to Croome, 12 March 1957.
[32] CAC, Potter to Croome, 12 March 1957.

noli me tangere, and 'good altar ornaments.' Once again 'the only serious opposition came from the Archdeacon who was against moving anything within or from the building.'[33] Sutherland was first involved in 1959. The scheme, with Potter's austere stone altar, Sutherland's picture, and Clarke's candlesticks and communion rail, was dedicated in 1961. If the Arundel screen was largely a work of restoration, this was Hussey's first major artistic achievement. There was, he writes, 'the expected small crop of letters to the local newspaper, most of them hostile'; the picture was 'damaged by an angry church goer not long after it was installed'.[34] Croome wrote that the chapel 'had more of a "prison cell" atmosphere to me than a devotional chapel.'[35]

There were two more major artistic projects. The first was the tapestry.[36] Moore first suggested involving John Piper. The earliest letter on the subject is dated 8 January 1963; by 3 April there are sketches, still so uncertain that Piper is only hesitantly and reluctantly allowing the Council of the Friends—the donors—to see them. But they were well received, and the designs matured. Early in 1965 there was a set-back, and a despairing Piper wrote, 'I found the Archdeacon's comments at this 11th hour unnerving, and I foresee the greatest trouble in meeting his demands. Why did he not make them in October when he saw the earlier sketches, since when the idea has crystallised . . .?' Mason, fortified, he claimed, by the opinions of three theologians, had detected a doctrinal deficiency in the Trinitarian symbolism of the tapestry. Fortunately Piper lighted on a solution. A white circle was added, symbolizing God the Father. The tapestry was unveiled in the autumn of 1966. It proved controversial: 'There were perhaps more words of disapproval . . . than of anything else that was done at Chichester during my twenty two years there.' But there was also appreciation: Canon Walter Marsh, the Vicar of Eastbourne, wrote of his 'excited delight on seeing the tapestry. The view from the west door, embracing pulpit, screen and hangings, is quite unforgettable.'[37] The last major artistic commission was a stained-glass window.[38] Hussey seems to have toyed with stained glass early, but only with the tapestry completed did he take the idea up seriously. He thought Chichester weak in glass, and was attracted to the 'great handler of

[33] CAC, Potter to Croombe, 12 Oct. 1957.
[34] *Fine Art Collections*, p. 21.
[35] CAC, Croome to Scott, 6 Nov. 1961.
[36] Hussey, ch. 12.
[37] WSRO, March, 10 Oct. 1966.
[38] Hussey, ch. 5.

colour', Marc Chagall. Plans developed slowly. Chagall expressed interest in 1969, but this last commission was installed only after Hussey's retirement. It cost £17,954, his most expensive commission. He undertook to raise the money himself, avoiding sources which might otherwise give to the restoration of the cathedral.

Alongside these there was a flow of musical compositions—a number of settings of the evening canticles, notably, perhaps, a Chichester service from Howells, a rumbustious rumba from Bryan Kelly, and a service from Walton, who had long before repented of his early refusal.[39] But Hussey's most audacious musical commission was undoubtedly the *Chichester Psalms* of Leonard Bernstein.[40] On the strength of a slight acquaintance, Hussey wrote to him, saying—a little patronizingly perhaps—they 'would not mind if it had a touch of the idiom of West Side Story.' Bernstein attended the performance at the Southern Cathedrals Festival in 1965.

Towards the end of his time at Northampton, Hussey had commissioned a cope from John Piper. Hussey tells how, when he wore it at Chichester, the canons felt drab, and demanded copes for themselves. These were designed by Ceri Richards. Piper was commissioned to design a set of eucharistic vestments, conceived to be worn against the backdrop of the artist's tapestry.[41]

There were smaller matters. At Northampton, Piper had designed a magazine cover, at Chichester he designed a poster for a flower festival; Reynolds Stone replaced the plain cover of the Friends journal and designed the format of the weekly service-lists.[42]

Near the beginning of his career Hussey had used the fiftieth anniversary of St Matthew's to announce his interest in the arts. Now he sought to use the ninth centenary of the cathedral in 1975 to close it with an explosion of creativity. The Walton Canticles and the Chagall window were the most obvious products of this; but there was also a festival (which has continued) and the volume *Chichester 900*, to which a number of Hussey's friends contributed, including Henry Moore, Kenneth Clark, whose contribution—'not without considerable embarrassment to its subject'—was a handsome tribute to him, and John Piper, who designed the cover.[43]

[39] Ibid., p. 40.
[40] Ibid., ch. 11.
[41] Ibid., pp. 127ff.
[42] Ibid., p. 92; WSRO, Piper, 27 Jan. 1966; Hussey, p. 130.
[43] *Chichester 900* (Chichester, 1975): Clark, pp. 68ff.; Hussey's comment, p. 3.

But the celebrations must have been something of a disappointment, for by then Hussey had to accept that some of his friends were unlikely to work for him again. There had always been some disappointments: at St Matthew's, in addition to Walton, those who declined his invitations included Vaughan Williams ('I have so many commitments');[44] T. S. Eliot, whom he asked to write a 'hymn', and who replied that 'a merely commissioned work has only to satisfy the commissioner . . . but I should have to put my own satisfaction first . . . If I can do it, you shall have it . . . I can make no promises',[45] and C. Day Lewis ('my cast of mind is too much an agnostic one').[46] At Northampton, too, he approached Stravinsky, but nothing came of it.[47] The question of Britten writing a Mass setting was first discussed in 1948. This, or another composition, recurs in their letters. But Britten's increasing busyness and, later, failing health, meant that nothing was written. The Mass is last mentioned in 1971: 'As for the mass this year I fear I have had bad news . . . we have had rather a bad time . . . if I find a solution to the vexed question of a mass in English, especially including congregational participation (about which I am very keen) and it fits in with my complicated schedules, I will let you know.'[48] Hussey continued to hope for something for the anniversary: 'In 1975 I may have recovered and be thinking once again of writing some music! especially for such an auspicious occasion', Britten wrote.[49] Hussey was also the victim of Moore's celebrity. In 1973 he asked him about a crucifix for 1975. 'I'm afraid, Walter, it really is impossible for me to give you a definite answer . . . time goes so quickly.' Moore also wrote saying, 'It is hopeless about the door handles. I am hopelessly behind.' These were for the glass doors on the west porch. Geoffrey Clarke finally designed them.[50] By 1975 Sutherland had become the hope for a crucifix, but, again, the work was never forthcoming.[51]

By this time Hussey's friends were distinguished and ageing. As they collected honours from the State, they inevitably became something of an establishment. His continued quest of them proclaims the highest aesthetic standards, but it was not the pioneering work of the North-

[44] WSRO, Vaughan Williams, 1 Feb. 1950.

[45] Ibid., Eliot, 20 Jan. 1945.

[46] Ibid., C. Day Lewis, 18 May (no year given).

[47] Ibid., Stravinsky, 20 March 1953.

[48] Ibid., Britten, 6 Jan. 1971.

[49] Ibid., 11 Feb. 1973.

[50] Ibid., Moore, 7 June 1973 (crucifix); 26 March 1973 (handles); for Clarke, see Hussey, p. 131.

[51] WSRO, Sutherland, 21 Jan. 1975; 14 April 1975; 11 May 1977.

ampton commissions, when he and they were young; he did not move on to a new generation of artists.

Reactions to Hussey were varied. At Northampton at least one fellow incumbent thought his pursuit of the arts made him arrogant and insensitive. He recalls how once at the St Matthew's Day lunch, to which he invited the clergy, Spencer Leeson, not long Bishop of Peterborough, was paying his first visit to St Matthew's. Welcoming him, Hussey said, 'Though he had visited many of the parishes in the diocese he might find his visit to St Matthew's the "bonne bouche" ... I expect [the clergy] thought "well that's Walter Hussey" but I for one thought it in very bad taste.'[52] At Chichester, some of the senior clergy found him shy and solemn and reserved.[53]

But with artists he was relaxed and responsive. Kathleen Sutherland wrote, 'You are the nicest house guest I have ever met. You do us so much good, we feel quite deflated when you go.'[54] All the artists he worked with were laudatory: hearing he was writing an artistic memoir, Sutherland wrote, 'I hope you quote someone who thinks you were the most sensitive enlightened and considerate patron an artist could ever encounter.'[55] And from the 1940s his artist friends had the sense that he was forging links which were broken: '... if only all Vicars had been so understanding as you are', Pears wrote, 'I don't believe the church would have lost so many of her artist sons.'[56]

The laity at St Matthew's trusted him. He was careful, before the two most controversial commissions, to prepare them. He wrote to Bell about the Moore, 'I do not feel I could fight with the PCC over it, or with the people who actually use the church. I want them to accept the gift willingly even if it is not exactly their idea.' They repaid him with their support: 'When the storm of protest broke, not one of them "ratted".'[57]

Hussey's appointment to the deanery of Chichester caused consternation among the antiquarians, who were dominant in the Cathedrals Advisory Commission. Duncan Jones was their ideal of a dean: his choice of architect and his taste in art were theirs. They viewed Hussey's first plan

[52] Communication from The Revd Grenville Morgan, Vicar of Dallington, Northampton, 1947–60.

[53] Communications from Dr J. N. D. Kelly, FBA (non-residentiary canon from 1948); and The Rt Revd Warren Hunt (Hon Assistant Bishop from 1977).

[54] WSRO, Kathleen Sutherland, 12 Nov. 1962.

[55] WSRO, Sutherland, 11 Aug. 1978.

[56] WSRO, Pears (undated, ?1940s).

[57] BC, Hussey to Bell, 19 July 1943; Hussey, p. 46.

for Spence to colour a medieval screen nervously. G. H. S. Bushnell wrote to Judith Scott: 'Raby thinks Blacking should be sounded. I only wish he were doing the job, it is just up his street, and I don't want to make Dean Duncan Jones turn in his grave!' And he added, 'The trouble is of course that the Dean has pushed Blacking out (like an ass).'[58] Blacking himself said, 'How thankful we should be that D.J. was spared to complete Webb's fine series of windows: think what might have happened under the new regime.'[59] Their role was purely advisory; they sensed the need to ingratiate themselves with Hussey. Judith Scott reported to Croome that she had helped Spence about colouring the screen: 'It was no good, I felt, to defer action until the Cathedrals Committee met, as he was obviously expecting to put the work in hand in a few days . . . can we stop a steam roller?'[60] But when they visited Chichester they were 'agreeably surprised by [Hussey's] co-operative attitude'.[61] Later relations improved, and they approved of the appointment of Potter, who, while admiring Hussey's artistic taste, partly shared their anxieties and saw vigilance about antiquities as part of his task.

It is difficult to resist the judgement that Hussey was a man of one talent, with marked limitations in other spheres. As a dean, he was not, in the round, distinguished. A well-informed obituarist of Lancelot Mason wrote of his 'great influence in Chichester where the Dean, Walter Hussey, was more than content for him to run the Cathedral.'[62] And although Bell's hope for 'a closer relation between the church and the arts' was abundantly met, his belief that Hussey would be good pastorally and in linking the cathedral and the city was more doubtfully fulfilled. In 1971 the Mayor and Corporation decided not to attend the cathedral on Mayor's Sunday. A former mayor was reported as having said, 'The psalms are high falutin' and the hymn tunes are dirges. We would like a service where there are more popular hymn tunes and a sermon to fit the occasion.' A correspondent in the *Church Times*, who had had 'the privilege of singing in [the cathedral] choir', more temperately wrote, 'Chichester cathedral, though excellent in some fields, is a cathedral which takes too narrow a view of its role.'[63]

[58] CAC, Bushnell to Scott (undated).
[59] CAC, Blacking to Scott, 10 Aug. 1956.
[60] CAC, Scott to Croome, 18 Jan. 1956.
[61] CAC, Scott to Croome, 6 Sept. 1956.
[62] *Daily Telegraph*, 14 Feb. 1990.
[63] For both see *Church Times*, 20 Aug. 1971.

Hussey was not a man of wide intellect. His appreciation of the arts was felt, rather than reasoned; in his book there is little rationale, little but platitudes about his convictions:

> How sad it was, I felt, that artists had become largely divorced from the church; sad because artists think and meditate a lot, and are in the broadest sense of the word religious. They create fine expressions of the human spirit which can symbolise and express worship, as well as conveying the truths of God to man.[64]

The low place of letters among his concerns is perhaps of a piece with this. The literary fastidiousness of a man who in an artistic memoir could employ the hackneyed phrase, 'I kept a low profile' is unlikely to be high, and it is noteworthy that although he was unembarrassed about arranging for *Rejoice in the Lamb*, with its strange words, to be performed after the Eucharist, literature 'posed a problem. It wasn't easy to see how it could be suitably woven into the life of the church.' Words from Auden or Eliot he can only think of as for setting to music.[65]

For all this, Kenneth Clark's description is just: 'aesthete, impressario and indomitable persuader'.[66] And he was finally generous, leaving most of his private collection to the public, and with bequests for the arts to the churches he had served, and for a lectureship in religion and art at Oxford.[67]

With all his limitations, his achievement was great. Because of it he went into retirement with an honorary doctorate of the University of Sussex and with an honorary FRIBA. His artistic friends hoped the State would honour him. Henry Moore wrote to James Callaghan, 'Since late renaissance times, religious art in Europe has slowly deteriorated in its standards until at the beginning of this century it was at a very low level of sentimental prettiness. Dean Hussey's help in raising the standard in England of Church art, I am sure, should be recognized in some way.'[68] In the 1940s the path he cut was a pioneer one. It is this that raises him from the mediocre to the memorable.[69]

[64] Hussey, p. 3.

[65] For Auden, Hussey, p. 83, and above: for Eliot, WSRO, Eliot, 20 Jan. 1945: 'I shall hope eventually to write something which I could offer you to be put to music . . .'.

[66] *Chichester 900*, p. 72.

[67] For Hussey's will see *Daily Telegraph*, 2 Dec. 1985.

[68] BC, Moore to Callaghan, 4 April 1977.

[69] I am grateful to the individuals and depositaries referred to above, and to the Dean and Chapter of Chichester, the executors of Hussey's estate, and to the Britten-Pears Foundation.

LIVERPOOL'S TWO CATHEDRALS

by JOHN NELSON TARN

LIVERPOOL was a great port in the eighteenth century and after the Industrial Revolution its growth was spectacular. This is reflected in the heritage of public buildings designed on a scale and with a richness of detail which surprises many visitors, but because the affluence of the city was so sustained, the people of Liverpool came to think of their city not so much as a provincial town, but as a great metropolis, and when they built, they usually built on a grand scale.

The Town Hall was designed by John Wood of Bath, and building began in 1749.[1] It was refurbished by James Wyatt after a fire in 1795. Externally it now looks rather diminutive, but inside is a suite of reception rooms, decorated and furnished in the French Empire style, which rivals any to be found in Britain. The Albert Dock complex, built to the design of a local man, Jesse Hartley, in the early 1840s, was conceived on a scale which matched the growing Atlantic trade, and St George's Hall, built on the Lime Street plateau from 1842 to 1854 to the design of Harvey Lonsdale Elmes, is one of the great neo-classical buildings of the world and Liverpool's answer to the growing north country desire to give expression to that sense of civic pride which drove one town after another to build town halls.

The streets which lead to the Pier Head, particularly Water Street and nearby Castle Street, are lined with fine commercial buildings, and Pier Head itself rivals the loop area in downtown Chicago or the Bund in Shanghai. Socially and economically Liverpool's history is linked with the potato famines in Ireland in the middle of the last century which led to so many Irish people coming to Britain. The west coast ports of Liverpool and Glasgow have retained a strong and vigorous Irish community, which in Liverpool strengthened the old Lancashire Catholic tradition and led eventually to the aspirations for the Metropolitan Cathedral.

Extreme poverty and conspicuous wealth have existed side by side for more than 150 years on Merseyside. Yet even during this century, when the economic prosperity of the city was already waning, the desire to

[1] There is a good and more detailed account of the public buildings in Liverpool in Nikolaus Pevsner, *Lancashire I, The Industrial and Commercial South – The Buildings of England Series* (Harmondsworth, 1969), pp. 141ff.

create monumental buildings—if the opportunity arose—has led to the construction of two great cathedrals, which continue that saga of building mania which seems so much a part of Liverpool's past. Neither cathedral was easily conceived. The first attempt to launch a project for the Anglican Cathedral came in 1887, seven years after the foundation of the diocese in 1880.[2] It was doomed from the start, because the site chosen, St John's Gardens, between St George's Hall and where is now the entrance to the first Mersey Tunnel, was cramped, and the design by Sir William Emerson was not universally admired. It was not until a new bishop, Francis James Chavasse, was appointed in 1900, and a new site on St James's Mount was finally chosen and acquired, that the project took off and, in 1901, architects were invited to submit their portfolios so that a group might be selected to take part in a second-stage competition.

The project now fired the imagination of people in the city, as well as the 105 architects who submitted entries. Although originally the brief had asked for a design in the Gothic style, this particular requirement was subsequently withdrawn after vociferous protests from the architectural profession. Designs were submitted in a variety of styles, and R. N. Shaw and G. F. Bodley, the assessors, selected five and ultimately recommended in 1903 that the design of Giles Gilbert Scott, then aged 22, should be recommended to the committee. His was an unusual and fairly idiosyncratic essay in Gothic, arresting in its form and dramatic in its silhouette. The competition design bears little resemblance to the building which was completed in 1978, and the young Scott, who was asked to work with Bodley for the first few years, until the latter's death in 1907, redesigned the building quite fundamentally in 1909 and continued to amend the design in detail, often quite radically, until his own death, at the age of 80, in 1960.

The Roman Catholic Cathedral has its roots much earlier in the nineteenth century when, following Catholic emancipation in 1829 and the restoration of the hierarchy in 1850, a cathedral to be built in Everton was designed in 1853 by E. W. Pugin, and the Lady Chapel actually built in 1856.[3] That fragment still stands today in St Domingo Road, Everton, but,

[2] References to the early projects for the cathedral are taken from the summary in Pevsner, *Lancashire I*, p. 187, and the main published history of the project: Vere E. Cotton, *The Book of Liverpool Cathedral* (Liverpool, 1964), see esp. ch. 1.

[3] Source material for the Metropolitan Cathedral is less readily available in summary form. For the early history of the diocese see Cyril Taylor, *The History of Liverpool's Catholic Cathedral, in Souvenir of the Solemn Opening of the Metropolitan Cathedral Crypt* (Liverpool, 1958), and for the

alas, in ruins. The need for suburban churches and schools delayed further progress on the cathedral, and it was not until the appointment of Richard Downey as Archbishop of Liverpool in 1922, at the remarkably early age of 47, that the project was revived. A nine-acre site originally occupied by the old Liverpool workhouse, near the University, and between Mount Pleasant and Brownlow Hill, was acquired, and Edwin Lutyens was appointed architect in 1930. He was an obvious choice at that time, since he was both a man of outstanding talent and at the height of his career. The foundation stone was laid in 1933 for a great baroque church, the very antithesis of the Anglican Cathedral, crowned by a dome, the whole project conceived on a gigantic baroque scale.

Work on the crypt went on until 1941, and then the project was halted by the war. After the war the built portion of the crypt, which then covered about half the site of the proposed cathedral, was completed and brought into use in October 1958.

The rest of the project was hopelessly unrealistic, and in 1953, under Archbishop Godfrey, Adrian Gilbert Scott was commissioned to scale down the Lutyens design.[4] Lutyens himself had died during the war. The Scott version was not admired and represented an unfortunate compromise. Godfrey was translated to Westminster in 1957, and his successor in Liverpool, John Carmel Heenan, decided to abandon the classical design, to hold a competition, and to build a modern cathedral at what amounted to breakneck pace. The competition took place in 1960 and attracted 300 entries, which in themselves make an interesting commentary on attitudes to church design at that time.[5]

The brief was for a church to seat 2,000 people, capable of being built within five years, and at a cost of one million pounds in 1960 terms. Heenan wanted the basic shell, and he asked that the design should relate to the existing Lutyens crypt. In many ways it was unfortunate that the brief was prepared and the competition held before the outcome of the Second Vatican Council clarified the liturgical arrangements which were to influence quite fundamentally the design of Catholic churches in subsequent years. The winning design by Frederick Gibberd was for a centralized church, more or less as it appears today. Gibberd had a large

---

context of the Lutyens design see Christopher Hussey, *The Life of Sir Edwin Lutyens* (London, 1950), ch. 18.

[4] This design is illustrated in the 1990 version of the cathedral guide.

[5] The 3 premiated designs and a selection of the rest are illustrated in *Architects' Journal*, 132 (1 Sept. 1960), pp. 313–33. For the finished design see the appraisal by Nicholas Taylor, 'Metropolitan Cathedral Liverpool', *Architectural Review*, 141 (June 1967), pp. 432–48.

and prestigious practice, but is, perhaps, best known as the architect-planner of Harlow New Town. The building was completed with considerable speed, bearing in mind its size and complexity, and was consecrated in 1967, while the Anglican Cathedral was creeping slowly westward decade by decade and had ten years and one more bay of its nave still to be built.

There are a number of general points which are worth making before turning to either cathedral in detail. The Anglican Cathedral (colour plate 7), despite its romantic silhouette and its Gothic clothing, was not a Gothic space, and in his efforts to find a resolution to the problem of accommodating a large congregation in a space unimpeded by columns and arches, Scott was led further and further away from the ideal traditional big Anglican church which at least in plan he had used for his competition entry. Neither is the Anglican Cathedral truly Gothic in its construction. Much of the building is load bearing, with a brick core encased in dressed stone, but there is a considerable amount of concrete and steel reinforcement to resist the stresses in building volumes which transcend anything achieved in the Middle Ages. But, nevertheless, the mixed constructional techniques were sufficiently traditional to allow Scott to vary the design throughout its development. By cladding the structure in a substantial stone skin, Scott was able to decorate the surfaces of the building using traditional techniques of carving into the stone, which he developed and extended in a very personal way.

If the Anglican Cathedral appears superficially to be a conservative building and, on closer analysis, can be discerned as increasingly radical and original conceptually, almost the reverse is true of the Metropolitan Cathedral (colour plate 8). One's first impression here is of a new architectural fundamentalism, radical both in appearance and in its centralized plan. But twenty years after its completion the plan itself is in many ways perceived as conservative and the architectural style peculiarly dated. Constructionally the Metropolitan Cathedral is quite straightforward; two great ring beams support the main roof and the lantern and are, in turn, held up by great sloping concrete beams, rather like guy-ropes, while the external walls which form the chapels and the porches are load-bearing structures, visually separated from the reinforced-concrete main frame by the surrounding bands of blue glass, which are such a characteristic of the building internally.

Gibberd designed only the shell of the building and left much of the decoration and ornamentation to be added when money was available in later years. This was quite different from the attitude taken by Scott, who completed each part in great detail before moving on to the next phase. In the Gibberd design very little of the decoration is integral with the structure or the primary finishes of the main shell, and the techniques for embellishment have to be entirely different from those of the Anglican Cathedral. To some extent, these techniques were not established at the outset, and the assimilation of works of art and the decoration of the building has proved to be a daunting and difficult task. There is an interesting comparison between Coventry and the Metropolitan Cathedral in Liverpool. There are many parallels in the constructional techniques, but at Coventry the scheme of decoration is more sophisticated and much of it has been incorporated in the basic design. I shall return to these problems later in this paper.

THE ANGLICAN CATHEDRAL IN DETAIL

The popular concept of Giles Scott is of the architect in later life, highly successful as a practitioner, President of the RIBA, and very much an establishment figure.[6] Some would add that he was born to greatness, the son and the grandson of formidable architects: it was natural that he should follow in their footsteps. To counter that, it is necessary to remember that although the first Gilbert Scott[7] had been one of the great forces in Victorian architecture and one of the first successful practitioners in the modern sense, his son, while probably more than his father's equal as a designer, had a less successful career and died after a long period of ill health in 1897. Giles and his brother Adrian, whom we have already met as the second architect of the ill-fated Roman Catholic Cathedral, were both articled to Temple Moore. He was an important and original late Gothic designer, who had himself been a pupil of their father. Giles was born in 1880; his formative years were, therefore, in that last decade of the century, which in spirit and attitude was far removed from the strait-laced moral world in which his father and grandfather had practised. They were heavily influenced by the crusading attitudes to architecture, religion, and morality which were propounded by Pugin, Butterfield, and Street.

The Gothic Revival style had gone through many phases during the

[6] There is as yet no biography of Scott. The most useful summary of his career is still the obituary notice: *RIBA Journal*, 67 (April 1960), pp. 221–2, which was written by Sir Hubert Worthington.

[7] See David Cole, *The Work of Sir Gilbert Scott* (London, 1980).

nineteenth century. By the last decade of the century it had long since ceased to be a suitable vehicle for pubic commissions, and there was already a powerful classical revival, which was to find its main outlet in Edwardian England. For ecclesiastical work Gothic was still one of the favoured styles, but its interpretation was now much more free. The early years of the new century were to see some of the most interesting and unique interpretations of the style: churches like William Lethaby's at Brockhampton,[8] in Herefordshire, and Edward Prior's at Sunderland, in County Durham.[9]

Scott himself seems to have been influenced by this new sense of freedom. We can see in the work of Temple Moore himself, particularly in one of his best churches, St Wilfrid's, Harrogate,[10] a scholarly understanding and a wide vocabulary of Gothic but, at the same time, a personal wilfulness about form. Scott was to demonstrate similar qualities. Equally, it is difficult to find much hint of *fin de siècle* qualities, or any reference to the naughty nineties, but there are certain touches of art nouveau decoration in the Lady Chapel at Liverpool. It is also useful to remember that Scott in his later career was the architect of a wide range of buildings, touching upon various architectural styles. In Cambridge, the University Library and Memorial Court at Clare, cheek by jowl and different in style, the one safely classical, the other bolder in form but a reticent and idiosyncratic version of the early Modern Movement. Both demonstrate a predilection for formal solutions. In Oxford, the New Bodleian was stylistically more quirky, but, in London, and perhaps most significantly, Battersea Power Station displayed a powerful endeavour to make an industrial building into a civic proposition. Again the design has a strong formal quality.

While Liverpool Cathedral was clearly designed in the first decade of the century, much of its development took place against the background of other and quicker compositions, and it is a reasonable proposition to argue that Scott, in addition to his scholarly delight in European Gothic, had a clear sense of classical order and, indeed, struggled to rationalize the cathedral design and to impose an ordered discipline upon its axial plan.

[8] This was illustrated and reviewed: Peter Blundell Jones, 'All Saints Brockhampton', *Architects' Journal*, 192 (15 Aug. 1990), pp. 24–43.

[9] A good contemporary account of this church is Dean Hawkes, 'St. Andrew's Roker', *Architects' Journal*, 181 (30 Jan. 1985), pp. 20–38.

[10] Again, no proper account of Temple Moore's architecture is available: see Nikolaus Pevsner, *Yorkshire, The West Riding – The Buildings of England Series* (Harmondsworth, 1959), p. 248.

There is a discernible and growing formalism, perhaps not overt but certainly latent in the design of his cathedral.

The competition design had a simple, traditional, cruciform plan which made little contribution to the development of large church planning. The external massing, however, was memorable, with the powerfully expressed triple clerestory windows of the nave and the unusual tower arrangement consisting of a rather stubby single western tower, centrally placed, not quite like Ely, and two grand towers over the transepts in the manner of Exeter. This must have appealed to the two assessors. But to our eyes it is a restless composition: the contradiction of direction in the design of the nave with the top-heavy, high clerestory windows jockeying for attention with the towers is not satisfactory, and the whole design fails to come together as a unity.

The practical arrangement once Scott was appointed was to invite one of the assessors, Bodley, to assist the young Scott in progressing the design.[11] It was an awkward arrangement, bearing in mind their difference in age, but it probably had an interesting effect upon the first stage of the project, although practical issues also began to influence the design. Chavasse wanted a substantial part of the Cathedral for use relatively quickly, so that there was a presence on St James's Mount, and for this reason the idea for the enlarged Lady Chapel developed. The form it took is recognizable from the 1904 drawings. Work proceeded quickly, and it was consecrated in 1910. Work began at the same time on the foundations of the eastern limb of the main cathedral, and on 19 July 1904 Edward VII laid the foundation-stone. At this point the general design seemed fixed.

It is difficult to know how much influence Bodley had upon the design of the Lady Chapel. In its basic form it has little precedent, except perhaps in a building like the Sainte-Chapelle, in Paris. It is effectively a single-cell building, with very narrow, low, passage aisles, which are to be found in some of Bodley's own churches, and were his answer to gathering people in one space while retaining the spirit of an aisled nave. There is a vestigial triforium and then tall, elegant clerestory windows and a delicate fourteenth-century style stone vault. The east end is apsidal, the general effect part-French, part-German, a hint of Scott's own later eclecticism. The west end, however, already displays Scott's own clear whimsical mixture of pointed and rounded arches. In its interplay of levels, in order to arrange the external entrance and internal connections with the main

[11] The most useful account of Bodley's work is in Basil F. L. Clarke, *Church Builders of the Nineteenth Century* (London, 1938; repr. Newton Abbot, 1969), pp. 209ff.

cathedral floor-level above, Scott plays spatial games, offering the visitor glimpses down into the chapel from a balcony before finally descending on to the chapel floor (plate 1). Only then do you discern that high above the balcony is yet another level containing the organ-loft. I think this shows the intuitive brilliance of Scott's mind working at its best on spatial geometry, and it hints at things to come later, in the revision of the main cathedral design. The detailing is intimate and rich, the text of the *Magnificat*, which is carved at the foot of the triforium is one place where there is a suggestion of art nouveau detailing. The stonework setting of the so-called Hallelujah door and the metalwork on the timber door itself are exuberant and enjoyable designs in the free-style idiom and are completely convincing (plate 2). The stained glass, of course, was replaced after the Second World War and is more translucent than apparently was the original, which was damaged in one of the air raids on the city. The gilded timber triptych above the altar has a curiously German quality. Already, in his basic approach to the design, Scott used the enrichment of the fabric in a broadly traditional way to provide the majority of the necessary decoration. All the decisions were in the hands of the architect, and the further addition of memorials and other works of art can only have a secondary role and a modest impact upon the internal space.

Clearly, while this first phase was being brought to a conclusion, Scott was increasingly unhappy, and we know that his relationship with Bodley deteriorated. Had Bodley not died in 1907, Scott was seriously thinking of resigning. To their credit, the Cathedral Committee immediately entrusted the whole job to Scott alone, and in October 1909 Scott submitted to them a new design. It is difficult to imagine how Scott must have felt on St Peter's Day, 28 June 1910, when the Lady Chapel was consecrated: he had still not obtained a view from the Committee about the new scheme; that was not to come until November of that year. It had in the end taken the Committee over a year to come to terms with what was being proposed.

When you look at the new drawings[12] it is not difficult to understand why the decision took so long. Scott's revisions were not of detail but of quite fundamental matters. The two transeptal towers, already some twenty feet out of the ground, were abandoned. In their place was a new and much larger central tower to the west of the proposed crossing, and

[12] The evolution of the new design is well illustrated and described in Cotton, *Liverpool Cathedral*, ch. 3. I have also drawn upon the unpublished study by one of my students, R. W. Hanson, 'The Last Triumph of Gothic' (Liverpool, B.Arch. dissertation, 1983).

Plate 1 The Anglican Cathedral, Liverpool, West End of the Lady Chapel, showing Scott's early use of different arch forms and his delight in the interplay of levels (photo: Author).

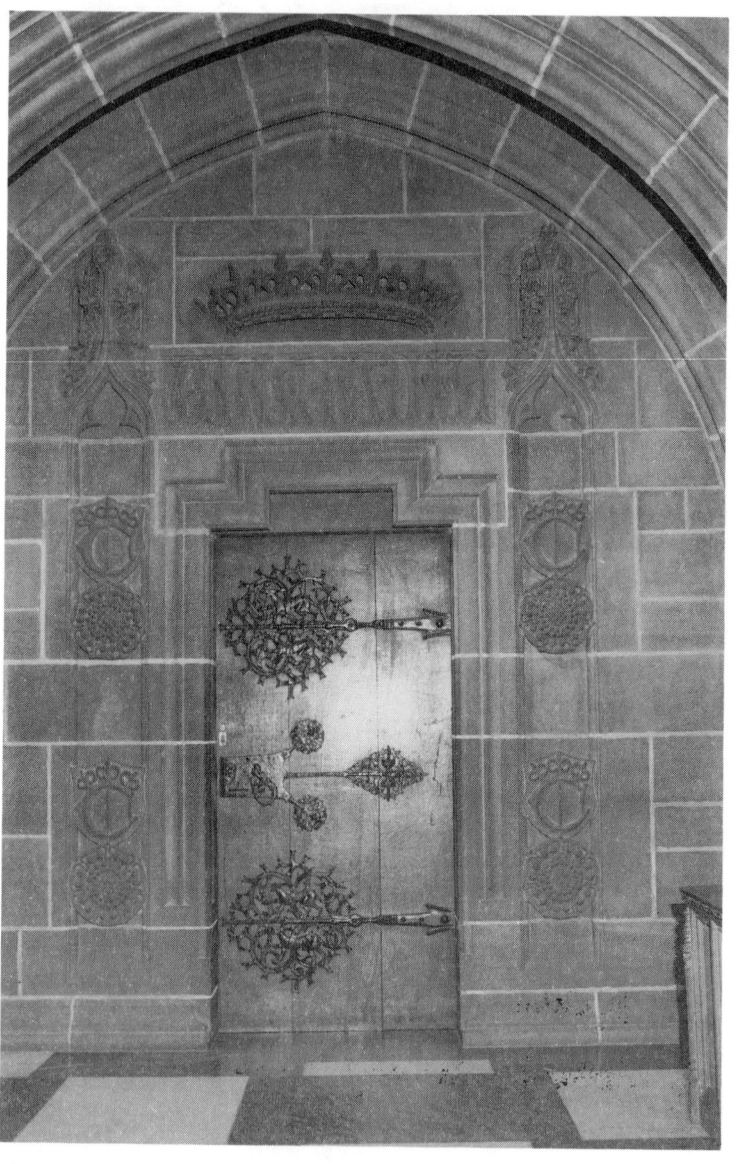

Plate 2 The Hallelujah Door in the Lady Chapel of the Anglican Cathedral: youthful exuberance in detailing (photo: Author).

beyond that another pair of balancing transepts and a three-bay nave, with a conventional roof line balancing the three bays of the choir already under construction. The first drawings of this design show a huge open space, stretching from the eastern to the western extremities of the two pairs of transepts, the full width of the choir and its aisles. A space free of columns, providing a great gathering area for the congregation. Effectively this was the nave, and the three bays of the nave proper were no more than an anti-space.

The new plan answered the original brief far better than did the original conventional plan, and, no doubt, this point was well taken by the Cathedral Committee. It nevertheless involved a certain amount of abortive work, and it gave Scott some very difficult problems to reorganize and rationalize what had been built. The lower levels of the eastern transepts were, of course, far too heavy now that they were not to carry towers, and the redesigning of the upper levels of the original crossing required some clever rearrangement of the vaulting subsequently to disguise the new plan form. But none of this has ever been impossible within Gothic construction, nor was it to be so now.

It should also be noted that the plan form is now basically symmetrical in both directions. If one disregards the various alternatives for the western narthex, the three bays of the nave were intended to balance the choir. The central space, with its double transepts, not only possesses a symmetry, but is the equivalent of the great domed space in a classical church. There is, indeed, one version of the plan which describes a circle underneath the central tower as though Scott thought of it as a domed space at some stage. No dome, however, was either possible or proposed externally.

The revised design could only be executed with modern constructional aids, the spans were far too great for traditional Gothic arches, and the sheer size of the tower above the intervening space transcends anything previously built. For some, this inherent dishonesty, where the stresses and strains of Gothic construction are resisted not by the mass of stone so much as by the tensions of reinforced concrete, causes intellectual problems, but it was not in the nature of Scott's attitude to Gothic to be that pure. He saw the opportunity and the potential to create a building which was essentially different from all its Gothic predecessors, and although it is a paradox that the architectural focus of the building beneath the under-tower space is not at the liturgical focus, it is, nevertheless, at the heart of the congregation and the dominant gathering space on great occasions. The concept is, however, essentially classical; in some ways more so than St Paul's, in London.

Once accepted, Scott developed the scheme quite consistently; subsequent changes are nearly all refinements. The central space was narrowed somewhat for technical reasons rather than for aesthetic ones, but the impact of the narrowing at the point where the two great triple doorways are placed strengthens the appearance of the internal space and in no way detracts from the basic spatial concept.

Work proceeded on the revised design of the eastern limb, which included the whole of the choir and the first pair of transepts, until 1924.[13] The choir has a similar arrangement to that first adopted in the Lady Chapel, with a broad central space and narrow passage aisles. The difference is that the aisles are treated internally like miniature transepts, compartmentalized from each other by buttress-like walls, through which the low aisle archways penetrate. They go up almost the full height of the building. This permits tall aisle windows and no traditional bay design of arcade, triforium, and clerestory. The effect, were it not for the disappointingly dark glass, would be to let light flood into the choir from both sides and enliven the red Woolton sandstone.

The east end is squared off in the northern English tradition, with a low ambulatory and a huge east window divided into two, almost deliberately creating a duality which is only resolved by the powerful central eye, one could hardly call it a rose, in the traceried head. The reredos is carved on to the structure of the building and picked out in gold. Here Scott uses Gothic shapes and forms inspired by some of the Spanish churches he had seen. He introduced four-centred flattened arches, which are half perpendicular and half Spanish, he again resorted to the interplay between the pointed arch and the semi-circular arch, and he treated the whole as a setting for traditional sculptural relief panels (plate 3). The sculpture is in detail and, at close hand, disappointing, but the overall effect is satisfactory. The development of the sanctuary, the high altar itself, and the surrounding detailing all seem to grow effortlessly out of the structure of the building. The use of marble and alternative stones for pavings and detailing is deceptively logical. Exactly the same technique is used for the choir-stalls, the bishop's throne, the pulpit, and the lectern (plate 4). Each develops out of the structure, and the detailed design is then extemporized, sometimes in stone, often in timber.

The designs are all different, drawing the stonework up to form a

[13] There is an interesting contemporary assessment of the design by C. H. Reilly, *Some Architectural Problems of Today* (Liverpool and London, 1924), ch. 23: 'Liverpool Cathedral', pp. 184–200.

Plate 3 The High Altar Reredos of the Anglican Cathedral, carried on to the structure of the building and Spanish in inspiration (photo: Author).

Plate 4 Anglican Cathedral Pulpit, entirely of stone, launched off the main crossing-pier (photo: Author).

plinth to make a setting for timber to form seats and reading-desks or a contrasting marble detail. Each is manipulated within the slightly whimsical spirit of Gothic, which we have already observed as a Scott characteristic. Nikolaus Pevsner describes the choir-stalls as 'feeble',[14] and one can understand what he means. There is an inevitableness, even a monotony, about some of the designs, and Scott's particular style in detail is much less robust than it is when he deals with conceptual forms. One needs to ask whether his conviction for Gothic detail is sustained into the furnishings; he certainly does not have the freshness of Pugin or Ruskin or the muscularity of Burgess. One longs for the whimsy and virility of the O'Shea brothers on the Oxford Museum, or the approach of Lethaby or Prior in their highly original churches mentioned earlier. An equally powerful comparison is between Pugin's original detailing of everything down to ink-wells and umbrella-stands in the Houses of Parliament and Scott's reconstruction of the House of Commons after the Second World War. The same lack of Gothic conviction and virility is evident.

Nevertheless, the overall impression of the eastern arm of the cathedral is of a resplendent unity and completeness. There is tremendous professional competence in the execution of the detail and absolute clarity in the articulation of the forms. The spirit of Gothic is observed and the skill of the craftsman is respected, if not perhaps his imagination. One looks in vain for the freshness of the carvers in the fourteenth-century chapter house of Southwell. In the first decade of this century the inspiration for that sort of individual creativity was absent and had been replaced by a much more mechanized view of detail design, although one which differed substantially from that of the mid-Victorian. Maybe that was because the scale of the total endeavour was so great, and the capacity for one designer to breathe life into so vast a project at all levels was so demanding. Yet Scott's own individuality is never in question, the decoration is used sparingly to enhance the scale of the rebuilding, to enrich it and humanize it, and there is clearly an overall artistic control which creates a sense of confidence in the design. But is that inspiration infused at all levels with Gothic sensibility?

After the completion of the eastern limb, work proceeded westwards through the central space to the western edge of the second pair of transepts. There are several variants on the design for the central tower which show Scott's concern to achieve a satisfactory profile and design. The height and the mass, as well as the elevational treatments, go through

[14] Pevsner, *Lancashire I*, p. 190.

lengthy development. The interior of the space was completed in the summer of 1941 and the tower itself the following February. Externally Scott arrived at a silhouette for the tower which has considerable character and great beauty. The great mass of masonry rises from amongst the transepts, and out of it gradually emerge the four tapering turrets, leaving the central tower to be resolved as a square with the corners chamfered off, but not to the point where it becomes an octagon. The turrets stop short of the corona, and there are vestigial pinnacles on the remaining eight points. The transepts are suppressed below the parapet line of the main choir roof, and Scott links them by two deep porches, with what by now are the typical long, slow, semi-circular arches. The external silhouette at which he finally arrived has an inevitability and a sense of repose and 'rightness' only possessed by truly great architecture.

Internally, the under-tower space is controlled much more by the overall architectural concept than was the case in the choir. The visitor is overwhelmed by the sheer scale of the space, and yet it is saved from becoming inhuman by exactly that same attention to ornament and detail which gave the earlier phase of the building its particular character. The triple doorways to the two transeptal porches, with their Spanish detailing and their tall, thin statues set under canopied niches, humanize the scale of the central space before the eye is led ever upwards by the long vertical lines of the crossing piers and the great south and north windows, which rise into the under-tower space itself. East and west of the huge arches spanning the full width of the building, lie the triple bays of the choir and nave, narrowed by their aisles, and emphasized to the east by the double organ-cases facing into the central space and across the choir. The rectangular plan of the central space is gathered together high overhead by a series of squinch arches, which prepare for the chamfering of the main tower and the development of the under-tower vault. The internal shape now begins to reflect the external form of the tower. Above, hidden from the eye, lies the ringing-chamber and then the belfry.

In 1942 Scott prepared his final designs for the nave and for the bridge between the nave and the central space and for the narthex. Building work did not resume until 1948, and then, slowly, the final three bays were completed, the first in 1960, the second in 1967, and the third in 1978. Scott himself died in 1960 and was buried outside the cathedral in what was to have been the narthex. Sadly this was the only piece of the original design not to be executed in accordance with the 1942 plan, but the main internal form of the building is complete, and while some will quibble over Frederick Thomas's west window design, the overall effect is much as Scott must have desired.

The 1942 design for the nave simplified the earlier scheme of the eastern limb, reducing the decoration and altering some of the window proportions. But essentially it is the concept Scott evolved in 1909. The nave itself has a lower floor-level than the rest of the building, while the aisles remain at the general floor-level. This gives an increased sense of height and, as in the medieval cathedral, all is not revealed when you enter the building. Between the nave and the central space lies the bridge, originally intended to carry a free-standing organ as it would be on a choir screen. As it is, it still provides an effective division between nave and central space. Here again is the long, slow, semi-circular arch, carrying the stone bridge and the timber gallery. Beneath it, the visitor climbs the steps and enters the central space and, in effect, enters the cathedral proper, with its long, unimpeded vista up to the high altar, beneath its gilded stone reredos, far away in the distance (plate 5). The experience, now that the building is completed, is unforgettable, and we can now begin to understand the nature of the cathedral which Scott sought to create, but never actually saw, except in his mind's eye.

Two of the four transepts have specific functions: that to the south-west is the baptistry, and the north-east transept houses the war memorials. The canopy for the font is a free-standing *baldacchino*, rather more vigorous than some of Scott's designs. Beneath it is a very simple font in marble, with low relief carvings by E. Carter Preston and a delightful mosaic pavement, with little fishes leaping through a wreath of waves (plate 6). The idea is fresh and relaxed, a welcome relief from the general architectural drama. Maybe the purpose inspired a gentleness and simplicity which is absent elsewhere—even in the canopy overhead. The war memorial transept demonstrates the appropriateness of Scott's style for the great formal occasion. The reredos and altar against the north wall echo in a more restrained way the design of the high altar. In the centre of the transept is the plinth which carries the Book of Remembrance. It is richly detailed in black marble, Hopton Wood stone, and bronze. Around the walls it has been possible to include other memorials carved into the stone.

These main liturgical furnishings and formal memorials set the mood for the cathedral. They demonstrate how the building can seem complete through its architecture alone, although it can receive further enrichment almost as afterthoughts. The need to create a war memorial chapel, for example, could be accommodated with apparent effortless ease. One is

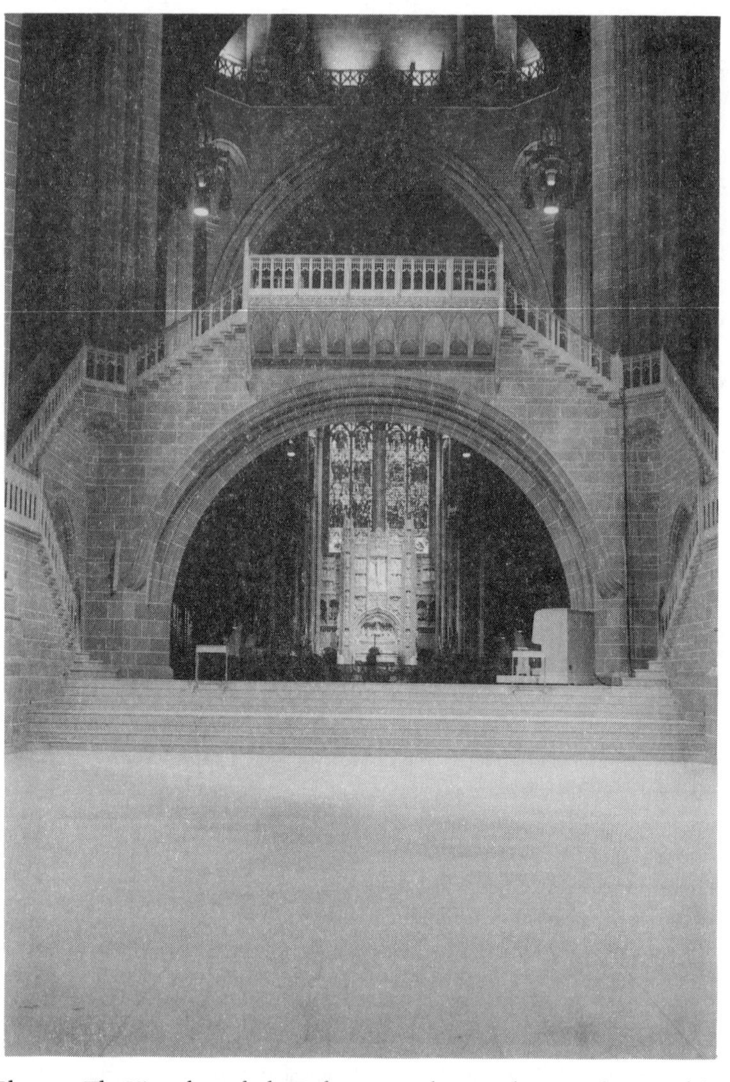

Plate 5 The View through the Dulverton Bridge into the Central Space of the Anglican Cathedral (photo: Author).

Plate 6 The Font of the Anglican Cathedral, carved by E. Carter Preston: a welcome relief from Scott's endless Gothic detailing (photo: Author).

tempted to say it was a useful way of justifying spaces, which had no more liturgical function than Gibberd's chapels at the Metropolitan Cathedral.

While it is clearly true to say that the building is its own ornament, its scale and the modelling of the internal surfaces permit addition and alteration in detail, because they can take place unself-consciously. As yet, of course, insufficient time has passed for the taste of many different generations to play a part in the appearance of the cathedral, but a number of additions and changes already have come about which are worth comment. The memorials begin with those to Bishop Ryle, the first Bishop of Liverpool, in the south choir aisle, and the 16th Earl of Derby in the south-east transept. Both take the traditional form of recumbent effigies, and both were essentially designed by Scott, although the recumbent figure of Bishop Ryle was, in fact, Carter Preston's first work in the cathedral. Very much later he designed in a rather different style the memorial to the first Dean of Liverpool, Dean Dwelly. In every way this is a much more personal tribute to the man who brought the cathedral alive liturgically. Behind the bishop's throne, again in the south aisle, is the memorial to the founder, Bishop Chavasse, appropriately holding in his hand the model of the cathedral.

When Scott designed the cathedral, his sense of order and balance led to the creation of two great porches between the pairs of transepts. Until 1978 the main entrance to the cathedral lay through the south porch overlooking the Mersey, but the north porch, which overlooks the quarry cemetery and across to Gambier Terrace, served no practical purpose. In recent years it has been turned successfully into the cathedral tea-room, linked to the cathedral shop, which now occupies the north-west transept. Doubtless Scott never dreamt of such a thing, but it brings to life a dead space, and it has opened vistas from the cathedral to the north, which are in themselves memorable. An imaginative idea which many would see as a positive improvement.

THE DETAIL DESIGN OF THE CATHOLIC CATHEDRAL

The fragment of the Lutyens cathedral, which takes the form of an aboveground crypt, is incorporated in the podium of the new cathedral, although it is neither complete nor finished in the way Lutyens intended. It makes an interesting study of the approach that the architect was taking in the last years of his career, not only to conceptual design, but to the detail he considered appropriate for a church which was a building type Lutyens worked on all too rarely. It makes an interesting comparison with

Scott's approach and is, of course, very different from Lutyens's own earlier church work at Hampstead.[15] It belongs much more to his civic commissions and perhaps most of all should be seen as a further development of the monumental concept of New Delhi.[16]

The fragments of the exterior are detailed in a simplified version of the baroque, almost abstract in detail and in scale with the design which would have risen above. The whole of the outside would have been in white Portland stone. Internally the structural material is brick, the detail granite. Lutyens would have plastered the brick, but the simple, cavernous vaults are to our eyes impressive in their own right. The effect is gloomy but heroic. Stylistically the design of the interior is in Lutyens's own version of classicism, sometimes rather idiosyncratic, always visually arresting. The detailing is also related very closely to the quality of granite, its hardness and the difficulty experienced in working it. The combination of the material and stylistic predilection has resulted in strong, simple shapes, which can be recognized in the detailing of altars and especially the pontificial chapel, the burial-place of the archbishops of Liverpool, with its great rolling-stone for a door. The visitor can only feel cheated that there is not more of this great building to explore (plate 7).

The decoration, so far as it goes, is integral to the construction, and in this Lutyens follows a similar approach to that of Scott's Anglican Cathedral. But Scott, by contrast, seems much more conservative in his attitude to Gothic than is Lutyens in his approach to classicism. Whether that impression would have been sustained in the complete building is doubtful, but the evidence we have suggests that the classical Metropolitan Cathedral would have been in the end a worthy successor to the Viceroy's House at New Delhi in Lutyens's total output. The surviving drawings, however, do not suggest it would have broken further new design ground beyond the abstract classicism Lutyens arrived at in India.

The Metropolitan Cathedral of the 1960s, which incorporates the Lutyens crypt beneath one half of the podium and then places the new building over an underground car park, which occupies the other half of the site, breaks quite different ground. I have already compared it with Coventry in its general approach, but there is more to be said about the detail design. Buildings of this type need to be conceived and realized according to a single design. There is little room for any fundamental

[15] There are two churches crowning the hill in Hampstead Garden Suburb, the parish church of St Jude and the Free Church, both 1908–10.

[16] Hussey, *Edwin Lutyens*.

Plate 7 Metropolitan Cathedral, Liverpool: Lutygens Granite Detailing in the Crypt (photo: Author).

manœuvrability, since the structure is finite, and there is not the latitude for second thoughts which was available to Scott. Nor, of course, was there the same length of time during which the design could gestate. The building is much more a statement about architecture, even though it is still capable of subsequent embellishment. The merits of Gibberd's design are essentially its clarity of form and the way the structure becomes a major influence on the appearance of the building. Like the great classical centralized churches, built as well as unexecuted, the round form is finite and has a latent perfection. The contrast between the main structure of the cathedral and the graceful lantern, with its tall and delicate crown, provides the visitor with one of the essential images of the building. It is as much part of the Liverpool skyline as is its Anglican counterpart. For those who live in Liverpool, the play of light on the lantern on an early spring morning is as beautiful as the sihouette of Scott's tower emerging from the mist in the autumn. The abstract forms of the surrounding chapels, set between the great mosaic-clad concrete ribs and themselves clad in Portland stone, give the drum of the building a sculpted form, at times unpredictable and surprisingly powerful and abstract, which contrasts strongly with the delicacy of the lantern.[17]

If the vertical massing works well, the sense of direction on the ground is much less clear. For various reasons outside the architect's control, the approach to the main west entrance facing on to Hope Street is oblique, which in itself is a curiously English characteristic of design, since we rarely favour the full-blown axiality of many of our European neighbours, but the west porch and the bell turret which surmounts it lack the power to give the entrance to the building a real sense of celebration. The external altar and its setting at the east end, overlooking the exposed roof of the Lutyens crypt, is much the least satisfactory of the outside features.

Gibberd projects the porch proud of the main drum and the surrounding chapels, bringing it forward by means of a linking vestibule and then finally crowning it with the triangular feature, a kind of architectural exclamation mark which houses the bells. Above the doors, he takes the opportunity to carve within the Portland stone cladding. The impact of the lower relief design is rather disappointing and, viewed from a distance, although it possesses clarity, the eye becomes quickly bored.

[17] Pevsner, *Lancashire I*, pp. 154–7, is particularly interesting on the Metropolitan Cathedral which, clearly, he did not much like. His assessment both of the exterior form and the interior space is an important assessment by an architectural historian of our earlier generation.

Beneath are the two powerful sliding doors in fibreglass, which are splendidly vigorous, even barbaric in a kind of Romanesque way (plate 8). They are normally slid back so that they look like panels, revealing the banal entrance screen in metal and glass. This looks for all the world like the entrance to a departmental store, and even though the hinged doors have now been replaced by revolving doors because of wind problems, the actual entrance is an anti-climax, and the lobby gives no hint of the space beyond. In part, this is a problem of inadequate detail, but Gibberd seems not to know what he wants this space to be, and the visitor is left completely unprepared for the experience which lies beyond. The one purpose the lobby does serve is to subdue the level of natural light entering the main building, so that when you pass into the central space, with its reduced level of lighting, you are in part prepared.

The impact of the central space is surprisingly powerful, lit from the pervading blue glass that surrounds the side chapels where they fit between the main structured ribs of the building, while high above, in the lantern, the superb, rich, jewel-like glass of John Piper and Patrick Reyntiens immediately draws the eye away from nearly everything else. The impact of the blue light varies considerably according to weather conditions, and its effect on the visitor is unpredictable. What can be said for it is that it helps to create the atmosphere of the space. The glazed lantern, which is an abstract conception of the Holy Trinity, represented as three white lights set in the colours of the spectrum representing the unity of God's nature, is, I suppose, an alternative treatment of the *Te Deum* theme of the rather disappointing east window of the Anglican Cathedral. A more effective contrast, of course, is with the west window of the Anglican Cathedral, but, without doubt, Piper has endowed the Metropolitan Cathedral with an integral artistic contribution to the design which, to a large extent, holds the whole composition together. At night, lit from the inside, the jewel-like colours of the glass shine out against the pale, floodlit shell.

The exposed concrete structure and the roughened rendering of the internal walls are grey and off-white in colour, largely washed by the blue light of the 'nave' windows. So the building possesses a monochromatic unity, which would verge on boredom were it not for the lantern high overhead. The contrast with Le Corbusier's church at Ronchamp, where the internal faces of the surrounding chapel are drenched in primary colours, and the more violent and strident use of light, can never be far from one's mind. Gibberd's chapels neither have the mystery nor the drama of Ronchamp. They are, of course, the victims of changing

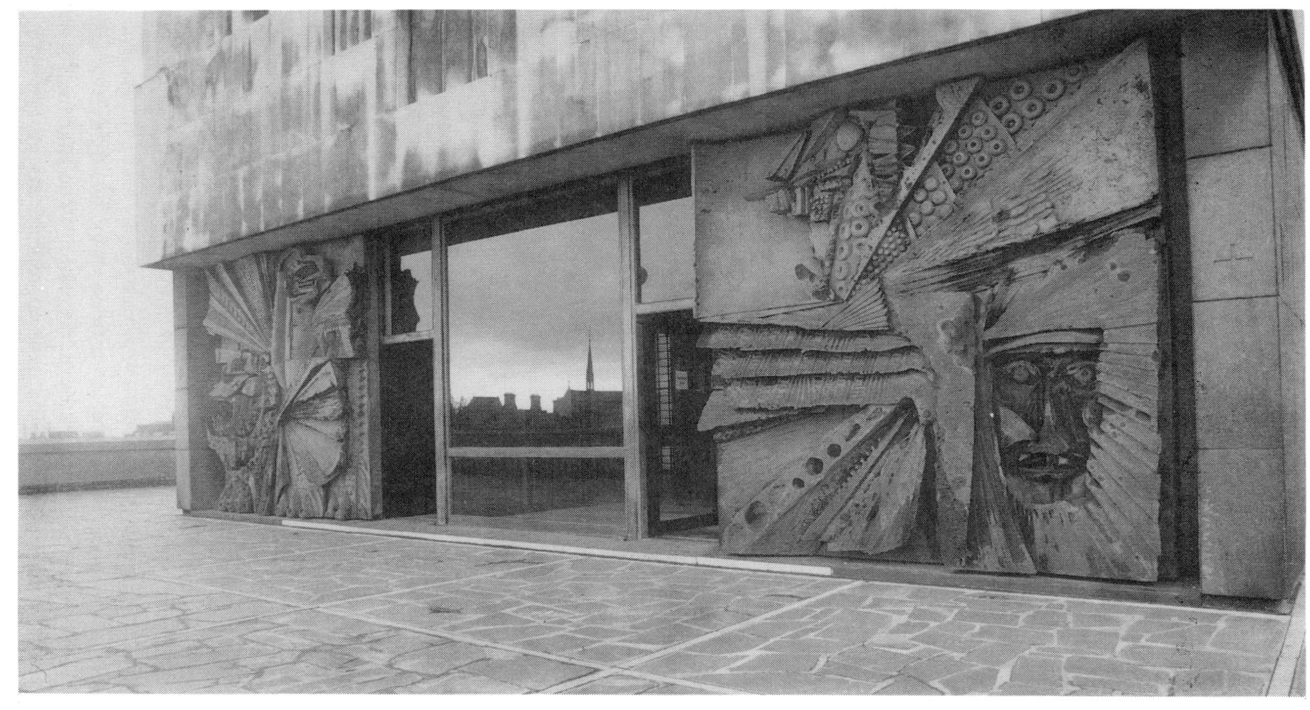

Plate 8 The Main Entrance of the Metropolitan Cathedral, with the doors by William Mitchell (photo: Author).

religious requirements: it is true to say that they are a series of chapels in search of a purpose, since they are no longer required to house separate altars. During the last twenty years, on the whole, they have been embarrassing spaces. Only three were defined functionally in the original design. The principal secondary space arranged axially to the east is the chapel of the Blessed Sacrament, where Ceri Richards was asked to design two triangular windows, a reredos, and a tabernacle (plate 9). Here we see the real problem of adding self-consciously works of art into the vast open spaces of a modern building. Gibberd chose in general not to break up the wall surfaces apart from their structural definition. However, in this chapel there is a canopy, structurally part of the east wall, below which Ceri Richards placed his reredos as a framed picture. The canopy looks more like a cooking-hood than a *baldacchino*, and the picture is lost against the prairie spaces around it. The tabernacle doors, which are in ceramic tile, are themselves beautiful to look at as works of art, but neither their setting nor the indication of their purpose are well worked out. The best that can be said is that the three items relate thematically and in colour to one another and give the chapel some identity. But the lasting impression is one of self-consciousness.

The second important sub-space is the Lady Chapel, whose outer wall comes to an apex in which at relatively high level stands Robert Brumby's statue of Our Lady with the Child Jesus (plate 10). Normally a pitfall in Catholic Church art, this is an unsentimental and hauntingly beautiful statue, softly lit by monochromatic glass by Margaret Treherne. Artistically both are more coherent and successful than the Blessed Sacrament Chapel.

Last in the designated spaces comes the baptistry, designed by Gibberd himself. It is a circular space, lit by small, low-level, slit windows, and enclosed with a simple grille and gates. The font is set at the centre of a radial floor design, a cylinder of skopje marble, plain in design with a metal cover. It is here that Gibberd's weakness for detail design is most apparent. The simplicity is not a thing of beauty but of boredom. Window-sills and skirting-boards that are reminiscent of local authority houses in Harlow New Town look entirely out of place in the great height of the chapel, and one longs for a contrast of forms, of colour and texture.

At the centre of the cathedral itself, underneath the great glazed lantern, is the high altar, on a sanctuary raised two steps above the floor of the cathedral (plate 11). In many ways the floor design, by David Atkins, is the most subtle and successful internal 'decoration'. The altar itself is a simple block of white skopje marble, more appropriate and satisfactory in

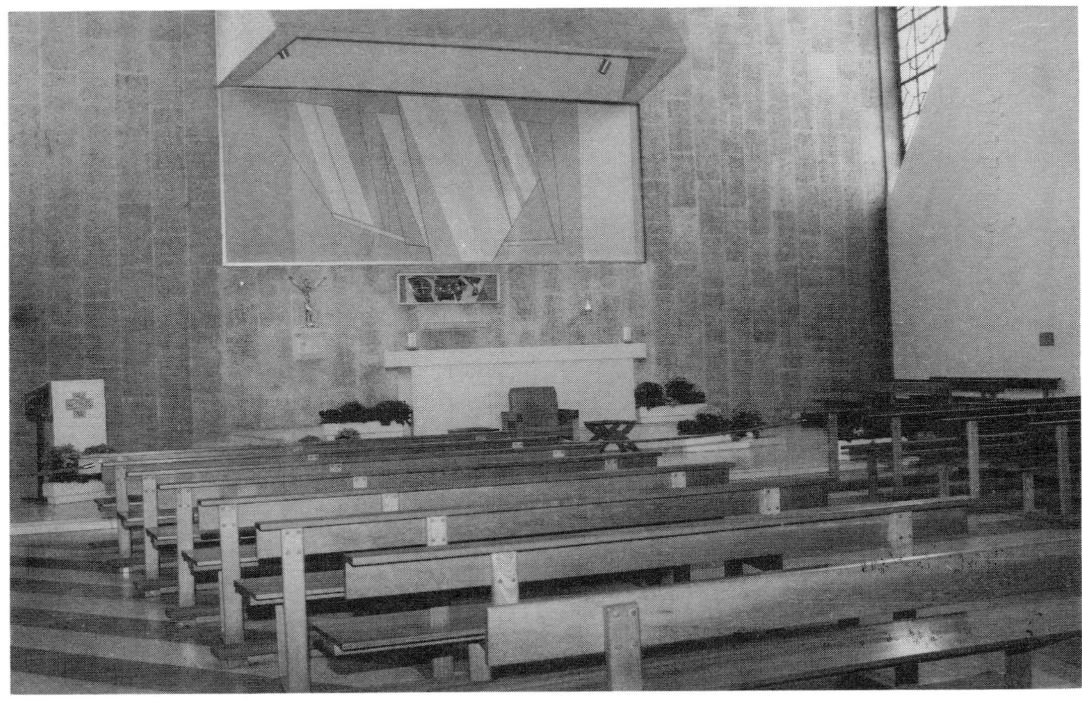

Plate 9 The Blessed Sacrament Chapel of the Metropolitan Cathedral, the work of Ceri Richards (photo: Author).

Plate 10 Robert Brumby's Statue of Our Lady and the Child Jesus in the Lady Chapel of the Metropolitan Cathedral (photo: Author).

Plate 11 The Sanctuary of the Metropolitan Cathedral: the floor developed by David Atkins, the candlesticks by Robert Gooden, and the crucifix by Elizabeth Frink (photo: Author).

its setting than was the font. Above is the great tubular steel *baldacchino*, designed by Gibberd himself, and originally intended to carry electric light like some ancient corona. Opinion differs about this significant climax to the design; there is a simple beauty about the high altar, with Robert Gooden's no-nonsense, chunky candlesticks and Elizabeth Frink's strong and unsentimental figure of the crucified Christ, which represent all that is best in the diversity and tension of modern design, linked to an appropriate simplicity in the architecture. The canopy looks like scaffolding to some, while to others it is an effective visual link between sanctuary and lantern above: it now appears very dated in design. If it were still possible to light it at night, the effect might be better, but the main criticism must be that in a building so large as this, the central focus, while it may not require the baroque treatment of Bernini in St Peter's, certainly requires more than Gibberd was able to invest in it if its liturgical meaning and its physical presence are to be fully realized. It is here, too, that the traditional problems of the centralized plan become acutely evident. The president's chair and the archbishop's throne, as well as the siting of the choir, have never been resolved with any degree of natural logic, and the building always seems to lack order. The ambivalence of the brief at a time of change in part is responsible for this, but the rest is an historic design problem associated with centralized churches, perhaps incapable of resolution.

The only other significant feature of the original design is the organ, mounted high on a gallery or bridge at the east end of the building, above the entrance to the Blessed Sacrament Chapel. In its well-arranged display of pipework, it is a satisfying and welcome piece of detail design, and one which in this form is entirely appropriate to a modern building. Rather as with the engineers in the early nineteenth century, the logic of technology can have a beauty of its own.

In this state of partial completion the cathedral was consecrated in 1967. The problems of defining the uses for apparently unnecessary side chapels and the further ornamentation of the building was left to posterity. Twenty years on, posterity has had some say. Time, too, has altered the perception of a building once so new and innovative. The cathedral is now in its own right a place of pilgrimage and has its own association with the great occasions of the city and the nation. Its image as a place of worship is known through television and the media to countless millions who have never seen it. Its function has been explored, and its interior has been embellished. It is in every sense a pilgrimage church, hallowed by the joys and sorrows of Liverpool. By general consent, the monochromatic quality of the concrete and the rendered walls was unsatisfactory, and, in the short term, a scheme of embroidered hangings, rather like over-scaled banners, some pictorial and some heraldic, have been installed as a counter-balance. To them has recently been added a fine mosaic by Meyer Martin, removed from Holy Ghost Church, at Ford, where it had filled the east wall, depicting Pentecost. The mosaic is a work of the 1960s, more or less contemporary with the design of the cathedral, and has found an appropriate setting. There were no pictorial images of the Stations of the Cross in the original design and no obvious settings for them. This leaves a significant design problem, and until such time as an appropriate and worthy set can be acquired, a temporary series for use during Lent has been provided by the cathedral embroiderers. Much of what we see in 1990 is, therefore, ephemeral. Various gifts in recent years have resulted in the furnishing of several side chapels. In these and other ways the introduction of a variety of designers continues the tradition established with Ceri Richards and the other members of the original team and avoids the potential monotony of an over-unified approach, which Scott achieved in his dominance over the Anglican Cathedral work. Time will tell whether these recent additions are considered worthy of the building, but they arise from a mixture of liturgical need and the desire to provide devotional settings, which either draw attention to the traditional purposes of a cathedral, or simply provide spaces of rest and quietness more intimate and in scale with the human being. Robin Mcghie, for example, has provided the housing for the holy oils and a painted wall panel for the chapel in which they are kept, but with the same problems that faced Ceri Richards.

Stephen Foster took a different approach and has carved on to the matchboarding which lines the chapel of St Joseph a low relief depicting scenes from Joseph's life (plate 12). This is the first and probably the most interesting attempt at integrating a design with the original finishes of the building, if not with the structure. The design deliberately spreads itself across the surface of the wall, and this might provide a way in which some further work could be executed.

Richard O'Mahony has furnished the chapel of St Anne as a place of private prayer and provided it with a timber entrance-door, which demonstrates that within the vocabulary of modern design it is possible to celebrate the entrance to a space appropriately. Gibberd left a tantalizing opportunity here, which Pevsner saw as a link with the Lutyens crypt.

The overriding impression, however, is of Gibberd's architectonic shell, and, curiously, while most of the subsequent additions have

Plate 12 Scenes from the Life of St Joseph, carried on to the timber lining boarding by Stephen Foster: Metropolitan Cathedral (photo: Author).

softened the impact of that shell and to some extent humanized its appearance, little has happened which augments the building in any profound way. Paradoxically, Gibberd's shell exercises the same authority as does Scott's, but in an entirely different way. One is forced to ask whether it is possible and whether posterity will seek to remove much of the temporary decoration and come to terms with the simplicity of the shell. But will it ever be perceived as the beauty of holiness? Will the liturgy of the twenty-first-century Catholic Church be celebrated in a building of puritanical simplicity, while the Anglicans come to terms with the triumphalism which today causes them so much embarrassment?

Liverpool School of Architecture and Building Engineering,
University of Liverpool

THE WESTERN DISCOVERY OF NON-WESTERN CHRISTIAN ART

by A. F. WALLS

CHRISTIANITY is in principle perhaps the most syncretistic of the great religions. Unlike Hinduism, it does not have a unifocal religious culture belonging to a particular soil; nor, like Islam, does it have common sacred language and a recognizable cultural framework across the globe. Historically, Christian expansion has been serial, moving from one heartland to another, fading in one culture as it is implanted in another. Christian expansion involves the serial, generational, and vernacular penetration of different cultures.

This inbuilt fragility of Christianity and its vernacular nature have particular implications for Christian art, precluding the establishment of a normative Christian art in the sense that there is a normative Islamic art, a Christian civilization in the sense that there is an Islamic civilization. There was nothing distinctive about the earliest Christian art except its subject-matter: it brought no style, form, or technique that was not already employed in pagan Roman art. Christian art needs vernacular expression, a sense of locality. The Word became flesh and spoke Aramaic; presumably with a Galilean accent.

The massive shift in the demographic centre of Christianity, most noticeable during the present century, has thus immense implications for the future of Christian art. It is likely that in 1900 over eighty per cent of professed Christians lived in Europe or North America, and that something approaching sixty per cent now live in Africa, Asia, Latin America, or the Pacific.[1] On the evidence of previous Christian history we can now expect a complete, though probably a gradual and certainly a multi-layered, change in the manifestations of Christian art. This paper is therefore mainly concerned with prehistory, and with the early signs of recognition of one of the major implications of the modern missionary movement.

Around 1500, when the Christian West first came into prolonged contact with the cultures of the southern continents, Christianity was

[1] Extrapolated from figures in D. Barrett, ed., *World Christian Encyclopedia* (Nairobi, 1982), esp. Global Table 2, updated by Barrett, 'Annual statistical table on global mission: 1988', *International Bulletin of Missionary Research*, 12 (1988), pp. 16–17.

geographically more concentrated on Europe than at any time before or since. It could celebrate its triumph throughout the Continent, east and west; in the Christianization of Finland and the Baltic and the ejection of Islam from Iberia. The European triumph coincided with a twilight period elsewhere. Outside Europe, Christianity, once widespread across Asia and north-east Africa, was reduced to small enclaves. By 1500 European Christianity possessed a coherent, largely homogeneous artistic tradition. Art was, generally speaking, Christian art. 'Secular' art certainly existed, but in an essentially subordinate role. There was a recognized range of appropriate themes of Christian art, and its iconographic register was settled. The Christianity which entered into engagement with the faiths of Asia and Africa was in confident possession of an artistic expression which had absorbed several vernacular European variations and had nowhere else to go. In Asia it met artistic traditions shaped by other faiths; in Africa artistic traditions that seemed uncouth and barbarous, perhaps childish.

By the middle of the twentieth century the European adventure was over. The achievement of independence by India in 1947 heralded the addition of dozens of new nations to the roll of nation states as Europe opted for a continental future. Vasco da Gama sailed home. By this time both the religious and the artistic map of Europe had altered beyond recognition. The engagement of Christianity with Africa and Asia had an unforeseen outcome; Africans and Asians proved to have been adhering to Christianity at the very time Europeans were departing from it. And the European art tradition—so coherent, so secure, so Christian in 1500—was now fragmented, hesitant, and overwhelmingly secular in theme and outlook. Even when employing a theme from the Christian repertory, such as crucifixion, it was likely to do so as an illustration of the human condition rather than as a statement about the transcendent. The unity of theme, the common register of symbols, was lost beyond recall. So was European assurance in the face of other art traditions; for a generation past, Europeans had been moved by the power and mystery of African and Pacific art, without being able to adopt its indigenous significance or identify its ritual or cosmological context.

In terms of Christian art, the year 1950 witnessed an event of prophetic significance; the Vatican exhibition of Art in the Missions, which probably is still the most considerable celebration yet held of Christian art of non-Western origin. Its creator was Cardinal Celso Costantini, then Secretary of the Sacred Congregation for the Propagation of the Faith (the 'Propaganda'), and already the author of the most substantial comprehensive work yet devoted to the artistic expression of Christianity in the non-Western world.[2] Before he turned to theology Costantini had begun work as an apprentice mason, bidden to read books on architecture and history of art. As a young priest he had brought artists and priests and others together in a Society of Friends of Christian Art, and he had combined parish and ecclesiastical duties with the directorship of a museum and the care of antiquities. From 1922 to 1933 he was Apostolic Delegate in China; years which according to his own account saw two revolutions, that of China itself and that of the missions. Among his contributions to the latter was an insistence that new churches and other Christian buildings reflect Chinese traditions in style and materials; he developed and published a substantial document of guidance on this. Equally significantly, he gathered a group of Chinese artists (none of them at that time Christians) to explore the painting of Gospel themes in Chinese style. Some of the group, notably Luke Ch'en, its most distinguished member, later became Christians.[3]

Costantini desired a renaissance of the arts which he saw emerging from reformation in the missions. The new generation of Asian Christian artists, he believed, presented a fresh vision of creation and of Christian faith, and Westerners, whose own aesthetic tradition was breaking down with fatigue, could turn to them (as to the Renaissance 'primitives') with relief.[4] However, it would not be right to think of him as primarily an aesthetic reformer. His own account of his years in China concentrates on his concern for a Chinese episcopate; at his arrival, despite three hundred years of Catholic presence, there was no Chinese among the fifty Catholic bishops in China. His concerns about art and architecture (and also about music and liturgy) were part of a wider concern about the overwhelmingly foreign aspect of Christianity in China.[5] The neo-Gothic cathedral jarred with Beijing palaces and pagodas; the neo-classical cathedral in Hankow spoke of Europe as much as the synagogue in Rome spoke of the Jews.[6] Modern Christians should follow the practice of the early Church; Confucius and the other Chinese sages provided the same sort of

[2] C. Costantini, *L'Arte Cristiana nelle Missioni* (Rome, 1940); *L'art chrétien dans les missions* (Paris, 1949).

[3] Costantini compiled five volumes of memoirs: *Foghe Secche* (Rome, nd); *Con i Missionari i Cina*, 2 vols (Rome, nd); *Ultime Foglie* (Rome, nd); and *Cum Petro in Christo* (Rome, 1957). A French abridgement of the whole appeared as *Réforme des Missions au XXe siècle* (Paris, 1960). The account of his life before his appointment to China is given in *Réforme*, pp. 13–24.

[4] Costantini, *Réforme*, p. 242.

[5] Ibid., pp. 27ff.

[6] Ibid., p. 239.

preparation for the Gospel that Greek philosophy did in the Mediterranean world, and offered a similar clothing for Christian thought. Instead of viewing local art as a threat to Christian integrity, and affirming Catholicism over against paganism by the consecration of alien styles, it would be well to return to the principles which Gregory the Great commended to Augustine of Canterbury,[7] and indeed to the Propaganda's original principles that missionaries should not transport France, Spain, and Italy with them.[8] The three vital principles are: evangelize, not colonize; respect the art and culture of the country; and remove foreign forms from sacred art.[9]

Costantini's appointment to the Propaganda brought these ideas to bear well beyond China. They assisted the development of the theology of adaptation which became the conventional wisdom in Catholic missiology in the period which produced the Second Vatican Council, and which made its own contribution to that event. The search for indigenous art forms was extended to other areas. In Nigeria, for instance, an experiment began which has been credited with the rescue, just in time, of traditional Yoruba woodcarving by bringing traditional carvers to work on Christian themes.[10] In India the hierarchy was generally supportive, and the Jesuit Fr H. Heras took initiatives which led to the development of interest in Christian painting, architecture, and scholarship, using Indian cultural resources.[11]

Behind Costantini's thinking is the idea of art as essentially a *language*. It is in a sense value free, neither 'pagan' nor Christian; it can be equally the vehicle for the expression of sentiment, prayer, or blasphemy.[12] In the same vein, the founders of the Nigerian experiment insisted—in contradiction of some loud voices of the time[13]—that traditional Yoruba art was 'humanistic' rather than 'religious', and thus could express Christian themes without danger of confusion with pre-Christian ideas.[14] Such

[7] Cf., of many passages, *Réforme*, pp. 223–36.

[8] Ibid., p. 238.

[9] Ibid., pp. 237–42.

[10] K. Carroll, *Yoruba Religious Carving: Pagan and Christian Sculpture in Nigeria and Dahomey* (London, 1967): cf. the foreword by the ethnographer W. B. Fagg.

[11] Cf. J. F. Butler, *Christian Art in India* (Madras, 1986), p. 124. Heras (1888–1955) was primarily a historian, but his work touched many aspects of Indian culture. See the tributes in *Indica* 25 (1988), pp. 83–91; and M. Lederle, *Christian Painting in India through the Centuries* (Bombay: Heras Institute, 1987).

[12] Costantini, *Réforme*, p. 243.

[13] Especially Ulli Beier, *Art in Nigeria 1960* (London, 1960).

[14] Carroll, *Religious Carving*, pp. 70–2.

simplicity of approach was hardly possible in dealing with Indian art; but such questions rarely surface in Costantini's exposition of the meaning of culture.

The Protestant world, without apostolic delegates or sacred congregations, reveals, on the one hand, a good deal of quite adventurous practice and, on the other, remarkably little public discussion and exploration of principles.

As far back as 1883 the Church Missionary Society opened a church in Peshawar, in the Punjab, not far from the border with Afghanistan. All Saints' Memorial Church was built on a grand scale, with a huge square façade, a central arch scalloped (as frequently in Islamic architecture), and smaller arches either side of it, each surmounted by a large star. Across the façade, in fine Arabic calligraphy, was set the words, 'Amen, Blessing and glory and wisdom and thanksgiving and honour and power and might, be unto our God for ever, Amen.' Each corner of the building had a slender minaret, and a great dome sat over the whole. Only the gilt cross over the dome proclaims that the building is not a mosque but a church. The interior was equally designed to provide landmarks for Muslims. A delicately-carved screen of local wood, in local style, by local craftsmen, was set behind the communion table, with an ambulatory across the apse behind it; and another screen across a transept allowed the purdah rule to be observed by women.[15] Another area of the church allowed space for observers who did not wish to uncover either head or feet. The walls carried biblical texts—in Arabic, Urdu, Persian, and English—in the way that Islamic buildings bear Qur'anic inscriptions; representational decoration was avoided. Altogether, All Saints', Peshawar, may seem an extraordinary production on the part of a rather conservative missionary society in the 1880s. Yet it seems to have attracted no great heart-searching or controversy; and the Society's magazine for the general home constituency felt confident in providing a full description[16] of the opening of this 'remarkable building in Saracenic style, designed to adapt a Christian place of worship to Oriental ideas'.[17]

That home constituency was even more aware of another building half a century later; the great cathedral built at Dornakal and designed by

[15] Photographs of exterior and interior in D. J. Fleming, *The Heritage of Beauty* (New York, 1937), pp. 67–8.

[16] *Church Missionary Gleaner*, Nov. 1884.

[17] E. Stock, *History of the Church Missionary Society*, 3 (London, 1899), p. 471.

Bishop V. S. Azariah, the Indian churchman best known outside India.[18] Azariah was well known as a spokesman for Indian Christian identity; a cathedral for a largely new Christian community must reflect that identity. But in India it is less easy than in China to adopt Costantini's principle of art as a language which is religiously neutral. An Indian cultural identity must surely mean Hindu cultural identity—unless it takes Islamic identity. Which of the traditions most readily accords with specifically Christian needs and symbols? Azariah's answer was to essay a deliberate combination of the two: an Indian Christian building should reflect the whole of the nation's past without being tied to any one of its separate traditions. Azariah's building thus has both Muslim domed minarets and Hindu open court;[19] the most obvious analogies are in the palaces of south Indian princes. This recalls another feature of Dornakal Cathedral, its grandeur of scale and concept. Yet the Christian community to be served consisted mostly of desperately poor subsistence farmers. Azariah wanted to bring a touch of splendour into these contracted lives. On the one hand, the great building was a declaration that Christianity was there to stay, whatever happened to the government of India. On the other, it was a sign that even the poorest Christians owned a share in magnificence. Azariah was facing and resolving in his own way an issue that has been raised more recently by the doyen of Indian Christian artists, Jyoti Sahi: the proper artistic expression of a Christian counter-culture in a setting where the dominant culture is associated with oppression.[20]

Church building, the provision of appropriate space for worship, obviously forces Christians into making artistic choices. But in India, in particular, pictorial art was raising theological issues of immense importance—and it was not only Christian artists who were raising them.

In the earliest phase of the Indian renaissance the figure of Christ as presented in the Christian Scriptures was an unmistakable influence. In the twentieth century art came explicitly into the sphere of the renaissance, with Rabindranath Tagore's university of Indian culture at Śantiniketan, and its school of art headed by Tagore's nephew Abanidranath.

Some of the outstanding artists who came from Śantiniketan use

---

[18] See C. Graham, *Azariah of Dornakal* (London, 1946). For the cathedral, see pp. 11f., 99f., 114f. Miss Graham rather stresses the Hindu aspect; but the minarets are unmistakable.

[19] Illustration in J. F. Butler, *Christianity in Asia and America = Iconography of Religions*, 24:13 (Leiden, 1979), plate XIX.

[20] Jyoti Sahi, 'Reflections on Biblical images/symbols in relation to Indian Christian spirituality', *Image*, 37 (1988), pp. 10–11.

Christian themes. Janini Roy, the greatest of them all, regularly painted Jesus; a Jesus who is greater than us, and who is not tied to a particular period; who walks on the water (like other deities he is at home in the elements, in air, in fire, in water). It is a Hindu reading of the Gospels. K. C. S. Panikkar (not a Christian but a former student at Madras Christian College) is another Indian renaissance artist who regularly paints the Christ figure; a Christ who belongs to India, for he stands with the other peace-makers, the Buddha and Gandhiji, giving his blessing to the poor, the sick, and the naked.[21]

But Christian artists went to Śantiniketan also; indeed one, V. S. Masoji (d. 1977), became a professor there.[22] Among the important early figures are the Roman Catholic Angelo da Fonseca[23] (who was associated with Father Heras, already mentioned) and the Anglican A. D. Thomas. The latter may be specifically mentioned at this point, since his paintings attracted some attention in the West through the publication in 1948 by the Society for the Propagation of the Gospel of *The Life of Christ by an Indian Artist*,[24] containing twenty-four pictures. Thomas attributed his inspiration to a verbal picture of Jesus by a Western missionary; that by E. Stanley Jones in *The Christ of the Indian Road*.[25] Thomas's portraits of Christ certainly present him as an Indian figure on the Indian road; but it is a serene, soft-coloured Christ. He has the smile of the Buddha, untouched by earth and all that earth can do.

The Indian Christian artist works in perhaps the most testing environment that Christianity has yet met. That environment includes a religious culture in which the divinity of Christ, and the superlative status of his teaching, and his right to worship, devotion, and love, can be readily conceded, so long as that recognition is not held to imply a unique or exclusive status or to demand a transition from one community to another. Christianity in India walks a tightrope: on one side the condition

21 On Roy and Panikkar see R. W. Taylor, *Jesus in Indian Paintings* (Madras, 1975), and cf. Butler, *Christian Art*, pp. 125–9.

22 Examples of Masoji's painting in A. Lehmann, *Afroasiatische christliche Kunst* (Berlin, 1966), plates 161–6.

23 See *The Art of Angelo da Fonseca* (Bombay, 1980). This booklet, written for an exhibition of da Fonseca's paintings at the Heras Institute, includes a statement by the artist and an account of his life and work by M. Lederle. Da Fonseca, born in Goa and brought up in Pune, lived from 1910 to 1967.

24 The pictures are also reproduced in A. Lehmann, *Die Kunst der Jungen Kirchen*, 2nd edn (Berlin, 1957). The SPG had earlier published *The Life of Christ by Chinese Artists* (London, 1943).

25 E. Stanley Jones, *The Christ of the Indian Road* (London, 1925).

of a foreign, alien, and entirely detachable institution; on the other, absorption as one more of the multifarious forms of Hinduism.[26] The Indian Christian artist has to expound the person of Christ in the land which both gave birth to one of the most powerful innovators in religious history, Gautama Buddha, and reinterpreted him as one of the incarnations of Viśnu. The image of Christ has long had a place in Indian art far outside the Church. Sacred pictures with salvation themes were a principal evangelistic instrument of the Jesuits at the court of Akbar, who loved paintings; in later Mughal painting the Christian themes take on a life of their own, independent of the traditional iconographic register.[27] The Indian renaissance takes Christ along Indian roads not mentioned in that register. Panikkar's portrayal of Christ alongside the Buddha and Gandhiji (and as Indian as they are) can be paralleled in dozens of popular bazaar prints.[28]

All this illustrates the quite considerable degree to which non-Western art over the last century (in church architecture and furnishing especially, but in other ways too) has been a means of exploration of the relations of Gospel and culture and of the relation of Christianity to other faiths. Indeed, artists and architects and church designers were facing these questions at a deeper level than that reached by many of the theological commentators, and sometimes raised issues before the high theologians reached them. But Christian art figures only marginally in the general discussions on the impact of Christianity on Africa and Asia during the period when the great demographic shift within Christianity was beginning.

Christian art does not seem to have reached the agenda of the great missionary conferences until the Tambaram meeting of the International Missionary Council (IMC) in 1938. It would indeed be surprising to find it in the conferences of the late nineteenth century; and the Edinburgh World Missionary Conference of 1910 was too much concerned with the impact of Western education and 'civilization' upon the non-Western world to take much account of the independent cultural heritages of the newer churches. And although the Jerusalem meeting of the IMC in 1928 paid attention to the religious consciousness of Asia, the question of how that consciousness might surface within Christianity was not at the

[26] The issues discussed at length by Taylor, *Jesus in Indian Paintings* and by Butler, *Christian Art* throughout their studies.

[27] Cf. the examples in F. zu Löwenstein, *Christliche Bilder in altindischer Malerei* (Münster, 1958).

[28] Examples in the Butler Collection, Centre for the Study of Christianity in the Non-Western World, University of Edinburgh.

forefront. Even at Tambaram the treatment is tentative and perfunctory. The clearest reference comes in the section on 'The inner life of the Church'. In the sub-section on worship, recommendation 7 begins:

> Having noted that there is in some of the younger churches extreme eagerness and in others extreme reluctance to use in worship indigenous forms of art, such as music and architecture, we urge the publication of literature at a price within the reach of all, giving examples of the music or other arts of different nations as used in the life of the Church, and passing on the inspiration and joy of bringing out native arts as an offering to our Lord.[29]

Here one scents the unmistakable odour of hot potato, especially as no suggestions are made as to who is to write and produce this economically priced literature. The impression of tentativeness is reinforced when the recommendation continues:

> We hope that some guiding principles on the connection of architecture with worship and witness may be made available for any church or mission desiring to study them.[30]

The only hint as to what these principles might be is a bibliographical footnote referring to two books by Daniel Johnson Fleming (to be mentioned later) and one article in the *International Review of Missions*. The footnote is clearly editorial; the article had not even appeared when the conference met.[31] With manifest relief at being able to be specific at last, the recommendation concludes with a reprimand to missionaries who are still eager to transplant the music, architecture, or art of their home churches, and an affirmation of 'the duty of helping the younger churches to express their Christian life in forms that are part of their nation's heritage'.[32]

Amongst the notes preserved from the preliminary papers for this section are commendatory references to T. C. Chao's Chinese hymn-book, with its use of Chinese tunes and other liturgical experiments in China, with the non-committal statement, 'There is also Dr K. L. Reichelt's *Ritual Book of the Christian Church among the Friends of the Tao* and

[29] *The Life of the Church International Missionary Council Meeting at Tambaram, Madras = Tambaram Series 4*, p. 6.

[30] Ibid.

[31] But the author, J. Prip-Møller, was a delegate at Tambaram and may well have had his say on the subject.

[32] *The Life of the Church*, p. 6.

Dr Chu Pao-yüan's *Book of Indigenous Worship Forms*.'[33] Another paper refers to Indian melodies used in Lutheran liturgies in Andhra,[34] and another carries a suggestion from the Congo Protestant Council that Christian worship might more closely reflect African rhetorical practice by employing antiphonal singing and interweaving song and speech as in traditional story-telling.[35] On the other hand, a multidenominational conference in South Africa concluded:

> It is difficult for us at the present stage to conceive of worship in the younger church in South Africa taking a form other than the present one. We cannot think what a form of worship more closely related to the life of the African people would be, though through time it may evolve.[36]

The thinness of treatment of art and architecture at Tambaram is quite in line with the modest appearance the subject makes in the missionary literature of the time. It is very little in evidence through the 1930s in the *International Review of Missions*, the IMC's own organ, and the principal Protestant missiological journal. The article referred to in the editorial note on the Tambaram report was by an architect, J. Prip-Møller.[37] Prip-Møller had worked with Karl Ludvig Reichelt in his endeavours to establish a setting in which Chinese Buddhist monks could approach and study the Christian faith, and had helped to construct the striking Hong Kong building for Reichelt's Tao Fong Shan institute.

The article reflects Chinese experience, pleading for entry into the 'spirit' rather than the 'details' of Chinese architecture. That involves more attention to how buildings are grouped, and how they fit into the landscape, and to the effect of shadow created by long, overhanging eaves, than to painfully copying curved roofs or multiple brackets. It may be true that some Christians are inoculated by missionary practice against their local styles; but it is surely more important to consider the effect on the far

[33] *The Life of the Church*, p. 8. Reichelt's controversial views (set out in, for example, *Truth and Tradition in Chinese Buddhism*, 1st Eng. edn (Shanghai, 1927), and posthumously in *Religion in Chinese Garment* (London, 1951), were expressed in equally controversial practice. See E. J. Sharpe, *Karl Ludvig Reichelt, Missionary, Scholar, Pilgrim* (Tao Fong Shan, Hong Kong, 1984); H. Eilert, *Boundlessness: Studies in Karl Ludvig Reichelt's Missionary Thinking* ... (Ringkøbing, 1974).

[34] *The Life of the Church*, p. 12.

[35] Ibid., p. 15.

[36] Ibid., pp. 15f.

[37] J. Prip-Møller, 'Architecture: a servant of foreign missions', *International Review of Missions*, 28, 109 (1939), pp. 105–15.

greater number of non-believers. The less the effect of foreignness is paraded before them, the more likely are they to reflect on the central concerns which are the reason for the Christian buildings' existence.

Among British contributions relating directly to the arts are an article in the Anglican review *The East and the West* from 1927 on 'African art and its possibilities' and a three-part series on 'The arts in the mission field' in *The Church Overseas*, a magazine of the Society for the Propagation of the Gospel, in 1931.[38] Edward Shillito, a Congregational minister of poetic attainments who did literary work for the London Missionary Society, produced a small book called *Craftsmen All*. A better-known book[39] by another LMS writer, Mabel Shaw, attracted attention by its accounts of African initiatives in worship within a girls' mission school in what is now Zambia. In 1933 the SPG published *Worship in Other Lands: a Study of Racial Characteristics in Worship*, put together by a member of the Society's home staff, H. B. Thompson, from examples supplied by SPG missionaries. The author expressed a hope that other missionary societies would take the story further from their own resources; none seem to have done so. Much of *Worship in Other Lands* is concerned with liturgical acts in the narrower sense, and the influence of Bishop W. V. Lucas of Masasi, with his somewhat archaizing ideas about African rituals,[40] is evident. But there are specific examples of architecture, music, drama, and the visual arts. Of its nature it is a thing of shreds and patches. It is slightly disturbing to find the Black Madonna of the frontispiece, carved in a mission workshop in South Africa, described as 'perhaps the most notable work of art that can so far be shown' from Africa. It is certainly African in facial features, but in other respects pure Percy Dearmer.

The strand of Anglican tradition represented in the SPG believed, as the preface of a manifesto volume of the time puts it, that Christianity could 'absorb and transmute all that is good and of permanent value in other religions, cultures, and institutions'.[41] In fact, it is fashionable to exaggerate the cultural insensitivity of the missionary movement of this period as a whole. And, as we have seen, there was by the time of the Second World War and the close of the Vasco da Gama era, already a substantial corpus of non-Western Christian artistic expression. Much of

[38] There were contributions on Africa (by W. V. Lucas, Bishop of Masasi), China, and Japan.

[39] Mabel Shaw, *God's Candlelights* (London, 1932).

[40] See his contribution, 'The Christian approach to non-Christian customs', in E. R. Morgan, ed., *Essays Catholic and Missionary* (London, 1928); repr. as late as 1950 in *Christianity and Native Races* (London).

[41] Morgan, ed., *Essays*, p. v.

the experimental work had been in church building; yet Prip-Møller in 1939 makes a plea for 'beautiful architecture' to take its place alongside the Chinese poetry, calligraphy, and music already being used to the glory of God.[42] Another contributor to the *International Review of Missions* says in 1942 of Indian music that, 'No missionary of my acquaintance is averse to its use. Most advocate it, even belligerently.'[43] His plea is for a far deeper understanding of it, rather than for its recognition and use.

Yet questions of art, whether in themselves or in their wider implications, figure little more in the literature of the post-war period, so concerned first with the autonomy of the Asian and African churches and then with Gospel and culture, than they do in the pre-Tambaram period.[44] There are some splendid studies of the earlier aspects of the Christian presence in the non-Western world—Mughal painting, Japanese Namban art, Congo ivories—and recent years have produced valuable accounts of development in particular areas, notably India.[45] But—if we leave aside Costantini's work and what it produced—only three writers in the whole of the twentieth century appear as consistently drawing attention to what was happening in Christian art in the non-Western world as a whole, and to its theological and artistic implications. They are the American Daniel Johnson Fleming, the German Arno Lehmann, and the Englishman J. F. Butler.

Fleming had recently graduated from college when, travelling in India, he saw All Saints' Church, Peshawar, and thought it was a mosque. It fixed his interest in 'the naturalization of Christianity in national homes of the spirit and the manifold expression of Christian experience as found in houses of God'.[46] In *The Heritage of Beauty* (1937) he gave photographs and commentaries of three dozen or so such houses of God, all but two or three of them Protestant, all over the world. Asia predominates, but Alaska and the Pacific are not forgotten, and there are some telling items

[42] Prip-Møller, 'Architecture', p. 115.

[43] M. Pitt, 'Take, for instance, Indian music', *International Review of Missions*, 31, 122 (1942), pp. 205–10.

[44] There is a rather embarrassed reference in the report of the World Council of Churches Assembly in 1961 to the close historical association of the Church with the arts and the open questions about art and society. The conclusion appears to be that the subject is important, but the Council currently without machinery for pursuing it. There is no reference to the possible contribution in this field of the newer churches: *The New Delhi Report: the Third Assembly of the World Council of Churches 1961* (London, 1962), pp. 181ff.

[45] The works of M. Lederle, R. W. Taylor, and J. F. Butler have already been mentioned: see nn. 11, 19 above.

[46] Fleming, *Heritage*, p. 17.

from Africa. (The latter included one by then already vanished, the first cathedral at Namirembe, Uganda; entirely an African hut in design, but of gigantic proportions.) Fleming, who was a professor at Union Seminary, New York, was aware that what was involved was not 'a relatively simple matter of the use of brick and mortar'.[47] The theme of much of his writing is the essential connection between the diversity of world Christianity and its catholicity. 'World Christianity' is a favourite phrase of his (his other books include *Marks of a World Christian* and *Ethical Issues Confronting World Christians*), and his view of the nature of Christian mission is essentially permeative. He also has a strong view of world citizenship (he wrote on *Ways of Sharing with Other Faiths* and *Contacts with Non-Christian Cultures*). But if a liberal (and there are frequent reminders of Hocking) he was not a naïve liberal. It is a feature of *The Heritage of Beauty* that sensitive issues raised by particular buildings are identified and succinctly set out. He is also concerned about aesthetic issues, and not simply in architecture. The *Heritage* includes one painting (by Luke Ch'en), and Fleming went on to produce *Each with his own Brush*[48] and to consider wider issues of religious symbolism.[49] He also had the prescience to see a new future within Christianity for indigenous African arts threatened with destruction by Western influences.[50]

Arno Lehmann had seen missionary service in India, and wrote an important history.[51] In his later work as Professor of Missiology at the University of Halle-Wittenberg he developed the systematic study of the Christian art of Africa and Asia (which for these purposes included the Pacific). A stream of studies proceeded through the 1950s and 1960s, especially dealing with pictures from Africa and Asia illustrating biblical incidents or themes. Whereas Fleming had emphasized architecture, Lehmann's chief concern was with painting and the plastic arts. Two encyclopaedic surveys (as well as an article in *Religion in Geschichte und Gegenwart*[52]) came from his later years: *Die Kunst der Jungen Kirchen* (1957)

[47] Ibid.

[48] Daniel Johnson Fleming, *Each with his own Brush* (New York, 1938).

[49] Daniel Johnson Fleming, *Christian Symbolism in a World Community* (New York, 1940).

[50] Fleming, *Heritage*, p. 85. On Fleming's theology and place in American mission history, see W. R. Hutchison, *Errand to the World. American Protestant Thought and Foreign Missions* (Chicago, 1987), pp. 150–8.

[51] Arno Lehmann, *Es begann in Tranquebar* (Berlin, 1955); tr. *It began at Tranquebar* (Madras, 1956).

[52] 'Malerei und Plastik VII: Christliche Kunst in den jungen Kirchen', *RGG*, 4, cols 702–4. For Lehmann's other articles see the bibliography in *Afroasiatische christliche Kunst*; tr. *Christian Art in Africa and Asia* (St Louis, 1969).

and *Afroasiatische christliche Kunst* (1966). Both are profusely illustrated. Lehmann, more than any other single person (with the possible exception of Costantini), documented the sheer extent and richness of modern non-Western Christian art, and the innovative nature of much of it. His achievement is the more remarkable in that the collection of data on which it was based was compiled in the German Democratic Republic.

John Francis Butler was appointed Professor of Philosophy at Madras Christian College in 1937, the year in which *The Heritage of Beauty* appeared. He later served with the Christian Literature Society for India, which dealt not only with books, but with the posters, pictures, and ancillary material used by hundreds of congregations and thousands of ordinary believers. In 1951 he returned to Britain, and never held another academic appointment. For most of the rest of his life he was a Methodist circuit minister, filling the studies of a succession of manses with books, journals, slides, and exemplars of what he called 'missionary art'. He used the term advisedly; 'missionary art', he argued, is the use of art in mission: the nationality of the artist is a secondary consideration. Over a thirty-year period came a stream of articles, both learned and popular, and a handful of books, some published, others remaining in manuscript.[53] Architectural historians sometimes noticed him when theologians did not.

Of the three pre-historians of the non-Western phase of Christian art (if the considerations with which this paper opened are valid), Butler is probably the most important. He has far more depth than Fleming, and more breadth of treatment than Lehmann. His approach was grounded in a philosophical interest in aesthetics and backed by a detailed knowledge of Western art and architecture. More than either of his seniors, he set the art of the churches of Africa and Asia in their context in the history of art and the history of Christianity. For the same reason, he was more aware than they of the special importance of Latin America in the story of Christian art, and of the aesthetic and theological issues involved in mixed traditions. He was interested in Mughal art, in Castiglione and the Jesuits in China, in 'Jesuit pottery', in Namban art. In his later work he came to argue that the theological problems of cultural transmission and syncretism in art should be posed historically. The questions facing Christian

[53] The most important books are *Christianity in Asia and America* in the Brill *Iconography of Religions* series, and the posthumous *Christian Art in India* both already referred to. See also his contributions to G. Cope, *Christianity and the Visual Arts* (London, 1964), and G. Frere-Cook, *The Decorative Arts of the Christian Church* (London, 1972). A collection of his articles is in the Butler collection at the Centre for the Study of Christianity in the Non-Western World, University of Edinburgh.

artists and decision-makers in Africa and Asia were endemic to Christianity, and Christian history revealed a succession of more or less successful solutions to analogous problems. His chosen title for an article with this thesis was 'Nineteen centuries of missionary art'.[54] The issues he raises range from the economic one of 'How is an Asian Christian artist to live?' to influence of 'international' styles in architecture and whether Africa and Asia can make better use of ferro-concrete than the West has done.

He also took up a question which Costantini had hinted at—whether non-Western Christianity might be the matrix for a new artistic renaissance. Butler once wrote an article entitled 'Can missions rescue modern art?'[55] In it he contrasts the old cultures of Africa and Asia—tired, perhaps, but the basis of national pride and self-confidence—with a dying culture in Europe. That culture has lost its ultimate values, its social solidarity, and any viable economic basis for the arts; Western art, accordingly, is in a perilous state. The churches of Africa and Asia seethe with problems, but by their possession both of the Christian faith and the resources of cultures of the non-Western world, they can provide the clash of ideas and techniques from which renaissance springs. It could well happen that missions would prove to be the source from which salvation came to modern art.

Butler lived to see the foundation of the Asian Christian Art Association in 1978.[56] The number of Asian countries which now have their own associations of Christian artists or societies for promoting Christian art attests the vigour of the movement. Whether or not salvation will come from the East to Western art, as he and Costantini envisaged, it is still impossible to know. But that a new phase of Christian art has opened, with its focus in the southern continents, is beyond doubt. Costantini, Butler, and Lehmann are among its few prehistorians.

Centre for the Study of Christianity in the Non-Western World,
University of Edinburgh

[54] The published title was 'Nineteen centuries of Christian missionary architecture', *Journal of the Society of Architectural Historians*, 21 (1962), pp. 3–17.

[55] J. F. Butler, 'Can missions rescue modern art?' *Hibbert Journal*, 56 (1958), pp. 371–87.

[56] The association arose with the support of the East Asia Christian Conference, later the Christian Conference of Asia, and the active promotion of the Sri Lankan churchman D. T. Niles. Niles commissioned Masao Takenaka of Doshisha University to collect work by Asian painters on Christian themes. Takenaka's *Christian Art in Asia* (Tokyo, 1975), was a manifesto volume. See R. O'Grady, 'The tenth anniversary of the Asian Christian Art Association', *Image*, 37 (1988), p. 2.